How to Teach Reading

How to Teach Reading

A Competency-Based Program

Albert J. Harris
Edward R. Sipay

LONGMAN

New York

London

HOW TO TEACH READING
A Competency-Based Program

Longman Inc., New York
Associated companies, branches, and representatives
throughout the world.

Developmental Editor: Nicole Benevento
Editorial and Design Supervisor: Linda Salmonson
Interior Design: Pencils Portfolio, Inc.
Cover Design: Albert M. Cetta
Manufacturing and Production Supervisor: Louis Gaber
Composition: Fuller Typesetting of Lancaster
Printing and binding: The Maple Press

Library of Congress Cataloging in Publication Data

Harris, Albert Josiah.
   How to teach reading.

   Bibliography: p.
   Includes index.
   1. Reading (Elementary). I. Sipay, Edward R.,
joint author. II. Title.
LB1573.H232   372.4'1   77–17722
ISBN 0–582–28048–6

Manufactured in the United States of America

To Those We Love

Contents

List of Figures

List of Tables

Preface

During the past decade it has become clear that better reading achievement requires better teachers of reading. The best reading teachers do not blindly follow a printed set of directions; they do understand children, are aware of the complexities of the reading process, and are competent at the many specific tasks that expert instruction involves.

This book may be used, at the advanced undergraduate or beginning graduate level, as the core of a competency-based course, in a conventional basic course on the teaching of reading in the elementary school, or in any combination of approaches that the instructor chooses. The eleven units that constitute part 1 provide a background of knowledge that students need about reading instruction. The modules that make up part 2 provide a framework for a competency-based course. Our aim has been to develop a plan that will help students become competent teachers of reading and at the same time will not overload either the instructor or the students.

Students should realize that the principles, theories, and procedures described in this text are founded on a large body of relevant research and theory, which has increased tremendously in recent years. The Bibliography of more than eight hundred items, the majority of which have been published in the 1970s, represents our selection of relevant and significant contributions. They are cited unobtrusively throughout the text by giving the author's name and the date of publication; with this information the full citation can be found in the Bibliography. Many of these references amplify the description of procedures that may be summarized briefly in the text and make it possible for the student who becomes interested in a specific procedure to find useful further reading about it.

The eleven units of part 1, some of which are substantially longer than conventional chapters, provide the knowledge about theory and practice that a teacher of reading requires. Unit 1 discusses the importance of reading, language and reading, factors related to reading achievement, theories and definitions of reading, and the objectives of reading instruction. Unit 2 is on reading readiness, the factors that influence it, how to evaluate it, and how to hasten its development. Unit 3 offers a comprehensive view of beginning reading instruction. Three meaning-emphasis approaches and five code-emphasis approaches are defined, with discussion of the strong and weak points of each. Attention is also given to the special problems of beginners who speak a divergent dialect or a foreign language. Unit 4 provides an overview of reading instruction in the primary, intermediate, and upper grades.

Unit 5 is concerned with planning and organizing differentiated reading instruction. After a discussion of basic principles of effective teaching, this unit takes up in detail teaching with various kinds of groups, whole-class instruction, individualized instruction, and sample one-week plans for different grade levels. It also describes the learning-center type of class organization and the contribution of administrative procedures to teaching effectiveness. Unit 6 deals with techniques for determining reading status and needs and for assessing progress. Considerable attention is given to newer trends, such as the use of cloze tests and criterion-referenced tests; and procedures for analyzing a child's reading performance are described.

Unit 7 is on word recognition. Both the whole-word method and decoding are described in detail, with emphasis on the combined use of graphic, phonemic, syntactic, and semantic cues. Unit 8 deals with the improvement of comprehension: vocabulary, reading in thought units, and the extraction of meaning from connected discourse. Attention is given to the nature of comprehension; the development of literal, interpretive, and evaluative comprehension skills; and the relation of rate to comprehension. Unit 9, on reading to learn, deals mainly with the study skills and habits needed in the middle and upper grades, with special attention to the problems of reading materials in mathematics, science, and social studies. Unit 10, on instilling the desire to read, considers what is often the most neglected part of the reading program. Among the topics treated are the factors that influence reading interests, ways to determine the interests of children, readability, and specific ideas for creating and fostering interest in reading.

Unit 11, on assisting children who have special needs, provides essential information about various kinds of "different" children to be found in today's classrooms. Disabled readers are defined, methods of studying their needs are described, principles of good remedial teaching are summarized, and specific materials for use with disabled readers are listed. A lengthy section considers the special problems and needs of educationally disadvantaged children. This section includes summaries of the major divergences between standard English, black English, and the oral English of speakers of Spanish, Chinese, and American Indian languages. The final sections of this unit describe the special reading needs of slow-learning children and of gifted children.

A competency-based course has four essential characteristics: (1) the objectives that students are expected to attain are specified at the beginning of the course so that students as well as the instructor know what is expected; (2) the course includes a variety of activities in which students can apply the knowledge gained; (3) the criteria to be applied in judging student performance are made clear in advance; and (4) the evaluation of student achievement is based on what students can do as well as on what they know.

Other characteristics are frequently part of a competency-based procedure, such as providing alternative ways to learn, alternative ways to demonstrate achievement of the objectives, optional as well as required objectives, preassessments to determine readiness or previously acquired acknowledge, time flexibility, simulations, and school-based experiences with children.

A competency-based course is organized into segments called *modules*. A module ordinarily has five components: a list of objectives, a plan for preassessment, required and optional learning activities, the specification of alternative ways to demonstrate achievement of the objectives, and the provision of assessment procedures during and upon completion of the module.

Part 2 of this book provides a framework for a competency-based course on the teaching of reading in the elementary school. A short introduction, which explains the general plan in greater detail than is possible here, is followed by eleven modules, which parallel the eleven units of part 1.

Eight of the modules (1, 3, 4, 5, 6, 7, 8, and 10) are usually required, and three modules (2, 9, and 11) may be included at the discretion of the instructor.

In preparing these modules we kept in mind the wide variations in courses on reading instruction in different institutions: differences in amount of credit given; in faculty load; in length of semester; in library facilities; in the availability of facilities for the use of recordings, closed-circuit video, and so forth; and in opportunities to observe schoolchildren and do things with them. For each module we have indicated that certain objectives are required and others are optional; activities involving interaction with children are all optional. We have provided many opportunities for students to simulate teaching and testing activities by practicing on one another; this should always be possible, whereas access to children sometimes cannot be arranged. We have left to each instructor the specification of learning activities and the devising of appropriate tests.

We wish to thank the many people who have helped us learn about competency-based instruction. Our gratitude is particularly strong to the members of the Commission on High Quality Teacher Education of the International Reading Association and its co-chairmen, Harry W. Sartain and Paul E. Stanton, for their excellent report entitled *Modular Preparation for Teaching Reading* (Sartain and Stanton 1974).

We want to acknowledge our indebtedness to those who were outstanding leaders in the field of reading when we were beginners: to Arthur I. Gates, William S. Gray, Nila B. Smith, Ruth Strang, and Paul A. Witty, who are gone, and to Donald D. Durrell and Emmett A. Betts, who are still productive workers. We have learned much from each of them.

We thank Edith Harris for her careful reading of the manuscript and many helpful suggestions. Donna Parent has been a careful and accurate typist. Our Longman editors have helped us in many ways to come closer to our aim of clear and unambiguous expression of ideas. We are grateful to the many publishers who have graciously allowed us to reproduce copyrighted material; an acknowledgment accompanies each figure.

How to Teach Reading

Paul E. Kotler

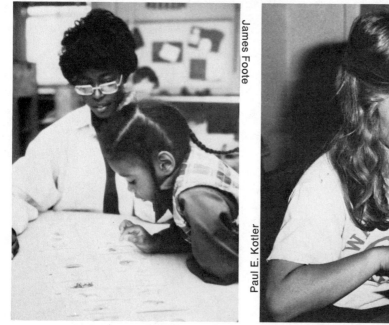

James Foote

Paul E. Kotler

UNIT 1

Reading:
Who Needs It?
What Is It?

Since the advent of television, prophets have been foretelling the fall of reading from its position as the main avenue to education and to occupational and social success. They have been predicting that pictures and the recorded spoken word will render reading superfluous. Before embarking on a serious study of reading and how to teach it, it may be well to consider whether reading still is necessary and worthwhile.

Thus, unit 1 begins with an examination of the importance of reading. Other major topics covered in this unit are language and reading; factors related to reading achievement; descriptions, definitions, and models of reading; and objectives of reading instruction.

IMPORTANCE OF READING

Imagine what life would be like if you could not read. True, you could obtain news and also be entertained by watching television. But you have to read many things each day—street signs, mail, food and medicine labels, advertisements, forms, questionnaires, and newspapers. The reading skill necessary for such everyday reading tends to be of high school level. Directions on an aspirin bottle require a tenth-grade reading ability; directions on a TV dinner, eighth grade; federal income tax forms, ninth grade; and most insurance policies, twelfth grade (Kilty 1976).

The attainment of reading competence is a major educational objective that must be achieved if the rest of the academic program is to be effective. Until you were able to use such learning tools as textbooks, reference works, and library materials, your educational opportunities were very limited. Despite advances in the use of audiovisual procedures, reading remains the main avenue for acquiring information. A child whose reading skills are inadequate is handicapped in all curricular areas. Of course, children must learn to read before they can read to learn. Reading is both a major part of the elementary school curriculum and an essential tool for mastering subject matter. Moreover, with the increasing emphasis on adult education and with continuing rapid changes in science, technology, and the kinds of jobs available, reading plays a leading role in continuing education and self-improvement.

You can also recognize the strong relationship between level of reading competence attained and the amount of education you will be able to complete; and with this, recognize that amount of education completed is significantly related to job level and salary achieved (Young and Jamison 1975). Thus your reading ability is an economic asset; illiteracy is a grave economic handicap.

Do People Read?

Most adults read quite a bit as part of their everyday living. They read a newspaper regularly, as well as one or more magazines. They read in doing tasks around the house, shopping, commuting; they read at school and on the job. The average American spends about 1.75 hours daily reading (Sharon 1973–74). Nevertheless, once formal schooling ends, relatively few American adults regularly read books other than the Bible; book reading in the United States lags behind several other countries.

Is Reading Necessary?

While television, radio, and the movies all can serve some of the same purposes as reading—they further recreational interests, satisfy curiosity, aid in understanding current events, supply information, and satisfy personal needs—reading has characteristics that other modes of communication cannot match. Reading is uniquely individual and flexible. Reading is the only form of mass communication in which a person can control the content and rate of presentation of the material. A reader can select reading material from a tremendous variety; can read where, when, and how he or she pleases. The reader sets the pace, pausing to reflect or reread, taking an intermission, skimming or taking careful notes. Reading is a preeminently private, personal, and self-controlled activity.

To the television program we need bring only a receptive mind and sit torpidly while the display of sound and image fills us. If others are watching, they are filled to the brim in precisely the same way, all of them, and with precisely the same sounding images.

The book, on the other hand, demands cooperation from the reader. It insists that he take part in the process.

In doing so, it offers an inter-relationship that is made to order by the reader himself for the reader himself, one that most neatly fits his own peculiarities and idiosyncracies.

When you read a book, you create your own images, you create the sound of various voices, you create gestures, expressions, emotions. You create *everything* but the bare words themselves. And if you take the slightest pleasure in creation, the book has given you something the television program can't. (Asimov 1974, p. 269)

Nor has automation eliminated the need for reading in obtaining or keeping a job. On the contrary, improved technology often requires higher levels of reading skill than many adults possess. Printed instructions have to be followed accurately or disastrous mistakes ensue. And in the military, such jobs as cook, carpenter, and clerk require minimum reading competencies of seventh- to ninth-grade level.

Has Reading Ability Declined?

It is easy to fall victim to the delusion that things were better in the "good old days." Actually, things weren't all that good. Fifty years ago, 20 to 40 percent of first graders had to repeat first grade, many pupils took two or three extra years to complete eighth grade, and thousands never got that far.

There is, however, plenty of room for improvement in reading. For example, thousands of people in military service who are high school graduates score below the seventh-grade level in reading (Sticht et al. 1972), and even college graduates sometimes have difficulty understanding application forms (L. Harris and Associates 1970). On the brighter side, the National Assessment Study found that a representative sample of individuals at four age levels read all types of materials better than the test makers had expected (Gadway 1972).

A comprehensive review of before-and-after test results led Tuinman, Rowls, and Farr (1976) to conclude that (1) a gradual improvement in reading competency took place between 1925 and 1965; and (2) the years 1965 to 1974 saw a leveling and perhaps a slight decline in average reading achievement. In consequence, they felt that many of the alarmist statements about the decline in literacy were without foundation.

Reading ability is essential for survival in our complex society. Our efforts to teach children to read have improved somewhat over the past half century, but further substantial improvement is possible. Perhaps the least successful aspect of our reading efforts has been in the area of getting both children and adults to read voluntarily.

LANGUAGE AND READING

Language has been defined as "the aspect of human behavior that involves the use of vocal sounds in meaningful patterns and, when they exist, corresponding written symbols, to form, express, and communicate thoughts and feelings" (*American Heritage Dictionary* 1969). Oral language has two aspects, speaking and listening; written language involves a writer and one or more readers. The active or productive aspects of language are speaking and writing; the receptive aspects are listening and reading. Reading is, therefore, one of the four main types of language activity. Its similarities to the other three types, and its differences from them, need to be understood by reading teachers.

Written and Spoken Language

Human beings were probably communicating through some form of spoken language several hundred thousand years ago; writing and reading were invented about 4,000 years ago. Speech usually develops before the age of two; reading and writing are learned several years later. Thus both in the history of humankind and the development of each person, oral communication precedes written communication.

Linguists reach differing conclusions on whether speech is primary, with written language only a representation of speech, or whether speech and writing are two equal and somewhat different forms of language. In general, linguists of the structural school tend to regard speech as primary; linguists and psycholinguists of the transformational-generative school tend to regard speech and writing as equal and somewhat different.

Language is more than speech. "Language is knowledge in our heads; speech is the realization of that knowledge in behavior. Language consists of all the words in a person's mental dictionary, and all the rules at his (usually nonconscious) command for combining these words into an infinite number of novel sentences and for interpreting the equally novel sentences that he hears. Speech, by contrast, consists of his actual utterances spoken to particular people in particular situations" (Cazden 1972, p. 3). An important aspect of language is "inner speech," which includes most thinking.

Linguists of the transformational-generative school, which has grown greatly in influence in recent years, emphasize that language has a deep structure and a surface structure. The deep structure consists of the essential meanings and can be expressed in a series of simple one-clause sentences. The surface structure is the particular way of stating the ideas; it often combines several ideas in one compound or complex sentence.

For example, consider the following sentences:

1. Peter tossed the meaty bone to his hungry dog.
2. Peter threw the bone, which had meat on it, to his dog, which was hungry.
3. The meaty bone was thrown by Peter to his hungry dog.

The three sentences above all convey the same ideas:

4. Peter had a dog.
5. Peter had a bone.
6. The dog was hungry.
7. The bone was meaty.
8. Peter threw the bone to the dog.

Sentences 4 through 8 represent the deep structure. The same ideas are conveyed by sentences 1, 2, and 3, each of which is a different surface structure that corresponds to the same deep structure. Linguists are engaged in studying the rules by which speakers and writers transform their meanings (deep structure) into the particular sentences they say or write (surface structure), and the rules by which listeners and readers respond to these sentences by discovering their meanings. After a rule has been learned, it can be used to generate or produce new sentences.

According to K. Goodman (1972, p. 151), "Written and oral language are alternative surface structures with the same underlying deep structure. In both listening and reading, the language user infers this deep structure without resorting to a shift from oral to written surface structure or vice versa. . . . It is only in the special case of oral reading that the reader is also interested in producing an oral signal and, even then, it appears that proficient readers decode graphic language for meaning and then encode (recode) an oral signal."

Many linguists do not agree with Goodman and others of the transformational-generative school. To Reed (1965), for example, reading is translating a set of printed or written symbols into the corresponding word sounds. Understanding or comprehending, to Reed, is not a necessary part of reading, but is a separate operation that is common to reading and listening.

Written and oral language have some important differences. Written language tends to be a concise, formally correct, and rather abstract mode of expression. Speech tends to be repetitious, colloquial, informal, and often incomplete in its sentence structure. Actually there are several levels of formality-informality, which De Stefano (1973) calls *registers*. For example, a teacher uses an informal register when talking to her own family, but a more formal register when talking to her pupils. She would use a still more formal register in a speech before a teachers' convention; this would probably approximate the formality of a written essay.

Despite these differences, the competence a child has developed in oral communication provides an important base for learning the beginnings of reading and writing. Among the deaf, language is conveyed by signs rather than speech, but language competence is still necessary as a base for learning to read. Preschool children who are slow in mastering speech are apt to have difficulty later on in learning to read (Ingram 1969). Reading involves the utilization of many language rules that a beginning reader has already learned in spoken language, as well as other rules that are specific to reading. In a sense, reading is built on a foundation of competence in speaking and listening.

Language: Innate or Learned?

There is a basic difference of opinion between linguists who believe that humans are innately predisposed to develop language competence [1] and the majority of psychologists, who believe that language skills, like other skills, are acquired bit by bit through the normal process of learning.

Linguists often refer to the writings of Lenneberg (1967), who assembled data indicating that important language milestones are reached by practically all children in a fixed sequence. This sequence cannot be accelerated by special training; rather, it appears to be closely related to the child's general biological maturation. They consider the disposition to develop language to be innate; the particular language that a child develops depends, of course, on his or her environment. N. Chomsky (1970) and his followers believe that a child comes equipped with an aptitude to learn the rules of the language to which he or she is exposed. These rules are not verbally explainable by the child, but are practices that are followed automatically. Thus, a young child who has grasped the rule that the past tense is indicated by adding *d* or *ed* is likely at first to overapply it and say *runned* for *ran* and *goed* for *went*. The irregular forms are mastered later.

These linguists also emphasize that the mastery of linguistic rules allows children to produce sentences that they have never heard and that they therefore could not have learned by imitation; children also understand sentences they have never heard before. In this sense they can be creative every time they speak or listen.

Many psychologists are skeptical about the emphasis that linguists place on the innate aspects of language development. They believe that what is innate is not a specific predisposition to develop linguistic rules, but rather a great potential for learning.

There are different schools of thought about how children learn. Some psychologists rely on the principles of operant conditioning; that is, they

---

1. Linguists distinguish between language *competence* and language *performance*. Performance is what an individual does in a particular situation; competence is what he is capable of doing. Competence is inferred from a series of performances.

consider reinforcement and imitation the main explanatory principles. To these psychologists, a child's earliest words develop when, out of the baby's random babbling, certain sounds such as *mama* or *dada* are reinforced (rewarded) by immediately giving the baby extra smiles and attention. These sounds are reinforced only when the proper person is present and are ignored at other times, and the baby learns to say them only when that person is present. When a bottle is presented, the adult may say "milk." If the baby makes a somewhat similar sound, the adult reinforces by giving milk and also with smiles, cooing, and so on. If the baby makes the sound at another time, milk may be offered. In that way the sound of the word becomes associated with the object. As the baby gets older, pronunciation becomes closer to adult pronunciation. Later, imitation of adult sentences is reinforced, and additional self-initiated repetitions speed the learning process. At first, any crude approximation of the intended word is accepted and reinforced; as children mature, utterances gradually have to become closer to adult utterances to receive reinforcement.

It would not be appropriate here to go into the several alternative psychological explanations of how children learn to talk. Suffice it to say that most psychologists are skeptical of the linguistic innate-factor theory about the acquisition of language.

Both the linguists and the psychologists may have part of the truth. It may be that we are innately predisposed to learn a language and that its early development follows a fairly fixed sequence. But this does not explain how particular words, phrases, and sentences are learned. Here it seems evident that particular language responses are acquired through such explanatory principles as attention-focusing instruction, imitative behavior, and reinforcement of correct responses. Differentiation and generalization are accounted for in different ways by different schools of psychological thought.

Athey (1971b) concluded, from a thorough review of the literature, that although various language theories have provided us with some useful insights, we do not yet have an adequate theory that clarifies the relationships between what we know about learning and what we know about language. This seems to be a correct conclusion.

Some Linguistic Terms

At this point it seems desirable to clarify the meanings of some of the technical vocabulary used by linguists in discussions of reading.

Phonology is the study of a language's sound structure. In phonology, the basic unit for linguistic analysis is the *phoneme*. A phoneme is the minimal sound unit that distinguishes one meaningful word from another. The sounds /s/, /h/, and /m/ are phonemes in English because changing /sat/ to /hat/ or /mat/ produces a word with a different meaning.[2] Certain variations in pronunciation, as between dialects, do not change the meaning and so are considered not to change the phoneme. For example, the /p/ at the beginning of a word like /pots/ is not identical with the /p/ at the end of /stop/; this can be proved by making records of the sound waves. But we consider them one phoneme since no change of meaning is involved. Variant sounds of a phoneme are called *allophones*. For example, when a southerner pronounces /I/ to rhyme with /ah/, the /ī/ and /ah/ are allophones. Allophones of the same phoneme do not change the meaning.

A *grapheme* is a written or printed symbol that represents a phoneme. Most graphemes are single alphabet letters. However, some letter combinations represent one phoneme each, and the combination is therefore a grapheme. Thus in the word *threw, th* is one grapheme, *r* is one grapheme, and *ew* is one grapheme.

Phonics is the study of the relationship of graphemes to phonemes as a means of *decoding* (determining the spoken words that correspond to particular written or printed words).

A *morpheme* is a unit of language that conveys meaning. If an utterance can be divided into two or more items each of which contributes meaning, those items are separate morphemes. A *free* morpheme is one that can be used independently; it is a whole word that cannot be further divided into meaning-bearing elements. A *bound* morpheme is one that must be combined with a free morpheme, and changes its meaning. For example, *boy* and *like* are free morphemes; the *s* in *boys* and the *ly* in *likely* are bound morphemes. Bound morphemes in English include prefixes, suffixes, and inflectional endings. The most common bound morphemes are five regular inflectional endings: *s* or *es* indicating plural; *'s* indicating possession; *s* representing third-person singular of a verb (*rides*); *d* or *ed* indicating past tense; and *ing* indicating the progressive form of a verb.

Many linguists use the term *morphophoneme* to represent a unit that is intermediate between a morpheme and a phoneme. For example, the /ē/ in extreme and the /e/ in extremity have different phonemic value but are

---

2. When a letter, letter cluster, or word is printed within slashes it represents the spoken sound or sounds; when it is in italics, it represents the written or printed form.

similar in meaning; the addition of *ity* changes the sound in a predictable fashion, as in *familiar, familiarity* or *obscene, obscenity*. Morphophonemes follow rules that are more complex than simple phoneme-grapheme relationships, and show that many so-called exceptions are actually governed by rules.

There are three kinds of intonational phonemes that are not directly represented by graphemes. Pitch, stress, and juncture are types of phonemes because changes in them are accompanied by changes in meaning. Children learn to use the intonation phonemes of pitch, stress, and juncture automatically in spoken language, but many children have difficulty in transferring this knowledge to reading. *Pitch* involves the raising or lowering of the voice as on a musical scale. For example, declarative sentences usually end with a falling pitch, while questions usually end with a rising pitch. An intermediate pitch usually indicates that the sentence is not yet ended. Compare the pitch of /home/ in the following sentences: Go home! Will you please go home? If you go home, take this with you.

Stress or *accent* refers to the relative loudness with which syllables in a word, or words in a sentence, are spoken. Stress is indicated in dictionaries by marks like this: ´, ´. The heavier the mark, the stronger the stress. Changing the stress within a word may change the part of speech it represents: con'vict, con-vict'. Changing the stress of words in a sentence may change the meaning. "Rob' ate the cake" indicates *who* did it; "Rob ate' the cake" emphasizes what he did, and "Rob ate the cake'" emphasizes the object of the action.

A *juncture* is a pause. We usually pause slightly between words, have longer pauses between phrases and clauses, and pause longest between sentences. Junctures are indicated by the blank space before and after each word. Children are sometimes confused because words may be run together without junctures in informal speech, as in *gonna* for *going to,* so that the printed term indicates a pause they do not hear. Changes in the juncture pattern within a sentence can change the meaning: (1) "Sue," said Rob, "go home." (2) Sue said, "Rob, go home." In this case the punctuation marks help to show the proper juncture pattern.

Syntax is the study of the way in which words are arranged in phrases, clauses, and sentences to convey particular meanings. Most of the time, syntax is used as a synonym for *grammar*. As used by linguists, grammar is a somewhat more inclusive term because it may include semantics as well as syntax.

Semantics is the study of meaning in language forms. Most of semantics is concerned with the meanings of sentence elements (words and phrases).

Lexical meaning refers to the meanings of single words.

The meanings of the above terms will become clearer as they are met repeatedly in the text.

Language Development in Children

Most children understand some words before their first birthdays and begin to say single words between 12 and 18 months. In these earliest one-word sentences the adult listener has to guess at the exact meaning. "Mik" may mean "I want milk," "I see the milk," and so on. By about 18 months most children begin to use two-word sentences: "Allgone milk" or "See kitty." From the age of 2 on, sentence constructions expand rapidly in variety and complexity, and vocabulary continues to expand at a rapid rate.

By about three and one-half years the average child has the competency to comprehend the major sentence forms found in adult speech, although the child does not yet speak like an adult. By about age five or six, most children have control over most of the elements of adult syntax, although grasp of difficult constructions continues to develop through preadolescence (Ruddell 1976).

In order to understand spoken or written communication, children must understand the meanings of the individual words (semantic or lexical meaning), the significance of word order (syntax), and intonation patterns. "In order to either utter or understand a sentence, a person must have a mental dictionary that contains the words in that sentence. He must also have a set of rules for combining dictionary entries into a meaning for the sentence as a whole" (Cazden 1972, p. 65).

Vocabulary and Mental Development

The vocabulary of an average child starts slowly, with a few words mastered by the age of 18 months, then expands rapidly and continues to grow at a fairly steady rate throughout childhood. There are, of course, very marked differences in rate of vocabulary growth. The average child entering first grade can understand between 2,000 and 3,000 words, and vocabulary increases about 1,000 words a year during the school years. Vocabulary growth is shown not only in the number of words understood, but also in the increasing precision of meanings and in the learning of alternative meanings for many words.

Much thinking is carried out in the form of "inner speech"; people have auditory images of sentences, they hear themselves think. This imagery is accompanied by tiny changes in the tension of the muscles in the larynx, throat, and mouth region that are used in speaking. The words with which inner speech is carried on are labels that represent concepts and ideas. To a great extent, if we cannot express a thought in words, we cannot think it. It should not be a surprise, therefore, that over and over again a good vocabulary test has been found to be the best single measure of verbal intelligence, closely correlated with other kinds of verbal intelligence measures. Since reading is a highly verbal activity, the size and accuracy of a child's vocabulary determines to a great extent the ability to extract meaning from what is read.

Not all thinking and reasoning is verbal. Mathematicians think in terms of the mental manipulation of mathematical signs and symbols. Architects and artists usually have strong visual imagery and can manipulate spatial representations mentally without expressing them in verbal terms. Some persons think partially in imagery of a series of muscular movements or action tendencies. Musicians may have vivid auditory imagery for melodic and harmonic sequences, and composers seem to be able to think in terms of "hearing" original melodies. Furthermore, there is some evidence that verbal reasoning is carried on primarily in the left half of the brain and nonverbal reasoning primarily in the right half of the brain.

The Writing System of English

The origin of spoken language is shrouded in antiquity, but written language is only a few thousand years old. Most early writing systems were in the form of picture writing. Gradually the pictures became stylized and more abstract and came to represent related ideas; a picture of a sun, for example, might represent a day. Chinese writing developed from primitive picture writing; each complex symbol represents an idea, which is represented by different spoken words in different dialects.

At some point someone discovered that written symbols could be used to represent sounds. Our present alphabet derives from the Roman alphabet, which was modified from the Greek alphabet ("alpha" and "beta" are the first two letters of the Greek alphabet), which in turn was probably based on the Phoenician alphabet. Our 26 letters (of which *c* and *x* are superfluous) can be combined in different patterns to represent hundreds of thousands of words.

Because there are over 40 phonemes in American English (the exact number varies from one dictionary to another) and only 26 letters, an exact correspondence cannot be made between phonemes and the graphemes that represent them. Most consonant letters represent one or two phonemes each, but each vowel letter, alone and in combination with other vowel letters, represents several different phonemes, and each vowel phoneme may have several possible spellings. For example, the long *e* phoneme /ē/ can be represented as in b*e*, s*ee*, rec*e*de, c*ei*ling, bel*ie*ve, l*ea*f, k*ey*. The letter *e* may represent various phonemes as in h*e*, b*e*d, gr*e*y, h*e*r, h*e*art, d*e*ceive, and is often silent at the end of a syllable or word. While the majority of printed words can be decoded (recognized) by pronouncing in sequence the phonemes most commonly represented by their graphemes, there are enough exceptions (estimated at about 20 percent) to make the decoding of English more difficult than decoding such languages as Italian and Spanish, in which phoneme-grapheme relationships are less variable.

Orthography means the particular method used to represent the sounds of a language by written symbols. The term "traditional orthography" (T.O.) is sometimes used to refer to the spelling system used in printed and written English.

There was a close relationship, in Anglo-Saxon and Old English, between phonemes and graphemes. For example, the *gh* in *through*, the *ed* in *laughed*, and the final *e* in *name* were originally pronounced. Over the centuries spelling tended to remain more resistant to change than pronunciation did. There were shifts in vowel values, some previously pronounced letters became silent, and words borrowed from other languages tended to retain their original spellings and pronunciations (*bouquet*).

There have been many proposals for a new orthography in which the correspondence of grapheme to phoneme would be perfectly regular. Some of these ideas, including one that received a large prize from the estate of the late George Bernard Shaw, involve completely new alphabets. Others, including one sponsored by the Simpler Spelling Association, retain the present alphabet but employ certain letter combinations to indicate particular phonemes. For example, *a* represents the vowel in *pat*; *ae* represents the vowel in *pate*, which would be spelled *paet*.

Many linguists oppose alphabet reform on the grounds that at the morphophonemic level, English orthography is quite regular. N. Chomsky (1970), for example, has stated that present orthography is nearly optimal for writing English, at least for skilled readers who get semantic and grammatical information about words from their written forms. Spelling may distinguish between homophones (words that sound alike), such as *knight* and *night* or *led* and *lead*. The close similarity in meaning of *relative* and *relation* is evident in their spellings, although their dictionary pronunciation respellings are quite dissimilar: rel'ə-tiv, ri-lā'shən. An alphabet that would exactly fit the pronunciation of one dialect may create problems for speakers of other dialects.

In view of this opposition from linguists, as well as the tremendous expense of shifting to a new alphabet, Sir John Pitman has proposed that a special alphabet should be used only for beginning readers, after which the children would make a transition to traditional orthography. The Pitman alphabet, called the Initial Teaching Alphabet or i.t.a., is discussed in unit 3.

Others wish to help children learn letter-sound correspondences by using one color for all graphemes that represent a particular phoneme. The *e* in *bed*, the *ea* in *head*, and the *ai* in *said* might all be printed pink. As with i.t.a., color cues would be phased out when no longer needed. In the earliest of these systems, *Words in Color*, consonant as well as vowel phonemes were given specific colors. More recent applications of the color-cue idea tend to use color only for vowel phonemes.

Reading for Children with Differing Language Backgrounds

Much attention has been given in recent years to the special problems of teaching reading to children who enter school speaking a dialect that differs from standard American English or for whom English is a second language and only imperfectly spoken. Substantial evidence exists that children with these kinds of language backgrounds have difficulty learning to read and on the average make poor progress in reading. Several explanations of this reading retardation have been offered and several ways to improve the situation proposed. These issues are discussed in unit 3 and are considered in greater detail in unit 11.

OTHER FACTORS RELATED TO READING ACHIEVEMENT

Numerous factors besides language are related to reading ability. They fall within three main categories: cognitive, physical-physiological, and cultural. Although we know that these factors relate to success in learning to read, we do not know exactly what the relationships are, or how the factors interact. The presence of a relationship does not in itself prove a cause-effect relationship.

Cognitive Factors

A substantial relationship exists between general mental development and success in learning to read. The correlations between IQ and reading scores start as low to moderate (.40–.50), rise to about .70 by fourth grade, and tend to remain at about that level. With a correlation of .70, variation in one trait accounts for about half the variation in the other trait. The other half of difference in achievement is probably accounted for by differences in motivation, in the quality of the educational program, in socio-economic conditions, and other factors.

In young children perceptual, reasoning, verbal, and numerical aptitudes are interrelated, so that the idea of general intelligence has considerable value. As children near adolescence, these abilities may develop at varying rates, producing lower correlations among them.

The intelligence tests commonly used in elementary schools usually give scores in terms of mental age (M.A.) and intelligence quotient (IQ). Mental age represents the average degree of maturity a child shows in understanding, reasoning, remembering, and so on. Thus a bright 8-year-old and a dull 12-year-old who both have M.A.s of 10 years are more like typical 10-year-olds in their ability to understand and reason than they are like children of their own biological ages.

The IQ, which is the M.A. divided by the child's chronological age, is an indicator of the child's rate of mental growth. The more the IQ is above 100, the faster the child's future rate of learning is likely to be; the more below 100, the slower. These scores, however, will not give a true picture of the child's mental ability if the child's background of experience and command of English are not reasonably comparable to the representative sampling of children on whom the test was standardized. Group IQ tests often present questions in printed form and therefore assume a reasonable proficiency in reading; the intelligence of a very poor reader may be seriously underestimated. Children with limited knowledge of standard English or from an underprivileged socioeconomic background may also not be fairly measured by intelligence tests.

Some children with average or even above-average intelligence have extreme difficulty in learning to read, particularly with word recognition and decoding. Children with low intelligence can learn to read, but usually do so at a later age and more slowly than average children. A child who misses the wide variety of information and varied practice in thinking and reasoning that reading provides may become increasingly handicapped on IQ tests. Such a child's IQ may decrease as he or she gets older.

Physical and Physiological Factors

The presence of a sensory handicap does not necessarily prevent a child from learning to read; many children compensate successfully for such handicaps. Nevertheless, sensory handicaps may increase the difficulty of learning the perceptual tasks in reading. In vision, the common defects of acuity that are correctible with glasses should of course receive attention, but they are less likely to interfere with progress in reading than difficulties in aiming, focusing, and binocular coordination of the eyes. School eye examinations usually do not detect the latter kinds of visual handicaps.

A partial hearing loss may make it difficult for a child to discriminate between phonemes that are similar, such as /t/ and /d/, /m/ and /n/, and /sh/ and /ch/. A child who cannot hear the difference will have difficulty associating each grapheme with its commonest phoneme. Children with partial hearing losses are likely to benefit from a reading program in which phonics is not emphasized.

Common illnesses of childhood are unlikely to interfere with reading unless no provisions are made to make up for skills taught during periods of absence. Certain chronic conditions that lower general vitality and energy, such as rheumatic fever and malnutrition, and certain endocrine disturbances, may interfere with efficient learning in general. There is no direct cause-effect relationship between poor muscular coordination and reading disability, although both may be indicative of an underlying neurological problem.

Brain functioning is very important in reading. When the quality of brain functioning is generally poor, the child is mentally retarded and learning to read is delayed and slow. When only part of the brain functions poorly, as may happen from brain injury at birth, from a head injury, or occasionally from a feverish disease such as scarlet fever, some functions may develop normally while others are severely affected. There also seem to be cases of children whose brains do not develop at an even rate; parts of the brain are delayed and irregular in their maturation. Such children are likely to have difficulty in learning to read (see Harris and Sipay 1975, pp. 262–69).

Social and Cultural Factors

The progress that children make in reading is related to home and neighborhood conditions as well as to schooling and the child's abilities. If the parents have had good educations, enjoy reading, have many books in the home, read to their children and tell them stories, take them on trips and vacations, and encourage them to watch TV programs of educational value, it is easy for their children to become good readers. Such parents help their children develop linguistic skills and the background of concepts and ideas on which good reading skills can be built. They encourage children to read by providing adult reading models and by expressing interest in the child's reading. They keep watch over the child's progress and confer with the teacher if difficulties arise.

Many children come from homes in which the parents can do little to help with schoolwork. Some parents have had insufficient education themselves. Other parents, whose educational experiences were unsatisfying and whose work demands little or no education, may place only slight importance on education in general and reading in particular. Many parents have high aspirations for their children, but they do not understand what they can do to assist in the child's education.

Neighborhood conditions are also important. The attitudes of the child's peer group toward schooling may be even more important than the attitudes of parents. Success in school may be incompatible with acceptability as a member of a gang.

Child Development

The development of children from infancy to maturity is generally gradual and progressive. Practically all abilities show continuous progress, although not necessarily at uniform rates. At any school age there are wide differences among children in every ability. Many have abilities that develop at similar rates, while a few show quite uneven growth patterns.

Maturation and learning are intimately interwoven. *Maturation* refers to aspects of development that are part of the organism's biological makeup and that take place inevitably if the environment is reasonably suitable. *Learning* means change in the individual as a result of experience. Without maturation, the child cannot learn; without experiences, the child has nothing to learn.

Professionals disagree about the relative importance of maturation and learning for education. Those who stress maturation tend to believe that what, when, and how a child learns depends primarily on his or her own growth characteristics and therefore stress the importance of adapting school practices and experiences to the growth rate of each child. They suggest waiting until the child shows "readiness" to learn and then allowing the child to set the pace of learning.

Those who stress learning regard children as adjustable creatures whose outstanding characteristic is their ability to profit from experience. They believe that an apparent lack of readiness to learn often is due either to a lack of motivation or to the school's failure to devise an optimal learning situation. Believing that such difficulties can be overcome, they advocate building readiness for learning rather than waiting for it to unfold.

Neither maturation nor learning should be stressed to the exclusion of the other. Excessive reliance on maturation may lead to unnecessary delays in instruction resulting from mistaken notions of a child's not yet being ready to learn. Ignoring maturation leads to ignoring marked differences in ability to learn and striving in vain for uniform achievement. A uniform standard puts undesirable pressure on the slow and stifles the able learner.

DESCRIPTION, MODELS, AND A DEFINITION OF READING

Reading is a very complex activity, and despite nearly a century of experimental study and theorizing, we are still far from fully understanding it. Differing viewpoints about the nature of reading have led to a wide variety of teaching programs. This section first describes the reading process, then summarizes some of the many models that attempt to explain how and why reading takes place, and finally offers a definition of reading.

The Reading Process

Sensation   The reading process starts with the focusing of the two eyes so that both center on particular marks on a contrasting background, usually black on white. Light reflected into the eyes from the page forms patterns of light and dark on the retina and produces chemical changes, which in turn induce patterns of electrochemical changes in thousands of fibers in the optic nerves. These patterns are conveyed to the brain, and the person is aware of seeing something. For this process to be reasonably efficient the print must be clear and of adequate size, the light sufficient, and the eyes able to focus clear patterns on the retina. During reading the eyes progress in a series of alternating pauses (fixations) and quick, jerky, sidewise movements (saccadic movements). The eyes see the print only when motionless during the fixations.

Perception   Sensation is merely awareness that something is there; perception involves meaningful interpretation of what is sensed. When a pattern of nerve impulses reaches the brain from the optic nerve, the pattern is somehow compared with the memory traces of similar patterns.

For example, a young boy has had many experiences that have helped him form his concept of an orange—experiences of taste, feel, color, size, weight, what it is like to peel one, etc. He has also learned to associate the verbal label *orange* with this collection of meanings called a concept and traces representing both the concept and its verbal label are stored in his memory. When the boy learns to recognize the printed word *orange*, memory traces of its visual form become linked or associated with the traces of both the verbal label and the concept it represents. When he sees the printed word again, and its pattern matches the memory trace of its form, the traces of the spoken word and its concept are aroused. The child says or thinks the oral word and is aware of its meaning. This combination of seeing and recognizing meanings is called perception.

Comprehension   Reading involves a series of perceptions taking place in rapid succession. Recognizing a triangle is perceiving it, and recognizing the printed word *dog* is perceiving it. But perceiving *dog* is reading when *dog* is part of a sequence of words used by a writer to express an idea, and the reader is trying to re-create that idea. Reading comprehension involves the use of one's knowledge of syntax and semantics to extract meaning from a series of sequential perceptions of words.

Success in re-creating the author's intended meaning depends partly on the degree to which the reader's concepts match those of the writer, and the syntactic patterns in the material are familiar. It also depends on the degree to which the author has supplied enough cues to minimize uncertainty about the intended meaning. The sentence "The dog jumped on me" is ambiguous. What kind of dog? Jumped with what kind of intention? We can amend that sentence to supply enough detail so that the meaning is far clearer: "The spotted hound, tongue lolling and tail wagging furiously, jumped on me and tried to lick my face."

The incomplete pattern of ideas provided by the first few words builds expectations of what is to come. If these expectations turn out to be correct, word recognition is aided; if incorrect, the reader is likely to misread a word or two before realizing that something is wrong and have to reread to get back on the track. Concepts represented by single words fit together in units of increasing size and complexity: phrase, clause, sentence, paragraph, whole selection.

Reaction   Readers react physically and emotionally as well as intellectually. When printed words are first learned, a young child tends to say them aloud. If encouraged to read silently, the child is likely to make observable lip movements without audible sound. At this stage the child can hardly "think" of a word's meaning without going through the motions of saying it, and hearing it inwardly. Gradually the child becomes able to think the word with less and less motor accompaniment. Tiny changes in the muscles of the throat and larynx accompany the imagery of hearing the word as if spoken by an inner voice. This kind of reading is called *subvocal* reading, since it is silent but involves some minimal traces of the movements of speaking. Most people continue to read subvocally all their lives. Only a few very superior readers achieve truly silent reading with no accompanying changes in the speech muscles, and even they resort to subvocal reading for difficult material.

Other types of muscular activity are also involved in reading. Usually the reader is physically quiet, and the main muscular response is moving the eyes to the next fixation point. Sometimes reading involves greater muscular activity, however. For example, an experienced driver who sees a STOP sign reaches for the brake automatically, sometimes before being aware of thinking "Stop." Some readers actually feel themselves performing the acts of characters with whom they identify, and an observer can see twitchings and changes of posture that are tiny representations of those actions.

Other combined emotional-physical reactions may be going on as well. When the book's hero is threatened with imminent danger the reader's pulse may quicken, breathing may become more rapid, and tension and some anxiety or apprehension may arise. When the hero triumphs the reader may feel relief, gratification, and a relaxation of tension. Feelings and emotions and their physical accompaniments are important parts of the reader's reaction.

Another type of reaction in reading is reacting evaluatively or critically to the ideas one reads. As we read we may stop to think about the ideas, or wait until we have finished reading. More commonly we have a running commentary as we read along, making such comments to ourselves as, "Cleverly put!" "That's really important." "A really funny line." "Rubbish!" We accept and reject, praise and criticize, delight in or are made furious by what we read.

Reading and Learning Reading provides a substitute for experience. Through reading, new words and ideas are learned; concepts are enlarged, refined, and clarified; information is digested and combined with what was known before; feelings of many kinds are intensified, weakened, or changed.

Reading is a way of learning, changing, and developing. Reading can enrich and ennoble; it can also delude and debase. The act of reading is itself neutral, but the ideas and feelings aroused while reading become part of the person's total background of experience; they become integrated with the traces of all related previous experiences. Reading allows individuals to learn from the experience of others and permits human knowledge to become cumulative.

Models of the Reading Process

In recent years there has been much interest in the development of theoretical models of reading. A model, in this sense, is "a tentative ideational structure used as a testing device" (*American Heritage Dictionary*).

The description of reading given above is a summary of the descriptive model of reading developed by W. S. Gray (1960). It attempts to describe, but does not attempt to provide a theoretical explanation of, what goes on in each of the various steps. More recent model makers attempt both a more detailed step-by-step analysis of the process and a theoretical explanation of the process.

Models differ according to the theoretical presuppositions of their makers. An important characteristic of a good model is that it leads to the formulation of specific hypotheses that can be tested experimentally. If the experiment does not come out as the model would predict, the model must be modified to take account of the new data. In this way a model can be improved and refined over a period of years.

Models may attempt to be comprehensive, accounting for all phases of reading. But most models are partial, restricted to mature reading or beginning reading, the perceptual or the conceptual aspects of reading, oral reading or silent, and so forth.

Most recent models of reading have been developed by psychologists, by linguists, or by psycholinguists. Out of the many models that have been developed in recent years, three are described in this section. Any summary of complex and difficult conceptions can be no more than adequate, so for full understanding it is necessary to study the model as presented by its originator.

Reading as Decoding   A number of writers of differing backgrounds have arrived at the common conclusion that reading is essentially the translation or decoding of graphic symbols into their speech equivalents. Adherents of this theory include psychologists like Staats (1968) and Gagné (1970), linguists such as Fries (1963) and Reed (1965), professors of English literature (Walcutt 1961), and neurologists (Crosby and Linton 1968). These writers agree that the task of the beginning reader is to translate or decode printed words into their corresponding spoken words. Comprehension is considered irrelevant for the beginning reader, who can therefore be started with single words or with word parts. Advocates of the "reading as decoding" type of model generally pay little attention to the development of higher-level reading skills and concentrate almost exclusively on decoding during beginning reading.

Such writers tend to agree on beginning instruction with word elements and words, paying little attention to meaning until substantial progress in decoding has been achieved. Nearly all would start with teaching young children to discriminate letter forms from one another, and then to asso-

ciate the form of the letter with its name or sound or both. There is disagreement among them on the relative merits of starting with letter name,
with phoneme, or both.

There is also disagreement on whether to abstract phoneme-grapheme
rules or generalizations from whole words, or to start with single-letter
phoneme-grapheme associations and then put them together (or blend
them) to produce the word. Most linguists object to the letter-by-letter
sounding and blending approach on the grounds that it involves gross distortion of the phonemes, since the phoneme in a word is quite different
from the phoneme one produces when trying to say it by itself. These linguists tend to begin with short, regular words of the consonant-vowel-
consonant pattern that contain a consistent letter-sound relationship (such
as *ban, can, man, tan*) enabling each child to develop his or her own generalization. On the other hand, letter-by-letter sounding and blending has
its advocates. Some of them take an extremely oversimplified stand, such
as the journalist Flesch (1955), who wrote: "Teach the child what each
letter stands for and he can read." Other, more sophisticated versions
attempt to detail a sequence of steps to be taught in series, going systematically from the simplest level to quite complex skills (Gagné 1970).

Reading as a Cognitive Activity   The viewpoint of cognitive psychologists is
represented by E. Gibson (1970), who considers reading to be the extraction of information from text. Learning to communicate by spoken language is a prerequisite for reading. Once a child begins the progression
from spoken to written language, three phases of learning present three
different kinds of learning tasks; and although they are roughly sequential,
there is considerable overlapping: (1) learning to differentiate graphic
symbols from one another; (2) learning letter-sound relationships; and
(3) using progressively higher-order units of structure.

Differentiation of written characters is logically preliminary to developing grapheme-phoneme relationships. Such differentiations are made on the
basis of distinctive features, which are usually pairs of opposites such as tall
versus short lines, straight versus curved lines, diagonals versus perpendic-
ulars, and so on.

When the letters can be distinguished from one another the decoding
process can begin. In addition to grapheme-phoneme correspondences for
single letters, there are important linguistic units consisting of combinations of letters that have consistent pronunciations, like *-tion*, and there

are complex linguistic rules that govern the phonemic equivalent of letters (extr*e*me, extr*e*mity). Many letter-sound correspondences are variable rather than constant. A "set for diversity" (not expecting a consistent one-to-one correspondence between letters and sounds), which can be developed by using both words that have constant letter-sound relationships and words that do not, may make it easier to decode words in which there are alternative possible phonemes for the graphemes (h*ear*, h*ear*t, p*ear*).

The third phase involves learning rules or principles of unit formation. The child becomes able to organize the information available and to read in larger, more efficient units. Gibson notes three kinds of structural principles in written text: (1) rules of correspondence between the phonological and graphological systems; (2) rules of orthography, or how sounds are represented by spellings; and (3) grammatical principles, which restrict the number of possibilities (e.g., in "Alice _____ the apple" the missing word must be a verb, and the number of words that make sense in the sentence is limited).

Recently Gibson has taken the view that there is no single reading process and therefore no single model for reading, and there is more than one good way to teach these processes (Gibson and Levin 1975). Rather than construct many different models, Gibson and Levin state general principles about the skilled reading process that apply in many reading situations and at different levels of proficiency.

1. Reading is an adaptive process that is active and flexible, the processing strategies changing to meet the demands of the text and the purpose of the reader.
2. There is a trend toward increasing economy in the mature reader.
    a. The reader tends to process textual material in the most economical way that he can, by:
        (1) selecting relevant information;
        (2) ignoring irrelevant information;
        (3) processing the largest units that are appropriate for the task;
        (4) processing the least amount of information needed.
    b. Efficient, adaptive reading is characterized by the reduction of information necessary to process the text.
        (1) The fewer the number of alternatives that could follow in the ensuing information as the reader proceeds, the less processing is needed.

(2) Alternatives are reduced by the application of rules and constraints, in the text as well as in the language. For example, in the sentence, "He will lead the horse," *lead* has to be a verb.

(3) Alternatives are reduced by using information already available, both possessed by the reader and already gained from the text, to comprehend new information. (Gibson and Levin 1975, pp. 474–80)

Reading as a Guessing Game   K. Goodman (1976b), who has been greatly influenced by transformational-generative linguistic theory, considers reading to be a psycholinguistic guessing game; that is, reading is a selective process that involves use of available minimal language cues selected from perceptual input on the basis of the reader's expectations. As this partial information is processed, tentative decisions about meaning are made to be confirmed, rejected, or refined as reading progresses. There is an intimate interaction between thought and language. Efficient reading results from skill in selecting the fewest, most productive cues necessary to produce guesses that are right the first time, rather than precise perception and identification of all elements.

According to Goodman, the reader uses only as much information as necessary to get to the meaning and that information is of three types: graphic, syntactic, and semantic. The graphic information is gained visually, the other two are supplied by the reader. Using previously acquired knowledge of language structure, the reader makes predictions of the grammatical (syntactic) structure and supplies concepts that fit into the structure. In turn, the syntactic structure and meaning allow the reader to predict what the graphic input will be. There is no need to notice every letter or even read every word; the reader can be highly selective, sampling the print to confirm or modify predictions. Readers use less graphic input as they become more proficient because they have more control over language structure, a better and more complete store of concepts, and better sampling skills.

The skilled reader decodes from the graphic stimuli directly into deep structure (meaning), not first to speech. In oral reading, he then encodes the meaning into speech (surface structure). Since comprehension is the main goal of reading, the skilled reader's oral reading may contain transformations in vocabulary and syntax that do not change the meaning. Such a reader may make miscues (observed responses that do not match expected responses) without altering comprehension. An analysis of miscues allows one to understand the reading process at work and may serve as a basis for planning instructional needs (K. Goodman 1973, 1976a).

The skilled reader's predictions are tested by asking if the reader's miscues are consistent with the syntactic structure and make sense in the sentence. Readers develop (1) sampling strategies to select the most useful and necessary graphic cues; (2) prediction strategies to get to the deep structure of meaning and to anticipate what will probably occur in print; (3) confirmation strategies to check the validity of their predictions; and (4) correction strategies to use when predictions are inaccurate, and additional graphic, syntactic, or semantic cues must be processed in order to get to the correct meaning.

Goodman (1976a, pp. 22, 23) has listed some of the implications of his model for the teaching of reading, as follows:

1. Where should reading instruction begin? Not with letters or sounds but with whole real relevant natural language we think.
2. What is the hierarchy of skills that should be taught in reading instruction? We think there is none. In fact, in learning to read as in learning to talk, one must use all skills at the same time.
3. Why do some people fail to learn to read? Not because of their weaknesses but because we've failed to build on their strengths as competent language users.
4. What should we do for deficient readers? Build their confidence in their ability to predict meaning and language.
5. Can anyone learn to read? Yes, we say. Anyone who can learn oral language can learn to read and write.

It may be noted that Goodman's analysis becomes relevant only after a reader has acquired at least beginning skills in word recognition. Goodman does not discuss the way in which the beginning reader becomes able to recognize words. He concedes that an alphabetical system is economical and convenient, but leaves it to others to attempt to explain how the reader becomes able to process graphic cues.

Other Models of Reading   Numerous other models attempt to explain reading. The interested reader will find good introductions to this field in the *Reading Research Quarterly,* Summer 1972 and Winter 1973 issues, and in Singer and Ruddell (1976). Among the most informative summaries are those of Williams (1973), J. F. Mackworth (1972), and Geyer (1972). Since these writers provide brief summaries of the ideas of many other writers and researchers, and since many of the concepts involved are abstract and unfamiliar, they require very careful reading.

A Definition of Reading

For the purpose of this book, *reading may be defined as the attaining of meaning as a result of the interplay between perceptions of graphic symbols that represent language, and the memory traces of the reader's past verbal and nonverbal experiences.* Reading is an active process in which the reader is trying to "make sense" of the written or printed message; reading is not a basically passive, receptive process. It is a grave error to define reading as word recognition, considering comprehension to be a general function of language; the meanings the reader finds guide anticipations of what is to come, and these anticipations influence perceptions of the words to come.

For beginning readers, speech often serves as a mediator between visual perception and meaning. They have to pronounce the words aloud in order to call up their meanings. Speech soon lessens in importance. Silent reading without obvious lip movements is usually achieved by the third grade, and the expert reader may be able to go from print to meaning with only the slightest traces of either the movements of speaking or the auditory images of hearing the language of the text.

The nature of reading varies not only with the skill of the reader but also with the reader's purposes and the characteristics of the text. Reading is a very complex activity that involves almost all psychological processes including sensation, perception, motor behavior, motivation, attention, emotion, cognition, and all kinds of memory. Since these psychological functions are far from perfectly understood, a true understanding of the reading process must await the further development of psychological and linguistic knowledge.

OBJECTIVES OF READING INSTRUCTION

To a large extent, our aims determine our achievements. Ill-defined goals result in vague results. This is especially true of reading instruction. In response to the question "What is the goal of your reading program?" some teachers would reply, "To teach every child to read." While well-intentioned, such a goal is too general to be useful. If asked to be more specific, they might add, "To teach the children to comprehend." To which one might respond, "Comprehend what and how?" The point is simple: if you don't know specifically where you are headed, you get there only by accident. Moreover, objectives should guide the choice of procedures and materials. Teachers can achieve the same planned objectives by different means; but without the same objectives, similar outcomes occur only by chance.

Some teachers slavishly follow a manual, without thinking about the meaning or purpose of the stated objectives or suggested procedures. When questioned about such practices, they respond that these are the objectives and procedures of the published program in use. Who are they to question the experts? This nonquestioning attitude has marked the teaching profession for too long. Intelligent teachers should not blindly accept a "cookbook recipe" approach to teaching reading. Once the decision is made as to a definition of reading, a program that is consistent with the tenets of that underlying philosophy should be developed or selected. Regardless of what materials and manuals are employed, teachers need to understand *why* something is suggested. Such understanding helps teachers decide whether or not the objectives or suggested procedures are needed by their pupils.

No one published reading series can or should serve as the total reading program. A total elementary school reading program should have three broad strands. In *developmental reading*, the primary general aim is learning to read; that is, to develop and to improve reading skills. It is in this strand that published reading series serve their primary purpose. *Functional reading* is concerned with the use of reading as an efficient tool of learning; that is, reading to learn. It is sometimes referred to as work-type reading or study skills. *Recreational reading* involves the development of interest in reading as a voluntary enjoyable activity, and with raising and refining reading taste and appreciation.

Emphasis on specific objectives should change as children's skills increase, but a balance among these three strands should be maintained throughout the elementary school.

Nearly all beginning reading instruction is developmental in nature. As children become better able to read independently, recreational reading becomes increasingly significant. Functional reading increases as the need to acquire information through reading grows as the reader advances in grade, so that by the intermediate grades it assumes greater instructional time than developmental reading. Decisions about the weight given to different objectives should be influenced by the needs and abilities of a particular group or child.

Whenever possible, reading activities should be planned to satisfy more than one objective. For example, in selecting material for developing specific skills one seeks enjoyable stories or interesting factual selections that suit the purpose.

Teachers need to understand the goals of a total reading program. Each of the broad purposes needs to be made clearer by developing it in detail, and these detailed objectives are made specific in planning lessons. The following is a somewhat more detailed statement of major goals within each of the three general strands of the reading program. These are stated in terms of what the learner should be able to do after relevant instruction.

I. Developmental Reading
    A. Basic or facilitating skills. The learner:
        1. Recognizes many words at sight
        2. Flexibly employs a variety of skills to recognize or to decode unknown words
        3. Reads silently with speed and fluency
        4. Reads orally with proper phrasing, expression, pitch, volume, and enunciation
    B. Reading comprehension
        1. Vocabulary. The learner:
            a. Demonstrates an extensive and accurate reading vocabulary
            b. Uses context effectively in order to
                (1) determine the meaning of an unfamiliar word
                (2) choose among alternate meanings of a word
            c. Interprets figurative and nonliteral language such as metaphors, similes, and figures of speech
        2. Literal comprehension. The learner:
            a. Grasps the meaning of increasingly larger units: phrase, clause, sentence, paragraph
            b. Selects, understands, and recalls main ideas
            c. Notes and recalls significant details
            d. Finds answers to specific questions

       e. Follows written directions accurately

       f. Recognizes or reproduces a series of events in correct sequence

    3. Inferential comprehension. The learner:

       a. Makes appropriate inferences ("reads between the lines")

       b. Anticipates and predicts outcomes

       c. Notes and explains cause-effect relationships

       d. Grasps the author's plan and intent

       e. Identifies the techniques that authors employ to create desired effects

       f. Critically evaluates what is read

       g. Extrapolates from what is read to reach new ideas and conclusions ("creative reading")

II. Functional Reading

    A. Locates needed reading material. The learner:

      1. Uses indexes

      2. Uses tables of contents

      3. Uses dictionaries

      4. Uses encyclopedias

      5. Uses other bibliographic aids

      6. Skims for information

    B. Comprehends informational material. The learner:

      1. Interprets technical and specific vocabulary correctly

      2. Applies the general comprehension skills listed above

      3. Uses the specific skills required by special subject matter, e.g.,

        a. Reading arithmetic problems

        b. Reading maps, charts, and graphs

        c. Conducting a science experiment according to printed directions

      4. Interprets headings, subheadings, marginal notes, and other study aids

      5. Reads content subject materials independently

    C. Selects the needed materials

    D. Records and organizes what is read. The learner:

      1. Takes careful notes

      2. Summarizes

      3. Outlines

    E. Displays appropriate study habits and skills

III. Recreational Reading
  A. Displays an interest in reading. The learner:
    1. Enjoys reading as a voluntary leisure-time activity
    2. Satisfies interests and needs through reading
    3. Selects material appropriate to personal interests and needs
  B. Improves and refines reading interests. The learner:
    1. Reads various types of material on a variety of subjects
    2. Reads materials that reflect mature interests
    3. Achieves personal development through reading
  C. Refines literary judgment and taste. The learner:
    1. Applies different criteria for various literary forms
    2. Appreciates style and beauty of language
    3. Seeks for deeper symbolic meanings

The objectives listed above can be further subdivided into highly specific and detailed objectives. Very specific objectives are commonly known as "behavioral" or "performance" objectives. Although most teachers will already have such objectives stated for them, those who wish to write their own, or to modify existing ones, may refer to such sources as Gronlund (1970).

A behavioral objective usually states (1) the conditions under which a specified behavior will occur (e.g., when shown ten unknown consonant-vowel-consonant three-letter words), (2) the type of behavior that is to occur as a result of instruction (the child will correctly decode); and, (3) the acceptable performance level (at least eight). Behavioral objectives must be stated in terms of learner outcomes (what the child should be able to do) rather than in terms of teacher behavior (what the teacher does with the learner to help him to achieve the desired competence). The latter are process objectives, which identify the means by which the teacher can achieve behavioral objectives.

Use of behavioral objectives follows the sequence (1) stating the objective; (2) pretesting to determine if the objective has already been met and, if not (3) selecting and using appropriate instructional procedures and materials; and (4) posttesting to determine if the criterion for mastery has been met.

A few points need to be made about using behavioral objectives. Behavioral objectives do not easily lend themselves to determining when outcomes in the affective domain have been achieved. It is much easier to determine if a child can select stated main ideas of paragraphs than whether or not feelings or attitudes have been altered. Writers do not agree as to what the objectives should be, nor to what degree each should, or *must*, be mastered. Not all behavioral objectives are equally important. Teachers must decide which objectives are the most necessary for successful reading, and accordingly stress them.

There is little, if any, evidence as to what level of performance indicates mastery. A criterion of 80–90 percent is commonly used, but since not all skills are equally important a uniform standard does not seem appropriate.

Teachers should not blindly adhere to a fixed criterion. If a child cannot meet the criterion after a reasonable time, the teacher must decide how important that skill is and whether or not the criterion is appropriate. Some teachers refuse to allow a child to go on to a new objective until the present one is met, no matter how long it takes. Such rigidity is correct only when the present objective is a necessary prerequisite for the next skill in the program, and even then judgment should be exercised. Certainly the achieving of more than one objective during a given time can be undertaken.

On the other hand, one cannot assume that once a criterion has been met, the skill has been mastered. In one large city in which the results of criterion-referenced tests were computerized, teachers punched out a space next to "stated behavioral objective" when the criterion had been met. Unfortunately, many teachers found that what had been "mastered" on Friday was "unlearned" by Monday; they had to be given kits with which the punched-out holes could be filled in. Such situations indicate the need for spaced review and continuing guided application, and show that meeting the stated criterion on a test does not necessarily demonstrate permanent mastery.

UNIT 2

Reading Readiness: What, Why, and How

Casual observation reveals wide variations among young school-age children in such physical characteristics as height and weight. But closer observation shows differences that are more significant for education in such factors as mental maturity, conceptual development, language facility, and perceptual development. In order to ensure that children will learn to read, and that their early attempts are successful, teachers must not only take into account these individual differences, but also how these factors are related to the methods and materials of instruction. This unit considers the concept of reading readiness, the factors associated with it, how it can be measured, and how readiness can be facilitated.

WHAT IS READING READINESS?

The concept of reading readiness, and the practices associated with it, began in the United States in the late 1920s when it was determined that 20 to 40 percent of first graders were not being promoted because they had not learned to read. Among the reasons uncovered for these failures was the idea that many young children were being forced into learning situations for which they simply were not yet ready. Thus reading readiness programs came into being for the purpose of preparing children for learning to read, thereby lessening the likelihood of failure in first grade.

But as often happens with educationally sound concepts, reading readiness practices themselves became rigid. Most children were given the same "readiness program" regardless of need. Such poor practices led to criticisms of the concept of reading readiness or outright suggestions to abandon it. We believe the concept is valid, but practices must be improved.

Reading readiness is the state of general development of children that allows them to learn to read without undue difficulty. A reading readiness program comprises the methods and materials used to help children who have not yet attained the needed level of maturity. The purpose of such a program is to help the learner be better prepared for learning to read. In practice, reading readiness is an interaction between the two—what the child brings to the task and what the task demands of him. As MacGinitie (1969) aptly pointed out, rather than asking if a child is ready to learn to read, it would be better to ask what he is ready to learn. To this question should be added, "Does he need to learn this?" and, "If so, what can be done to facilitate this learning?" Answers to such questions are not obtained easily. Arriving at reliable answers is complicated by the complexity of readiness within the child and the lack of agreement as to which skills are central to the development of readiness.

Readiness within the child is composed of a complex of many interrelated factors. Readiness is not an either-or proposition. There are all degrees of readiness, from very high to very low, and there is no magic point that clearly separates the ready from the unready. At present, we do not know what general level of readiness is an absolute minimum for success, let alone can we specify the level of proficiency in any given factor below which success is unlikely. Moreover, different beginning reading programs probably require differing levels of specific skills. Unfortunately, we have not yet progressed to the point where we can state with certainty that if you want a learner with given attributes to learn a given task, you should present certain materials or information in a given way at a predetermined pace. Perhaps we may never be able to do so. But we cannot wait for all the answers before acting. We must use currently available information and do the best we can for each child.

FACTORS ASSOCIATED WITH READING READINESS

Many factors associated with reading readiness also are related to reading ability and to learning in general. This reflects the way in which reading readiness factors have been established. Most commonly, the factors have been identified by determining the extent to which different measurable characteristics of children are related to later success in reading, particularly at the end of first grade. Correlation coefficients with reading scores generally are accepted as a means of estimating the importance of a factor; the higher the r, the more important the contribution of that factor. Correlations do not necessarily indicate a cause-effect relationship, however. When two variables are highly related, one cannot say that one caused the other; or if one did, which was the cause and which the effect. It is also possible that both variables were caused by a third factor. As yet we do not have a very clear understanding of the specific roles and interactions of the various predictors. Nor have our attempts at prediction been especially accurate (MacGinitie 1969).

This section summarizes the available evidence and opinion regarding the factors thought to be important in learning to read. Much of what is stated concerning these factors also applies to later reading achievement, although the relative importance of the factors changes with the learner's age.

Because readiness is a composite of many different kinds of abilities and previous learnings, a child may be advanced in some aspects of readiness, but be average or low in others. All factors are not equally important, and no one factor by itself assures success or failure in beginning reading. It is not necessary for the child to have "adequate" skills in all the factors associated with reading readiness.

How well a child succeeds also depends on the extent to which the instructional program is geared for that child's particular needs. A program's content and pace greatly influence degree of success. Success and enjoyment in the initial stages of learning to read are extremely important. Repeated failure can have a long-lasting effect. Early loss of self-confidence and a feeling that reading is difficult or distasteful can contribute strongly to later reading problems.

Cognitive Factors

General Intelligence   A close relationship between general intelligence and reading ability is to be expected because general intelligence implies comprehension, interpretation, concept learning, problem solving, memory, and reasoning—all abilities important for successful reading (Downing and Thackray 1971).

Mental age (M.A.) is a measure of the level of mental maturity; the intelligence quotient (IQ), a measure of the rate of mental growth. Both are related to reading readiness and reading achievement. M.A. tends to be a slightly better indicator of learning in the near future; IQ the better long-range predictor.

Correlations between intelligence or learning capacity tests and first-grade reading achievement tend to vary with the intelligence tests and reading tests employed, the populations sampled, and the reading programs used. Typical of other findings were the fifteen USOE first-grade reading studies in which the correlations between intelligence scores and first-grade reading ranged from .45 to .56 with a median of .50 (Bond and Dykstra 1967). The size of these correlations indicates that although intelligence is substantially related to learning to read, (1) other factors must also be operative; and (2) the reading achievement of an individual child cannot be predicted with accuracy from an intelligence test score.

A mental age of six years or six and one-half years is *not* a prerequisite for learning to read. This once commonly held belief was based mainly on the Morphett and Washburne study (1931), which had a number of limitations. Even Washburne (1941) did not say that such a mental age was an absolute minimum for success, but rather that it was safer not to try to teach children to read before they reached an M.A. of six. It is impossible to set a definite minimum mental age for reading because so many other factors are involved in learning to read. Reading progress is influenced by instructional reading approaches, pacing of instruction, the appropriateness of the difficulty of the materials and tasks, and the quality of instruction, as well as by pupil abilities. Children with mental ages below six can and do learn to read. But because most American children who fail to learn to read in first grade have mental ages below that point, it is *desirable* (but not essential) for a child to have a mental age of at least six when formal reading instruction is initiated. Adjusting the reading program to individual needs decreases the relative importance of intelligence as a factor for success. That a given mental age is not an absolute prerequisite is illustrated by the fact that in England, where reading instruction is initiated at age five, a mental age of five or five and one-half is considered necessary for success in *traditional* reading methods (Downing and Thackray 1971).

Slow learners [1] can learn to read close to their capacity when appropriate adjustments are made in the reading program. On the other hand, some very bright children have specific handicaps that lower their readiness. Nevertheless, since most first graders in the United States enter school at the age of 5 years 9 months or older and about 75 percent have IQs of 90 or above, most children are intellectually ready for reading when instruction is initiated because they will have attained a mental age of six or over by that time.

Samuels and Dahl (1974) state that we can reduce the correlation between intelligence and achievement by (1) simplifying the learning task; (2) ensuring that prerequisite skills have been mastered; (3) developing motivational procedures to keep the child on the task; and, (4) allowing a sufficient amount of time to master the task. An even stronger stand is taken by K. Goodman (1975, p. 629), who states, "Our success in teaching reading depends not on the basis of their intelligence, but on the basis of how relevant school is and how willing or able they are to learn our way."

Although the nature-nurture argument continues, most educators and psychologists believe that intelligence (and intelligence test scores) are influenced by both heredity and environment. For children raised in an environment that differs markedly from that of the sample upon whom an IQ test was normed, the test may not be a fair measure of either current intellectual functioning or potential for learning. Nevertheless, Lessler and Bridges (1973) found that IQ scores can predict differences in future achievement fairly well within a group of disadvantaged children. Similarly, Henderson et al. (1973) found that performance IQ scores contribute to the prediction of success in reading for black males.

Specific Mental Abilities   Traits such as attention and memory are closely interrelated in most young children and are not clearly distinguishable from general intelligence. Yet it is possible for a child with average or better intelligence to have a specific deficit, such as poor auditory or visual memory, or the inability to concentrate on or attend to the learning task. Such deficits in specific aspects of mental functioning may interfere with progress in learning to read.

1. Teaching reading to slow learners and gifted children is discussed in unit 11.

Attention is a prerequisite for learning, since only what is attended to is learned. Children are bombarded with a tremendous amount of sensory stimulation, auditory, visual, touch, etc., and can attend at one moment to only a small part of this intake. From the array of incoming stimulation the child must focus on one main whole or pattern. The rest is background, hazily perceived and largely ignored. Most of the time we can attend to about four to seven subunits within the whole, pattern, or sequence. This selective attention apparently improves up to early adolescence. We cannot be certain what a child is attending to; at best we infer attention from observed responses. When a child does poorly on a test or task, the low score may indicate lack of the ability or abilities required or may result from the child's poor attention to the task.

General Conceptual Background   A rich conceptual background is helpful in reading because it provides the basis for comprehension and reaction. Conceptual development becomes more important beyond the beginning stages of reading. Beginning reading materials usually employ vocabularies and concepts within the experiences of most six-year-olds. By the time they have reached first grade, or even kindergarten, most of today's children have had real or vicarious experiences from which they have developed general information, ideas, and concepts that are adequate for beginning reading instruction.

But as with most abilities or traits, marked differences in clarity of ideas and grasp of meaning appear as reading instruction proceeds. If important concepts are lacking or inaccurate, it is the teacher's responsibility to help children to develop them. Some concepts should be established prior to teaching reading; others can be developed concurrently with reading instruction. Attention to general conceptual background is particularly important when the children's background is quite different from that of most schoolchildren.

Cognitive Clarity   Downing (1973) has proposed the idea that many children do poorly in beginning reading instruction because they are confused as to what reading is all about. The young child cannot see what a reader does and may misunderstand what reading is and why the reader does it. With proper instruction this cognitive confusion should gradually clear up. If it persists it may remain a major impediment to learning to read.

Specific Concepts   Many words that teachers tend to use freely in beginning reading instruction represent concepts that are not understood, or understood only partially, by many children. One of these is *word*. Downing and Oliver (1973–74) found that many preschool, kindergarten, and first-grade children applied the term *word* to isolated phonemes and syllables as well as to spoken words. Until about age six and one-half, they also tended to confuse phrases, sentences, and some nonverbal sounds with words; after that age such confusions tended to disappear (probably as a result of instruction). A study of auditory and visual language concepts of kindergarten children indicated that such commonly used concepts as *word, letter, sound of the letter, first, last,* and *middle* were not well understood (Hardy, Stennett, and Smythe 1974). By the end of the school year these concepts were well understood. Even first graders have difficulty understanding the meaning of *word* (Kingston, Weaver, and Figa 1972; Holden and MacGinitie 1973). If a first-grade teacher asks: "What word begins with the same sound as *toy* and *to* and ends with *an?*" the child may not be able to understand the question because he does not yet have a correct concept for one or more of the following: *word, begins with, same, sound, ends with.*

Segmentation   The understanding that oral language consists of sentences that are divisible into words, which in turn are divisible into subunits called sounds, is a difficult set of concepts that many children have not developed when they enter school. This set of concepts is called *segmentation*. The idea that "Howdoyuhdo" is a group of four words while "television" is one word is not easy to grasp. Young children can analyze words into syllables fairly easily, have difficulty analyzing sentences into words, and usually are unable to segment spoken words into phonemes (Gibson and Levin 1975). Rosner (1974) has claimed that auditory analysis of phrases into words, words into syllables, and phonemes within word context can be taught to four-year-olds.

MacGinitie (1976, p. 375) states that "we should expect young children to have difficulty conceiving of a meaningful utterance as being analyzable into parts. He may have even greater difficulty analyzing a printed statement than separating a spoken utterance. It is a long way back from this printed representation, through an analysis of it, to a meaningful utterance that he finds difficult to conceive of as analyzable in the first place."

The relation of skill in segmentation to success in learning to read is still only partially explored. It seems probable that skill in segmentation may be more important for some methods of teaching word identification than for other methods. We do not know as yet if training in segmentation as a readiness activity makes it easier for children to learn to read, or if it has a beneficial effect on later reading as compared with the training in word analysis that is embedded in beginning reading instruction.

Perception

Perception is the interpretation of sensory experience. We perceive when we are aware of the melodic pattern of a sequence of notes, identify a shape as belonging to our next-door neighbor, or recognize a delightful odor as that of orange blossoms. Perception is an active process in which the nerve impulses from the sense organ reach the brain, their patterns in space and time are compared with the memory traces of somewhat similar excitations experienced in the past, and the result is the identification of something meaningful.

Visual Perception   There are many aspects of visual perception including the perception of size, shape, relative position, distance, color, and optical illusions. Most of these do not seem relevant to the act of reading.

The *Frostig Development Test of Visual Perception* (Follett)[2] is a widely used test for preschool and primary children that has five subtests: eye-hand coordination, figure-ground, form constancy, position in space, and spatial relations. Most of the stimuli are geometric forms. The total Frostig score has substantial correlations with success in first-grade reading, but recent studies have cast doubt on the value of this test. The diagnostic value of differences among a child's subtest scores is questionable (Mann 1972). Frostig scores are not independent of intelligence, and when differences in intelligence are partialled out, most of the correlations between Frostig subtests and reading drop to near zero (DuBois and Brown 1973).

Correlations between visual perception and reading are *relatively* high for kindergarten and first grade, but decrease steadily with increasing age and grade level. There also is evidence to suggest that many children learn to compensate for perceptual inadequacies as they mature (Chester 1974). Therefore, visual perception would seem to be more important during the initial stages of reading than later.

---

2. The full names and addresses of all publishers mentioned in this book can be found in Appendix A.

Visual Discrimination Most of the visual perception tests that are used in the measurement of reading readiness are tests of visual discrimination—the ability to detect similarities and differences among visual forms that are somewhat alike.

A child may have adequate visual acuity, that is, be able to see clearly, but be weak in visual discrimination. Many young children do not pay much attention to the details of visual stimuli and have difficulty noting the similarities and differences between and among printed symbols. Visual discrimination is important in reading readiness because it is hard to recognize a word like *house* if there is difficulty differentiating it from other printed words of different length or configuration (*he, happy*), or words that more closely resemble it (*mouse, horse*). Some children tend to rely on the initial letter(s) of a word and ignore the rest of it. Even kindergarten children do not appear to match words only on the basis of single letters, however, although initial and final letters are more likely to be matched correctly (Calfee, Chapman, and Venezky 1970). Also there is a tendency to make reversal errors because many young children are not yet sensitive to directional orientation. Reversals may involve letters, (*b-d*) or words (*saw-was*). Such errors are more likely to occur when the stimuli are presented in isolation than when set in context that provides additional cues. Although first-grade children with marked reversal tendencies make less than normal progress in reading (Jansky and de Hirsch 1972), most of these children overcome the problem in first or second grade. For those who need it, instructional emphasis on left-to-right direction helps.

Based on a review of the literature, Barrett (1965) concluded that visual discrimination of letters and words has a somewhat higher relationship to first-grade reading than discrimination of geometric forms and pictures, but that several tests using the latter had predictive validity that warranted additional study. Most of the recent tests of visual discrimination require matching of letters and of words.

The majority of kindergarten children could discriminate visually one letter from another even when the items were selected as difficult based on feature analysis and common reversal tendencies; however, word matching was more difficult for them (Calfee, Chapman, and Venezky 1970). Paradis (1974) found that many middle-class preschoolers and most kindergarteners could successfully perform visual discrimination tasks drawn from the reading readiness materials of seven widely used reading series. He also found that pre-first graders had little difficulty visually discriminating pictures and letters, but did find words more difficult. Visual discrimination of words improves up to the third grade, but little thereafter (Mackworth and Mackworth 1974).

Visual-Motor Ability   The ability to copy or reproduce visual forms involves both visual discrimination and fine motor coordination in the handling of pencil or crayon. Tests of visual-motor skill show moderate correlations with success in beginning reading and are not highly correlated with visual discrimination tests.

The *Bender Visual-Motor Gestalt Test* (Psychological) has been the subject of much research in relation to beginning reading. This test is administered to one child at a time, by a trained person who is usually a psychologist. A series of irregular designs involving straight and curved lines, open and closed figures, dots, and little circles is presented to the child one at a time. The child is asked to copy them. The Bender test score tends to improve during the primary grades. When the test has been administered before reading instruction begins, it has moderate correlations (about .40 to .50) with success in beginning reading. Only when Bender performance is very poor can later reading performance be predicted with some confidence (Keogh and Becher 1973).

Group-administered tests of visual-motor ability are included in several currently used reading readiness tests. These subtests, which all require the copying of progressively more complex visual forms, have correlations with later success in reading comparable to those of the Bender. It may be that visual-motor ability will turn out to be more predictive of handwriting ability than of reading ability.

Visual Memory   Visual memory primarily involves the recall of visually presented stimuli. Logically, it should be related to reading achievement because children must remember printed letters and words. The limited research regarding its relationship to reading readiness and beginning reading, however, is far from conclusive. For example, although Benenson (1974) found that a specific visual memory test had little predictive utility, Whisler's study (1974) indicated that visual memory training resulted in significant improvement in visual discrimination and reading ability.

Auditory Perception   There are many aspects of auditory perception. In music, for example, one should be able to distinguish higher from lower notes; louder from softer notes; time intervals of various lengths; and patterns of rhythm, melody, and harmony. Those aspects of auditory perception that would seem relevant to learning to read involve the perception of speech sounds. Two aspects that have attracted much attention are auditory discrimination of words and phonemes, and auditory blending.

The *Wepman Test of Auditory Discrimination* (Language) is an individually administered test in which the child listens to two words and reports if they are alike or different. Some pairs are alike. The difference pairs differ in only one phoneme, as /cat/ or /pat/, /run/ or /rub/, /pet/ or /pat/. There are several other tests of this type. Usually the directions are recorded to provide uniform administration. Group tests of auditory discrimination require children to listen to a word, then listen to three or four other words, and then choose the ones that begin the same as the first word or rhyme with the first word. Most reading readiness tests contain a subtest measuring auditory discrimination.

The *Roswell-Chall Auditory Blending Test* (Essay) presents the child with a word that has been pronounced with pauses between the phonemes, as /p/ . . . /a/ . . . /n/. The child is asked to put the sounds together and say the word. Several other blending tests follow the same principle. Blending and segmentation, which were discussed earlier (see p. 39), would seem to have in common the need for understanding the idea that spoken words are composed of sounds that can be considered separately or put together.

Research has shown that many children who have difficulty learning to read do poorly in auditory discrimination or blending or both, and that these perceptual deficits may last for several years. But when tests of such abilities are given to groups of unselected children and compared to reading scores, the correlations with reading tend to be low. According to Hammill and Larsen (1974), who put together the results of 33 research studies, the median correlation with reading in grades 1–3 was only .29 for auditory discrimination of phonemes and only .31 for sound blending. Such correlations, while a little better than pure chance, indicate that such auditory tests are almost useless for predicting success or failure in learning to read.

Some tests do better than the results combined by Hammill and Larsen. The Roswell-Chall had a median correlation of .47 with reading, according to Hammill and Larsen. The Auditory Discrimination subtest of the *Macmillan Reading Readiness Test* (Macmillan) correlated .65 with the reading scores of 313 first graders (Harris and Sipay 1970). Even when two auditory perception tests seem very much alike they tend to have low correlations with each other, and it makes a difference which of them one uses.

The significance of auditory perception probably varies with the instructional method. Auditory skills seem highly relevant when instruction stresses phonics, and much less relevant when a predominantly visual method is employed. Moreover, if a teacher carefully teaches and reviews the auditory discrimination and blending skills that seem to be needed, children who were originally very low in those skills may do much better than their low scores seemed to indicate.

Many linguists have pointed out that a child who has learned to speak clearly must have adequate auditory discrimination. But *having* the ability is one thing; *applying* it in learning to read is something else. The ability consciously to abstract a beginning phoneme (or ending phoneme, or middle phoneme) from a whole spoken word, and compare it with a phoneme similarly abstracted from another word, goes quite far beyond simple comparison of the sounds of two words. The ability to abstract is a cognitive ability that many young children have not yet developed well by the time they are five or six years old. It is an aspect of cognitive development.

It is usual for speakers of divergent dialects and children for whom English is a second language to do poorly on typical auditory discrimination tests. Some linguists (Baratz 1970, Labov and Cohen 1973) have insisted that such performance is the result of the children's tendency to hear words as they are pronounced in their dialect or native language. So, for example, a speaker of black English may not hear a difference between /pen/ and /pin/ because no differentiation exists between /e/ and /i/ in that dialect; similarly, *whole* and *hold* may be called the same because many final consonants are elided in that dialect. Bryen (1976) found that when linguistically unbiased tests were used, there were no significant differences among white, black, and Puerto Rican children in auditory discrimination.

Knowledge of Letter Names   Most reading readiness tests contain a subtest in which the child listens to the name of an alphabet letter, then locates the letter among several possible choices and marks it. Usually both lowercase and capital letters are tested. Quite consistently, the scores on such tests of letter-name knowledge have had higher correlations with reading scores than other readiness subtests.

It would seem to be a reasonable assumption, therefore, that children would learn to read more easily and quickly if they were taught the identification of letters before they began learning to read. Many current reading programs provide for teaching letter identification during the readiness stage. But several research studies have shown that when one group is systematically taught to name letters before reading and a group of comparable ability is not, the first group does not read better at the end of the first grade (R. J. Johnson 1970, Samuels 1971).

This apparently paradoxical result can be explained. The readiness test, given before instruction, shows the result of spontaneous or incidental learning in advance of systematic instruction. The child who does well must already have reached a satisfactory level of development in such abilities as visual discrimination of letter forms, auditory discrimination of letter names, interest in learning, and associative learning. Nearly all first graders can learn to name letters if given enough time and patient instruction. The presence or absence of spontaneous learning is predictive, but it does not seem to matter whether systematic instruction in letter names is given before or during beginning reading instruction.

Language Readiness

The development of language in children has been discussed in unit 1 and is briefly summarized here. Receptive and expressive language abilities provide a basis for reading ability. The beginning reader interprets writing or print by saying or thinking a meaningful utterance, which may or may not match exactly the words on the page. Linguists inform us that most children entering first grade have mastered most of spoken English and are linguistically competent to learn to read.

The most significant aspects of language development for reading readiness are understanding of word meanings (lexical meaning) and maturity of sentence structure (syntax). Since the vocabulary of beginning reading materials is restricted to a few hundred words, while most first graders already understand the meanings of at least 2,000 words, a limited meaningful vocabulary is not usually a handicap in beginning reading. Sentence structure is more likely than vocabulary to be a handicap in learning to read. The more immature the child's understanding and use of syntactical patterns, and the greater the difference between his or her own oral language patterns and the kinds of sentences used in the reading materials, the more likely the possibility of some interference with learning to read.

Language and cognitive development are interdependent, and most thinking seems to take place in the form of inner speech. There is, therefore, a strong relationship between language development and the child's intellectual development. When a child's oral language is retarded, and the child has had normal opportunities to learn language, this may be one aspect of generally slow mental growth. If intelligence is normal, one may suspect a hearing deficiency or a neurological problem. Such handicaps can occur in children who speak a divergent dialect as well as in children who speak standard English.

Apparently many children who speak a divergent dialect can understand standard English quite well. But sometimes there is such a marked difference between the spoken language of their culture and that of the teacher that it almost seems as though the teacher is speaking a foreign language. Such actually is the case with children whose first or only language is not English. If children cannot express their ideas in words and sentences understood by the teacher, or cannot understand the teacher's language, communication and learning are severely limited.

Attitudes and feelings are also involved. If the teacher regards the child's dialect as a defective and inferior version of standard English rather than as a separate dialect that the child is using correctly, the child's willingness to speak in the classroom may be severely inhibited and he or she may develop negative attitudes toward school in general.

Speech. Indistinct speech and other impediments such as lisping or stuttering may be related to some problems in learning to read. However, reading instruction need not be delayed or avoided. The reading program can be planned with the speech therapist. "Mispronunciations" caused by the speech problem should be accepted by the teacher, oral reading in the presence of other children kept to a minimum, and teaching of symbol-sound association involving speech sounds with which the child has difficulty delayed. Retarded speech development in children of at least average intelligence usually is caused by defective hearing or a neurological problem. The question of whether speech impediments are significantly related to reading disability has not been answered to everyone's satisfaction (R. J. Smith 1974a).

Physical and Physiological Factors

Conflicting conclusions have been drawn regarding the relationships between physiological factors and reading ability. Among the possible explanations for such a situation are: (1) physiological factors have little to do with the process of learning to read; (2) the research studies have lacked rigor; and (3) the reviewers' biases may have entered into their interpretations of the findings (R. J. Smith 1974a). A discussion of a number of possible physical and physiological factors follows.

Chronological Age   In itself, chronological age is not an important factor in readiness. It is of significance, however, because of rapid developmental changes that usually occur at this age level. Older children tend to be more advanced in readiness than younger children, not simply because they are older, but because they usually have learned more and attained a higher level of general development. Reading instruction typically is initiated at age five in England, six in the United States, and seven in Sweden. Yet no matter at what age instruction is begun, there are wide ranges in readiness and in reading achievement by year's end. Chronological age is a convenient but inaccurate indicator of reading readiness. Other variables play a more important role.

In many communities the minimum age for entering first grade is 5 years 9 months in September, so that there is an age range of almost a year. The oldest child is about 15 percent older than the youngest, and has had that much more time for developing and learning. While some younger children are more advanced than some older children, the youngest first graders are usually among the less mature when the school year begins. Some of them will develop at a faster than average rate and will be among the more advanced by the end of the year; others will remain comparatively immature.

Sex Differences   Because girls on the average mature physiologically faster than boys, develop language facility earlier, and often spend more time in sedentary activities, it is commonly believed that they are ready to learn to read sooner than boys. At least one of these bases has been challenged— sex differences in language. Older studies that showed female superiority considered only speech development; more recent studies make the theoretical distinction between speech and language competence. When phonological, syntactical, and semantic development are considered, the question of sex differences in language development remains an open one (Cherry 1975).

Sex differences on measures of reading readiness tend to be small and do not always favor girls. But primary-grade girls tend to score higher on reading achievement tests, and fewer girls than boys need remedial reading. Among the hypotheses offered for the superior reading achievement of girls are: (1) early reading materials are geared more to girls' interests;

(2) almost all primary-grade teachers are women, who have a better understanding of girls, who may be less tolerant toward boys' behaviors, and to whom it is easier for girls to relate; and (3) boys are less motivated to learn to read in certain subcultures where reading is not considered a masculine activity.

Perhaps as Kolczynski (1974) suggests, the most reasonable hypothesis to account for sex differences in reading involves an interaction of biological and cultural factors. There is evidence that such differences are more likely related to cultural influences (D. Johnson 1973–74) or sex-role expectations (Dwyer 1973, 1974) than to biological factors.

But the whole controversy may be irrelevant for actual classroom practice. Regardless of whether mean differences favor girls or boys, the range of individual differences within each sex in any readiness factor or reading skill is far greater than average differences between the sexes. Some boys are more ready to learn to read than some girls, and vice versa. The child should be treated as an individual, not as a "boy" or a "girl."

Neurological Factors   Although it is probable that neurological dysfunctioning or immaturity may cause some cases of unreadiness or reading disability, the appearance of such problems in the typical classroom is rare. Crossed dominance (the preferred hand and eye on opposite sides) is not significantly related to reading (Robbins 1966; Stephens, Cunningham, and Stigler 1967). But, directional confusion (shown by inability to identify left and right) and delay in establishing a consistent hand preference are related to reading (A. J. Harris 1957, Cohen and Glass 1968, Clark 1970). Of course, such relationships are not necessarily of a cause-effect nature. Yet knowledge of them provides some useful information for teachers. Learning the left-to-right sequence needed for reading is easiest for consistently right-handed children, a little harder for the definitely left-handed, and hardest for those who have not developed a preferred hand. Children who have difficulty distinguishing left from right and in following the correct directional sequence of our writing system are more likely to have persistent reversal difficulties.

The kinds of neurological immaturity or damage that produce delay in reading readiness cannot be diagnosed by teachers. A neurological problem can be suspected, however, if a six-year-old has difficulty with tasks requiring finger dexterity (e.g., tying shoes, cutting with scissors), cannot copy a drawing of a square, has not established a dominant hand, is generally clumsy, seems unable to learn left-to-right directional sequencing or scanning, is overactive, and has a very short attention span. No one of these symptoms alone indicates a neurological deviation. When the symptoms are severe, occur in combination, and persist, the child should be referred to a pediatric neurologist.

Sensory   Visual and auditory defects can interfere with perception of written or spoken words, and with learning in general. Early detection is important. Many first graders are far-sighted (hyperopic), so it often is suggested that they should not be given work that requires near-point vision (e.g., reading) for extended time periods. As for other visual defects, it is impossible to state their exact relationship to reading ability. Although some studies have found little or no relationship, others have indicated a relationship between certain types of visual defects and reading difficulties. Furthermore, some children apparently can compensate for visual problems provided they are not too severe and are not accompanied by other problems.

Teachers should be alert to such signs of visual problems as excessive tearing, redness of the eyes, frequent headaches, and comments that the pictures or print look blurred. There is little the classroom teacher can do to overcome most visual difficulties. When a visual problem is suspected, the child should be referred for a thorough visual examination. The Snellen chart test is not adequate for detecting those visual problems that are likely to affect reading ability adversely. Use of large-print books and preferential seating can help the visually impaired child to function in the classroom. The print of most first-grade books is large and clear enough even for most children who have defective visual acuity.

Acoustically impaired children are repeatedly found to be poorer readers as a group. But, as in the case of defective visual acuity, the extent to which partial hearing losses interfere with reading ability varies from child to child. High-frequency hearing losses may create problems in hearing and discriminating among certain consonant sounds and therefore forming letter-sound associations and distinguishing the meanings of some words. Again, the teacher's role is to refer suspected cases for a thorough auditory examination and to assist the child by preferential seating, making certain that oral instructions or directions are understood, and perhaps by using a reading approach that does not place great emphasis on phonics.

Poor auditory acuity or discrimination is suggested by the persistence of infantile speech in first grade. Other possible symptoms of auditory problems include inflamed or running ears, frequent requests to have statements repeated, cupping the hand behind the ears, cocking the head to one side, scowling or other intense effort in listening, a general appearance of dullness, and indistinct speech. A child with an undetected hearing loss is unaware that he or she does not hear as others do; there is no basis for comparison.

Physical Development   Although there is evidence that all aspects of the changing structure and functioning of the developing human organism are somewhat interrelated (R. J. Smith 1974a), there is practically no direct causal relationship between success in reading and such physical factors as height or weight. Therefore, little information can be gained regarding reading readiness from any index of physical maturity that is readily usable by teachers.

General Health   General health affects reading ability indirectly. Frequent or prolonged absences due to illness or physical problems may disrupt learning if no attempts are made to teach the child the important skills that have been missed. A child who is sleepy, tired, or hungry will not be alert for any learning. Any chronic health condition that impairs strength and vitality may diminish the child's ability to attend and to expend the effort needed for learning.

Whenever health or physical problems are suspected, the child should be referred to the proper professionals, usually via the school nurse. If parents are slow to follow up on recommendations, someone needs to explain to them the relationship between the particular problem (e.g., poor vision, lack of sleep) and the child's school performance. If nurses or counselors are unavailable, teachers can take the initiative to request that the child receive free or low-cost meals, or medical or other services.

Social, Emotional, and Cultural Factors

Emotional and Social Maturity   Children are as varied in their personalities as they are in cognitive and physical characteristics. Immature social adjustment and emotional development are among the reasons why some intellectually ready children have disappointing starts in reading.

Self-reliant children can carry on everyday classroom activities with little teacher direction and can solve their own problems. Extremely dependent children often make excessive demands on the teacher's time and attention, and may stop trying unless given much personal attention. Self-confident children are likely to approach the learning task with greater relish and less fear of failing, and to recover more quickly from any setback.

Emotional self-control also is important. Some first-grade children still display the volatility and emotional instability characteristic of preschoolers. Temper tantrums, rapid changes in mood, and crying at the slightest provocation disrupt the learning situation for everyone, particularly for the child who engages in such behaviors.

The ability to participate actively and cooperatively in group activities is important because a great deal of group instruction takes place in first grade. Group participants need to pay attention, listen actively, follow directions, act in concert, take their turns, allow others to take theirs, and share. Socially or emotionally immature children can be taught readiness skills and to learn to read if special adjustments are made for them.

Since many children take a while to adjust to school, the first few weeks of the school year often are devoted to helping them settle down and learn classroom routine. If behaviors such as restlessness, timidity, helplessness, and aggressiveness continue to prevent a child from participating effectively in learning activities, the problem should be regarded as serious. Maladaptive behavior that persists beyond the first few weeks of school should be discussed with the child's parents. If they are unable or unwilling to provide corrective measures, the teacher should pursue the problem with the school principal or psychologist. Some problems require diagnostic study and treatment that no teacher can provide.

Anxiety   Generally, children with average anxiety perform well in reading. However, highly anxious children perform better in a structured than in an unstructured reading approach (Chester 1974, Merryman 1974). Nekas (1973) found that regardless of success or failure in learning to read, low-anxiety children became significantly more anxious, and high anxious children became less anxious, after reading instruction. A little anxiety may help the learner to achieve, but high anxiety is likely to have an adverse effect on learning.

Interest in Reading   As a result of such previous experiences as having been read to and looking at picture books and illustrations, most first graders are eager to learn to read. Others have little desire to do so because they would rather play or are afraid that learning to read is a sign of growing up, something they would prefer not to happen for various reasons; or because they expect learning to read to be difficult, if not impossible. Such preferences or fears often are related to social or emotional immaturity.

A challenging part of teaching is arousing and nourishing an interest in reading in children who do not display such an interest. Learning to read easily and successfully reinforces favorable attitudes toward reading. Failure tends to build negative feelings toward the task and also reinforces a poor self-concept, which in turn adversely affects willingness to try to learn.

Cultural and Socioeconomic Factors   As Dulin (1974) pointed out, sociological factors function both before reading instruction is begun and during schooling. A wide range of sociological variables function as predisposing conditions as to when, what, why, and how well the child reads. During reading, these factors affect the meaning the reader brings to the printed page and takes from it. When intelligence is partialed out, the range of educational individual differences is markedly influenced by sociological and cultural factors.

The adequacy of a child's experiential background is largely determined by the general cultural level of the home. Regardless of socioeconomic status, the home can foster favorable development by providing such things as a linguistically rich atmosphere, reading to the children and taking them on trips, and giving them a feeling of security and self-confidence. Parents who have favorable attitudes toward education often stimulate and encourage intellectual pursuits. Many children do not come from homes that have provided such experiences. Nevertheless, it is incorrect to assume that a child from an economically poor home is necessarily educationally disadvantaged.

Children from homes of low socioeconomic status (SES) tend to score low on reading readiness tests. For example, Telegdy (1974) found that when compared to high SES children, almost four times as many low SES children were not ready to learn to read according to the readiness test scores. Socioeconomic status and social class, which often are intertwined, are related to reading readiness and achievement, but that relationship is not necessarily a cause-effect one, especially when individuals are considered. A general classification such as SES or social class is comprised of many interacting factors that might contribute to reading success or failure. Many reading readiness handicaps can be overcome, and with good teaching the reading achievement of low SES primary-grade children can approximate national norms (A. J. Harris, Morrison, Serwer, and Gold 1968).

In order to lessen the negative impact of cultural and socioeconomic factors on school success, compensatory education programs such as Head Start have been initiated. Available evidence suggests that effective prekindergarten programs, those with specific structured cognitive activities, result in significant initial gains in intelligence test scores, language proficiency, and reading readiness (Stanley 1972, McDaniels 1975). These initial gains tend, however, to dissipate if primary-grade programs are not also adjusted. The television program "Sesame Street" also seems to improve the reading readiness of children who watch it regularly.

The general idea of readiness applies to all levels of reading development, not just to the initial stages of acquisition. Considering the child's readiness to learn should be a part of good planning at all levels. The implications of the readiness idea for planning reading instruction at all levels are discussed in unit 5.

EVALUATING READINESS FOR BEGINNING READING

In some cases, a child's readiness to learn to read is obvious. Children who are already reading stand out, as do many of those for whom reading instruction at this time would result in almost certain failure. General readiness for successful learning by other children can be evaluated by using intelligence tests, reading readiness tests, or teacher observation and judgment, singly or in combination.

Intelligence Tests

Group intelligence tests that do not require any reading ability are often administered in kindergarten or the early part of first grade. A child who obtains a very low score or is thought to be brighter than the test suggests should be retested individually or in a small group (and his or her performance monitored) with an alternate form of the test or with a different group test. If the test score is still very low, an individually administered intelligence test should be given by a qualified psychologist.

As previously pointed out, success in learning to read is only partly dependent on mental ability. A high M.A. or IQ alone does not assure success, nor does a low score preclude it. Intelligence test scores are not particularly accurate in predicting an individual's reading achievement. Nevertheless, the teacher may use the following as a rough guideline: Children with a mental age of approximately six years are probably ready to learn to read without undue difficulty provided they do not have specific handicaps. For children far below this point, an adjusted program or delayed start is suggested.

Reading Readiness Tests

Reading readiness tests attempt to measure factors that have been found to be related to success in beginning reading. To some extent, they resemble group intelligence tests used at the same grade level, but unlike intelligence tests, they deliberately include certain types of acquired knowledge.

Although the content of readiness tests varies considerably, and no one test contains them all, the following factors are most commonly found in such tests: (1) visual discrimination, (2) auditory discrimination, (3) knowledge of word meaning, (4) listening comprehension, (5) letter-name knowledge, (6) visual-motor skills (copying designs), (7) visual memory. An annotated list of the readiness factors sampled by various tests is provided by Mavrogenes, Hanson, and Winkley (1976). Of these, only visual discrimination is sampled by all readiness tests. An often unmentioned but important requirement for good performance on readiness tests is the ability to attend to, comprehend, and carry out oral directions.

The preceding list makes apparent the fact that readiness tests do not sample all the factors associated with success in learning to read. Moreover, although correlations between readiness test total scores and later reading test scores are high enough to allow good prediction for a group, they are not high enough to allow accurate prediction for individuals.

Reading readiness test performance is correlated with mental age. Engin, Wallbrown, and Wallbrown (1974) found that M.A. accounted for 57 percent of the variance of the total score on a commonly used readiness test, thus being the most important single factor. Readiness test scores are better predictors for children with M.A.s of 6.5 or above (Bilka 1972). These three facts indicate that great faith should not be placed in readiness test scores alone when making decisions about individual children.

Not all reading readiness tests are equally valid in predicting success in reading, nor are their scores equally reliable. Predictive validity may be in-

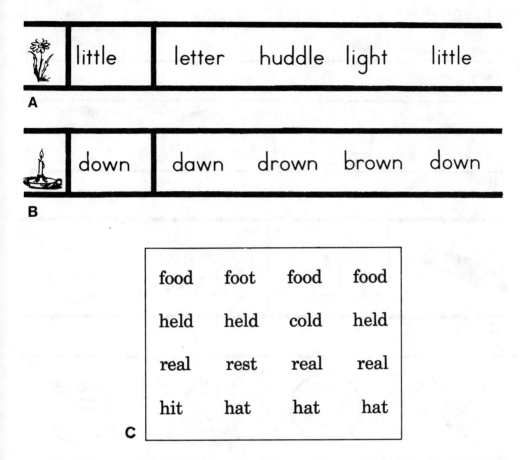

FIGURE 2.1.   Items from readiness tests of visual discrimination. In items *A* and *B* the child is to draw a line through the word that "looks just like the word in the little box." In item *C* the child is to put an *X* on the one word that is different. Note the difference in the way the two tests sample visual discrimination.

Items *A* and *B* are from the Matching Words subtest of *Prereading Battery,* form B, by Theodore Clymer and Thomas C. Barrett, © copyright, 1967, Personnel Press, Inc., Princeton, N.J. Used with permission. Item *C* is from the *Gates-MacGinitie Reading Tests: Readiness Skills,* © 1966 by Teachers College Press, Columbia University. Reproduced by permission of the publishers.

fluenced by the reading program employed (Pikulski 1973). Furthermore, prediction will be influenced by what is done for the child, particularly for low scorers. The more effective the attempts to overcome readiness handicaps are, the less likely it is that a low score will predict failure.

Selecting the best test for a particular school involves careful study and

FIGURE 2.2. Items from readiness tests of auditory discrimination. In item *A* the child is to mark the pictures *(flag, fork, fly, frog)* that begin with the same sound as the cue word *(flower)*, which is spoken by the examiner each time a picture is named. In item *B* the child is to mark the pictures *(step, bed, net, head)* that rhyme with the cue word *(said)*. In item *C* the child puts a cross on the pictures (all of which are previously named by the examiner) that begin with /k/-/k/. In item *D* the child is to mark each picture that "has the m-m sound at the end." Note the differences in the ways the auditory skills are sampled by the two readiness tests. Both tests have brief teaching sessions to help children understand the directions.

Items *A* and *B* are taken from the Auditory Discrimination subtest of the *Macmillan Reading Readiness Test*, rev. ed. Copyright © 1970 by the Macmillan Publishing Co., Inc., 1965, 1970. Items *C* and *D* are from the *Murphy-Durrell Reading Readiness Analysis*, Phonemes Test, copyright © 1964, 1965 by Harcourt Brace Jovanovich, Inc. Reproduced by permission of the publishers.

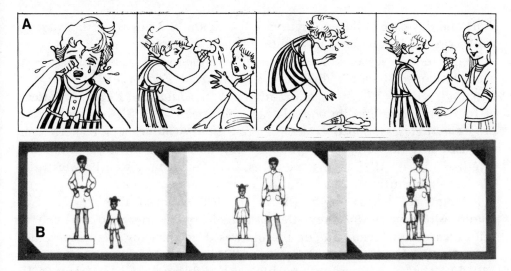

FIGURE 2.3. Items from readiness tests of language skills. In item *A* the child is to put an *X* on the "picture that shows what made her cry" after being told that Suzy was crying. In item *B* the child is to mark the picture that shows "the girl beside the woman is standing on a box."

Item *A* is taken from the Comprehension Unit, Cause-Effect and Prediction A of the *Pre-Reading Assessment Kit*, copyright © 1972 by the Ontario Institute for Studies in Education; published by McGraw-Hill Ryerson Limited, Toronto, Canada. Item *B* is reproduced from the School Language subtest of the *Metropolitan Readiness Tests*, Level II, Form P, copyright © 1974 by Harcourt Brace Jovanovich, Inc. Reproduced by permission of the publishers.

tryout. Guidelines for selecting a readiness test are provided by Harris and Sipay (1975), and reviews of readiness and other reading and reading-related tests may be found in Buros (1968, 1972) and Farr and Anastasiow (1969).

Great care should be exercised in interpreting an individual's subtest scores. Subtests rarely have a reliability of .90 or above, which is desirable if differences in subtest scores are to be used for planning instruction. Determining instructional needs from subtest scores alone is a questionable practice.

Among the more widely used readiness tests are *Clymer-Barrett Prereading Battery* (Personnel), *Gates-MacGinitie Readiness Skills Test* (Teachers), *Macmillan Reading Readiness Test* (Macmillan), *Metropolitan Readiness Test* (Harcourt), and the *Murphy-Durrell Reading Readiness Analysis* (Harcourt). The individually administered *Walker Readiness Test for Disadvantaged Preschool Children* (USOE) was standardized on Head

Start and day-care children. Figures 2.1, 2.2, and 2.3 illustrate the ways in which various factors are sampled by a few of these tests.

Semistandard lessons accompanied by systematic observations have been developed, two of which are *Kindergarten Evaluation of Learning Potential, KELP* (Webster) and *Let's Look at Children* (ETS). A battery of fourteen group and individual tests comprise *CIRCUS: Comprehensive Program of Assessment Services for Pre-Primary Children* (ETS). Even if one uses only the core tests of this battery, administration time is lengthy (Raths and Katz 1975). In some cases, however, it may well be worth the time if reliable information useful for instruction is obtained.

Attempts to identify "high risk" or "at risk" children also are forms of readiness testing, in that they attempt to identify children who are likely to fail in learning to read. Among the indexes developed for this purpose are those by Banks (1970), Hoffman (1971), and Jansky and de Hirsch (1972).[3] The selection criteria for high-risk children usually misclassify 10 to 20 percent of the children.

The charge has been made that readiness tests are biased against minority and disadvantaged children. This charge has been greatly exaggerated, according to studies by Davis and Personke (1968), Mishra and Hurt (1970), and Lessler and Bridges (1973). Of course, interpretation of readiness test performances should be tempered by knowledge that these children may not have had certain experiences prior to the administration of the test. A linguistic-capacity index predicted the reading achievement of Spanish-speaking first graders about as well as most readiness tests might (Fowler 1973).

Occasionally readiness tests are given following a readiness program, particularly in kindergarten. In first grade, readiness tests are usually administered two or three weeks after school begins. The delay allows the children time to become accustomed to first grade, yet occurs early enough to allow the teacher to make use of test results in planning instruction.

Teacher Observation and Judgment

There is some evidence (Long and Henderson 1974) that teachers place more faith in reading readiness test performance than they do in their own

---

3. These indexes are described and evaluated by Harris and Sipay (1975, pp. 34–37).

observations of a child. Teacher observations and judgments are not only important because of the need to assess factors that are not sampled by standardized tests, but also because there is a need for a continuous on-going evaluation of pupil progress.

Studies have shown that teacher estimates predict future success in reading about as well as reading readiness tests do (Heilman 1972). Identification of high-risk children by teachers also has been shown to be fairly effective (Ferinden, Jacobson, and Linden 1970; Keogh, Tchir, and Windeguth-Behn 1974; Schaer and Crump 1976).

Competent, experienced teachers can judge the readiness of most of their children fairly well after a few weeks. The accuracy of teacher judgments tends to improve with the number of observations made. Even experienced teachers, however, can be misled about a child. Verbal youngsters may seem brighter than they are; bright but shy, self-effacing children, less ready than they are. Well-behaved girls may be rated higher than boys who act up. What children are able to do is a more reliable basis for judgment than how they look or behave. Open-minded teachers who keep written notes about children are less likely to make inaccurate decisions than those who form quick general impressions based on casual mentally noted infrequent observations.

Reading Readiness Rating Scales

Using a readiness scale can help teachers to clarify their judgments and make them more specific. In a study by Keogh and Smith (1970), 90 percent of the children rated by teachers on a reading readiness scale achieved in the predicted direction. Harris and Sipay (1970) indicated that a rating scale correlated higher with a reading readiness total score than any other subtest, and predicted reading achievement about as well as some other subtests.

Rating scales have been devised (e.g., Banks 1970 [4]) or can be found as part of readiness tests (e.g., *Macmillan Reading Readiness Test*). Although checklists such as that prepared by Sanacore (1973) may provide useful guidelines, it should be remembered that simple "yes-no" choices may be misleading. There is often a range within which a factor may fall, and not all factors are equally important.

---

4. A copy of this *Kindergarten Behavioural Index* also appears in Harris and Sipay (1975, p. 36).

A readiness rating scale is shown in figure 2.4. The items to be rated have been discussed previously in this unit. In making the ratings, the teacher should rely mainly on the accumulated information gained from daily classroom observations. Judgments should be reevaluated periodically because original opinions may be inaccurate, and effective instruction should result in positive change.

Each factor is rated on a scale from –2 to +2 by checking the appropriate place. The number of checks in each column is multiplied by the value of the column. Thus, as in figure 2.4, if the –2 column has two checks, the column total is –4. The algebraic sum of the column totals yields the total score. Plus scores indicate above-average readiness; zero scores, average readiness; and minus scores, below-average readiness.

The basis for the ratings shown in figure 2.4 are shown in figure 2.5. The total score (–5) indicates the child was a little below average in readiness and specific ratings suggest where help was probably needed. His inconsistent handedness probably was related to the reversals and difficulty with left and right. Since some preference was shown for the left hand, the teacher encouraged its use. He also was given extra practice in left-to-right direction and visual discrimination of letter and word forms. None of the other ratings was low enough for concern, and since general immaturity is not unusual for a child so young, it probably would improve throughout the year. With an above-average IQ, his prognosis for success was average, and after brief training in the indicated areas, reading instruction was initiated while practice in these areas continued.

Ratings can be usefully combined with testing to help teachers discover the specific needs of children. Teachers can then concentrate on overcoming specific weaknesses, making reading readiness activities functionally useful.

Suggested Procedure for Determining Readiness for Reading

The following may provide insurance against rushing some children into instruction for which they are not ready or delaying reading instruction for other children unduly.

1. If the school's policy is to administer a group intelligence test or readiness test in kindergarten or near the beginning of first grade, note particularly the scores of those who did very well or very poorly.
2. As soon as most of the children seem to have settled into classroom

Name Henry   Age 5–10   Rated by _____   On 9/20   Total Score −5

	RATING				
	Low		Average		High
Factor	−2	−1	0	+1	+2
Cognitive					
M.A.	___	___	X	___	___
IQ	___	___	___	X	___
Attention	___	___	X	___	___
Specific concepts	___	___	___	X	___
General conceptual background	___	___	___	X	___
Letter-name knowledge	___	X	___	___	___
Auditory discrimination	___	X	___	___	___
Visual discrimination	X	___	___	___	___
Visual perception	___	X	___	___	___
Language					
Vocabulary	___	___	___	X	___
Sentence structure	___	___	___	X	___
Listening comprehension	___	___	X	___	___
Physical/Physiological					
Ability to identify left and right	___	X	___		
Consistent hand preference	X	___	___		
	None	left	right		
Muscular coordination	___	X	___	___	___
Visual acuity	___	___	?	___	___
Auditory acuity	___	___	?	___	___
Speech production	___	X	___	___	___
General health	___	X	___	___	___
Social/Emotional/Cultural					
Self-reliance	___	X	___	___	___
Self-control	___	X	___	___	___
Group participation	___	___	X	___	___
Interest in being read to	___	___	___	X	___
Interest in learning to read	___	___	X	___	___
General cultural level of the home	___	___	___	X	___
Intellectual stimulation of the home	___	___	___	X	___
Column totals	−4	−9	___	8	0

FIGURE 2.4.   A reading readiness rating scale.

Factor	Rating	Basis
Cognitive		
M.A.	0	Average, since child's CA is only 5–10
IQ	+1	IQ of 114
Attention	0	Usually focused on task
Specific concepts	+1	Most terms well understood
General conceptual background	+1	Displays wide range of information
Letter-name knowledge	−1	Could name only 5 letters
Auditory discrimination	−1	Understands rhyme, but cannot discriminate among some speech sounds
Visual discrimination	−2	Extreme difficulty on readiness subtest and workbook exercises
Visual perception	−1	Marked reversal tendency
Language		
Vocabulary	+1	Above average use in Show and Tell and
Sentence structure	+1	classroom responses
Listening comprehension	0	Understands directions and stories
Physical/Physiological		
Ability to identify left and right	−1	Often confuses terms when referring to them himself
Consistent hand preference	−2	Often shifts hands, but tends to use left slightly more
Muscular coordination	−1	Not well coordinated on playground or classroom activities
Visual acuity	?	Not checked, but seems adequate
Auditory acuity	?	Not checked, but seems adequate
Speech production	−1	Slight lisp, difficulty pronouncing /l/, /r/, /w/
General health	−1	Not particularly strong or vigorous
Social/Emotional/Cultural		
Self-reliance	−1	Needs more teacher's help than peers
Self-control	−1	Occasionally cries
Group participation	0	Participates, shares, waits turn; but doesn't volunteer
Interest in being read to	+1	Asks to have stories read
Interest in learning to read	0	Displays normal interests
General cultural level of the home	+1	Both parents college graduates
Intellectual stimulation of the home	+1	Both parents attended first conference and revealed strong interest in child's learning

FIGURE 2.5. Bases for ratings on the rating scale shown in figure 2.4.

routines, fill out a rating scale such as the one in figure 2.4 for each child. Code each child's form as indicating general readiness, general unreadiness, or readiness with some specific weaknesses.

3. Try some informal reading lessons using a modified language-experience approach. From sentences suggested by the children, develop a simple experience chart. Read it to the children, first as a whole, then line by line, and finally word by word, pointing to each word as it is pronounced. Give volunteers an opportunity to try to read lines or any words they can identify. These sessions should be informal, allowing each child to join, remain with, or leave the group. Note particularly those who learn words, and those who avoid participation. See unit 3 for more detail about the language-experience method.

Putting together the results of tests, the rating scale, and the sample lessons, most of the children will fit into one of three main categories: (1) Children who are obviously ready or are already reading. Reading instruction should begin immediately for them; requiring them to go through a typical readiness program probably will bore them, dull their desire to read, and may induce undesirable behavior. (2) Children who are obviously unready. A readiness program tailored to their needs in content and pace is suggested. After a few weeks their rating scales should be marked again, using a different color, as a basis for recording improvement and modifying their programs. It is also desirable to give those classified as needing further readiness work some sample lessons using a method that contrasts with the method described in step 3 above, in stressing sound-symbol associations as a basis for decoding words, rather than whole-word visual recognition. Some children can do much better with a phonic approach than with a visual approach. (3) Children who are generally ready but who need help in one or more specific areas. For those who are strong in other areas, and whose weaknesses are not severe or numerous, reading instruction can begin and practice in the weak areas can be given concurrently. For others, reading instruction may have to be delayed somewhat longer. For some of these children it may be simply a matter of arousing their interest in learning to read.

If any of the children who were placed in the reading group fail to make progress, move them temporarily into the readiness group, try to discover and work on their specific areas of unreadiness, and when they and some other children seem to be ready, start the group on reading. It is very important to prevent the frustrating effects of prolonged failure.

DEVELOPING READING READINESS

A reading readiness program prior to formal reading instruction will allow many children to make easier and faster progress in learning to read. But not all children should be given the same readiness program. Children who already can read do not need any of the typical readiness program. If ready to learn more advanced reading skills, they should be given the opportunity to do so. Those with highly developed general readiness who have been missed on the first screening should be identified after a very brief time in the readiness program, with reading instruction beginning for them shortly after. Other children will need a concentrated and extended readiness program.

The success of a readiness program depends greatly on how well the teacher individualizes instruction. Time and effort are wasted when children are given tasks they can already perform well or which require skills they do not yet possess. It is important that the child neither be bored nor fail often during the early stages of learning to read.

Although maturation plays an important role, teachers should not just wait for readiness to evolve. When specific weaknesses are noted, efforts should be made to improve important skills and attitudes that can be developed. Teaching procedures and the child's program should be adjusted to help the child to compensate for those problems that cannot be overcome by direct teaching.

Readiness skills are not equally important. Some skills need not be taught prior to teaching beginning reading; they can be presented concurrently with reading instruction.

It is advisable for many children to begin their readiness programs in the latter part of kindergarten. Readiness programs for kindergarteners or first graders with very low general readiness should include activities directly related to the later development of reading skills that will be taught in the particular reading program employed.

Children with High General Readiness

The concept of reading readiness was advanced to give children who were not ready the opportunity to start gradually and proceed slowly, experiencing success instead of failure. It was never intended to justify a reading readiness program for all children.

Some children already have started to read when they enter school. Alert teachers spot these early readers quickly and can help them to develop more advanced reading skills. Such children should be allowed to participate in reading lessons, if they wish, and allowed to proceed at their own pace.

After the first few weeks of first grade, teachers often can identify children who seem ready for reading. The sooner these children are introduced to reading, the better. No purpose is served by requiring all children to complete a certain amount of readiness work, such as finishing a readiness workbook, when some of them have nothing to gain from it.

Although these generally mature children are ready to learn to read, some still may benefit from improving certain readiness aspects, such as conceptual background and language facility. In such cases, they can be given experiences similar to those provided for the less generally ready children.

Children with Low General Readiness

Slow learners, often identified through below-average intelligence test scores or very low readiness test scores, are likely to be retarded in language and conceptual development, low in perceptual abilities, and emotionally and socially immature. They are apt to need longer than the usual few weeks to get ready, and when reading instruction is begun, their learning rate is likely to be slow. There is no educational magic that can transform truly slow learners into normal learners, but we can provide them with appropriate readiness and reading programs.

We cannot measure intelligence and other aspects of readiness with high accuracy, and the relationship between readiness factors and beginning reading ability is far from perfect. Every child, *regardless of test scores*, should be given an opportunity to learn to read. This can be done most easily with a language-experience approach. Children who show little or no progress with this approach can be continued with simple but appropriate readiness and beginning reading activities long after other children have started to use reading texts. Teachers who prefer to get into the first reading text of a series early can move along very slowly, providing ample repetition and readiness activities until the children are ready to move ahead.

If there are a sufficient number of children with low general readiness, it may be advisable to have a transition class, readiness first grade, or pre-primary class such as the one described by Shohen (1974). In such classes a specially trained teacher works to develop readiness and beginning reading with a smaller number of children than are usually found in a first-grade class.

Children with Specific Weaknesses

Many children are ready in many respects but have some specific weaknesses that may create real difficulty in learning to read. Most teachers will have available to them the reading readiness program that is part of the reading program being employed in their school. Rather than use these suggested methods and materials in the same way with every child, the teacher should select for each child those which seem appropriate.

Often a few children can benefit from the same kind of help, and it is economical of teacher time and effort to work with them in a group. Usually this kind of group work starts before reading instruction is begun, and if still needed it can continue as a supplementary activity after children have started to read. More detailed activities for developing readiness can be found in the references listed in module 2 and in the manuals accompanying the readiness and first texts of most published reading series.

Not all of the factors associated with reading readiness can be improved by direct instruction. For instance, the intellectual experiences of attending school probably help children's intelligence to develop, but since these experiences are fairly similar for most children, their standing relative to other children tends not to change much; lack of such experiences may cause the child's IQ to decline. For some factors, particularly health handicaps and serious personality maladjustments, all the teacher can do is refer the child to specialists, follow through on their recommendations, and make whatever facilitating adjustments are possible. Factors such as socioeconomic status are beyond the influence of the school; but teachers should understand the implications of these factors in dealing with children. Other factors, as indicated in the preceding sections, are of doubtful importance for most children. Suggestions for developing certain factors have already been made. The following suggestions pertain to factors commonly found in need of improvement that have an influence on reading ability beyond the initial stages of reading acquisition.

General Conceptual Background The development of conceptual background should be tied closely to language development. Before, during, and after the children have experienced vivid firsthand experiences, important verbal labels should be brought to the children's attention and used in oral or written language. Class trips and direct participation in activities are useful for developing concepts if they are well planned and conducted. Because many concepts cannot be gained at first hand, vicarious experiences such as the following should be provided: motion pictures, television, filmstrips, pictures, charts, and story telling and reading aloud by the teacher.

Language The child's understanding of certain concepts and their accompanying verbal labels is important for learning. Concepts such as "right," "left," "top," "bottom," are best developed in presenting tasks that require knowledge of them. Even if they do not have a direct impact on reading ability, increasing a child's expressive and receptive language skills can be beneficial. The teacher can provide a good language model and encourage children to expand their speaking and listening skills.

Teachers can develop a relaxed atmosphere that encourages children to talk. They can present pictures or other objects and ask the children to discuss them or make up stories about them. They can involve the children in discussing class trips and holidays in large or small groups. There can be regularly scheduled "sharing periods" or "show and tell." They can put on plays and puppet shows.

Vukelich (1974) described a procedure intended to aid both the child's conceptual development and ability to express ideas. By using a succession of leading questions, the teacher helps children learn to label, describe, generalize, and categorize objects and experiences. Listening comprehension can be increased by reading suitable interesting material to the children, then asking questions about it (at times focusing on specific skills, such as the main idea) or discussing the story.

Attempts to change dialect language patterns have been somewhat successful (Rentel and Kennedy 1972, Strickland 1973a); however, such changes have not resulted in increased reading readiness or achievement scores. This simply may indicate that comprehension of language is separate from the ability to speak in certain patterns.

Visual Perception During recent years, many schools have used specific workbook materials to improve visual perception skills as a way of improving reading readiness. One of the most widely used sets is the Frostig-Horne *Frostig Program for the Development of Visual Perception* (Follett). This provides graded series of exercises in the five aspects of visual perception tested in the *Frostig Developmental Tests of Visual Perception* (see p. 40). The practice material consists mainly of geometric forms.

There have been many studies of the efficacy of the Frostig perceptual program, and they lead to the following conclusions: (1) the program, when used in kindergarten or first grade, results in improved scores on the Frostig tests; (2) it does not consistently result in improved scores on conventional readiness tests; and (3) it has failed to show any beneficial effect on first-grade reading, as compared to similar amounts of time spent in readiness and reading instruction (H. M. Robinson 1972a; Hammill, Goodman, and Wiederholt 1974).

Similar results have been found for programs which stress sensorimotor training. Such programs may include activities such as walking along a narrow beam, jumping on a trampoline, or doing floor exercises such as "angels in the snow." Reviews of many studies of such programs fail to show any consistent benefit to readiness, intelligence, or academic achievement (Klesius 1972; Hammill, Goodman, and Wiederholt 1974).

Visual Discrimination   On the other hand, there is good reason to believe that training in the visual discrimination of letter forms and printed or written words is desirable for children who show weakness in this area. As noted, training in the naming of letters is included in either the readiness program or in beginning reading instruction (it does not seem to matter which). Before a child can learn to name a letter, he or she must be able to differentiate it from other letters. While many entering school can already do this, others need help. Recent work by educational psychologists indicates that directing the learner's attention to distinctive features results in fewer discrimination errors and a faster learning rate in learning letter names.

Three types of distinctive features of graphic forms seem fairly well established, at least with capital letters: (1) break vs. close (*C-O*); (2) curve vs. straight (*U-V*); and (3) diagonal vs. horizontal (*M-H*) (Guralnick 1972). In distinctive-feature training, letters are presented in contrasting pairs and the distinctive features are highlighted. Thus *P* and *R* would be presented with the diagonal stem of *R* in red to emphasize the difference (which would gradually be faded out; the color would be made less and less red) and calling attention to this feature by using informative verbal labels. It is better to highlight one distinctive feature than to add redundant information, such as color-coding the entire letter. Making *b* blue and *d* red may be counterproductive because the children may focus on the color and not on the particular distinctive feature. Distinctive features may be isolated and presented alone until the discrimination is learned. Gradually those features are added, so that by the time the whole letters are presented, the discrimination is well established (Ross 1976). Learning distinctive features is enhanced through use of three-dimensional materials (Towner and Evans 1974).

Few children have difficulty in matching pictures or geometric designs. Such exercises, often found in readiness workbooks, are of doubtful value. Most children who are weak in visual discrimination will need help dealing with printed letters and words. As many useful exercises as are needed can be selected from published workbooks or duplicating masters, and teachers may devise additional ones.

Simply giving the children numerous exercises will not help them to overcome weaknesses. Instruction in how the letters or words are the same or different often is needed. Children also must understand concepts such as "letter," "word," "same," "different," "begin," "end," in order to perform the tasks. The exercises that follow require skills that are likely to transfer to learning to read. Directions in these exercises are given orally.

1. Single letters
   a. Mark the two letters if they look just the same (different)
      t t, a y, c e, m m
   b. Mark the letter that looks just the same as the first letter
      o: x m o l
   c. Mark the letter that does not look just the same as the others
      b b d b
   d. Mark all the letters that (do not) look just like the first letter
      n: m n h u w n
2. Words
   a. Mark the two words if they (do not) look exactly alike
      rag bone, top top, miss mess, saw was
   b. Mark the word that looks just like the first word
      make: fake mate mike make
   c. Mark the word that does not look exactly the same as the others
      bell ball bell bell

3. Letter position and sequence
   a. Mark the word(s) that begins (ends) with the same letter as the
      first word
         take: top   have   tell   make
   b. Mark the word(s) that has the same letter(s) in the middle as the
      first word
         hat: cap   hot   how   man
   c. Mark the word that is exactly the same as the first word
         spot: pots   stop   tops   spot

Each of the above items can serve as a model from which several pages
can be prepared, starting with very easy and obvious comparisons and
gradually calling for more demanding visual discriminations. As with any
such task, the more closely the wrong answers resemble the correct response, the more difficult the item. Visual discrimination exercises are used
to help children perceive visual similarities and differences, not to teach
letter names or word recognition. Learning to identify letters by name follows naturally. Once printed words are introduced, pointing out and comparing how they differ visually provides a form of visual discrimination
training.

Left-to-right Direction   By convention, English is read from left to right, and
the sequence of letters within words follows the same pattern. Children
who have difficulty with following the left-to-right sequence can be assisted
by:

1. Teaching the concepts of "left" and "right," starting with establishing
   which hand is which, progressing to other body parts, and finally pro-
   jecting these concepts to other objects. Teachers can direct attention to
   the fact that they are writing from left to right, or have children put up
   pictures in a left-to-right sequence.
2. Running the hand or pointer smoothly and slowly under words and
   phrases from left to right, when reading material to children from the
   chalkboard or chart.
3. Encouraging children to look at words by starting at the left and going
   steadily to the right, when careful inspection is needed. Color coding
   the first letter, word, or left margin "green for go" and the last letter,
   word, or right margin "red for stop" may assist some children. Naturally sentences should be one per line.

4. Providing practice in visually discriminating words that have reversible letter sequences, such as *on, no; tan, ant, nat.*

Many reading readiness workbooks contain exercises for developing left-to-right progression by arranging pictures in the correct order or interpreting pictures that already are arranged from left to right to form a story. While such exercises may serve to develop other skills such as picture interpretation and language (these uses often are recognized as indicated by the fact that they are combined with other objectives for the exercise), they operate on a level far below that needed by most children who have difficulty with left-to-right direction.

Auditory Discrimination   Training in auditory discrimination is usually a component of published reading readiness programs, and because of this there is a tendency for all children to receive the same training, regardless of need or value. How then are teachers to individualize their programs? The easy answer is: if a child is not learning a task for which auditory discrimination is judged important, then specific training in auditory discrimination appears to be called for.

Training in auditory discrimination should involve distinguishing speech sounds from one another. Although some readiness programs provide practice in deciding which of two tones is higher in pitch, or louder, or longer in duration, and some provide practice in identifying sounds made by particular animals or birds, there is no evidence that such discriminations are relevant to reading or have any beneficial effect on progress in reading.

Auditory discrimination exercises can be developed using the kinds of items in recent auditory discrimination tests as models. They can include such activities as the following:

1. Listening to two words that differ in only one phoneme (initial, final, or medial) and deciding whether they are the same or different.
2. Listening to two words with particular attention to the initial phoneme (or final or medial phoneme). For example: Raise your hand if the two words begin with the same sound: *man* and *tan, man* and *meat, man* and *sand, man* and *money.*
3. Listening to words and deciding whether or not they rhyme. For example: *sing* and *thing, sing* and *sand, sing* and *ring, sing* and *south.*

While there seems to be no harm in including some auditory discrimination practice during readiness work prior to reading instruction, most of the practice can be made an integral part of the teaching of the phonemic values of letters and letter groups, during reading instruction.

Interest in Learning to Read   To stimulate children's interest in wanting to read, teachers can do many things.

1. Signs and labels around the room excite curiosity, but they should not be overdone so as to confuse or overwhelm children. Most children enjoy being able to recognize their own names and those of others, as well as learning what signs and labels mean. In playing store, the clerk has to obtain a labeled product, the customer must determine if a brand-name product is available. Games in which the child responds to printed words can motivate. At first only single verbs (e.g., stand, sit, jump) need be used.
2. Teachers can read interesting stories and poems to children, show them illustrations, and then leave the book on the library table. Children are likely to seek out the book and look at the pages and pictures.
3. Notices, rules, weather charts, committee lists, experience charts, classroom newspapers, etc., convey the idea that it is necessary to read in order to obtain information. Of course, the teacher should read these to the children.
4. Since nothing succeeds like success, it is extremely important to ensure that the earliest reading experiences are successful and satisfying.

Effectiveness of Reading Readiness Programs

Research findings regarding the effectiveness of reading readiness programs are mixed. A rather wide-ranging readiness program enabled culturally different kindergarteners to score higher on a readiness test than those who did not receive such training (Stanchfield 1972). However, as with many other readiness studies, there is no indication as to the program's impact on later reading achievement. Studies that have compared various types of programs have not found any significant differences in effects (Quorm 1974, Roettger 1976). But as with studies that compare reading approaches, lack of significant mean differences does not tell us which programs were or were not effective for children with certain weaknesses or attributes. A study by Spache et al. (1966) indicated that the effectiveness of the readiness program appeared to increase as the pupils' ability decreased; the bottom quarter benefited, the rest did as well or better without a readiness program. But Belmont and Birch (1974) found that supplementary perceptual or remedial programs for low scorers on a reading readiness test were no more effective than a placebo treatment or no intervention at all. In light of the lack of conclusive evidence in either direction, it seems reasonable to suggest that teachers continue to attempt to overcome specific weaknesses that may handicap children in learning to read.

Early Reading

Should four- or five-year-olds be taught to read? Based on his review of the research, Ollila (1972) concluded that the whole issue of early reading remained unsolved but that (1) most studies indicated that children who have an early start in reading achieve higher than their later-starting peers, mantaining that advantage, especially if later instruction is adjusted; (2) caution should be exercised because so little is known about effects of early reading on eyesight; and (3) early reading seems neither to create nor prevent reading disability, boredom, school adjustment, or psychological problems.

A more recent well-designed longitudinal study by Durkin (1974–75) followed the reading achievement in grades 1–4 of children who had participated in a two-year pre-first-grade program in which reading was taught as part of a language arts program. Although the reading achievement of these children exceeded that of the control group at each grade level, the differences were significant in only the first and second grades. This finding, that there was no lasting advantage to early reading, conflicted with her earlier findings with children who had learned to read outside of school (Durkin 1966). Durkin (1974–75) hypothesized that "characteristics of a family that fostered preschool reading ability would continue to foster achievement, with or without an appropriate instructional program."

Attempting to teach all nursery school or kindergarten children to read has little to recommend it. On the other hand, those who are ready to read and *want* to learn to read should not be denied the opportunity.

UNIT 3

Learning to Read

Throughout our nation's history, children have been taught to read in various ways (Huey 1908, N. B. Smith 1965, Mathews 1966). America has gone through periods when the prevailing beginning reading instruction relied mainly on an alphabet-spelling method (*see-ay-tee* says *cat*), teaching whole words, intensive phonics, sentence or story methods, or silent reading for meaning. As the weaknesses and excesses of each method were recognized, dissatisfaction and agitation led to change, although some teachers clung to established procedures, thus continuing "older" methods long after they were unfashionable.

These trends were followed by the development of reading methods that attempted to combine the good features of one-sided approaches while avoiding their weaknesses. The resulting "basal reader" programs also attempted to employ what was known about child development and learning theory in their methods and materials. More recently, there has been a resurgence of "phonics-first" programs, reintroduction of old ideas under new titles, and the introduction of new programs that have been influenced by psychologists, linguists, and psycholinguists.

New methods emerge, glow, and fade; older ones are modified and revised. Yet no single method has proven to be the long-awaited panacea. Most children learn to read regardless of methodology, and some fail in every program. Comparative studies strongly suggest that the teacher's skill, the learning environment, the characteristics of family and community, and the child's abilities are more important than the particular reading program employed.

There are marked differences among beginning reading programs in regard to initial emphasis; structure; vocabulary employed and the basis for its choice; story content; scope, sequence, pace, and emphasis of reading skills; and instructional materials. Successful teachers of reading not only know their pupils and the strengths and limitations of the reading program being employed, but also are acquainted with other methods and materials that might be employed in teaching those who are not profiting from instruction.

Although recent changes in published programs have tended to blur the lines of distinction (Popp 1975), beginning reading programs may be classified into one of two general approaches depending upon whether the main emphasis is placed on comprehension or on word identification. Meaning-emphasis programs initially place primary stress on obtaining meaning from the written form of language; code-emphasis programs on "cracking the code," that is, on the ability to decode or work out the pronunciation of written words. This basic difference influences the methods and materials of the resulting programs. There has been a tendency of late for programs to place more stress on the formerly less emphasized aspects of reading (e.g., meaning emphasis programs now introduce phonics much sooner and in larger doses). But whatever the initial emphasis, programs generally become increasingly similar as they progress through the grades.

Wide variations exist among programs grouped under a general approach, and some do not fit neatly into any one category or subcategory. Space does not allow extensive description of all the currently available reading programs and their diverse methodologies, but the major types will be described. Those interested in more information can consult sources such as Kerfoot (1965), Vilscek (1968a), Aukerman (1971), Laffey (1971) and Popp (1975). Reading programs employed in England have been summarized by Southgate and Roberts (1970).

MEANING-EMPHASIS APPROACHES

Three approaches that place primary emphasis on reading for meaning are discussed below: eclectic basal-reader programs, language-experience programs, and individualized reading. Use of one does not necessarily preclude use of the others; in fact, using more than one approach in combination may strengthen the developmental reading program.

Basal-reader Programs

Basal-reader programs provide the framework for the major part of reading instruction in most American elementary schools. A basal-reader series is not just a set of texts. It is a detailed, organized method for developing reading skills, with materials written to conform to the method, and the details of method planned for use with these specific materials (A. J. Harris 1972).

Materials   Most basal-reader series include the following materials for use in the primary grades: (1) a series of texts, starting with one or two readiness workbooks and progressing through two to four preprimers,[1] a primer, a first reader, a low and a high second reader, and a low and a high third reader; and (2) a teacher's guide for each text. Optional materials usually include: (3) a workbook to accompany each text; (4) placement and mastery tests; (5) large word, phrase, and story cards for group instruction; (6) related exercises that may be duplicated; (7) supplementary paperback story books that use the reader vocabulary; (8) dictionaries; and (9) related audiovisual materials.

Three thin paperbacks, called preprimers, usually are the first actual reading materials employed. They may be used right after the initial readiness program or after a language-experience program has been in use for a short time. In many series the preprimer and primer stories center around the experiences of one family. The amount of reading in preprimers increases from one word per page to a maximum of about eight lines, each line being a complete sentence. The story line is largely portrayed through pictures, and much of the reading matter is dialogue among the characters. Despite restrictions imposed by a limited vocabulary, which often is

1. These terms are employed in this book to indicate the difficulty levels of readers used by children. Most current basal series now label their texts by levels to discourage the belief that a grade-level designation indicates that the book should be used only in that grade and because reading is now taught in some kindergartens and in nongraded schools. For example, what was formerly labeled a "primer" or "1¹ reader" is now designated as "Level 6" or "Book 6" if it follows two readiness books and 3 preprimers. However, because not all programs contain the same number of texts, level designations by the various publishers are not directly comparable. Therefore the need to use the older terms in this book.

introduced at a rate of not more than one or two new words per page and is abundantly repeated, well-written preprimer stories have interest, suspense, or humor for first graders. The recent trend is to use more natural oral language patterns in beginning reading materials. The language does not seem as stilted and repetitious to children as it does to critical adults.

The primer is usually the first hard-covered book. It contains a richer vocabulary than it did in the 1960s, as is the case with basal readers in general. As the vocabulary expands, the language becomes more varied and natural and conveys more of the story, while the illustrations become relatively less important (see figure 3.1).

Some recently published series distinguish between words that most children probably will not be able to identify independently and those that they should be able to identify, with varying degrees of teacher assistance, by using previously taught word-recognition skills. The term "new word" means that the word is introduced for the first time in that basal series. Some children may already be able to identify it, and its meaning is probably already known by most.

Preprimer and primer stories no longer deal exclusively with a single white middle-class family. Almost all series have introduced ethnic and cultural pluralism, with a few stressing multiethnic characters and urban settings. Regardless of the character's ethnic or cultural background, or the story's setting, the families are most often middle class (Blom, Waite, and Zimet 1970). There is no evidence that the introduction of ethnic and cultural pluralism has resulted in improved reading performance (Messmore 1972–73), as desirable as the practice is for other reasons. The family-home theme is gradually replaced by anthropomorphic animal stories, old folktales, factual and fanciful stories, space-age stories, and poetry.

The teachers manual may be bound with a copy of the child's edition or may be a separate book. In the latter case, the reader pages are reproduced in reduced size, with the teaching plans printed near them. These manuals explain the general methodology and give detailed, specific lesson plans for each selection.

A correlated workbook is usually available for each reader level. Because workbooks are optional material, most teachers manuals contain exercises that are similar to the workbook pages and can be reproduced. Some workbook pages may prepare the children for the story they are about to read, but most involve follow-up activities.

"We can't do it," said Tiger.

"It won't work," said Squirrel.

"We can't get her out," said Rabbit.

"What's going on?" asked Mouse.

"We can't get Lion out of here,"
said Rabbit.

"I can help!" said Mouse.

"Go away," said Squirrel.
"You'll just be in the way."

"I want to help," said Mouse.

FIGURE 3.1.   A page from a primer in a basal-reader series. From *Honeycomb* by William K. Durr et al., p. 42. *Houghton Mifflin Reading Series.* Copyright © 1976 by Houghton Mifflin Company. The original is in color and larger. Reproduced by permission of the publisher.

Workbooks vary greatly in the attention given to the various reading skills, and in their adaptability for independent use. At the first-grade level most workbook activity has to be guided and supervised. Although the added practice with vocabulary and skills is often helpful to many children, good readers may become bored by practicing skills they have already mastered. It is not necessary for every child to do every workbook page, and some children may require more guided practice and repetition than the workbook provides.

Workbook pages should be promptly corrected, returned, and discussed as needed. A child's performance on these and other exercises can provide valuable information. Children who complete the work on a few pages covering the same skill(s) rapidly with few or no errors should be excused from future exercises on those skills. Errors should be analyzed to determine probable weaknesses, and should be used as a basis for corrective lessons. Teachers should not expect that simply providing workbooks or worksheets teaches skills; they are merely tools. Direct, skilled teaching is required for learning skills.

Instructional Procedures   Most basal-reader series have fairly similar general instructional plans. Typically there are three main steps, which are repeated for story after story: (1) preparation, (2) guided reading and re-reading, and (3) follow-up activities.

Preparation. Preparation for a new selection involves three things. The first is motivation and arousal of interest, which usually is more important when a new unit or group of stories is being introduced. The second is the introduction and explanation of concepts that may be unknown or unfamiliar. The third is the presentation and teaching of new words, which also may serve as review and application of previously taught decoding skills. New concepts and recognition of the words are often taught together.

The extent to which interest needs to be stimulated, concepts developed, and new words pre-taught varies from child to child. Knowing the children's background and the extent of their skill development helps teachers to decide how much of each step is needed.

Guided reading and rereading. Teacher-led discussion of the story title, first picture, possible story content, etc., usually precedes the reading of the story. Then the teacher asks a motivating question or two, and the children read the selection silently, in part to find the answer(s). The amount read silently may range from one or two lines at the preprimer level to a complete selection at later reader levels. These amounts also should depend on the children's reading ability at any level, with the better readers allowed to read larger units than the ones suggested by the manual. After silent reading, the teacher leads a discussion of answers to the motivating question(s). Oral reading for various reasons usually follows silent reading.

Follow-up activities. There are two types of follow-up activities: skills development and enrichment. Specific plans for developing various reading skills are contained in the manuals, and practice of the skills is provided by workbook and worksheet exercises. The relative importance given to these skills and the amounts, kinds, and usefulness of the suggested activities vary considerably among basal series.

Various kinds of enrichment activities are recommended in the manuals: stories or poems to be read to the children or by them, language development, songs and music, creative art or handiwork, and dramatization. Specific selections are listed, and recommended poems and songs may be reproduced.

Variations in basal-reader methodology. The best way to understand how reading is taught with basal readers is to study representative lessons at about the same reader level in two or three series—using the manual, text, and workbook—and going through the complete instructional sequence for a selection. Among the most frequently used basal reading series are those published by Allyn & Bacon; American Book; Ginn; Harcourt Brace Jovanovich; Harper & Row; Holt, Rinehart and Winston; Houghton Mifflin; Macmillan; Rand McNally; and Scott Foresman. It is helpful to be able to observe expert teachers conducting similar reading lessons and to discuss the lessons after the observations.

Inexperienced teachers find the very specific directions given in the manual very useful, but they should not attempt to do everything suggested, particularly in the follow-up activities. As they become more experienced and confident, teachers become more selective in following a manual, using it as a resource that contains many useful ideas rather than a set of directions to be followed rigidly. Teachers are expected to select appropriate activities based upon the needs of their pupils.

There are other variations among basal series besides differences in vocabulary load and story content. They vary in such things as the emphases placed on different objectives, the amount of oral reading suggested, and the placement of skills development in the lesson plans. Some series attempt to assist teachers to adapt instruction to individual differences. Most often this takes the form of providing separate lesson plans for children of varying abilities, or offering additional suggestions for slow or accelerated groups. Other variations include giving plans for both a "basic reader approach" and a "modified basic reader approach" that includes considerable emphasis on use of experience stories; and having separate sets of materials and programs for developmental, functional, and recreational reading.

Advantages. Basal-reader programs provide carefully planned, systematically balanced instructional programs. The teacher's time and effort are conserved by providing a well-designed series of graded texts, assorted other materials, and manuals that provide detailed teaching suggestions. As with any tool, these programs must be used flexibly.

More Than One Basal Series   Questions arise regarding the use of more than one basal series in a classroom or school. Because basal series vary in difficulty, easier series may be more appropriate for slow learners and more challenging series for advanced students. More than one series should be available if they differ sufficiently to accommodate such individual differences.

Is it better to go straight through one series of basal readers or to read the materials of more than one series at one level before going on to the next level? Teachers who opt to use materials from more than one series do so to provide extra skills practice, including reinforcing a sight vocabulary, or for independent reading. If skill development is the purpose, teachers must ask themselves whether they are attempting to push children through the first program at too rapid a pace. When children are deficient in a number of skills or have difficulty understanding the stories, this may well be the case.

A child need not go through an additional reader just to practice certain skills. It is more efficient to provide specific exercises for overcoming weaknesses. Selecting appropriate lessons is facilitated by the use of cross-referenced lists of objectives and keyed lists of commercially available texts (including basal series) and materials that are part of published reading systems (Zweig, CTB/McGraw-Hill, Random House). In making such decisions, consider whether the material lends itself to the teaching or practice of the desired skills; and if the child is to use the material independently, whether its level of difficulty is appropriate. It also may be possible, if skill development is not too deficient, to use the material at the next higher level in the same series as a vehicle for reteaching those skills, even though the manual may not call for such instruction.

As for reinforcing sight vocabulary, concern need be given only to high-utility words. Words that do not occur frequently need not be mastered. If books from other basal series are used to reinforce sight vocabulary, they must have considerable vocabulary overlap with the text in use, particularly at the lower levels. Insufficient vocabulary in common may make a text at the same designated level from another series more difficult for the child than proceeding to the next higher level in the same series. Since up-to-date comparative vocabulary lists are not readily available, teachers must make their own comparisons. It may be more feasible to utilize optional materials that accompany the basal program and use the same vocabulary, or to develop material employing the desired vocabulary. In the latter case, copies of the material could be kept on file for future use.

For inexperienced first-grade teachers, it is safest to proceed through the preprimers, primer, and first reader in a given series rather than to intersperse texts from other basal programs. This will ensure coordinated vocabulary and skill development.

A somewhat related question involves using a text at a grade level other than that suggested by the publisher. The child's reading ability, not the grade he is in, should be the determining factor. A reader usually employed in first grade may be appropriately used with a second or third grader who has a reading problem. Conversely, children should be allowed to utilize above-grade-level texts if they are ready for their use.

Basal-reader Content   Basal readers, particularly first-grade ones, have been criticized as having meager vocabulary, unnatural language structure, and dull or biased story content. In order to allow children to concentrate on learning the mechanical skills of reading, writers of beginning reading materials tend to use words, ideas, and expressions familiar to most children, as well as words that are likely to be met frequently in reading. Limiting the words that can be used necessarily restricts the literary quality of the stories. But, as indicated, the downward trend toward less total vocabulary has been reversed since the mid-1960s, and more natural language patterns are being employed. These two factors have led to stories that are more interesting and less repetitive. There also has been a recent increase in nonfiction selections and a significant increase in the use of children's literature (Popp 1975). It should be remembered, also, that repetition is not necessarily undesirable in stories for young children. Moreover, having a limited number of words to learn makes it easier for children to learn to read.

Much recent criticism has been aimed at sexism in basals and other texts. Critics have shown that significantly fewer females have been depicted or mentioned; males are portrayed in more occupations, and females are often cast in stereotyped roles; males are shown as being active, intellectual, persevering, while females are passive, docile followers (Gough 1974, Britton 1975). Basal readers did not change significantly in these respects from 1966 to 1971 (Schnell and Sweeney 1975). To combat sexism in reading materials, guidelines for writers have been developed by publishers (McGraw-Hill 1975) and professional organizations (National Council of Teachers of English 1976).

Most recently published basal-reader programs teach decoding skills earlier, more intensively, and more effectively than their predecessors. Much of the criticism that basals give insufficient attention to decoding is no longer justified. If some teachers fail to teach the skills as detailed in the manuals, the teaching rather than the program is at fault. When basal-reader lessons do not seem to cover decoding skills thoroughly enough, the use of supplementary phonic material may be helpful. If supplementary phonics material is used, care should be exercised lest the children become confused by differing approaches, wording of generalizations, and so on.

Most of the other complaints against basal readers reflect their misuse rather than any inherent limitations. Poor teaching practices such as considering the basal series to be the total reading program, rigid grouping practices, lack of individualization, and indiscriminate use of workbooks or exercise assignments can happen with almost any program.

Language-experience Programs

Language-experience programs attempt to take advantage of the relationships among the language arts—listening, speaking, writing, and reading. All forms of language are considered essential and are viewed as mutually reinforcing. By integrating language skills, it is hoped that the child will conceptualize:

"What I can think about, I can talk about.
What I can say, I can write (or someone can write for me).
What I can write, I can read.
I can read what others write for me to read." (Allen 1968, p. 1)

Language-experience programs take a variety of forms. Whatever similarity exists is in the sources of the basic instructional and reading materials and the general procedures for their development and use. Basically the approach involves having the children relate an experience that is written down, first by the teacher and later by the children as their writing and spelling skills increase. The resulting experience stories are used in various ways.

Instructional Methods and Materials   A language-experience approach may be utilized alone or in combination with another approach, in the initial stages of reading acquisition only, or through the primary grades. Experience stories also may be used with individuals or groups to bridge the gap between the prereading period and reading the first text in a published series or the initial stages of an individualized reading program. They also may be the main material in a continuing language-experience program.

Almost any event can be the basis for an experience story or chart: pets, birthdays, holidays, science experiments, classroom events. Field trips can provide material for three or more stories—planning the trip, stating what happened, and what was learned on the trip. But not all experience stories are suitable for teaching reading. Some are excellent experience records, good for language development and enrichment, but are much too complicated for effective use as beginning reading material. The vocabulary may include too many new words. Such charts may be read to the children; however, it is not advisable to attempt to teach recognition of all the words.

During the prereading stage, experience charts may be used as part of the readiness program, as an observational-testing tool, and as a technique for arousing interest in language and learning to read. Under the teacher's guidance, the children discuss an interesting experience, then formulate a title and a series of sentences that summarize the experience. Discussion of what should go into the story provides practice in thinking, speaking, and listening. Children can be helped through questions (e.g., "How shall we start our story?") and guiding statements (e.g., "Think about what the firemen did first") to express their ideas in complete sentences and to compare alternative statements in order to select the most appropriate one. These written records enhance the importance of the experience for the participants and help to crystalize new concepts and word meanings.

The teacher usually runs her hand under the line from left to right as she reads the material to the children. This helps them learn that each one-line sentence says something definite, that written words may occur in a sequence that corresponds to the spoken words, and that we read from left to right, top to bottom. Even though there usually is no direct attempt to teach word recognition at this stage, some children may begin to identify a few words. It should be realized, however, that children often memorize entire stories and can "read" (recite) them without looking at the printed stimuli. Word identification can be checked by presenting the words in varying sequences or in isolation. If the basic purpose is to demonstrate the relationship between spoken and written language, the children's rendition should be recorded and read to them verbatim. Translation of a dialect into standard English can wait until after the children are learning to read.

Experience stories also can be used as a lead-in to a published reading program or to an individualized reading program. In the former situation, the teacher makes an effort to include in the experience charts many of the words that appear in the first reading books.

If the experience stories are used as a lead-in, the teacher can edit the stories. This may occur either as they are being dictated or when the original is being placed in permanent form. The possible danger of editing is that children may realize that what they are saying is not really being considered and may feel manipulated. It may curtail their verbal enthusiasm. The impact of editing can be lessened by establishing a proper classroom environment, asking for statements until one contains the desired word, telling the children the purpose of the editing, and editing sparingly. Some teachers, who plan to move into an individualized reading program or continue with a language-experience program, also exert some vocabulary control, using a list of high-utility words (see p. 254) as a guide. When not used as a lead-in, there usually is little attempt to control the vocabulary or sentence structure. This practice is based on the belief that the children will employ language that they understand, thus providing the only control necessary.

Children keep a "word bank" or "word box" containing on individual cards the words from individual or group stories, or words that they ask the teacher to write for them. Alphabetizing can thus be introduced in a very practical way. At first these words are written by the teacher, with the children gradually assuming increased responsibility for doing so. These words are tested periodically, usually about once per week.

The classroom environment must stimulate the desire to express oneself.

As the facilitator, the teacher must structure a room that is alive with things to do and to talk about with others (Shohen 1973). Either the teacher focuses attention on some experience, or a child or group expresses the desire to write about something. The experience story is composed by the child with as much help from the teacher as necessary. If used with a group, the teacher records the spoken language in manuscript on the chalkboard or chart paper. For individuals, a small chart or regular-sized paper may be used. The story is then read aloud by the teacher during the early stages of instruction, and later by the children. If the stories are to be used for teaching reading, the teacher or aide prepares two or three copies, one of which is on a large sheet of ruled paper. A second copy is made on oaktag, or similar thin cardboard, which can be cut up into sentence, phrase, or word cards. Copies for individuals usually are typed and placed in their "reading books." Children practice reading these individual stories before reading them to the teacher or other children, or they are read silently by the author or other children.

Using the large ruled-paper copy, mounted on an easel, the teacher reads the story to the group line by line during the early stages of instruction. After the story is read in this way two or three times, the children are given the opportunity to volunteer to identify the lines. Guiding questions are asked, such as "Who can read the sentence that tells what kind of pet we have?" and, "Which sentence tells us the pet's name?" When all the children have read the sentence silently, one child comes to the chart and frames the line with his hands or runs his hand under the line as he reads it aloud.

Generally, it is preferable to ask questions that require thinking ("Which line tells what the fish did?") than to tell the children exactly what is on the line, phrase, or word card and ask them to find it ("Who can find the line that tells us that the fish ate the worm?"). In answering the first type of question, the children read silently, having to think about meaning. When the correct response is selected, they can be asked to read it aloud, and the teacher can note and correct inaccuracies. Some children begin to identify words; others see only the general characteristics of the words, such as their varying length.

A cardboard copy of the story is read orally by the teacher, compared with the original, and cut into sentence strips as the children watch. Various activities can be carried on with the sentence strips. For example, the strips can be placed in random order along the chalkboard ledge. Then the teacher asks, "Who can find the strip that tells the name of our story?" The title is found by a volunteer, read aloud, and placed on the top level of a pocket chart or flannel board. Each succeeding sentence in the original story is similarly located, read, and placed in position. Other procedures are to ask for the sentences in random order; or to ask the children to place the sentences in correct sequence, using the original as a model.

These line strips, or another cardboard copy, can next be cut into two- or three-word phrase cards, matched with the original, identified, read aloud, and arranged in sentences in the pocket chart. These phrase cards can also be used to formulate new sentences. Phrase strips can be cut into separate word cards (aiding the development of sentence segmentation ability), and assembled into phrases and sentences (e.g., I like cats). Calling the children's attention to the fact that each card has a word on it helps to develop the concept "word." New sentences can be formulated with these words, as well as sentences found in the original story. Similar procedures can be used by children using their individual word banks.

At times it is desirable to have the experience stories illustrated by the children. When the topic is favorable, the children can all draw or paint illustrations, one of which is chosen to place on the chart. After sufficient progress in writing ability has been made, children can make their own copies of the group story or can write and illustrate individual stories.

After several children learn some of the words in the experience stories, they are grouped to begin reading instruction. When used as a lead-in to a basal series, if many of the preprimer words are known, the pace for reading the preprimer stories can be increased, since less time is needed for introducing words. Some teachers simply have the children read and discuss the complete story in one or two sessions. However, the teaching of important reading skills should not be slighted. Meanwhile, the teacher continues with experience stories with the rest of the class and also gives special readiness practice as needed. As additional children show that they are ready for formal reading instruction, another reading group is formed. If an individualized reading program is being employed, each child proceeds at his or her own pace. Children continuing in a language-experience program continue to write stories and use them as reading material.

Experience charts can be used long after children have learned to read, regardless of the type of reading program employed. They can be narrative or descriptive stories. They can be of temporary interest or bound and kept for later reading. As children reach more mature levels of reading, experience charts become records of group planning and of group or individual compositions.

Advantages   Among the advantages of language-experience programs listed by Allen (1968) and Dallman et al. (1974) are (1) the relationships among the language arts are made evident; (2) children are more likely to understand the nature and flexibility of English as they work and rework their own language; (3) children are motivated to improve their communication skills as their writings are read by others; (4) ability grouping is not required, or recommended, thus overcoming the stigma such grouping might produce (although in practice, grouping may occur for specific skill development or when experience stories are not used exclusively as the instructional materials); (5) learning to read is easy and interesting because the learner's own vocabulary, language structure and patterns, and experiences are employed in the reading materials; (6) children acquire a reading vocabulary whose value they easily recognize; (7) spelling and writing skills are also fostered and developed; (8) skills are developed as they are needed, thus making learning them relevant; and (9) experiences are made more meaningful by having them recorded.

Research findings comparing language-experience with other approaches are conflicting (Vilscek 1968b); and although the language-experience approach is recommended for use with the disadvantaged by some writers (Serwer 1969, Cramer 1971, Garcia 1974), research regarding such use is limited and inconclusive (Hall 1972). Downing (1974) argued that the language-experience approach offers a vehicle for the development of cognitive clarity (see p. 38). He stated that although the first, and most important, language concept a child must develop is of the purposes of the written form of language, many beginning readers have only a vague idea of its usefulness. The language-experience approach not only provides them with concrete demonstrations of the communicative and expressive purposes of written language, but also with opportunities for developing specific concepts such as "word" and "sentence."

Possible Limitations   Because a language-experience program lacks the preplanned systematic structure of other reading programs, its success is greatly dependent on the skill, ability, and knowledge of the teacher. Although some commercial material is available, a great deal of teacher initiative, planning, and time is necessary to implement a successful language-experience program. Specific reading skills are introduced and reinforced as the teacher perceives the need. Therefore the teacher must be able to determine individual needs, must know the skills that need to be taught, and must plan or select procedures and materials for teaching them. The use of a skills checklist (see p. 234), behavioral objectives, and criterion-referenced tests may help overcome some of the limitations imposed by a lack of structure. The teacher also must have the ability to organize as well as be organized.

Other possible limitations lie in the materials used and the time necessary for recording and developing them. Although reading about their own experiences may stimulate interest, children may get tired of the restricted content of experience stories. The best way to overcome this problem is to provide other appropriate reading material as soon as the child can read independently. Similarly, not relying exclusively on experience charts can also cut down the time needed for developing materials. As for the lack of control of vocabulary and sentence structure, the teacher can revise judiciously. It is also quite likely that high-utility words will occur with sufficient frequency in the experience charts and stories or other material read by the children. If not, exercises can be developed to teach and practice these words.

Time must be allocated to record and reproduce stories. Group stories are less time-consuming than individual stories. Because the teacher must record and reproduce stories, more time is needed at first, but decreases as the children become able to write their own stories. Children also should be allowed to read stories written by other children. Use of a teacher's aide to record and reproduce stories or to give assistance in writing stories can relieve some of the limitations imposed by time. A procedure for using a cassette tape recorder in the development of early reading material has been described by L. B. Smith and Morgan (1975). Time also can be saved by grouping for instruction when appropriate, and by using commercially available materials for skill development. The *Breakthrough to Literacy* (Bowmar) materials and a series of three kits, *Language Experiences in Reading* (EBE) for grades 1–3, are available.

Individualized Developmental Reading

The term "Individualized Developmental Reading" (IDR) is used to distinguish such programs from other forms of individualized reading (see p. 160). Its underlying philosophy states that when given freedom of choice, children will select appropriate material and read it at a pace that is appropriate for them. IDR programs almost defy a common description because as Jacobs (1958, p. 4), an early leader in the movement, wrote, "It

is not feasible or desirable to present a simple, single methodological formulation of what is right in individualized reading which every teacher should
follow." Rather, each child's reading program is different because it reflects
the child's personal interests, needs, ability, and progress. IDR does not
have a preplanned systematic instruction program, such as is found in
basal readers, but uses individual reading in a variety of materials as the
methodological core rather than as a supplement. In a completely individualized developmental reading program, no two children may be reading
the same thing at the same time.

IDR programs are based on three tenets: seeking, self-selection, and
pacing. According to the *seeking* principle, "children tend to seek nurture
according to their growth needs and their abilities to perform tasks successfully and with satisfaction" (Olson 1949, p. 326). Thus they are given
the opportunity to explore a wide variety of reading material. *Self-selection*
means that children can choose whatever material they want to read and
read it at their own rate in accordance with the *pacing* principle. In actual
practice, seeking is limited by the materials available to the children, and
many teachers provide guidance in selection of reading material.

A few IDR advocates believe that if a child does not learn to read, the
best thing to do is to wait for readiness to occur, no matter how long it
takes. They consider remedial help to be a form of forcing, and therefore
a violation of the pacing principle. On the contrary, most reading authorities believe that simply waiting is not in the child's best interests. There are
ways to stimulate reading readiness and interest in learning to read, and
corrective or remedial assistance has proven to be beneficial to many children, particularly if provided early (Schiffman 1970).

Instructional Procedures   The general procedure is as follows. Each child
selects something to read and reads it silently during the reading periods,
with assistance from the teacher or a designated helper as the need occurs.
The teacher holds five- to ten-minute individual conferences with each
child, usually once or twice a week. Preparation for reading is almost completely eliminated, and reading usually is guided by the child's interest
rather than by any specifically stated purpose. Rarely is there rereading for
specific purposes. Reading skills are taught, either individually or in groups,
as they are needed.

During the teacher-pupil conference, the teacher is expected (1) to
find out what the child has read since the last conference; (2) to discuss

what has been read, which includes (a) questioning to evaluate the child's comprehension and recall and (b) giving the child the opportunity to state a personal opinion about the content and reaction to it; (3) to listen to the child read orally a small sample of the material; (4) to give the child an opportunity to talk about what to read next; (5) to note any difficulties or needs that become apparent; (6) to give help with words or ideas, teach or reinforce reading skills, ask questions that stimulate thinking, and in general supply assistance as needed; and (7) to write a concise summary of the conference. Not all of these objectives can be met, or should be attempted, in each conference.

Teacher-pupil conferences are an essential and valuable part of IDR. They provide the means for evaluating pupils' reading ability and giving them needed assistance. Although the conferences do not occur frequently, children are said to gain a great deal of satisfaction from having the teacher's exclusive attention. Some writers assert that the number of minutes of personal attention each child receives equals or exceeds that which any one child would get in daily group reading lessons. It is also claimed that teachers obtain a more comprehensive evaluation of the child's reading abilities when attending to one child exclusively than in the more frequent but briefer pupil responses during group sessions.

Most advocates of IDR recommend that the program should include some group and whole-class activities. When several children display a similar need, a temporary group is established and meets regularly with the teacher until the members have accomplished the purpose for which the group was created. Then the group is disbanded and another special-need group is started.

Whole-class activities are usually of the audience type, providing an opportunity for sharing activities such as reading portions of a favorite story, a panel discussion of a book read by several children, dramatizations, and so on. Some teachers introduce new reading skills on a whole-class basis.

Advantages   Theoretically, Individualized Developmental Reading makes it possible to provide maximum flexibility in adjusting reading instruction to individual abilities, interests, and needs. Pupils usually show an interest in reading and favorable attitudes toward it, and often read much more widely than in other programs. Moreover, it is claimed that the child strives for self-improvement and makes rapid progress when not compared with others and therefore neither frustrated nor hindered by group standards.

Teachers report that they get to know the children better, and that the extra effort required is worthwhile.

Possible Limitations   A number of factors can hinder an IDR program, not all of which are inherent weaknesses in the approach. Most of the possible limitations can be overcome or lessened as indicated below.

Teacher competence. A successful IDR program requires a higher level of teacher competence than is needed to obtain good results with a pre-planned program. The teacher must know, or have available, a sequence of developmental reading skills in order to be able to judge whether a child is doing well at his or her own reading level or is being held back by specific gaps in skills. Teachers should be perceptive of children as individuals, sensitive to their needs, and able to furnish encouragement, reassurance, and support to each child. They also should be able to discover specific needs on the basis of small samplings of children's reading. All these characteristics are desirable in any teacher, but those who rely on preplanned programs can get along with lower qualifications.

The most frequently asked question about IDR programs involves the teaching of reading skills. The lack of a preplanned skill sequence can be overcome if teachers are clearly aware of these skills, include them as important objectives, plan definite individual or group learning activities to develop them, and test to determine how well the skills have been mastered. Even when little attention is given to the direct teaching of skills, some children seem to acquire them; others, however, never seem to learn them. Teachers may wish to employ the suggestions for skill development made for a language-experience program (see p. 89) or use individualized reading skill kits, skill development workbooks, or programmed texts. Self-teaching materials can help each child to develop the necessary skills at his or her own rate and to concentrate on those skills in need of additional practice.

A teacher cannot possibly be knowledgeable enough about all the available reading material to ask specific questions about its content. When unfamiliar with a work, the teacher must revert to general comprehension questions that could be asked of any story, such as, "Which character did you like best?" "Why?" "Tell me the story in your own words," "What lesson can be learned from this story?" "Could this story really have happened?" "Why?" Spache and Spache (1973, pp. 205–6) list 19 such questions, and Veatch (1966, pp. 156–58) lists over 50 questions.

The literature (MacDonald, Harris, and Marin 1966) suggests that first-grade teachers are generally not very competent diagnosticians. So even though they may know what skills should be taught, they may not be aware that a child has a weakness, or what is causing that weakness.

Materials. It is often stated that for a successful IDR program, the number of available books should be at least three times the number of children in the class, with a wide range in content and difficulty. Relatively few classroom collections meet this standard.

School or public libraries that loan collections for classroom use can assist in overcoming this possible limitation. Any classroom collection should be changed periodically. If finances are available, a number of teachers can place their orders together so that a wide range of materials would be available for circulation. Inexpensive paperbacks can extend the budget. Materials for specific skill development usually are not mentioned in the IDR literature, but they would seem necessary if skills are to be learned adequately.

Class size. When there is a limited amount of time for teacher-pupil conferences, the more children there are, the smaller share each child gets. A class size of more than 25 would seem unfavorable for IDR, particularly in the primary grades. In a large class the teacher has to reduce either the duration or the number of conferences, or can use IDR with only one or two groups rather than with the whole class.

Maturity of the children. Other things being equal, the older and more mature and competent the children, the greater the likelihood of a successful IDR program. Of all the grades in which IDR might be employed, the first grade would seem the least suitable. Young children often are unable to continue with independent activities. Therefore, during much of the year, they would be dependent on the teacher for guidance and direction. Beginning reading has been successfully taught in an IDR program; but this seems to require a superior, resourceful, well-organized teacher. IDR makes more sense after children become capable of doing genuinely independent reading. Older children are better able to find material they can read by themselves. Also, they are able to sustain attention for longer periods of time and do not need as much assistance from the teacher.

There is some question as to whether many children select appropriate reading material on their own. For instance, only one-third of the children in Mork's study (1973) chose material at their measured instructional level. The lower the child's reading ability, the less likely it was that he or she would select material of appropriate difficulty. Mork also found that a five-minute guidance session was not effective in improving their selections. Apparently, more than brief teacher guidance is required.

Recordkeeping. A good recordkeeping system is essential in IDR. The teacher's records for each child should include a cumulative record of what the child has read, including titles, dates started and completed, number of pages read, and comments based on observations made during the conferences. Periodic use of skills checklists such as those found in Heilman (1972, pp. 400–401) and Harris and Sipay (1975, pp. 206–10) helps to avoid overlooking needs or problems. Children should also keep records of their reading as well as maintain a "word bank" of sight words, a vocabulary notebook, a list of reading skills they are trying to improve, and progress charts for skills being developed.

Classroom management. Commonly, several children who are to have conferences are seated near the teacher. As one conference is finished, the child returns to his seat and the next child moves to the chair next to the teacher. While the conferences are being conducted, the rest of the class are either reading silently or working on some meaningful activity assigned by the teacher. Children who are just learning to read must be provided with independent nonreading activities.

Conferences should be held on a regular rotating schedule, with the participants clearly notified in advance, perhaps by placing their names on a conspicuous list. Allowing time for some whole-class and group sessions, and assuming that the reading period will vary between 1½ and 2½ hours daily, it will probably take three to five days to confer with all the children. Some teachers who have a strong commitment to the pacing principle favor waiting for the child to request a conference. However, the children who most need help and stimulation are likely to be the ones most reluctant to ask for conferences.

Although much of the reported research involving individualized reading is faulty (Duker 1968), the general findings seem to indicate that an IDR program can be successful under favorable conditions. Nevertheless, less capable pupils and those with special problems are less likely to be successful than in a structured program (Sartain 1969). Teacher-pupil conferences could well be incorporated profitably into any reading program. And since "seeking, self-selection, and pacing" are well adapted to recreational reading, an individualized approach to recreational reading can become an integral part of total reading programs. Teachers interested in IDR must ask themselves if they have the qualifications and resources necessary for an IDR program. If the answer is affirmative, it might be a good idea to start with only one group.

CODE-EMPHASIS APPROACHES

Decoding skills are emphasized initially in code-emphasis programs. Three types of code-emphasis approaches are discussed below: phonic, linguistic, and special alphabet.

Phonic Programs

Although phonic [2] programs place emphasis on learning symbol-sound associations and applying phonic generalizations, they vary greatly in content and methodology. Among the important points on which they differ are (1) whether instruction begins with consonants, with vowels, or with combinations; (2) whether short or long vowel sounds are considered first; (3) whether a synthetic procedure (word parts are blended to form words), a whole-word phonic procedure (attention is paid to the sounds within words but not sounded in isolation), or a combination is employed; (4) how many generalizations are presented, which ones, and how they are worded; (5) the sequence of skills; and (6) when and how to introduce meaningful material. When meaningful material is introduced, the vocabulary usually is controlled by using only words that can be constructed of the phonic elements already introduced. After all the decoding skills in the program have been introduced, there is almost no vocabulary control. A number of words that are exceptions to phonic generalizations (e.g., *the, one*) must be taught as sight words.

There are two main types of phonic programs: those intended as a supplement to basal-reader or other meaning-emphasis programs; and those designed for use in place of a basal-reader program. Supplementary phonic programs are discussed on pages 289–93. Four basal phonic programs are briefly described below.

2. *Phonology*, the scientific study of speech sounds, includes phonemics and phonetics. *Phonemics* is the study and discrimination of a language's sounds (phonemes). *Phonetics* deals with the production, combination, description, and written representation of speech sounds. *Phonics* is the study of the relationships of *phonemes* to their written symbols (graphemes). Therefore the correct term to use when discussing decoding is *phonics*, not *phonetics*. The adjective form is *phonic*.

The *Keys to Reading* program (Economy) has a readiness book and five books for first grade, two texts each for grades 2 and 3, and one each for grades 4–8. All have accompanying manuals and supportive materials such as tests, workbooks, and duplicating masters. Although the program attempts to develop a balance between decoding and meaning, the early emphasis is on decoding. Eighty-three phonic generalizations are introduced, most of them in first grade. Readiness for word analysis is developed by having the children identify sounds and their written representations in word and story contexts. Long vowel sounds, followed by short vowel sounds, are introduced before consonants.

The general procedure for presenting letters and the sounds they represent includes the following steps:

---

(1) Show a letter or combination of letters and help the pupils name each letter displayed. (2) Say a sound represented by the letter or letter combination and show the children how to make the sound. (3) Have the pupils repeat the sound several times. (4) Help the children associate the sound with the letter or letter combination that represents it. (5) Write the letter on the board and let the children examine the configuration.

The following steps are suggested for helping pupils analyze one-syllable words: (1) Have the children look at the whole word. (2) Let them determine what sound the initial letter or letter combination represents. (3) Ask the children to count the vowel letters in the word and to note their position.[3] (4) Have the pupils decide what vowel sound the word will have. (5) Have them determine what sound the final letter or letters represent. (6) If a letter represents more than one sound, have the pupils decide which sound with the other sounds in the word forms a recognizable word. (7) Have the children combine the sounds in the word quickly and smoothly. (8) Have the pupils identify the word as one that makes sense. (9) Let a pupil illustrate the meaning of the word by using it in a sentence. (T. L. Harris, Creekmore, and Matteoni 1975, pp. 13–14)

Basic Reading, a phonic-linguistic program (Lippincott) has texts from the preprimer through the eighth-reader level (four for first grade, two

---

3. The program teaches generalizations about determining vowel sounds by the number of vowel letters in a word and their position.

Red runs fast.
Fran runs fast.

Fran can not get Red.
Red is in his nest.

FIGURE 3.2. A page from a primer in a phonic-linguistic series. From Glen-McCracken and Charles C. Walcutt, *Book A*, p. 42. Lippincott's Basic Curriculum Series. Copyright 1975 by J. B. Lippincott Co. The original is in color. Reproduced by permission of the publisher.

each for second and third grades, and one each for the other grades) with accompanying manuals, workbooks, supplementary reading materials and teaching aids, filmstrips, and criterion-referenced tests. Auditory and visual discrimination exercises are part of the lessons beginning with the preprimer. Tactile-kinesthetic reinforcement is emphasized. The program begins by teaching the symbol-sound association for short *a* (lower- and upper-case letters are presented simultaneously) followed by the association for *n*. At that point the children are taught that *an* is composed of /a/ and /n/. The following procedure is followed several times: listen to the word, identify the sounds, name the letters, pronounce the word. Children then manipulate felt or flannel letters to form the word, and are told that letters are a way of writing down sounds so that we can read words. Next the children are introduced to the words *an*, *Ann*, and *Nan* on a page in their texts. See figure 3.2 for a sample page.

The important point in this initial procedure is that at no time do you have children "sound out" the word. Nor do you have the children isolate the sounds to discover the word. Rather, you begin with the whole spoken word, then help the children hear its sounds, then present the letters that represent these sounds. Your goal is to have the word recognized, that is, seen as a whole and understood as a whole. The child can learn to recognize a word without sounding it out, and can, at the same time, be aware of the sounds that are in the word and the letters that spell these sounds. (McCracken and Walcutt 1975, pp. 11–12)

The more than 100 phonic elements that are taught in approximately 90 lessons in first grade, are reviewed in 12 lessons in the low-second reader level. A more complete description of the methods and rationale for the program may be found in Walcutt, Lamport, and McCracken (1974).

Apparently, adjustments for differences in learning ability are made by requiring that different numbers of words be learned.

In teaching the 44 sounds and presenting more than 2,000 words at the Grade One level, we present adequate material to keep the bright pupil well occupied. But the slower learning pupil need not study and master every one of the words that appear in the word lists because not all these words are necessary for successful reading of the accompanying stories. The pupils work with the word lists until they become familiar with the phoneme-grapheme relationships involved and can recognize them in new or unfamiliar words. (McCracken and Walcutt 1975, p. xviii)

The word lists include some words likely to be unfamiliar to young children, such as *ramp, ram, pod, punt,* and *grunt.* Symbol-sound associations for consonant blends as units (e.g., *tr, ft*) are not taught because "a child can hear a blend as easily as a syllable, we do not approach blends as special problems or as items that have to be presented individually as blends" (McCracken and Walcutt 1975, p. xiii).

The *Open Court Basic Reader* program (Open Court) has three foundation workbooks, a reader for first grade, two readers each for grades 2 and 3, and one each for grades 4–6, manuals, storybooks, and supplementary materials. Two main stated purposes are to teach children to read independently by the end of first grade and to provide selections of literary quality. The foundation program, designed for use in the first half of first grade or remedial use, has three stages. Stage one consists of teaching listening skills, letter names, and writing letters. In stage two, symbol-sound associations, blending techniques, and dictation skills are introduced, and simple stories and poems composed of words formed from these sounds are read. The remaining sounds are introduced in stage three, so that by midyear, 43 sounds (with 90 spellings) have been introduced. As each new sound and its possible graphemes are introduced, the child hears and says the sound, and sees and writes one or more of its corresponding graphemes. A synthetic phonics approach is used (sounds are blended to form words) in which long vowel sounds are taught first. Other language arts are incorporated into the program.

Distar (SRA) is a very highly structured program based on the belief that children, particularly the disadvantaged, can overcome their "language deficiencies" and learn to read if taught properly. Using the manual, the teacher and children are programmed—the teacher as to what wordings to use, how to signal the pupils to respond, when and how to reinforce correct responses and how to handle incorrect ones; the children as to how to respond (many oral responses are required). Symbol-sound associations are taught first, followed by instruction in blending the phonemes ("Say it fast"). The program, which involves a great deal of drill and repetition, also includes presentation books, short-story books, "take-home" worksheets, and criterion-referenced tests embedded in the material.

Successful use of *Distar* with disadvantaged children has been reported by Guinet (1971) and Ogletree and Dipasalegne (1975). But according to the latter authors, only 5 of the 21 teachers who used Distar found it effective for all children, the rest saying that it was less effective for slow learners. Because they disliked the structured format, or because the program failed to develop comprehension skills, or because children became bored with the repetition and drill, 18 of the 21 teachers modified the program.

It would seem that Distar's structure may be both a strength and a weakness. Those in need of a highly structured learning situation may profit from the program. However, the lack of flexibility can cause problems for both the teacher and pupils.

Advantages   The main advantage of an early emphasis on decoding is that children tend to become independent in word identification sooner than they might in meaning emphasis approaches. Children in code-emphasis programs also tend to score higher on standardized word-recognition tests; however, this advantage tends to disappear by third grade.

Possible Limitations   There is the danger that decoding may be overemphasized to the detriment of comprehension. If teachers do not provide meaningful selections and check comprehension through questioning or discussion, children may think that reading is simply pronouncing the words correctly. Some children also may attempt to decode all or most words, even those they can recognize at sight.

There is also much doubt that all the phonic generalizations found in some programs are really worth teaching. Some are applicable to very few words, others have many exceptions. Trying to learn a large number of generalizations may confuse some children; others can verbalize the rules, but never apply them to unknown words. Blending phonemes is particularly difficult for some children. Many of these programs assume that once a skill is introduced it will be mastered; adequately spaced review is not always built into the program. Also, the pace of learning symbol-sound associations and generalizations is too rapid for some children. Just as not all children can learn to recognize words through a whole-word approach, not all can learn through a phonics approach. Finally, there is the danger that children will rely too much on a single approach to unknown words, rather than employing syntactic and semantic cues in addition to graphic ones.

Teaching by Syllables   Some writers have recently advocated teaching initially by syllables rather than by phonemes, based primarily on the belief that the syllable is more easily discernible within the spoken word than the phoneme is. The syllabary program reported by Gleitman and Rozin (1973) begins with teaching the association of oral syllables with a few pictures and written one-syllable words. It therefore is really a rebus-syllabic program. A twenty-two-element syllabary is combined to form two-syllable and polysyllabic words, which in turn are used in sentences. Gleitman and Rozin (1973) reported success with the program, as did Harrigan (1976), who used a similar approach. Jones (1970) used a "closed syllable method" —one that begins with a vowel and ends with a consonant (*et*), semi-vowel (*ay*), or "silent e" (*ate*)—to teach reading to primary-grade Alaskan children. In this program, which employs 80 graphonemes,[4] words are used in which the graphoneme is stable (e.g., *eat*, n*eat*, s*eat*, but not gr*eat*). Later, decoding skills are taught using the graphonemes as the main units. For example, r*un* and h*er* are placed on the board, and the children told that since they can read these words, they can read the word *under*. Attention is called to the graphonemes in known words (they are underlined) and the same elements in other words. Although the program appears greatly to resemble the old "word family" approach, there are some differences in methodology.

Such approaches may be appropriate for children who have difficulty learning the associations for single phonemes, or blending them, but their limitations are apparent if one compares words such as *family*, *among*, and *famous*, in which the *a* followed by *m* represents a different phoneme in each word.

Linguistic Programs

Linguistic reading programs place their main emphasis on decoding in the early stages of reading instruction. Although no two linguistic series

---

4. "Graphoneme" is a word coined by Jones to refer to what linguists call a "spelling pattern," and what teachers have for many years called a "word family."

Six Pet Cats

Miss Hull had six pet cats—Muff, Cuff,

Huff, Puff, Ruff, and E. Nuff.

Miss Hull had the cats in a pen.

Miss Hull fed the cats well.

The cats got big, but the pen did not.

So the cats did not fit in the pen.

"Jim Bell, at the Red Mill Inn, has a

big pen," said Miss Hull.

"I will sell the cats to him."

FIGURE 3.3.   A page from the third book in a linguistic series. From *SRA Basic Reading Series, Six Ducks in a Pond*, p. 4, Level C. © 1976, 1970, 1965, 1964 by Donald E. Rasmussen and Lenina Goldberg. Reprinted by permission of the publisher, Science Research Associates, Inc.

agree closely on details, they usually have these factors in common: (1) They begin with teaching letter names, not sounds. (2) At the beginning they restrict vocabulary almost entirely to words that have consistent relationships between grapheme and phoneme. (3) They present three-letter words of the CVC pattern in groups that have a common spelling pattern, as *ban, can, Dan, fan, man, ran, tan* (see figure 3.3). (4) They teach a few irregular high-utility words as sight words, in order to be able to write some meaningful sentences. Other irregular words are taught later as needed. (5) They do not teach phonic generalizations, but expect children to note the similarities of words containing the same spelling pattern and to develop their understanding of the relationship between spelling and sound. (6) They give ample practice in comparing words that have minimal contrasts; in other words, that differ in only one phoneme and one grapheme, such as *tin* and *pin, tin* and *tan,* or *tin* and *tip.*

Besides the usual differences in content, linguistic reading programs differ on such points as whether or not to use nonsense words, and whether or not to employ illustrations. They also differ on amount of attention given to words arranged in lists as compared to meaningful sentences, the sequence in which spelling patterns are introduced, and the amount of practice given on particular elements. Some programs try to get into stories as quickly as possible; others remain with words and unrelated sentences for quite a while.

The *Merrill Linguistic Readers* series (Charles E. Merrill) has an alphabet book, three paperbacks, and three hard-covered readers without pictures in addition to accompanying teachers manuals, workbooks, and supplementary materials. Unlike most other linguistic programs, silent reading precedes oral reading in the lessons. Three major kinds of spelling patterns are used in the program: (1) consonant-vowel-consonant; (2) consonant-vowel-consonant-final *e*; and (3) patterns in which medial single vowels are contrasted with vowel combinations (e.g., *met-meet*).

The *Palo-Alto Program* (Harcourt) contains 20 paperback readers and workpads, writing activities to precede reading, six teachers manuals, and assorted supplementary materials. It differs from most linguistic programs in that more sight words are taught, a synthetic sounding-blending approach is used to teach decoding, and syntax is controlled beginning with kernel (basic) sentences and progressing to more complex forms. The program also attempts to develop factual comprehension early in the learning process. Attention is given to vowel combinations (e.g., *ay*) and spelling patterns such as *old.*

The *Miami Linguistic Program* (Heath) is strongly influenced by structural linguistics (Robinett 1965) and was designed primarily for use with bilingual or non-English-speaking children in grades 1 and 2. Oral-aural exercises in English are presented prior to reading instruction. There are 21 paperback readers with accompanying workbooks and manuals, as well as placement tests. Unlike other linguistic programs, only seven different words are used in the first book. Although the early story characters are animals that behave like humans, later stories involve folktales, myths, adventure, and realism. Other language arts are incorporated into the two-year program.

Advantages   The advantages of linguistic reading programs are basically the same as those claimed for phonic programs, the principal difference being that their authors claim that the use of spelling patterns enhances the acquisition of word recognition and decoding skills. Some children may be aided by the consistent symbol-sound associations and extended practice provided by such programs.

Possible Limitations   Many of the limitations listed for phonic programs apply here, as well as some other possible problems. Linguists do not agree as to what contributions linguistic programs make to the teaching of reading (Wardhaugh 1969). In fact, some question whether there even is such a thing as a "linguistic" reading program (F. Smith and Goodman 1971). As Pikulski (1976a) pointed out, linguistic principles have been translated into diametrically opposed ideas as to how reading should be taught. Linguistics has not provided a definitive answer as to how or when word recognition should be taught.

The slow rate at which new words are introduced and the frequent repetition may bore some children, as may the stilted language and artificiality of early stories. Use of minimally contrasting trigrams may confuse children who need more varied graphic information to learn words. Other children need to be taught symbol-sound associations because they cannot abstract them on their own, just as some may need to have sounds isolated for them. There also is the question as to whether it is better to establish an early "set for diversity" (Levin and Watson 1962) so that children do not incorrectly generalize that letters represent only one sound each.

According to Gunderson (1972), no current linguistic reading program (1) provides the teacher with definite means of determining children's oral language readiness; (2) gives the teacher the means of building upon present oral language skills; (3) gives the teacher instruction in the aspects of linguistics needed for understanding oral and written language; (4) provides the diagnostic and instructional materials needed for continual development of oral language proficiency; and (5) contains reading content developed in accordance with natural oral language patterns.

Special-alphabet Programs

Because English has an imperfect and often arbitrary spelling system, with many irregularities in the correspondences between letters and the sounds they represent, there have been many efforts to modify the alphabet in the hope that such modifications would make it easier to learn to read and spell.

i.t.a.   One line of effort has been to adopt an alphabet in which each symbol always represents the same sound, and each sound is signaled by only one symbol; in other words, there is a 1:1 symbol-sound correspondence. There are many such alphabets, of which the Initial Teaching Alphabet (i.t.a.) is the best known. The Initial Teaching Alphabet is *not* an instructional method, but a 44-character alphabet with some interesting features: (1) capital letters are the same shape as lower-case lettters, only larger; (2) there is a separate symbol for each of the 44 sounds of English; (3) many present letters are retained; and (4) the new characters were designed to facilitate the transfer to use of the conventional alphabet (traditional orthography or T.O.), mainly by retaining the upper halves of T.O. letters (see figure 3.4). It has been most widely utilized in Great Britain in a basal-reader program employing an eclectic methodology similar to that found in American basal readers. In the United States, the most widely used i.t.a. program, the *Early to Read* program (Fearon-Pitman), employs an early language-experience approach and a phonic decoding emphasis. In both cases, i.t.a. is seen as a transitional alphabet and is used only in the initial stages, with a transition made to T.O. spellings.

Advantages   The major advantages in learning to read an alphabet with consistent symbol-sound associations are (1) quantitatively, there is much less to learn in acquiring the ability to pronounce correctly the written

girls and boiz lern

tωo reed with ita

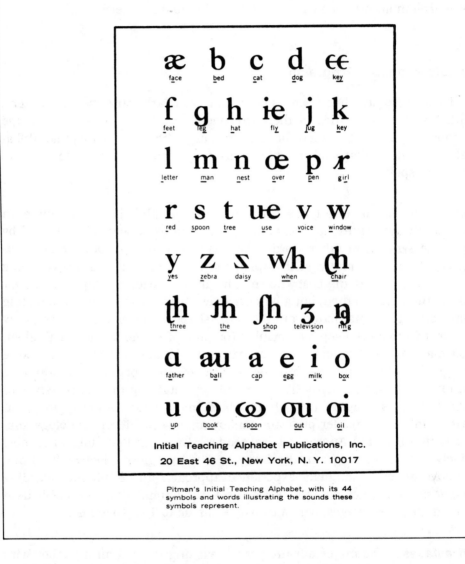

Pitman's Initial Teaching Alphabet, with its 44
symbols and words illustrating the sounds these
symbols represent.

FIGURE 3.4. The 44 i.t.a. symbols, and words illustrating the sounds these symbols represent. Reprinted by permission of Fearon-Pitman Publishers, Inc.

words in one's native language; and (2) qualitatively, what has to be learned is less complex (Feitelson 1976). Thus, using a transitional modified alphabet should make it easier to learn to read. Since spelling is easier, children are more inclined to express themselves in writing.

Transition from i.t.a. to T.O. is accomplished without difficulty by children who can read i.t.a. fluently and with understanding (Southwell 1973). The Bullock Commission found no adverse effects of i.t.a. at later stages of reading development (Downing 1976), nor did it adversely affect the spelling ability of middle-grade children studied by Petty, Murphy, and Mohan (1974). Robertson and Trepper (1974) reported successful use of i.t.a. with bilingual Mexican-American children. According to Downing (1973), beginning with i.t.a. facilitated cognitive clarity regarding the tasks of learning to read, and subsequently this cognitive clarity helped children to cope with the complexities of traditional orthography.

Possible Limitations As with all other reading methods, most children learn to read with i.t.a. Nevertheless, others do not (D. Johnson 1974). Some children have difficulty making the transition to the conventional alphabet.

The early advantage of learning to read with a system that is consistent in its sound-symbol correspondences does not guarantee later proficiency in reading. According to Warburton and Southgate (1969, p. 283), "after about three years of schooling, the reading attainments of most children taught initially by T.O. are approximately equal to those of children whose initial medium of instruction was i.t.a." "By about the fourth grade, regardless of a language's correspondence system, children vary in reading ability" (Gibson and Levin 1975, p. 174). Since the meanings of homophones (*whole-hole, one-won*) are identified through their spellings, use of a medium that removes this cue (*hoel, wun*) may create some problems. Use of context cues, however, may lessen this possible limitation. Linguists (N. Chomsky 1970) also suggest that a phonemically regular alphabet could deny readers cues to the similarity of meaning of words that are pronounced differently, with accent shifts and changes in vowel sounds (*courage-courageous, telegraph-telegraphy*); but such cues are more useful to skilled readers than to those just learning to read (Francis 1970).

Another possible limitation involves the number of available books written in i.t.a. Southwell (1973) claimed, however, that over two thousand different books were available by 1973. Such books would be necessary only until the children have made the transition to T.O.

Color Systems   There also are systems that retain the traditional alphabet but use colors as cues to the sounds that letters represent. One hue usually is assigned to all letters that may represent a given sound. Thus the *ee* in *meet, ea* in *meat,* and *e* in *be* would be printed in the same color. The best-known program that employs such a modification is *Words in Color* (Educational Solutions), which uses 47 hues (some letters are two-colored) as cues in its synthetic phonic approach to teaching reading. Materials include 21 wall charts in color, 8 phonic charts, colored chalk, 3 primers, a word-building book, a series of story books, and worksheets. None of the printed material from which the child reads is in color. A synthetic phonic method is used. Sounds are taught in isolation, then blended together mainly through "visual dictation" in which children respond orally to the letters as the teacher points them out in rapid succession. Letter names are never mentioned.

The advantages and possible limitations cited for other modified alphabets also apply to color modifications. The one advantage they may have is that they retain the traditional alphabet, thus making the transition easier. Nevertheless, it is difficult to determine the effect of color cues alone because the program also involves various methodology differences. One special limitation is the probability that some children, particularly boys, who are more likely to be color-blind, might have difficulty discriminating among the colors. About 8 percent of boys have varying degrees of color-blindness.

INDIVIDUALIZED SKILLS-EMPHASIS PROGRAMS

Programmed Materials

Programmed materials are constructed so that learning can take place in very small steps. The learner actively responds, probably will be successful, and obtains almost immediate feedback about the correctness of responses. Theoretically the child should be able to use the materials almost independently and proceed at as rapid a pace as possible.

Two series of programmed readers (McGraw-Hill, BRL) are on the market, and a number of other programmed materials are available for independent use or with teaching machines. The programs that use consumable paperback books primarily employ a phonic/linguistic method for teaching decoding. The programming is linear; that is, each step is done in

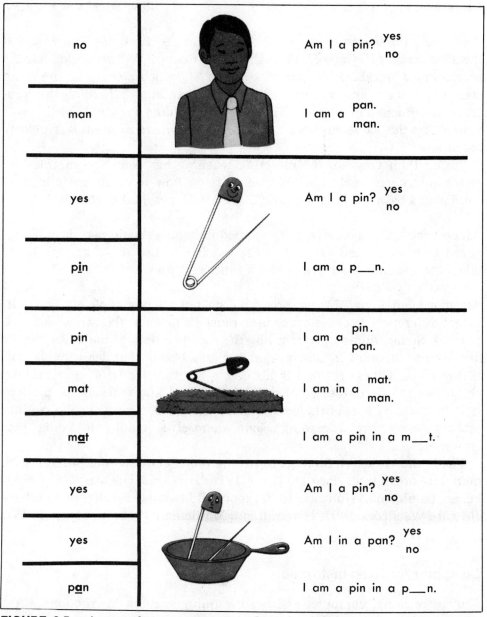

no	Am I a pin? yes / no
man	I am a pan. / man.
yes	Am I a pin? yes / no
p<u>i</u>n	I am a p__n.
pin	I am a pin. / pan.
mat	I am in a mat. / man.
m<u>a</u>t	I am a pin in a m__t.
yes	Am I a pin? yes / no
yes	Am I in a pan? yes / no
p<u>a</u>n	I am a pin in a p__n.

FIGURE 3.5. A page from a programmed reader. The correct answers in the left-hand margin are supposed to be covered until the child makes a response. Then the child slides the marker down to determine if the response was correct. From Cynthia Dee Buchanan, *Programmed Reading, Book 1* (3rd ed.), p. 8. New York: Webster Division, McGraw-Hill Book Co., 1973. Original is in color and larger. Reproduced by permission of the publisher and Behavioral Research Laboratories.

sequence without any deviations. A sample page from the *Programmed Reading* series (McGraw-Hill) is shown in figure 3.5. This series has 23 programmed workbook readers, a series of story books that use the same vocabulary, tests, and manuals. For more information regarding this program, see Buchanan (1968). The *Sullivan Reading Program* (BRL) was written by the same authors as *Programmed Reading* and is similarly organized.

Rather than program the material, teaching has been programmed by giving tutors extremely specific directions on how to teach an individual child with a basal-reader program (Ellson, P. Harris, and Barber 1968).

Advantages   Theoretically, programmed materials should permit individualized instruction and also allow the teacher to use the time previously taken for teaching repetitive tasks for other purposes.

Possible Limitations   Linear programs do not allow completely for individual differences because every user must go through the same sequence of tasks. Some children get bored by the repetitiveness of the tasks; others look at the answers in advance; the manual says that learning is still taking place. Unless reading is also done in other kinds of material, the child does not encounter connected discourse of any real length, particularly in the early part of the program. Lastly, not all aspects of the reading process (e.g., critical reading) lend themselves readily to being programmed.

The limited research findings regarding the effectiveness of programmed materials are mixed. Two studies (Della-Piana and Hogben 1968; Feldhusen, Lamb, and Feldhusen 1970) reported favorable results; three others did not (Woodcock 1967, Hammill and Mattleman 1969, Lumsden 1975).

Computer Assisted Instruction

More recently, computer-assisted beginning reading instruction (CAI) programs have been developed. In one program (Atkinson and Fletcher 1972), the visual material is presented on a televisionlike screen, with the auditory stimuli presented by a synchronized tape recorder. The child records answers by touching a spot on the screen with a light-pen, and the computer determines the correctness of the response. A more recent version reduces cost by substituting a typewriter for the light-pen. The program is primarily of the linguistic type, stressing decoding. Programming is of the branching type in that items or frames can be omitted or repeated, or additional practice to overcome a particular weakness can be selected and presented by the computer. Other CAI programs have been described (Serwer and Stolurow 1970, Golub 1974). The Edison Responsive Environment "talking typewriter" also uses a computer (Moore and Anderson 1967), as do some instructional management systems such as PLAN (Flanagan 1971).

The advantages and possible limitations of CAI are similar to those listed for programmed instruction, with a few differences. Computers offer impartial instructions and make it easier to have branching programs that truly allow for individualized instruction. The voice used in recording the audio material is warm and seems friendly. It uses many forms of verbal support, praise, and encouragement and never loses its temper. While imperturbability is desirable, some children need and seek personal contact with a teacher. The human aspect of teaching should not be overlooked.

Favorable results with CAI (Atkinson and Fletcher 1972) and programmed teaching (Ellson et al. 1968) have been reported. These programs have been designed as supplements to normal classroom instruction. Because of the potential for individualizing instruction, future developments in programmed and computerized programs should be watched carefully. In general, programmed instruction has been as effective as traditional instruction and may result in decreasing the amount of time needed to achieve specific educational goals. CAI has been shown to be effective as a supplement to regular instruction (Jamison, Suppes, and Wells 1974). As the cost of computers comes down, the feasibility of using them to teach increases.

Diagnostic and Prescriptive Reading Instruction

There has been increasing interest during recent years in what is most frequently called "diagnostic and prescriptive teaching." Plans of this type have also been called "skills management systems" and "objective-based systems." They represent applications of the systems idea, which was originally developed to increase military efficiency, to teaching.

In developing plans for such a system, the first step is to assemble a detailed and comprehensive set of learning objectives. These are stated in behavioral terms, and each objective is written to indicate what the pupil can do when he has mastered the objective. The second step is to develop a set of pretests, placement tests, and posttests or mastery tests. The third step is to locate teaching materials, key them to the objectives, and place them in sequences for learning. Preference is given to materials that can be self-administering and self-checking; for this reason, preference is often given to programmed materials. If not enough published practice material can be located, additional material is written for the program.

A child who is placed on the skills continuum (perhaps at different levels in various skill areas) in accordance with placement or pretest results works independently on assignments covering a skill that has not been mastered. When the child feels ready, a posttest is administered. If the posttest is passed, the child takes the next pretest; if the posttest is failed, more practice, perhaps of a different nature, is provided. Mastery tests covering broader skill areas are given periodically, and review work is assigned as needed.

The teacher's role involves (1) selecting, administering, and scoring tests; (2) drawing diagnostic conclusions; (3) assigning appropriate practice materials from a resource file; (4) keeping records; (5) giving individual or group help as needed; and (6) providing motivation and maintaining order. Except for administering tests, a computer could perform the first four items.

Among the management systems currently in use are: *Fountain Valley Teacher Support System* (Zweig), *Individually Prescribed Instruction (IPI)* (Glaser 1968, Beck and Bolvin 1969, Scanlon 1970); PLAN (Flanagan 1971); *Read on* (Random House), SCORE (Westinghouse Learning); and *Wisconsin Design for Reading Skill Development* (Otto and Askov 1972; Interpretive Scoring Systems). Although there are some basic similarities in these programs, they also differ significantly. Many of these systems and others are described by Prager and Mann (1973), Thompson and Dziuben (1973), Rude (1974), and Stallard (1977).

Advantages Among the purported advantages of diagnostic/prescriptive instruction are: (1) instruction is highly individualized; (2) instructional effort is not wasted because the pupils get tasks that are not too easy or too difficult for them; (3) the tests provide a basis for reporting specific progress; (4) the system allows all concerned to operate within an established set of guidelines; and (5) criterion-referenced tests that clearly indicate instructional needs replace global, diagnostically useless, norm-referenced tests (Johnson and Pearson 1975).

Possible Limitations   There are several possible limitations: (1) The testing program and recordkeeping may be too heavy for teachers to handle unaided (Carner 1973). Although extra help in the form of computer assistance, machine scoring of tests, or a teacher aide or clerk can lessen the burden, the extra expense may cause a distinct problem. (2) There is also the danger that use of the approach can become mechanical. Systems approaches can become quite rigid. Not all children learn in the same way and not all skills are equally important. A teacher may consider all objectives absolutely necessary for all students, regardless of their abilities, and as the only route to learning to read (Popp 1975). (3) It is more important to learn why a child cannot meet a criterion than simply whether he or she passed or failed; assigning another exercise without finding out why the child did poorly in a test or exercise can lead to blind repetition of the same type of error. (4) There is a strong temptation to stress skills that are highly specific and easy to test, such as decoding skills, and to slight skills such as inferential comprehension, which are harder to teach and to test. (5) The total demand on teacher time and effort may be excessive.

BEGINNING READING INSTRUCTION FOR DIALECT SPEAKERS OR NON-ENGLISH SPEAKERS

Many children classified as "disadvantaged" either speak a dialect that differs in varying degrees from standard English or do not speak English fluently or at all. A few do not even understand spoken English when they enter school. Although other factors also contribute to the poor progress in reading made by many such children, language factors are frequently cited as important contributing or causal factors.

Dialect Speakers

Five alternatives have been offered as solutions to the "dialect problem." First is the recommendation that such children be provided with beginning reading materials written in their own dialect (Baratz 1970). Use of a language-experience program could accomplish this aim. This opinion is based on the assumption that material that approximates the child's spoken language will be easier and more interesting to learn to read. Apart from the practical problems occasioned by commercial attempts to produce materials that reflect various dialects and words employed by subcultures (e.g., *pop* vs. *soda*; *tote* vs. *carry*) (Mitchell 1972, Y. Goodman and Sims 1974, Simons 1974a) and other problems (Venezky 1970), there is strong parental opposition to this idea. Black parents, for example, generally are opposed to practices that they feel perpetuate or encourage the use of dialect. So they tend not to accept the use of black English in school, especially in reading and writing (Hoover 1975), and are likely to believe in overt correction of young children's oral language (Schwartz 1975). There also is evidence that black children are not any more successful comprehending material written in their own dialect than written in standard English (Nolen 1972; I. Ramsey 1972; Hall, Turner, and Russell 1973).

A second approach involves teaching standard English as an alternate dialect necessary for effective communication (Erickson 1969, Davino 1971). A program in which the content is printed both in black English and in standard English has been described by Gladney (1972), but evidence regarding its effectiveness is lacking. A third remedy would have children learn to speak standard English before learning to read it (Venezky 1970), which seems sensible; however, there is no research evidence that such a procedure has the desired effect (Simons 1974a). Fourth is the suggestion that materials be written in standard English, but in a style which minimizes dialect and cultural differences (Venezky 1970). This seems unrealistic because it would limit the words and structures the author would be permitted to use. Lastly is the recommendation that teachers accept and approve children's rendition of written standard English into their own dialect (Goodman 1965). Research findings as to which of these approaches is the most desirable are not available.

Although massive intervention with first-grade disadvantaged children may not have been as successful as hoped (Goolsby and Frary 1970), good teaching can result in reading achievement by disadvantaged children which is close to national norms whether the instruction emphasized basal readers, supplementary phonics, or language-experience (A. J. Harris, Morrison, Serwer, and Gold 1968). Perhaps a successful reading program for such children might involve helping teachers to be knowledgeable about children's dialect, initial use of a language-experience program, a structured skill-development program, and acceptance of dialect speech, all under a skilled teacher's direction. Children's dialects should not be belittled or criticized as defective, lest they view such behavior as a personal reflection of them and their culture with the result that they reject reading. Reading comprehension depends on comprehension of standard English rather than on habitually speaking standard English, and many children understand it quite well while continuing to speak their dialect.

Non-English speakers

There are many children in the United States whose native or strongest language is not English. Until fairly recently, most of them were placed in reading programs in which English was the language of instruction, with materials written in English. Instructional materials reflecting the cultures of such children have been developed, in the hope that such materials would be more understandable and interesting, as well as reflect their heritage. Non-English-speaking children either (1) are taught to read first in their native language, with receptive and expressive English-language skills taught concurrently or after reading has been started; or (2) are taught to understand and speak English before beginning reading instruction in English. Although there is a trend toward increased bilingual education, present research findings do not clearly favor either of these approaches (Hatch 1974). Teaching children to read English as a second language is complicated by such factors as phonological interference (e.g., reading *fit* as /feet/) and difficulty in predicting English syntax (Hatch 1974). Refer to unit 11 for a more detailed discussion of the reading problems of children from different language backgrounds.

WHICH BEGINNING READING APPROACH IS BEST?

Chall (1967), who reviewed the research on beginning reading conducted prior to the mid 1960s, concluded that code-emphasis programs tended to produce better results than the meaning-emphasis programs typified by the basal readers of the 1950s and early 1960s. She also concluded that the research findings did not favor any one code-emphasis program. The author herself qualified the first general conclusion, so it should not be accepted as an endorsement of all code-emphasis programs or a statement that all children should be taught to read by using a code-emphasis program.

The 27 Cooperative First-grade Reading Studies sponsored by the U.S.

Office of Education compared a variety of reading programs. The findings of these studies were summarized in the May and October 1966 and 1967 issues of the *Reading Teacher* and by Stauffer (1967). Results of 15 of these studies that compared overlapping methods were coordinated by Bond and Dykstra (1967). Among the more significant findings they reported were:

1. . . . It is likely that Basal programs should develop a more intensive word study skills element, while programs which put major emphasis on word recognition should increase attention paid to other reading skills.
2. Reading programs are not equally effective in all situations. Evidently factors other than method, within a particular learning situation, influence pupil success in reading.
3. . . . The tremendous range among classrooms within any method (wide differences in achievement were obtained by teachers supposedly employing the same program) points out the importance of elements in the learning situation over and above the methods employed. To improve reading instruction it is necessary to train better teachers of reading rather than to expect a panacea in the form of materials.
4. Children learn to read by a variety of materials and methods. . . . Furthermore, pupils experienced difficulty in each of the programs utilized. No one approach is so distinctly better in all situations and respects than the others that it should be considered the best method and the one to be used exclusively.

The second-grade findings were similar to those of the first year (Dykstra 1968a), and although they appeared to support Chall's conclusions, Dykstra (1968b) cautioned that there was not clear evidence that the early emphasis on decoding was the only or even primary reason for the relative superiority of code-emphasis programs. In seven of the eight studies that followed the original subjects through the third grade, there was no consistent significant difference in final reading achievement for any of the methods compared. Thus, although they had limitations (Sipay 1968, Corder 1971, Lohnes and Gray 1972, Lohnes 1973), the most recent large-scale studies in the United States indicate that no one program produces consistently superior results. Nor did any program eliminate failure. Rather, the quality of the community, school, teacher, and pupils far outweighs methodology.

In Great Britain the Bullock Commission (Department of Education and Science 1975) arrived at similar conclusions, stating that no one method, medium, approach, device, or philosophy holds the key to the process of learning to read.

Gross comparisons of beginning reading programs have not yielded a great deal of useful information. What may be good for most children may not be suitable for *all* children. Most children learn to read regardless of the program employed; some fail in every program. Furthermore, current published reading programs are becoming increasingly alike.

The suggestion has often been made that schools should try to find a child's strongest aptitude, and teach the child by a method that stresses that aptitude. Psychologists use the term "aptitude-treatment interaction" to express this idea. In reading, efforts have been made to see if matching aptitude and method produces superior results. Children with better visual perception than auditory perception have been taught with a visual method, and children with stronger auditory perception by a phonic method; control groups with similar test scores were taught without regard to stronger aptitude. Seven studies to date have failed to find any average benefit when method matches aptitude in beginning reading (H. M. Robinson 1972b). It may be that the aptitude tests used in these studies were inadequate and that when better tests are used, the results may be different; but for the present, the idea doesn't work.

It is reasonable to conclude that for most children, best results can be obtained by using a balanced, eclectic approach. In such an approach equal stress can be placed on word identification and comprehension, and multisensory cues can be taught from which the child can select and use whatever cues are most helpful in learning to identify words. If the program employed in a school does not have these characteristics, the teacher has the responsibility of providing the needed balance and diversity. When a child continues to fail in a reading program that emphasizes a particular approach or medium, a different approach to teaching that child should be tried.

UNIT 4

An Overview of the Elementary School Reading Program

This unit provides an overall view of reading programs beyond the initial stages of reading instruction. It is divided into three sections: reading in second and third grades, reading in the middle grades, and reading in the upper grades. Each section considers the three strands of a total reading program.

READING IN SECOND AND THIRD GRADES: FOCUS ON SOLIDIFYING BASIC READING SKILLS

The second and third grades are vital in a reading program because during these years rapid progress in important basic reading skills is essential. By the end of the primary grades, children should have developed word-recognition, decoding, vocabulary, and comprehension skills that allow them to read not only their reading texts, but also simple content subject texts and reference materials, and a wide variety of library books. In these grades, developmental reading lessons form the major part of the instructional program in reading (averaging about an hour and a half a day),

118

although both functional and recreational reading increase in importance as compared to the first grade.

It is a great mistake to assume that all children entering second grade are ready for "second grade" reading activities. It is likely that some children will still be functioning at the primer or first-reader level or even lower. Others will be capable of handling material above the second-reader level, and one or two may not even have started to read. Second-grade teachers must be prepared to meet these challenges.

At the beginning of the third grade, the range of general reading ability is even wider. Many entering third graders can already read successfully at the third-reader level, some at the fourth-reader level or even higher. Nearly half are probably below third-reader level, with a few still struggling with first-grade material.

A successful reading program starts where the children are. It must give every child opportunities to develop his or her reading skills and abilities. When teaching is very effective, the rapid progress made by the most able learners widens the distance between their skills and those of their most limited classmates. Relatively uniform progress tends to signify a reading program that fails to meet the needs of the most competent learners.

Basal-reader Programs

The following discussion considers "on-grade" materials; however, as indicated, children should use materials that are suitable for their general level of reading ability and conceptual background, regardless of the grade in which they are placed.

Materials   In structured programs such as basal-reader and some phonic programs, there usually are two books (readers) each for second and third grade. Whereas in much first-grade material the pictures tell a major part of the story, illustrations in second- and third-reader materials depict events in stories that are complete without them.

Content of the reading texts is increasingly varied. Some stories were written for the book, while others are shortened or simplified versions of previously published stories, often by well-known authors. The stories are usually grouped in a number of units, each with a central theme. By the second-reader level in some series and by the third-reader level in others, the stories tend to become further removed from the "here and now" themes characteristic of first-grade texts. Story length gradually increases, and plot complexities tend to get more involved in each successive book. Naturally each set of readers is somewhat different in content from any other.

The words used in the stories are controlled to varying extents. With phonic programs that introduce all or almost all decoding skills in their program in the first grade, there is virtually no vocabulary control. Other phonic and linguistic programs continue to restrict vocabulary to words that contain phonic elements or spelling patterns previously introduced. Basal readers' vocabularies continue to be controlled, although to a lesser extent than in first-grade texts. There are wide variations among the basal series as to the number of new words introduced at each level, the pace at which they are introduced, and the cumulative total vocabulary.

Total vocabulary and rate of introducing new words are not the only factors that determine the difficulty of a reading text. Words with unfamiliar meanings are harder to learn than familiar spoken words whose printed forms are new. Difficulty also depends in part on the sentence structure, the complexity of the plot, the children's conceptual and experiential backgrounds, and the sheer length of the story.

Accompanying material usually includes teachers manuals and workbooks. Some manuals give very detailed plans; others supply only a general plan for the story and leave it to the teacher to work out the details. When manuals suggest a rich variety of activities for each story the teacher must be intelligently selective. Otherwise progress through the text would be slow, and few children would profit from doing everything suggested. Preparation can be shortened, especially with the better readers. Not all comprehension questions have to be asked or discussed in detail, oral reading can be selective, and enrichment activities are optional.

Supplementary materials vary and may include separate correlated story books, filmstrips, and duplicating masters. A few basal series have "transition" books that can be used with children who are not quite ready to progress to the next higher reader level.

Of the various kinds of activities, the ones that deserve most faithful adherence at the second- and third-reader levels are those concerned with the development of reading skills, particularly with independence in word identification (recognition, decoding, and meaning). The word-identification skills that intensive phonic programs introduce in the first grade are introduced over a two-year period in most basal-reader programs. By the end of second-reader level, most of the same ground has been covered. In the past, basal readers have been criticized for their weak decoding programs, but if the suggestions in current manuals are carried out, most children steadily improve in their ability to decode unknown words successfully.

Decoding   As taught with basal readers, decoding involves the combined use of three strategies: context (syntactic and semantic cues), morphemic (structural) analysis, and phonics. Children are given practice in making intelligent use of the meaningful setting in which new or unknown words appear. Morphemic analysis means dividing a word into meaningful parts (morphemes) that can be recognized or analyzed as subunits. This includes dividing words into roots, prefixes, and suffixes, and separating compound words (doghouse) into their components. If long and short vowels have not been introduced earlier, their symbol-sound associations and generalizations, as well as most consonant blends (*st, bl*) and digraphs (*sh, wh*) are introduced at the second-reader level. Vowel principles involving two vowels (*oi, ow*), silent consonants (*kn, wr;* called "digraphs" in some programs), and the introduction of syllabication may occur at either the second- or third-reader level in basal-reader programs.

Word Recognition and Word Meaning   The vocabulary used in first-grade basal readers is restricted almost entirely to words that are part of most children's speaking vocabularies so as to allow instruction to concentrate on the development of word-recognition skills. Such may not be the case with code-emphasis and individualized reading programs. In basal-reader programs this is still largely true at the second-reader level, although some unfamiliar concepts and words are introduced. A transition takes place at the third-reader level, with a shift of emphasis from word recognition to word meaning.

By the third-reader level, children usually can recognize over a thousand words at sight and have the decoding skills to figure out many more words. Word recognition is no longer a major problem for those who have made normal progress.

The expansion of content at the third-reader level brings with it an increasing number of new words whose meanings are unfamiliar. There also are many technical terms needed for reading content textbooks, the meanings of which have to be taught. The total number of words of unknown meaning is larger than the number that teachers can take the time to introduce properly, so that the selection of the particular words for direct teaching is also a problem.

Language-experience Programs

In schools that start reading instruction with a language-experience approach there is usually a shift during first grade to either a structured basal-reader approach or to individualized developmental reading. The readers may be eclectic, phonic, or linguistic.

Schools that do not make such a shift during first grade usually do so at the beginning of second grade or soon afterward. Very few schools continue with experience stories as the main reading materials beyond first grade. Language-experience procedures are likely to be continued as a way of recording plans and information gained, in such content fields as science and social studies.

Individualized Developmental Reading

Children who have started to read in an IDR program usually continue in such a program through second and third grades. They have already learned the routines of such a methodology. The range of individual differences in reading competence and in desire to read becomes increasingly wide. Many IDR teachers teach specific decoding skills only as they recognize individual needs for such instruction. Others systematically cover a decoding skills program, using workbooks or programmed material. Still others supplement individualized reading with a diagnostic/prescriptive decoding program.

Children who begin reading in a language-experience program are often moved into an IDR program sometime during first grade or, in relatively few schools, at the beginning of second grade. Less commonly, children whose first-grade reading was in a carefully preplanned program using eclectic, phonic, or linguistic readers are moved into an IDR program in second or third grade. Whenever the shift to IDR takes place, the teacher has to spend some time patiently getting the children accustomed to the new routines.

Phonic and Linguistic Programs

Because of the heavy emphasis on decoding in phonic beginning reading programs, the decoding practice in second- and third-grade reading levels in such programs is mainly review and practice in application. The increasing number of words met that are exceptions to phonic generalizations causes problems. Some are taught as sight words. Others require use of a strategy to apply the most likely generalization, then try the resulting word in a sentence to see if it makes sense; if not, try an alternative generalization. Some children who fail to grasp phonics in first grade are ready to do so a year later, and review of first-grade phonics gives them a chance to learn and apply what they could not master before. Decoding, however, receives much less emphasis in second and third grades than in first grade, for most children in phonic programs.

The readers in phonic series become collections of short selections, many of them adaptations of traditional folk and fairy tales. There is little vocabulary limitation, and new words are usually taught only if their meanings are expected to be unfamiliar.

Much the same is true of linguistic programs, in which children are expected to formulate their own decoding rules. Those who have successfully completed the first-grade levels are considered to be ready to decode most words they meet. The emphasis shifts toward reading for meaning. For children in either a phonic or a linguistic program who have not mastered first-grade goals, the second-grade teachers are expected to continue with them from where the previous teacher left off.

Individualized Skills-emphasis Programs

When programmed reading is the heart of the first-grade program, children finish the year at greatly varying points in the series. Some will have completed most of the materials intended for grades 1 and 2, while others may be less than halfway through the booklets usually completed by first graders. Each child is expected to continue in second grade from his or her first-grade stopping place.

As children near the end of the programmed sequence, emphasis shifts over to connected reading. In some schools they enter a basal-reader program; in others, an IDR program; and in still others, a diagnostic/prescriptive program. The strong decoding emphasis of beginning programmed material must be counterbalanced by a shift toward major emphasis on reading for meaning and pleasure if children are to finish third grade with well-rounded reading skills and with favorable attitudes toward reading.

In diagnostic/prescriptive programs the second-grade emphasis is often very heavy with decoding, with page after page of workbook-like practice on more advanced decoding skills. The main difference from programmed reading is that in a typical programmed reading series all the children go through the same instructional sequence at different rates; in a diagnostic/prescriptive program children who show they have mastered a skill do not have to do further practice on it. In both types of programs an increasing stress on reading for pleasure is needed to offset the sometimes boring sequence of practice pages and tests.

Independent Reading

As children become more competent readers and more capable of reading independently, the role of independent reading can be enlarged. There is an ever-growing variety of materials that can be read successfully by children with no more than beginning second-reader ability. Picture books with few or no printed words also are available for children just beginning to read. As children progress through second- and third-reader levels, the reading matter they can use for independent reading continues to expand in variety and interest, and much reading is done "just for fun."

Children who read extensively improve their reading skills in the most natural way possible. Doing a large amount of easy reading builds speed of word recognition and fluency. Reading somewhat challenging books helps children acquire new ideas and concepts and stimulates them to think and reason.

Recreational reading should be considered an important part of the total reading program. Suitable materials for it need to be provided. A central school library with a trained librarian is a valuable asset. Each classroom should have its own collection of at least fifty books, varying widely in difficulty, style, and content. Teachers often get many of the books from the central school library or the public library. Each child should have a library book handy for use when assignments are finished early, as well as in periods designated for independent reading. Much recreational reading also can take place at home, but time for independent reading in school should be definitely scheduled. In the sample teaching plan outlined in figure 5.3 (p. 170), a major portion of the reading program is devoted to independent reading on two of the five school days, and opportunities for such reading occur on the other three days.

Independent reading allows children to read in a highly individualized way. Each child can select reading material and go through it at his or her own pace. Recreational reading helps to compensate for the limitations of grouping, in which the best readers in a group may experience little challenge, and the poorest in the group may have to exert strenuous effort just to keep up.

Functional Reading

The use of textbooks in content areas such as English, spelling, arithmetic, science, and social studies is begun in some schools as early as first grade and in most other schools starts in second grade and continues throughout elementary school. Content texts are often more difficult to read than basal readers at the same grade level. Each subject has its own special vocabulary that has to be learned. In addition, content texts often employ less control over general vocabulary and sentence structure than basal readers do and tend to be harder to read. Some content texts are frustratingly difficult even for children with average reading ability.

Several alternatives to the textbook study assignment can improve content learning by children with limited reading skills. They include: (1) Use of a project or unit plan in such areas as science and social studies. Each of several committees contains children with widely varying reading skills and uses library resources of many kinds and difficulty levels. (2) Reliance on oral presentations and listening skills, live or by use of recordings. (3) Use of a variety of audiovisual materials to develop concepts and present information. These may include motion pictures, filmstrips, and film loops, silent or with accompanying sound tracks, and recordings of reference books and texts. (4) Adaptation of a developmental reading lesson plan to the use of content textbooks, with preparation, guided reading, and discussion. These procedures are discussed in some detail in unit 9.

Special Issues in the Primary Grades

Oral Reading   Oral reading plays an important role in primary-grade reading programs. It can contribute to the child's development in many ways because oral reading: (1) provides the teacher with an assessment tool for appraising important reading skills such as word recognition and phrasing; (2) gives the reader practice in communicating with an audience; and (3) provides the audience with practice in listening. Oral reading is one activity in which personality characteristics such as shyness are clearly evident and is a medium in which sensitive teachers can help children toward better social adjustment. An insecure child should not be forced to read in front of peers. Shy children with adequate reading ability can be helped to make the transition by having them read parts behind a screen for a puppet show or shadow play (see Weiger 1974 for suggestions on making and using puppets).

In the usual pattern of developmental reading lessons, children read the selection silently before they are asked to reread part of it orally. This provides an opportunity to concentrate on obtaining meaning, and when necessary, to decode a word, try out phrasing, or correct an error or miscue without embarrassment. Oral reading after silent reading tends to be more accurate, more fluent, and more expressive than if it were done at sight.

In some situations, however, unrehearsed oral reading is desirable. It is useful in diagnosis because it can provide a clearer picture of the child's word-recognition skills. Children who are fluent readers sometimes enjoy oral reading at sight as a variation from the usual procedure.

Oral reading can be undertaken for a variety of purposes in the primary grades.

Diagnostic session. It is desirable to have a diagnostic oral reading session with a child individually from time to time, to check on the child's needs and progress. While the rest of the class is engaged in some self-directing activity, the teacher calls one child to a spot apart from the class and records his or her performance. As Mays (1974) pointed out, errors committed during silent reading cannot be detected or corrected.

Purposeful rereading. Teachers manuals suggest a variety of ways to motivate oral rereading and to help it from getting monotonous and boring. Some of these are: (1) to show how the characters feel as they speak, which not only improves oral reading performance, but also gives an idea as to the reader's comprehension of the material; (2) to find the place where a character feels a certain emotion; (3) to prepare a dramatization of the story; and (4) to make the characters sound real. In a discussion that follows silent reading, asking the children to find and read aloud the particular sentence or paragraph that gives the answer to a question or that served as a basis for a response is a natural way to bring oral reading into the total lesson plan.

Two oral reading practices, which are sometimes combined, should be avoided. The first involves having children take turns orally rereading the whole story. Such a practice rarely serves a useful purpose. Children get bored rereading a story unless there is a special purpose; after a while many will not bother to read it silently the first time. If the purpose is supposedly for assessment, diagnosis is best done in a one-to-one situation. The second practice is having the rest of the group "follow along" in their books as one child reads orally. This does not provide an audience situation or assure that the "followers" will "learn the words" because they may not be looking at the same word that is being pronounced by the child who is reading orally. For good readers, being required to follow along at the slower pace of oral reading may have an adverse effect on reading rate and interest. Even more damaging is the practice whereby the group try to catch the child making a mistake in oral reading. (The child who detects the error then gets to read.) Such a situation is anxiety-provoking, particularly for the poor reader, who is most likely to make errors.

Oral reading is more constructive when parts of the story are reread for specific purposes after prereading it silently and when it is done in a group in which differences in reading ability are not great. Group oral reading can sometimes be carried on with a group chairman or leader, freeing the teacher for other activities.

Audience reading. When oral reading is a genuine process of communication, the audience does not read along silently while one child reads orally. The audience listens attentively.

Instead of using the reading text, children should be given the opportunity to read to the class or group an interesting passage from something they have read independently. They are expected to practice until they can present it with fluency and good expression. It is advisable, at times, for the teacher to listen to make sure the reading is satisfactory before allowing the child to read to an audience. A weekly audience reading period helps to motivate independent reading, provides an incentive for improving oral reading skills, and affords an enjoyable listening experience.

Another kind of audience reading occurs when a group presents a favorite story or play dramatically, or as in a TV or radio broadcast. There is an announcer, and each character's part is read by a different child. Each group can have a turn presenting a story to the rest of the class. Stories with a good deal of dialogue, radio scripts, and children's plays can be presented effectively in this way. The performance can be tape-recorded, and later the children can listen to their performance and evaluate it.

A large number of plays are available from PLAYS, Inc. or can be located in the index compiled by Kreider (1972). Excellent suggestions for using drama reading can be found in Henning (1974) and Larson (1976). The use of high-interest readers as a basis for teaching reading through drama has been described by Batinick (1975).

Choral reading. Oral reading in unison is particularly well adapted to the reading of poetry or other rhythmical material. When the whole class or group reads aloud together, the better readers set the pace and the less able readers join in, being helped with phrasing, rhythm, and interpretation. After the selection has been read in unison, it is possible to assign certain lines as solo parts and other lines to particular groups. With appropriate balance of solo and choral effects, some high and low voices, some parts read loudly and some softly, some slowly and some at a fast pace, choral reading can provide many of the values of choral singing, and at an age when most children are not yet ready for singing in harmony. Bamman et al. (1971) present useful ideas on choral reading and interpreting poetry orally.

Children often need direct instruction in oral reading skills (see p. 224 for a checklist.) Teachers can present a good model of oral reading and can call attention to what they are doing to read well orally. Instruction and practice can be given in proper phrasing, use of voice, posture, and so forth. For example, to demonstrate how intonation affects meaning, sentences can be read orally but with stress placed on different words. Each rendition is explained: "*Tom* broke the red window. Tom *broke* the red window. Tom broke *the* red window. Tom broke the *red* window. Tom broke the red *window*."

Eye-voice span. Teachers can demonstrate an interesting fact about oral reading. As the teacher reads aloud, a child, who has been instructed to do so, covers the page. Usually the teacher is able to continue reading part of the material that has been covered. This demonstrates the eye-voice span, the number of words (distance) the eyes are ahead of the voice.

A wide eye-voice span allows children to read orally at sight with good comprehension, phrasing, and expression. It also allows children to look up at the audience without pausing or losing the place.

The eye-voice span is normally the amount a person can read in one second (Geyer 1968). Its length also has been measured in terms of the number of words, being approximately 3 words for second graders and 4.5 words for fourth graders (Levin and Turner 1966). The eye-voice span tends to increase with age and improved reading, and is influenced by the meaningfulness of the material.

There is the possibility that the eye-voice span can be increased with specific practice. Children can work in pairs, one reading orally while the other uses a cover card. The number of words in the eye-voice span can be counted and a progress record kept.

Silent Reading

Many children who are just learning to read find it very difficult to read silently, mumbling or reading orally quietly instead. Learning the written forms of words involves associating them with their spoken form and meaning. Saying the word aloud helps many children to make this association. Teachers should not stress completely silent reading before the children have achieved some security in word recognition. The transition from quiet oral reading, to silent reading with observable lip movements, to silent reading without lip movements does not have to be made by all children at the same time.

By the time children are reading at the second-reader level, they should be able to read silently, and lip movements usually can be given up by children by the third-reader level, if not sooner. All that is generally necessary is to suggest that the child is now ready to read in a more grown-up fashion, without saying the words out loud or with lip movements. If this does not work, it is wise to wait a few weeks and try again.

Neither should the crutch of finger pointing be taken away too early from children who need it. For some children, pointing to each word or moving the finger under the line of print helps them to keep their places; without it, their eyes roam around the page. Insisting that they stop finger pointing may interfere with their progress. Children who persist in pointing should be allowed to do so.

A transitional technique is the use of a card as a marker, which is placed under each line in turn. As with lip movements, the use of pointing or a marker can usually be stopped safely when children are at the second- or third-reader level, if the child has not already stopped without teacher intervention. The need to do so much earlier has been exaggerated by some writers.

When reading silently or orally, the material should be held approximately 12 to 18 inches from the eyes, except for extremely near-sighted children. Children who deviate from this guideline, or who tend to tilt or cock their heads to one side when reading, may need a visual examination. Moving the head from side to side should be gently discouraged. Proper reading posture involves sitting with a reasonably straight back, with the book either flat on the desk or held in a nearly vertical position.

READING IN THE MIDDLE GRADES: FOCUS ON READING TO LEARN AND FOR ENJOYMENT

Learning to read has been largely accomplished by most children, although by no means finished, by the time they enter the fourth grade. Range and variety should be the outstanding characteristics of reading programs in the middle and upper grades. Both recreational and functional reading become increasingly important, and reading becomes a necessary tool for learning from content-subject texts and reference materials.

The term "middle school" means different things in different school districts. It may include two, three, or four grades, with grade 5 the lowest and grade 8 the highest. Cutting across the traditional sequence of a six-grade elementary school followed by a three-grade junior high, the middle school idea has not yet jelled into a fixed pattern.

The youngest children in a middle school are usually preadolescents, 10 to 12 years old. Their oral language differs only slightly from adult language. Their abstract reasoning ability is still developing, making concrete examples still necessary for many of them as a base for logical reasoning. The older middle school children, 13 or 14 years old, and some of the 12-year-olds, are going through the many changes of puberty. Whether these young teen-agers are in a middle school, a junior high school, or the upper grades of an eight-grade elementary school, they are encountering radical physical and physiological changes. They are likely to be emotionally volatile, and their intellectual development is sometimes erratic. They are striving to develop basic attitudes and values. Often the need to be accepted by their peers makes conforming to peer standards and values more important than the combined influence of parents and teachers.

The following characteristics have been described as desirable for a middle school reading program: (1) it should improve reading skills and help pupils to achieve personal satisfaction from reading; (2) it should help to satisfy the felt needs of the pupils; (3) it should include regular teacher-pupil conferences, and personal records of reading progress kept by each pupil; (4) it should help to improve the efficiency of the pupils in studying; (5) it should help the pupils to experience vicarious attitudes, concerns, feelings, and values; (6) it should provide a widening base of general information; and (7) it should make available reading materials which are widely varied in topics and levels of readability.

Nevertheless, as Duffy (1976) points out, middle school theory sometimes is far ahead of actual practice. Rather than presenting a unique educational structure designed to meet the preadolescent's and early adolescent's special needs, many middle school reading programs are just copies of junior high school programs. Typically they are departmentalized, and often they are part of the English program.

Teaching reading in the middle school is covered in greater detail by Duffy (1974), Hafner (1974), and Smith and Barrett (1974).

Developmental Reading

Most basal-reader series and phonic or linguistic programs that extend beyond third grade have one book for each of grades 4 through 6. For the most part, the texts are collections of short stories or excerpts from longer selections, arranged in six to eight thematic units. Story themes run the gamut, with an increase in nonfiction and settings far removed in time and distance from the child's immediate world. Illustrations are less profuse and include photographs, maps, and schematic drawings. Most reading texts contain glossaries by the fourth-reader level, if not sooner.

Most reading series have greatly relaxed their vocabulary control by the fourth-reader level. Instead of the guiding principle being one of whether children can recognize or decode words that have not been previously used in the series, the guideline becomes more one of word meaning. The care with which authors provide context cues to make it easier to infer the meanings of unknown "new" words varies considerably.

The difficulty of a story is not entirely a matter of the frequency of unknown words, sentence length, or unfamiliar ideas. Sentence structure also is important because as sentences become longer and more complex, there are more inversions in word order, parenthetical phrases and clauses, conditional statements, uses of the passive voice, and unusual expressions. Not only do plots become more complicated, but also some characters speak in a way typical of a particular region, culture, or era.

Workbooks that accompany each reader usually are designed as reinforcing and skill-developing tools which are recommended for use as related reading. It is typical for middle-grade workbooks to have a correlated vocabulary but independent content. Decoding skills are reviewed, and additional principles of syllabication and morphemic analysis are introduced. Emphasis is given to teaching dictionary skills, word meanings, and specific comprehension and study skills.

Basal-reader Methodology Middle-grade basal-reader manuals tend to have the same general organization as those for the primary grades. Each starts with an overview and explanation of the general plan, then provides a teaching plan for each story.

Preparation for the new selection is likely to be briefer than in the primary grades. The "new" words are listed, and some manuals indicate the specific decoding skills that children can apply to them. The teacher usually is advised to encourage pupils to use their decoding skills, context cues, or the glossary to identify unknown words and discover their meanings. Essential new concepts may require explanation, and a guiding question or two is given to motivate the first reading.

Guided reading and interpretation generally call for silent reading first, often of a fairly long whole selection in one session. In working with groups it usually is necessary to assign one group a fairly long selection for silent reading while the teacher works directly with another group. After the silent reading there is a check on comprehension, which may involve written answers or oral discussion or both, in response to written or oral questions. Rereading may involve oral or silent reading, and varied purposes for motivating rereading are provided.

The teaching of related skills shows some change of emphasis. In the fourth reader, primary-grade phonic and word-recognition skills are reviewed, and syllabication and morphemic analysis, often begun at second- or third-reader level, are reviewed and further developed. Practice is given in locating words in the glossary and dictionary as well as in interpreting definitions and selecting the definition that fits a particular context. Further refinement of syllabication, morphemic analysis, and dictionary skills is provided at the fifth- and sixth-reader levels. Synonyms, antonyms, and homonyms are given special attention, and words are classified in a variety of ways. The meanings of common prefixes and suffixes are studied.

Related practice in comprehension skills tends to be specific. Some exercises involve reading for main ideas; others stress reading for significant details; still others, reading to discover cause-effect relationships, and so on. Although most reading in the middle grades is assimilative in character, some attention is usually paid to developing the ability to read critically.

There also may be some attention to reading rate. Directions for simple tests of reading rate may be given in the manual, and suggestions may be provided for individualized work with the exceptionally slow reader. Timed practice exercises for improving rate also may be recommended.

Basal readers for the middle grade are vehicles for the systematic and sequential development of basic reading skills. Experienced, capable, creative teachers often can improve on the lesson plans given in the manuals. This does not absolve them from covering, in their own ways, the important and needed skills called for by the manual. Slavishly adhering to a manual may result in dull and uninspired teaching; totally ignoring it may result in many important reading skills not being taught.

Individualized Developmental Reading   In grades 4 through 6 the conditions that allow an IDR program to be successful are easier to meet than in the primary grades. Nearly all children have reached a level of reading competence sufficient to allow truly independent reading, at least of very easy material. Children are more mature and capable of continuing independent silent reading for long periods. There is a larger number of suitable books and a greater variety of content. Most children can select suitable books for themselves and can comprehend fairly complicated plots.

The amount of reading that most children do between conferences with the teacher in such a program makes it difficult to check their comprehension with any adequacy. The method tends, in consequence, to encourage a quick, superficial reading; a once-over-lightly. Unless other procedures are employed to develop comprehension skills, the child in an IDR program may become a fast reader who gets the main ideas but notes and recalls few details. Independent developmental reading needs to be combined with procedures that help to develop the skills of careful reading and study.

Individualized Skills Development   Abundant materials can be utilized in an individualized way to improve comprehension skills in the middle grades. Boxes of materials, usually called "reading laboratories" or "reading kits," provide short informational selections that are followed by comprehension questions, to be answered on separate paper. Usually the box contains about 10 levels of difficulty, with about 15 selections at each level. Answer keys are provided, which children can take to their seats, use to correct their own answers, and enter the score on a personal chart or graph. Some kits also include short selections for use in improving rate of reading. Kits to improve listening comprehension are also available.

Several graded sets of workbooks can be used for individualized or group practice, mainly of comprehension skills. One series of programmed workbooks for middle grades provides six levels of difficulty and covers decoding, vocabulary development, and comprehension. Details about the materials available for building comprehension skills can be found in unit 8.

These types of individualized practice materials are intended to be used as part of a reading program, not as a total program. Their use can be combined effectively with either a basal-reader program or an IDR program.

Vocabulary Development   Middle-grade materials include many words that children probably have never heard used in speech, and perhaps never will. For example, in reading stories about knights, children are likely to encounter archaic words like *forsooth* and *methinks*, and types of armor such as *cuirass* and *chain mail*. The meanings of such terms often can be inferred successfully without using a dictionary. If children expect that they will not have to read the word aloud or use it in their speech, they are likely to be satisfied with an approximate pronunciation, perhaps only later recognizing that a word they hear pronounced correctly is one they have met previously in print. Many children gradually acquire reading vocabularies that outgrow their speaking vocabularies.

Vocabulary development occurs in three main ways in the middle grades. First, important new words, particularly those occurring in content areas, are discussed and explained by the teacher. The meanings of such key words as *longitude, oxidation,* or *improper fraction* cannot be left to guesswork or to a dictionary definition. Second, many new words are absorbed effortlessly while reading, when the context makes their meanings clear. Third, children proficient in the use of the dictionary turn to it frequently to get an exact statement of a word's meaning or to check its pronunciation. Training in the intelligent use of context and the efficient use of dictionaries is important for vocabulary development. Provisions should be made for listing important new words and reviewing them periodically.

Oral and Silent Reading

Many children quickly learn to read silently; others take years to reduce oral responses from quiet mumbling to inaudible lip movements to truly silent reading. Although primary-grade teachers usually try to get children to give up lip movements, a substantial minority continue them into the middle grades. The habit can be overcome most easily by motivating children to try to read without lip movements while reading very easy material.

Even good adult readers, when confronted with difficult reading material, tend to slow down and move their lips. Therefore, at times, persistent lip movements and audible whispering are symptoms indicating the need to use material that is less difficult for the child.

Most children begin to read faster silently than orally when they are at the third-reader or fourth-reader level. To reach average silent reading rates in the middle grades, children must be able to read faster than they can talk. Persistent lip movements are a deterrent to such development. Research seems to show that, in the middle grades, encouraging a large amount of independent reading does as much to speed up reading as does spending an equivalent amount of time in practice exercises intended to promote phrase perception and speed up reading (A. J. Harris and Sipay 1975, p. 574).

Oral reading serves the same purposes in grades 4 to 6 as in the primary grades: diagnosis, listening practice, communication, and personality development. The varieties of oral reading recommended for the primary grades on pages 126–29 also are appropriate for the middle grades. Various types of genuine audience situations, in particular, provide motivation for practicing and polishing oral reading skills. Some excellent silent readers need considerable help before they are able to read orally with clear diction, suitable phrasing, and expression.

Comparative research studies on whether elementary school students read better orally or silently have produced conflicting results. Recently Rowell (1976) found that both third and fifth graders obtained higher comprehension scores when reading orally.

Sustained silent reading, that is, uninterrupted silent reading for a definite time period, was described by Hunt (1970) and has been advocated by a number of writers. However, two studies done on the intermediate grades have indicated that sustained silent reading did not increase comprehension (Oliver 1973) or reading skills in general (Evans and Towner 1975). Yet despite these findings it may be that such a practice may have advantages not measured by reading tests, such as developing an interest in reading.

Recreational Reading

The marked individual differences among children in expressed reading interests are greater and more striking than those related to sex or age differences. Some children have immature reading tastes, while others are precocious. Some have very narrow interests; others will read almost anything. Some read several books a week, while for others reading is near the bottom of their leisure-time activities. Yet forcing a book on a student may lead to an apathetic attitude or outright hostility. Teachers are better advised initially to allow children to employ self-selection from among approved books, and later gently recommend specific titles.

An extensive library is needed to cater to this great variety of interests and maturity levels, to say nothing of the wide range of reading ability found at each grade level. Convenient access to a central school or public library helps to amplify classroom resources, and fostering membership in the public library is important.

Home conditions are not always favorable for reading as a leisure-time activity. Lack of privacy, peace and quiet, and a negative attitude toward reading discourage many children from taking books home. So, although many children do read extensively at home, it is unsafe for the school to rely on this. The school must provide time as well as materials for independent recreational reading. The plan that is outlined in figure 5.4 reflects the need for independent reading periods.

Functional Reading

Both research reading and the reading of textbooks grow in importance as children progress through the middle grades. For research reading, children need to learn location and study skills; for textbook reading, they need help in adapting their reading skills and habits to the special requirements of each subject area, as well as in acquiring the specific skills needed for each. In all kinds of functional reading, they need to be selective and able to organize and summarize the information they find.

Location skills start with learning to find entries quickly in an alphabetical order. Usually this starts with a glossary or dictionary; later, it is extended to the varied requirements of locating items in indexes, encyclopedias, and a library card file. Some help in classification, in order to be able to choose alternative possible entries for a particular kind of information, also is needed. Once the relevant pages are located, rapid skimming to find the particular needed fact or to get an overview can be developed with practice.

Inability to read textbooks independently is one of the most common problems faced by middle graders. Reading textbooks presents some special problems. There are many technical words and heavy concept density. Many children need to be shown how to use headings, subheadings, and marginal notations. Guidance is needed in the interpretation of different types of maps, charts, graphs, tables, and other graphic illustrations. The analysis of arithmetic problems requires a different kind of reading than that employed in reading about a historical sequence of events or a science experiment. In general, adaptations of reading skills to the demands of specific textbooks should be done during subject-matter periods and cannot be assumed to be taken care of by developmental reading lessons.

The beginnings of learning to select and organize ideas start with the construction of the first experience charts for beginning readers. Every time that plans are formulated and listed, or a group's or committee's findings are summarized, another step is taken in learning how to condense, classify, and organize ideas and information. In the middle grades this informal training is supplemented by specific instruction and practice in outlining. In a series of graded steps, starting with a complete outline of a selection and then progressively providing less and less help in subsequent selections, children can be taught how to find the logical skeleton of the author's plan and how to develop their own outlines.

READING INSTRUCTION IN THE UPPER GRADES: REFINEMENT OF READING SKILLS

The seventh, eighth, and ninth grades are handled differently in various administrative plans. In some school systems, these three grades form the junior high school. Others have the seventh and eighth grades as part of the elementary school, with ninth grade as the first year of high school. Still other systems have a four-year or five-year elementary school followed by a four-year or three-year middle school.

Provisions for the teaching of reading in the upper grades are varied. For a long time it was assumed that a child who got that far in school knew how to read, and reading was assigned rather than taught. Literature was read and analyzed and textbooks were studied, but reading skills as such were not considered in need of further development.

During the 1930s and 1940s the growing awareness that a large number of upper-grade students were unable to do the assigned reading resulted in the development of many remedial reading programs in these grades. Children with normal IQs and low reading ability were given special instruction in small groups. Little or nothing was done for good or average readers, or for those poor readers whose IQ scores were low (often on group intelligence tests that required more reading ability than they possessed).

The past three decades have seen an increasing acceptance of the idea that the reading requirements of modern life demand reading skills at a higher level than can be attained in the first six grades. Reading programs have been developed at senior high school and college levels as well as in the upper grades, and there has been an increased effort to combat adult illiteracy. Stress is placed on developmental reading, with the central idea that every student can be helped to improve his reading ability. Refinement of the reading skills of able students as well as those with inadequate reading ability is now considered an important educational objective.

Departmentalized instruction, which is usual in the upper grades, creates some important differences from the self-contained classrooms commonly found in the first six grades. Instead of one teacher who is responsible for all reading instruction, several teachers share the responsibility. The English teacher often has the major responsibility for developmental and recreational reading, and the various subject teachers should each be responsible for helping pupils read effectively in their content areas. When English and social studies are combined in a core program, the core teacher is responsible for both developmental reading and some teaching of study skills.

The extremely wide range in reading ability (for example, in seventh grade a range from third to twelfth grade in reading ability is not unusual) commonly is reduced by sectioning English or core classes according to reading test scores. The class is likely to be scheduled as a unit for other subjects, also. In a small school with just one or two classes at each grade, the problem of dealing with individual differences is intensified.

Developmental Reading

Developmental reading ordinarily takes up one or two English periods per week, with a variety of materials used. Sometimes a basal reader is employed that is an extension of the series used in preceding grades, and strongly resembles the fifth and sixth readers. The accompanying manuals provide lesson plans for reviewing and extending the reading skills taught in the middle grades. With slow classes, middle-grade basal readers are sometimes used; however, many texts now contain material of interest to this age level but are designed to develop reading skills usually taught in the middle grades or lower.

A second type of material is a series of readers that in form and content are primarily literature anthologies. In using these books, literary appreciation and vocabulary enrichment are frequently stressed.

A third kind of material is a reader designed expressly for reading skill development. One recent book of this type contains sixteen chapters, each designed to develop skills in a particular area (Gainsburg 1978). There are also several series of paper-covered workbooks that give practice in sharpening reading comprehension skills, developing vocabulary, and improving rate of reading. Some of these are designed so that reading, answering, correcting, and discussing one exercise takes about a period. More explicit information regarding these and other materials is given in the units that cover these topics in detail.

Also available are kits for individualized practice materials, including exercises suitable for a wide range of reading abilities. Another type of material, which may be used with slow learners or poor readers, is written for teen-age interests at lower levels of readability, and can be used to develop reading skills.

Recreational Reading

Seventh- and eighth-grade pupils tend to do more independent reading than at any other time in their lives. Most of them have attained levels of reading ability that allow them to read with ease materials covering a wide range of maturity and difficulty. Television watching tends to decline, and the combination of heavy homework assignments and increased social activity that occurs in senior high school has not yet arrived. So upper-grade students have time to read, and with suitable opportunities and encouragement, will use a substantial share of their spare time reading.

In these grades, a sharp distinction is sometimes made between literary appreciation and recreational reading. For literary appreciation, a few "classic" selections are read by the entire class and then analyzed in terms of plot, characterizations, description, use of language, imagery, underlying theme, and the like. Recreational reading is usually independent reading, done outside of school. Often children are given a list of approved titles from which to choose. Outside reading often is checked by some form of written or oral book report. A minimum number of books is required; reading beyond that is voluntary.

One problem with this approach is that there is often a conflict between the intellectual and the emotional outcomes. Too many pupils have discovered that the more a selection is analyzed, the less it is enjoyed. By using challenging questions, fostering stimulating discussions, and using dramatizations and role playing, some teachers succeed in intensifying the enjoyment of literary selections while building literary insight. The search for clues to a character, the interpretation of figurative language, the challenge of attempting to predict the outcome, the identification of words that create vivid images or depict subtle moods and emotions—these activities can be exciting or boring, depending on how they are taught. Similarly, book reporting needs to be planned with its probable impact upon the desire to read in mind. A combination of brief written reports with some opportunities for oral discussion of outside reading is usually preferable to long written analyses.

Functional Reading

In the upper grades, most reading in the content areas is textbook reading, with some independent research reading for individual and group projects and reports. Textbook reading is usually difficult for the majority of the pupils because these texts contain abstract concepts, complex sentence structure, and difficult vocabulary. Guidance in how to use the particular textbook is the responsibility of each subject-matter teacher. It is not safe to assume that all that is needed is to tell the class how many pages to read.

The technical vocabulary of each subject requires careful consideration. Which words are essential? Can their meanings be derived from context; is a dictionary definition informative enough; or does the word warrant direct explanation and illustration in class? Can visual aids be used to show and clarify the meanings of technical terminology? If so, where can they be obtained?

Many children find that the school time available for studying their textbooks is insufficient. If children are allowed to take the text home, they have an opportunity to reread, to look up words, and to write notes or a summary. Or if the book is very difficult for them, a member of the family can read it to them or with them.

GENERAL PRINCIPLES FOR TEACHING READING

There is no one plan for teaching reading that meets the needs of every situation. Not only do children differ in a variety of traits, as do teachers, but school policies and the availability of reading materials also vary greatly. Each teacher tries to follow a program that is adapted to his or her pupils, makes efficient use of available materials, and is suited to that particular teacher's teaching abilities.

Although specific application differs according to circumstances, six general principles should be incorporated into any reading program:

1. *Reading must be an enjoyable activity.* Every reading program should attempt to develop the habit of reading for fun. Provision must be made for encouraging large amounts of silent reading in interesting materials of suitable difficulty. Programs that consist mainly of drill on word recognition and comprehension skills will not accomplish this goal.
2. *Systematic instruction must be given in specific reading skills.* Primary-grade programs should focus on developing a basic reading vocabulary, decoding skills, and reading for meaning. Above the primary grades, emphasis should be given to continually expanding vocabulary, refining comprehension skills, and mastering study skills and habits.
3. *The reading program must be balanced and contain varied activities.* Unless a program has a reasonable balance between decoding and meaning, oral and silent reading, specific practice and independent reading, and recreational and informational reading, it will produce children whose reading skills reflect the imbalance.
4. *Provisions must be made for individual differences.* Children vary widely in every significant trait—intelligence, language and conceptual skills, maturity, interest, and handicaps to learning. In order to be successful, a reading program must be flexible enough to provide differing pupils with types of instruction from which they will profit.
5. *Attention must be given to children whose general level of reading ability is below what can reasonably be expected of them.* Time must be

devoted to helping these students improve their reading abilities. Whether remediation is given individually or in small groups by the classroom teacher or a special teacher, it should be based on an intelligent diagnosis of each child's needs.

6. *There should be a planned articulated reading curriculum from kindergarten through high school.* Clearly stated objectives arranged by skills and by levels will allow teachers to know where each child stands along a continuum. Instruction can be adapted to individual needs without losing sight of overall goals.

UNIT 5

Planning and Organizing for Differentiated Reading Instruction

When teachers are asked what aspects of teaching reading give them the most concern, over and over again they bring up questions about dealing with individual differences. Some are concerned with problems of organization: what is the best way to divide my class into groups? Some are bothered about planning: how can I give each group or each child the amount of time they need? Some have management questions: while I work with one group, how do I keep the other groups profitably busy? Some have problems relating to materials: should I use an above-grade basal reader with my highest group? Some are worried about child morale: how can I keep up the morale of children in the lowest group? Teachers recognize that meeting the reading needs of all the children involves many difficult decisions.

This unit first considers issues that influence the effectiveness of teaching, using any form of class organization. In the second section, practical issues of grouping and teaching reading to groups are discussed. Several forms of individualized reading are considered in the third section, and useful types of whole-class reading activities are described in the fourth section. In the fifth section, several illustrative plans for combining group, whole-class, and individualized reading are presented and discussed. The sixth section describes the learning center as an alternative form of classroom organization. In the final section, administrative contributions to differentiated reading instruction are discussed.

SOME PRINCIPLES OF EFFECTIVE TEACHING

Instructional Time

Reading specialists recommend that the time devoted to developmental reading in first grade should be about 90 minutes a day, and time devoted to all other reading activities (experience chart reading, independent reading, using content textbooks, weekly newspapers, etc.) should be a little under an hour, giving a total of about 2.5 hours for reading per day. Recommended time for developmental reading should decrease grade by grade to about 60 minutes in fourth grade and 40 minutes in upper grades, while "other reading" should increase to 80 minutes in fourth grade and 100 minutes in seventh grade (Brekke 1963).

An analysis of the time actually spent by first-grade teachers (as revealed by the daily logs they kept) showed that the number of minutes per day of direct reading instruction correlated substantially with average pupil reading achievement ($r = .55$), while time spent on supportive activities such as story telling, discussion, writing, art related to reading, and dramatization did not show a significant correlation with reading achievement. There was a general tendency for teachers who spent more time on the activities distinctively characteristic of their method of instruction to get better results than teachers who spent less time on those activities. For example, time spent on basal-reader lessons and sight-word teaching correlated positively with achievement for basal-reader teachers; while time spent on writing, dramatization, social studies, and science correlated positively with achievement for language-experience teachers (A. J. Harris and Serwer 1966a).

Above the first grade, the time per day spent in reading by pupils probably has more bearing on their improvement than the teacher time spent with them. Silent reading and various kinds of skill-building exercises are usually carried on while the teacher works with another group. Moreover, time spent on an activity that is frustratingly difficult, or practice on a skill already well learned, may have a negative effect on pupil attitudes and achievement.

Research evidence is lacking on the complex interactions that determine whether time spent in reading is spent usefully or wasted. However, it seems only common sense to conclude that provision for sufficient time for various kinds of reading in the classroom is one of the minimum essentials for obtaining good results.

Rosenshine and Berliner (1977) have developed the concept of "academic engaged time" as a major determiner of the effectiveness of instruction. This concept includes two main elements: content covered, or students' opportunity to learn; and student engagement, which is the amount of time the student spends actually working on the tasks assigned. They cited research which indicates that "the more successful teachers directed activities without giving their students choices, approached subject-matter in a direct, businesslike way, organized learning around questions they posed and occupied the center of attention. In contrast, the less successful teachers made the students the center of attention, organized learning around the students' own problems, and joined or participated in student activities." The successful teachers tended to teach with large groups. These authors pointed out that when children work independently without supervision, a much higher proportion of the time is wasted than in a supervised group, so that academic engaged time tends to be low.

Motivation

It is usually not necessary to spend much time developing motivation for an otherwise well-planned reading activity. When children find that the things they are expected to do are interesting, and the difficulty level allows them to succeed but requires some effort, they tend to engage actively in the tasks. Poorly planned lessons invite straying attention and disorder.

A teacher's habitual tendency to respond to pupils' responses with praise or with blame also influences pupil performance. A simplistic interpretation of the principle of reinforcement might lead one to expect that the more frequent the use of approval or positive motivation, the better the result. It is more complicated than that; minimal reinforcement through use of such comments as "Right," "Uh Huh," and "Okay" tends to be accompanied by relatively good achievement, while frequent use of stronger praise is not. "Praise is more effective when a reason for it is given, such as praising pupil planning or pupil interpretation of ideas. Accepting a pupil's idea and using it by restating it, applying it, comparing it to another idea, or using it in a summary tends to be a characteristic of teachers whose classes achieve well" (A. J. Harris 1969). The use of a "warm" voice has been found in several studies to be negatively related to reading achievement. Most children of elementary school age resent the kind of sugary manner that is often used with tots and prefer to be treated in a more grown-up fashion.

Teachers who tend to resort to frequent strong criticism get poor results. Teachers must identify wrong responses as incorrect, but this should be done in a matter-of-fact way that does not indicate disparagement or disapproval of the child. Teacher reaction is readily sensed by children from bodily attitude, facial expression, and tone of voice as well as from verbal comment, so how the teacher feels about a child may be quite evident even when the teacher guards her verbalizations (Emans and Fox 1974).

Children's motivation is also influenced by their expectations and those of their parents. Entwhistle found that lower-class children in first grade tend to have unrealistically high expectations, while their parents tend to have low expectations for them. "If one expects to win 50¢ and wins $5, this is positive, whereas if one expects to win $50 and wins $5, the same event may be negative. To get a low mark when one expects it may not lead to unhappiness. Most persons would agree, however, that to get a low mark when one expects a high mark is a punishing state of affairs" (Entwhistle 1976, p. 86). Low parental expectations often accompanied high absence rates, which disrupted schooling.

Teachers' expectations of what children can do influence their placement of children in groups, the assignments or tasks that groups are expected to handle, the kinds of questions that teachers ask, and so forth. Sometimes teachers place children in low, medium, or high ability groups on the basis of little objective evidence. Regardless of the basis for placement in groups, it is important for teachers to be on the alert for signs that a child may have been placed in an inappropriate group; the work may be either so hard as to be continually frustrating or so easy as to invite boredom.

Teachers sometimes convey to children the impression that they value a high group more than the lower groups, or that they don't think a low group can do much. Such an attitude can become a self-fulfilling prophecy in that each group may accept what it perceives to be the teacher's evaluation and try, or not try, accordingly. "We're the sparrows; we ain't supposed to learn much."

Teachers may also influence learning by the questions they ask. Some teachers ask questions requiring thoughtful or original responses only of a high group, asking the other children questions limited to a literal, factual nature. These other children do not get the necessary guided practice in learning how to reason while reading (Emans and Fox 1974).

Securing and Maintaining Attention

Attention is a prerequisite for learning. The ability to concentrate one's attention on the task at hand involves maintaining focus on particular stimuli and disregarding or ignoring other competing stimulation. Children who can maintain focus and ignore distractions may do better in school than their aptitude scores would lead one to expect, while children who are easily distractible may do much worse than expected (Samuels and Turnure 1974).

Teachers cannot expect perfect attention at all times, but they are responsible for managing so that most of the children are attending to their tasks most of the time. Among the things that teachers can do to help children maintain attention are: (1) show enthusiasm in one's own manner; (2) find novel ways to present material, particularly in reviewing; (3) involve as many children as possible actively in the lesson; (4) with younger children particularly, and with restless children, provide tasks that often require motor responses as well as verbal responses; (5) with distractible children, avoid crowding the room with decorations, artwork, etc., that may distract their attention from the task at hand; (6) provide independent activities that are interesting and not frustrating, and check frequently on what those working independently are doing.

Planning and Conducting Reading Activities

The great majority of elementary school teachers in the United States and Canada utilize basal readers as the core of their developmental reading programs. Whether these readers are eclectic, linguistic, phonic, or use a special alphabet, the teachers manuals provide detailed lesson plans, the nature of which has been described in units 3 and 4. Research has shown, however, that teachers using the same readers with similar pupils differ greatly in the results they obtain. Differences among the average scores obtained by classes in the same instructional method are usually far greater than the differences between the overall averages for contrasting methods (Bond and Dykstra 1967).

The printed lesson plans often provide more suggested activities than there is time for. The teacher has to select which parts of the plan to use, keeping in mind long-range as well as immediate objectives, the present skills and needs of the children, and the time available. Practice on skills already mastered can be omitted, while other skills may require more practice than the manual provides.

Some of the ways in which a teacher can improve the efficiency of pupil learning are:

1. Plan a schedule of reading activities at least a week in advance. Many teachers find it useful to plan in blocks of three to six weeks.
2. Develop efficient routines for passing out and collecting materials. Distribute materials just before they are to be used.
3. Have one or more specific objectives for each activity. Keep these objectives in mind and help the children to focus on them.
4. Check on knowledge of prerequisites and reteach them only when necessary.
5. Keep to a minimum the time spent on motivational readiness. If motivation seems lacking, try to find out why—material too difficult or uninteresting, skill already well known, etc.
6. Avoid getting so involved with the means (e.g., an attractive display of materials) that the objective of the lesson (e.g., learning a new phonic generalization) is forgotten.
7. When planning a series of lessons, keep in mind the need for sequencing, such as proceeding from the concrete to the more abstract, from simple to complex, from quite easy to progressively harder, from small doses to larger ones, from much supervision to little supervision, etc.
8. Eliminate activities that are irrelevant to the objectives of the lesson, even though they seem attractive.
9. Make verbal explanations easy to understand by including clear and relevant examples, using the chalkboard when possible. (You can't explain the differences among *hole, whole,* and *hold* without putting the three words on the board or chart.)
10. Form the habit of evaluating lessons, particularly those that do not seem to work, to get ideas about what went wrong and how the next lesson might be improved.

A self-checklist for evaluating a directed reading activity is shown in figure 5.1. It can be modified to suit the teacher's needs. Additional suggestions about planning efficient reading lessons are provided by Kerber (1974, 1976), and Durkin (1975).

	Yes	No	Comments

I. Objectives
  a. Do I expect children to gain knowledge of certain facts or understanding of a phenomenon or a process from this lesson?
  b. Do I expect children to learn a reading skill(s) from this lesson?
  c. Do I expect children to develop certain attitudes and/or appreciations as a result of this lesson?			

II. Readiness and Motivation
  a. Did I build on children's experience in order to prepare them for the present lesson?
  b. Did I introduce new words in a meaningful way?
  c. Did I set purpose(s) for this lesson?
  d. Did I use any films, filmstrips, display, etc.? Were any needed?			

III. Development
  a. Was silent reading guided?
  b. Were questions at different levels of thinking ability?
  c. Was the discussion well conducted and did it lead to better understanding of the lesson?
  d. Was the rereading done for a purpose?			

IV. Review a. Was the review brief and relevant?			

	Yes	No	Comments
V. Assignment and Follow-up			
a. Was the assignment related to the objectives?			
b. Were the directions clearly given?			
c. Was the assignment differentiated to meet the needs of the groups and individuals?			
d. Was the lesson related with content areas?			
e. Were the objectives achieved?			
f. Can I relate this lesson to next lesson?			

On the whole this lesson was: Poor ☐   Satisfactory ☐   Excellent ☐

FIGURE 5.1.   Self-evaluation of a reading lesson (Narang 1975). Copyright © 1975 by the National Council of Teachers of English. Reprinted by permission of the author and the publisher. Part I is completed before teaching; the other parts, after the lesson is completed. Not all items are applicable to every lesson. It also may be wise to list the specific objectives in Part I and to determine if they were met.

Readiness for Learning Activities   Considering learner readiness is part of lesson planning at all levels, not just during the initial stages of reading instruction. Since it is a factor teachers should consider in any reading or reading-related lesson, they may wish to use the questions that follow as guidelines for determining readiness. Answers to any of the questions will be influenced by the purpose of the lesson, the children's level of ability, and whether or not the material is written so as to allow children to apply their skills. For example, a teacher may preteach the meanings of some key words if the terms are not explained fully in the selection or if the children do not possess the skills needed for using the context clues made available to them by the author of the selection. On the other hand, if the needed skills have just been taught and the teacher wishes to assess how well they have been grasped, she might choose to have the children read the selection without any preteaching of vocabulary. Not all the questions that follow are applicable to every reading activity.

1. What ideas or concepts in the lesson or material are likely to be unfamiliar or to confuse the children? Should they be explained beforehand or will they be clarified by reading the selection?

2. What words in the selection are likely to be difficult for the children to recognize or to decode, or whose specific meanings are probably unknown? Should they be pretaught, or will the children be able to figure them out?
3. Is it desirable to spend a little time arousing curiosity and interest?
4. Are special skills needed for reading this type of material efficiently? If so, have the children mastered the skills, or do they need further help in their application?
5. Is the difficulty of the material suitable for each child? If it seems inappropriate, are alternative materials available? If it seems too difficult and alternative materials are not available, what can be done to help the children cope with it?

INSTRUCTING CHILDREN IN GROUPS

Types of Groups

One way of coping with the wide range of reading abilities typically found in every grade is to group children for various purposes. Grouping children for instruction is efficient because it saves time and energy. However, using only one type of group or one grouping procedure alone has limited value. Different groupings should be used concurrently in various parts of the total reading program.

Grouping by Reading Levels Grouping children by their general level of reading ability (instructional level) is the most commonly employed form of classroom grouping, and when more than one form of class organization is used, it is usually given the largest time allotment. Each group utilizes a different reading text in a published series. The value of such a form of grouping is that the material is of a suitable level of difficulty for instructional purposes, and it allows the group to follow a sequential skills development program. Ability grouping of this type has encountered a great deal of criticism—few changes are ever made in groups ("Once a bluebird always a bluebird!"), it sets up a caste system, contributes to the poor self-esteem of the low group, and does not fully meet individual needs because instruction is geared to the average children in the group. But these limitations can be lessened greatly by also employing other forms of grouping and classroom organization. For example, the stigma of being in a low group is less likely to occur if children function as members of more than one kind of group, and if the teacher makes it clear that she values their efforts as highly as those of more competent readers.

Noting that the research findings regarding the effectiveness of ability grouping are mixed, Wilson and Ribovich (1973) offer an interesting variation. In "open grouping" a child meets regularly with his or her own reading group; but during independent reading time is allowed to take part in any group session. Movement among groups is facilitated by informing all the children as to what each group will be working on that day.

Specific-needs Groups   Certain specific instructional needs may be shared by children whose general level of reading ability varies widely. Instruction for needs groups may be diverse, ranging from overcoming specific word-recognition problems (e.g., confusion of words beginning with *wh* and *th*) to oral reading with natural expression, to understanding implied main ideas.

Generally, it is best to have only one or two special-needs groups at a time and to meet with each of them once or twice weekly until the common weakness is overcome. If all but one or two children have mastered the skill, individual help can be given to them after the group has disbanded. When one specific-need group has been disbanded, another can be formed for a different purpose.

Even when administrative plans attempt to reduce the range of reading abilities in a class, children who score within a narrow range on a reading test (e.g., 2.0–2.9), or who are judged to be functioning at the same reader level, usually differ widely in the degree to which various reading skills have been mastered. Thus a group using a low third reader for instructional purposes may contain some children who require a review of decoding skills, some who are word-by-word readers, and some with weak specific comprehension skills. Each of these problems may be found in children from more than one general reading ability group. In the fifth or sixth grade, special groups might be established for accurate but slow readers, for rapid but inaccurate readers, or for those who need to be more flexible in their reading rate.

Interest Groups   Several members of a class who share a common interest can form a group or club, regardless of their levels of reading ability. They can meet every two or three weeks to discuss common problems or questions, exchange information, recommend useful reading to one another, and read independently about their interest or hobby. Several interest groups may operate in a class at the same time, with membership entirely voluntary. Pupils may belong to more than one such group at a time. Interest groups meet infrequently, take little class time, and require little teacher planning, so they can be included in the organization plan with little extra effort.

Project Committees   When a class chooses a topic for a major project, some time is first spent in discussing and deciding what major areas should be investigated. They may want to learn about a certain culture's clothing, food, shelter, customs, history, and geographic conditions. This provides work for six committees, each taking responsibility for one main question. Every child is assigned to one committee, usually by the teacher, considering both children's expressed preferences and the desirability of having a wide range of reading ability in each committee.

Within each committee a list of specific questions is drawn up. Each member may take certain questions, or the whole committee may work on all the questions. The teacher has the responsibility for providing appropriate reference material and as much guidance and direction as needed. Fairly mature books and references can be used by the best readers. Even the least capable readers, who may be able to do little more than study illustrations carefully, usually can contribute some useful ideas to the group report.

Number of Groups

The number of groups one should have varies with the makeup of the class (e.g., age, reading ability, maturity), their needs and interests, and the teacher's skill in group management. At times it is sufficient to divide a class into two groups for reading instruction: those who can profitably use the on-grade reading text and those for whom it is too difficult. Those in the upper group who finish assignments quickly can have extra time for independent reading, and those who struggle to keep up with the lower group can be given individual help. Of course, if the material far outstrips the ability of several children, such a plan is not suitable.

A two-group plan also may be used in the rare class in which all the children are reading at the same instructional level. In such situations, although the class is using material of the same level (not necessarily the same material), groups can be formed to facilitate adjustment to differences in rate of work and to foster teacher-pupil interaction, which is more likely to take place in a group than in a whole-class situation.

The pupils who are below grade level in reading are sometimes so varied that the teacher is unable to find a reading text that is reasonably satisfactory for most of the group. When this is the case, the most obvious solution is to separate them into two groups, using different levels of reading material. If this does not solve the problem, individualized reading programs for those who do not fit into the lowest group may be preferable to separating them into more subgroups.

Children who are reading far above grade level also present a problem. Some teachers prefer to keep them in the highest ability group to give them social participation in the reading program, and to keep class organization simple. These excellent readers complete assignments quickly and have extra time for a variety of enrichment activities. This may be a viable solution if only one or two children fall into this category. If there are more, it is preferable to form another group and provide them with more difficult material and challenging instruction. This suggestion is based on the belief that superior readers should not be held back from improving their reading abilities. A third and equally acceptable plan is to give them an almost completely individualized reading program. They would join only those group activities from which they could profit or to which they could contribute, using most of their time for independent reading and for developing reading skills that are usually taught at grade levels beyond the children's actual grade placement.

There is no magic to having three reading groups, and there are other ways to organize reading instruction. Decisions about the number of reading groups to have and how to set them up should be made after the reading abilities and past experiences of the children have been studied. It is better to start with a simple grouping organization and expand it later, if necessary, than to start with multiple groups and find that the management problems are overwhelming.

To set up ability groups, first study the following information: (1) the children's performance on standardized or criterion-referenced tests and tests that accompany the published reading series employed; and (2) the reading group each child was in last, and how successful the child was in that group. (The last teacher's placement of the child may not have been accurate.) Then set up the number of groups you think you can manage successfully. Once these ability groups are functioning fairly smoothly, branch off into the other types of groups.

Factors Influencing Group Efficiency

Group Size   The number of children in a group necessarily will vary with the class size and the number and types of groups used. Deciding this issue usually is a compromise between two desirable but mutually contradictory principles. On one hand, it is desirable to keep the organization plan simple and manageable; on the other, groups should be small enough to allow individual attention and frequent participation.

In general, the more individual help the children need, the smaller the group should be. Children about whose group placement the teacher is doubtful should be started in the lower of two ability groups under consideration. If a change is needed, it is better for the child's morale to move from easier to harder material than the opposite. Interest groups and project committees can be of any workable size. Small groups of two to four children can work well for certain types of practice, such as testing sight vocabulary or playing reading games. In this form of "team learning," one of the children must know the answers or be provided with them, and the children should be compatible. Use of "pupil partners" initially requires a great deal of teacher direction, and the procedures should be demonstrated to all pairs of children (Whisler 1976).

Group Flexibility   There are two main ways to keep grouping flexible, both of which are desirable if not carried to extremes. One is the concurrent use of more than one kind of reading group. For example, some of the limitations of grouping by instructional reading levels can be counteracted by having project committees and specific-needs groups, each containing children with a range of reading proficiency.

The other kind of flexibility is the willingness to change group placements and assignments whenever there is good evidence that the change will benefit the child. Some children outgrow the group in which they start, or were misplaced initially; others are frequently absent or find it difficult to keep up. When considering a change in groups, it is desirable to discuss it with the child to learn how he feels about it, and to give those feelings serious consideration. One child may feel quite relieved at the opportunity to move to a lower group where he can be "on top" for a change, while another may plead for the opportunity to demonstrate that he can handle the work of the higher group.

Group Names   Referring to a child as a "good" or "poor" reader is likely to convey the impression of a value judgment. Children cannot help being less competent than others in reading any more than a short child can help not being tall. It generally is bettter to use such terms as "higher" or "lower," "more competent" or "less competent," or "faster paced" or "slower paced." Some children are more competent readers than others, but all are equally worthy when performing to the best of their abilities. When a teacher demonstrates as much enthusiasm about a successful effort in the lowest group as about the work of the most capable reader, children accept their group placements as natural and helpful. Demonstrating approval for only the capable readers leads children to regard placement in a low group as punishment.

Usually the children in a class are clearly aware of the differences in reading ability among groups. It is desirable to choose group names that do not imply differences in value or importance. One good procedure is to allow the groups to choose their own names, so that in a class studying about Indians, each group can select the name of a tribe. Groups can be named casually according to the color of the reading book they are using, by the name of the text, or by the name of the group chairperson. In the latter case the group name would change with each change of chairperson. The main point is to avoid names that are likely to build or reinforce inferiority feelings.

Physical Arrangement of the Classroom   Movable chairs and desks make it possible to rearrange the classroom to suit a variety of reading activities. Many primary-grade teachers like to have a semicircle of chairs near the chalkboard, to which each group comes for many teacher-directed reading activities. If more than one row is used, the shorter children should be seated so they can see the board or chart. For group discussion and oral reading, a circle, semicircle, or hollow rectangular arrangement allows each child to see all group members. For independent reading it is desirable to minimize interpersonal contact, and an arrangement in rows tends to work well.

Every classroom should have a library area. This should contain a wide variety of books and other materials, a colorful display of books or other reading materials, and a table and chairs for browsing and sampling books.

Storage space for sets of readers and other reading materials is necessary. Use of visual aids requires accessory equipment such as darkening shades and a convenient screen. If visual aids are used by one group or child, a viewing corner shielded by folding screens can be set up.

Reading Materials   Assembling materials needed to differentiate reading instruction effectively takes time. New teachers usually have to use materials found in the classroom, and this may limit the plans one can use. Teachers are more likely to obtain desired materials when they know what they want and ask for them several months in advance.

In order to allow for a rich and varied reading program, the following types of materials should be available in the classroom:

1. Appropriate sets of readers or other materials for each group, with enough copies (usually a maximum of 15) to supply one for each child in the group. A sequence of at least two readers should be available for each group. Each group should use material appropriate for instructional purposes.
2. Workbooks that accompany the reading series. These simplify the assignment of group reading to be done without the teacher and introduce or provide practice on specific reading skills. Without them, the teacher has a heavy burden of preparing and/or duplicating seatwork pages.
3. A collection of reading games and puzzles that can be used independently by individuals or very small groups.
4. A classroom library of at least 50 books covering a wide range of difficulty and topics. The collection (books, magazines, etc.) should be changed every few weeks if possible.
5. Reference books, including picture, elementary and advanced dictionaries; and, above the primary grades, an encyclopedia set, atlases, an almanac, etc.
6. Materials for specific skills practice, which may be commercially purchased, teacher-made, or collected from a variety of workbooks. It is helpful if these are organized so as to be self-administering and self-checking.
7. If the class is working on a project or unit, a collection of materials of varying difficulty that provides useful information on the topics.
8. Audiovisual materials and equipment, which may be shared with other classes.

Of course reading can be taught with less quantity and variety of materials; but the richer the materials, the greater chance the teacher has to obtain superior results.

Group Assignments

Teachers must plan work for other groups while the teacher is working with one group. In doing so, teachers should consider the following points: (1) the assigned activity must be one that can be carried on without the teacher; (2) directions must be clear and explicit; (3) those who finish an assignment early should have additional things to do; (4) the use of helpers, who can answer questions and give directions to the group, lessens the number of times the teacher is interrupted.

When a group is unable to carry on reading activities without the teacher, it is necessary to provide nonreading activities that can be carried on independently. These should be quiet activities such as related artwork, caring for classroom pets, or use of an interest center. Once children have learned to read, recreational or research reading can be part of the plan.

It generally takes a few weeks of patient training with young children before routines are assimilated; older children adapt to them more easily. Usually the children who are in the groups not working with the teacher learn their activities during the assignment period. They can be taught to obtain needed equipment or material, work quietly, clean up, and put things away.

In planning the length of reading periods, the teacher should take into consideration the length of time that the children engaging in independent activities can maintain attention, as well as the attention span of the group working with the teacher. Children who are carrying on activities without the teacher may finish an assignment before the period is over. Each group can have a list of additional things to do, which has been worked out in discussion with the teacher and then listed on a chart. When a series of suggestions is in view, such as the following chart used in a fourth grade, interruptions are kept to a minimum:

Sue's Group

1. Look up the new words in the glossary.
2. Read the assigned pages in the reader.

3. Read and answer the questions on the board.
4. Read a library book, draw a picture about the story, or study your spelling words.

Pupil Leaders

Some kinds of reading activities carried on without the teacher require someone to decide whose turn comes next, how long it should last, if an answer is acceptable, and so forth. This authority can be handled by a group chairperson whose tenure is rotated among members of the group. The most competent readers enjoy being group leaders or helpers, but the privilege should not be restricted to them. In a buddy system, a capable reader is teamed with one who has reading difficulties and is seated near him to make it easy to give help.

A helper from a more advanced group can serve as a resource person for a reading group, supplying words, correcting errors, and in various ways making it possible for the group to carry on a reading activity that would otherwise require the teacher's involvement. Rotating the privilege of being a group helper or leader among a number of children minimizes the tendency to identify them as "teacher's pets" and avoids depriving any child of a major portion of individual reading time.

Teachers should help prepare chairpersons and helpers before they assume their roles. If a chairperson or helper is incompetent, or becomes officious, bossy, or unnecessarily critical, the teacher should discuss with the "offender" how to become a more competent helper. If improvement is not forthcoming, the helper will have to be replaced, but the child should be given an opportunity to learn. Ehly and Larsen (1975–76) offer suggestions for selecting, training, and supervising peer tutors.

Teacher Aides and Paraprofessionals

The use of aides, paraprofessionals, and volunteers in the classroom has increased in recent years. These assistants have diverse backgrounds and preparation for their roles and responsibilities. Some are high school graduates, others have graduate degrees; some are paid, most are volunteers. When used effectively, these people can be of great assistance to the teacher in individualizing instruction. Such personnel are more likely to be effective if (1) they are carefully chosen; (2) they are given adequate preparation for their job, and receive supervision while on the job; and (3) both the aide and the teacher are clearly aware of their roles and responsibilities and those of the other person as well.

Plans for conducting a workshop for adult tutors are outlined by Sanacore (1974b). Use of paraprofessionals and tutors is discussed further in unit 11 (pp. 447–48).

INDIVIDUALIZED READING ACTIVITIES

Reading can be individualized in ways other than in the individualized developmental reading program described in unit 3. The individualized reading approach can be applied to various components of the total reading program.

Individualized Reading Skills Practice

The concept of a reading program in which the teacher makes a careful analysis of each child's reading skills and provides a skills development program tailored to each child's needs is not new (Cole 1938), but the recent availability of materials has made such programs much more feasible. In an individualized reading skills program, materials are organized so that each pupil obtains the exercise needed next, does it, corrects it with a scoring key (it may be self-scoring), and consults with the teacher if help is required. The systems approach, computer-assisted instruction, and programmed material are forms of individualized reading skills practice (see pp. 108–13), as are sets of materials constructed specifically for this purpose (see pp. 290–93, 356–58).

Individualized Progress in Basal Readers

Teachers who employ an Individualized Developmental Reading program sometimes use basal readers or some other published reading series, but not in the way suggested in the manuals. Several such types of programs have been briefly described by Sucher (1969).

In applying a modified systems approach to a basal reader, Bruton (1972) chose some major objectives, stated them in behavioral terms, and constructed pretests and posttests for them. Exercises directly related to the objectives were removed from the workbooks, mounted, and arranged in sequence. A somewhat similar approach, using sequentially ordered task cards that indicate assignments, has been described by Criscuolo (1976). For those children who need them, additional exercises can be obtained from other sources and kept on file. Some school systems have set up their own lists of behavioral objectives and provided teachers with cross-referenced sources (e.g., various workbooks, basal series, skill kits) that indicate the pages that can be used for developing specific skills. Some publishers (e.g., Zweig, Random House) have produced such reference sources for use with their materials.

Individualized Recreational Reading

For years the recreational reading program in the elementary school has focused on encouraging a large amount of independent, pleasurable reading in which children are allowed freedom of choice. Extensive individualized recreational reading provides an abundance of reading experience that helps to build fluency and increase rate of reading. However, its promise of developing a lasting interest in reading as a leisure-time activity has yet to be realized because many teachers have not included time for it in their schedules. The rapid growth of school libraries and of publication of children's books in recent years gives evidence to the stress placed on wide reading in the elementary school. This strand of the total reading program is discussed in detail in unit 10.

Individualized Functional Reading

Individual projects and reports often are used as an enrichment procedure. Each child works independently, selecting a topic, locating sources of information, taking notes, and preparing an oral or written report. One of the major functions of school librarians is to help teach how to use library resources for individual reports. Individualized research reading is more appropriate in the middle and upper grades than the primary grades.

WHOLE-CLASS ACTIVITIES

It is neither necessary nor desirable to teach all reading activities in groups or individually; a number of activities can be conducted effectively with the whole class. Activities in which the whole class functions together help to establish a feeling of belonging and participating in each child (especially for those in the low groups), help to build a spirit of class unity, and aid in breaking down the "group caste system." By reducing the number of periods for which the teacher must plan and teach, whole-class activities lighten the teacher's workload.

Introducing New Ideas and Skills

Among the activities for which whole-class participation is appropriate are the introduction of new concepts, ideas, and word meanings; the use of visual aids to develop conceptual background; new decoding skills; alphabetizing, locating information, using the dictionary; and so on. These may be specifically needed at the time by one group, but can benefit the rest of the class also. Not all children will learn with equal speed, so reteaching probably will be necessary for many children, but the first presentation is likely to be of some benefit even to the least capable readers. The guiding principle in selecting whole-class activities of this type is: how transferable are the skills or how useful the concepts regardless of the children's general level of reading ability?

Current Events

Reading about current events really begins with the development of the first experience story with children who are just learning to read. In the primary grades, and to a lesser extent in the middle grades, summaries of current whole-class experiences that are placed on charts for all to read and discuss continue to be useful reading materials.

Weekly newspapers such as *My Weekly Reader* (Xerox Educational) and *Junior Scholastic* (Scholastic) are published for use in specific grades. Some teachers prefer to order two or more graded editions. After each group reads the edition of appropriate difficulty for them, the whole class discusses the topics that are common to the editions, and each group contributes information found only in the different editions. Other teachers order only the on-grade edition for the entire class, the main purpose being to lessen the stigma of low reading ability. The less capable readers read as best they can (often with the aid of the teacher or a helper) and participate in the group discussion.

A daily newspaper may be used in the sixth grade and with advanced fourth and fifth graders. Having the class or group read and compare contrasting or conflicting accounts of the same event in different newspapers is particularly helpful in developing critical reading skills.

Audience Reading

Most children love being read to, so that children in any grade can form an appreciative audience for reading by their classmates. In having children read to their peers, the following guidelines should be observed: (1) only the performer has a copy of the material, and the others listen as a genuine audience; (2) the material should be unfamiliar and of interest to most of the audience; and (3) the performer(s) should rehearse to the point where the presentation is fluent, expressive, and easy to understand.

A book club meeting in which each of several children reads an especially interesting portion of a favorite book provides a popular type of audience reading situation. Alternatively, one group may present a dramatization of a story they have read. Extensive memorizing can be avoided if children's plays are presented like radio scripts, with the parts read rather than recited from memory. Having to perform before one's classmates often motivates children to improve the quality of their oral reading, but children should not be forced to perform. Practice sessions can be taped, with each child assessing his or her own performance.

The audience also benefits from the experience. Audience listening can strengthen a child's listening comprehension skills and help to broaden the range of topics in which to become interested.

Choral Reading

Choral reading is a kind of whole-class reading that is particularly useful for developing appreciation of poetry.[1] It is also quite helpful to shy

---

1. The technique of choral reading is discussed on p. 128.

children and less capable readers. They are less likely to be inhibited when their voices are merged with those of their classmates than when reading alone before their peers.

Textbook Reading

Textbooks in the content areas often are too difficult for many of the children who are supposed to use them. Teachers who are restricted to one prescribed text in certain curriculum areas have to adopt various expedients to cover the needed content. Careful preparation, guided preliminary silent reading, purposeful oral rereading, and full discussion form a usable lesson-plan outline for using content textbooks. Most of the oral reading can be done by the more competent readers, and those not able to read the book on their own can learn by listening. In such cases, it also would be wise to teach listening skills. The main drawback to such a procedure is that oral reading of the whole text is very time-consuming and probably boring to the more capable readers. Useful ideas for aiding those unable to read texts in the content areas are given on pages 378–80.

Use of textbooks on a whole-class basis is usually a matter of necessity rather than preference. When the text is so difficult that only a few pupils can read it, the teacher may have to write and duplicate a simpler version or rely on lecturing and placing summaries or outlines on the board for children to copy. It also may be possible to obtain, with the help of a librarian, a variety of materials written at easier levels that cover the same or similar topics as the text.

COMBINING ORGANIZATIONAL PROCEDURES

It is advantageous for both teacher and pupils to employ group, individual, and whole-class activities in a combined program. Although many activities are done in groups, some reading is conducted on a whole-class basis, with recreational and functional reading being highly individualized.

Individualized reading procedures can be combined with other kinds of reading organizational plans. Individual teacher-pupil conferences can be incorporated into any reading program. An individualized developmental reading program can be used with only one or two groups, especially if the range of reading abilities in a "group" make it impossible to choose a reading text that is reasonably satisfactory for most of its members. Groups can take turns using an individualized reading approach. For example, if a teacher had four groups, each group could use individualized reading every fourth week. Other ways of combining individualized and more conventional procedures include alternating the two by months, weeks, or days; or by having individualized reading on one or two days every week.

No one pattern of class organization is best for all classes. Teachers must determine which plan best suits the needs of their classes and their own capabilities.

Time Allotments

As noted, satisfactory teaching of reading in first grade usually requires a minimum of 90 minutes per day for basic instruction. If groups are employed, each group should have a daily instructional period of at least 20 minutes. Additional time, 45 to 60 minutes, will be needed for developing and reading experience stories; reading to the children; reading the weekly classroom newspaper; meeting a second, third, or fourth time with reading groups; working with small special-needs groups; and for individualized reading. Insufficient time allotments make it impossible for teachers to cover the full instructional program. When this happens, there is a strong temptation to get through the books on schedule, at the expense of developing specific reading skills or using supplementary reading activities.

As the grade level and reading ability increase, the time needed for developmental reading instruction slowly decreases. Time allotments for other reading activities should increase so that the total amount of time devoted to all reading activities remains about the same, approximately two hours daily.

Whatever the grade level, teachers must judge the length of time appropriate for reading activities in their particular classes. If enabling tasks (e.g., getting and putting away materials) leave too little time for instruction or reading, the period is too short and thus is inefficient. When periods are too long boredom and fatigue set in. In general, periods requiring intense concentration on difficult tasks should be comparatively brief; easy, pleasurable activities can be much longer. The teacher should make adjustments as needed. If an activity proceeds rapidly and the objective is met, it should be terminated. Restless behavior and increased noise level often signal that an activity should be brought to a close. While total inflexibility is not desirable, lengthening a period because children haven't clinched a concept, or are enjoying the activity, means shortening the subsequent period. Sometimes stopping when enthusiasm is still high makes motivation easier the next day. The psychology of learning suggests that in planning the reading program, it is desirable to interpolate nonreading activities between reading periods or follow one type of reading activity by another quite different one.

One other point about time should be considered in planning. If one or more children indicate a desire to learn a particular reading skill, the teacher should attempt to use that "teachable moment" rather than wait until the skill is called for by the manual or predetermined plan.

First Grade   Early in the year first-grade teachers become aware of marked differences in readiness and rate of learning to read. These differences can be handled with a combination of the three main ways already discussed.

Before either group or individual reading instruction can be undertaken, children must learn to carry on a variety of activities without the teacher's help. While this competence is being acquired, the teacher is conducting readiness activities and developing experience stories mainly with the whole class. Early in the fall, considerable emphasis should be placed on helping children learn to plan their activities and work independently. Nonreading activities that can be carried on while the teacher is with another reading group should be relatively quiet ones, such as painting, drawing, coloring, looking at picture books, doing puzzles, playing quietly with toys, or caring for pets or plants. The need for walking quietly, speaking softly, and using equipment without a fuss (respecting the rights of others) can be discussed with the children, who can help define their own roles of conduct. These rules could then be placed on a chart, possibly entitled "Thinking of Others."

During most of first grade, many children are not capable of reading by themselves. The teacher needs to guide their reading step by step. As the year progresses, the more capable children become able to read without teacher guidance.

A one-week plan, representative of successful group instruction near the middle of first grade, is shown in figure 5.2. There are three reading periods for groups daily, each approximately 20 minutes long, and each group has at least one period with the teacher. The low and middle groups generally engage in nonreading activities when not with the teacher, although activities such as cutting and mounting pictures for a picture dictionary or playing simple reading games may be used. With these groups the regular sequence includes preparation, guided reading and rereading, and guided workbook activity that involves practice on specific skills. Phonic skills and enrichment activities are provided during the daily whole-class activity.

The high group is capable of some independence. After preparation for a story they can read ahead silently without teacher guidance, and after the story has been discussed and parts reread they can use the workbook with only preliminary directions. Toward the end of the year, the middle group often is able to function in this way also.

Use of daily whole-class periods in this plan is a departure from the plans in most teachers manuals. Phonic principles are taught to the whole class, partly to save teacher time and effort, but mainly because a child who learns words slowly through a whole-word approach is not also necessarily slow in learning to use phonic principles. If a decoding-emphasis program is being employed, the whole-class activity might well involve teaching sight words. Various enrichment activities also are planned largely on a whole-class basis because of the tendency to neglect them, particularly with the lower groups.

In addition to the general ability groups, it is necessary from time to time to bring together a few children who need extra instruction or guided practice on some particular reading skill; these children may come from one or more of the regular groups. At times some children should be moved to either a higher or lower group. Group instruction needs to be supplemented with alertness to the special needs of individual children and resourcefulness in finding time to give them special attention.

Grades Two and Three   Compared with first grade, group management is somewhat easier in second and third grades. The children generally are more mature and have greater attention spans. Children are more self-reliant, thus need less-frequent teacher assistance. While the teacher works with one group, the others are able to carry on alone. It is not necessary for the teacher to work with each group every day, and time allotments for independent reading can be increased. Some group activities can be lead by a pupil, and temporary special groups can be set up and disbanded as necessary. On some activities, such as reviewing words and playing reading games, children can work in pairs or in small groups of three to six. The reading program can be somewhat more varied and flexible than in the first grade.

Minutes	Low Group	Middle Group	High Group
5–10	Whole class: Daily directions and assignments for each group		
	MONDAY		
20	Nonreading activities	*T* Preparation for new primer story	Recreational reading; draw picture of event in story
20	*T* Develop and read experience story	Prepare picture dictionary	↓
15	Nonreading activities	Nonreading activities	*T* Preparation for new story
15	Whole class: Symbol-sound association *f* = /f/		
10	Whole class: Read story to class		
	TUESDAY		
20	*T* Preparation for preprimer story	Nonreading activities	Silent reading of new story; supplementary reading
20	Preparing word cards	*T* Guided reading and discussion of new story	↓
20	Preparation of picture dictionary in teams from both groups	Same as low group	*T* Discussion and purposeful rereading of story
20	*T* Guided reading of preprimer story	Related workbook	Related workbook
20	Whole class: Teacher reads poems; children recite known poems and rhymes, listen for rhyming words		
	WEDNESDAY		
10	Whole class: Review symbol-sound association of *f*		
15	Whole class: Introduce symbol-sound association *m* = /m/		
25	*T* Develop and read experience story	Worksheet to reinforce skills	Related workbook, individualized reading
20	Nonreading activities	*T* Purposeful rereading; guided use of workbook	↓
20	Nonreading activities	Nonreading activities	*T* Check and discuss workbook, introduce new story
20	Whole class: Choral reading of duplicated poem read by teacher on Tuesday		

Minutes	Low Group	Middle Group	High Group
		THURSDAY	
20	Whole class: Develop and read experience story		
20	*T* New basic sight words	Recreational reading	Recreational reading
20	Read picture books Listen to tapes	*T* Guided practice in writing their own individual experience stories	
20	Nonreading activities	Work on individual experience stories	*T* Reading and discussion of new story
20	Whole class: Review symbol-sound association for *f* and *m*; introduce *p* = /p/		

Minutes	Low Group	Middle Group	High Group
		FRIDAY	
20	Sight word games with high group	*T* Preparation for new primer story	Team with low group for sight word games
20	Nonreading activities	*T* Guided reading and discussion of story	Silent reading of new story. Recreational reading for early finishers
20	*T* Auditory discrimination (5 min.) Guided use of workbook	Recreational reading	Recreational reading
20	Nonreading activities	Recreational reading or non-reading activities	*T* Purposeful rereading and discussion of story
15	Whole class: Review symbol-sound associations for *f*, *m*, and *p*		
15	Whole class: Group dramatization of story, or teacher reads story		

FIGURE 5.2. A three-group plan for first grade. *T* indicates the group with which the teacher is working for that period. The reading periods can be partly in morning and partly in afternoon, with nonreading activities interspersed.

The general one-week plan shown in figure 5.3 includes developmental and recreational reading activities, but not functional reading. Functional reading activities are best conducted with content material being used for such instruction. Systematic reading instruction on a three-group basis is scheduled three times a week. On the other two days there are provisions for a library visit, independent reading, specific-needs group work, individualized help, and individual teacher-pupil conferences.

Workbook pages are done without teacher supervision, but are checked by the teacher within a short period of time. Teaching of related skills and purposeful rereading, both oral and silent, are provided regularly for each group. While the teacher is working with one group, the other groups have

Minutes	Low Group	Middle Group	High Group
5–10	Whole class: Daily directions and assignments for each group		
	MONDAY		
25	*T* Preparation for new story Guided reading and discussion	Silent reading of story introduced on Friday; related workbook	Silent reading of story introduced on Friday; draw illustration for story
25	Related workbook Draw illustration for story	*T* Discussion and purposeful rereading; check workbooks	Recreational reading
20	Recreational reading or reading games	Individualized skill practice assignments	*T* Discussion and purposeful rereading of story
15	Whole class: Choral reading		
	TUESDAY		
10	*T* Whole class: Discussion of behavior, book selection, etc., in library		
30	Whole class: School librarian introduces new books. With librarian and teacher guidance, children select books to read in class		
20	*T* Specific needs group: Decoding words containing vowel diphthongs	Rest of class has independent reading	
20	*T* Specific needs group: Selecting main idea		

Minutes	Low Group	Middle Group	High Group
		WEDNESDAY	
25	Play reading games	T Related skills Preparation for new story	Plan and rehearse dramatization with group chairperson
25	T Check workbook Purposeful rereading Related skills	Silent reading of new story Related workbook	↓
30	Recreational reading	Recreational reading	T Discuss dramatization Related skills Preparation for new story
15	Whole class: Review combining semantic and syntactic cues		
		THURSDAY	
20	T Special needs group: Syllabication ⎫ Rest of class reads		
40	Individual teacher-pupil conferences ⎭ independently		
30	Whole class: Audience reading of favorite part of library books High group presents dramatization		
		FRIDAY	
30	T Preparation for new story Guided reading and discussion	Recreational reading	Silently read new story Related workbook
30	Related workbook Supplementary reading	T Check workbook Discussion and purposeful rereading	Recreational reading
30	Individualized skill practice assignments	Write individual experience stories	T Discussion and purposeful rereading Check workbook
30	Whole class: Weekly newspaper		

FIGURE 5.3. A three-group plan for third grade. T indicates group with which teacher is working. All the reading activities need not occur in a continuous block of time; other instructional periods may intervene.

a sequence of assignments or list of permissible activities that they pursue independently; not all activities done during these times need be directly related to reading instruction. Dramatization of a story, shown for only the high group in figure 5.3, should be done at times with all groups. On most days there is some kind of whole-class reading activity. Seven different types are listed in the plan, and these do not exhaust the possibilities.

This kind of plan, combining systematic, sequential instruction by groups with a substantial amount of independent recreational reading, and including whole-class activities and provisions for working individually with children, is preferable to plans that involve only reading by groups or plans that rely mainly on independent reading without a planned, sequential skill development program.

The plan suggested in figure 5.3 can and should be modified to fit particular situations. One way is to combine the middle and high groups (if they both can handle the same material) with the superior readers finishing group assignments quickly and having more time for recreational reading. It is not necessary to meet with each group every day, particularly with the top group, but the low group is more likely to need daily teacher direction. With a generally slow class, a plan more like that shown in figure 5.2 may be more appropriate. As with any general plan, it takes careful and conscientious preparation to fit in all the needed activities and to keep them running smoothly.

Group sessions need not be of equal length, but most will take about 20 to 30 minutes. This means that a plan as described above requires about 90 minutes a day. Considering the central importance of reading improvement and mastery of basic skills in these grades to provide a foundation for the heavy reading requirements of the later grades, such a time allotment is not excessive. Skimping on time for reading instruction in the primary grades only creates later problems.

Middle and Upper Grades   In most schools, middle- and upper-grade teachers have to deal with a wide range of reading abilities, with a span of five years or more not uncommon. Some schools attempt, through administrative arrangements, to reduce the range of reading ability with which teachers must deal in giving reading instruction. Such plans are discussed in the concluding section.

A one-week plan for a fifth grade class with a wide range of reading abilities is shown in figure 5.4. This plan calls for four groups, with the very high group (reading at seventh-reader level or above) being placed in an individualized reading program. The least capable readers in the low group will need some individual help in addition to group activities. In this plan, group and whole-class instruction and activities are combined with a substantial amount of individualized independent reading. Since the teacher need not meet with every group daily, the plan suggests three teacher-led periods per week for the low and middle groups and two a week for the high group. A period for individual teacher-pupil conferences is scheduled for the very high group. These can be increased, however, by giving more time to the reading program.

At this age level all groups can usually work independently. Preparation, guided reading, discussion, rereading, skill development and practice need not always proceed in that usual sequence, and workbook use may pre-

Minutes	Very Low Group	Middle Group	High Group	Very High Group
	MONDAY			
5	Whole Class: Daily directions and assignments for each group			
20	*T* Preparation, silent reading	Silently read the story introduced on Friday Related workbook pages	Independent reading	Individualized reading
15	*T* Guided rereading	Continue workbook		
15	Related workbook	*T* Discussion and purposeful rereading		
20	*T* Whole Class: Read and discuss weekly newspaper			
	TUESDAY			
20	Word recognition and decoding practice and games	*T* Preparation for new story	Silently read new story, no preparation	Individualized reading
20	Independent reading	Silent reading of new story	*T* Discussion, purposeful rereading, related skills	
15	*T* Specific-needs group: Use of context clues			
15	*T* Specific-needs group: Words with several meanings	Rest of class reads independently		

Minutes	Very Low Group	Middle Group	High Group	Very High Group
		WEDNESDAY		
20	T Check workbooks Preparation for new story	Related workbook pages	Exercise on critical reading, written responses	Individualized reading
20	Silently read new story	T Check workbooks Discussion and purposeful rereading	Independent reading	
30	T Whole Class: Use of dictionary pronunciation guide and abbreviations			

		THURSDAY		
25	Related workbook	Plan and rehearse story dramatization under direction of group chairperson	T Discussion of critical reading exercise	Individualized reading
20	T Check workbooks, discussion and purposeful rereading	Independent reading	Independent reading	
15	T Specific-needs group: Use of context cues (same group as Tuesday)	Rest of class reads independently		
15	T Specific-needs group: Inferred main ideas			

		FRIDAY		
30 AM	Whole Class: Recreational or research reading			T Individual teacher-pupil conferences
30 PM	T Whole Class: Book club meeting, dramatization; interest groups			

FIGURE 5.4.   A four-group plan for fifth grade. T = teacher works with group.

cede or follow. The high group may use special material that allows them
to develop higher-level comprehension skills. Related skill development
activities and enrichment come at various times, and some are conducted
on a whole-class basis. Twice a week the entire class has independent reading at the same time, freeing the teacher to have a series of individual conferences or work with specific-needs groups.

The duration of periods for each group is somewhat flexible but is usually between 15 and 30 minutes, allowing for a daily total of from 60 to 75 minutes in the fourth grade. In the other middle and upper grades, the daily plan can be quite similar, but with less total weekly time devoted to developmental reading for those who have made adequate progress. Groups can be merged for some activities.

An alternative plan calls for only two groups, a smaller low group using appropriate material at their instructional level, and a larger group using material that is on or above grade level. The more able readers complete the group assignments early or are excused from them; they read independently or act as helpers for classmates. Such a plan is easier to operate than a three-group or four-group plan and allows an increase in the number of group sessions per week or additional time for individual conferences. Of course, it is necessary that the assigned reading material be of suitable difficulty for instructional purposes, and that differentiated instruction take place.

READING CENTERS

One way to provide for differentiated reading instruction is to organize a number of reading centers (alternatively called *reading stations*) within the classroom. Each station or center provides space, furniture, equipment if necessary, and materials for a different kind of activity. Since many centers cannot accommodate more than five or six children at a time, this sets a maximum to the size of groups. If 30 children are in the class and at least one center cannot accommodate more than six children, one needs a minimum of five centers. It is desirable to have one more center than there are groups. For some activities two or more groups can be combined, and some whole-class activities can be part of the plan.

The nature of the centers can be varied. The choice of what centers to set up is made by the teacher partly on the basis of her understanding of the emphases needed to improve the children's reading, and partly on the basis of available supplies and materials. When the class has accomplished the objectives for which a particular center was set up, that center can be discontinued and one with a different set of objectives can be organized.

At a second-grade level, a representative list of centers might include: (1) decoding skills, (2) basal reading with teacher supervision, (3) comprehension exercises, (4) vocabulary development, and (5) a center for free-choice independent reading. Related centers for creative writing, individualized spelling, and individualized math could also be included. If some children are immature, a center for quiet play may be desirable.

At a middle-grade level the nature of the centers would be somewhat different. Comprehension, vocabulary, and independent reading centers would still be relevant. A basic study-skills center, a rate-building center, a critical reading center, and a center for work on a current class project are possibilities. Some teachers set up centers or stations for work on specific kinds of comprehension emphases, such as main idea or sequence of events or following directions. Related centers for independent work in writing, spelling, and math can easily be fitted into the plan.

Aside from a center for teacher-guided activities and a center for independent reading, materials for a center should so far as possible be self-administering and self-scoring. Programmed booklets and workbooks fit in well. So do reading laboratory kits containing sets of reading exercises on cards, with accompanying scoring keys. Other skill-building materials can be adapted to reading center use by preparing duplicate pages with the answers written in, to serve as answer keys. Alternatively the teacher can prerecord directions and answers on cassette tapes so the child can listen to the directions, turn the recorder off, do the exercise, then turn the recorder on again to check the answers. Workbooks can be used repeatedly if the children are trained to write their answers on separate paper.

Audiovisual equipment can provide added variety and enrichment. This can include one or more tape recorders, a set of several earphones to allow a group to listen to a recording simultaneously, slide, filmstrip, overhead, and movie projectors, and a device such as the *Language Master* (Bell & Howell). If projectors are used, it is desirable to have screens that can block off the projection corner from the rest of the classroom.

In diagnostic/prescriptive teaching, small groups are convenient for rotating children through several types of reading activities, in which each child has individualized assignments. A simple rotating group scheme is shown in figure 5.5. There are five groups, six reading centers, and two reading periods a day. For the first period on Monday Group 1 is in Center A, and that group is assigned to each of the other centers in the following periods. Group 2 starts in Center B and follows the same sequence through the other centers; Groups 3, 4, and 5 follow the same sequence of centers, each one step behind the preceding group. After Center F, each group starts over again at Center A.

Some teachers who use learning centers prefer to give children consider-

Group	Monday Period 1	Monday Period 2	Tuesday Period 1	Tuesday Period 2	Wednesday Period 1	Wednesday Period 2	Thursday Period 1	Thursday Period 2	Friday Period 1	Friday Period 2
1	A	B	C	D	E	F	A	B	C	D
2	B	C	D	E	F	A	B	C	D	E
3	C	D	E	F	A	B	C	D	E	F
4	D	E	F	A	B	C	D	E	F	A
5	E	F	A	B	C	D	E	F	A	B

FIGURE 5.5. A simple rotating assignment schedule for five groups and six centers.

able leeway in choosing their activities. Teacher-pupil conferences can be used to review progress and set specific goals and emphases for the next one to four weeks. These goals can be formalized in a written contract. The specific activities to be completed for each objective can be checked off as they are completed, or progress can be evaluated at the end of the period. A large schedule chart can be posted, with each center having the number of lines corresponding to its capacity. Pupils sign their names under the center they want; if it is full, they have first choice for it the next period.

Vacca and Vacca (1976) recommend a combination of teacher assignment (groups by reading levels), free choice by pupils, and random assignment. Teacher assignment is used for such activities as guided reading in a basal reader and basal workbook. Free choice is used for free reading, creative writing, use of audiovisual equipment, and skill games. Random assignment is used for visits to the school library, skill-kit exercises, and so forth. Whole-class activities include audience reading and listening and sustained silent reading during which the teacher can hold individual conferences.

In a plan using reading centers the teacher's role is radically changed. Relatively little time is spent in direct instruction. The teacher's role emphasizes organizing, managing, diagnosing, guiding, and serving as a resource person and helper. Two of the main problems are (1) collecting, preparing, and arranging materials; and (2) keeping adequate records. Both can consume large amounts of time.

ADMINISTRATIVE PROCEDURES

A number of different kinds of administrative procedures have been recommended and tried out in efforts to make it easier for teachers to deal with individual differences.

Postponing Beginning Reading Instruction   For more than 75 years, suggestions have been made that one could eliminate or greatly reduce failure in learning to read by postponing beginning reading instruction until the age of eight, nine, or ten. These suggestions have been based on the idea that fewer children at those ages would be unready for beginning reading instruction and children in general would be capable of faster and easier learning. However, age alone does not appear to solve the problem. Children begin learning to read at age five in England and at age seven in Sweden. Yet they still have reading disability cases in Sweden, as Americans do when instruction is typically begun at age six, and a wide range of individual differences occurs in all three nations.

Nonpromotion and Acceleration   General policies of retention, "100 percent promotion," or acceleration have not proven particularly successful. Each case should be considered individually. If a decision is to be made regarding whether to retain a child in a grade, a number of factors must be considered. If the child is not promoted, what efforts will be made to provide him with a more appropriate reading program? If he is sentenced to another year of the same thing in the same book with an unsympathetic teacher, it is probably better to promote him. On the other hand, if the child is promoted and the new teacher expects him to do "on-grade" work, other problems arise. In any case, the decision also should be based upon what the retention might do to the child emotionally and socially. Some children (and their parents) would be devastated by being kept back; others would welcome the idea, particularly if they are young or immature. Their feelings must be taken into account. Acceleration for the advanced reader is usually considered only if the child is quite mature physically and socially as well as academically.

Homogeneous Grouping   Homogeneous grouping involves assigning children to classes so as to place children with similar abilities in the same class. A truly homogeneous group is rare, if not impossible. When children are grouped according to any one attribute or combination of factors, they invariably differ in others. For instance, children grouped according to general reading ability differ in their decoding skills, their depth and breadth of comprehension, their interest in reading, and their rate of reading. Research has shown that the effects of homogeneous grouping on academic achievement have been inconclusive and that children assigned to low classes have lower self-esteem (Esposito 1973).

Cross-grade and Cross-class Grouping   In an effort to reduce the range of reading ability with which the teacher must deal, children are divided into reading classes, all of which meet at the same time. In small schools such a plan, often referred to as a Joplin Plan, ranks the pupils across a number of grades (e.g., grades 4–6) according to reading ability and splits them into reading classes, each usually with a range of about two years in reading ability. In larger schools each grade having a number of sections may be so divided.

If there are differentiated instruction, increased reading materials, conferences between the children's teachers, and enthusiastic administrative support, highly satisfactory results can be obtained. Nevertheless, the plan has several possible limitations. Teachers are tempted to treat the class as homogeneous and to rely on whole-class instruction. If reading is taught as a discrete subject it is not likely to be coordinated with other language arts or work in the content subjects. Unless the different teachers communicate, the child's needs may not be accommodated. Rigid time schedules as to when children must leave and return to their regular classrooms pose some problems. Young children may find it difficult to switch teachers and teaching styles.

Although Cushenbery (1967) concluded that the Joplin Plan's advantages outweighed its disadvantages, other reviewers (Newport 1967, W. Miller 1971) indicated that once the newness wore off, reading gains tended to disappear. The plan gives teachers the opportunity to meet individual needs better, but apparently the opportunity is not always used to advantage.

Nongraded Schools   In a nongraded plan, usually found only in the primary grades, children are classified mainly on the basis of reading ability. The primary reading curriculum is divided into eight to twelve levels, with each teacher usually having no more than three adjacent levels in her class. A child who successfully completes one level moves to the next higher level at any time during the school year. Children move through the levels at different speeds. Most children complete the primary program in three years, some take four years, and a few only two years. Nongraded plans have not resulted in improved reading achievement (DiLorenzo and Salter 1965, McLoughlin 1967). The nongraded idea seems to have fallen short of its hopes and no longer receives the attention it once did.

Split-half Classes   Another administrative plan involves having half the class come an hour or so earlier in the morning and leave an hour before their classmates, who begin and end school an hour later. Favorable results of its use have been reported in Denmark, where the plan has been used for 15 years (Lundahl 1976). Although the plan presents teachers with the opportunity to work with fewer children at a time, reduced class size alone apparently is not the answer. Theoretically, having significantly fewer children in a class should allow teachers to increase individualization of instruction. But if the teacher does the same thing with a class of 15 that she does with a class of 30, class size is not a factor. Similarly, while generally important, the amount of time devoted to teaching reading, by itself, is not a significant factor. It is what is done with the time that is important. Based on his review of the research, Arnold (1976) concluded: (1) it is not possible to state that small classes, in general, are highly desirable, since other factors may be more influential and powerful; (2) although class size may be a significant factor in developing countries, it is not the most important factor; (3) individual or small-group instruction is beneficial to many disabled readers; (4) small classes are most important in the early grades; and (5) other factors being equal, teacher training and morale are important.

Departmentalization   Based on the belief that teachers cannot be equally proficient in all areas, some middle grades are departmentalized. The advantages claimed for such a plan are that (1) having a special reading class assures that time will be provided for teaching reading, something that might be slighted; and (2) the reading teacher may be better informed about teaching reading than one who is responsible for all the subjects. Its disadvantages are similar to those listed for cross-grade grouping (Smith and Barrett 1974). Departmentalization is almost universal above the sixth grade.

Open Schools   In an open school, which appears to be an American attempt to emulate the British informal infant or junior schools, planned curriculum sequences are largely replaced by child-centered and child-initiated learning activities. According to Downing (1975), the open school is a style of education, a philosophy, not a facility. There is still room for walls and rooms in a school with an open philosophy. This viewpoint was substantiated by Seidman (1975), whose study found that open climates did not occur significantly more frequently than closed climates in open-space schools.

The open school is based on the assumption that children essentially want to learn and will cooperate in doing so, and operates on four practical principles: (1) The school becomes a workshop organized around a variety of learning centers. There is limited and planned freedom of choice, and there are no rigid externally imposed schedules. Self-discovery and self-discipline are keys to its success. (2) As a "learning facilitator," the teacher not only must supply an abundance of activities and materials, but also must keep track of a wide range of activities. Teachers work alongside children in shared learning activities. (3) In this child-centered plan every activity is planned so it can begin where the child is when he or she comes to it. A smoothly functioning language-experience approach often is thus an essential component of an open school. (4) "The educated life is for here and now" implies education is something to be enjoyed now, not in the future. Therefore reading and writing activities should be relevant and functional to the children.

In open schools, reading instruction tends to be a combination of language-experience and individualized reading procedures, with relatively little systematic skills development (Watters 1971, Moss 1972). However, many teachers group for reading instruction, making use of basal readers and programmed texts, and provide more structure than found in the British primary schools (Wiener 1974, Rogers 1976).

Studies regarding the effectiveness of open schools are limited, but the available evidence suggests that (1) children in traditional classrooms were more proficient readers; (2) behaviorally immature children had more chance for success in a traditional classroom; (3) there was no evidence that well-integrated children had a learning advantage in an open class (Bell, Switzer, and Zipursky 1974); (4) distractible boys do more poorly in an open classroom (Reiss and Dyhalo 1975); (5) after 2½ years, an open-school environment did not have a differential influence on the affective development of children; and (6) children in an open school had a conspicuous deficiency in academic skill areas (Wright 1975). Yet as the latter author pointed out (p. 463), "mastery of basic skills such as reading may be more essential to the child who is attempting to work independently than they are to the child who is working in a more fixed learning environment." The open school does not seem to be an improvement so far as reading performance is concerned.

From this brief overview of administrative arrangements, it seems safe to conclude that no arrangement can do more than give teachers an opportunity to teach well and that good and poor teaching can occur in any school. The active support and help that a concerned principal can supply is, however, a major assist to teachers, and its absence can hurt teacher morale and impair teacher performance (A. J. Harris 1976).

UNIT 6

Determining Needs and Assessing Progress

In order to adjust reading instruction to individual needs the teacher must determine each child's levels of reading ability and specific reading strengths and weaknesses. Knowing the child's levels of reading ability allows the teacher to select suitable reading material. Knowing which skills have or have not been mastered enables the teacher to individualize skill development. Both types of information help the teacher to group children, and provide information that can be used to assess their progress in reading.

The first part of this unit is devoted to ways of assigning children to groups and determining if material is suitable for instructional purposes. In the second section, ways for determining how well a child is reading are discussed. This is followed by suggestions for determining specific needs. The final sections are devoted to evaluating recreational and functional reading.

ESTIMATING CHILDREN'S LEVELS OF READING ABILITY

A question teachers often are asked is, "How well can this child read?" In response, many are prone to reply, "She scored 3.6 on the reading test" or "He's in the fourth reader, or at level twelve." Such replies only partially answer the question. One of the first steps in obtaining useful information about children's reading ability is to ask the right questions. Knowing what information to obtain enables teachers to select the appropriate measures.

There are basically two situations in which teachers need to know at what reading level pupils are functioning: (1) selecting materials for various purposes and (2) determining the particular reading skills individual children need to learn.

One of the first questions teachers must answer involves selecting material that is suitable for instructional purposes. Of course, if a language-experience or individualized reading approach is used exclusively, this problem theoretically does not exist because the teacher usually assumes that the material the child produces or selects is of suitable difficulty. When in doubt, however, users of these approaches still may employ the techniques described below.

Teachers must attempt to match, as closely as possible, a child's general level of reading ability with material that is neither too difficult nor too easy. Much reading instruction is done in groups. Assuming that all the members of a group will be using the same material, there are two main questions: (1) is this material suitable for use with Group X? and (2) does this child belong in Group X?

Well-kept cumulative records can provide initially useful information. Such records should indicate which material(s) have been used for reading instruction, results of achievement tests that accompany the reading series, report-card ratings and teacher comments, and scores on standardized tests. If a class is promoted intact, the former teacher may pass on a list of the reading groups as well as information about their progress. This combined information can be a first step in grouping children by their general level of reading ability. Although one cannot be certain that the next reading text in the published series (assuming the group has completed the preceding text) is suitable for their reading instruction, or that each child has mastered all the skills introduced in the program up to that level, checking that text for suitability is a logical place to start.

A Quick Screening Test

Once tentative groups are organized, the next step is to make a quick check of the suitability of the group's text for each child in the group. Children may have been misplaced in a group or their reading ability may have fallen behind or spurted ahead. For example, if a high second reader is to be used with the lowest group, all the children in that group would be screened with that reader. The following technique, which yields a rough estimate, may also be used for (1) locating less-able readers whose reading abilities need a more thorough evaluation or diagnosis; and (2) making a quick check of content subject texts.

1. From near the beginning of the text, select a paragraph that has not yet been read.
2. Schedule about a half hour for testing.
3. Tell the children that you want to find out how well they can read so that you can help them to learn to read better.
4. Have one child at a time read the passage orally at sight; always test apart from peers if at all possible.[1]
5. Excuse any child who is unwilling to try; provide any help the child needs while reading.
6. When each child has finished, rate performance:
   S = Satisfactory: the book appears suitable; reading is fluent and quite accurate.
   D = Doubtful: suitability is uncertain, more information is needed.
   U = Unsatisfactory: unwilling to try; needed help on more than two or three words; was excessively slow, hesitant, or repetitious; or displayed obvious signs of tension and uneasiness.

Because comprehension is not checked, the teacher may later discover that a child whose word-recognition skills are satisfactory has difficulty understanding what is read. A rough estimate of comprehension may be made during the screening by asking the child to relate the paragraph in his or her own words or by asking a few comprehension questions.

Pupils reading at and above the third-reader level can also be tested silently at another time. After the teacher provides a little background for the selection and a motivating question, the whole group silently reads the same three or four pages. A child who has finished the selection closes the book; in this way the teacher can note who are the slowest readers. If the questions have been mimeographed, the child can begin writing the answers as soon as reading is finished. Alternatively the teacher can wait

1. If not, the teacher should select a few alternate passages so that the children will not benefit from hearing the others read the passage.

until all have finished and ask the questions orally, with written answers. In either case, short objective questions are preferable. Comprehension scores of less than 60 or 70 percent or extremely slow reading probably indicate that the book is too difficult for that child. Children who are rated as "Doubtful" or "Unsatisfactory" can be similarly tested in lower-level material a day or so later, or an informal reading inventory may be administered.

Informal Reading Inventory

An informal reading inventory (IRI) is a series of graded selections. One or more representative selections are taken from each book in a published series, or the range of selections may be restricted, from two levels below grade level to two levels above it.

A well-constructed, well-administered, and well-interpreted IRI can yield more satisfactory information about the suitability of material for a child and the child's general level of reading ability than can either a quick screening test or a standardized reading achievement test. The IRI technique may be adapted for use in checking the suitability of any piece of reading material.

Because using an IRI is time-consuming, teachers should consider its use only with doubtful or extreme cases, or let the reading specialist do it (Hollander 1974). Some published reading programs make available what amounts to an IRI. If these tests have proven satisfactory, a new one need not be constructed. Knowing the techniques for administering and interpreting an IRI is useful to classroom teachers in their daily instructional activities.

Construction From each text to be sampled, choose two selections: one to be administered orally, the other as an alternate oral test or for testing silent reading or listening comprehension. Each selection should be as representative of the book as possible in difficulty, content, and language. Representative samples may be chosen randomly, but a more accurate estimate of difficulty can be made by applying a readability formula (see pp. 407–10) to at least five samples from the book. The two selections that most closely approximate the book's average readability score are chosen.

It is advisable to choose a selection from the beginning of a story, so that less background has to be provided. At the preprimer level, selections of about 50 words are usually sufficient, as are 100-word selections at the primer and first-reader levels, and 200-word selections above that. Each selection should end with the end of a sentence.

Some teachers like to give a word-recognition test before deciding where to start a child in the IRI. The teacher can construct a series of word-recognition tests by taking 10 to 20 words at random from the list or glossary at the back of each book in the series. These can be typed or printed in column form (see figure 6.1) or the lists in the figure can be used as they are. Or a published series of word lists based on a specific series such as those in the *Macmillan Placement Test* (Macmillan) could be used. Start the child with an easy list. If the child reads 80 percent or more of the

Preprimer	*Primer*	*1st Reader*	*2nd Reader*
and	around	again	bake
ball	book	began	cupcake
dog	father	could	field
get	him	fire	glove
here	know	hand	magic
look	new	kind	place
not	pet	name	second
see	she	please	stick
to	thank	sleep	trip
will	went	those	yourself

3rd Reader	*4th Reader*	*5th Reader*	*6th Reader*
among	airport	barbecue	aircraft
cape	blend	cheat	blister
desk	council	determination	cower
fold	fifteen	fertilizer	environment
hut	hero	hint	helm
metal	memory	literature	mammoth
polite	pleasure	occasional	perilous
scream	seal	radiant	representative
statue	terror	sum	sponge
tribe	wealth	voyage	wallop

FIGURE 6.1. Ten-word lists at eight reader levels. Taken from *Basic Elementary Reading Vocabularies* (First R Series), by Albert J. Harris and Milton D. Jacobson. Copyright © Macmillan Publishing Co., Inc., 1972. The difficulty levels are not indicated on copies presented to the pupil. An equivalent form may be found in A. J. Harris and Sipay (1975, p. 221).

words in a list correctly, try the next higher level; if the score is below 80 percent, try the next lower list. Oral reading in the IRI may be started at the level below the highest level at which the child scores 80 percent or more on the word list. Although giving word lists takes a little time, it may help to lessen the number of levels to be tested in the IRI. Specific errors made are useful in the qualitative analysis of the child's decoding skills, as they show how the child identifies words when deprived of meaningful context.

Prepare an introduction for each IRI selection. This statement should provide a brief background for the selection, a motivating question, and directions as to what and how (orally or silently) to read.

If specific comprehension questions are to be asked, formulate five to ten good ones. It is better to have a few good questions than many weak ones. Use both factual and inferential questions, with fewer inferential questions at the lower reading levels. Avoid trick questions and confusing wording, and try to gear the questions to the difficulty of the book. Any question that can be answered with a simple yes or no should be followed up with a "How do you know?" type of question; the two parts are counted as one question. More specific suggestions for formulating questions have been presented by Valmont (1972). Care should be taken in formulating the questions because they can greatly influence IRI results. For example, when Petersen, Greenlaw, and Tierney (1976) used three different sets of questions with the same passage, they found that 37 of 57 children tested had their instructional levels assessed as being at two different reader levels, and 8 children were assessed at three different levels.

Because it is difficult to frame a given number of good questions on short selections, and because variations in question difficulty make exactness of score questionable, some teachers prefer to use a free-response comprehension check ("Tell me the story in your own words"). This necessitates listing the concepts or events in the selection so they can be checked off as the child relates the story. Ideas not mentioned by the child can be checked by asking specific follow-up questions.

There are three ways to record a child's performance on an IRI. If the teacher is interested only in determining what level of material is suitable for instruction, no record form is necessary. All that is needed is a sheet of paper with the child's name on it, and the date, reader levels, and criteria noted down one side. Next to each selection, the teacher simply tallies the child's errors as they are made, and the number of comprehension questions answered correctly. If the child's performance is to be analyzed, a record must be kept of responses on either of two forms.

Name _____ Rob _____ Date _____ 2/8 _____

Reading Levels: Independent _4_   Instructional _5_   Frustration _6_

4th Reader, pp. 30–31 (201 words) WPE 2 (99%) Comp. 10 (100%)

Said	*For*	*Told*	*Omissions*	*Additions*
toll	toil	tourniquet		

Repetitions / to self-correct *Fluency*   Very fluent
ride for *raid*

5th Reader, pp. 15–17 (218 words) WPE _6½_ (97%) Comp. 8 (80%)

Said	*For*	*Told*	*Omissions*	*Additions*
rusty	rustle	scythe	assault	
dī sēz'	disease	cougar		
old	ancient			

Repetitions ///   *Fluency*   Misphrased at times

6th Reader, pp. 19–21 (204 words) WPE 21½ (89½%) Comp. 5 (50%)

Said	*For*	*Told*	*Omissions*	*Additions*
torpedōō	torpedo	auxiliary	initial	
rested	restricted	periscope	infamous	
expectations	exceptions	unidentifiable	decks	
unproved	unprovoked	negotiate		
resolve	resolution	cruisers		
furry	fury	chamber		
terrible	trivial	sonar		
the	a	submerge		
		conning		
		depth		

Repetitions ⅃⅂⅂⅂/   *Fluency* Very slow; tension movements

FIGURE 6.2. Rob's performance on an informal reading inventory ás shown on a listing/tally form. Word perception was scored according to the modified scoring procedures indicated on p. 197. The WPE (Word Perception Errors) are first indicated as the number of errors made; the percentage that follows indicates the percent of correct word perception.

Name_____ Sue _____   Date_____ 8/29 _____

Level 11 Golden Treasure, pp. 119-120

WPE: No more than (9)__3__Comprehension: At least (7)____8_____

Introduction. This story tells about an animal that makes
wonderful pet. Read (orally) (silently) from here to here to find
out some of the things you should know before you get one as a pet.

_____

A puppy should be about eight weeks old when you

take him (away) from his mother. When you see a

puppy that you like, make sure he's a healthy one.

A healthy puppy has a shiny coat and bright eyes.

A new puppy is like a new baby. People and places
                        P
might scare him, so you must be very gentle with

him. Don't play too hard with him, and when he gets

tired, let him take a nap.

You can make a bed for the puppy out of a box. Put
        (blanks)
some old blankets or towels in the box. Make sure

the bed is in a quiet place so the puppy can sleep.
                            radio
Don't put the bed near a radiator or on a cement floor.

It shouldn't be too hot or too cold.

_____

_____1. How old should a puppy be before you get him as a pet?
         (about eight weeks)

_____2. Name two ways to tell if a puppy is healthy.
         (shiny coat and bright eyes)

FIGURE 6.3. Sue's performance on one selection of an informal reading inventory (mimeographed form). Only part of the 190-word selection and two of
the comprehension questions are shown. Her performance was scored according
to the modified procedures shown on p. 197. The symbols indicate that (1)
away was omitted = ½ miscue; (2) *he's* was pronounced as "he is" = ½ miscue;
(3) *scare* was pronounced for her = 1 miscue; (4) *blankets* was first pronounced
as "blanks" but was self-corrected in the repetition = 0 miscues; and (5) *radiator*
was mispronounced as "radio" = 1 miscue.

The content was reproduced from *Golden Treasure. Reading Unlimited*, Level
11, *Scott Foresman Systems*, revised by Ira E. Aaron, A. Sterl Artley, Kenneth
Goodman et al. Copyright © 1976, 1971, by Scott Foresman and Co. The original page is in color. Reprinted by permission of the publisher.

The first, Listing/Tally Form, is similar to the one shown in figure 6.2. On it are recorded the name of the book, level of the selection, pages on which it is found, the criterion, and the child's name and date. Space is provided for recording the mispronunciation errors (*Said* column) and the expected response (*For*), words pronounced for the child (*Told*), omissions, additions, repetitions, and the teacher's judgment as to the suitability of the material (*Level*). Remarks also can be noted about voice, nervousness, phrasing, etc.

Figure 6.3 illustrates the other kind of form, a mimeographed copy of the selection on which the teacher directly records the child's performance. The mimeographed copy should be double-spaced to allow room to record the miscues. It is a good idea to place the answers you are willing to accept in parentheses after each comprehension question. In that way you will be more consistent in scoring the comprehension check. Also, indicating the type of comprehension question aids later interpretation. Use of a mimeographed copy saves time during testing because the expected responses are already recorded, and knowing where the miscues occurred can be of value in analyzing the child's reading performance. Listing the errors later on as in figure 6.2 will aid the teacher in determining if any patterns emerge.

Administration   Select a time when about twenty minutes without interruption are available, and a place where the other children cannot hear the testing. Be sure that all the pages are marked and materials are ready to use. Put the child at ease; tell him you are going to have him read from some books to see which one seems just about right for him. Also tell him you will be asking some questions about what he reads. If a word-recognition test has been prepared, begin with a low list. Present each list in increasing order of difficulty. Stop when the child responds correctly to less than 80 percent of the words on the list. Failure to respond acceptably to a word within 3 seconds is considered to be an error. Begin testing oral reading at the level below the highest reader level at which 80 percent of the words are read correctly. If a word-recognition test is not used, initiate IRI testing at least two levels below the child's grade level or at a level which should be very easy for the child.

After the introduction to the selection is read to the child, he reads orally at sight [2] from the book. As he does, the teacher records his performance

---

2. The findings of studies regarding the effect of rereading on word recognition are mixed (Gonzales and Elijah 1975).

Type	Recording Symbol	Sample
Word pronounced for child after 5-second hesitation	Write P above the word	*p* believe
Mispronunciation	Write response above expected response	*tǎm* tame
Substitution	Write response above expected response	*cat* kitten
Omission	Encircle word or part of word	⟨stop⟩ capi⟨ol⟩
Addition	Mark place where addition occurred with a caret and write the added material above	the ˄*big* dog quick˄*ly*
Repetition	Draw a wavy line under the material repeated	all along
Self-correction within 5 seconds	Place parentheses around the recorded error	(*cat*) kitten
Reversal	Same as mispronunciation; may be changed sequence of a word, part of a word, or a sequence of words	*dairy* diary *spot* stop *are they* they are
Ignoring or misinterpreting punctuation marks	Draw an X through the mark	cats×dogs× and lion×
Phrasing, hesitations	Draw a slash for each slight pause (less than 5 seconds)	He ran/into the/room
Dialectal rendition	Write response above expected response; add a capital D	*fis* D fist *rided* D I rode

FIGURE 6.4.   Recording oral reading on a duplicate copy of the material.

either by tallying, listing, or recording the errors, using the symbols shown in figure 6.4 if a mimeographed copy is used. The following types of mis-cues [3] must be tallied or recorded: mispronunciations, words pronounced for the child, omissions, additions, repetitions, reversals, and self-correc-tions. Teachers also may wish to record other reading behaviors discussed later in this unit. When the child has completed the selection, the teacher asks him to tell the story in his own words (free response), asking supple-mentary questions if the child's account is incomplete or hazy, or asks the specifically prepared questions. Oral reading testing continues at the next higher level if the criteria are met. If the error or comprehension criterion (or both) is failed, oral reading testing is terminated.

Silent reading testing is begun one reader level below the highest level at which oral reading criteria were met. For example, begin testing silent reading at the high-third-reader level if the highest level for successful oral reading was fourth-reader level. Continue testing at each higher level until the child's comprehension falls below 60 percent. Both oral and silent read-ing may be timed (in seconds) if the teacher wishes to compare reading rates in both modes (the selections must be almost equal in length and con-tent). Above the second reader level, silent reading should be faster. Al-ternatively, only silent reading may be timed.

Listening comprehension (auding) also may be checked. Auding is be-gun at the lowest level at which the child failed to meet the comprehen-sion criterion for silent reading (or for oral reading, if silent reading is not tested). Testing continues at each higher level until comprehension falls below 60 percent. As with oral and silent reading, the comprehension questions are asked and answered orally.

Interpretation   Over thirty years ago, Betts (1946) introduced the idea of three levels of reading competence. The *independent level* is the highest level at which the child can read easily and fluently with few errors and very good comprehension. Generally, material at this level is suitable for recreational reading, but the child should also be allowed to read material above and below the estimated independent level. At times high interest, motivation, or experiential background allows a child to read indepen-dently material at or even above his or her usual instructional level. The

---

3. Miscues are defined and discussed on page 229.

instructional level is the highest level at which the child can read satisfactorily with guidance from the teacher; errors are not frequent and comprehension and recall are satisfactory. Material at the instructional level should be used for most teacher-directed activities. At the *frustration level,* the child's reading skills break down, fluency disappears, errors are numerous, comprehension or recall is weak, and signs of tension or anxiety appear. It is very unlikely that reading skills will improve if the child is constantly given material that is too difficult. The *listening comprehension level* is the highest level at which the child understands the material. It is used as a rough estimate of the child's potential for improving level of reading ability.

A variety of criteria for determining these levels have been suggested over the years, but there is still no consensus. Many reading teachers employ the criteria proposed by Betts (1946, pp. 449 ff.) His main criteria for the instructional level were (1) a minimum comprehension score of 75 percent; (2) accurate pronunciation of at least 95 percent of the running words; (3) ability to anticipate meaning; and (4) freedom from tension in the reading situation. For the frustration level he proposed a comprehension score of below 50 percent, inability to pronounce 10 percent or more of the running words, slow, halting reading, and signs of tension and emotional upset. Obviously there is a gap between the instructional criteria and the frustration criteria, requiring subjective judgment.

The best research study to determine criteria for IRIs is still the one by Cooper (1952). IRIs were administered in autumn to 1029 children by a staff of 18 experienced examiners; each child was tested on the reader with which he or she was being taught. Silent reading tests were given in November and May so that progress in reading could be measured. A group IQ test was also given. Complete data were available for 819 pupils. The most suitable instructional level was taken to be that at which the most growth in reading took place, and the frustration level was identified as showing a significant drop to an unsatisfactory amount of reading growth.

Cooper's findings showed that (1) For both primary and intermediate pupils, gains in reading achievement tended to decrease as the difficulty of the instructional texts increased. (2) The percentage of word-perception errors was a satisfactory measure of the difficulty of a text for that child. (3) At primary levels (grades 2 and 3) materials in which pupils correctly recognized 99 percent of words resulted in greatest gains; materials in which 95 to 98 percent of the words were recognized were of questionable instructional suitability, with the degree of suitability decreasing as percent of errors increased; and materials with 94 percent or less correct word recognition were undoubtedly too difficult and frustrating. (4) Intermediate pupils were able to tolerate a slightly wider range of difficulty; materials with 97 to 99 percent correct word recognition appeared to be most suitable; materials with 91 to 96 percent correct word recognition appeared to be of questionable suitability, with suitability decreasing as percent of errors increased; materials with 90 percent or less correct word recognition were undoubtedly too difficult.

With regard to comprehension, primary-grade pupils who read materials that were properly adjusted to their reading abilities obtained average comprehension scores of 70 to 85 percent. Intermediate-grade pupils who read materials properly adjusted to their abilities achieved average comprehension scores of 60 to 70 percent. The lower limits for satisfactory comprehension, then, seemed to be 70 percent for primary materials and 60 percent for intermediate materials.

Certain symptoms increased steadily and sharply as degree of difficulty of material increased. These included word-by-word reading, inadequate phrasing, reading slowly and haltingly, ignoring punctuation, head movements, finger pointing, strained high-pitched voice, and other physical symptoms of marked insecurity and tension. Cooper's interpretation was that the presence of any two symptoms to a noticeable degree, when combined with a borderline performance in either word recognition or comprehension, is an indication that the material is frustrating for the child. The noticeable presence of more than two symptoms, even when criteria were met, was also interpreted as indicating that the material was unsuitable.

Criteria for the IRI based on Cooper's data are summarized in table 6.1. The instructional level is divided into two subcategories: most suitable and questionable. The questionable range is not sharply separated from the frustration level but rather shades gradually into it. When word-perception falls within the questionable range, the material is probably frustrating if the comprehension score is low or there are noticeable qualitative symptoms of disrupted fluency and tension (see above). It may be considered instructional if comprehension is satisfactory and qualitative symptoms are minimal or absent. These findings held good for both boys and girls, and for children with above-average, average, and below-average IQs.

If criteria based on Cooper's results are used, oral reading should be scored as Cooper scored it. Word-perception errors include substitutions, mispronunciations, words pronounced by the examiner (after a hesitation of 5 seconds), omissions, and reversals. Additions, hesitations, repetitions,

TABLE 6.1.

Criteria for the Instructional Reading Level

	Most suitable (%)	Questionable [a] (%)	Frustration (%)
Word perception			
Primary grades (2–3)	99	95–98	94 and below
Intermediate grades	97–99	91–96	90 and below
Comprehension			
Primary grades (2–3)	70 and up		below 70
Intermediate grades	60 and up		below 60
Qualitative symptoms:			
Word-by-word reading, inadequate phrasing, slow and halting reading, punctuation ignored, finger pointing, visible tension, strained high-pitched voice			Any two symptoms combined with a borderline performance. More than two symptoms even when criteria are met.

[a] The "Questionable" category probably indicates the instructional level for most pupils, but the upper limits of it suggest the frustration level for some pupils. The lower the percentage of acceptable word perception, the less suitable the material is for the pupil. The comprehension score and the noticeable presence or absence of qualitative symptoms of frustration will nearly always help to decide whether a questionable word-perception performance is indicative of the pupil's instructional or frustration level.

Source: Cooper (1952).

and ignoring punctuation are not counted. All errors are given equal weight.

Cooper's children lived in a small New England city in which "there appeared to be no serious difficulties related to bilingual problems in the schools," and apparently the question of making scoring adjustments for speakers of nonstandard dialects did not come up. In giving an IRI to children who speak a nonstandard dialect such as black English, it would seem reasonable not to count miscues (responses that differ from the text) that are the dialect equivalent of the text. This would include miscues such as saying /hōl/ for /hold/ or /he goin'/ for /he is going/.

Cooper's criteria do not provide a clear differentiation of the independent reading level from the instructional level. Materials that a child can read with no more errors than those allowable for the most-suitable category and with superior comprehension and good fluency would seem suitable for independent reading. A child who is very much interested in the subject matter can sometimes cope with material near the upper range of the instructional level when reading independently.

Other research workers, employing different criteria, have come out with different recommendations from Cooper's. Powell (1973), for example, considered that any material on which the child did not show observable symptoms of emotional strain and tension was instructional. On that basis he recommended the following percentages of miscues for the instructional level: preprimer-second grade, 6–13 percent; grades 3–5, 4–8 percent; sixth grade and up, 3–6 percent; for comprehension, at least 70 percent at all grades. Obviously someone using Powell's criteria will come out with different ratings of materials from those obtained with Cooper's criteria. Our preference is for Cooper's criteria for developmental reading materials. For content texts and materials more importance should be given to comprehension and less to errors or miscues.

Although Cooper's scoring and the scoring on most published oral reading tests count all word-perception errors equally, common sense suggests that some errors are of minor importance and should be given less weight than others. Harris and Sipay (1975, p. 173) proposed a modified scoring as follows:

1. Count as one miscue each: (a) any response that deviates from the printed text and disrupts the intended meaning; (b) any word pronounced for the child after a five-second hesitation.
2. Count as one-half miscue each: any response that deviates from the printed text but does not disrupt the intended meaning.
3. Count as a total of one miscue, regardless of the number of times the behavior occurs: (a) repeated substitution such as *a* for *the*; (b) repetitions (that are not self-corrections).
4. Do not count as miscues: (a) miscues that conform to cultural or regional dialects; (b) self-corrections made within five seconds; (c) hesitations; (d) ignoring or misinterpreting punctuation marks; (e) repetitions made for self-corrections.
5. Count repeated errors on the same word as only one miscue, regardless of the type of error made.

If the above scoring recommendations are followed, the total of word-perception errors will be lower than with Cooper's scoring, and consequently error percents in the questionable range will often represent frustration rather than the instructional level. The comprehension score and presence or absence of visible signs of frustration aid in forming the correct decision.

If both oral and silent reading have been tested, and the instructional levels in these two modes disagree, a problem of interpretation arises. In selecting material it is advisable to give more weight to the oral instructional level in primary grades, and more weight to the silent instructional level in intermediate and upper grades.

Teachers should be aware that use of an IRI is not foolproof. For one thing, different criteria combined with different material may result in different placements (Forese 1974). In a study by Page and Carlson (1975) in which 17 reading specialists rated the same performance, 6 rated it at the independent level, 5 at the instructional level, and 6 at the frustration level! Even personality variables such as reflectiveness and impulsity may influence the number and type of miscues (Hood and Kendall 1975, Fisher 1977).

The criteria used to determine the instructional level should be adjusted to serve particular situations. For example, if educationally disadvantaged children are tested, it may be more prudent to use a 50 or 60 percent comprehension criteron rather than 70 percent, with the expectation that a great deal of needed experiential background will be developed prior to reading the material. Comprehension is often influenced by what the reader brings to the printed page.

Even if the sample selections are truly representative of the *average* difficulty of a reading text, there will be some selections in the book that will be easier and others harder than the IRI selection. The teacher is advised to keep a record of how closely the IRI results match daily performance. Informal reading inventories based on a particular set of books are less likely to result in making accurate choices of other materials. This is especially true when an IRI based on a reading series is used for selecting content subject material. The instructional approach also must be considered. For example, a test based on an eclectic basal-reader series is probably not a valid measure for a child who has been instructed with a linguistic reading series. Because of variation in such factors as vocabulary and story content, it is advisable to base the IRI on the actual materials being considered for use.

Standardized reading achievement test scores tend to indicate grade equivalents higher than the most suitable instructional level. However, a number of factors (e.g. the standardized test used, the criteria employed in the IRI) can influence such comparisons (Sipay 1964). When standardized and IRI results disagree, more credence should be given the IRI *if* it has been well constructed, administered, and scored.

Cloze Tests

The instructional level or the suitability of material also may be estimated by using a cloze test in which the reader must write in words that have been deleted. Part of a cloze test is shown in figure 6.5.

Construction   Cloze passages may be selected at random or some effort may be made to choose representative samples. The latter may be done as suggested for the IRI on page 186, or five or six passages can be selected randomly, made into cloze tests, and administered to a number of children for whom the material is intended. Compute the mean percentage of correct response for each selection, then find the average of the means. Use the selection whose mean score comes closest to the average of the means.

A cloze passage should be at least 250 words long if every fifth word is

All eyes looked up. _____ was too late to _____. It was too late _____ anything. There was another _____ crack. Loud! A huge _____ of rock trembled and _____ in the roof directly _____ them. Small stones tumbled _____ on them through the _____. There was another rumble. _____ great mass above them, _____ enough to cover them _____, moved again. The dust _____ stones poured down. It _____ all over. The great _____ of stone was coming _____!

John Henry took a _____ forward. He rose above _____ crouching men, and bending _____ head down, pressed his _____ against the falling roof.

Deleted words in order of deletion: It, run, for, sharp, sheet, shuddered, above, down, cracks, The, large, all, and, was, slab, down, step, the, his, shoulders.

FIGURE 6.5.   Part of a cloze test. Reprinted from *John Henry and his Hammer* by Harold W. Felton by permission of Alfred A. Knopf, Inc., copyright 1950 by Alfred A. Knopf, Inc., New York City. Taken from *Finding the Way*, p. 115. Copyright © Allyn and Bacon, Inc., 1973. Reproduced by permission of the publishers.

deleted, as is commonly the case, because at least 50 deletions are needed to obtain a reliable measure. If deletions are more spread out (every seventh or tenth word), the passage must be correspondingly longer. Use of a cloze test with young children presents some problems, apart from the fact that they are not used to the task involved. First, it is difficult to obtain a 250-word selection at the first-reader level or below. Second, deleting every fifth word may make the task too difficult for young readers. Deleting up to every tenth word is often suggested for them. If this is done, however, the passage would have to be 500 words long to obtain 50 deletions, many more words than stories contain. Therefore, teachers may have to be content with shorter and less reliable measures at lower reader levels. Lastly, young children, as well as some older children, may have difficulty spelling the words or even writing them. In such cases, the cloze test can be administered individually with the responses given orally, or the teacher can provide assistance in spelling, or approximate spellings can be accepted. The selections are duplicated with equal-length spaces replacing the deleted words. Like the IRI, the range of selections may be narrow or wide, depending on the situation and purpose for testing.

Administration   It is a good idea to give pupils some guided practice in how to perform the task before administering a cloze test; the same is true of any type of test with which the children are unfamiliar. Tell the children they are to read the whole selection and think about what words fit best in the blank spaces. Then they are to reread the selection and write in the missing words. Time allowed should be generous.

Scoring and Interpretation   Most writers suggest that only the exact word deleted should be accepted in scoring because accepting synonyms lessens the interexaminer reliability (examiners may differ about which synonyms to accept). However, teachers must decide for themselves whether or not they are willing to accept synonyms. Another possibility is to use a modification called the maze procedure in which the reader selects, from three words below the space, the one that best completes the thought.

Bormuth (1968) reported that correct responses between 44 and 57 percent indicate the instructional level; scores below 44 percent are indicative of the frustration level, and above 57 percent, the independent level. Rankin (1971) similarly found that cloze scores between 44 and 58 percent predicted comprehension scores of 75 to 90 percent, a criterion commonly used to indicate the instructional level. If these standards are used, every fifth word must be deleted and no synonyms are acceptable. And just as studies have demonstrated that standardized reading tests and IRIs do not yield similar scores, two studies (Sauer 1969, E. J. Hodges 1972) have found that cloze test scores do not closely approximate the instructional level as determined by other measures.

Like any test, cloze tests have limitations. Their results can be influenced by which words are deleted. For example, it may be more difficult to arrive at the exact words for nouns, main verbs, and adjectives than for other parts of speech. Furthermore, the context may not indicate exactly what word belongs in a space, or certain words (e.g. noun markers such as *a* and *the*) may be chosen frequently for deletion because they occur in the fifth position. When use of a cloze passage indicates that many of the deletions are either too easy or too difficult, try starting with a different first deletion and delete every fifth word from there.

Because the cloze procedure is usually administered silently, no information is obtained regarding miscues or other oral reading behaviors. Of course, administering the test orally can overcome this limitation. Nor does the cloze test allow one to obtain information regarding strengths and weaknesses of certain types of comprehension (e.g. factual or inferential). In short, the cloze test provides limited diagnostic information.

On the other hand, the cloze test does provide a good measure of the ability to use syntactic and semantic (context) cues. Its other advantages include: (1) it is easier and quicker to construct, administer, and interpret than an IRI; (2) it does not require as much expertise to construct, administer, or interpret; and (3) results are not influenced by comprehension questions of unknown difficulty. Teachers must decide what information they want and select the most appropriate procedure. Those interested in learning more about the cloze procedure are referred to the annotated bibliography prepared by R. D. Robinson (1972) and the excellent discussion of its uses and limitations by Rankin (1974a).

Whatever tests are used, the teacher should consider children's daily performance in rechecking the suitability of reading materials. If initial placement is inaccurate, adjustments should be made.

HOW WELL IS THIS CHILD READING?

When we ask how well a child is reading, we nearly always have in mind one of three questions: (1) How does this child compare in reading with other children? (2) How does this child's reading compare with his or her estimated potential reading ability? or (3) Has this child mastered specific reading skills? Ordinarily standardized tests are utilized to answer the first and second of these questions, and criterion-referenced tests are employed to answer the third question.

Standardized Reading Tests

Standardized reading tests are intended for use in a wide variety of schools and attempt to measure basic reading achievement independent of any particular instructional materials or methods. They have manuals that provide exact directions for administering and scoring the test. They may be scored by hand, using a scoring key that gives the answers, or they may be sent away to be scored by machine. Teachers are expected to administer the test strictly according to the directions in the test manual. Failure to do so invalidates the test results.

Norms   When such tests have been given and scored according to the manual, the tables of norms supplied in the manual may be used to interpret the results. Usually three kinds of norms are provided: grade equivalents, percentiles, and stanines. Sometimes standard scores are also given. The norms are based on the scores of thousands of children, selected to represent a cross section of the child population in the appropriate grades, who took the test as part of the standardization process.

Grade equivalents are based on the median scores of the sample groups from several grades. By looking up a child's raw score (number of correct answers) in a table one can find the corresponding grade equivalent. A grade equivalent of 3.6 means that the child's score is equal to the median score of children in the sixth month of the third grade.

Percentiles and stanines are based on comparisons with the range of scores of children in the same grade. A percentile score of 35, for example, means that the child's score is higher than the scores of 35 percent of the same-grade children who were used in developing the norms, and below the scores of 65 percent of those children. Percentiles are easy to understand. They suffer the disadvantage that the percentile scale is not one of equal intervals. Because many more scores are near the average than are near the extremes, a difference of five points of raw score near the average may mean a big difference in percentile scores, while a difference of five points of raw score near the upper or lower end of the distribution may make very little difference in the corresponding percentiles.

Stanine scores divide the full range of the score distribution into nine intervals, each including a range of scores equal to one-half the standard deviation of the scores. The lowest stanine is 1; 4, 5, and 6 are low to high average; and 9 is highest. Stanines are equal intervals and are better for certain statistical purposes than percentiles.

Some reading achievement tests also have standard-score scales. These scales make it possible to compare rates of gain across grades, since the points on the standard-score scale are supposed to represent equal differences.

Because standardized tests put so much emphasis on the use of norms, they are sometimes called *norm-referenced tests*. They are intended to be used for comparing the results in one school system, school, or class with other systems, schools, and classes. The average for a class is a more accurate measure than the score of an individual pupil. Norm-referenced tests also provide a basis for deciding how much pupils have gained in reading between one testing and another, and whether they are achieving reasonably close to their capacity.

Most standardized reading achievement tests contain word-recognition and comprehension subtests in the early primary grades; above that, vocabulary (word meaning) and comprehension subtests. Some contain all three types of subtests, and a few include a decoding subtest. Samples of some subtests are shown in figures 6.6 and 6.7. Usually there are two or more comparable forms of the test to allow for retesting.

Interpreting Test Results Some standardized reading tests are labeled *diagnostic*. As opposed to reading *achievement* or *survey* tests, whose main purpose is to give a fairly accurate measure of a pupil's general level of silent reading ability, diagnostic tests, better called *analytical*, have the potential of providing a profile of skills. However, care should be taken in interpreting their subtest results, particularly for individuals, because the subtests may not possess sufficient reliability. Subtest reliabilities should be above .90 for individual use and the subtest intercorrelations should be below .65 (this indicates that the subtests are really not measuring exactly the same thing). The difference between the child's subtest scores should also be substantial, such as a minimum of two stanines, to be meaningful.

It also should be realized that no reading test in and of itself can be truly diagnostic. Tests can provide information, but diagnosis is a logical, involved process that is carried out by someone skilled in determining exactly what factors are causing or contributing to the child's reading problem.

As test users, teachers should understand two concepts: *reliability* and *validity*. *Reliability* is an indicator of the test's consistency. A test's reli-

---

Block of stone

A. pile
B. step
C. chunk
D. pillar

Hollow

A. blank
B. empty
C. fallen
D. holy

A

Bob wanted to scare his little sister. He pretended to be a

6 kitten   lamb   lion.
   ○   ○   ○

He let out a loud

7 laugh   roar   sigh,
   ○   ○   ○

but his sister was not

8 fooled   tired   disappointed.
   ○   ○   ○

B

FIGURE 6.6. Samples of reading vocabulary and comprehension test items for the primary grades. For item *A*, the child is to select from the four choices the word that means most nearly the same as the underlined word. For item *B*, the child is to fill in the space under each word that best completes the sentence.

Item *A* is reproduced from *The Nelson Reading Skills Test*, Level A, Form 4, copyright © 1977 by Houghton Mifflin Company. Reprinted by permission of Houghton Mifflin Company. All rights reserved. Item *B* is reproduced from the *Stanford Diagnostic Reading Test*, Red Level, copyright © 1976 by Harcourt Brace Jovanovich. Reproduced by permission of the publishers.

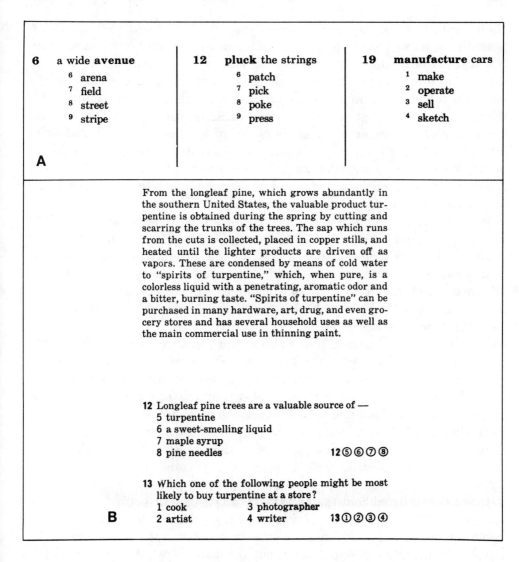

6   a wide **avenue**
    6   arena
    7   field
    8   street
    9   stripe

12   **pluck** the strings
    6   patch
    7   pick
    8   poke
    9   press

19   **manufacture** cars
    1   make
    2   operate
    3   sell
    4   sketch

A

From the longleaf pine, which grows abundantly in the southern United States, the valuable product turpentine is obtained during the spring by cutting and scarring the trunks of the trees. The sap which runs from the cuts is collected, placed in copper stills, and heated until the lighter products are driven off as vapors. These are condensed by means of cold water to "spirits of turpentine," which, when pure, is a colorless liquid with a penetrating, aromatic odor and a bitter, burning taste. "Spirits of turpentine" can be purchased in many hardware, art, drug, and even grocery stores and has several household uses as well as the main commercial use in thinning paint.

12 Longleaf pine trees are a valuable source of —
    5 turpentine
    6 a sweet-smelling liquid
    7 maple syrup
    8 pine needles   12 ⑤ ⑥ ⑦ ⑧

13 Which one of the following people might be most likely to buy turpentine at a store?
    1 cook   3 photographer
B   2 artist   4 writer   13 ① ② ③ ④

FIGURE 6.7. Samples of reading vocabulary and paragraph comprehension test items for the intermediate grades. Item *A* is reproduced from the *California Achievement Tests, Reading*, Level 3, with the permission of the publisher, CTB/McGraw-Hill, Monterey, CA. Copyright © 1970 by McGraw-Hill, Inc. All rights reserved. Printed in the U.S.A. Item *B* is reproduced from the *Stanford Achievement Test, Reading*, Intermediate Level I, Form A, copyright © 1972 by Harcourt Brace Jovanovich. Only two of the six questions pertaining to the selection are shown. Reproduced by permission of the publishers.

ability indicates how much a score might vary if the test were given repeatedly, or how much faith you can place in the stability of the test score. If a test is not reliable, faith cannot be placed in the test results because they might fluctuate greatly from one administration to another. No test is perfectly reliable; a number of factors prevent this from happening. And the average scores of groups are more reliable than one individual's score. For individual assessment a test should have a *reliability coefficient* of at least .90 for a single age or grade level or a *standard error of measurement* of not more than 3 months for grade-equivalent scores. The lower the standard error of measurement and higher the reliability coefficient, the more reliable the test.

Remember, an obtained test score is not an exact measure; the child's true score should be thought of as falling within a range of scores. For example, if a test with a standard error of measurement of 0.3 for grade-equivalent scores were administered a number of times to a child who obtained a first score of 3.1, two out of three of his or her scores would fall between 2.8 and 3.4 (3.1 ± 0.3). One of six scores would fall below 2.8 and one of six would be above 3.4.

Validity is an indicator of how well the test measures what it is supposed to measure. Validity is judged on the basis of answers to three questions: (1) How well does the test correlate with already established tests? (2) How closely does the content and makeup of the test correspond to the subject matter or skills one wishes to measure? and (3) How closely does the rationale of the test agree with the theoretical construct of the abilities to be measured? These three types of evidence—statistical validity, content validity, and construct validity—are all important in judging the validity of a test.

It should be noted that the validity of a test cannot be higher than the test's reliability, but it can be much lower than the reliability. A highly reliable test may be a valid measure of something one is not at present interested in measuring, but a very poor measure of what one is trying to measure. The validity of a test varies according to the purpose for which it is being used.

In appraising a reading test, teachers should not hesitate to compare the makeup, vocabulary, and language of the test, and the kinds of questions asked, with the characteristics of the reading material that the pupils have been using. One should allow, however, for the fact that a standardized test should have some questions easy enough for the poorest readers in the grades for which it is recommended, and some questions to challenge the ablest readers. Evaluative reviews of published tests may be found in the various editions of the *Mental Measurement Yearbook* (Buros 1968, 1972, 1978).

Although standardized tests are generally quite good in placing pupils in rank order of reading ability, a number of points should be considered in interpreting standardized test scores, particularly the scores of individuals. Any test is only a sample of behavior from which the degree of skill or knowledge possessed is inferred.

One problem is that different tests have been standardized on different samples of the population, and their norms are not completely in agreement. The Anchor Test Study (Loret et al. 1974) provides tables for translating scores on any one of eight intermediate-grade standardized reading tests into scores on any of the other seven tests and furnishes new national norms for the tests. The grade scores for some tests seem to correspond fairly well to the instructional level, while the norms on other tests seem more typical of the frustration level.

One must be quite careful in interpreting scores that are near the bottom of the scores obtainable, or near the top. A sixth-grade child, for example, may obtain a grade equivalent of 3.0 on a test on which he had only one right answer (probably by guessing), simply because that is the lowest possible grade score on that test. Conversely, a very proficient reader may be unable to demonstrate his or her full ability because he or she is limited by the highest possible score on the test. A solution to this limitation is to give the pupil the level of test that matches estimated level of reading ability. Thus, a sixth grader estimated to be reading at the second-reader level would be given the primary level rather than the intermediate level of the test.

Guessing is a factor in test scores that is difficult to evaluate. Competent readers obtain most of their correct answers by reading and thinking, gaining relatively little from successful guessing. The weaker the child's reading ability, the more likely it is that the silent reading test score is artificially raised by successful guessing. Careful observation during testing enables teachers to pick out many of these children. Also, checking the answer sheets may reveal excessive guessing. When the questions are easy for them, most children get almost all the items correct; when encountering more difficult questions, they make more incorrect responses than before. Excessive guessers start making errors very early and tend to have a high proportion of wrong answers on easy as well as hard items.

It also should be realized that in measuring growth or reading achievement, children with the lowest scores are most likely to show the most gain as compared to previous tests. Those in the middle will show less gain, and those with the highest initial test scores probably will show the least gain.

Furthermore, Tuinman (1973–74) has shown that children can answer some questions on multiple-choice achievement tests without even reading the selections. A number of test items are written so that they can be answered from past experience or from cues within the test questions; they are not "passage dependent." Tests also should be checked to determine how closely they sample the reading skills being taught. Other problems in the measurement of reading skills have been discussed by Tuinman and Blanton (1974).

As pointed out previously, errors of measurement occur in any test. Moreover, factors such as extreme anxiety, lack of motivation, a severe visual problem, or just having a bad day can influence a child's test performance. Reading tests should be used as only one piece of information in decision making. Informal tests and daily performance must also be considered.

Standardized tests are sometimes criticized as biased against urban non-standard-English speakers. But black and white urban children did not perform significantly differently on black dialect versions of standardized silent reading tests than they did on the standard English version (Hockman 1973, Marwit and Neuman 1974). In oral reading, third-grade speakers of a Newfoundland dialect did significantly better on the standard English version of the test than on the same test written in their dialect (Walker 1975).

Apparently, oral language dialects do not greatly interfere with written language performance. Neither do the wide variety of language patterns found in reading tests seem to affect test performance. Jongsma (1974) found that there was no significant difference in the comprehension performance of fourth graders when they read the original tests as compared to those rewritten to follow more common language patterns.

Dialect speakers, however, may be penalized on oral reading tests if dialectal renditions are counted as errors. For example, Hunt (1974–75) found that 46 percent of the errors made by a group of inner-city third and fourth graders on the *Gray Oral Reading Test* were attributable to dialect. But, even though there was a statistically significant difference between the mean scores (1.8 vs. 1.9) when scored by the standard procedure and without the dialect errors, the difference was only a tenth of a year—hardly of any practical significance. Furthermore, comprehension is not considered in the Gray test score.

Granted that standardized test contents do not adequately reflect the life experience and dialect of inner-city nonstandard-English speakers, a basic question becomes, "Should they?" MacGinitie (1973b) contended that reading tests should measure the pupil's ability to cope with materials used in school. Special tests *might* allow urban children to obtain higher scores, but as Hill (1974, p. 11) remarked, "Unless we can assume that the inner-city student will not compete with others for jobs or for further educational opportunities, unless we are willing to accept responsibility for not encouraging him to expand his personal fulfillment through broader intellectual exposure and personal challenge, it would be flagrantly dishonest of us not to make him aware of what he hasn't mastered and yet needs to learn in order to participate and compete successfully." Modifying tests so minority-group children will obtain higher scores will not guarantee that they will learn more; the educational program, not the tests, needs to be changed (Fitzgibbon 1974). If children do poorly on reading tests because they lack experiental background or reading skills, something should be done to help them overcome those limitations. If a child scores poorly on a test because it is conceptually foreign to him, the test score should not be considered a true indication of that child's total reading ability. Nor should a poor reading test performance be regarded as indicating a lack of potential for improving reading skills.

Criterion-referenced Tests

Criterion-referenced tests (CR) indicate whether or not a testee has mastered a specific skill according to some predetermined standard. CR tests are commonly associated with behavioral objectives and can be useful in individualizing reading instruction. If a child can demonstrate mastery, there is no need to teach or practice that skill.

An example of a criterion-referenced standard is as follows: Given ten unknown monosyllabic words containing the short sound of a, the child will correctly decode at least eight words. In a sense, the IRI and cloze tests are criterion-referenced because the learner's performance is judged by certain standards rather than compared with the performance of others, as in norm-referenced tests.

Various reading programs employ sets of criterion-referenced tests, many of which have been described by Prager and Mann (1973), Niles (1973), and Klein and Kosecoff (1973). Many of the commercially available CR tests have been described and their limitations pointed out by Thompson and Dziuben (1973). Those who wish to construct their own CR tests may refer to such sources as Gronlund (1973).

Criterion-referenced tests also have limitations and unresolved problems. There is no firm agreement as to the nature of mastery or how to measure it (Meskauskas 1976). Another unresolved problem is determining what criterion to set as passing. Arbitrarily set criteria of 80 or 90 percent are usually employed, but there is little evidence as to which criteria indicate mastery, or whether there should be a varying criterion depending upon such factors as the importance of the skill for learning other skills. Some sets of CR tests appear to measure so many separate skills that one wonders if all are really necessary for learning to read, and if all are of equal importance, or if having to go through a specified sequence of skills may hinder efforts to develop strategies other than those outlined by the program (Popp 1975). Some writers question whether CR tests can adequately measure such complex domains as reading comprehension. Others point out the dangers of not considering appreciations and attitudes because their measurement does not readily lend itself to criterion-referenced tests; and of believing that performance on a short test is truly indicative of mastery.

Questions of reliability and validity apply to CR tests as well as to standardized tests. CR tests are usually short, containing 5 to 10 items. A good 10-item test rarely has a reliability coefficient higher than .80, and a well-written 5-item test usually has a reliability coefficient of .60 to .70. These values are lower than the desirable minimum for accurate individual measurement and indicate that pass-or-fail scores that are close to the criterion are of doubtful accuracy. Validity questions also come up. For example, a CR test on syllabication may measure knowledge of rules rather than ability to use syllables to decode words. Permanence of mastery is also an issue.

Standardized Oral Reading Tests

A standardized oral reading test contains a series of selections of increasing difficulty. Testing is initiated at a level thought to be easy for the child and continues until the material becomes too difficult. As the child reads orally at sight, the examiner records performance on a printed record form.

Differences among these tests exist as to what are considered errors, how they are scored, their content, the type and number of scores, and the number of alternate forms. For example, the *Gray Oral Reading Tests* (Bobbs) yield one grade-equivalent score based on the number of word-recognition errors on each selection, and time taken to read it. Four factual questions are asked for each selection, but the results are not included in the test score. The *Gilmore Oral Reading Test* (Harcourt) gives separate scores for accuracy, factual comprehension, and rate. The *Spache Diagnostic Reading Scales (DRS)* (CTB) is scored like an IRI and allows one to estimate the child's independent and instructional level. Unlike the IRI, however, Spache defines the independent level as the highest level at which the child can read silently with at least 60 percent comprehension. Oral reading tests are part of the *Gates-McKillop Reading Diagnostic Tests* (Teachers) and the *Durrell Analysis of Reading Difficulty* (Harcourt), each of which (as does the *DRS*) contains a number of other tests that may be useful in the detailed analysis of disabled readers. There are also three published reading inventories that are very similar to the IRI in format and scoring: the *Standard Reading Inventory* (Klamath), *Classroom Reading Inventory* (W. C. Brown), and *Reader Placement Inventory* (Economy).

If the staff does not have the knowledge or time to construct a good IRI, a standardized oral reading test or inventory may be employed. Each school should experiment to learn which test gives the most accurate and useful results for their needs.

Informal Assessment and Tests That Accompany Programs

Informal assessment includes observations, checklists for systematized observations, anecdotal records, teacher-made tests, brief skill tests found in manuals, and workbook assignments. Such forms of assessment are needed to obtain information that is not available from other sources and to provide a more accurate estimate of the children's reading skills and abilities—the more behavior sampled, the more likely the assessment is to be accurate.

Published reading series often make available tests to accompany their program. These are usually "tailor-made" to measure the skills taught in that particular program at various stages. If they are well constructed, they should give a more accurate picture of children's progress and needs in that program than any standardized reading achievement test could. Tests that accompany reading programs may include readiness tests, mastery or achievement tests that are given at the end of a unit or book, and what amounts to an informal reading inventory. Some of these are norm-referenced and present norms based only on users of that program; most of them are criterion-referenced.

Reading Capacity

In order to determine if a youngster is making acceptable progress in reading, it is necessary to estimate at what level the child might reasonably be expected to function. Children whose reading ability is significantly below their potential for learning and their grade level are defined as *disabled readers*. It is important to distinguish cases of reading disability from children whose reading is below grade level but close to what might be expected of those with slow or limited mental development. Although both should be given help, the *disabled reader* is a better prospect for improvement than is the *slow learner in reading*. Slow learners should not be expected to read "at grade level" nor should their needs and capacity to learn reading skills be ignored.

There are also *underachievers in reading*, those bright children who although reading at about grade level are operating far below their potential. Disabled readers need special reading help, while underachievers usually require stimulation and motivation rather than extra help with basic reading skills.

The simplest procedure for comparing a child's reading performance to his (her) estimated capacity is to subtract his reading-grade score from his mental-grade score. Mental grade is easily computed if one knows his IQ (as determined by a satisfactory intelligence test) and his chronological age, as follows: (1) Multiply his IQ by his CA and divide by 100; this gives his estimated present mental age. (2) Subtract 5.2 years from the M.A. to obtain a corresponding mental grade. For example, a child who is 10 years 6 months old (10.5 years) and whose most recent IQ is 90 has an estimated present M.A. of 9.45 and an estimated mental grade of 4.25.

A probably more accurate estimate of capacity can be obtained by combining M.A. with CA, giving M.A. twice the weight of CA. Reading expectancy grades based on this principle are shown in table 6.2. To use this table, find the column nearest the child's CA and the row nearest the child's IQ. Where this column and row intersect, one finds the reading expectancy

TABLE 6.2.

Reading Expectancy Grades for Selected Combinations of
Chronological Age and Intelligence Quotient

IQ	\multicolumn{13}{c}{Chronological Age}
	7.2	7.7	8.2	8.7	9.2	9.7	10.2	10.7	11.2	11.7	12.2	12.7	13.2
140	3.9	4.4	5.1	5.7	6.4	6.9	7.7	8.2	8.9	9.5	10.2	10.7	11.5
135	3.6	4.2	4.9	5.4	6.1	6.6	7.3	7.9	8.6	9.1	9.8	10.3	11.0
130	3.4	3.9	4.6	5.1	5.8	6.3	7.0	7.5	8.2	8.7	9.4	9.9	10.6
125	3.2	3.6	4.3	4.8	5.5	6.0	6.7	7.1	7.8	8.3	9.0	9.5	10.2
120	2.9	3.4	4.1	4.5	5.2	5.7	6.3	6.8	7.5	7.9	8.6	9.1	9.7
115	2.7	3.1	3.8	4.2	4.9	5.3	6.0	6.5	7.1	7.5	8.2	8.6	9.3
110	2.4	2.9	3.5	4.0	4.6	5.0	5.7	6.1	6.7	7.2	7.8	8.2	8.8
105	2.2	2.7	3.2	3.7	4.3	4.7	5.3	5.8	6.3	6.8	7.4	7.8	8.4
100	2.0	2.5	3.0	3.5	4.0	4.5	5.0	5.5	6.0	6.5	7.0	7.5	8.0
95	1.7	2.2	2.7	3.2	3.7	4.1	4.5	5.2	5.6	6.1	6.6	7.0	7.5
90	1.5	1.9	2.4	2.8	3.4	3.7	4.3	4.7	5.2	5.6	6.2	6.5	7.1
85	1.2	1.6	2.2	2.5	3.0	3.4	3.9	4.3	4.8	5.2	5.7	6.1	6.6
80	1.0	1.4	1.9	2.2	2.7	3.1	3.6	4.0	4.5	4.8	5.3	5.7	6.2
75	1.0	1.1	1.6	2.0	2.4	2.8	3.3	3.6	4.1	4.5	4.9	5.3	5.8
70	1.0	1.0	1.3	1.7	2.1	2.5	2.9	3.3	3.7	4.1	4.5	4.9	5.3
65	1.0	1.0	1.1	1.4	1.8	2.1	2.6	2.9	3.4	3.7	4.1	4.4	4.9
60	1.0	1.0	1.0	1.1	1.5	1.8	2.3	2.6	3.0	3.3	3.7	4.0	4.6

grade, near enough for most purposes. For example, if a child is 8 years 10 months old, the nearest CA column is 8.7; if his IQ is 118, the nearest IQ row is 120. Reading down the 8.7 column till it reaches the 120 row, the reading expectancy grade is 4.5.

For a difference to be meaningful, the reading grade should be at least 9 months lower than the mental or expectancy grade in the primary grades, a year lower in grades 4 and 5, and at least 18 months lower in grades 6 and up. To illustrate, suppose that two fifth graders both have reading grades of 3.9. Child A has a reading expectancy grade of 5.6 and is, therefore, a disabled reader. Child B, with a reading expectancy grade of 4.1, is reading about in accord with his estimated capacity.[4] Of course, if a child of average intelligence is functioning far below grade level in reading, there

4. For a more detailed treatment of the measurement of reading capacity, see A. J. Harris and Sipay (1975, pp. 145–57).

is no need to apply a formula to determine that the child needs special assistance.

Measuring capacity and comparing it to reading ability has a number of limitations. Both capacity and reading levels vary with the measures employed, and there are unsolved measurement problems in applying expectancy formulas. There also is the possibility that the intelligence test score is an inaccurate measure of potential. Most group intelligence tests above the primary grades require reading ability, so that disabled readers cannot demonstrate their learning potential. Estimates of potential also should be tempered by knowledge of the child's conceptual and experiential background, familiarity with standard English, amount and quality of education, and motivation. Whenever there is any doubt about a group intelligence test score and such information is needed in decision making, the child should be given an individual intelligence test such as the *Wechsler Intelligence Scale for Children* (Psychological) by a competent psychologist.

Reading capacity also may be estimated from the child's level of listening comprehension. This may be done through the use of a teacher-made or commercially produced informal reading inventory or a standardized listening comprehension test such as the ones included in the *Durrell Listening Reading Series* (Harcourt) and the *Sequential Tests of Educational Progress (STEP)* (ETS). If a child's instructional level is significantly below grade level and his or her listening comprehension is two or more years above instructional level, it is reasonably certain that the child has a reading disability. A one-year difference points in the same direction, but its meaning is more doubtful.

WHICH READING SKILLS HAVE BEEN MASTERED? WHICH READING SKILLS NEED TO BE TAUGHT?

Answers to these two questions enable teachers to individualize reading instruction. All the previously mentioned sources of information should be used. For the purposes of determining specific reading strengths and weaknesses, standardized reading achievement tests offer the least useful information, except for information regarding the child's reading vocabulary. More valuable information for planning the program comes from criterion-referenced tests and use of daily informal measures and observations.

Teachers tend to rate children's reading in a global fashion (Olshavsky,

Andrews, and Farr 1974). What they need to acquire is the means for assessing specific strengths and weaknesses.

Reading Behaviors

The following discussion is useful not only in testing but also in observing reading behaviors during daily lessons. Behaviors that children manifest while reading orally and silently can reveal information about their reading strategies and abilities. Of the two modes, oral reading yields more diagnostic information because more behaviors are directly observable. In observing these behaviors, two points should be considered: (1) it is much more important to understand what probably caused the behavior (so the cause rather than the symptoms can be treated) than simply to note it; and (2) not all behaviors are necessarily undesirable.

General Behaviors   Some general behaviors may occur during either oral or silent reading, among which are finger pointing, head movements, possible symptoms of visual problems, and inappropriate rate. *Finger pointing* may take various forms. Word-by-word pointing may be (1) habitual (probably so if it occurs on material that the child reads easily); (2) caused by weak word recognition; or (3) needed to keep the place (the child loses the place if prevented from pointing). If the latter two are ruled out as causes, an attempt can be made to wean the child from finger pointing by first allowing him or her to use a marker, then gradually reducing its use. Moving the finger under phrases (this may aid phrasing) and under lines of print or to the beginning of the next line suggests that the child is having difficulty keeping the place. This crutch probably helps the user to avoid omissions of lines or phrases or faulty return eye sweeps. Finger pointing may be a needed crutch, particularly for young children, and should not be discouraged prematurely.

Head movements usually take the form of moving the head laterally from side to side. This behavior may interfere a little with reading speed. Calling the child's attention to head movements and gentle reminders to read "just with your eyes," or having the child place a hand on his or her chin, often helps overcome this problem.

When reading, the material should be held approximately 12 to 18 inches from the eyes. Marked deviations from these distances, as well as such behaviors as moving the material back and forth from the eyes, sharply tilt-ing the head to one side, holding the book at odd angles, or covering one eye may indicate visual problems. Although these behaviors may not inter-fere greatly with reading ability, the child should be referred for a visual examination.

Inappropriate rate may involve either reading too slowly or too rapidly. Very slow reading may be caused by (1) poor word recognition or poor comprehension (conversely, an excessively slow rate may contribute to comprehension problems because it makes it more difficult to relate one idea to another); (2) inattention, particularly during silent reading when the reader is not forced to attend; (3) compulsivity, the habit of making sure that every word is inspected carefully; (4) simply never having been in-structed in speeding up reading. Reading too rapidly usually results from nervousness, from a desire to get through the task as quickly as possible, or from the mistaken belief that reading rapidly is desirable even at the cost of comprehension.

Interpreting Oral Reading

Knowing what constitutes an excellent oral reading performance provides the teacher with a set of standards against which each child's reading can be compared. Teachers who regard each oral reading sample as an oppor-tunity to discover specific facts can use each situation as an occasion for discovering needs. For example, noting that Tom's voice is tense, that he makes numerous repetitions and mispronunciations, and that he blushes when corrected, can provide a starting point for helping him. Asking ques-tions such as the following is the first step in finding solutions: Is the book too difficult for him? Should he be in a lower group? How can he be helped to be more secure in oral reading? What causes the repetitions and mis-pronunciations? Is there some pattern to his miscues? How can he be helped to feel less embarrassed when he makes a mistake? Would it be better to have him read orally alone to me until he becomes more secure?

A tape recorder can help greatly in recording and analyzing oral reading. While the child is reading, the teacher need write down only behaviors that will not appear on the tape (e.g., finger pointing). The tape can be played later, and replayed if necessary, and a written analysis made at that time. It is also helpful to invite children to listen to their recorded readings and to encourage them to help evaluate their performance and set goals for improvement. Tapes of the same child's reading made a few weeks or months apart usually arouse real interest in children and provide a dramatic, clear, and useful basis for appraising progress.

During oral reading the child's fluency, phrasing, and expression should be noted. Oral reading should be smooth, with words grouped in appropriate thought units; these phrases are indicated by appropriate pauses and inflections. Word-by-word reading and inadequate phrasing may be due to weak word recognition or may be a symptom of comprehension difficulty. If these behaviors occur during testing on material that is not frustrating for the child, they may be due to the fact that oral reading is done at sight. If daily performance indicates that they do not occur after the child has preread silently, there is no need for concern.

The voice should be of appropriate volume and indicate acceptable enunciation and expression. Subtleties in meaning often are conveyed by inflections of the voice and emphasizing one word or another. Thus the simple question "What are you doing?" can be spoken so as to express a polite request for information, a sarcastic comment, or an exasperated demand. Lack of inflection and emphasis may indicate comprehension difficulties or contribute to them. The child's voice can be revealing. Is it too loud or soft, pitched too high or low, tense or relaxed? Is there evidence of a dialect, speech defect, or foreign accent? If the voice volume is loud even in a non-reading situation, the child may have a hearing problem. Changes in the voice also may indicate that the material is too difficult for the child or may be due simply to nervousness.

Oral reading also allows teachers to observe the child's word-recognition skills and possibly, decoding skills. Responses that deviate from the printed stimuli are referred to as *word-recognition errors*, or *miscues*. The latter term, introduced by K. Goodman (1969), is more appropriate because not all deviations are "errors" in that they simply may reflect the reader's dialect or reading strategies. Dialect variations should not be considered reading errors; this applies both to the way in which words are pronounced (most variations occur on vowel sounds) and changes in sentence structure (e.g., *He be* for *He is*).

The following types of miscues should be noted during testing and daily activities: *Mispronunciations* [5] may involve whole words (*ear* for *hat*), word parts (*kit, hit, had, him,* for *hat*), or *reversals* (*was* for *saw, girl* for

5. Some writers distinguish between mispronunciations and substitutions, with the latter implying that the response made sense and did not distort meaning.

grill). Reversals also may involve single letters (*d*ig for *b*ig) or word order (*I am* for *Am I*). Mispronunciations that distort the intended meaning are much more serious than those that allow the reader to maintain it. For example, *hog* for *hat* is much more serious than *kitten* for *cat*. Distinguishing between major and minor miscues is taken into consideration in the scoring procedure outlined on page 197. Reversals are almost always serious because they alter meaning. Among the causes of mispronunciations are weak word-recognition and decoding skills, excessive reliance on word parts or inattention to them, overreliance on context or weak use of it, or the anticipation that certain words are likely to occur next in a given sequence or story.

Words pronounced for the child after a five-second hesitation should be noted. They indicate that the words are not in the pupil's sight vocabulary and that the pupil is unable or unwilling to decode them. The need to have many words pronounced suggests that the child is not using context cues. Whether or not the child can use these cues needs to be determined.

Omissions may take the form of whole words, word parts, or groups of words. The seriousness of an omission depends on the extent to which it changes the intended meaning. For example, leaving out a single letter may simply reflect a dialect (*two dog* for *two dogs*) or may affect meaning (*pat* for *pact*).

Additions, inserted words or word parts, usually are minor miscues and reflect anticipation of a word occurring in a given sequence. Like some omissions and mispronunciations, some additions are made to correct for previous miscues (e.g., *the dog eats* for *the dogs eat;* because *dogs* was miscued as singular, the singular verb form was given).

Repetitions may involve word parts, single words, or groups of words, but only the latter is usually considered an error. A repetition may occur (1) to correct a miscue (the child realized the word did not make sense or sound right); (2) to aid comprehension or regain the train of thought; or (3) to stall for time while attempting to decode a following word. The first two are desirable behaviors and usually should be encouraged. However, a marked number of repetitions may indicate that the material is difficult for the child. In the scoring system we suggested on page 197, no matter how many repetitions occur, they are counted as only one miscue. However, if the criteria in table 6.1 are used, repetitions are not counted as word-perception errors.

Miscues that are self-corrected within five seconds, hesitations, inadequate phrasing, and ignoring or misinterpreting punctuation marks should be noted, but should not be counted as errors in scoring. Self-corrections are desirable and should be encouraged.

Silent Reading In addition to the previously mentioned general behaviors, two behaviors that should also be noted during silent reading are *lip movements* and *vocalization*, both of which tend to slow down reading rate. If they occur in young children or if they occur occasionally in older children there is not much need for concern. In the former case, the children have not had much experience reading silently and have not yet fully made the transition from reading everything orally. In the latter case, the vocalization may aid comprehension; however, marked lip movements or vocalizations may indicate that the material is too difficult. Giving the child easier material will overcome the problem. If they occur with easy material, gently reminding the child not to move his lips or having him put his finger on his lips may help.

Comprehension Specific strengths and weaknesses in comprehension can be observed as children try to answer questions of various kinds, orally or in writing, on both oral and silent reading. Some children can only answer questions about details and then only when the answer is explicitly stated in the selection. Others grasp main ideas that are directly stated, but flounder when the main idea must be inferred; some have difficulty with both. Some cannot interpret beyond what is directly stated; others can "read between the lines," respond to what is implied, anticipate developments, predict outcomes, and read critically.

Some standardized and criterion-referenced tests indicate what type of comprehension each item or subtest measures. Care should be exercised in interpreting the results of these tests. Almost all of them contain too few items of any one type to provide a reliable measure, and in some cases the items apparently are mislabeled. There is also the question of whether reading comprehension is a unitary skill or is composed of different types of skills. This point is considered in more detail in unit 8. Daily reading lessons and workbook performance provide the most detailed information regarding comprehension.

Some children are *context readers*; that is, they rely too much on context when they encounter unknown words. Their reading may be fairly fluent and rapid, but tends to be inaccurate, often skipping, adding, or substituting words; it is also marked by inattention to details. Using semantic and syntactic cues as aids to word meaning is desirable, but a child who does not have or use other methods of decoding unknown words will run into difficulty. Context readers often score considerably higher on comprehension subtests than they do on vocabulary or word-recognition tests. Such children generally need training in word-recognition techniques and in reading more carefully and accurately. However, care must be taken lest they get the wrong idea and start to concentrate on every printed word, thus slowing down their reading. Word-identification skills must be combined with semantic and syntactic cues.

Reading paragraphs or longer selections is a difficult task for some children. They usually can comprehend items of one or two sentences, but have difficulty obtaining meaning from longer and more complex selections. Many children who have this problem are word-by-word readers who cannot see the forest because of the trees.

Reading Rate   Rate of silent reading is best measured on material of the same level of difficulty rather than on material of increasing difficulty. In the latter, inability to comprehend the more difficult passages may complicate the interpretation of test results. Standardized or informal rate tests can take either of two formats: (1) a large number of short paragraphs with a time limit for completing them; or (2) a selection of a few hundred words with the children timed on how long it takes them to complete the test. In informal tests, the selections should be long enough to take average children about five minutes to complete. After the children are told to read at their usual rate and that they will be asked comprehension questions, they all begin to read. As they are reading, the teacher prints a new number on the board every ten seconds (1, 2, 3, etc.). As the children complete the exercise, they look up and copy the number on their paper. The number of words read per minute is computed by multiplying the number of words in the selection by six and dividing by the number recorded from the board. Thus if the selection is 500 words long, the rate of a child who records a 10 on his paper is 300 words per minute ($\frac{500 \times 6}{10} = \frac{3000}{10} = 300$).

It is advisable to check comprehension when testing rate because some children "cover" the material rapidly with little or no understanding of what they read. Silent reading *accuracy* can be computed by dividing the number of correct comprehension items by the number of answers attempted.

Comparing rate and comprehension is likely to be informative, particularly in the middle and upper grades. Those with low rate and high comprehension probably can benefit from training to read faster. Those with high rate and low comprehension need exercises that stress accurate reading or versatility. When both rate and comprehension are low, try first to determine why comprehension presents a problem.

Excellent readers often are both fast and accurate, but they also adapt their rates to their purposes for reading, their background on the topic, and the requirements of the material. A reader who wishes simply to obtain an overview or enjoy the material should read it rapidly. When one does not have the conceptual background, a new topic may have to be read slowly and carefully. Material that contains many important details and requires very high accuracy (such as is found in science and math texts) may have to be read quite slowly. Easy narrative material may be read very quickly. Flexibility is the key.

Inflexibly rapid readers tend to be more successful in grasping central thoughts than in noting and remembering details. They usually enjoy narrative material, both fictional and historical, and do well with it. When factual information is presented in highly organized and somewhat condensed form, as is characteristic of many content subject texts, inflexibly rapid readers tend to hit the high spots only and obtain a rather sketchy and inaccurate account.

Consistently slow readers are sometimes slow because they have difficulty rapidly recognizing or decoding words; in these cases, the word-recognition or decoding problem is primary. For others, inadequate comprehension is the cause of the slow rate. There are many slow readers, however, whose word recognition and comprehension are good. But they tend to read as though every word were extremely important; they are afraid of missing something.

Vocabulary   The ability to understand the meanings of printed words is closely related to reading comprehension. Therefore, it is advisable to measure children's reading vocabularies periodically (reading vocabulary involves word meaning and subsumes word identification).

Most standardized reading achievement tests and some tests that accompany reading series beyond the early primary grades have vocabulary subtests. These vocabulary subtests differ in format. In some the stimuli are single words, in others the key word is set in varying types of phrase or sentence context. Directions may require choosing synonyms or antonyms. The biggest limitation of these tests is that they sample only the child's ability to understand one meaning of the word. Yet a great many English words have many possible meanings. Take *bar*, for example. Dale and O'Rourke (1976) reported comprehension scores for fourteen different meanings of *bar*. They found that *bar* meaning a piece of candy or soap, or a drinking place, is understood by most fourth graders, while *bar* meaning excepting ("bar none"), or a sandbar, or to fasten ("bar the door"), is not understood by the majority of tenth graders. So it makes quite a difference which meaning is tested, and a child who knows the most common meanings of a word may be unable to interpret that word when employed in one of its less frequent uses. Skillful readers use the syntactic and semantic cues in the sentence to select from among the meanings they know, or to infer a new meaning if none of the ones they know seems to fit.

Teachers can make informal tests patterned after standardized tests to sample children's understanding of words they encounter in their reading or context subject texts. Occasionally, it is interesting to determine how many meanings children know for certain words. As with other reading skills, daily activities present excellent opportunities for assessing a child's understanding of printed words.

Word Recognition and Identification   The ability to recognize words is a prerequisite for reading with understanding. A distinction is made in this book between "word recognition" and "word identification." Word recognition includes the use of both sight vocabulary and decoding to determine what a printed or written word represents. Word identification includes both word recognition and identification of meaning.

Nearly every standardized silent reading test contains a subtest of either word recognition or word identification. In a typical word-recognition test the teacher says a word and the child chooses one out of several printed words that matches it. In a word-identification test the child sees a printed word and must choose the answer with a corresponding meaning; the choices may be among pictures in the lower primary grades or among word choices in more advanced tests. Word-identification tests are often called "reading vocabulary" tests. Poor performance on a word-identification or reading vocabulary subtest may be due to either a lack of word-recognition skills or ignorance of the corresponding meanings.

Tests of word recognition or identification sometimes do not give an accurate estimate because the words used in the tests may not be representative of the ones the children have been taught; this is more true of tests for first and second grades than at higher levels. More importantly, the way in which the skills are sampled in any group test differs from the task required while reading. Some children score well on multiple-choice tests but cannot respond correctly when asked to pronounce the printed word. More useful estimates of word-identification ability can be obtained from children's daily reading. If a child makes few miscues during oral reading and shows generally good comprehension there is little need to appraise word-identification skills, as they are obviously adequate.

Some children are so capable at inferring the identity of words from context that real weaknesses in word recognition do not show up clearly. Of course, a child who renders a paraphrase of the text with no change in meaning should be commended for good comprehension before being asked for the exact words in the book. To get an estimate of ability to recognize words when context is ambiguous or otherwise unhelpful it is advisable to test the child with words that are presented in isolation, without any meaningful context.

Word lists such as the ones in figure 6.1 can be used to test word recognition. Teachers can construct similar lists based on the vocabularies of the materials used in instruction. A test of the total vocabulary of a book or workbook can be constructed by using a random-sampling technique to get a cross section of the words used in that book. For example, one can decide in advance to take the third word on the second line of every fifth page; if there are duplicates or proper nouns, take the next following word. A 20-word or 25-word test with the words selected in this way gives a surprisingly good cross section of the total vocabulary in the book. If one wants to test the new words rather than the total vocabulary, take a random sample from the new word list or glossary at the back of the reader. It is desirable to have available word lists from two levels below to two levels above the book in present use.

It is advisable to administer a word-list test in privacy. One can start with the list based on the child's present text and go down if it proves difficult, go up to a higher level if it proves easy. Testing should be discontinued on a list if the child misses four words in succession. Give a child who errs on a word a second try at it; if the child gets it right on the second attempt, count it as half an error. If a child hesitates on a word for three seconds, go on to the next word and count it an error. Write mispronunciations in; place parentheses around self-corrected errors; draw a line through a word not attempted.

Since there is no benefit from context, interpretation is somewhat more lenient than word-identification miscues made during connected reading. Rough standards are not more than 20 percent errors on new vocabulary

	Rob	Sue	Cheryl	Joel	Maria	Tom	Fred
Generally inadequate sight vocabulary							
Errors on high-utility words							
Inadequate use of context Miscues alter intended meaning							
Doesn't attempt to correct miscues							
Relies on context excessively							
Doesn't attempt to decode							
Has difficulty Dividing words into parts							
Making symbol-sound association							
Blending sounds/syllables into words							
Uses inefficient decoding technique Looks for little words in big words							
Spells							
Overrelies on configuration, size							
Overrelies on one part of word							
Poor fluency Word-by-word reading							
Inadequate phrasing							
Numerous repetitions							
Ignores punctuation							
Inappropriate rate							
Inadequate use of voice							
Finger pointing							
Head movements							
Possible visual problem							
Weak comprehension Main ideas							
Facts							
Inferences							

FIGURE 6.8. A checklist for recording oral reading weaknesses.

and not more than 10 percent errors on total vocabulary, for the instructional level.

It is an excellent idea to ask a child who is struggling with a word to think out loud so the teacher can understand what the child is trying to do and possibly gain insight into exactly what goes wrong. A great deal can be learned about a child's difficulties in decoding by listening as the child tries to solve words that are not recognized immediately. This may disclose the process the child is attempting to use and how successful the attempt is, as well as the results.

Oral reading provides particularly useful opportunities for analyzing a child's word-recognition and decoding skills. The checklist shown in figure 6.8 may be used as a guideline. A single check indicates presence of the behavior; a double check, marked presence. The list may be shortened by using only the main headings. Using such a checklist can help the teacher set up specific need groups by showing which children have similar needs.

Efficient readers use a variety of decoding methods when words are not recognized immediately or the context does not reveal the word. They use morphemic analysis, dividing the word into meaning units. Or they divide the word into parts to which they can apply their phonic skills, then blend the parts in a left-to-right sequence to form a word. Almost all attempts are checked to see if they make sense in the sentence.

When a teacher listens to a child's oral reading, it is sometimes very difficult to decide how the child is attempting to solve unknown words and what causes the particular miscue. But if the errors are written down as they occur or are taped and later recorded, it does not take long to assemble enough miscues to get an idea of where the child's difficulties lie. The miscues can be analyzed when the teacher has time to ponder them. Having a written record also makes it easy to compare the frequency of different kinds of behaviors and to decide what kind of help the child needs most urgently. For example, an analysis may reveal that the child is not using context, is relying on it excessively, or is unsure of common high-utility words whose recognition is necessary for fluent reading and comprehension. The problem may include a lack of the ability to syllabicate or make symbol-sound associations for certain types of word elements (e.g., vowels, consonant blends) or for specific elements (when *c* represents its hard or soft sign; short *a*).

Looking for similarities in the miscues helps to decide what problem(s) the child is having as indicated by the following four examples. The samples shown in each are typical of the miscues made by the child. These patterns are not mutually exclusive. More than one of these patterns may occur in a child's miscues.

1. *absent, differ, mingle, naval, cushion.* The one thing these words have in common is that they have two syllables. Therefore, the teacher should pursue the hypothesis that the child has difficulty syllabicating words. The next step would involve an informal test of about 3 to 5 items on each spelling pattern (see page 101) to determine which syllabication generalizations the child has not mastered, or in which spelling patterns he or she finds it difficult to "chunk" elements (find parts that go together).

2. *antique, cafe, depot, scythe, view.* All these words contain elements that represent sounds typically not signaled by these letters (e.g., if *cafe* followed the "rule," it would be pronounced as /kāf/). Such words are not amenable to decoding, but must be recognized at sight. A number of high-utility words (e.g., *the, one*) fall into this category.

   Putting the response and stimulus next to each other, and underlying the element(s) in which the error probably occurred, will aid in revealing patterns. For example:

Said	*For*
antīkū	antique
kāf	cafe
dēpot	depot
skith	scythe
vīū	view

3. p*ou*t, *oo*ze, gl*oa*t, ord*ea*l, m*ai*nt*ai*n. As the italics indicate, this problem appears to be making symbol-sound association for vowel combinations in general. At times, they occur as only certain elements (e.g., vowel diphthongs such as *oi*). If a general problem is uncovered, testing should begin either with the elements already introduced; or if all or most have been introduced, with the most common and consistent vowel combinations (see pp. 564–65).

4. /kup/ for cash; /dot/ for den; /bun/ for bag; /rip/ for rap; /stab/ for stun. This pattern of errors suggests two possibilities. The first is that the child is relying too much on the initial element and guessing the rest of the word; the second is that the child is having difficulty making correct symbol-sound associations for short vowels, and the final consonant errors are secondary to this. These possibilities can be

checked out by calling the child's attention to the error on the vowels and asking him or her to try again. If the child then responds correctly, the first possibility is the more likely cause of such miscues.

It should be remembered that the words that children encounter influence their miscues. Decoding strengths or weaknesses cannot be displayed if the stimuli do not require their applications; e.g., difficulty with consonant blends will not show up if few or no unknown words contain such elements. Children with extensive sight vocabularies can show their decoding skills only if tested on words they cannot recognize at sight. Because real words might be part of a child's sight vocabulary, some published decoding tests use nonsense syllables (*tox, geck*).

Group-administered decoding (phonics) tests yield little useful diagnostic information, mainly due to the way in which they must be administered. In such tests, the task usually is similar to the following: From a number of possible choices (*c m b t*), the child marks the printed stimulus that represents the sound they hear at the beginning (middle, end) of the words pronounced by the teacher (*b*ad, *b*eg). In short, the task involves matching a sound with a symbol (sound-symbol association). Many children do well on such tests but are unable to perform the more difficult task of going from the printed symbol to its spoken counterpart.

If group decoding tests are employed, teachers should examine the task required by the subtests. Tests may not really measure what their title implies or may require more skills than the title suggests. Some tests measure skills that have little or no relationship to decoding ability (McNeil 1974).

There are some short survey phonic tests on the market such as the *Roswell-Chall Diagnostic Reading Test* (Essay) or the *Phonics Criterion Test* (Dreier); both are individually administered. More comprehensive word-analysis tests such as the *Sipay Word Analysis Tests (SWAT)* (Educators) are available, but their administration may be too time-consuming for classroom teachers. Nevertheless, they provide models for teacher-made tests, and their use can be restricted to children who have serious decoding problems.

Simple phonic skills tests can be constructed by teachers and given to a child in five minutes or less. Which decoding skills are sampled will depend on the child's particular problems and what skills have been introduced. Words that are unlikely to be known by the child or nonsense words can be used to determine how a child goes about attempting to break them up into some usable parts. The child is asked to divide words into parts or syllables and tell what he or she is doing and why. ("If you were going to figure out what this word says, what parts would you divide it into? Why?")

Symbol-sound association knowledge may be tested by presenting the elements in isolation (e.g., *b, bl, a, oa*). These phonic elements can be typed in nonalphabetical order on a sheet of paper with a carbon or mimeographed copy used as a record blank, or they may be placed on separate cards. The single letters or letter groups should be well separated, with double spacing between lines. The testing is administered by indicating to which letter(s) the child is to respond and asking the child what sound it (they) makes. If the element represents alternate sounds (e.g., *g, a*), the child can be asked what other sound it can have, if the first response was correct. Since some children are taught phonic elements in whole words, they may have difficulty responding to letters in isolation. These children may be asked to say a word that has the sound in it. Knowledge of when letters that represent various sounds are most likely to signal a given sound may be tested by presenting pairs of words (*tot-tote, gam-gem*) or other combinations (*lope-lop-lo*).

Some children learn symbol-sound associations but have difficulty blending the sounds into whole words. To test a child's auditory blending ability, pronounce a word sound by sound, being careful not to distort the sounds. First, tell the child what you are going to do, then ask what word you said. A brief series of words will do, such as *u-s, m-e, m-e-n, t-a-ck, b-at, su-m, hap-pen, neigh-bor*. If a child has real difficulty with blending the type of item shown in the first six above, breaking words into larger parts such as syllables is likely to be more helpful than a letter-by-letter phonic procedure.

Closely related to blending is the ability to listen to a word and identify the phonemic parts that can be discerned within it; this is called *segmentation*. Segmentation is auditory analysis while blending is auditory synthesis; both are important aspects of the part-whole relationship. It is not clear as yet whether segmentation is a necessary prerequisite ability for blending. I. Y. Liberman et al. (1974) used a simple form of segmentation test with young children, in which the child was asked only to listen to a word and tap a number of times corresponding to the number of parts heard. They found that segmenting by syllables was much easier than segmenting by phonemes. Near the end of first grade 90 percent were successful with syllable segmentation, while only 70 percent succeeded with phoneme segmentation. The degree to which this ability can be improved with specific training has not yet been ascertained.

There also may be a need to check a child's ability to combine decoding skills. This can be done by presenting whole words that are unlikely to be recognized at sight (*loam*) or nonsense syllables (*mog*) and asking the child to say the word.

If after a reasonable length of time a child still has difficulty learning words through the procedure being employed, an alternate approach may be advisable. The efficacy of various word-identification procedures for a particular child may be determined through sample lessons as suggested by Harris and Sipay (1975, pp. 228–33).

Miscue Analysis

Miscue analysis is based on the belief that reading is a language process in which the reader attempts to construct meaning from the written form of language. Everything the reader does is assumed to be caused by this psycholinguistic process, and thus unexpected responses during oral reading may reveal how students use reading strategies (K. Goodman 1976a).

Not all miscues are considered "errors." Basically, miscue analysis involves determining if the miscues: (1) reflect the child's dialect or a speech impediment; (2) result in changes in intended meaning; (3) are semantically acceptable; (4) are gramatically acceptable; (5) look like the expected response; (6) sound like the expected response; (7) are corrected. The measures are analyzed and serve as a basis for developing lessons designed to teach or strengthen reading strategies. For example, if the majority of miscues were grammatically acceptable but changed the intended meaning, the lessons would focus on closer attention to word meanings. Classroom teachers probably would find the detailed classification procedures set forth by K. Goodman (1969) or even the less detailed ones presented by Y. Goodman and Burke (1972) too laborious. There is also some difficulty in classifying miscues because there appear to be overlapping categories. Much of what classroom teachers will find useful can be determined using the above seven points. Those interested in learning more about miscue analysis and its uses are referred to the above citations and to K. Goodman (1973a) and Burke (1975).

Miscue studies have led to the following conclusions:

1. Young readers utilize both grammatical and semantic language cues (children were able to read in context at least two-thirds of the words they were unable to recognize in isolation).

2. Even young readers tend to substitute words that serve the same grammatical function as the stimuli.
3. There is a tendency for young children to produce more miscues that are syntactically acceptable than semantically acceptable.
4. Readers of all ages and abilities "edit" the written text and produce language more acceptable to the reader when the printed matter provides inappropriate language cues. (Y. Goodman 1976)
5. Miscues on easier material reflect more attention to contextual and less attention to graphic cues; there are proportionally more corrections on the easier material. (Williamson and Young 1974, Hood 1976)

HOW SUCCESSFUL IS MY RECREATIONAL READING PROGRAM?

In recreational reading, the important areas of evaluation include the amount of reading done, the adequacy of comprehension and recall, the honesty of the child's reporting, the suitability of the books chosen, and the child's attitudes and feelings about reading.

Amount of Reading Done

The amount of reading children claim to have done is easily ascertained. How to keep records of recreational reading is discussed in the concluding section of this unit and in unit 10. Such records may reveal the amount of independent reading reportedly done, but quantity is not the most important consideration.

One of the main goals of the recreational reading program should be to develop a love for reading. The question then becomes, "To what extent do children choose reading as a leisure-time activity?" Some children really enjoy reading, and read almost everything they can get their hands on. Others take it in stride, neither being enthusiastic about it nor disliking it; these children will read if something strikes their fancy, someone encourages them to do so, or if there is nothing else to do. Still others actively dislike reading and manage to waste a good deal of the time assigned for recreational reading. These children often are the less able readers who find reading a laborious task. Teachers usually can observe indications of feelings about recreational reading if they are alert to the importance of doing so.

Adequacy of Comprehension and Recall

There are a few standardized tests of literature, only one of which, *A Look at Literature* (ETS), is meant for the elementary level. These are divided into two types: (1) recall of information about selections and (2) understanding of material just read (the material is part of the test). The main limitation of the recall-type test is the fact that not all literature programs require reading of the same works. Therefore, each test must be reviewed by the school to determine how closely the test content matches that of their recreational reading or literature program. The understanding-type literature tests resemble reading achievement tests except in content. Their biggest limitations are the tendency to deal with low-level inferences and to try to force a single interpretation on the testee. They neglect trying to learn how children liked the story, how it made them feel, and what images it created (Purves 1976).

Discussing what they have read with children and observing children's reactions while reading offer the best opportunities for teachers to determine how well children understood what they read and what effect it had on them.

Honesty of Reporting

Since recreational reading usually is not checked as frequently or as thoroughly as other types of reading (and shouldn't be), it is only natural that some children, valuing praise more than reading, should try to receive maximum credit for reading. This is most likely to occur in classroom atmospheres in which competition is stressed. One honest way to "look good" is to limit one's reading to books with many illustrations and little reading matter. The teacher is well advised, therefore, to keep track of the number of pages read, as well as the number of books. A less straightforward way of padding the record is to skim a book without really reading it, trying to get just enough of the content to be able to provide the expected kind of report. Asking fairly searching questions encourages reading with some care. Such questioning, or any form of evaluation, must be tempered, however, so that the child is not "turned off" from reading.

Suitability of Material

Many children choose a wisely varied reading diet, some of it easy, some of it challenging, most of it comfortable, with a range of topics. A few good readers restrict their choices to books that are so easy that the child has little to gain from them. Some poor readers consistently select books that are above their frustration levels because they do not want to admit their limited skill. Even though a wide freedom of choice should be allowed, teachers should be alert to children who consistently choose books whose difficulty is inappropriate for them, or who have narrow reading interests. Ways of coping with these situations as well as the problem of literary quality are covered in unit 10.

HOW SUCCESSFUL IS MY FUNCTIONAL READING PROGRAM?

Standardized Tests

Some achievement-test batteries contain various content subject tests. With the exception of mathematics, they tend to stress factual knowledge. A few tests measure work-study skills such as the ability to interpret maps, charts, and tables and use of reference skills.

Teacher-made Tests

In evaluating functional reading skills, teachers have to rely primarily on their own resources. A great deal can be learned by paying careful attention to the signs of difficulties children may show during directed reading activities in various content texts and materials. Some developmental reading manuals and workbooks contain practice exercises for developing specific study skills and other skills that are useful in reading in content areas. These exercises may be used directly or can serve as ideas for teacher-made exercises. The real test, however, is the extent to which children can utilize these skills in reading their daily assignments.

Middle- and upper-grade teachers may want to test specific skills that have been recently taught. These may include the meanings of technical terms; location skills such as finding entries in dictionaries and encyclopedias; and outlining skills. Exercises used in the development of these skills also indicate which children have understood and successfully completed the assignment and which have not. For the latter group, talking with each child about the difficulties experienced in doing the exercise may be more revealing than any amount of further testing. A useful procedure is to ask the child to do again the items he got wrong, giving his reasons and explaining his steps. This kind of simple explanation often discloses the heart of the difficulty and indicates what additional teaching is needed.

HOW CAN I KEEP TRACK OF ALL THIS INFORMATION?

Keeping adequate records is indispensable if children are to be understood and treated as individuals. Few of us have such remarkable memories that we can keep track of the details about each child without writing things down. Recordkeeping can become a heavy burden unless care is taken to organize it efficiently.

In devising a recordkeeping system, the following should be kept in mind: (1) the records should provide a maximum of information with a minimum of writing; (2) records should be organized so that important points can be easily noticed; (3) records should emphasize items that have instructional significance; (4) a uniform sequence of items makes it easy to compare records of different children, or to compare summaries made at different times on the same child; and (5) a good recordkeeping system will call the teacher's attention to the kinds of information needed.

Using a Checklist

One way of simplifying recordkeeping is to use a checklist. In the preceding sections of this unit a large number of specific items have been discussed, on which it would be desirable to have a written record. A checklist makes it possible to record information on many points with a minimum

Name _____ Date of Rating_____

Stand. Rdg. Test. Date _____ Reading Grade _____

    Scores: Wd. Recog. _____ Vocab. _____ Comp. _____ Total _____

IRI. Date _____ Levels: Indepd. _____ Inst. _____ Frust. _____

Intell. Test Date _____ IQ _____ Estimated present M.A. _____

Reading Capacity. Teacher estimate _____ Listening comp. _____

Rating. Normal progress _____ Slow learner in reading _____

    Mild reading disability _____ Severe reading disability _____

    Underachiever _____

Reading Group. Group name _____ Reader level _____

    Work seems: Too hard _____ About right _____ Too easy _____

Comprehension Problems. Generally poor _____ Difficulty with:

    Main ideas _____ Inferences _____ Details _____ Conclusions _____

    Sequence _____ Directions _____ Critical reading _____

    Too literal comprehension _____ Other _____

Reading Vocabulary Problems. Generally inadequate _____ Difficulty with:

    Polysemantic words _____ Selecting appropriate meanings _____

    Other _____

Word-recognition Problems. Generally inadequate sight vocab. _____

    High utility words _____ Irregular words _____ Omissions _____

    Additions _____ Reversals with: _____ Confuses word

    pairs: _____ Fails to correct miscues when meaning is changed _____

    Use of context: Excessive _____ Inadequate _____ Substituted words:

    Similar meaning _____ Slightly changed meaning _____ Spoil meaning _____

    Grammatically correct _____ Grammatically incorrect _____

Decoding Methods. Does not try _____ Spells _____ Looks for little words _____

    Attempts to sound out, using: Single letters _____ Phonograms _____

    Syllables _____ Relies too much on: Configuration _____ Length _____

    initial _____ medial _____ final _____ Elements. Lacks flexibility _____

Decoding Weaknesses. Dividing monosyllables into usable parts _____

    Syllabication _____ Morphemic analysis: Compound words _____

    inflected endings _____ prefixes _____ roots _____ suffixes _____

    Symbol-sound associations: Consonants _____ Cons. Blends _____

        Cons. digraphs _____ c + g _____ Short vowels _____ Long vowels _____

        Open syllable _____ Final silent *e* _____; Vowel digraphs _____

        Diphthongs _____ Silent letters _____

    Blending: Sounds into syllables _____ Syllables into words _____

General Reading Behaviors. Finger pointing _____ Moves head _____

    Visual problems _____

Oral Reading Problem
 Fluency. Word by word _____ Poor phrasing _____ Hesitations _____
  Ignores punctuation _____ Misinterprets punctuation _____
  Repetitions _____ Rate: Too fast _____ Too slow _____
  Loses place _____ Short eye-voice span _____
 Voice. Monotone _____ Nervous or strained _____ Too loud _____
  Too soft _____ Too high _____ Too low _____ Enunciation _____
  Slurs words together _____ Speech impediment _____ Dialect _____
  Foreign accent _____
Silent Reading Problems. Moves lips _____ Vocalizes _____ Spotty atten-
 tion _____ Rate: Too slow _____ Too fast _____ Lacks flexibility _____
Independent Reading. Enjoys _____ Accepts _____ Dislikes _____
 Comprehension: Poor _____ Scanty recall _____ Reports honestly _____
 Tends to exaggerate _____ Special interests: _____
 Books read _____ No. pages read _____
Functional Reading. Difficulty with: Technical vocabulary in:
 Math ____ Social studies ____ Science ____; Locating information ____
 Using reference materials _____ Note taking _____ Outlining _____
 Study habits _____ Study skills _____
 Math text: Too easy _____ About right _____ Too hard _____
 Social studies text: Too easy _____ About right _____ Too hard _____
 Science text: Too easy _____ About right _____ Too hard _____

FIGURE 6.9. A checklist for recording information about a child's reading ability and skills.

of effort, since for most items all one needs to do is decide which entries
to check.

A checklist that summarizes the main points discussed in this and other
units is shown in figure 6.9. The first few lines provide space for recording identifying data and for listing the most recent test scores and measures of reading capacity. Specific places for recording judgments about
overall performance, oral and silent reading, comprehension, word recognition, decoding, and recreational reading are provided in the rest of the
form. It is easy to make the most important items stand out by checking
them with red.

Teachers may use this checklist or formulate their own. Mimeograph-
ing such a form will save time. If the teacher is unable to fill out certain

parts on the checklist, she can use her judgment as to whether that information is really necessary. The skills that are checked as deficient provide leads to particular skills on which group or individual instruction can be centered.

Often when a checklist is first used, it is filled out only for those children who have the most trouble in reading. But if the teacher takes the trouble to complete a list on the average and superior readers, she may be surprised to find that even the best readers have some specific areas in which they could use some help.

Probably the most efficient way to use a checklist is to go down the list of underlined headings checking at the left only those that are of concern. Details are then filled in only for those headings.

Other Types of Records

Some teachers like to prepare a file folder for each child in which various kinds of records are kept; others prefer a loose-leaf notebook. Whatever is used, the child's reading record should include (1) the kinds of information found in figure 6.9; (2) cumulative records of the child's recreational reading; and (3) for disabled readers, a summary of possible contributing factors and remedial recommendations.

In addition to summaries, there should be provision for filing little notes. For this, it is helpful to have a 3-×-5-inch or 4-×-6-inch pad or index cards handy. Whenever the teacher notices something about a child's reading that she does not want to forget, she quickly can jot down the child's name, date, and one or two comments. These jottings should be sorted once a week, or more often, into the children's folders or parts of the notebook. About every three or four weeks, the teacher should go over the accumulated notes for each child and from them make additions or changes in the child's summary and plan lessons accordingly. Information recorded in this way is far more likely to be used than if the teacher relies on memory.

UNIT 7

Word Recognition

As we saw in unit 3, many different approaches are used in beginning reading programs. Helping children to learn to recognize words is a central problem for all these approaches and is examined in greater detail in this unit.

There has been some inconsistency in the way commonly used terms in this area have been used. We will try to be consistent in employing the following terms as defined here:

Decoding. The use of a variety of cues and skills, including morphemic and phonic analysis, to discover what a printed or written word represents, when it is not recognized at sight.

Sight vocabulary. Words that a reader can recognize quickly without resorting to phonic or morphemic analysis. The words may have originally been learned through use of decoding techniques or as sight words.

Word recognition. Includes both decoding and sight vocabulary.

Word identification. Includes word recognition and the determination of word meaning.

Phonic method. A teaching method that initially emphasizes learning grapheme-phoneme correspondences and using those associations in decoding words.

Whole-word method. A teaching method that initially emphasizes learning to associate whole printed or written words with their spoken equivalents.

Morphemic analysis. A decoding procedure in which a word is analyzed into meaningful components such as root words, prefixes, suffixes, and inflectional endings.

Before taking up specific methods of teaching word recognition in detail, three points seem to be worth noting. First, there are great differences between skilled readers and children who are just learning to read in the ways in which they identify words. Skilled readers recognize most words instantly and need to work out the pronunciation or meaning of a word relatively rarely. Their skills have been so well learned that they are automatic; word recognition requires little or no attention, which can therefore be concentrated on getting the meaning. Unskilled readers, whether beginners or older children with reading difficulties, have to figure out many words. This requires their main attention, so that comprehension suffers. Because the limits of human attention suggest that we can focus main attention on only one thing at a time, automatic word-recognition skills are important for reading comprehension. One of the goals of reading instruction is to make the application of word-recognition skills automatic so that it requires little or no attention (Samuels 1976).

Second, a distinction needs to be made between teaching procedures and the way skills are used by the child. Word recognition skills are usually taught one at a time, but have to be used in combination, and not all skills need to be used for most words. It is much harder to determine what skills a child is actually using than to describe the teaching procedures to which the child has been exposed. Some children taught by a whole-word method compare words and develop and apply their own phonic generalizations. Some first graders taught by a phonic method tend to use a whole-word method of word recognition (Barr 1974–75).

The third point concerns the continuing controversy as to whether children should be started with a whole-word or a phonic approach. This debate is nonproductive for a number of reasons, among which are: (1) neither method is successful with all children; (2) neither method is used exclusively in any program with which we are familiar; and (3) after two or three years of schooling there is little difference in the average performance of students taught by the two approaches. Although the initial emphasis differs, children in both types of programs learn to decode unknown words and eventually develop an extensive sight vocabulary.

Compared to children taught initially with a whole-word method, beginning readers taught with a phonic method are less likely to guess at an unfamiliar word. They are more likely to be successful with words having regular grapheme-phoneme relationships than with irregular words. Their substitutions are likely to have graphic similarities to the word presented, but may not make sense in the sentence. Such children may make little use of semantic and syntactic cues. Good readers taught by a phonic method are more likely than poor readers to make nonsense errors; they begin by making no response to an unfamiliar word, shift to making nonsense errors, then shift to meaningful substitutions (Barr 1972, 1974–75, 1975; Nelson 1974).

Children taught initially with a whole-word method are likely to guess at unfamiliar words, relying heavily at first on context cues, sometimes with little visual resemblance to the stimulus word. The substituted word may be another word recently taught. As they acquire phonic and morphemic skills they tend to apply them, or to make no response. As they become competent readers they increasingly combine both contextual and graphic cues (Biemiller 1970).

The Committee on Reading of the National Academy of Education (1975, pp. 14–15), in commenting on the debate over the respective merits of meaning-emphasis and code-emphasis programs, stated:

To the extent that it has been assumed that a teaching method must be oriented exclusively toward *either* phonics *or* sight-word recognition, the concern with this controversy has been misguided. From research on the reading process, we know that *both* 'phonic' and 'sight-word' approaches must be included in any comprehensive teaching procedure. Children learning to read need both a knowledge of letters and their sounds and an ability to recognize words at sight. A teaching procedure may fail with a child if in the long run it plays down either of these aspects of learning to read. What is important is a proper balance between them.

Even when children are taught by the same program, such factors as intelligence, language facility, prior experience, and concentration produce great differences in the rate at which word-recognition skills develop. Furthermore, cues that may be relied upon heavily in the initial stages of learning may become less important and less useful at a later period of development.

Effects of Pacing

The number of repetitions provided in teaching tends to be related to the pace of instruction; the faster the pace, the fewer the repetitions. Even when the same methods and materials are used, teachers can vary the pace and the number of repetitions. Bright children who acquire sight vocabulary easily can be excused from exercises that primarily repeat and reinforce new vocabulary. Slow learners can be given the full workbook and worksheet program, plus additional teacher-made exercises, to provide enough repetitions. Barr (1973–74) found that when the same pace was used for all children in a class, teachers tended to adapt the pace of instruction to the slower learners. Children of average and above-average aptitude learned fewer words and had a narrower range of word-recognition skills than similar children in classes where instructional pace was differentiated.

Slow pacing and ample repetition may not be a complete answer to the learning problems of slower learners, but such children can be frustrated by too rapid an instructional pace, as well as by material with a heavy load of unfamiliar words. Fast learners can become bored and lose interest when the pace is slow.

Instructional pace is also important in code-emphasis programs. In one of the Cooperative First-Grade Reading Projects, a phonic-linguistic method was compared to a conventional basal-reader program. The phonic-linguistic materials exposed children to several times as many words in the first grade as the basal program did. The phonic-linguistic method produced higher average reading scores for those who did not fail, but also resulted in a much higher rate of failure in first grade, 20 percent as compared to 6 percent (Hayes and Wuest 1967). It may have been the pace of instruction rather than the method of teaching words that was mainly responsible for the differences.

There are no set guidelines for determining the correct pace for individual children or for groups. A good teacher is alert to the reactions of the children, provides for differences in rate of learning, and modifies the pace as needed.

The Words

Some words are easier for children to learn than others. Words that a child wants to learn tend to be mastered quickly. Words with rich meaning and strong emotional overtones, such as "mother," tend to be easily learned (Adams 1974). Concrete words such as names of things and action verbs are usually easier to learn than abstract words such as "the" and "is" (Kiraly and Furlong 1974). This suggests that when presenting abstract words, teachers should use them in phrases with concrete words. Words that suggest imagery also tend to be learned more easily than other words.

The physical characteristics of the printed word are also significant. Although short words are generally easier to learn than long words, a word of distinctive length and shape and rich meaning, such as "elephant" or "astronaut," tends to be learned more easily than most short words. Words in lower-case letters are more easily distinguished from one another than words in capitals.

THE WHOLE-WORD METHOD

This section deals with the whys and wherefores of the whole-word method, both in the development of an initial sight vocabulary and beyond that stage of development.

Why a Whole-word Method?

Among the reasons given for using a whole-word method are those that follow. First, most children can learn words through this method. Even preschoolers successfully employ it on their own ("What's that word say?") or with parent or peer instruction in learning the words on such things as food containers and signs. Second, a number of words in our language are irregular or contain irregular elements; the letters in these words represent sounds other than those they most commonly signal. For example, if one were to apply the usual phonic generalizations to words like *one* or *was*, the words would be pronounced as /ōn/ (as spelled by *own*) and /waz/ (rhymes with *has*). Such words, and there are many of them among the high-utility words, must be learned as wholes at any stage of reading development.

Third, the whole-word method may be preferred in the initial stages of reading instruction because it is believed that teaching children a number of words they can respond to at sight will enable them to get involved in real reading sooner than if a phonic method were employed.

At one time, basal-reader programs taught 50–75 sight words before introducing any phonic skills. This is rarely the case today. More generally, as soon as the children learn two or three words that have a common component (e.g., *me, milk, mother*), they are taught that symbol-sound association (e.g., *m* represents /m/). As the child's word-identification skills improve, decreasing emphasis is placed on the whole-word method, except for irregular words or words that cannot be decoded by the skills the children possess.

Readiness for the Whole-word Method

It seems logical that since printed words are seen, visual discrimination, perception, and memory abilities facilitate the acquisition of a sight vocabulary. Visual discrimination helps the learner to differentiate one printed word from another. Visual memory aids in recalling printed words. Visual perception influences the other visual abilities. A person can have clear perception and still not have very vivid memory. On the other hand, the memory image cannot possibly be clearer than the original perception. A child who perceives a word in a vague and hazy way cannot call up a memory image of it that is any clearer than the original perception. Clear perception is, then, a minimum essential for good visual memory.

Durkin (1974) has pointed out three other readiness factors for the whole-word method. The first involves form constancy; that is, children must understand that a word remains the same word regardless of its size or style of type or writing (e.g., book, Book, BOOK, *book*).

Second, although letter-name knowledge is not a necessary prerequisite for learning to read, such knowledge makes it easier for teachers to call attention to certain features of words. Lastly, children must understand what constitutes a printed word and that this printed form equals a spoken form. This also entails knowledge of graphic boundaries when words appear in context; that is, a word is set off by spaces larger than those between letters, but shorter than those between sentences. Some young children do not possess the concept of "word."

Whole-word Methodology

Basically, the initial teaching strategy for the whole-word method involves getting the learner to associate the printed form of a word with its spoken form and with the concept of the word that is already stored in memory. Words may be presented in context or isolation.

Many published reading programs that employ a whole-word method suggest initially introducing new words [1] in sentences so that children can use the context as a possible aid to word identification. The sentences, often with the new words in isolation above them, are presented visually on the board, on a large card, or by arranging word cards to make the sentence on a chart holder or flannel board. All the other words in the sentence should be in the children's sight vocabulary so they can concentrate on the new words. Depending on the program, the sentence is read first by the teacher and then by the pupils; or the teacher develops some background and the sentences are first read independently by the children. Children are encouraged to look at the word carefully while saying it, in order to learn to associate the printed word with its spoken counterpart. Again depending on the program, the teacher may also point out how previously learned word-recognition skills may be employed in identifying new words. The required associational tasks are made less complicated for the children by using words whose common meanings are understood by most children their age.

Further practice may be given by such activities as calling upon children to "frame" new words with their hands as they pronounce them; to match the isolated word on a card with the same word in the sentence; to select the word spoken by the teacher from a number of word cards; and to choose the correct sentence in response to an oral question.

Whole words may also be presented initially in isolation. The spoken form may be presented by a person or audio device (e.g., "This word says _____"). In self-instructional or programmed materials, the word may be thought or said by the learner in response to a picture accompanying the printed word. This requires that the picture evoke the appropriate oral word for its printed form. If the picture is ambiguous, the child may learn an incorrect association; for example, when a picture of a "cap" is thought to be a "hat."

In order not to confuse children or mislead them into learning an incorrect association, the oral stimulus must be spoken clearly. At times, children with deviant dialects or auditory problems may "mishear" the

---

1. "New" means that the word is introduced for the first time in that particular program. For exact procedures by which new words are introduced in a particular program, refer to the teachers manual that accompanies the text.

word. This can be checked by asking the child to repeat the oral word while looking at its printed form.

Whether the word is presented in isolation or context, the child must be looking at the printed word as its spoken counterpart is presented. Sometimes the whole-word method is referred to as the "look-say" method; but more accurately it could be entitled the "look-while-you-say" method. Unless the pupil gets a clear impression of the printed word, it is not likely to be remembered.

Is Context Helpful?   There is a difference of opinion as to whether words should be first introduced in context or isolation. Those who believe in the use of context feel that the context will aid word recognition and that children normally will meet new words in context and not in isolation, so the setting is more natural. On the other hand, there are those like Biemiller (1970) whose findings suggested that encouraging the early use of context and picture cues is not advisable because the child's first task in learning to read is mastery of the concept that one spoken word corresponds to one written word. His belief is that the longer a child stays in the early context-emphasizing phase of word recognition without showing an increase in the use of graphic information, the more likely the child is to be a poor reader by the end of the school year.

Picture clues. Because the vocabulary in almost all published reading programs is restricted by use of various criteria, the story line in beginning reading materials must be told, or heavily supported, through the use of pictures on almost every page. Such pictures provide the reader with information as to how the story characters would say the printed words found on the page. These pictures also may provide clues or reminders for word recognition. For example, the names of new story characters usually are presented near a picture in which the character is easily identified. Nouns are easily illustrated, as are action verbs like *run* and *jump*. Words denoting direction (*up, down*), place (*in, out*), or comparisons (*small, big*) can be illustrated by contrasting pairs of pictures, perhaps accompanied by arrows. Picture clues can supply occasional reminders when a child forgets a word; however, children must be taught to use cues properly and not to rely on them too much.

Singer, Samuels, and Speroff (1973–74) conducted a study that attempted to resolve the seeming conflict between Samuels' focal attention theory (pictures and context clues deter the acquisition of reading responses because they enable children to identify the word without focusing on its graphic features) and Goodman's belief that contextual presentation facilitates word recognition. The sample of first and second graders scored best when words were presented alone, next best on word and picture presentations, third on words presented in sentences, and poorest on words in sentences accompanied by pictures. Thus, their finding was that efficiency in learning words was significantly greater when words were presented in isolation than in the other conditions, and was interpreted as supporting Samuels' theory.

Yet it may well be that, used judiciously, picture clues can aid some children in acquiring an initial sight vocabulary or can add to their existing sight vocabulary. However, if a child constantly looks for pictures and pays little attention to word details when encountering unknown words, the teacher should cover the pictures so the child is forced to focus on the printed word.

As for the difference of opinion between Samuels and Goodman, it may be that during the initial stages of acquisition, attention should be focused on the printed symbol. But once a sufficient sight vocabulary has been acquired, context can and should play an increasingly important role.

Should words be presented in context or isolation? A reasonable answer is: both, depending on the purpose and the words. As Durkin (1974) suggested, there are three situations when words should be presented in the context of a phrase or sentence: (1) abstract words that have no meaning of their own (e.g., *and, that*); (2) homographs, words with the same spelling but different possible pronunciations and meanings (e.g., *bow*); and (3) polysemantic words, words that have multiple meanings. In the latter two cases, the context should clearly indicate which meaning the teacher wants the children to acquire, which is usually the one they will encounter in the story about to be read. A sentence such as "He took a *bow*" would not be helpful, whereas one like "In her hair, she tied a little red *bow*" would be.

Helping Children to Remember Words

Once words have been introduced, there are many things that can be done to help children remember them. The key is the opportunity to meet the word in print repeatedly, and in differing contextual settings. New words are included in the stories found in published reading programs, but teachers should be aware that the number of times a new word appears in future stories varies considerably.

Follow-up or preparatory exercises may include reading sentences containing the new words, and workbooks can give additional practice in which the word is matched with a picture, used to complete a sentence, or has to be differentiated visually from other words that resemble it. Teachers construct or find similar exercises for those who need additional practice, while children who have mastered the words are excused from such exercises. Games and a great deal of easy silent reading also help to fix the sight vocabulary.

There is no proven exact number of times that a word must be seen by children of various abilities before it is learned. A very few individuals have extraordinary visual memory, which allows them to recall verbatim whole pages that they have seen but once. For nearly all children, however, a single exposure is not sufficient for learning. The number of exposures needed for mastery will depend upon such factors as the learner's visual memory, how well the child attends to the stimuli (not scanning the printed word for relevant cues is likely to influence learning adversely), and how important and meaningful the word is to the learner.

Repetition is used as a means of helping children "overlearn" the words so that they are remembered and recognized rapidly. Nevertheless, repetition alone will not suffice to establish a sight vocabulary. Studies of the learning process have shown that learning best takes place when (1) the learner is motivated; (2) the learner is ready in terms of developmental maturation and necessary previous experiences or skills; (3) the learner can distinguish the desired response from incorrect responses; (4) the desired response is reinforced, but not others; and (5) enough repetition takes place to provide for some permanence of retention. Repetition is helpful when the other conditions are present. But if the learner is one who is not interested in learning, or one who cannot discriminate differences among similar printed words, or if nothing happens to let the learner know if a response is correct or not and incorrect responses are repeated, repetition may simply strengthen the confusion.

When a new word is first introduced, having children attend to the details of the word aids them in distinguishing it from other printed words and in recalling the word. One way to get children to attend to a word's component elements is to have them contrast a known word or words with the word to be learned. It also is helpful to have similarities pointed out. At first the comparisons can be made by the teacher; as the children catch on to the technique, they can be asked to discuss the comparisons. In initial contrasts, the differences may be quite marked ("Look at our new word 'mother.' Does it look anything like these other words we know, 'at,' 'me,' 'said'?). Then words that are more alike can be contrasted. Thus, after having printed two words one under the other on the board $\left(\begin{smallmatrix} \text{little} \\ \text{look} \end{smallmatrix}\right)$, the teacher can say, "Look carefully at these words. How are they different? How are they the same?" A more difficult task involves contrasting words that are minimally different graphically, such as *hot* and *hat* or *hat* and *had*.

In learning new words, children are apt to generalize on the basis of the first letter in a word. This suggests the need to direct their attention to the sequence of letters. During this stage of development it is advisable to demonstrate the importance of letter sequence in words. This may be done by printing two words on the board as above (e.g., *cat-act*) and pointing out that although exactly the same letters are in both words, the order in which they appear from left to right (move your hand under the word in this direction) does effect what the word "says." Similar exercises with readily reversable words (e.g., *saw-was*) may help to prevent some problems.

Perception and Word Recognition

We naturally tend to perceive a whole as a unique recognizable quality which is more than just the sum of its parts. For example, we learn to recognize a person's face without being able to describe exactly any facial feature. The term *Gestalt* refers to this unique total quality.

Babies' perceptions tend to be vague, crude, and largely undifferentiated. As children develop, they become increasingly able to make differentiations and to recognize similarities. They become able to discern the parts within the whole and to detect minor differences that formerly were not noticed. Skilled perceivers can recognize the unique Gestalt of a face or of a printed word, and at the same time are aware of the distinctive features within it. They shift their attention from the whole to its parts (analysis) or from the parts to the whole (synthesis); their perceptual approach is flexible and versatile.

Figure-ground   Usually when we are looking at something, part of what we perceive (the figure) stands out from a more vaguely defined background (the ground). The figure tends to have clear boundaries and definite form; its details are easy to notice, and it occupies the center or focus of the perceiver's attention. The background seems more vague; its details are shadowy and receive only marginal attention.

In reading, clear perception is facilitated when printed material has a marked contrast between black, clear type and an unobtrusive white or almost white, nonshiny paper. Letters within words are printed close together to make it easy to perceive the word as a unit, and the spaces between words and lines allow each word to be seen as a clear figure against a background. For example, thispartofthesentenceisdifficulttoread because there are no spaces to mark the word boundaries. Children's attention to a word or word part can be enhanced by making it stand out through underlining, by writing it larger or with bolder lines, or by using color.

Closure   Closure is the tendency to perceive an incomplete form as if it were complete. Thus, we can look at a picture in which lines have been left out and "see" it as if it were a complete image. In other words, we tend to complete an incomplete form. All of us do not have the same closure ability; some require many more visual or auditory cues than others in order to recognize an object or word. Good readers do not have to perceive every part of a word clearly in order to recognize it, nor do they have to be able to recognize every word in a sentence to gain meaning from it.

Good readers can read successfully when the lower half of words is hidden

When the top half is hidden it is harder to read.

Y— c–n –ls– r—d w–th—t th– v–w–ls.

–o—o–a——— a–e –o–e e—e—ia–. (Consonants are more essential)

In reading the above sentences, closure makes meaningful reading possible. The first sentence usually does not cause much difficulty for good readers because more visual cues are provided by the upper halves of letters than by the lower halves. The second sentence is more difficult because much less visual information is available in the lower halves of letters. Except perhaps for the word "also," the third sentence is easy to read; but because consonants usually carry more information than vowel letters, the last sentence is almost impossible to understand.

Closure also takes place in connected reading whenever the context helps a reader to overcome a difficulty. Consider the sentence:

It was cold, so Carol put on her c _ _ _.

All the words preceding the omitted word suggest that Carol put on something to keep her warm. The initial letter and configuration rule out a number of possibilities, such as "gloves"; but they strongly suggest "coat." This ability to achieve closure, and the inclination to seek closure, are basic to the theory upon which the cloze procedure is based (see p. 199).

Some children depend too heavily upon the closure effect and pay insufficient attention to the details of print. These context readers rely excessively on context and let their expectations take priority over their perceptions to the point where their reading becomes quite inaccurate. Although their reading usually makes sense, often the meaning is different from what the author intended.

Other children make insufficient use of closure. They seem to be constrained to look at all the details and at every word. In their absorption with details, they may fail to integrate the successive perceptions into a meaningful whole. When they misread words, they often do not seem to notice that the result does not make sense. Neither over- nor under-reliance on closure is a desirable reading behavior.

Sequence is yet another aspect of perception which, in reading, is spatially imposed on the reader. In our culture words are formed by letters going left to right, and words are read from left to right, with a right-to-left diagonal return sweep at the end of each line of print going down from the top of the page. The habit of examining print systematically from left to right is therefore important in learning to read.

Word-recognition Cues

Three main sources of available information may aid word recognition —graphic, semantic, and syntactic. Although they are discussed separately, they most often are used in combination when a child encounters an unknown word.

Graphic Cues   Almost 100 years ago, as a result of his experiments dealing with the ability to recognize words and letters that were flashed very quickly, Cattell (1886) concluded that words are read as wholes, not letter by letter. Indeed, if children had to depend on the letter-by-letter sounding out of words it would be almost impossible to read a selection for meaning the first time because their short-term memories would be overtaxed and processing would not be automatic (F. Smith 1971). Cattell's finding has been confirmed a number of times since then, and experiments have shown that it is much more difficult to read words when the letters that form them are presented sequentially one at a time than when whole words are available for the reader to scan (Gibson and Levin 1975).

Word length and configuration cues. Word length may provide some cues to word recognition in the initial stages of reading acquisition. Thus, a child just learning to read may distinguish between two words that both begin with the same letter (*me-mother, at-astronaut*) by their differences in length, but have difficulty with such words of similar length (*me-my-may*).

The outlines or general shapes of some words such as grandfather or elephant have distinctive appearances that may make it easy to discriminate them visually and to recall them. Words that are very similar in shape, length, and component letters (*want-went, what-that*) often cause problems for beginning readers. Many beginners do not notice the small differences in words and are sometimes insensitive to differences in letter sequence (*was-saw*).

When children are first acquiring a sight vocabulary, such cues as configuration and word length may aid recognition and recall. As more and more words share the same visual characteristics, the potency of such cues is sharply diminished. Beginning readers who continue to rely largely on configuration tend to become increasingly confused as the number of words with similar general appearance increases. Skilled readers are not dependent on shape or length cues because they have learned that there are many words with similar visual characteristics, and other cues must be employed.

Recent research has tended to suggest that configuration cues are not often used in word recognition. These findings are open to question because their use of only words of equal length removed a major factor in configuration (length). Nevertheless, children should not be taught to rely on word length or configuration cues.

Letter cues. Tachistoscopic research has tended to show that initial letters are the principal graphic cues used for word recognition, with final letters next in importance. Gibson and Levin (1975, p. 197) have pointed out, "There are several reasons for this very reliable finding. When the subject is allowed only one rather fast look, the letters in the center may undergo a masking effect; perception of the letters on either side will reduce their visibility." Gibson and Levin have also speculated that the beginning of a word is more predictable by skilled readers, and that the ends of words get more attention than the middles because they carry more information.

The letters themselves provide visual cues. Certainly the ascending and descending features of lower-case letters assist in word recognition;

words in lower case are more easily recognized than the same words in capital letters. Information about letter constraints reduces uncertainty and facilitates word recognition (Gibson and Levin 1975). These letter constraints involve such things as where consonant clusters are likely to occur, the number of vowels that can follow one another, and the fact that specific letters are much more likely to be followed by some letters than others.

Semantic Cues   When words appear in context, two additional cue systems are available to the reader as aids to word recognition—semantic and syntactic cues. Semantic information involves meaning cues and includes knowledge of word meaning, of how words are related to one another, and an understanding that certain sets of words appearing in the same context "fit together" (*whale* with *water, boat*) while others do not (*farmer* with *fish, boat*) (Pearson 1976). Basically, the information is derived from the meaning of the material surrounding the unknown word. Semantic cues act to limit the words that could make sense in that context. In the sentence, "He ate the _____," the unknown word apparently is something that can be eaten. If we added the clause "which was red and juicy," the possibilities would be further delimited. And, if the preceding sentences indicated that the unknown was picked from a tree and was intended for making a pie, the uncertainty is even further reduced. By asking himself, "Does this word make sense?" the child is making use of semantic cues.

De Lawter (1975) found that only half of the miscues made by the second graders in her study fitted the context. This led her to suggest that children should be taught to realize that they are not reading if the words they say or think do not make sense. Pearson (1976) has suggested that children who think that oral reading does not have to make sense in the same way as speech can be helped by purposely reading to them sentences or paragraphs containing anomalous words. The children are told to stop the teacher whenever they hear something that does not make sense.

Syntactic Cues   Syntactic cues, which usually function in combination with semantic cues, involve grammatical constraints. The cues are provided by word order and the functions of the words. By using oral language ability to monitor a response, the child can tell if the response is grammatically acceptable. Only certain types of words fit our language patterns and only certain sequences of words are acceptable. The child who asks himself, "Does it sound right?" is making use of syntactic cues.

Self-corrections are a positive indication that the child is reading for meaning; such reading behaviors should be encouraged. Recht (1976) found that the number of self-corrections increased from second grade up to grade 6, then leveled off. The type of miscue most often corrected involved responses that were partially acceptable both syntactically and semantically (e.g., substituting *spending* for *speaking* in "He was speaking to Julia"). Recht speculated that such miscues were most frequently corrected because they disrupted meaning or structure. Miscues such as *a* for *the* were usually not corrected because they did not disrupt either sense or grammar and they tended not to be noticed. If the responses were totally unacceptable, the readers often could not correct them because they were unfamiliar with the word, unaware that the error occurred, or were not receiving enough information to evaluate the miscue effectively.

The use of certain words signals what is likely to follow. For example, markers such as *a* or *the* signal that the following word will probably be a noun or part of a noun phrase.

Efficient readers maximize their reliance on semantic and syntactic cues in order to minimize the amount of "print to speech" processing (use of grapho-phonemic cues) they have to do. They predict what will occur next in print and attend to only enough grapho-phonemic cues to verify these predictions (Pearson 1976).

Children should be instructed that when they encounter important words that are not recognized, they should keep on reading, or reread the sentence, in order to see if the context aids word recognition. They also should be encouraged to guess what the word is, and to test the guess for graphemic, semantic, and syntactic suitability. Furthermore, they should be taught to make use of various types of context cues. Such cues are discussed in unit 8 because they are more useful in determining word meaning than in word recognition.

In order to strengthen children's integrated use of grapho-phonemic, semantic, and syntactic cues, practice exercises must emphasize meaning. Exercises such as the following can be selected or constructed, with the answers and available cues being discussed after the children have completed the exercise:

1. Context cues alone, but with multiple choice (Fred was so sad that he began to _____).
     laugh   cry   cram
2. Context cues alone, as in the cloze procedure.

3. Context plus beginning letter (Rob drank the m_ _ _).
4. Context plus beginning and final letters (Marie liked to eat c_ _ _y).
5. Context plus word length as indicated by the number of letters in the word (It got hot when the _ _ _ came out).

Which Words Should Be Taught?

As indicated, irregular words should be taught through a whole-word method. The same is true for words that children could not recognize independently with the decoding skills they possess.

Not all the words found in any published reading program or on any word list need be learned by the children. Regardless of the method by which words are first introduced, however, children need to recognize certain words rapidly. There is a relatively small number of words that occur very frequently in the materials used for reading instruction and in reading material in general. Because instant recognition of these high-utility words facilitates the reading process, the teacher should assure their mastery. Some words occur only occasionally in reading materials. Much less emphasis need be placed on their acquisition.

Use of a basic word list can help teachers decide which words should receive the most attention. Two recent, comprehensive word lists based on frequency of occurrence in print are useful for elementary school teachers. *The Basic Elementary Reading Vocabularies* (A. J. Harris and Jacobson 1972) are based on reading and content subject texts found in the first six grades. The *American Heritage Word Frequency Book* (Carroll, Davies, and Richman 1971) is based on a wide variety of educational materials for grades 3 through 9. There are also numerous shorter lists, derived in various ways, that agree to varying extents as to the "important" words. Descriptions and comparisons of many of these current lists may be found in A. J. Harris and Jacobson (1973–74), Hillerich (1974), and Monteith (1976).

CORE PREPRIMER LIST

a	daddy *	green	look	ride	want
and	did	have	make	said	we
are	do	he	me	see	what
at	dog *	help	mother *	something *	who
ball *	down	here	my	stop	will
big	for	I	no	that	with
blue	fun *	in	not	the	work
call	funny	is	play	this	you
can	get	it	ran	to	
come	go	little	red	up	

CORE PRIMER LIST

about	car *	home *	of	show	tree *
all	eat	house *	on	sit	two
around	fast	into	one	so	us
ask	father *	jump	out	some	went
away	fish *	know	paint *	soon	word *
bike *	from	let	pet *	take	yellow
birthday *	goat *	like	put	thank	yes
boat *	good	man *	run	then	your
book *	has	may	saw	they	
but	him	new	say	too	
cake *	his	now	she	train *	

CORE FIRST READER LIST

after	cat *	girl *	live	prize *	think
again	catch *	give	long	rabbit *	those
airplane *	children *	gone *	lost *	race *	three
along *	coat *	good-by *	made	rain *	time *
am	cold	got	many	read	told *
an	color *	grass *	maybe *	ready *	tomorrow *
animal *	could	guess *	men *	right	took *
another *	cow *	had	met *	road *	town *
any	cry *	hair *	miss *	rocket *	toy *
as	cut	hand *	money *	sang *	truck *
baby *	dark *	happy *	more *	sat *	try
back *	day *	hard *	morning *	school *	turtle *
bag *	didn't *	hat *	must	seen *	TV *
balloon *	does	head *	name *	shoe *	under
bark *	don't	hear *	never	should *	very
barn *	dress *	hello *	next *	sing	wagon *
be	drop *	hen *	night *	sister *	walk
bear *	duck *	her	nothing *	sleep	was
bed *	fall	hill *	off	sound *	water *
bee *	far	hold	oh *	stay	way *
before	farm *	hop *	old	step *	were
began *	fat *	horse *	or	still *	wet *
behind *	feet *	how	other *	stopped *	when
better	fight *	hurry *	our	store *	where
bird *	find	I'll *	over	story *	which
black	fire *	ice *	own	street *	white
box *	first	if	pan *	sun *	why
boy *	five	it's *	party *	surprise *	window *
bring	fly	just	peanut *	talk *	wish
brown	food *	kind	penny *	tell	won't *
build *	found	kitten *	picnic *	than *	would
bus *	four	last *	picture *	their	zoo *
by	fox *	laugh	pig *	them	
cage *	friend *	leg *	please	there	
came	game *	letter *	pocket *	these	
can't *	gave	light	pony *	thing *	

FIGURE 7.1. Harris-Jacobson Core Words for first grade. Words that are not also in the Dolch Basic Word List are marked with asterisks. Taken from *Basic Elementary Reading Vocabularies* (First R Series), by Albert J. Harris and Milton D. Jacobson, copyright © Macmillan Publishing Co., Inc., 1972. Quoted by permission of the authors and the publisher.

One of the older, but frequently used, word lists is the *Dolch Basic Sight Vocabulary* (Dolch 1960) that contains 220 words, none of which are nouns. Although some authors feel the list is outdated, Lowe and Follman (1974) found that all but a few of the first 150 Dolch words occurred on four current lists, and Johns (1976) calculated that the Dolch 220 still accounts for over 55 percent of the words found in materials for grades 3 through 9.

As shown in figure 7.1, most of the Dolch 220 are at the first-grade level, with only about 15 percent at the second-reader level, and a few at the third-reader level. The 45 Dolch words not found in the 332 first-grade words shown in figure 7.1 are indicated in figure 7.2.

always	drink	much	six
ate	eight	myself	small
because	every	once	start
been	full	only	ten
best	goes *	open	today
both	going *	pick	together
buy	grow	pretty	upon **
carry	hot	pull	use
clean	hurt	round	warm
done	its *	seven	wash
draw **	keep	shall	well
			write

FIGURE 7.2. Dolch 220 Basic Words that are not in the Harris-Jacobson Core Words for first grade. Inflected forms of H-J first-grade words are marked with one asterisk; H-J third-grade words are marked with two asterisks. The other words are H-J second-grade words.

Increasing Word-recognition Speed

Once words have been introduced, the more nearly instantaneous and automatic the recognition process becomes, the more efficient reading can be. Children who struggle with word recognition cannot devote the major share of their attention to obtaining meaning. Rapid and accurate word recognition allows the reader to proceed with speed and fluency, and to concentrate on interpretation. Two basic ways of improving speed of word recognition are discussed here, and two others in unit 8 under Reading Rate.

A large amount of easy, pleasurable reading provides the most natural way of obtaining abundant practice on high-utility words. Words that are seen over and over again become so familiar that they are recognized instantly. When children are eager to find out what is going to happen, they tend to read as fast as is comfortable for them. This is one of the reasons why a good total reading program includes a substantial amount of silent recreational reading.

Flash-card exercises in which previously taught words are exposed briefly is the second procedure. In successive sessions, the teacher gradually shortens the exposure time, being careful not to greatly exceed the children's speed of perception. In presenting flash cards, the card to be shown should be held in one hand. The other hand holds a blank card, which is raised to expose the word and lowered again. It is not a good practice to show the card briefly, then remove it; this creates a need for pursuit movements of the eyes.

Because hand-held flash cards or teacher-made devices do not allow exact exposure times, some teachers use commercial *tachistoscopes*. A tachistoscope is a device that can be set for a variety of exposure times that may range from one second to 1/150 of a second. Some of these devices use slides; other employ filmstrips. Small spring-powered tachistoscopes that are hand held, but not as accurate, are available for individual practice.

In addition to their use in increasing speed of recognition, word cards are also often used to present new words, to review words, and to build phrases and sentences. Large cards are employed with groups, smaller ones with individuals. While flash cards have some valid uses, recognition of a word on a card does not guarantee its recognition in context. Some children are able to respond correctly because they recognize some extraneous visual cue, other than the printed word, on the card. They remember the card but not the word, perhaps because the card has a torn corner or a smudge on it.

If flash cards are used, the following principles should be observed: (1) use them only for promoting quick recognition of known words or for testing word recognition ability; (2) replace any flash card that is distinguishable by some visual cue other than the printed word; (3) provide ample opportunity for children to find and read the word in connected discourse; (4) be sure not to cover part of the word with your hand when exposing it; (5) flash cards should not be used frequently, and then for no more than five minutes or so at a time; (6) try to make their use more interesting by varying the way in which flash cards are presented (e.g., make a game or contest of it), as just showing the cards time after time can become a dull routine that does not command full attention.

Helping Children Acquire an Initial Sight Vocabulary

Some children are very slow at building a sight vocabulary when a whole-word method is employed. They continue to confuse words of similar appearance and repeated practice brings little, if any, improvement. If introducing fewer new words per lesson and allowing more time for mastery before introducing additional words does not help, it may be that a phonic or syllable method may be more effective in teaching the child to read. For teaching nonphonemic words to such children, or for children who have difficulty learning through any other method, a kinesthetic or visual-motor method may be advisable. It may be that the child does not perceive the word clearly and therefore cannot form a clear memory image. It is necessary, therefore, to help him to improve the clarity and accuracy of his perception.[3]

Kinesthetic Method   Some children who are unable to remember words that have been taught visually or phonically can get started in reading when emphasis is placed on tracing words, written in large letters, over and over again with the fingers while pronouncing them (Fernald 1943). This *kinesthetic* method is based on the early psychological observations that some individuals are aided in recalling visual forms by tracing their outlines. It is frequently called the VAKT (visual-auditory-kinesthetic-tactual) method. As a complete program, the kinesthetic procedure is slow and requires a large amount of individual help from the teacher or aide. Its main use has been in remedial reading programs for severely disabled readers. The technique, however, can be modified for use with only certain words or pairs of words (*that-what*) that cause problems for a child. The method has been summarized by Harris and Sipay (1975, pp. 393–96).

Visual-motor Method   Many children who do not need the kinesthetic method can be helped greatly by a word-study procedure that combines visual study with writing. This VAK (visual-auditory-kinesthetic) method can be used with an individual or a group.

---

3. Recently there has been a great deal of interest in visual perception. A number of visual-perceptual and visual-motor tests, as well as numerous visual-perceptual training programs using nonverbal stimuli, are available. While such training may benefit certain children, there is little valid research evidence to indicate that it has any marked effect on reading ability in general.

New words are taught as needed for connected reading and at a pace suitable for the child or group. Each word is introduced in meaningful context and the appropriate meaning is checked or taught. After the word has been presented orally and visually, the steps are as follows:

1. Hold up the word card and pronounce the word. The children are encouraged to look carefully at the word in a left-to-right fashion and to try to see it as a whole, while pronouncing it several times.
2. Each child shuts his eyes and tries to "see" the word (form a visual image). He then opens his eyes and compares his image with the word on the card.
3. The card is removed and each child attempts to write the word from memory, in the same script as the card.
4. The card is shown again and each child compares his reproduction with the original. If any differences are found, the child looks at the card again, paying particular attention to the part of the word that was not remembered correctly. The teacher may need to assist the child by pointing out the differences.
5. If there have been any inaccuracies, the process of looking, saying, trying to form a visual image of the word, checking, and writing from memory is repeated, until the child can write the word correctly from memory.
6. Reading the word in meaningful contexts and reviewing it on subsequent days help to fix the word in memory and to provide transfer to genuine reading.

In this procedure, children should pronounce the word as a whole or, if a long word, by syllables. Spelling the word orally is not allowed because it leads to rote auditory memory and does not help to form a visual image of the word as a whole. It is better for the letters to be seen as parts within the whole than to be remembered as a sequence of separate spoken units. After some weeks of practice with this method, many children improve their ability to perceive and remember word forms and can shift to visual study without writing, supplemented by their developing phonic knowledge.

Adapting the Word-study Method to the Individual   In light of the marked individual differences in perception and imagery, it would be surprising if all children learned to recognize words most easily in the same way. No method of learning words has been discovered that works well with all children. Each method works well with many children and poorly with some. If after a reasonable trial a child is not doing well with the word study procedure being employed, a different method better suited to the child's abilities should be tried.

Correcting Word-recognition Errors   How much emphasis should be placed on accurate word recognition during oral reading? Or, put another way, to what extent should a teacher correct oral reading errors or miscues while the child is reading? There is some evidence that reading comprehension and rate suffer when children are corrected during oral reading (Pehrsson 1974) and that children generally do not retain words that are pronounced for them (Eberwein 1975). Such a finding is not surprising. Rarely does learning take place after one exposure.

If the errors or miscues are not numerous and do not interfere with obtaining the author's intended meaning, there is no need to become concerned. Frequent and disruptive errors may simply indicate that the material is too difficult for the learner. Providing more suitable reading material usually solves this problem. Noting and analyzing the child's performance may provide diagnostic information that can be used to plan a corrective program suited to individual needs.

In most teacher-directed reading lessons, silent reading should precede oral reading. This is not to say that everything read silently should be reread orally. Rather, in most daily reading activities, children should be allowed to preread silently whatever they will be asked to read orally. This should give them the opportunity to understand the material, which in turn should assist them in phrasing, proper use of the voice to impart the mood of the story, and so forth. It also gives them time to decode any unknown words.

If during oral or silent reading an unknown word is causing a problem for a child, the teacher should either quickly say the word or assist the child to apply known word-recognition skills. In making such a decision, the following guidelines may be employed:

1. Tell the child the word quickly if:
    a. previously learned decoding skills and the context are not sufficient to allow the child to recognize the unknown word, or
    b. the situation is provoking a great deal of anxiety in the child.
2. Provide cues to assist the child who has been taught the skills necessary to decode or recognize the word.

Reversals Although a wide variety of explanations are offered as to the cause of reversals, as yet there is little evidence that any one is more valid than the other. There is evidence, however, that reversals are not unusual in young children and should not be a cause for concern unless they persist beyond the better part of the second grade. Reversals account for a relatively small proportion of reading miscues and seem to occur more frequently on certain letter and word forms than others. For example, Liberman et al. (1971) found that at least twice as many errors occur on *b* as on *d* or *p*.

According to Y. Goodman (1976), the context influences reversal errors. In context, *was* is occasionally substituted for *saw*, but rarely is the reverse true; *was/saw* substitutions are much more likely to occur in subject-verb-object sentences (*I saw an elephant*) than in a subject-verb-adjective sentence (*I was happy*). Also, whether or not a child is likely to make reversals is at least partially dependent on the task involved. For example, writing a letter or word from memory is more likely to produce reversals than reading it.

A child who makes a high percentage of reversals can be helped in a variety of ways. (1) For children with adequate auditory segmentation and blending ability, a synthetic phonic method (sounding and blending) may be taught. (2) A kinesthetic or visual-motor procedure may be used for the specific letters and words which the child tends to reverse. (3) The left-to-right direction can be emphasized in a variety of ways, such as underlining the first letters of words with green ("go"), encouraging the child to finger point as he or she reads, and exposing a line of print from left to right by moving a cover card to the right, or opening a zipper placed over the line. (4) The child who has been taught to check reading for meaning learns to correct most reversals without teacher aid.

Materials for Improving Sight Vocabulary

Teacher-made Materials Materials that help children to reinforce and expand their sight vocabularies are useful in the primary grades, and above that for children still reading at primary-grade levels. These words are taken either from the children's current reading material or from a list of high-utility words. In addition to the use of flash (word) cards, other materials can be made.

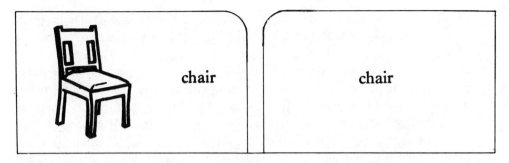

FIGURE 7.3. A sample picture-word card. The front view is shown on the left; the back view on the right. Taken from Picture-Word Cards (Dolch 1941). Reproduced by permission of the publisher, Garrard Publishing Company.

Picture-word Cards For supplementary practice or for independent learning by some children, picture-word cards similar to the one illustrated in figure 7.3 can be made by the teacher or children. The word is printed on one side of an opaque card; an illustration of the word and the printed word appear on the other side. In reviewing the words, the child tries to name the printed word, then turns the card over and checks the picture to see if the word chosen was correct. For independent learning, the child first looks at the picture, then focuses on the word while saying it out loud softly. Later, he uses the preceding procedure for self-testing.

Exposure Techniques Children can be exposed to printed words in a variety of ways that may indicate to them the importance of written language and the ability to read it, and reinforce and expand their sight vocabularies. These include use of labels, bulletin boards, a simple class newspaper, picture dictionaries that children themselves may construct, and above all, the opportunity to do a great deal of recreational reading.

Games and Exercises Games and exercises can be constructed that one child or a small group of from two to six can use without the teacher. The following types of teacher-made materials are recommended:

1. *Word-O.* Oaktag or other thin cardboard is cut into 5-×-8-inch boxes, each of which is ruled to make 25 boxes, or fewer (usually 9 or 16) if 25 is too many. If there is an odd number of boxes, the center one is "free." Review words are printed in differing sequences in the boxes.

All the review words are also printed on separate small cards from which the leader randomly chooses. The game is played like Bingo or Lotto.

2. *Racing.* In many commercial games a marker is moved along a path, with the first player to get "home" being the winner. Usually the number of spaces a player may move is determined by spinning a wheel or tossing dice. Sometimes there are penalty squares. Any commercial game of this kind, or homemade equivalent, can be adapted to word review by a simple addition. Word cards are placed in a pack, face down. Before a player can move his marker, he has to pick a word card and read it; if unable to do so, he forfeits his turn.

3. *Individual word cards.* Unlined 3-x-5-inch index cards are cut into five 1-x-3-inch strips. When a child hesitates over a word or does not recognize it, the review word is printed on the card and given to the child. If the word can be illustrated, the child can draw, on the reverse side, a picture that serves as a reminder. Each child keeps his words in three labeled files, each kept together by a rubber band or placed in a separate envelope. The child puts a new word in the "Don't Know" pile and tries to learn it so it can be moved to the "Know" pile and finally to the "One-look" pile. Each time a "Don't Know" word is recognized without help, a check mark is placed on the back of the card. When a card has three checks on it, it is moved to the "Know" pile. The "Know" pile is reviewed to build automatic instant responses. Three instant responses, noted by checks, indicate that the card can be moved to the "One-look" pile. Children can work in pairs, each testing the other.

4. *Fish pond.* Select word cards from those currently being studied. Place a paper clip on each card and spread the cards, face down, on a flat surface. Each child in turn picks up a card by fishing with a small horseshoe magnet strung from a short stick. If the child recognizes the word, he keeps the card; if not, he is told the word and it is put back in the "pond". Several children can play this game, preferably with one being able to recognize all the words.

5. *Spin the wheel.* A large oaktag wheel is fastened to a backing by means of a two-pronged brass pin. Some teachers prefer to make a new wheel for each group of words; others choose a more lasting setup, making radial slits near the outside and inside rims, in which word cards can be inserted. An arrow marked on the backing points to a word when the wheel stops spinning. Each child has a turn to spin the wheel and read

the indicated word. Score can be kept in a variety of ways, and well-matched teams can have exciting competitions.

Commercial Materials   Materials that may be purchased and can be used for building a sight vocabulary include:

Basic Sight Vocabulary Cards (Garrard). The Dolch 220 high-utility words on individual cards. The same words in larger print are in *Popper Words*, Set 1 and Set 2, each containing 110 words.

Picture Word Cards (Garrard). The Dolch 95 common nouns are pictured on one side of each card, with the printed word on the other side.

High Frequency Words (Ambassador). The 100 *High Frequency Words* account for 53 percent of the words found in 110 widely used trade books in grades 1 and 2; the *100 High Frequency Nouns* account for approximately 45 percent of all the nouns used in the same books.

Picture Word Builder (Milton Bradley). Pictures of 36 familiar objects on cards die-cut so only the correct word can be inserted to complete the matching word-picture.

Word Demons (Educators). A card game similar to the game of *Authors*; contains many common nonphonemic words.

Big Deal (Educators). Six card games can be played using sets of words at 10 levels of spelling complexity.

Language Master (Bell and Howell), *e f i Audio Flashcard System* (Electronics Futures), *Audio-Q-Motivator* (Teaching Technology), *Electronic Card Reader* (Mast). Commercially prepared or teacher-prepared cards (blank cards are available) are used with these machines. A child can look at the word(s) printed on the card, attempt to recognize it, place the card into the machine, and then hear the word pronounced. The child also can record responses and play the card back in order to compare it with the response prerecorded on the magnetic tape on the card.

Sources of Reading Games and Exercises   There are several books that present a variety of games and exercises that may be helpful in developing specific reading skills; see Wagner and Hosier (1970), Herr (1977), Dorsey (1972), Mattleman (1973), Thompson (1973), Burie and Heltshe (1975), Russell, Karp, and Mueser (1975), and E. Spache (1976).

New materials for teaching and practicing reading skills are constantly becoming available commercially. Reviews of many of these occur periodically in such journals as the *Reading Teacher*, the *Journal of Reading, Language Arts*, and the *Journal of Learning Disabilities*. Guidelines for evaluating new materials have been provided by Bleil (1975,) Ball (1976a), and Watson and Van Etten (1976).

TEACHING CHILDREN TO RECOGNIZE WORDS INDEPENDENTLY

This section deals with decoding. At first glance the definition of decoding used by linguists, that of translating written or spoken language to meaning (Hodges and Rudorf 1972), is basically different from the definition used in the field of reading instruction. But when one recognizes the purpose for decoding, the definitions seem less distant. In this book, *decoding* means determining the oral counterpart of an unfamiliar printed word through the use of various skills. The purpose for doing so is the expectation that recognition of the spoken form will trigger meaning, if the meaning is in the child's understanding vocabulary.

Children learn to decode words either as their initial reading instruction in code-emphasis approaches or a little later as part of the word-analysis programs in meaning-emphasis approaches. Even though most teachers follow the procedures in the manuals that accompany the reading program in use, they should understand the principles that underlie the decoding methods used in their reading program and recognize any shortcomings it may have. They also must recognize that the decoding part of the program is very important. Moreover, teachers should know which decoding skills each child possesses and should deviate from the program outlined in the manual when necessary to provide for individual needs.

Some Useful Terms

Some linguistic terms that are often used in discussions of decoding, such as phoneme, grapheme, and morpheme, were defined in unit 1 (see pp. 9–10). Other terms that teachers need to understand when reading about decoding are the following:

Prefix. A meaningful beginning that modifies the meaning of the root word to which it is attached (*re*write, *un*happy, *super*vision).

Suffix. A meaningful ending that modifies the meaning of the root word to which it is attached (farm*er*, teach*able*).

Inflectional ending. A suffix that indicates: a change in number (box*es*) or tense (play*ed*), possessive (Tom'*s*), comparison (dark*er*, dark*est*), present participle (walk*ing*), or third-person-singular verbs (he rid*es*).

Affix. A prefix, suffix, or inflectional ending.

Digraph. A two-letter combination that represents a single sound. The most common consonant digraphs are *ch, ph, sh, th,* and *wh.* Vowel digraphs include *ee, ea, ai, oa, ie.*

Blend. A combination of two or more phonemes in which the sound of each phoneme can be distinguished. Consonant blends are represented by clusters of two or more consonant graphemes; such clusters include *bl, cr, st, spr.*

Diphthong. A blend of two vowel phonemes; also the letters that represent them. The most common are /oi/ as in *boy* and *boil* and /ou/ as in *out* and *cow.*

Blending. The process of mentally combining a succession of phonemes or phoneme combinations into a larger unit such as a syllable or word.

Syllable. A unit of language consisting of one vowel or diphthong which may or may not be preceded or followed by one or more consonants, and may constitute a word or a part of a word; also, the graphemes that represent a spoken syllable (*a, be, an, man, stand* are syllables as well as words).

Phonics. The study of the relationships of graphemes (letters) to the phonemes (speech sounds) they represent, and the use of these relationships in identifying printed or written words.

Teaching Word Recognition in Code-emphasis Programs

In unit 3, four beginning reading programs called "phonic" and three designated as "linguistic" are briefly described. These programs, and others that have been described by the same labels, differ among themselves in many significant ways. (1) Some rely primarily on teaching single grapheme-phoneme relationships and blending; others avoid pronouncing consonant phonemes in isolation by having children note visual similarities and differences among whole words and compare them to auditory similarities and differences, or by teaching consonant-vowel combinations (*ca*-n) or vowel-consonant combinations (c-*an*). (2) Some start with consonants, others with long vowels, short vowels, or consonant-vowel or vowel-consonant combinations. (3) Some teach many generalizations or rules about grapheme-phoneme relationships; others provide examples from which the children are expected to generate their own generalizations. (4) Some require an extended period of drill on word elements and words in isolation or list form before introducing any meaningful reading, while others provide some practice in reading for meaning from the beginning. (5) Some require teaching the class as a whole, while others emphasize making provisions for individual differences.

It is evident, then, that there are important basic disagreements among code-emphasis programs. This makes it impossible to write a short generalized description of such programs. About the only characteristics they seem to have in common are an early priority on decoding skills over meaning, and early vocabulary limitation to words selected to fit the grapheme-phoneme relationships being taught.

Teaching Word Recognition in Meaning-emphasis Programs

Most of the eclectic basal-reader programs that are widely used employ an analytical type of decoding program.

Phonic Principles Are Developed from Sight Words   Before a grapheme-phoneme relationship is taught, several words containing it, usually in the initial position, have been learned as sight words. Realizing, for example, that the sound they hear at the beginning of *my*, *mother*, and *make* is represented by *m* helps children generalize that *m* represents /m/. When the common grapheme and phoneme have been identified in known words, they can be found in other words. Some children, however, cannot abstract such generalizations on their own; the sound the letter represents may have to be isolated for them.

Phonic Principles Are Developed Inductively   With the help of the teacher, children are led to discover the relationships between letters and sounds for themselves. Thus, they look at several printed words that have a common visual element and listen for the sound the words have in common. In this way, they find that the common grapheme represents the common phoneme, and the relationship is verbalized. Once a principle has been derived in this way, it should immediately be applied to unfamiliar words in isolation and in context. Of course, children who cannot learn easily through inductive reasoning should be taught by using a deductive process; that is, they should be taught the principle and helped to apply it to examples.

Whole-word Phonics   The whole-word phonic procedure was devised to avoid the distortions that arise when sounds are pronounced in isolation (e.g., *b* stands for /buh/). Such distortion can make it difficult to blend the sounds into a recognizable whole (/buh/-a-/tuh/ = bat). Known words in which the phoneme is easily identified are employed. Usually an easily pictured word is used as a cue word, which in turn suggests the sound. Thus, if a child forgets the sound represented by *b*, the teacher says something like, "This word begins like *bat*," instead of, "The word begins with /b/ or /buh/. Or, the child can use the picture cue accompanied by the letter.

A child who has learned the symbol-sound association for *m* = /m/ and knows the word *boat* as a sight word can decode the new word *moat* by thinking, "It begins like *man* and the rest is like *boat: boat, moat*." This skill is known as *consonant substitution* and is taught in many programs. The substitution technique is also used when a new word is similar to a known word except in its ending (ma*n*, ma*d*) or its vowel sound (p*a*t, p*o*t). Of course, the child must perceive the similarities and differences between the known and unknown words and be able to make the necessary symbol-sound associations, as well as have some blending skill, in order to employ the substitution technique. As vowel symbol-sound associations are learned, emphasis shifts from consonant substitution to rapid blending of the sounds in one-syllable words.

Sequence   In most meaning-emphasis programs, the sequence in which grapheme-phoneme relationships are introduced is based on the combined use of three main principles: (1) the associations are taught in order of assumed increasing difficulty; (2) several sight words that have the phonic unit in common are already known; and (3) opportunity to use the principle in decoding new words, and to read these words in context, should follow immediately. Most programs begin with consonants because their symbol-sound associations are more consistent than vowels, and introduce them in the initial position because graphic cues in this position are very useful. At the preprimer level many initial consonants and some final consonants are introduced, and before the end of the primer practically all single consonants, some consonant blends and digraphs, all the short vowels, and some inflectional endings have been introduced. The pace of the phonic program is increased at the first-reader level and tends to include many consonant clusters and digraphs (including silent consonants), long vowels, and perhaps some vowel digraphs and diphthongs. In the second readers, the program is rounded out with the remaining common consonant clusters, diphthongs, less common vowel digraphs, and alternate sounds for single letters (*c*, *g*) and vowel combinations (meat, head; now, crow), and *r*-controlled vowels.

Morphemic analysis often begins at the preprimer level with the final *s* for plurals. Most other inflectional endings are taught in first grade. Syllabication is often begun at the second-reader level and carried through the third-reader level at which time many dictionary and accenting skills are taught.

Phonics Combined with Context   When a tentative pronunciation of a new word has been worked out, the reader should ask three questions: (1) Does it sound like a real word? (use of language cues); (2) Does it sound right? (use of syntactic cues); and (3) Does it make sense in this sentence? (use of semantic cues). If, in the early stages of phonic instruction, children are depending heavily on configuration cues and are learning initial consonants, they should be encouraged to use the initial consonant in conjunction with the size and shape of the word and the meaning of the sentence. Children who are attentive to meaning can use partial phonic cues combined with configuration and context to recognize words correctly. Basically, what the child learns to do is to use as many cues as are needed to reduce uncertainty. For example, in the sentence "The boy ate the _____," the unknown could be a variety of words, but syntactic cues (noun marker "the"; object of the verb) indicate that the unknown word is a noun. If the initial letter were *m*, the choices are further delimited; and the configuration ⌐‾‾‾⌐ and number of letters _ _ _ _ help to eliminate other possibilities. Other graphic cues such as the final *t* and the vowel sound for *ea* may be utilized if known.

Adhering to phonic generalizations without attending to meaning or allowing for phonic exceptions creates many difficulties for a young reader. The English language has many pairs of words that sound alike, look alike, or both, yet have different meanings. *Homographs* are spelled the same but have different pronunciations and meanings (*bow, lead, desert*). Only in a meaningful context can one decide whether *bow* rhymes with *cow* or *low*, or means a hair decoration, a weapon, a part of a ship, or a bending of the body. *Homonyms* are words that sound alike but have different meanings and may be spelled alike (a country *fair*, a *fair* day) or differently (*stake*, *steak*). *Homophones* are words that sound alike but differ in spelling and meaning (*sum, some*). Context determines what meaning is intended.

Ordinarily *g* followed by *e*, *i*, or *y* represents its soft sound /j/, but if an exception like *girl*, *gear*, or *anger* is in the understanding vocabulary of a child who is attending to meaning, he or she is not likely to be misled. Context also aids in determining the pronunciation of phonic units that may represent more than one sound. Whether the *ea* in *meat* should be pronounced as in *mean, head, break, beauty, beard, early, bear, or heart* is not likely to bother a child who knows that the sentence deals with food and who also expects irregularities in the alphabetic representations of English sounds.

Readiness for Phonics   In order to make associations between letters and the sounds they represent, children must have adequate visual and auditory discrimination. A child who has difficulty differentiating between and among letter forms (visual discrimination) or has difficulty noting the differences among phonemes (auditory discrimination) is likely to have problems learning grapheme-phoneme correspondences. Instruction in these skills begins during the reading readiness stage and often continues through the phonics instructional program. However, many children enter school already possessing adequate auditory and visual discrimination skills. Since we do not know what minimal levels of each skill are necessary for learning phonics, the best current advice is to observe children's performance on the exercises given them. If the children have little or no difficulty in auditory and visual discrimination tasks prior to phonics instruction, such readiness activities can be terminated or greatly abbreviated for them. If they readily learn to make symbol-sound associations, there is little or no need to continue auditory or visual discrimination activities.

Practice in visual discrimination, such as that discussed on pages 247–49, should be provided for those who need such training. The technique of developing auditory discrimination may be summarized as follows: present several spoken words that contain the element to be heard; get the children to focus their attention on the sound that is common to the words; give practice in discriminating words containing the sound from words that do not; encourage the children to think of other words that contain the sound; and provide rhymes, riddles, or incomplete sentences that can be com-

pleted with words containing the sound. The usual sequence in the development of auditory discrimination of phonemes is as follows: initial consonants, rhymes, final consonants, medial vowels.

The following example using /m/ illustrates the technique summarized
above. Similar exercises can be used to teach auditory recognition and discrimination of final consonants and vowels.

1. Say a sequence of words (*monkey, man, milk, may, me*). Ask how they
   are alike.[4] If necessary, explain that they start with the same sound,
   and repeat the sequence of words.
2. Play a listening game in which the children signal one way when the
   teacher says a word that begins like *man* and another way if it does not.
3. Ask the children for additional words that begin like *man*. When one
   child suggests a word, ask another child if that word begins like *man*.
4. Give incomplete oral sentences or riddles, such as
   We wake up in the _____. (morning)
   What shines in the sky at night? (moon)
5. If children tend to confuse two sounds, such as /m/ and /n/, provide
   extra practice in discriminating between them. Remember that in some
   dialects there is no difference between sounds many of us hear as different. In such cases, auditory discrimination training to overcome
   such "problems" may be fruitless.
6. Provide seatwork with pictures that can be named. If the name starts
   like *man*, the children mark the picture. See figure 7.4.

To develop the perception of rhymes, children can listen to simple rhymes,
poems, and couplets, and pick out the words that rhyme at the ends of the
lines. They also can be given rhymes and jingles in which the last word is
omitted, their task being to supply the missing word. Ability to hear the
sounds that rhyme is fundamental to the building of one-syllable spelling
patterns like *best, nest, rest.*

Teaching Symbol-sound Associations

While there are many ways to teach symbol-sound association, the following steps using *f* = /f/ as an example, are recommended:

4. Remember that in order to perform certain tasks, children must understand concepts such
as *alike, same, different, first, last,* and *middle.*

	fix	bat	bead	man
	fi<u>sh</u>	ba<u>th</u>	bea<u>ch</u>	ma<u>tch</u>

whi <u>ch</u> th (ch)	pa —— sh th	pa —— tch sh	bru —— sh th
bir —— th sh	ca —— tch th	tra —— ch sh	pea —— ch th
sla —— sh ch	pi —— sh tch	chur —— ch th	tee —— sh th

Can you circle the right word?

1. There are twelve of these on a ruler. inches itches
2. This is something to serve food on. ditch dish
3. This is a trail through the woods. patch path
4. This tells the time of day. watch wash
5. People in a parade do this. marsh march
6. This helps to lock a door. latch lash
7. You take this to get clean. bath batch
8. This is something you spend. catch cash

FIGURE 7.4. Page from a phonics workbook. First the children name the pictures and tell which consonant digraph replaces the single consonant in each set of pictures. Next, they name the two digraphs printed in each box and circle the one that completes the word. Finally, they circle the word that is best described by each sentence. Taken from *The New Phonics We Use*, Book D, p. 13. Copyright 1972 by Rand McNally & Co. Reproduced by permission of the publisher.

1. *Auditory recognition and discrimination.* As much training as the teacher thinks is necessary is provided in becoming aware of the sound and discriminating it from other phonemes.

2. *Cue card.* A large cue card with a picture representing the cue word (in this case *fish*) with the letters *F* and *f* below it. The card is discussed and the children are told that the letter *f* represents the sound /f/ that they hear at the beginning of *fish*. Usually the card is posted so that the children may refer to it.

3. *Printed words.* The teacher asks the children for reading words that begin with the same sound as *fish*. As each word is proposed, the teacher prints it on the board (under the preceding one so the similarity can be easily recognized) and asks, "Does it begin like fish?" If the answer is affirmative, the child traces over the beginning *f* with colored chalk (or circles or underlines it).

4. *Letter name and sound.* While pointing to the letter, the teacher says, "The name of this letter is *ef* and its sound is /f/. Do you hear the /f/ in *fish*? Listen to the /f/ at the beginning of each of the other words (the list is repeated, slightly exaggerating the /f/).[5]

5. *Immediate reinforcement.* The children suggest other words that start with the letter *f* and the /f/ sound. After the teacher prints the words on the board, the child traces over the *f* and says /f/ or the word exaggerating the /f/.

6. *Guided practice.* After the association has been taught, practice should be provided in which the children use this skill in decoding unknown words both in isolation and context. Exercises that have the child mark pictures that begin with the sound of a given letter, or tests that ask a child to mark the letter that "stands for" the sound heard at the beginning of one or more spoken words, actually require the child to make sound-symbol associations (hearing a sound and associating a letter

---

5. Whether letter names should be used in such exercises is a point of disagreement. In our opinion, it seems psychologically sound and educationally practical to introduce the letter name and sound at the same time. It is important, however, to make clear to the children, most of whom already know the letter names, the distinction between letter names and the sounds letters represent.

The main argument against pronouncing sounds in isolation is that they become distorted, mainly through the addition of an "uh" or schwa sound that interferes with blending. But it is primarily the unvoiced consonants, *b, c, d, h, k, p,* and *t,* with which this problem can occur. With practice, teachers and children can learn to whisper the consonants with little or no extra vowel sound, and the principle of closure allows most children to identify the word even when there is some phonemic distortion. They can often respond to the "near sound."

with it). This is useful in spelling, but of little value for reading. Decoding a word requires the children to make symbol-sound associations;
that is, they must start from the grapheme and determine the phoneme
it represents. Many children who can perform quite well in making
sound-symbol associations have difficulty making symbol-sound associations.

The procedure outlined above can be generalized and used, with appropriate modifications, for teaching other phonic units. The unit should first
be heard within several words and seen in printed words. Its name (or the
names of the letters that form the unit) and the sound it (they) represents
can be introduced, and further practice can be given in hearing it, saying
it, seeing it, writing it, and if necessary, distinguishing it from other graphemes or phonemes. Much of this practice should be on words containing
the association and should involve meaningful reading (see figure 7.4).

An alternate instructional strategy has been proposed by Resnick and
Beck (1976):

1. The teacher models (pronounces) the isolated sound.
2. The children imitate the model.
3. The teacher models the sound again, pointing to the symbol.
4. The children imitate the model sound, while looking at the symbol.
    Concurrent with the children's imitation, the teacher mouths the sound
    silently in order to establish a cue or prompt.
5. The children produce the sound to match the symbol, without a spoken
    model, but with a silent mouthing cue.
6. The teacher fades the silent mouthing cue as the children produce
    the sound.
7. The children make the symbol-sound association independently.

The question of sequence in teaching phonics has been discussed above.
In meaning-emphasis programs the principle of teaching a grapheme-phoneme relationship when two or more words that provide examples of it
have been learned is generally followed, so that sequences vary according
to the words needed to tell the stories. In code-emphasis programs many
different sequences are in use, and there is no definitive research to indicate a significant advantage for any of them.

Gibson and Levin (1975, p. 324) emphasize the need to help children
develop a "set for diversity"; that is, to expect that graphemes do not al-

ways represent the same phonemes. Accordingly, they recommend that "if more than one phoneme is represented by a single grapheme, the child should be introduced to both correspondences very early in training." This seems to imply that when a vowel letter is introduced, both the short and the long sounds should be introduced simultaneously or in fairly rapid succession. Most programs do not do this, preferring to avoid the possible confusion created by an overload of new ideas.

In meaning-emphasis programs the words learned provide the basis for a set for diversity almost automatically. Among the Core Preprimer Words (see figure 7.1) there are 15 words containing *a*. In seven of these words the *a* represents a short sound, as in *and*; but there are also *a, make, are, ball, call, want,* and *what,* as well as *play* and *said.* Thus if one introduces short /a/ at primer level, the child has already had much experience with words in which *a* represents other phonemes. It is therefore easy to get across the idea that when in doubt try the short sound first, and if the resulting word doesn't fit the sentence, try alternative sounds for *a.*

Many teachers have incomplete or faulty knowledge of phonics and other decoding skills. Some of them learned to read in programs that did not emphasize phonics. Others learned words so easily that they made little use of the phonics they were taught and so they gradually forgot. They may apply phonic and morphemic principles automatically and correctly when they read, but be unable to verbalize the rules they follow. Mazurkiewicz (1975a, 1975b) found that teachers, and even professors who taught courses in reading instruction, generally had inadequate knowledge of phonics and other decoding skills. For this reason, a concise summary of grapheme-phoneme relationships is provided in Appendix B (see pp. 558–65).

Auditory Segmentation and Blending

Segmentation (the ability to analyze a sentence into words or to analyze a spoken word into subunits such as syllables or phonemes) has been discussed as an aspect of reading readiness (see p. 39). Understanding segmentation is probably a prerequisite or corequisite for the development of skill in blending. The development of auditory segmentation and blending can go hand in hand.

One approach to segmentation is for the teacher to pronounce a sentence and ask how many words are in it. Then the teacher says the sentence again, this time with noticeable pauses between the words, and the children clap their hands at each word. The sentence is spoken again with pauses, and this time the children count the words. If errors are still made, the process is repeated with a different sentence and longer pauses.

For segmentation of spoken words, the teacher can start with words of three or four syllables, pronouncing each word as a whole and then by syllables (e.g., *tel-e-graph, el-e-va-tor*). The children count the word parts they hear. Then monosyllabic words can be pronounced in two parts (*ca-t, br-ing, m-ate*) and the parts counted. Later, monosyllables can be pronounced with short pauses between adjacent phonemes, if that is part of the methodology being used. Understanding spoken words as consisting of recognizable parts should be a preliminary to visual segmentation of printed words, which is discussed later in this unit.

Auditory blending can be started with a polysyllabic word pronounced with pauses between the syllables, or with a monosyllabic word pronounced in two parts, with a pause between. The teacher explains that the parts fit together to make a word, and asks what the word is. If some children have difficulty, the teacher pronounces the word by parts again, slowly at first, then faster and faster, and finally as a whole. The children can be asked to pronounce the word, first as a whole, then by parts, then again as a whole. This is repeated with many words. As with segmentation, the teacher uses words that are easy to blend at first, and gradually increases the difficulty of the task. Controlled studies indicate that ability to blend phonemes into whole words is significantly related to reading ability (Balmuth 1972; Chall, Roswell, and Blumenthal 1963; Richardson, DiBenedetto, and Bradley 1977).

The carryover from auditory segmentation and blending to visual segmentation and blending is discussed later in this unit.

USING GRAPHIC INFORMATION IN DECODING

When context and minimal graphic cues do not allow children to decode unknown words, it becomes necessary to use additional grapho-phonemic information. First, the word is mentally divided into some component parts that will be useful to the child. Using previously learned associations, the sounds represented by each part are thought or said. Then the resulting phonemes or larger units are mentally blended into a whole word. This three-stage process—analysis, symbol-sound associations, blending—is often taught as part of the phonics program. The complexity of the task is often not appreciated, however. All the steps are performed mentally; except for words syllabicated at the ends of lines, at no time during the reading act is the word actually seen in parts. Moreover, the child must hold responses in memory at each step while performing the next step in the process, and finally must reassemble them in correct sequence.

Because there is little sense in analyzing words into some component parts if you cannot determine what sounds the letters represent, and because if you do not know what sounds are represented by the letters, there is nothing to blend together, symbol-sound associations are taught before analysis and blending skills.

Analysis Skills

Skill in dividing an unknown word into some component parts can aid word recognition and perhaps word meaning. Such divisions may occur in monosyllables as well as words of two (disyllabic) or more (polysyllabic) syllables.

Monosyllabic Words   Children who are exposed to intensive phonics programs are more likely to receive direct instruction in how to go about decoding monosyllabic words than are those instructed in a meaning-emphasis approach. In code-emphasis programs that stress single-letter phonemes, children are taught to start at the left and say (mentally or out loud) the most probable phoneme for each grapheme. While this procedure may be helpful in decoding short monosyllabic words, its usefulness decreases when words contain consonant or vowel clusters and the word is comprised of more than three or four letters. Some phonic programs have the child first look for a vowel-consonant phonogram, sometimes referred to as a *word family* (e.g., *at, en*) or a consonant-vowel pattern (*ca*), which is treated as a unit. The ability to recognize spelling patterns that consistently represent the same pattern of sounds (e.g., *ight, all, ook, old, eigh, ame*) can facilitate word recognition and ease the decoding burden. Looking for "word family" patterns may be helpful if the child realizes that they are more likely to represent the same sound pattern when they occur at the end of a syllable. Nevertheless, the practice of looking for a "little word" in a "big word" can be particularly misleading because the sound sequence that the spelling represents in the little word may not be the same as in the big word, and the combination of letters that would be a word by itself may be neither a syllable nor a meaning unit when these letters happen to occur in a long word (*in* in *final*; *very* and *on* in *everyone*).

Morphemic Analysis Morphemic analysis of words means analyzing them in terms of their morphemes (meaning units), in contrast to analyzing words into syllables (see below) and/or into graphemes (see above) and their corresponding phonemes. Thus, morphemically analyzing the word *international* results in a prefix *inter*, a root word *nation* (which is pronounced differently—the *a* becomes /a/—than it is when it stands alone; see the discussion of morphophonemics on page 9) and a suffix *al*. In a word like *provision*, the prefix, root, and suffix each consist of one syllable, so that the syllables are meaning units also. Many prefixes (*inter*, *super*), root words, and suffixes (*able*, *ity*) contain more than one syllable.

When a word has been divided mentally into its meaningful parts, the reader can often recognize these at sight because they have become familiar in other words. Many middle-grade children "see" *calmness* as consisting of *calm* and *ness*, each of which is recognized at sight. If morphemic analysis does not work, the word is then divided by applying phonic principles. The importance of developing competence in morphemic analysis is clearly evident when one looks at the vocabulary found in intermediate- and upper-grade textbooks. For example, McFeely (1974) found that almost half the social studies words he examined contained either a prefix or suffix.

In most meaning-emphasis and some code-emphasis programs, the first step in morphemic analysis is learning to recognize the root words and inflectional endings in such words as *runs, fishes, jumped,* and *looking*. Such analyses often begin as early as the preprimer level. By the first-reader level, children are also taught to divide compound words into the two words that each contains: *something, birthday, airplane*. Compound words are of three types: (1) sum of its parts (houseboat); (2) related to but not completely represented by the meaning of its components (shipyard—it is not clear that this is a place where ships are built or repaired); and (3) meaning not literally related to the meaning of its parts (moonshine) (Moretz and Davey 1974). Compound words usually should be introduced in context because of the aforementioned reasons and because compound words frequently have multiple meanings (doghouse).

Sometimes the root word is modified when certain suffixes are added. Some children have difficulty recognizing these inflected forms so that the relationship of the inflected form and the root must be pointed out to them. Among the more commonly taught generalizations in this area (usually taught in spelling) are:

1. When words end with a final silent *e*, the *e* usually is dropped when adding suffixes or inflectional endings that begin with a vowel (*like-liking*).
2. When a one-syllable word ends with a single consonant other than *x*, the final consonant is doubled when adding a suffix (*big-bigger*).
3. When the final *y* in a word is preceded by a consonant, the *y* usually is changed to *i* when adding a suffix, other than *ing*, that begins with a vowel (*baby-babies, fly-flying*).

Some omissions of inflected endings in oral reading simply reflect the reader's dialect. Because inflected endings often carry important meaning cues, however, careless inattention to them can adversely influence comprehension.

As early as the second-reader level, words with prefixes and suffixes begin to appear with increasing frequency. Instruction in the meaning significance of the affixes may begin at the third-reader level.

Suffixes help to indicate both grammatical function and specific meaning. When *act* changes to *actor* and *action*, the latter two words are both noun forms, one indicating a performer and the other indicating function. Because morphemic analysis is often more helpful in clarifying meaning than in recognizing words, the study of roots and affixes is taken up in greater detail in unit 8.

Two morphemic-analysis generalizations are worth teaching (developing):

1. Divide between words that form a compound word; other divisions may take place in either or both parts.
2. Divide between the root word and an affix; other divisions may take place within the root word or affix.

Syllabication   By the second-reader level many new words have more than one syllable. Therefore, most meaning-emphasis programs introduce the beginnings of syllabication during the second-reader level and reinforce and extend this knowledge in the later grades.

Syllabication is often introduced by making children aware that some words are made up of more than one syllable. They also learn the concept that every syllable has one vowel sound. The teacher pronounces sight words as a whole and then syllable by syllable; the children can beat time to the syllables. Later they listen to new words and try to count the number of syllables. After the concept of "a syllable" has been established children may be asked to note whether the vowel sound in each syllable is short or long. This is done to provide background for the teaching of generalizations concerning the effect of vowel position on vowel sounds. Practice in pronouncing and writing words by syllables is also stressed in some spelling programs, and it is desirable to coordinate instruction in syllabication so that reading and spelling practice can be mutually reinforcing. Syllabication generalizations can be used to help recognize previously introduced words as well as to decode unknown words.

Teachers sometimes forget that the real purpose of teaching phonic, syllabication, and morphemic generalizations is to assist the child in decoding unrecognized words, rather than to assure that the child can parrot back these generalizations or is able to indicate in a workbook which generalization should be applied according to the teachers manual. Generalizations should be taught so as to give children useful procedures for recognizing unknown words they encounter while reading. Application of generalizations, rather than verbalization, should be the goal.

The following simplified syllabication generalizations are suggested as the ones worth teaching:

1. Usually divide between two consonants that are not a digraph or a cluster.[6]

---

6. Knowledge of what comprises common digraphs and clusters is necessary in order to apply this generalization. The qualifier in this generalization is more applicable to digraphs than to clusters because many words are divided between letters that commonly form clusters (e.g., *st* is a common cluster, but *s* and *t* are divided in *blis-ter*). However, it would really matter very little if the word were divided keeping the letters that commonly form the blend together (e.g., *blist-er*) because the reason for syllabication is to assist the reader in approximating the printed word's oral counterpart. In the example given, a reader who understood the word would probably come up with the correct pronunciation. A reader who chose to place the *st* with the second syllable probably would decode the word with a long *i* sound since it ends the syllable. If the word is in a revealing context, however, most readers will quickly make the adjustment to the short *i* sound.

Some programs teach two generalizations, one involving unlike consonants; the other, double consonants (the same consonant is repeated). At least one program suggests dividing *after* double consonants since they usually represent one sound and the preceding vowel is short. Programs that have children divide between double consonants also teach them that the second consonant is usually silent. In either case there are exceptions, the most

2. A single consonant between two single vowels may go with either syllable.
3. Final *le* and the consonant preceding it usually form the final syllable.
4. If the root word ends with *t* or *d*, the final *ed* usually is a separate syllable.

Teaching children to syllabicate has come under criticism lately (Groff 1971, Waugh and Havell 1975). Yet the fact remains that, properly taught and utilized, syllabication generalizations can provide the learner with some guidelines for dividing long words into units that will trigger recognition or to which phonic skills can be applied. For example, syllabication often provides cues to vowel sounds. Three phonic principles regarding vowel values often taught in conjunction with syllabication and accenting are:

1. When an accented syllable ends with a single vowel letter, that letter usually represents its long sound. Syllables that end with vowels are called *open* syllables.
2. When an accented syllable ends with a consonant other than *r*, a preceding single vowel letter usually represents its short sound. Syllables that end with consonants are called *closed* syllables.
3. The vowel sounds in many unaccented syllables are diminished to the point where they sound very much alike (like a short *u*) and often are represented in dictionary respellings by the schwa (ə).

Because these generalizations are not perfectly reliable, children should be taught to be flexible in their use. If their first approximation does not result in a word they recognize, they should try an alternate vowel sound. Thus, in applying syllabication generalization 2 above, children should be told that if they decide that the consonant goes with the preceding syllable, they should try the short vowel sound first. If that does not result in a known word, they then should try the long vowel sound in the first syl-

common being with *cc* (*success*) and *gg* (*suggest*), in which each letter in the double consonant represents a different sound.

Somewhat similarly, the word *farmer* is an example favorable to morphemic analysis in which the division comes between the root and the suffix. A child who divides between the two consonants will probably recognize the word after blending *far* and *mer*. The danger in such cases is that *not* dividing into meaning units may badly mislead readers in their quest for meaning if the word is not in their understanding vocabulary (e.g., *far* and *mer* does not readily indicate the meaning of the word whereas *farm* and *er* does).

lable. As for syllabication generalization 4, children may be simply taught that sometimes *ed* is pronounced as a separate syllable; and if the word is in their speaking vocabularies, they will probably pronounce *ed* as a separate syllable when the occasion warrants it. There is little need to inform them also that *ed* may represent /t/ or /d/ because they will automatically provide the correct sound if the word is in their speaking vocabulary.

Seymour (1973a) has suggested use of the term "word division" rather than "syllabication" because dictionary syllabications are not particularly appropriate for decoding, and the process is not directed at pronunciation of completely new words, but at the recognition of words already in the reader's understanding vocabulary. While this may be generally so, there are times when a child needs to decode a completely new word.

Two practices have extremely limited, if any, positive value:

1. Having children draw lines between the syllables of known words. If the word is recognized, it can be syllabicated by saying it slowly. The only value to such an exercise is to demonstrate that the generalizations have applicability. Exercises that use words that fit only one generalization often can be done without thinking of the generalization. Even if the child is able to indicate with slashes where unknown words of various types should be syllabicated it should not be assumed that the child can, or will, actually apply these skills in arriving at the oral counterpart of a printed word.
2. Telling children to divide a word "as you would say it." If they can pronounce the word, they obviously can recognize it, so why bother to decode it. The only justifiable limited uses for such a practice are in the early stages of instruction to alert the child to the fact that words are composed of syllables, and for spelling.

Accenting   Accent is the emphasis given to a syllable in a word, or to a word in a sentence, that makes it stand out in comparison to the other syllable(s) or words. In most two-syllable words one syllable is accented; in words of three or more syllables, one syllable has a primary accent (´), and another may have a secondary accent ('). In a compound word both parts may be given equal stress. Children should have some experience in listening to words to distinguish primary and secondary accents and unaccented syllables, but this is mainly to prepare them for using a dictionary.

Generalizations about accenting are not very helpful in decoding. If the word is already in the child's listening vocabulary, the child will accent the word correctly. If the word is completely new, there are only two generalizations about accents that may be useful:

1. More often than not, the first syllable of a two-syllable word is accented.
2. Usually affixes are not accented.

The only way to be certain if an unknown word is accented correctly is to use a dictionary. Children should be made aware that shifts in accent can influence pronunciation and meaning (*de-sert', des'-ert; rec'-ord, re-cord'*).

Phonic Generalizations

There are great differences among reading programs in the emphasis placed on phonic generalizations. Some programs teach a great many generalizations; others expect children to develop their own generalizations inductively; still others teach a few rules, relying on sight word learning to take care of phoneme-grapheme relationships that are either variable or rare.

A number of research studies have shown that many of the once commonly taught generalizations are not particularly useful in decoding (Clymer 1963; Bailey 1967; Emans 1967; Burmeister 1968, 1971; McFeely 1974). A generalization is probably not worth teaching if there is a high percentage of exceptions to it or if it applies to only a few words or mainly to uncommon words.

One of the controversial generalizations states that when two vowel letters appear in sequence, the first usually represents its long sound and the second is usually silent. This applies with high consistency to only four common vowel digraphs (*ai, ay, ee,* and *oa*), and even these have exceptions (s*ai*d, qu*ay*, r*ee*nter, br*oa*d). A different version, "When two vowels go walking hand in hand, the first one does the talking," allows the first vowel to represent either its long or short sound (sp*ea*k, br*ea*d) and thus has fewer exceptions, but still has many exceptions in which the second letter is the one heard (st*ea*k, p*ie*ce). It is, therefore, advisable to teach vowel digraphs one at a time and avoid a broad generalization which has so many exceptions.

Another controversial generalization states that when a syllable ends with a single vowel letter, a single consonant letter, and a final e(VCe), the vowel usually represents its long sound and the *e* is silent. Although Clymer (1963), Bailey (1967), and Emans (1967) found that this "final silent *e*" generalization worked only about 60 percent of the time, Burmeister (1971), who used a much larger body of words, found it to be much more useful. The major exception is the suffix *-ive*, in which the *i* usually represents its short sound (*detective*).

There is a close relation between vowel values and syllable structure. In a closed syllable (ending with a consonant) the vowel is usually short, while in an open syllable (ending with a vowel letter) the vowel is usually long.[7] *R*-controlled vowels (as in c*a*r, h*e*r, s*i*r, f*u*r, f*o*r) provide a special class of exceptions for which specific, limited generalizations can be taught. Vowel sounds are also influenced by accent; most generalizations about long and short sounds do not apply in unaccented or unstressed syllables, in which any vowel letter can represent the schwa sound (ə), which is like a brief short *u*.

Phonic generalizations apply within syllables but not across syllables. Thus *ea* is not a digraph in r*ea*ct, *sh* is not a digraph in mi*sh*ap, *th* is not a digraph in po*th*ole. In such words the child has to be aware of the desirability of dividing the word into morphemes before applying phonic principles.

There is some evidence that children often do not apply phonic and syllabication generalizations when decoding unknown words. Hardy, Stennett, and Smythe (1973) found that first and second graders consistently searched for and manipulated familiar words or word parts in attempting to decode nonsense words. Such behaviors may be a function of the instructional program. According to Glass and Burton (1973) successful decoders in the second and fifth grades associated sounds with letter clusters rather than utilized generalizations. Of course, what some successful decoders do may not be what *all* children should learn to do.

Glass (1973), who believes that decoding should be taught separately from reading and should be learned using words presented in isolation, has developed a procedure that is meant to replace the teaching of syllabication skills. Basically, the procedure involves exposing the word card, saying the word, and identifying the spelling of clusters within the word. The whole printed word is always kept in view, with no part of it ever be-

---

7. Although long *u* is usually taught as meaning the vowel in c*u*te, there are about as many words in which the sound is like o͞o as in fl*u*te. It seems desirable to teach children that the term "long *u*" can represent both of these sounds.

ing covered. Target clusters are frequently identified by both letters and sounds. To illustrate for the word *longest*, the suggested procedure is (in terms of what the teacher says):

1. In the word "longest," what letter makes the /l/ sound?
2. What letters make the "ong" sound?
3. What letters make the "long" sound?
4. What letters make the "ongest" sound?
5. In the word "longest," what sound does the *l* make?
6. What sound does the *o n g* make?
7. What sound does the *l o n g* make?
8. In the word "longest", what sound does the *e s t* make?
9. What sound does *o n g e s t* make?
10. If I took off the /l/, what sound would be left?
11. If I took off the *l o n g*, what sound would I have left?
12. If I took off the "est" sound, what sound would be left?
13. What is the whole word? (Glass 1973, pp. 27–28).

Seymour (1973a) has presented the following useful suggestions for planning for a lesson on decoding multisyllabic words:

1. Present only words that have not been read before.
2. Be sure the words are composed of structural and phonological parts the children have been taught.
3. Give the children an opportunity to decode each new word by dividing it into known structural parts, decoding each part, and combining the parts into a whole word.
4. Check whether the children have really decoded the words by requiring their use in sentences: Because it was cold, mother put another _____ on the bed. (blizzard blossom blanket)

By the time children are introduced to syllabication, they usually can recognize and pronounce many syllables at sight. By this time, they have also usually developed considerable speed in mentally sounding and blending a sequence of phonic units. As they go through a word from left to right, pronouncing it by syllables, the big uncertainties are whether vowel sounds are long or short and where to place the accent. Often, the context provides enough cues so that configuration and sounding the first syllable or two are sufficient for correct recognition. If the first pronunciation tried does not provide a meaningful word that fits the context, a resourceful reader tries the accent in a different place and alternative vowel phonemes. A word that is within the reader's speaking or understanding vocabulary should be recognized in context if the reader comes fairly close to the correct pronunciation.

Blending

Auditory segmentation and blending have been discussed above. In auditory blending a child listens to a word as it is pronounced by parts and tries to put the sounds together to determine what the word is. In reading, the task is more difficult and complicated, because (1) the child has to look at an unfamiliar word and divide it mentally into usable visual units such as single letters, clusters, spelling patterns, or syllables; (2) using previously learned symbol-sound associations the child thinks the phonemic equivalent for each part in left-to-right sequence; (3) the child has to hold these phonemes in mind until the process is finished (short-term memory); (4) the child then has to synthesize or blend the sequence into a word; and (5) if the result is not a recognizable word or does not fit the meaning of the context, the child should try it again, with alternative accents and phonemes.

This process is a difficult one for many six-year-olds. The larger the units that can be used, the easier the process. For example, a child who can recognize *school* and *room* should have no difficulty blending them to get *schoolroom*. The fewer the units to be blended, the easier. Thus *bring* is not hard to blend if divided into /br/ and /ing/, but quite hard to blend if separated into single phonemes /b/, /r/, /i/, /n/, /g/.

Some children are able to segment a word into phonic units and can pronounce each part separately, but seem unable to blend them into a word. In such cases, additional practice in auditory blending may help. If it doesn't, it is desirable to emphasize a visual or kinesthetic procedure with that child and confine blending to compound words and syllables. Others who seem unable to blend fail because they cannot segment the word into usable parts, or having done so, do not know the needed symbol-sound associations. When a child seems unable to blend, one should try to determine if the problem is in segmentation, in symbol-sound associations, or truly in blending.

Some phonic programs take blending for granted and do little, if anything, to train blending ability. Others use specific and very different procedures, many of which have been described by Whaley (1975).

In the Distar program (see p. 99), as the teacher touches a letter the children say the sound and continue saying it "right into the next letter" she touches; emphasis is also placed on "say it fast."

Another procedure utilizes modeling or demonstration by the teacher. The teacher has large letter cards for use in a chart holder. The teacher places the cards for a word so that they touch, and says the word. She then moves the letter cards apart and pronounces the phoneme for each as she touches them in sequence, about a second apart. She then moves the cards closer together and pronounces them with barely perceptible pauses. Finally she moves them so they touch again and pronounces the word. At each step the children imitate what the teacher has just done, using small letter cards on their desks or tables. Then individual children are given the opportunity to repeat the procedure without teacher help. After the procedure has been well learned the teacher stops providing a model.

It should be noted that young children have short memory spans; many six-year-olds cannot keep in mind a sequence of more than four items. Thus words containing more than four phonemes should be segmented into letter clusters, spelling patterns, or syllables when possible, so as to minimize the number of units to be kept in mind.

In the program proposed by Resnick and Beck (1976), children are taught to use a successive blending procedure rather than a final blending procedure often used in intensive phonics programs. In successive blending, as soon as two sounds are produced, they are blended and successive phonemes are added as they are produced (/k/, /a/, /ka/, /t/, /kat/). In a final blending procedure, blending is postponed until the very last step (/k/, /a/, /t/, /kat/). The main advantage claimed for successive blending is that it reduces the memory load since no more than two sound units need to be in mind at any one time. A child taught via this program would go through the following steps in independently decoding *cat*:

1. Point to *c* and say /k/.
2. Point to *a* and say /a/.
3. Slowly slide a finger under *ca* and say /ka/.
4. Quickly slide a finger under *ca* and say /ka/ quickly.
5. Point to *t* and say /t/.
6. Slowly slide a finger under *cat* and say /kat/ slowly.
7. Circle the word with a finger and say, "The word is cat."

Durkin (1976, pp. 106 ff.) recommends a blending procedure that gives priority to vowels. In each syllable the vowel is pronounced first, then the preceding consonant is added to it, then the final consonant is added. In one of her examples, the word *alcove* is sounded and blended as follows:

$$a \rightarrow al$$
$$\bar{o} \rightarrow c\bar{o} \rightarrow c\bar{o}ve$$

This procedure has a major drawback—it disrupts the systematic left-to-right sequence that nearly all reading authorities recommend. It would seem to be particularly disturbing for children who have any tendency to make reversal errors.

Durkin's justification for the procedure is that pronouncing a consonant without linking it to a vowel distorts the phoneme, and that this is particularly acute for the stop consonants, *b, d, g, k, p,* and *t.* A similar argument is used by some linguists and reading specialists to oppose sounding by phonemes. They state that it is impossible to pronounce consonants in isolation without adding an extraneous and interfering schwa sound to them. Thus they state that sounding *bat* by phonemes produces /buh/,/a/,/tuh/ and that these sounds when blended do not produce *bat.*

Actually this argument is exaggerated. Many consonants can easily be pronounced without adding an extraneous schwa: *f, l, m, n, r, v, w, y, ch, j, sh, s, zh, z, th.* Stop consonants are produced without an added schwa when they occur at the ends of words or syllables; listen to *rob, road, lack, weep, met, hug.* Teachers can learn to pronounce them without an extraneous vowel by whispering them. This is somewhat easier to do for the unvoiced stop consonants such as *p* and *t* than for the voiced stops, *d* and *g*; the latter should probably not be used for blending practice until the technique has been fairly well learned.

One more blending procedure avoids pronouncing consonants without vowels and retains the left-to-right sequence. Both consonant-vowel and vowel-consonant combinations are taught. With a simple CVC word, the initial CV combination is pronounced, then the final VC combination (the vowel being pronounced twice), then blending consists of merging the two similar vowel phonemes. This would be a very popular procedure were it not for the very large number of CV and VC combinations that have to be learned. Thus, *cat* is blended as follows: /ka/, /at/, /kat/.

As proficiency is gained in sounding and blending, the process becomes increasingly rapid and automatic, to the point where children become able to pronounce an unfamiliar syllable or word without an awareness of thinking the separate parts and blending them. The good reader also automatically recognizes larger units, including prefixes, roots, and suffixes of more than one syllable: *super/impos/ition*. In this way the competent reader easily produces a reasonable (but not necessarily correct) pronunciation for many unfamiliar polysyllabic words. Pronunciation will be correct if the word is in the reader's listening vocabulary or can be verified by looking it up in a dictionary.

When Should Phonics Be Taught?

For many years, a research study by Dolch and Bloomster (1937) was used as justification for placing the bulk of phonic instruction at second- and third-grade reading levels. Research in the 1960s demonstrated that different kinds of code-emphasis programs can be used successfully with first graders. But, as we have seen in unit 3, research has failed to show a consistent advantage for either code-emphasis or meaning-emphasis programs. By the end of third grade in the Cooperative Reading studies sponsored by the U.S. Office of Education, the differences attributable to the method of teaching were small, inconsistent, and not statistically significant. The learning abilities of the children, the characteristics of their homes and neighborhoods, and the kinds of teaching they received were more important in determining the results.

One reason why some teachers are ineffective in teaching decoding is that their own knowledge of phonics is incomplete and inaccurate. A second possible reason is insensitivity to the learning rates of individual children. Tovey (1972) found that in first-grade classes, high-ability children generally received phonic lessons that were too easy for them, while the rest were given lessons that were too advanced for them.

A third problem is inherent in the lesson-plan sequence of some basal-reader programs. In those series, phonic instruction comes after silent and oral reading. Teachers who feel hard pressed to "cover the book" in a specific period of time are tempted to skip part of the lesson plan, and when that happens, it is usually the follow-up part of the plan that is neglected; thus the planned program may be satisfactory but the execution may be skimped. Furthermore, in such a plan phonic instruction is based on developing inferences from previously learned words, and there may be very little practice in applying those principles to new words. To be functionally effective, phonics should be taught with immediate application to unfamiliar words, and the time to do this is in the preparatory part of the lesson when new words are introduced.

It may be expected that when a phonic unit is first introduced, some children will not learn the skill, let alone master it for permanent retention. If the phonic principles are frequently reviewed and applied, most of these children will catch on somewhat later. Meanwhile, the ones who can grasp the skill the first or second time can use it profitably.

An alternative is to identify those children who could profit from such instruction, and to teach them phonic skills in separate groups or individually. Teachers who want to amplify the phonic program given in their reader manuals can develop a sequence that fits the readers they are using by employing the principles of phonic instruction discussed above. Some may prefer to use commercially published supplementary phonic materials, such as those described below in place of the phonic instruction found in the particular reading program being employed. Similar alternatives are open for the teacher using a language-experience approach or individualized developmental reading.

Materials for Developing Decoding Skills

A number of phonic materials are designed for use parallel to a basal-reader series or language-experience program, or as a supplement to it. These can be used with a whole class, groups, or individuals. A supplementary phonic program can be quite useful in remedial or corrective work, and in teaching children who seem to need a more intensive phonic basis than some basal readers provide.

A supplementary or parallel phonic program should have the following characteristics: (1) there should be a good teachers manual or set of directions; (2) phonic units should be introduced at a reasonable rate, in a defensible sequence; (3) the system should avoid much reliance on practice with sounds in isolation; (4) there should be a substantial amount of practice in using phonics in combination with sight recognition and context in meaningful reading.

Those interested in employing an objective-based word-analysis skills program may refer to Cheek (1974) or to such commercially developed programs as the *Wisconsin Design for Reading Skill Development* (ISS). However, care should be exercised in the use of the criterion-referenced tests associated with such programs. For example, in studying one such test, Roundabush (1974) found that since mastery of an objective is usually measured by a test of only five to ten items, errors of measurement may sometimes turn failing performances into passing scores, or satisfactory mastery into a failing score. He also pointed out that some objectives for which tests are provided (for example, counting the syllables in words) may not be significantly related to success in reading.

Decoding Games and Devices   The following are commercially available materials for teaching and practicing decoding skills:

Go Fish (Kingsbury). Provides sound-symbol practice with single and double consonants; played like rummy; two sets.

Vowel Dominoes (Kingsbury). Played like dominoes, but requires short vowel sounds.

Doghouse Game (Kenworthy). Contains 12 cards each with 35 word-ending patterns to which initial consonants and blends are added.

Consonant Lotto (Garrard). Involves matching pictures whose names start with the same initial consonant as the cue word.

Vowel Lotto (Garrard). Involves matching pictures that have the same vowel sounds.

What the Letters Say (Garrard). Aids in learning the association of sounds with letters.

Group Sounding Game (Garrard). Fifteen lotto-type games, each for 6 players, covering the phonic elements usually taught in the primary grades.

Take (Garrard). Involves matching cards that represent words with the same beginning sound, middle, or ending.

The Syllable Game (Garrard). Three sets of cards going from two-syllable to four-syllable words.

Phonetic Quizmo (Milton Bradley). Phonic lotto game.

Reading Laboratory 1: Word Games (SRA). Forty-four word games in individual packets.

Phonic Rummy (Kenworthy). Matching games with phonic elements.

Junior Phonic Rummy (Kenworthy). Matching game using 110 frequently occurring short-vowel words.

Phonics We Use Learning Games Kit (Rand McNally). Ten separate games for teaching various phonic elements.

Phono-Word Wheels (Steck-Vaughn). Five sets of word wheels covering initial consonants; blends, digraphs and endings; initial blends; suffixes; and prefixes.

Webster Word Wheels (Webster). Set of 63 word wheels for practice with consonant blends, prefixes, and suffixes.

Phonic Word Builders (Ideal). Small cards containing consonants, phonograms, and end-of-word combinations which may be used for making words.

Embeco Word Builder (Milton Bradley). Anagram lower-case letters printed on heavy cardboard.

Embeco Phonetic Drill Cards (Milton Bradley). Word-family phonograms on large cards, each with hinged smaller cards containing initial consonants; different words are made by turning the hinged cards.

Phonetic Word Analyzer (Milton Bradley). Wheel with interchangeable disks by which consonants and blends are matched with stems to form words.

Fun with Words (Dexter and Westbrook). Six boxes of small cards, each presenting 3 riddles with phonic and meaning cues, many of which are in rhyme.

Workbooks, Kits, and Programs   Among the good phonic workbooks and kits that are not part of a particular published reading program are:

Building Reading Skills (McCormick). Series of 6 workbooks developing decoding skills sequentially with emphasis on meaningful content.

Eye and Ear Fun (Webster). Series of 5 workbooks with emphasis on exercises that combine meaning, picture, phonic, and structural cues.

New Phonics We Use (Rand McNally). Series of 7 workbooks much like *Eye and Ear Fun*, but somewhat more gradually paced.

Phonovisual Method (Phonovisual). Consists of a large Consonant Chart, a large Vowel Chart, smaller versions of both for individual use, several workbooks, and other materials.

Breaking the Sound Barrier (Macmillan). Emphasizes a thinking approach in the application of phonics.

Macmillan Reading Spectrum: Word Analysis (Macmillan). Series of 6 programmed, self-checking workbooks, for use in the middle or upper grades.

Speech to Print Phonics (Harcourt). Cards for presentation by the teacher and response cards for the pupils; requires combined use of phonics and word meaning; but does not use printed context.

Durrell-Murphy Phonics Practice Program (Harcourt). A large number of cards each providing self-directing and self-checking seatwork.

Time for Phonics (Webster). Workbooks teaching phonics with use of picture and context cues; more suitable for primary grades.

Reading Essentials Series (Steck-Vaughn). Series of 8 workbooks stressing phonic and structural analysis skills; presents opportunity for applying skills in context.

Merrill Phonics Skilltexts (Charles E. Merrill). Series of 6 workbooks for developing phonics, structural, and contextual skills; provides for a great deal of review.

Functional Phonetics (Beckley-Cardy). Provides considerable auditory discrimination training; emphasizes initial consonant-vowel combinations.

New Structural Reading Series (Singer). Phonic-linguistic program in 8 worktexts emphasizing discovery, insight, and application in context.

Phoenix Reading Series (Prentice-Hall). A three-level program for "reteaching" phonics to intermediate-grade children. Uses photographs and contemporary themes.

+ *4 Reading Booster* (Webster). Kit containing various materials for developing decoding skills; also places emphasis on comprehension.

Individualized Directions in Reading (Steck-Vaughn). Criterion-referenced remedial reading system; deals with decoding and comprehension.

Diagnostic/Prescriptive Program for Word Analysis (Bobbs-Merrill). Kit containing brief tests and follow-up materials for teaching 51 decoding skills.

Multimedia Materials   Increasingly programs are combining tapes or records with various forms of reading materials. Some also have comprehension programs. The following list is far from inclusive.

Learning with Laughter (Prentice-Hall). Series of kits each containing a filmstrip, tape or record, assorted games, and a manual.

Consonant Sounds and Vowel Sounds/A Self Instructional Modalities Approach (Milton Bradley). Each program has a number of taped lessons, accompanying response sheets, and materials the children can manipulate.

Mast Programed Instructor (Mast Keystone). Instrument for using 35-mm. film strips. Child responds to frame by writing on the response tape, presses the answer button, and compares his response to the one on the screen.

Target (Field). Self-instructional kits containing behavioral objectives, pretests, duplicating masters, cassettes, and a manual.

Listen-Look-Learn (Ideal). Six sets of phonic lessons; duplicated workbooks or erasable lesson cards accompany recordings.

Phonics Program and Word-Picture Program (Bell and Howell). Various
sets of prerecorded cards for use with the *Language Master*.

Directional Phonics (TTC). Filmstrips, tapes, magnetic cards for use with
the *TTC Magnetic Card Reader*.

Systems 80 (Borg Warner). Modified branching programmed lessons requiring use of hardware that may be purchased or rented.

CAI Remedial Reading (Harcourt). Computer-assisted instructional programs for junior and senior high school students.

UNIT 8

Helping Children to Improve Comprehension

In the preceding unit attention was focused on the development of word-recognition and decoding skills. The present unit is concerned with obtaining appropriate meanings from printed or written material, which is the heart of reading.

The first part of the unit deals with word meaning. Words are the basic units of language, and knowing what most of the words in a sentence mean is a necessary prerequisite to understanding the thought which the sentence is intended to convey. The rest of this unit is concerned with comprehension of meaningful reading material. The major topics discussed are the nature and types of comprehension, learning to read in thought units, developing specific comprehension skills, and relating reading rate to comprehension.

DEVELOPING AND EXPANDING READING VOCABULARIES

Relationship of Reading Vocabulary and Comprehension

Although reading comprehension involves much more than simply knowing the meanings of individual words, an understanding of the author's words is a minimal essential for reading comprehension. Scores on reading vocabulary tests correlate very highly with reading comprehension scores, and most reading tests contain a vocabulary subtest that is given substantial weight in the total score.

Concepts, Words, and Vocabulary

A word is a verbal label for a concept. The concept represented by a word is the generalized meaning that the word comes to have. A concept is refined through many experiences in which an appropriate interpretation or use is reinforced and inappropriate ones are not. Thus, initially any furry animal may be called "doggie." Gradually the child learns that dogs come in various sizes, shapes, and colors; but that cats are not dogs. Although he cannot verbalize the difference, the child can understand simple discriminating statements, such as, "Dogs bark, but cats meow." Direct experience provides the basis for early concept formation. Even later in life, verbal explanation is secondary; it helps to clarify experience but cannot completely replace it.

Concepts, and accordingly words, can have emotional as well as intellectual content. The concept *dog* can evoke fear or pleasure, depending upon one's past experiences. As a word is repeatedly heard or spoken, it becomes firmly associated with the accumulating complex of meaning it evokes; it becomes the symbol that represents the concept. Despite the fact that no two people have had identical experiences and therefore have formed somewhat different concepts, there are enough basic similarities for the word (e.g., *dog*) to be useful in communication.

Concepts that are too broad become trimmed to appropriate size through the process of differentiation. If a preschooler calls a pond a big puddle, someone will probably say, "This is a pond; it is too big for a puddle." In this way, the child's concept of *puddle* is refined and a concept of *pond* is started.

Concepts also grow from specific to general to abstract through accumulated experience and increased mental maturity. An eight-year-old is likely to think of a word such as *dishonesty* in light of personal experience (stealing an apple). Gradually the meaning comes to include some specific acts and exclude others, until to the adolescent *dishonesty* should come to mean any form of intentional deception or illegal acquisition of property. But even when agreement on a generalized meaning is widely accepted, problems arise in specific applications. For example, when does a gift become a bribe and thus become dishonest? The more abstract and general a concept, the harder it is to obtain a concensus about its application.

Levels of Abstraction   Kindergarteners usually know the meaning of *red* and *blue* due to their past experiences with various objects of such colors. They have abstracted the color as a quality that can occur in many objects. Colors are first-level abstractions because they can be abstracted directly from perceptual experiences.

The concept of *color* is gained when a child realizes that *orange, purple,* etc., are all "members of a family" and all are colors. Therefore, since *color* is an abstraction from abstractions, it is a second-level abstraction. If we ask in what way second-level abstractions based on perceptions (loudness, hue, brightness) are alike, there is no one English word that represents the concept of such a third-level abstraction that includes all attributes of perceptual experience. Because there is little use for such a concept, a word to represent it has not been devised.

Concepts that represent immediate experience or are first-level abstractions tend to be easily learned by children. Second-level abstractions are relatively difficult. In teaching their meanings, one has to create links with the child's own experience. Third-level abstractions are still harder, and cannot be developed until the second-level abstractions on which they rest are understood.

In defining words, children display several levels of conceptual development. The lowest level involves definitions that are expressed only in terms of function or use (A *ball* is to play with). More maturity is displayed by some description with a statement of function (A *ball* is a round thing you can bounce). A still higher level is revealed when the child states the category to which the concept belongs and one distinguishing characteristic (A *ball* is a round toy). Adult-type definitions state the category and one or more truly distinguishing characteristics (A ball is any of various rounded movable objects used in sports and games). Use of a synonym (*honesty* means integrity) is another mature way to define words.

Intelligent, educated adults have their concepts organized into categories that are arranged in a hierarchy of increasing abstraction or generalization. Children think of a cat as a milk-drinking, purring animal that catches mice. A zoologist also knows that the cat is a small domesticated feline which is a carnivorous, mammalian, vertebrate animal. At each level of generalization, the zoologist knows both the basic common characteristics of the category and the contrasting characteristics that distinguish one category from another (vertebrate vs. invertebrate). The zoologist's knowledge is rooted in experience; but it has been refined, organized, and fitted into an hierarchical framework of ideas.

Types of Vocabulary

A listening (understanding) vocabulary is acquired first and tends to remain the largest type of vocabulary, at least through the primary grades. The speaking vocabulary develops later and more slowly than the listening vocabulary. At approximately 12–18 months of age, the child begins to say understandable single words. During this period, one-word sentences like "milk" may have a number of meanings, such as "I see the milk," "I want some milk," or "You look at the milk." F. Smith (1972), a linguist, stated that contrary to popular belief, children do not learn words and then find meanings for them. Rather, they invent words, which may or may not be closely related to adult language, to meet their own particular requirements and to represent quite complex deep structures. By about eighteen months, children begin to put together two words that are meaningful to them. Thus, the child says, "Allgone milk" or "See kitty." The next three to four months are marked by more two-word than one-word sentences, and an occasional three-word saying. After that oral constructions expand rapidly, with the child forming increasingly complex statements. By about 3½ years, a child does not speak like an adult, but has the competency to produce and comprehend all of the sentence forms found in adult speech (F. Smith 1972). By about age five or six, children have control over most adultlike grammar, but development of syntactical control extends through the elementary grades.

As children learn to read, they begin to recognize printed words that represent words already in their listening and speaking vocabularies. These words, which are understood as well as recognized, form their reading vocabulary. The writing vocabulary usually begins about the same time as the reading vocabulary, but increases more slowly. All the words in a child's listening, speaking, reading, and writing vocabularies comprise his or her meaningful vocabulary.

Size of Meaningful Vocabulary   Estimates of the size of children's vocabularies differ, but the best available evidence was summarized by Dale (1965). His data suggest that children finish first grade with an average meaningful vocabulary of approximately 3,000 words, and are likely to add about 1,000 words a year thereafter while in school. So, average third graders know the meanings of approximately 5,000 words, and the average sixth-grade child understands about 8,000 words. It is very difficult to obtain accurate data as to the exact number of words a child actually "knows." Since many English words have multiple meanings and usages, how many of these must be known before a word is "known"? Knowing the most common definition of a word, as commonly measured by vocabulary tests, does not necessarily mean that a word is known in all its meanings.

Of course, there will be wide individual differences at any grade level. Intellectually gifted intermediate-grade children, particularly those who read widely, sometimes develop vocabularies comparable to or exceeding those of their teachers.

Possible Reasons for Meager Vocabularies   One possible reason for a small meaningful vocabulary is below-average intelligence. It should be recognized, however, that a low IQ score on a group intelligence test that requires reading ability may simply reflect lack of reading ability rather than low intellectual functioning.

Other causes of vocabulary weakness are a lack of intellectual stimulation and lack of experience in using language. Children who have led very restricted lives are not likely to have developed the conceptual background and accompanying words that are in the repertoire of the average child. Limited knowledge of English or acquaintance with standard English may also contribute to the problem. This point should be considered in interpreting intelligence test results, even those administered individually. A low IQ score may reflect the child's lack of experience with the language employed by the test rather than a poor potential for learning. Auditory and speech handicaps also interfere with acquiring a meaningful vocabulary because they cut down conversational opportunities.

As children progress through the grades, they increasingly meet printed words that are outside their listening and speaking vocabularies. As they develop concepts for these words, children often add them to their other types of vocabulary. Therefore, weak reading ability can hinder growth of concepts and meaningful vocabulary.

Helping Children to Improve Their Reading Vocabularies

There are various approaches for providing children with skills that enable them to determine the meanings of printed words, and to increase their reading vocabularies. Teachers will have to decide which procedures to use in their classes because research findings regarding the relative effectiveness of different ways of teaching vocabulary are inconclusive (Petty, Herold, and Stoll 1968).

Increasing Listening and Speaking Vocabularies One way to improve children's reading vocabularies is to increase their listening and speaking vocabularies, so that when the children decode the printed forms of these words, their meanings are available. Concepts, and the words that represent them, are best developed through vivid firsthand experiences. If such experiences are impossible, then vicarious experiences such as audio-visual aids and reading to the children may be provided. In providing experiences, sensory contact alone is not sufficient for developing concepts. The teacher must know which concept she wants the children to acquire. Then the children's attention should be guided so that the concept and its verbal label are clearly understood and reinforced.

The following principles may be applied in teaching concepts: (1) establish the proper word label for the concept or attribute; (2) place emphasis on significant differentiating characteristics; (3) provide examples and instances of the concept in an appropriate sequence; (4) encourage and guide the child in the discovery of the essence of the concept; and (5) provide for application of the concept (Rentel 1971).

Vocabulary Control Although beginning reading materials mainly employ words whose meanings are known by children, there is less vocabulary control exerted in recent material than was the case in the 1950s, particularly above the primary grades.

Children can obtain meaning from material that contains some words whose meanings are unknown. The occasional rare word usually is not a great hindrance to comprehension. Nouns and verbs are most essential for meaning; other parts of speech can often be supplied by the reader. Learning the meanings of unknown words does not, however, automatically occur when the gist of the passage has been grasped. If unknown words make up a substantial percentage of the reading material, one may be able to abstract some meaning, but is unlikely to learn the meanings of the unknown words. As a rule of thumb, the unknown words should not exceed 5 percent.

Context Cues

It would be impossible to teach directly all the words to which children are exposed. Teachers must select the most essential words for direct teaching and provide children with skills that will enable them to increase their reading vocabularies independently. In selecting which word meanings to teach directly, the following guidelines may be used: (1) Is the intended meaning unknown to the child? (2) How important is the concept to understanding the material? and (3) What is the likelihood that the word will soon be encountered again?

Children who read widely can learn a great many words by inferring from context. In fact, there is evidence that for some children extensive reading is just as productive as direct vocabulary instruction in increasing reading vocabulary (Meyer and Cohen 1975).

Children often apply their word-recognition skills to an unknown word to obtain a tentative pronunciation. If their response does not approximate any word in their meaningful vocabulary that makes sense in the sentence, they infer its pronunciation and meaning as well as possible and go on reading. If the word is encountered repeatedly in print, the original inferred meaning is revised and refined to fit differing contexts. Becoming aware of the word's meaning may trigger the realization that the word has been heard before but not seen in print. Some children use a dictionary if they are dissatisfied with the estimated meaning or pronunciation.

The context in which a word is set often determines its meaning (He put the arrow in his *bow*; She put a *bow* in her hair), but it does not always reveal a word's meaning, or even its pronunciation (He took a *bow*). At times more than one sentence must be employed as a context cue. Use of context can assist children in recognizing unfamiliar words, determining the meanings of unknown words, and deciding which meaning of a polysemantic word is most appropriate.

An author can help children learn word meanings from context. After making new key words conspicuous by using italics or bold type, the author can explain or define the term in one of the ways indicated below. In selecting content subject texts, teachers should consider the care that has been given to making new terms understandable.

Research findings (H. A. Robinson 1963; Rankin and Overholser 1969; Klein, Klein, and Bertino 1974) suggest that many fourth-grade children find it difficult to derive word meaning from context. Regardless of how well texts are written, most children need systematic instruction in using context cues. Simply telling children to read the whole sentence and then guess the word's meaning is inadequate. During the initial stages of instruction, the context should be as revealing as possible.

Illustrating, discussing (not only the answers, but how they were arrived at), and providing guided practice in use of the following types of context cues should help children to utilize them.

1. *Synonym.* A more common synonym for the unfamiliar word may (1) appear in parentheses—*avarice* (greed); (2) appear in apposition— He did not *repent,* regret, his actions; (3) be embedded in a sentence— Tom was *exhausted* and Fred was tired too. At times the use of a synonym is too subtle for children to apprehend easily—Rare books cost more because they are *scarce* and in demand.

2. *Antonyms.* The unfamiliar word is contrasted in the sentence with an antonym whose meaning is more likely to be known—Dolores *hastened* to complete the job, but Alice did not hurry. A key to the use of this technique is recognition of such "thought reversing" cues as *but.* An author who thinks a word meaning is quite important may employ a synonym-antonym technique—Mary's speech was *concise*; it was brief, but John's speech was too long.

3. *Definition.* The unfamiliar word is defined: (1) in parentheses—The *caboose* (the last car on the train); (2) in apposition—*Polygamy,* the custom of having more than one wife at a time, is still practiced; (3) embedded in a sentence—The male principal of a private school often is called the *headmaster,* or in a subsequent sentence—Blood flowed from the *lesion.* This wound, etc.; (4) by supplying examples (usually introduced by such words as "such as")—*Odd numbers,* such as 1, 3, 9; (5) by a restatement (often introduced by "that is")—She was *wan*; that is, very pale; and (6) in a footnote.

4. *Experiential background.* The cue is based on the child's past experiences, either with life in general (The horselike animal with black and white stripes is a *zebra*) or language (Nickie was as quiet as a *mouse*). Past experience with language also leads the reader to anticipate words occuring in certain positions, or in a given sequence, or in conjunction with other words.

5. *Summary.* The preceding information is summarized by the unfamiliar word—First they saw an elephant. Then they saw lions and tigers in cages. Adam liked the *zoo.*

6. *Reflection.* The general situation or mood of the sentence or paragraph

provides the cue—The eerie music made me shudder. And when the candle went out, a strong feeling of *trepidation* came over me.

The ability to use context cues depends upon factors other than direct instruction. Reasoning ability is necessary, so teachers often must lead children through a series of reasoning steps. Children with weak word-recognition skills find it difficult to use context cues because too many words remain unrecognized. A meager understanding of vocabulary lessens the chances that a synonym or antonym will provide a cue to the meaning of an unknown word. Past experiences and the concepts derived from them influence the ability to use context, just as the ability to understand relationships influences ability to use the total passage.

Development of a chart following a group discussion may aid some children in recalling what they should do when they encounter an unknown word. Such a chart might be as follows:

1. Read the whole sentence.
2. Think of a word that makes sense in the sentence and fits the letters.
3. If necessary, reread the sentence before it, and read the following sentence.
4. Change the first guess if it does not seem to fit.

When a child uses context successfully the meaning he or she achieves may be correct but incomplete. Consider this sentence: The general was sure that his *mercenaries* would fight more skillfully and bravely than his armed peasants. It is easy to infer that mercenaries are soldiers, but the specific characteristic that distinguishes them from other soldiers (fighting for pay for a foreign country) cannot be inferred from information in the sentence.

Semantic Problems   Even though there are over a half million English words, most communication can be carried on with a relatively small number. For example, Ogden (as cited by Richards 1968) listed 850 words that can be used to express practically any idea that does not call for highly technical terminology. Dolch's list of 220 high-utility words (Dolch 1960) makes up more than 50 percent of the running words in practically any reading material.

One of the problems with English is the fact that many words have more than one meaning. For instance, the polysemantic word *run* is listed in a college dictionary as having 104 separate meanings; even an elementary dictionary lists 46 meanings for it. Word meaning also may range from the concrete to the abstract (a candy *bar*, a sand*bar*, being admitted to the *bar* [which may have two meanings], and Tennyson's "Crossing the *Bar*").

Those interested in determining at what grade level the various meanings of a word are understood by most children may refer to Dale and O'Rourke (1976). Their data, for example, indicate that although 86 percent of fourth graders knew that a *bar* was a place for drinking, only 67 percent of sixth graders knew it could mean a block or barrier, and only 68 percent of high school seniors knew that *bar* is a synonym for *sand bank*.

The problem of alternative meanings is complicated by *homographs*, words that are spelled alike but have different meanings and perhaps pronunciations (*lead*). To further complicate matters, there are *homonyms*, words with the same pronunciation but with different meanings and usually different spellings (*hale, hail*).

Errors in reasoning may occur when a speaker or writer shifts from one meaning of a word to another without noticing or indicating a shift in concepts. Interpretation errors occur when a listener or reader interprets a word as representing a concept different from the one intended by the speaker or writer.

When a printed word has more than one possible pronunciation or meaning, the context in which it is set helps the reader to select the one that fits. Consider the following sentences:

> Amy wanted to run home.
> Jimmy hit a home run.

Although the words *home* and *run* have quite different meanings in the two sentences, most readers automatically select the correct meanings. Of course, understanding the second sentence requires some knowledge of baseball; and if the particular concept is unknown (There was a *run* on the bank), comprehension is hampered.

With an abundance of previous experience involving hearing and saying the word and experiencing it in a variety of meanings, the necessary background is available and the immediate context helps the reader to get set for a particular meaning that fits. Skilled readers know that many words can represent a variety of meanings, and utilize the context to find out which concept the word represents in that particular setting.

The ability to use context may be assessed through use of the cloze procedure (see unit 6, pp. 199–201) using material of appropriate difficulty. Another technique involves having the child guess what a nonsense word probably means. At first, the nonsense word should represent an obviously known word (Ben put some *lom* in his coffee to make it sweet). Later the possible meaning can be less obvious (Joseph drank the *bap*). Moretz and Davey (1974) proposed using a series of sentences, each of which can succeedingly be used to refine the original hypothesis. For example:

1. Helen enjoys eating *zot*.
2. She has to use a sharp knife to cut the *zot*.
3. Francis and Robby like their *zot* well done, but Helen likes hers almost raw.

Explanation and Discussion   Prior to having children read new material, the teacher often selects the words that probably need explanation. In doing so, common words that are used in other than their common meanings should not be overlooked.

To encourage the use of context, these words are usually put on the chalkboard, charts, or cards in phrases or sentences that are read by the children. Then the teacher explains or checks the children's knowledge of each word's meaning, shows illustrative material if available, and gives examples of its use. Finally, in order to check their understanding, the children are asked to suggest additional sentences in which the words can be used.

Although explanation and discussion is a useful procedure, several possible dangers are to be avoided. *Verbalism* (see below) is likely to result if words are explained briefly in terms of other words, without any attempt to relate them to the children's experience. Children should be encouraged to indicate what other meanings a word can have and to discuss which is the most appropriate one for the given context. The number of new words that must be explained in one lesson should not exceed the absorptive capacity of the children. If the number seems excessive, the material probably is too difficult for instructional purposes.

Some teachers do not preteach new words, but ask the children what words gave them trouble after they have read the material. The stated rationale for such a procedure is that (1) it saves time because children will ask about fewer words than the teacher probably would introduce; and (2) the children are more likely to be motivated because learning arises from a felt need. Although this procedure may work well with skilled motivated readers, children with reading problems or uninterested students may either be unaware of their needs or reluctant to admit their weaknesses.

Verbalism   *Verbalism* means vagueness, emptiness, or faultiness of understanding concealed by the use of seemingly appropriate words. At times, school learning involves the memorization of verbal statements that are misunderstood or only partially understood because they have no real connection with the child's experience. Teachers often can recount humorous experiences occasioned by a child's faulty or incomplete understanding (e.g., after being told that *frantic* meant *wild,* a child referred to the "frantic flowers"). Many important concepts in the content subjects are difficult for children to understand because they are highly abstract and have been introduced without sufficient reference to experience.

Teachers often must go beyond mere verbal definition. For example, defining an isthmus as a narrow strip of land connecting two larger bodies of land may result in some unusual conceptions, particularly among children who equate land with dirt and bodies with people. Rather, a teacher should point to such a "land bridge" on a map while introducing the verbal definition. Better yet would be first showing a slide or picture of an actual isthmus. After being shown one example on the map, the children can inspect other maps to find other examples.

The abilities to grasp ideas quickly, to detect the underlying common characteristic that an abstract term represents, and to apply this concept correctly in new situations are very closely related to general intelligence. There are large differences among children in ease of development of concept formation and in learning the meanings of words that represent concepts. Bright children do not need as many examples and illustrations as do other children. But all children need an experiential foundation for clear, accurate concepts; without this one gets verbalism.

Individual Word Study   Children can be encouraged to be curious about new words, to write them down, to look up their meanings and to learn them. The more that children engage in independent reading, the more important it is for them to learn the meanings of new words on their own. Some children prefer to have notebooks, with pages for each letter of the alphabet. Others prefer a separate index card for each word; the cards are kept in alphabetical order (guide cards may be helpful) in an inexpensive filing box. A new word is written on one side of the page or card, and the pronunciation (if needed), definition(s), and one or two illustrative sentences are written on the back. The words should be reviewed periodically.

A resourceful teacher can find many ways to motivate and sustain an interest in individual word study, not the least of which is demonstrating an interest in words herself. Children can be "word detectives" on the trail of strange or interesting words. They can keep individual progress charts of the number of new words learned. Children can report on interesting new words during discussion periods. Occasional team competition can revive lagging interest. Games and contests (Bougere 1968; Lake 1967, 1971; Platts 1970; Dale and O'Rourke 1971, Wagner, Hosier, and Cesinger 1972; and Mallett 1975) may help to stimulate and maintain enthusiasm. Chance (1974) presented ways for using a learning station approach for vocabulary development.

Roots and Affixes   Research suggests that building vocabulary by means of studying prefixes, roots, and affixes is more appropriate for junior and senior high school than for elementary school children, and even then it is more beneficial for brighter students. It takes considerable intelligence to understand why *reporter* (back-carry-performer of the act), literally "one who carries back" should mean "a writer of news stories." The emphasis should be upon recognizing roots and affixes and understanding their possible effect on meaning. Memorizing long lists of affixes is not very productive.

Prefixes. About a quarter of the most common English words, and a higher proportion of those less common, begin with prefixes that have relatively constant meanings. Some of the more easily recognized ones (e.g., *re*tie, *un*broken) are usually taught in the primary grades. A relatively small number account for most of the common words containing prefixes (Stauffer 1942):

ab (from)	abnormal, abuse
ad, ap, at (to)	admit, appear, attract
be (by)	beside, behind
con, com, col (with)	conductor, commercial, collection
de (from)	deduct, defense
dis (apart, not)	disappear, disarm, disrupt
en, em (in)	engage, enjoy, embrace

ex (out)	exit, export
in, im (in, into)	income, impose
in, im (not)	incorrect, impure
ob, of, op (against, away, from)	obstruct, offend, oppose
pre, pro (before, in front of)	prepare, predict, projectile, promote
re (back)	refer, remodel
post (behind)	postpone
super (over, above)	superior, supervisor
trans (across)	transportation
sub (under)	submarine, subject
un (not)	unarmed, unbroken

Root words. According to Breen (1960) there are 82 Latin and 6 Greek roots that occur ten or more times in children's vocabulary. The most common Latin roots are:

fac, fact, fic (to make or do)	factory, fact, fiction
sta, stat (to stand)	static, station
pos, pon (to place, put)	post, opponent, position
fer (to bear, carry)	transfer, ferry, infer
mis, mit (to send)	submit, admission
tend, tens (to stretch)	tendon, tension, extend
vid, vis (to see)	vision, provide
mov, mot (to move)	move, motion
spect, spic (to look, see)	inspection, conspicuous
ven, vent (to come)	convention, event
par (to get ready)	prepare, repair
port (to carry)	export, transport

Suffixes. There are many suffixes in English, the majority of which have more than one meaning. Teaching only the most common meaning of a suffix may create some confusion later for the learner. Suffixes that are both fairly common and have a reasonably constant meaning include:

er, or, ist, ian (performer of)	teacher, sailor, dentist, physician
tion, sion (act of)	temptation, decision
ry, ty, ity (condition of)	finery, safety, purity
al (pertaining to)	formal, musical

ble, able, ible (capable of being)	adaptable, forcible
ment (result of, act of)	judgment, management
ful (full of)	careful, wonderful
man (one who)	policeman
ic (pertaining to)	comic, terrific
ous, ious, eous (like, full of)	joyous, laborious, nauseous
ence, ance (state of)	repentance, persistence
ly, y (in the manner of)	truly, windy

Burmeister (1976b) lists bound morphemes found in four different content areas and suggests ways of using them for increasing reading vocabulary.

Figurative Language   Idioms are ambiguous (Edwards 1974). They can carry either literal or nonliteral meaning depending on the intent of the author. To be understood, an idiom must be known as a unit or deduced from context. Its meaning cannot be arrived at by literal analysis. English is rich in such idiomatic expressions as *blue laws, palm off,* and *lost his head.* When idioms are unfamiliar to children, they should be taught like new words. Children often enjoy depicting the humor in a misunderstood idiom (He hit the roof). Edwards (1975) and Forester (1974) list many common idioms and suggest many ways to teach their meanings. Workbook exercises such as shown in figure 8.1 also may be used.

Similes and metaphors abound in poetry, and their interpretation is worth developing. Some children easily catch on to the meanings of figurative expressions; others have trouble understanding anything that does not have a strictly literal meaning. Not every child understands what is meant by a sky "like a bluebird's wing." Confused or unclear meanings can be clarified in discussion. Sometimes children can be strikingly original when encouraged to think up similes and metaphors on their own. Turner (1976) has suggested a number of techniques for raising children's awareness of figurative language, and sensitivity to it.

Verbal Relationships   Words become efficient tools when their relationships are understood and they have been mentally arranged into categories according to similarities, contrasts, and part-whole relationships. It is helpful for children to learn to classify words under headings, to know synonyms and antonyms, and to understand functional relationships. The kinds of items found in commercially prepared or teacher-made exercises include:

Synonyms
1. A placid person is: calm, pale, passive, unhappy.
2. Another word for *motionless* is: coiled, lasting, still, angry.
3. List all the words you can think of that mean about the same as *big*. Use each in a sentence that brings out its particular meaning.
4. Write a word that means the same as *beautiful*.

Antonyms
1. The opposite of noisy is: loud, quiet, sound, bang.
2. A mouse is tiny, but an elephant is _____.

   Read each sentence carefully to find the idiom that it contains. After each sentence three meanings are given. Choose the meaning that best fits the sentence. Write the letter that stands before this meaning.

   1. By the end of the summer, *time hangs heavy* with us.
      a. Time passes slowly.
      b. Time weighs too much.
      c. Time seems too short.

   7. News of Andy's heart attack comes like a *bolt from the blue*, for he seemed quite well two days ago.
      a. The news is as impossible as thunder in a clear sky.
      b. The news is as unexpected as thunder in a clear sky.
      c. The news hit us like a metal bolt falling out of the sky.

FIGURE 8.1. Part of a practice exercise on interpreting idioms. Taken from Lee C. Deighton, *Vocabulary Development*, revised edition, *The Macmillan Spectrum of Skills*, Level 3, pp. 96–97. Copyright © Macmillan Publishing Co., Inc., 1964, 1973. Reproduced by permission of the publisher.

3. A hostile person is not: active, homely, antagonistic, friendly.
4. Write a word that means the opposite of *enormous*.
5. Do these words have the same or opposite meanings? *increase-reduce*.

Classification

1. Put all the vehicles in one column and all the parts in another column: train, wheel, axle, engine, boat, motor, wagon, rudder, bicycle, brake, seat.
2. List as many things as you can under each of these headings: vegetables, fruits.
3. A *fin* is part of a: bird, fish, plant, clock.

Analogies

1. President is to country as mayor is to: state, city, nation, territory.
2. Glove is to hand as shoe is to _____.
3. Run: walk: : fast: slow, dance, march, talk.
4. Horse: pony: : cow: _____.

In finding answers to questions such as these, a child has to organize concepts and seek the relevant relationships. This is practice in reasoning as well as vocabulary development.

Fine Shades of Meaning Children often fall into the habit of using the same small number of words repeatedly. They do not realize that more exact communication is possible through the use of a variety of words. One of the best ways to stimulate such an interest is to discuss how one can communicate more precisely. If a child says a person is "nice," the teacher could follow up by asking, "Does 'nice' mean 'friendly'? 'Kind'? 'Physically attractive'?"

A tool useful for helping children learn to use more varied and precise language is the thesaurus, a book that contains listings of synonyms, related words, and antonyms. Thesauri suitable for use in the elementary school are available. After an unfamiliar synonym is found, its exact meaning can be checked in a dictionary.

Word origins. Many English words have interesting histories, which enhance their meanings. Some words commemorate real people (quisling, lynch, gerrymander) or mythical people (tantalize, vulcanize, erotic). *Alphabet* comes from the first two letters of the Greek alphabet, *algebra* traces back to Arabic, and *check* comes from the Persian *shah* (meaning king, through the game of chess). Many words have come practically without change from Latin or Greek: melody, radiant, hypocrite. Others have been

BONFIRE

a fire of bones

In the Middle Ages, funeral pyres for human bodies were a necessity in emergencies of war or pestilence. *Bonefires* (fires of bone) they were called. Later, when the custom of burning heretics at the stake became common, *bonefires* was the name applied to the pyres of these victims. The same term was used to designate the burning of articles under proscription, such as heretical books. Later, its meaning was extended to open-air fires for public celebration or for sport — but by this time in the less gruesome spelling *bonfire*, which today is a comparatively harmless word in spite of its grim history.

FIGURE 8.2. Example of the use of a word's origin to develop a clear and vivid meaning. From *Interesting Origins of English Words*, © 1961 by G. & C. Merriam Co., publishers of the Merriam-Webster Dictionaries. Reproduced by permission of the publisher.

borrowed without change from other modern languages: reservoir, kindergarten, piano.

Using such sources as *Interesting Origins of English Words* (Merriam) (see figure 8.2) and *What's in a Name?* and *Podunk and Such Places* (Barnell Loft), teachers can select a few interesting derivations and use them to arouse curiosity about the origins of other words. Bright children can enjoy tracing the origin of words, as well as profit from it. Serious study of word origins is not very practical before the upper grades, and then mainly for the more gifted students.

Using the Dictionary Dictionary use may be initiated with simple picture dictionaries as early as first grade. Commercially prepared or child-made dictionaries can provide practice in using alphabetical order and in interpreting very simple definitions and illustrations.

As children mature, successively more complex dictionaries can be introduced. At the third-reader level and above, many reading series have glossaries in the back of the readers. These brief dictionaries can be used to practice the skills of locating words in alphabetical order, using a pronunciation guide, and interpreting definitions.

The major dictionary skills that should be introduced by the middle grades or sooner are (the first two are further subdivided to illustrate that subskills are needed):

1. Learning words in alphabetical order
   a. Learning the sequence of the alphabet
   b. Determining which letter precedes and follows a given letter
   c. Alphabetically arranging a list of words that all start with different letters
   d. Alphabetically arranging a list of words that start with the same letter
   e. Alphabetically arranging a list of words that start with the same two letters
   f. Opening the dictionary at a point near the word
   g. Using the guide words
2. Using the pronunciation guide
   a. Recognizing division between syllables. Entry words are not always syllabicated in the same way as their phonetic respellings (farm-er, fär'-mər).
   b. Interpreting primary and secondary accent marks
   c. Understanding the pronunciation key and marks
   d. Pronouncing the phonetic respellings
3. Interpreting typical dictionary definitions
4. Selecting the definition that fits a given context
5. Looking up the meaning of an unfamiliar synonym given as the definition
6. Relating derived forms to the basic word
7. Interpreting information about word origins
8. Distinguishing acceptable current usage from obsolete, archaic, slang, dialect, or colloquial usage

Teachers should study carefully the pronunciation guide of the dictionary in use, because there are important differences among dictionaries

Choosing the Right Definition _____

When you look up a word in the dictionary, you often find that the word has several definitions. You need to read all of these definitions. Then pick out the one that best fits into the sentence you are reading to give it the right meaning.

Read the story below. On your paper, copy the letter for each blank. Fill in the best meaning for each underlined word in the story. The definitions are given in the box after the story.

Ramon ran to the window and raised **(a)** the shade. Thank goodness it wasn't raining! It was rare **(b)** to have rain this time of year, but Ramon had been worried that the picnic might be spoiled.

Ramon lived on the low, grassy plains **(c)** of Venezuela. From his window he had a plain **(d)** view of vast grasslands, with a range **(e)** of mountains in the distance.

When he got downstairs, his mother was at the range **(f)** cooking potato salad for the picnic. "It's plain **(g)** food, but it's good," she said.

"Where's Dad?" asked Ramon.

"He's out on the range **(h)** rounding up some cattle," Mom said. Ramon's father raised **(i)** cattle for a living.

Soon the rest of the family had gathered for the picnic. All Ramon's cousins were there. By the time Dad got back, everyone was hungry.

The steaks were ready in a few minutes, for Dad liked them rare **(j)** . The kids were having such a good time that Dad had to raise **(k)** his voice when he called, "Let's eat!"

plain
1. a broad stretch of level land
2. open, clear, not blocked
3. simple, not fancy

raise
1. to cause to rise, lift
2. to make larger, greater, louder, etc.
3. to cause to grow, produce

range
1. a row or line, especially of connected mountains
2. open land over which cattle graze
3. a cooking stove

rare
1. not often found, not common
2. not completely cooked, partly raw

FIGURE 8.3. Exercise to develop the ability to select the correct dictionary definition. Taken from Nila B. Smith, *Be a Better Reader*, Level B, Basic Skills Edition, p. 169. Copyright © 1977 by Prentice-Hall, Inc. Reproduced by permission of the publisher.

in the phonetic symbols used. For example, some dictionaries use a schwa (ə) for most unstressed vowel sounds while others have a different symbol for each letter that represents an unstressed vowel sound. In two different dictionaries, *future* is phonetically spelled as fū'-chĕr and fyōō'-chər. Children can easily become confused when they encounter two differing sets of phonetic symbols in the materials they are using. There is a trend to use fewer phonetic symbols in dictionaries.

A good dictionary definition has two elements: (1) it states a class or category to which the concept belongs; and (2) it gives one or more descriptive characteristics that distinguish this concept from other members of the category. A dictionary defines a *fanatic* as "a person with an extreme and increasing enthusiasm or zeal, especially in religious or political matters." The category is "person"; the rest tells how fanatics differ from other persons. Children can be helped to analyze definitions, construct their own definitions for familiar words, and compare them with those given in a dictionary.

Synonyms often are given as definitions. This is sufficient if the synonym is already understood or is clearly and understandably defined. Learning synonyms is one good way to enlarge one's vocabulary, especially when the dictionary explains fine distinctions or nuances, as among *old, elderly, aged, mature, venerable,* and *superannuated.*

Just as with other reading skills, children show differences in their ability to learn and employ dictionary skills. Because not all children will be working at the same level, dictionaries of varying degrees of difficulty should be available in the classroom. Teachers may find it necessary to provide group and individual instruction and practice in dictionary skills. Practice exercises can be found in many reading workbooks (see figure 8.3), and some dictionaries also provide lesson plans. Probably the most effective learning occurs when the application of these skills is of practical utility to the child.

Materials for Developing Reading Vocabulary

The following materials may be useful in helping children to increase their reading vocabularies:

Macmillan Reading Spectrum: Vocabulary Development (Macmillan). Series of 6 programmed workbooks for grades 4–6; allows for individualized practice.

Wordly Wise (Educators). Series of 9 workbooks for grades 4–12. Each book contains 30 lessons which have several kinds of exercises.

Scope/Visuals (Scholastic). Series of spirit masters for use with junior high students who are reading at a fourth- to sixth-grade level. Covers homonyms, dictionary skills, multiple-meaning words, and figurative language.

What's in a Name? and *Podunk and Such Places* (Barnell Loft). The first set of 6 books focuses on people's names; the latter set on names of places. Useful for introducing etymology.

Wordcraft Vocabulary Programs (Communacad). Two (grades 4–6, 6–8) of the four available levels are suitable for use in the elementary and junior high school.

Target Green (Field). Lessons on word classification, use of context, homonyms, homographs, synonyms, antonyms, roots and affixes; for grades 4–6. *Target Orange* emphasizes use of a context, derivatives, figurative language and connotations; for grades 7–9.

Fun with Words (Dexter and Westbrook). Series of gamelike exercises for developing interest in word meanings; 6 levels.

Synonimibles and Phantonyms (Curriculum Associates). The first contains 125 puzzles with clues in which two given synonyms must be related to an unknown third. In the latter, the antonym is concealed in the clue sentence; 110 puzzles at 5 levels. Suitable for intermediate grades.

Homonym Cards, Antonym Cards, Homophone Cards (DLM). Three games in which the basic task is matching pairs of pictured words.

Press and Check Bingo Games (Milton Bradley). Four bingo-like games for affixes, homonyms, synonyms and antonyms, and abbreviations and contractions.

The Plus Ten Vocabulary Booster Program (Webster). Structured vocabulary-building program for aiding intermediate graders with content-subject vocabulary. Contains workbooks, literature text, tapes, and mastery tests.

THE NATURE OF READING COMPREHENSION

What Is Reading Comprehension?

The ultimate goal of reading instruction is to develop individuals who comprehend what they read. Words occur in smaller groups (phrases, clauses) and larger groups (sentences), which in turn are organized into paragraphs and series of paragraphs. Certain subskills must be acquired in order to extract information from printed material. First, the learner must be able to recognize and decode individual words. Once word-recognition and decoding skills have been learned, the child must be able to obtain the meanings of these printed words rapidly, relying on memory or inferring from context. The learner must be able to detect the syntactic relations that hold between words, and to relate the resulting information to previous knowledge.

It is generally agreed that reading comprehension is a complex process involving high-level cognitive skills. It is not a purely passive, receptive process, but an active process in which the reader brings general knowledge and specific knowledge in the area discussed by the writer to bear on the pattern of words symbolized by the print. Many writers have emphasized the importance of what the reader brings to the printed or written word. Their point of view is typified by Dale (1976, p. 4): "I define reading as putting meaning into printed symbols in order to get meaning out of these symbols." Y. Goodman and Greene (1977) stated the same idea somewhat differently: "The more we observe the reading process, the more we realize that readers who work on getting meaning bring all of their knowledge of language, all of their relevant life experiences to bear in an effort to make sense out of a heretofore unfamiliar story."

Recently an increased number of theoretical models of reading comprehension have emerged (see Singer and Ruddell 1976), but these models are yet to be empirically tested. Because so much is still unknown about reading comprehension, our instructional procedures and materials continue to be based upon accumulated experience more than on research evidence.

Linguistic Views of Comprehension   The relationship between the spoken and written forms of language has been discussed in unit 1 (see pp. 4–7). There are differences of opinion among linguists concerning what language is, how it is acquired, and how to describe it (R. E. Hodges 1972). Many linguists assume that reading comprehension is heavily dependent on the comprehension of spoken language. Thus they recommend that reading comprehension can be improved by increasing the ability to understand spoken language, or suggest that the key is to get children to apply to reading the processes they already use for understanding spoken language.

Unfortunately, theoretical models of language that might provide a basis for a theory of reading comprehension have not yet been developed to the point where they can be translated into teaching methods and materials. For example, O'Donnell and King (1974) found a substantial relationship between skill in discovering deep structure of sentences and reading comprehension, but their efforts to develop a procedure for helping children to discover deep structure were not successful. As for teaching listening comprehension in order to improve reading comprehension, Kennedy and Weener (1973) found that if the goal was to improve reading comprehension, time spent on reading comprehension practice had more payoff than a similar amount of time spent in developing listening comprehension; but there was some carry-over from listening to reading.

K. Goodman and F. Smith have emphasized that reading is a process in which the reader formulates hypotheses or guesses about meaning, and as he or she reads ahead the hypotheses are either confirmed, or rejected and revised. It does not seem important to Goodman whether, in oral or silent reading, the reader produces the exact words of the writer so long as the reader responds correctly to the deep structure of meaning and produces an equivalent surface structure for that meaning. But linguists have not as yet demonstrated how we can get children to improve their ability to discover deep structure.

Logical Analysis of Reading Comprehension There also have been attempts to classify types or levels of reading comprehension logically. Bloom's taxonomy (Bloom et al. 1956), which is a classification of hierarchically arranged educational objectives, was adapted by Barrett (R. J. Smith and Barrett 1974) to produce a classification of reading objectives. Barrett's taxonomy used four main comprehension headings: literal recognition and recall,[1] inference, evaluation, and appreciation, each of which had further subdivisions. For example, literal comprehension tasks involved recognition or recall of details, main ideas, sequence, comparison, cause-effect relationships, and character traits. It seems evident that some of these may be directly stated in the material or may have to be inferred, so that whether a particular instance is literal or inferential needs to be judged. Beatty (1976) also modified Bloom's taxonomy to establish eight categories of reading comprehension skills: recall, translation, apprehension, extrapolation, application, analysis, synthesis, and evaluation.

---

1. An earlier version (see Clymer 1968) differentiated between recognition and recall, and included "reorganization" as a main heading.

A very widely used classification (N. B. Smith 1972) employs four main headings, often with an implied hierarchical order: (1) literal comprehension (getting the primary stated meaning); (2) interpretation (probing for greater depth of meaning); (3) critical reading (evaluating and making a personal judgment); and (4) creative reading (going beyond the implications derived from the material).

Reading comprehension also has been operationally defined in terms of a number of explicitly stated behaviorial objectives (for example, see Chester 1976). Some authors, like Otto (1976), are convinced that the way to improve reading comprehension is to help pupils to sharpen specific skills that are related to the process of comprehending.

Statistical Analysis of Reading Comprehension   Attempts have been made to analyze reading comprehension by giving many different kinds of comprehension tests to a large group of high school students and analyzing the results by the statistical technique of factor analysis. Three different analyses of the same data came out with somewhat different conclusions.

The data were collected and first analyzed by F. B. Davis (1968, 1971), who reported two vocabulary factors (recalling word meanings, and drawing inferences about a word from context), and three comprehension factors (obtaining the literal sense meaning of details; weaving together the ideas in context; and recognizing an author's purpose, attitude, tone, mode, and techniques). Spearritt (1972), reanalyzing Davis's data, found four factors: recalling word meanings; drawing inferences; following the structure of a passage; and recognizing a writer's purpose, attitude, tone, and mood. R. L. Thorndike (1973–74) also reanalyzed Davis's data and found only two factors: word knowledge and reasoning in reading. Spearritt had acknowledged that while he was able to distinguish three comprehension factors besides vocabulary, they were highly intercorrelated.

Similar analyses have not been performed at the elementary school level, but we can draw some conclusions from the correlations reported among the subtests of reading tests. In the first and second grades the correlations between word recognition and comprehension are very high; this relationship diminishes as one goes up the grades, but is still substantial (around .60) in the upper grades. Correlations among different kinds of comprehension tests are high but not quite as high as the reliabilities of the separate tests, suggesting that there is some differentiation, even though in general a child who is quite high on one comprehension test is likely to be high on other kinds of comprehension tests.

Implications of Models of Reading Comprehension   It would be impossible to cover all the models of comprehension, let alone their implications, in this unit. Many have been summarized by Harker (1975), who concluded that all of the available models of reading comprehension attempt to describe the process without suggesting ways in which the process can be taught.

If reading comprehension involves a variety of skills it is easy to conclude that practice should be given for each type of skill. If it is reasoning while reading (aside from vocabulary knowledge) one might conclude that what is needed is training in reasoning. We are not sure how to improve a child's ability to reason, or to what extent it is possible to do so. Such training needs content to reason about, and in the absence of information to the contrary, that content might as well be reading content. Reasoning about a science experiment may involve different cognitive skills from understanding the sequence of events leading up to a war. The use of a variety of reading materials and types of questions provides a broad base for transfer or application of reasoning in many kinds of reading situations.

Factors That Influence Reading Comprehension

The ability to think, reason, and solve problems—in other words, general intelligence—has a strong relationship to ability to understand while reading. Nevertheless, a number of other factors also influence the ability to comprehend.

A minimum essential for reading comprehension is an adequate sight vocabulary and the ability to use decoding skills in conjunction with context cues. Research indicates that good comprehension requires fairly automatic word recognition (Seifort 1976). The more attention is required in a struggle to figure out the words, the less attention can be paid to the search for meaning. Many poor comprehenders are concerned with recognizing or decoding each word and fail to use the relationships between words that could speed up the recognition process. As N. H. Mackworth (1977, p. 11) has put it: "The child who reads one word at a time is unable to make any predictions as to what will come next. His entire verbal brain is occupied with the one word. Therefore, his comprehension will be poor and there will be no activation of an internal model of a forthcoming word."

Of course the child's meaningful vocabulary, discussed at length earlier in this unit, is a very important factor in comprehension. This includes understanding of the alternative meanings of polysemantic words and skill in determining which of several meanings of the word fits the present context.

Ability to grasp the meaning of word groups of increasing size—phrases, sentences, paragraphs—develops along with word-recognition skills and reading vocabulary.

At all levels of maturity, degree of mastery of language puts realistic limits on reading comprehension. Once word recognition is no longer a major problem, children's reading comprehension is likely to approximate their listening comprehension because it is unlikely that they will understand printed material that they could not understand if it were read to them. Thus children's language competence is an important factor for reading comprehension.

People's experiential backgrounds affect comprehension in that the concepts formed through past experiences influence their interpretation of what they read. Prior concepts aid comprehension by allowing the reader to bring meaning to the printed page. The more similar the author's and reader's experiential background, the more complete the communication can be. A lack of experience can seriously hamper comprehension. For example, a rural child who has never seen a traffic light probably will have difficulty understanding a story about how a child used such a device to cross the street safely. At times restricted concepts also interfere with comprehension.

Interest is a potent factor in comprehension, especially for poor readers (Vaughn 1975). This variable is considered in detail in unit 10.

Still another factor affecting comprehension is cognitive style, which is the individual's preferred and habitual way of responding to situations calling for some sort of intellectual behavior. One dimension of cognitive style that has been much studied is field independence-dependence. The field-independent individual is able to analyze his or her perceptions and identify significant details without much assistance; the field-dependent person often requires the help of specific guidance and direction (Davey 1976, Blanton and Bullock 1973). Another dimension is global-analytical. The global person tends to get the overall picture or general idea without paying much attention to details; the analytical person concentrates on details, sometimes to excess. Still another dimension is reflective-impulsive; reflective children are likely to consider alternatives before responding, while impulsive children often respond with the first possibility that comes to mind. Kagan (1965) found that reflective children have some advantage in early reading, but it seems probable that in the later stages of reading, either extreme may be detrimental.

A Comparison of Listening and Reading Comprehension

The comprehension of spoken and written language requires (1) sufficient mastery of the language in which the message is framed; (2) an adequate level of mental ability that allows the listener/reader to follow the reasoning presented; and (3) active attention by the listener/reader.

There are also differences between listening and reading comprehension. (1) In reading, printed words must be recognized if meaning is to be acquired. (2) Whereas, to a large extent, listeners have the material organized for them by the speaker's phrasing, expression, and intonation, readers must organize the material into meaningful units. Also, nonverbal cues such as facial expressions and gestures are available to the listener. (3) In listening, the rate is controlled by the speaker; in reading, by the reader. (4) Unless the speaker is willing to repeat (or the message is recorded), the listener does not have the same opportunities as the reader to pause, reflect, or review a certain point. This requires the listener to be more constantly attentive than the reader.

Whether one comprehends better when reading or listening seems to be related to one's level of reading ability. Although individuals vary, a review of the research led Tinker and McCullough (1975) to conclude that (1) at the lower grade levels and for below-average readers, listening comprehension tends to be equal to or better than reading comprehension; and (2) for skilled readers, reading comprehension tends to be equal to or better than listening comprehension. Swalm (1974) found that there were no significant differences between comprehension in the two modes for average second- through fourth-grade readers.

Those most likely to benefit from instruction and practice in auding (listening with understanding) are children who are just learning to read, and poor reading comprehenders whose reading problem seems related to an inability to understand spoken language. Children with word-recognition problems, particularly older severely disabled readers, also should benefit from some instruction in auding. Such children often can learn content-subject concepts through listening. If disabled readers do not acquire concepts continuously as they progress through school, they are likely to encounter reading comprehension problems in the later grades even after they overcome their word-recognition problems because they will have large gaps in their knowledge.

Suggestions for teaching listening comprehension may be found in Russell and Russell (1959) and Wagner, Hosier, and Blackman (1962); its possible impact on reading has been discussed by Lundsteen (1971). Among the various commercially available materials for developing listening comprehension are the *SRA Reading Laboratories,* which present a four-step listening technique (TQLR): Tune-in, Question, Listen, and Review.

To facilitate transfer from listening to reading comprehension, Cunningham (1975) suggested using two parallel lessons. In the first, the children listen and respond in certain ways; in the second, which follows immediately, the children read and respond in the same ways. A sample lesson presented by Cunningham has a six-step process for developing the ability to sequence: (1) a purpose is set for listening; (2) the material is read to the pupils; (3) the major events are written on strips of paper and rearranged in correct sequential order by the children; (4) the children are given passages to read and are told they should read in order to be able to put the events in order; (5) after they have finished reading, the children are given mimeographed sheets on which they must rearrange events that are not in sequence; and (6) the class shares their results and explanations.

LEARNING TO INTERPRET THOUGHT UNITS

A phrase is a group of two or more words that forms a meaning unit with the significance of a single part of speech. A phrase can be used in the role of a preposition (*in regard to*), an adjective (*of great value*), an adverb (*in a hurry*), a verb (*used to go*), or a noun (*eating pie*). Many phrases can be replaced by a single word without changing the meaning. Thus, the indicated phrases are approximately equivalent to *about, valuable, hurriedly, went,* and *pie.*

Improving Phrase Reading

Emphasis should be placed on the phrase as a unit of meaning rather than as a perceptual unit. Eye-movement photographs show that average readers in the sixth grade make about 1.2 fixations (pauses) per word. Therefore, even allowing for the probability that some unfamiliar words require more than one look and thus influence this average, it seems evident that most children do not perceive phrases in one fixation. If phrase cards are used for recognition practice, more exposure time should be allowed than if a single word were being used because two or more fixations will probably be required.

Oral reading provides the opportunity to determine whether children read in phrases and use inflection and accent appropriately, thereby indicating that they are probably reading for meaning. Word-by-word reading can adversely affect comprehension because it not only breaks up the natural meaning units, but also puts a strain on short-term memory. If new visual information arrives from the eye to the brain before the brain has processed the preceding input, either the first or second bit of information may be disregarded. Short-term memory can hold only about five or six units, so a word-by-word reader, who tends to read more slowly and haltingly than a fluent reader, tends to forget the first part of a sentence before the end of it is reached. A child who has "chunked" a ten-word sentence into four phrases will usually have no difficulty recalling the content of the sentence, while a child who has read it as ten separate words will probably find that short-term memory has been overtaxed.

Faulty phrasing, in which a child joins words that belong in separate phrases and pauses between words that are part of the same phrase, naturally goes with poor comprehension. It shows a failure to obtain the correct meanings for important words, failure to grasp the syntax of the sentence, or both.

The phrasing ability of most children develops naturally in the setting of reading for meaning. There are, however, some children who need assistance before they can make any progress in phrasing appropriately. Teachers should encourage children to read sentences in the same way as they would speak them, thereby helping them to understand the relation between spoken and written language. Children should also be shown how placing emphasis on different words within a sentence can alter the meaning (See unit 6, p. 217). It is helpful for teachers to provide a model by reading a sentence or two to children and then ask them to continue reading in the same way, or to take turns reading alternate sentences, or to read in unison with her.

Children can be made aware of phrases by asking oral and written questions, such as the following, which require an answer in phrase form:

1. Where would you go to buy bread? _____ to the store _____ to the street
   _____ to the school
2. Robins usually build their nests (1) _____ in the water (2) _____ in a
   tree (3) _____ in the ground.
3. Which of these are places where a family is most likely to live? _____ in
   an apartment _____ in a factory _____ in a cottage.

Grouping material in phrases for the child may improve the comprehension ability of previously poor comprehenders who have adequate word-recognition skills (Cromer 1968; Oakan, Wiener, and Cromer 1971). The teacher can construct or use workbook exercises in which the phrases are separated by spaces (Fat cats   run slowly) (see figure 8.4) or underlined (Jack ran to the door). The child is instructed to read until he comes to the space or not to pause until he comes to the end of an underlined part. For further suggestions for overcoming inadequate phrasing, consult Harris and Sipay (1975, pp. 463–66).

Comprehending Sentences

Sentences are the natural units of meaning in both spoken and written language (Huey 1908). An essential concept that beginning readers need to grasp is the idea that sentences are composed of separate words, which can be arranged in a great variety of sequences to express different ideas. Some young children are unaware that sentences are composed of separate words. Some are also unaware of the spoken or written boundaries of words.

Children should be encouraged to read dialogue as if the characters were speaking. When words are pronounced at about the same rate and with the same voice stress and inflections that the character would use, meaning comes as easily as if the reader were listening. As long as the material employs words the children understand and can recognize, and uses familiar sentence patterns, the reading of sentences presents no particular problems. Difficulties begin to occur when the complexity of sentence patterns in the reading materials exceeds that which the children are accustomed to hear and speak.

Studies suggest that young children can better comprehend reading material which closely resembles their own language patterns or the sentence patterns that appear frequently in oral language. Such findings have

The players / are divided / into two teams. / On a table / at one end / of the room / is placed / a dish of /shelled corn / and a knife. / The leader / of each team / puts as many / kernels / or grains / of corn / as he can / on his knife / and carries them / to the goal / at the other end / of the room. / There / he must drop / the kernels / of corn / into a cup. / He then returns / and gives the knife / to the second member / of his team, / who carries / as many kernels / of corn / on his knife / as he can / and so on / until each one / of the team / has tried. /

When all / have finished, / the kernels of corn / in each cup / are counted. / The team / that has / the most kernels / of corn / wins. /

FIGURE 8.4. Part of a workbook exercise intended to develop efficient phrase reading and to diminish frequency of regressions. Taken from Ullin W. Leavell and Betty D. Via, *Challenges to Meet*, p. 117. The Reading Essentials Series, copyright © 1973 by Steck-Vaughn Co. Reprinted by permission of the publisher, Steck-Vaughn Co.

led to recommendations that children would benefit from control over sentence patterns (Tatham 1970). Theoretically this control could be accomplished most easily by using a language-experience approach. It should be realized, however, that using familiar or common patterns alone may not increase comprehension. Jongsma (1974) found that the performance of fourth graders did not significantly differ on the original form of a standardized reading-comprehension test and on a rewritten version containing high-frequency oral-language patterns.

Generally, active sentences (*Joel saw Cheryl*) are more readily understood than those written in the passive voice (*Cheryl was seen by Joel*). Many readers, especially the young, often do not recognize the subtle difference in emphasis ("Joel" in the first sentence, "Cheryl" in the second).

Other sentence structures may cause children problems.[2] Malicky (1975–76), who found that first- and second-grade children had more difficulty understanding sentences in which specific items were deleted (*They think that I am small* vs. *They think I am small*), concluded that

---

2. A measure of sentence complexity has been devised by Botel and Granowsky (1972).

many of the short, fragmentary sentences found in beginning reading materials were difficult for young children to understand. Even some older children have difficulty understanding that "you" is implied in the imperative, "Climb the tree." and even more difficulty with echoic questions such as "Climb the tree?" (Wolfram 1976). As Pearson (1974–75) found, grammatical complexity is often an aid rather than a hindrance to comprehension and recall. For example, reducing sentence length may reduce grammatical complexity. Consider: Because the chain broke, the machine stopped. This equals: The chain broke. The machine stopped. But the second version places a new burden on the child—inferring the cause-effect relationship which is indicated by *because* in the more complex sentence.

Poor readers had difficulty understanding sentences with embedded clauses (The boy who hit the girl ran away) but not sentences with conjoined clauses (The boy hit the girl and ran away) (Menyuk 1976). According to Guthrie (1973), comprehension of verbs and function words in reading sentences silently is determined more by syntactic cues, while comprehension of nouns and modifiers is based more on semantic cues. In his study, good readers and disabled readers made the same types of errors in a sentence comprehension task, but the poor readers made more of them.

Although understanding individual sentences is important and provides a minimum basis for comprehension, in order to become a skilled reader one must not only be able to understand the relationships of words within sentences, but also the relations between sentences and paragraphs. The meaning of printed material is cumulative, building from the relationships of words in sentences to relationships of sentences in a paragraph, and relationships of paragraphs in a selection. The reader must understand these relationships and be able to relate the content of each level to the meaning of the whole.

Neuwirth (1976) pointed out that three features appear in every written sentence. These features, which may facilitate comprehension, are not only predictable, but also redundant in that the information provided by one overlaps or duplicates that provided by the others:

1. *Syntactic cues,* which involve word order and the knowledge of the relations this indicates. In the sentence "A boy kissed a girl," the word order allows the reader to comprehend who did what to whom.
2. *Pattern markers* (e.g., inflections and function words), which signal

the grammatical functions of words and the relationships between words. For instance, the general relational structure of a simple type of sentence is revealed in "A (subject) (verb)ed the (object)."

3. *Punctuation and capitalization,* which indicate the limits of grammatical units by setting off phrases, clauses, and the beginnings and ends of sentences.

As the skilled reader scans each sentence, the syntax indicates units such as phrases and clauses by which information may be "chunked"; this requires fewer units to be stored in memory. The chunks of meaning already absorbed provide a context for predicting the meanings of subsequent chunks.

Checking the Ability to Comprehend Sentences   Children who find it difficult to understand single sentences usually become readily apparent during daily reading lessons when they cannot answer the comprehension questions or perform the workbook exercises. More formal checks may be made by having the children match sentences with pictures as is done in standardized sentence comprehension tests. Another technique (Simons 1971) involves having the child choose which two of three sentences have the same deep structure. For example:

1. The boy hit the ball.
2. The boy was hit by the ball.
3. The ball was hit by the boy.

Similar items may also be used as a teaching device.

Improving Ability to Understand Sentences

Reading interesting stories to children is one way to build listening comprehension of longer and more complex sentences. Hopefully, increasing the ability to understand spoken sentences will facilitate the comprehension of similar written sentences. As most children increase their word-recognition skills, enlarge their sight vocabularies, learn to read in phrases, and utilize punctuation, their ability to comprehend printed sentences improves.

When children exhibit difficulty in understanding sentences, reasons for their difficulties should be sought and corrected. If weak word recognition or word meaning is not interfering, weak comprehenders can be provided with simple sentences and asked specific questions that focus their attention (Who? What? Where? How? When? Why?).

Signal Words   Understanding the use of signal words which introduce, connect, order, and relate individual ideas to larger concepts aids comprehension. Signal words include conjunctions, prepositions, connectives, and phrases which serve similar functions. Among the signal words likely to be encountered by children are:

More information to follow: also, and, another, as well as, besides, finally, furthermore, in addition to, in conclusion, moreover.

Opposite idea to follow: although, as a matter of fact, but, either . . . or (implies alternative), even if, however, in spite of, instead of, nevertheless, on the other hand, rather, still, yet.

Cause indicated: as a result of, because, due to, in order to, on account of, since.

Effect indicated: as a consequence, as a result, consequently, so, so as to, so that, therefore.

Exceptions to follow: all but, except.

Conditions to be met: after, as soon as, before, following, if (also may indicate a supposition), provided that, should, while, without, unless, until.

Comparison to be made: as, before . . . after, like, once . . . now, some . . . others, than.

Examples to follow (These words are often followed by *is* or *are*): examples, for example, kinds, ordinal numbers (e.g., (1) . . .; (2) . . .), others, several, some, such as, the following, types, ways. (Wright 1965)

Teaching children the use of signal words may be begun at about fourth-reader level, using examples found in their reading materials. From first through fourth grade, children may have difficulty understanding conjunctions, particularly *when, so, but, or, where, while, how, that,* and *if* (Stoodt 1972). Understanding the conditional (*if-then*) is difficult for fourth graders, especially when the effect must be inferred (Klein 1975). Children in grades 4–6 may have problems understanding clauses introduced by *thus, which, however, although,* and *yet* (Robertson 1968). Even some junior high school students do not know the meanings of various function words including prepositions, coordinate conjunctions, correlatives (neither/nor), and relative pronouns (Marcus 1974).

Difficulty in understanding complex or compound sentences may be due to unfamiliarity with the meanings of connectives, such as the following, which often introduce dependent or subordinate clauses (note that many are also listed above as signal words):

Who, which, what, that, from, whom, to which
How, like, so as, so that, in order to
Because, as soon as, before, while, as, after, following
If, unless, provided that, whether, should
As well as, all but, hardly, except, without, although
However, moreover, therefore, nevertheless.

Rodgers (1974) listed, in order of frequency, the 20 connectives that occurred most frequently in content-subject texts used in grades 6 to 12 and whose meanings were essential to expressing the relationships between expressed ideas: *but, if, when, because, however, as, although, thus, then, while, for example, since, also, therefore, so, even, perhaps, yet, such as, in fact.* Connectives that performed only a joining function (e.g., *and*) were not considered in this study.

Apparently the position of a connective in a sentence influences performance. For example, Rodgers found that *although* was understood by half the children in his study when it occurred in the initial position, but was understood by only one-third of the same students when it occurred in the middle of a sentence.

Children can be aided in locating the subject and main predicate, an essential for comprehension, in complex and compound sentence structures. For instance, for the sentence "By paying a small fee, a farmer can have water pumped to his fields, while he looks on," children can be asked, "Who pays the fee?" and "What does the farmer get for his money?" Children also can (1) be asked to express the same idea in different words; (2) be given guided practice in constructing sentences using particular connectives or signal words; or (3) be asked to restate a complex sentence in several sentences, one for each separate idea expressed.

DEVELOPING READING COMPREHENSION

Assessing Comprehension

Accurate, reliable assessments of a child's reading comprehension are not easy to attain. What we usually do to measure comprehension is take a sample of behavior and assume that the child's responses are an indicator of usual ability to comprehend. What we often forget is that this small sample may not be truly indicative of the child's ability to read other materials of different interest value, content, and difficulty, or to read for different purposes.

Standardized norm-referenced tests, criterion-referenced tests, and mastery tests that accompany a published reading program are often used to assess comprehension. One limitation of standardized tests is that some items are not passage dependent (Pyrczak 1975, Tuinman 1973–74); that is, the child may be able to answer some of the questions without even reading the selection. Pyrczak and Axelrod (1976) cited three reasons why an item may lack passage dependency: (1) it deals with common knowledge, so can be answered from experience alone; (2) the answer may be revealed by material in previous questions on the same passage; and (3) the correct answer may stand out because it is longer, more precisely stated, or otherwise distinctive.

Another technique that may be used to assess or to monitor comprehension is the maze technique (Guthrie et al. 1974). Basically, it involves selecting a series of 120-word passages from graded materials that have not been previously read. Each sentence is modified by deleting every fifth or tenth word and providing three choices for it. This modified cloze test is read silently by the children, who are to select the appropriate word from among the three choices (the correct answer and two incorrect answers, one of which is the same part of speech as the correct answer, the other a different part of speech).

Teachers should not wait until a standardized test or mastery test is given before assessing comprehension. There should be ongoing assessment, the frequency of which will depend upon how well the child has mastered the skills; the weaker the skill or ability, the more frequent the need for assessment. Daily reading lessons provide an excellent opportunity to sample a child's ability to comprehend written language. Comprehension questions may be answered orally or in writing. After the questions have been answered, they can be compared during a group session, and the answers about which there is some disagreement or question can be discussed as to why certain responses are correct, why some are more acceptable than others, and why others are unacceptable. If a child is having difficulty answering questions, the reasons for the difficulty should be determined.

Comprehension Questions

Some teachers are content to ask only the exact comprehension questions found in the teachers manual. Although these questions can be used as a basis for checking comprehension, teachers should go beyond what the manual suggests and gear the questions to the needs of children.

It is not easy to formulate good comprehension questions. Poorly worded, vague, or misleading questions are difficult to answer. Useful suggestions for formulating questions are provided by Hunkins (1972, 1976) and Shuman (1976).

Many questions should be based on covergent thinking—there being one correct answer, or a response that is clearly the best of the alternatives offered. Acceptable answers to such questions need not be discussed; when problems arise, the teacher should explain how one can arrive at the answer. Other questions do not have one correct answer, but allow a variety of acceptable responses; they encourage divergent thinking. In such cases, children should be encouraged to discuss why they made a given response. When children have difficulty with divergent thinking, teachers should explain why one answer may be just as acceptable as another, or more acceptable.

Literal comprehension, the most basic level of comprehension, makes the least demands on reasoning ability. The most frequent type of question asked by teachers calls for the recognition and recall of factual information (Guszak 1967, Ruddell and Williams 1972, Schafer 1976). Perhaps this situation exists, at least in part, because factual questions are easiest to formulate and answer. There is nothing wrong with understanding what the author said. Rather, it is excessive reliance on literal comprehension questions that is inappropriate.

High reading groups are more likely to be asked questions requiring inferences, evaluation, explanation, and conjecture; lower groups are asked mainly factual questions. Though such practices may be somewhat in keeping with children's abilities, there is the danger that factual questions may be overemphasized to the point of making reading a dull question-answer period. Children in low reading groups should be afforded the opportunity to develop their comprehension beyond the strictly factual level.

The results of types of teacher questions on student achievement are still not clear (Rosenshine 1976), but it seems reasonable that one should attempt to include both lower- and higher-level comprehension questions. According to Medley (1977), certain limited research findings suggest that children of low socioeconomic status tend to make more progress in reading when they are asked a high proportion of easy factual questions, while middle-class children tend to do better with a high proportion of challenging questions that involve reasoning and judgment. For children with limited intelligence or reasoning ability, more factual questions may be employed; for the gifted, many less.

Some writers use the terms "factual questions" and "reading for details" almost interchangeably, often implying that the answers to both types of questions are directly stated in the text. While this may be true for some items (*Sentence*: Judy's hat was red. *Question*: What color was Judy's hat?), details are not always directly stated. Even some questions beginning with "why" and "how" actually involve literal rather than inferential comprehension because the author has explicitly stated the answer to the question (*Statement*: George went to the store to buy meat. *Question*: Why did George go to the store?). At other times, details must be inferred or the reader must understand certain relationships in order to be able to answer a question that has been labeled "factual" or "detail." Whether a question (and therefore the type of comprehension involved) is factual or inferential will depend mainly upon how the information needed to answer the question is worded in the reading material and the wording of the question.

The simplest type of factual question to formulate and answer involves repeating the exact words of the selection (*Sentence*: A bustle is a wire contraption that fits under a woman's dress. *Question*: What is a bustle?). It is possible to answer such questions merely by recalling the printed words without understanding their meaning. A child who continually responds with *verbatim* answers from the text should be encouraged to put the answer in other words. If the child is unable to do so, the teacher should suspect that either the child really does not understand the material or does not possess the language skills necessary for demonstrating comprehension.

Questions that are paraphrased versions of the text usually are more difficult to formulate and answer than verbatim questions. However, they are more revealing of whether or not the material was really understood. Of course, the ability to answer paraphrased questions is in part dependent upon whether the questions as well as the text are within the child's language ability.

A number of factual detail questions can be formulated for a single sentence. For example, the following questions can be generated about the sentence "Maria walked quickly into the room":

1. Who walked into the room?
2. What did Maria do? (The answer may also include the answers for questions 3 and 4.)
3. How did Maria walk?
4. Where did Maria walk?

Which question(s) the teacher elects to use should depend upon its relative importance to understanding the selection. In the above example, was it important to know who performed the action? If so, question 1 should be asked. Or, if the fact that Maria walked quickly had a bearing on meaning (perhaps a cause-effect relationship), question 3 should be presented.

At times the answer to a detail question depends upon the ability to understand a relationship. The most obvious of these is the pronoun referent (*Statement*: Tom called out loudly, then he sat down. *Question*: Who sat down?). Some children have difficulty understanding pronoun referents, especially when the pronoun precedes the noun in the selection or when the noun and pronoun do not appear fairly closely together. Other detail questions require an understanding of the relationship between the facts given in two sentences (*Sentences*: In walked the stranger. Suddenly the noise stopped. *Question*: Why did the noise stop?). Some writers would classify this as an inference question because the child must understand the implied connective "because."

Factual comprehension often is defined as using the author's words to comprehend; inferential comprehension as using the directly stated information and experiental background, through reasoning, to obtain an implied meaning. But differences between factual and inferential questions are not always clear-cut. Furthermore, questions within a given category may vary in difficulty. For instance, a question may require a simple inference or some very complex reasoning.

Although it is not always possible to give every question a label upon which all will agree, the teacher can always ask, "What must the child know or understand in order to be able to answer this question?" Instruction and practice in making inferences, even to the point of step-by-step procedures for arriving at an acceptable inference, are needed by some children. Many types of comprehension questions (e.g., main ideas, details, sequence, cause-effect) range from those whose answers are explicitly stated in the text to those requiring a high level of inferential reasoning. Two individuals can read the same selection and understand it to varying degrees.

It is often prudent to open questioning with a very general question such as "What was this story about?" and then ask more specific factual and higher level questions. Often it is a good idea to involve more than one child in answering a question. Thus, after one child has given an answer, another child can be asked, "Do you agree or disagree? Why?" Expecting this kind of question helps to keep all members of the group attentive. In a spontaneous discussion, children should be allowed to challenge another child's response, if they can justify their point.

Questions need not always be posed by the teacher; children should also be given the opportunity to formulate and ask questions. Such practice can be helpful in learning to formulate questions oneself—a skill that must be encouraged and developed because the teacher is not always going to be present to ask a "motivating question." Another technique involves reciprocal questioning (Helfeldt and Lalik 1976). Every time a child successfully answers the teacher's question, the child can ask the teacher a comprehension question. The possible value in such a procedure may lie in the active involvement of students in formulating questions, a task that requires comprehension.

Reading for Specific Purposes

Even though there is some question about the statistical independence of types of comprehension, some evidence suggests that specific practice tends to result in improved performance in the practiced skill (Calder and Zalatimo 1970). Even though the types of comprehension are listed separately, they do not function independently. Rather, they are interdependent and overlapping. Moreover it cannot be assumed that a child who can perform a skill at a given level of difficulty in a particular type of material will successfully do so in all types or levels of reading material. For instance, a third-grade child may be able to select and recall main ideas in the third reader but have difficulty doing so in the third-grade science book. Or, at fourth-reader level, the child may encounter difficulty because the ideas or language structure employed in the material are more complex and further removed from the child's fund of concepts and language patterns than those in lower-level materials.

It would be impractical to attempt a discussion of all the various types of comprehension listed in the literature. The types discussed below are generally considered to be important.

Understanding Main Ideas   The ability to find out the most important thing an author is trying to say—the main idea or central thought—is perhaps the most valuable comprehension skill. Without it, the reader gets lost in a mass of details. Yet even college freshmen have demonstrated weakness in this area (Coomber 1975). Selecting the main idea involves comparison and selection. One must distinguish between essential and nonessential information, and between the most important idea and details.

Children can learn to select the main idea of a paragraph and to understand how the rest of the paragraph often explains, illustrates, or elaborates the central thought, and how these parts fit together. Children who can successfully select main ideas from a multiple-choice format may not be able to generate responses with equal success (Van Blarecom and White 1976). Children who can state the main idea in their own words usually are also able to select main ideas. Inferred main ideas are more difficult to comprehend than are those which are found in a topic sentence.

There are several types of paragraph organization. In one pattern the main idea is given in the first sentence, with the rest of the paragraph consisting of illustrative details, examples, or amplification. Another pattern starts with a number of specific examples or details, leading to a general or summary statement in the final sentence. Less frequently the topic sentence containing the main idea is found in the middle of the paragraph, or is stated in both the first and last sentences. In some paragraphs there is no topic sentence, so that the main idea must be inferred from the details that are presented. Occasionally, a paragraph contains only illustrative information and does not have either a stated or implied main idea. When a chronological sequence of events is described, as in history, a summarizing statement may come at either the beginning or end of the paragraph or be missing. Materials intended to persuade or to demonstrate a cause-effect relationship usually employ the premise-conclusion or "if-then" format.

Among the practices which may help to develop the ability to understand main ideas are:

1. *Key or topic sentences.* In discussing the difference between a topic sentence and other sentences, paragraph structure (the organization through which the author attempts to communicate) is analyzed. Children learn that the topic sentence is usually the most general statement in the paragraph. Once skill in selecting the main idea in a single paragraph has been established, similar practice can be given with short selections consisting of a few paragraphs. Skill in determining this type of main idea is often more difficult than that required in reading a single paragraph because it requires the ability to understand the relationships among the "main ideas" of all the paragraphs.

2. *Supplying several sentences.* The children select from several sentences the one that sums up the main idea, then discuss the reasons for their choices.

3. *Constructing good paragraphs.* Learning how to write good paragraphs may enable the child to understand how to analyze those encountered in reading. More should be done to capitalize on the interrelationships among the language arts. Aulls (1975) reported his experiences using the writing of stories to improve reading comprehension. The procedure of improving reading comprehension through teaching a categorizing process (Gerhard 1975) appears to rely heavily on writing paragraphs.

4. *Titles and headings.* An author usually tries to suggest the main theme in the selection's title. In informational material, main ideas are often indicated in the headings and subheadings. The usefulness of the "author's outline" should be discussed with children.

5. *One-sentence or one-phrase summaries.* Asking children to state the gist of a passage or selection in one sentence or phrase is a challenging way to get them to try to distill the essential idea from the many details (see figure 8.5). At times, the theme can be summed up in a single word (e.g., greed). A news article can be placed on the chalkboard and criteria for choosing the best headline can be developed in discussion. Questions can be worded in various ways: What is it all about? What is the main idea? What would be a good title? What question is the author answering? In interpreting narrative material, understanding of main ideas often can be assessed by asking how a central character felt at a critical point.

6. *Introductory and concluding paragraphs.* In well-written explanatory selections an introductory paragraph or section often indicates the

1. Long ago men began to make boats. Some men tied logs together to make rafts. Others made boats out of baskets. There were boats made of skins and dug-out logs.

_____

_____

4. Trees give us places to play and climb. But they give us even more. They give us wood for homes and boats and paper. Some trees give us fruit to eat.

_____

_____

5. You can make butter at home. Get some cream and put it in a jar. Close the lid of the jar tightly. Then shake. If you like salty butter, add a little salt.

_____

_____

6. Birds may be different colors, but they are alike in many ways. They all have feathers. They all have wings. They have only two legs and no outer ears.

_____

_____

FIGURE 8.5.   Part of an exercise to develop the ability to understand main ideas. After reading each paragraph, the pupil writes its main topic on the lines following the paragraph. Taken from *A Discovery Book to Accompany More Than Words,* Josephine Wright and Marilyn W. Crosby, p. 44. Copyright © Macmillan Publishing Co., Inc., 1966, 1971, 1974. Reproduced by permission of the publisher.

author's purpose or explains the scope of the selection, and a concluding paragraph or section summarizes. Reading these introductions and summaries can enable one to obtain an overall impression of the material.

7. *Skimming for general impression.* Once the reader has set a purpose for reading, a very useful procedure is skimming through an entire selection rapidly to get a total impression. Skimming can be helpful in obtaining an idea of the scope and content of a chapter that is to be studied carefully afterward; in getting an idea of the author's main point without bothering about details; in sampling material to decide whether it would be useful, interesting, or of suitable difficulty. The distinction often made between skimming and scanning is that in scanning the reader is looking for a specific bit of information such as a date or answer to a specific question.

Grasping the Author's Plan   Good writing is organized writing because the author knows what he or she wants to say, thinks about the sequence, relative importance, and interrelatedness of the specific ideas to convey, and plans the writing accordingly. When discernible, the author's plan can be an aid to comprehension.

In most children's books, the author's intent is fairly clear. The intent may be to inform, entertain, or influence the reader in some way (these intents are not mutually exclusive). Realizing the author's purpose for writing can help a reader comprehend and evaluate the material. Fictional narratives tend to move ahead in simple chronological sequence, rarely including the flashbacks or other time inversions found in material read by older children or adults. Expository writing is usually well organized, with an introduction, a body, and a summary. Headings and subheadings help the reader to distinguish between major and minor topics and reveal the plan or organization.

Sometimes, however, the author's intentions are not so obvious. Children often fail to understand humorous exaggerations, irony, or satire in which the author expects the reader to know that the meaning is the opposite of what seems to be said. Even adults can miss an author's intent when it is not openly stated. In response to a satire in which a nonexistent research study was cited as showing that one can train babies to read before they are born (Sipay 1965), the writer received abundant correspondence that clearly indicated that the article's satirical nature was not understood, despite a footnote that stated, "Don't be too quick to believe everything you read!"

Good literature usually contains deeper meanings below the surface. Is *The Adventures of Huckleberry Finn* just a series of varied episodes or is it a savage criticism of some aspects of American society? Even when children are reading primarily for enjoyment, they can be helped to discover some of the ways in which the beliefs of authors are disclosed in their writings.

Finding Answers to Specific Questions   Many occasions arise when the reader wants to find the answer to a specific question. At times this requires careful reading and analytical reasoning; for example, learning how photosynthesis works. Reading is successful when the reader determines that he or she has the answer to the question. Because children often have difficulty determining which information is pertinent to their questions, specific guiding questions should sometimes precede reading. Written or oral answers to these questions, followed by discussion, provide a means of assessing success and correcting mistakes.

At times one wishes to find a specific piece of information. Very rapid reading to find such information as a date, name, telephone number, etc., is called *scanning*. As learners run their eyes rapidly over the material, total meaning is not absorbed. Rather they notice only the desired information which almost seems to stand out as if in bold print. Practice in scanning is best provided by using the kinds of material (texts, reference books, newspapers, telephone books) in which such information normally occurs.

Teachers can formulate a suitable number of questions of the who, which, what, when types, the answers to which can be found in the reading material. The questions are presented before the children begin scanning, and they are encouraged to find and note the answers as quickly as possible. After the exercise the answers can be discussed, and those who need help can be assisted in overcoming whatever prevented them from obtaining the answers rapidly.

Noting and Recalling Details   There are many times when it is important to be able to note and recall details. This is especially true when studying; that is, attempting to assimilate as much of the content of the reading material as possible. The ability to understand details is basic for achieving higher levels of comprehension. Children should attend to the important details in the material. Too often their attention is focused on insignificant details by teachers' questions.

Some children are quite able to obtain a general idea or the central theme when reading, but have little or no interest in absorbing details. Such readers do well when reading fiction, but experience difficulty in reading science and social studies material.

Children should be helped to learn important details in relation to the major ideas they support. Relating details to main ideas can be fostered by proper questioning. First, the main idea is identified. Then several kinds of questions can be asked: How is this shown? What evidence is there for it? Where or when does it apply? What are the exceptions? How many kinds are there? What applications are given? Such relationships can be tied in with teaching outlining skills (see unit 9, p. 387).

Grasping the Sequence of Events   A series of events often is related in narrative material whether fictional or not, and in historical accounts. In order to understand such a format, one must be able to note and remember the order in which the events took place and to comprehend, at least partially, the cause-effect chain linking each event with the preceding and following events.

The most natural way to develop ability to grasp a sequence is to ask for a retelling of the story. Children who cannot report a sequence from start to finish can be guided step by step: What happened first? Then what happened? What happened after . . . ? Did Henry hit Bob before or after Bob called him a name? (Such questions also help establish cause-effect relationships.) To be able to understand and relate sequence, children must have the concept of time sequence and understand words that indicate the sequence, such as *first, then, next, as a result of, lastly, finally*. The answers to sequence questions may be directly stated facts or implied.

A way of testing sequence that is often used in workbooks and tests presents the events of a story in a scrambled order. After reading the selection, the children are to renumber the events in the order in which they occurred in the story. A similar exercise has them rearrange strips of paper on each of which is written an event. When using such exercises or tests, the teacher should be aware that if a child errs in placing one event, even though the other events are correctly placed in sequence, they will not be numbered correctly. Thus children may appear to be weaker in sequencing ability than they actually are.

Anticipating Outcomes   Closely related to the ability to grasp the sequence of events is the ability to think ahead while reading. Anticipating outcomes involves forming hypotheses as to what is going to happen (based upon what has preceded in the selection, and one's life experiences), and testing and revising these guesses as the reader goes along. We use context not only to infer the pronunciation or meaning of unfamiliar words but also to project the story. If it were not for anticipation, there would be no such thing as a surprise ending.

Guiding questions can be used to encourage and aid children to predict what is likely to happen. The reason for making these predictions should be discussed. Then the children read ahead to determine if they were correct or not. Sometimes a guiding question is given before reading a story; but it is more effective to let the children read part of the story and then predict how it is going to continue. They also can think up alternative endings, and see how closely they come to the one given by the author. Some workbooks provide brief unfinished stories and ask the child to choose among possible endings or to complete the story (see figure 8.6).

Part A: Working Together

Michael was proudly bringing home the vase that he had made at school. It was a tall vase with a wide opening at the top, and he had worked very hard to be sure the bottom of it was level, so it would not tip. When he got home, his uncle was just going into the house with a bunch of flowers that he had cut in the garden. When Michael showed his uncle the vase, his uncle said that he thought it was the finest one he had ever seen. What do you think happened?

Things to remember about predicting outcomes:

• You should understand that being able to predict outcomes will increase your enjoyment of what you read.

(1) Notice all the facts that are given and the ideas that are suggested by the writer.

(2) Use those facts and ideas to predict the events that will occur next in the story.

Part B: Checking What You Have Learned

_b_ 1. Julie and Sarah were on the train, riding home from work. They were busily talking together about a very important meeting that they were planning. The conductor did not come through the car and announce their stop as he was supposed to do. They did not even notice that the train had stopped at their station. What do you think happened to Julie and Sarah?

a. They got off at the right stop.
b. They missed their stop.
c. They decided that they would never again ride on a train.

_c_ 2. Bud could not find his new hockey stick, and he accused his sister of losing it. She had used it earlier in the week, but she told him that she had returned it to his room the same day. Just then Lester came in with Bud's hockey stick in his hand. He thanked Bud for having let him use it the night before. "What do you say now?" his sister asked. What do you think Bud did next?

a. He shouted at Lester for using his hockey stick.
b. He lost his hockey stick.
c. He apologized to his sister.

FIGURE 8.6. Teacher-directed exercise to develop the ability to predict outcomes. Taken from *Reference Handbook for Medley,* p. 233, by William K. Durr, Vivian O. Windley, and Anne A. McCourt. Copyright © 1976 by Houghton Mifflin Company. Reproduced by permission of the publisher and reduced.

Having children devise their own endings for incomplete stories also helps to develop the ability to anticipate outcomes. Comparing their versions with one another and the author also may help them to develop what some have entitled *creative reading*—going beyond understanding of the reading matter to arrive at new ideas or conclusions. Other procedures that encourage this form of divergent thinking involve having the children use the plot of a given story, but change the setting to a different time and/or

34. Secret Messages in Code

It is easy to send a secret message if you use a code. Only those who know the code can read it. A good example of a simple code is the Rail-Fence Code used during the Civil War in our country.

Follow these directions:

1. A captain got this message from the war front:

   B   I   G   B   O   N   P   E   D   E   P
       R   D   E   L   W   U   S   N   H   L

   Copy this code on your paper. Be sure you put the letters in exactly the same order and space them in the same way.

2. Draw a line with your pencil from the first letter in the first line to the first letter in the second line. Continue these lines up and down until all the letters in the two lines are connected. The zigzag lines you have drawn will look like a split-rail fence.

3. Following your pencil lines, write all the letters in a *single line*. The first letter is B, the second is R, the third is I, and so on.

4. At this point the captain had decoded the message. He marked the letters into words, and read the message. Now you read the message and write it on your paper, spacing the words.

5. Here are two more messages. Can you decode them?

   N   E   M   R   B   L   E   S
       E   D   O   E   U   L   T
   T   O   U   D   E   M   N   I   L   D
       W   H   N   R   D   E   K   L   E

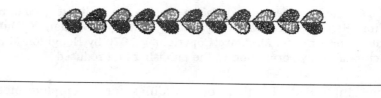

FIGURE 8.7. Exercise to develop the ability to follow printed directions. From Arthur I. Gates and Celeste C. Peardon, *Gates-Peardon Reading Exercises*, Intermediate-FD, *Can you follow directions?* Copyright © 1963 by Teachers College Press, Teachers College, Columbia University, p. 34. Reproduced by permission of the publisher.

place; and changing a given event in the story and encouraging the children to conjecture how it might have influenced the rest of the story. Other examples of creative reading activities are described by Smith and Barrett (1974).

Following Printed Directions Ability to follow a set of printed directions accurately and in the correct order is a valuable asset in everyday life. In school, this ability is important in many kinds of activities: doing a workbook page, conducting an experiment, following a recipe. Adults make even more use of this ability—reading directions for using a new microwave oven, reading the printed instructions for fixing the transmission on a new car, reading and completing an application, reading a paper that describes a new professional technique.

Practice in following directions accurately should make use of the kinds of material in which this skill is important. Many content-subject texts, particularly arithmetic and science, require skill in following directions and thus can be used for instruction and practice. Selections may be chosen from such sources as Scout handbooks; simple cookbooks; directions for constructing models, puppets, performing magic tricks, or playing games. The best practice, and test, is to let children carry out the activity, with a good result being its own reward. When this is not practical, questions can be formulated and provided in duplicated form, or workbooks may be used (see figure 8.7).

Pikulski and Jones (1977) offered a number of suggestions for writing directions that children can read: (1) use high-frequency language patterns; (2) present information in small steps, with repeated use of the same language pattern; (3) make repeated use of nouns rather than pronouns; (4) use words whose meanings are understood by the children, or develop their meanings prior to the activity; (5) use pictures or illustrations where appropriate; (6) number the directions and order them in separate sentences; (7) typewritten directions, generous use of blank space, and careful arrangement of print on the page make directions more readable; and (8) make the activity interesting.

Remembering What One Reads While inherent differences in memory exist, teachers can help children improve their efficiency in remembering. Some relevant principles have already been enumerated: (1) actively look for main ideas; (2) focus on the important facts; and (3) try to relate important details to main ideas. Material is remembered in proportion to the degree to which it is understood. Also important is the intent to remember. Recall should be selective because none of us can remember everything. A single reading is usually not sufficient; the material one wants to be able to remember must be repeated enough times to be able to recite it correctly without consulting the text. Retention is also aided by note taking, outlining, or summarizing (see unit 9, pp. 385ff). There also should be spaced, periodic review of the information.

F. Smith (1975) contends that it is always desirable to read for comprehension before trying to memorize. He states that the effort to cram details into long-term memory directly, without first determining how they fit into the total picture, clogs short-term memory and thus interferes with comprehension.

In determining whether children can remember what they have read, it should be understood that most daily reading lessons as well as reading tests only sample immediate recall. There is little need, and therefore little intent, to remember such information for any length of time. A child may answer questions quite adequately on material that has just been read, but have difficulty remembering that information overnight. Longtime retention requires repetition and review.

If children are always allowed to look back to find the answers or if recall is constantly aided by use of multiple-choice questions, children can get into the habit of not paying careful attention during their initial reading. To help overcome the habit of always looking back for answers, a guided recall procedure (Manzo 1975) can be employed about once a week: (1) After appropriate readiness has been established and a specific purpose has been set, the children are told to read and remember all they can. (2) As each child finishes, the material is turned facedown. When all have finished, the class is asked to relate what they remember, with the teacher recording this information in abbreviated form on the board. (3) The children are allowed to reread the article to encourage recognition of details which were either not recalled or incorrectly remembered. (4) The children attempt to organize what they remember into a summary or informal outline. (5) The teacher raises specific questions which require synthesis of new and old information. Alternatively, after the children turn the material down or close the book, they write as much as they can remember, then compare results.

Reading Critically   Enlightened citizens in a democracy must learn to distinguish trustworthy information from slanted or biased accounts. For example, accounts of the same events in newspapers may vary according to the editorial policy of the paper. They must be able to evaluate what they read; that is, they must be able to read critically. In today's world we are bombarded from all sides by reading matter that attempts to influence behavior and shape ideas. The trusting reader who believes that something is true simply because it appears in print is a potential victim for anyone with something to sell.

To be able to read critically, one must be able to think critically. In turn, critical thinking requires an open mind, experiential background, knowledge of how and where to find information and how to judge its accuracy, reasoning ability, and something about which to think critically. The biased or close-minded cannot think critically because they reject or refuse to listen to alternatives to their own fixed beliefs, which are often influenced by emotions. Likewise, it is impossible to judge the accuracy of material if one does not possess knowledge in that area. Since we cannot be expert in all fields (and experts themselves rarely agree), it is necessary to know how and where to find the desired information. Next one must be able to understand the relationship between existing knowledge and new information or ideas, as well as be able to reason through or analyze new material.

These skills and attitudes are of little use if children have limited or no opportunity to think or to read critically. Teachers must take advantage of situations that arise and also arrange situations that require children to evaluate what they hear and read. A classroom atmosphere that encourages a questioning attitude should be developed, without going so far as to produce skeptics who challenge everything.

Critical thinking and critical reading must be learned as a way of reacting in many situations beginning early in life, continuing through the elementary school, and intensifying in high school and college. There are skills related to critical reading that can and should be taught. For example, children should learn to distinguish fact from opinion. Some suggestions for doing so are given below; others may be found in King, Ellenger, and Wolf (1967), Lee, Bingham, and Woelfel (1968), and Stauffer and Cramer (1968). Nevius (1977) has outlined activities for developing logical thinking skills in young children.

Comparing different versions. Trust in the necessary truth of printed sources of information can be altered when the reader compares two versions of the same topic discussed from contrasting points of view; e.g., John Brown as a "savior" and as a "madman." When newspapers of differing political or philosophical viewpoints are available, their contrasting treatments of partisan issues can point up the need for critical evaluation and careful comparison. Often children are amazed the first time they encounter mutually contradictory statements in print. Even history varies with the author's perceptions and biases. The American Revolution is not treated alike in British and American texts; nor is the Civil War (the War Between the States) in texts used in the North and South. Current issues ("saving the environment" vs. "the need for energy") can provide interesting topics. Because exposure to varying points of view may irritate parents or influential community members, many schools have been reluctant to provide children with such experiences. Yet this kind of experience is important if future citizens are to be able to determine intelligently what to believe about important issues.

Evaluating sources. In judging how much faith probably can be placed in a source, a reader can employ the following guidelines. The background and reputation of the author certainly help to determine the probability that what is written is accurate, though this is not an infallible indicator of reliability. Closely related to this is the reputation of the publisher, or the magazine or journal in which the material appears. We are more likely to place faith in an article concerning hemispheric dominance written by an eminent neurologist that appears in a scholarly journal than one written by a journalist for a popular magazine. Children can learn how authors' backgrounds influence their writing and can look up well-known authors in encyclopedias and biographical sources such as *Who's Who in America* or *Contemporary Authors.* Similarly, children should learn to check the copyright date of a publication. Authors do change their minds and new information makes some former "facts" obsolete.

Considering new ideas. Another type of critical reading involves considering new ideas or information in light of one's own present knowledge and beliefs. Thoughtful readers ask themselves: Is it reasonable? Is it possible? They do not automatically accept or reject an unfamiliar idea, but they do become alert when disagreements occur between their previously accepted ideas and new ideas.

The word *propaganda* simply means promoting a particular doctrine or set of ideas; in itself there is no implication of wrongdoing. Only when the propagandist intentionally distorts and subtly misrepresents should the reader be alert for possible signs of falsification. There are several well-known propaganda techniques that older children, with help, can learn to recognize:

1. *Name-calling.* People or ideas can be made unpopular by identifying them with an unpopular label (e.g., Communist, radical, atheist) whether the label fits or not.
2. *Glittering generalities.* Political victories have been built on slogans such as "a chicken in every pot," so vague as to be almost meaningless.
3. *The plain-folks device.* Here the writer or speaker tries to get his audience to accept him as one of themselves and to regard his opponents as outsiders.
4. *Testimonials.* The endorsement of an idea, a person, or a product by a well-known and respected individual loses its validity when the endorser does it for pay and obviously is not expert on the subject.
5. *Identification with prestige.* Names of prominent people are frequently used to give authority to a particular idea.
6. *The band-wagon effect.* The idea that "everybody's doing it" persuades many people to follow suit, and so majority support is often claimed long before it is attained.
7. *Card-stacking.* This refers to the many ways of distorting facts and misusing statistics to favor a particular conclusion. One of the commonest is the "dangling comparative"—"twice as fast," "three ways better," etc.—without specifying faster than what or better than what. Surveys and opinion polls have at times been planned in advance to favor a particular outcome.

The teacher who recognizes the dangers of ignorance and gullibility about propaganda techniques can easily collect and have children bring in current samples for discussion. Research in the area of the affective effect of certain propaganda techniques is meager, but Dulin and Greenwald (1975) found that use of loaded words, name-calling and identification with prestige or dislikes do influence readers. Unfortunately, knowing about propaganda techniques does not ensure that people will recognize them or necessarily be immune from being influenced, but at least it gives them a chance.

An illustration of how propaganda techniques have been employed and how they can be detected is given by Swineford (1975). A three-step procedure for teaching critical listening regarding advertisements (Tutolo 1975) may be adapted for reading: (1) set up a standard of highly conscious criteria in the listener's minds, then discuss to which needs (self-actualization, esteem, love, safety, physiological) the advertisement is making an appeal; (2) sift the evidence and make a critical judgment using the above noted types of propaganda techniques or guidelines; and (3) draw a conclusion or act on the judgment made (e.g., decide whether to buy or not).

Other Procedures for Guiding the Development of Reading Comprehension

In addition to the use of questions and the development of specific types of comprehension, other procedures or techniques may prove useful in guiding the development of reading comprehension.

Directed Reading-Thinking Activities   Stauffer (1969) advocated a *directed reading-thinking activity* (DRTA) that is based on the assumption that children will be motivated, interested, and will understand better if they set their own purposes for reading and practice making predictions regarding the possible outcomes. The pupils preview a selection to identify purposes for reading it, are encouraged at several points to conjecture how the story will develop, and check their anticipations by reading. The teacher assists the children by raising questions that help them to set purposes, to recognize their "errors," and to answer their own questions. Individualized reading-thinking activities that can be interspersed with group DRTA have been described by Stauffer and Harrell (1975). A modification of the DRTA (Hoskisson 1973) involves three basic steps:

1. *Predicting.* The teacher begins the discussion with such questions as "What will a story with this title probably be about?" After a brief discussion, the children make predictions, with the teacher asking questions such as "Why do you think that idea is a good one?"
2. *Reasoning.* After reading, the children check their hypotheses by answering such questions as "Were you right?" and "What do you think now?"
3. *Proving.* The predictions are tested by questions such as "What in the story makes you think . . . ?"

Schwartz and Sheff (1975), who advocated and illustrated a very similar approach, suggested that the various types of specific comprehension skills are applied *concurrently* as the children try to understand each whole paragraph or selection. When children are helped to decide their own purposes for reading, they may participate more eagerly in the discussion than when questions are taken verbatim from a manual.

The Cloze Procedure as a Teaching Device   The cloze procedure (see unit 6, pp. 199–201) has been used to encourage first graders to apply their understanding of how language works to written language (Gove 1975) and to develop critical reading in third to fifth graders (Gomberg 1976), as well as for a variety of other purposes. Lopardo (1975) suggested that an every fifth-word deletion pattern be used when the objective is to focus attention on comprehension, and that selected deletion patterns be used to focus attention on specific types of reading skills. Thus, to help children weak in function words (articles, prepositions, conjunctions), the particular type of function word would be deleted. For example, John poured the milk _____ his glass. For vocabulary development, children can be instructed to insert synonyms or antonyms. Or, inflected endings can be emphasized. For example, Yesterday Cindy walk____ softly.

The following guidelines for using cloze as a teaching device have been presented by Pikulski (1976b):

1. Carefully define your instructional objectives.
2. Lead the group through practice exercises before asking children to complete a cloze exercise individually; children are often frustrated because they are uncertain as to what the "right answer" is.
3. Begin with relatively easy activities and move to more challenging ones. You may want to use as few as one or two deletions at first.
4. Discuss the children's responses with them. Discuss why in some cases only one response is correct, and why in other cases, there are several possible responses, but one may be better than the rest. Encourage the students to decide which responses are qualitatively better and to compare their choices to the author's.

Other techniques. Another instructional strategy proposed for enhancing reading comprehension is training children to use imagery—to form mental pictures of the story as they read (Levin 1976). A study by Kulhavy and Swenson (1975) involving fifth and sixth graders indicated that using imagery increased the amount of content remembered over time.

Henry (1974) has set forth a detailed, complex plan for teaching reading as concept development in which he defines reading as "making one's way through printed and written language in such a manner as to seek out a number of relations and to put this growing set of relations into a tentative structure." And a few specific samples of comprehension strategy lessons based on miscue analysis may be found in Y. Goodman (1975).

The preceding section dealt with instructional strategies that may improve reading comprehension. Techniques for attempting to make materials easier to comprehend are also covered in unit 9 on pages 378–80 and in unit 10 on pages 407–10.

RELATING RATE TO COMPREHENSION

The degree of relationship between rate and comprehension varies with the age of the readers, the kinds of materials used, the methods used to measure these two factors, and the child's purpose for reading. Regarding the latter, for example, Samuels and Dahl (1975) found that fourth graders read significantly faster when reading to obtain a general overview than when told to read for details.

In the primary grades there is a fairly high relationship between rate and comprehension, since both are mainly dependent on speed and accuracy of word recognition. Children who recognize words slowly or inaccurately and often have to reread to correct mistakes are not only slow in getting through the material but also have difficulty in getting the ideas. The latter is due partly to misread words, but mainly to the many interruptions in their train of thought, and to the focusing of attention on words, reducing focus on meaning. Speed improves naturally as reading becomes increasingly accurate and fluent.

Correlations between rate and comprehension vary with the type of material read, but in general are low. There is a slight tendency for fast readers to comprehend well and for slow readers to comprehend less well, but it is not certain which is the cause and which the effect, and there are many exceptions to this generalization. Above the primary grades one finds all possible combinations of rate and comprehension: rapid-accurate, rapid-inaccurate, average-accurate, average-inaccurate, slow-accurate, and slow-inaccurate.

There are many possible reasons why a pupil may be a slow reader, such as weak word recognition, faulty reading habits (e.g., lip movements, head movements), poor comprehension, and inflexible rate. Rate is also influenced to some extent by the rapidity with which one can take in or comprehend ideas. Before attempting to improve rate, it is advisable to determine why the learner is reading slowly. For a comprehensive discussion of how to diagnose and improve rate, refer to A. J. Harris and Sipay (1975, pp. 544–75). Those interested in learning more about rate of comprehension may also refer to the articles annotated by Berger and Peebles (1976).

One way to increase rate in the intermediate grades and above is having the children read selections under timed conditions. The knowledge that they are being timed and will have to answer comprehension questions provides strong motivation to increase rate without loss of comprehension.

Another method for increasing rate is the use of controlled reading or pacers. There are special types of projectors that use filmstrips for exposing the reading material at any of a wide variety of rates. However, individual differences in speed of comprehension, level of comprehension, and interests make it difficult, if not impossible, to select suitable material and an appropriate rate of presentation for a group. For individual practice there are also several kinds of pacing devices, all of which use regular reading material in book or workbook form and employ a shutter, screen, or beam of light that comes down the page at a preset rate.

With any method that employs pressure for more rapid reading, the big problem is transferring the speed acquired in the practice setting to normal reading. Many students do well in practice sessions, without much carry-over into their regular reading. Nor, as the Swalm and Kling study (1973) suggested, should one expect an increase in rate to result in improved comprehension. The experimental evidence indicates that in the elementary school, a well-conceived reading program that provides for an abundance of independent reading and timed exercises produces as much long-range improvement in rates as is generally attained with special instruments or machinery. Attempts to increase the span of perception (the amount seen in a single fixation) are not particularly productive.

When children are both slow and inaccurate, the material used is probably too difficult for them. The slow rate and poor comprehension may reflect word recognition or vocabulary difficulties or unfamiliarity with the language patterns. Such children usually need easier material through which they can be helped to improve their word recognition, reading vocabulary, and comprehension skills.

Children who read slowly but very accurately often can learn to read considerably faster without loss in comprehension. For them, a series of timed reading exercises with comprehension checks often brings a sub-

• 73 •

There are atomic submarines in the United States Fleet. The first of these ever built was the Nautilus. Substance the size of a baseball provides the ship with enough nuclear power to travel under water around the world. Once, it traveled more than 5000 miles under water in a little over fourteen days. Much of this time, it could not come to the surface because it was traveling under ice, making a trip to the North Pole.

Seeing what looked like an opening above it, the Nautilus tried to rise to the surface. But this was not a real opening. It was clear ice which bent the periscope of the Nautilus as it attempted to pass through.

Those who manned the Nautilus lived in a comfortable 72-degree temperature during the entire trip. As the crew stepped ashore back in the States a sailor exclaimed, "Gee, it's awful cold!"

1. The best title for this selection is (a) Submarines (b) The Nautilus (c) The Arctic (d) Atomic Power

2. This trip was a (a) scientific experiment (b) pleasure cruise (c) regular occurrence (d) war mission

3. The Nautilus (a) stayed under ice (b) bent its periscope (c) traveled in only two oceans (d) was bitterly cold inside

4. The water near the Pole was (a) frozen to the bottom (b) often covered with thick ice (c) covered with thin ice (d) free of ice

5. Once, when the ship tried to surface, it (a) was wrecked (b) surfaced with ease (c) could not surface (d) collided with an iceberg

6. At the end of the trip, the men (a) were sorry to return (b) thought the weather was cold (c) wanted to stay in the submarine (d) were glad to be where it was warm

7. Probably these trips were made (a) cautiously (b) hurriedly (c) very slowly (d) with little planning

8. The crew members were (a) comfortable (b) frightened (c) irritable (d) seasick

No. right	0	1	2	3	4	5	6	7	8
G score	2.6	5.0	5.5	6.1	6.9	7.6	8.3	8.9	9.6

FIGURE 8.8.   Exercise to coordinate rate with comprehension. From William A. McCall and Lelah M. Crabbs, *Standard Test Lessons in Reading,* Book C, p. 73. Teachers College Press, copyright © 1926, 1950, 1961, Teachers College Press, Columbia University. Reproduced by permission of the publisher.

stantial improvement in rate (see figure 8.8). The material used should be easy for them. Often they need to be convinced that they can read faster and still be able to understand the material. Each child charts his or her own rate and comprehension. If comprehension remains satisfactory, the child is encouraged to read the next exercise a little faster; if comprehension drops, the child is advised to try to maintain the same rate while trying for better comprehension.

The rapid-inaccurate reader needs experiences in which, by taking comprehension tests, he becomes aware of his weak comprehension and interested in improving it. Often the desire to improve comprehension is sufficient to bring about better attention to meaning. A graph or chart showing the child's rate and comprehension scores in successive practice exercises provides an incentive for continuing to improve. Stress is not placed on slowing down rate because it is desirable to retain as much speed as possible as is consistent with adequate comprehension.

Flexibility in Rate [3]

Both rapid and slow reading rates have their utility. Rapid reading is an advantage when a large amount of material has to be covered, and the learning of generalizations, getting main ideas, and understanding implications are more important than mastery of details. Slow reading is advantageous when the material is quite difficult or requires an exact and complete comprehension, as is the case in much scientific and mathematical materials. Just as the consistently fast reader may miss important details, the consistently slow reader may be wasting valuable time as well as handicapping comprehension.

The skilled reader varies reading rate according to his or her purpose for reading, background in the subject matter, and the nature of the reading material. Four main rates can be distinguished: skimming, rapid reading, normal reading, and careful reading. The kinds of situations in which each is appropriate are listed in figure 8.9. Fourth graders can be taught to be flexible in their reading rates (T. Harris 1976).

Children can be helped to vary their rates of reading according to the situation. The desirability of employing different speeds for different kinds

---

3. For an excellent discussion of the problems in defining and measuring reading flexibility, see Rankin (1974b).

Skimming		Rapid		Normal		Careful	
Work	Recreatory	Work	Recreatory	Work	Recreatory	Work	Recreatory
To get gist of material To find a reference To locate new material To refresh memory To answer a question	Looking over books, magazines, etc., to get gist of thought To pick out a story to read Reading pictures To review a familiar book or story	To get general idea of content To find specific reference To locate material To review familiar material To get information for temporary use	Reading of familiar narrative for relaxation Informational material for pleasure or relaxation At movies Reading pictures To reread familiar material	To get details of material To get main thought Reading new material When material is of ordinary difficulty To solve a problem To answer a question To find a new problem To locate a reference To locate new material To commit to memory To supplement thought	For relaxation To keep in touch with current events To know a new story To satisfy sense of humor For devotional purposes To memorize	To master content including details To evaluate material To raise questions To answer questions or problems To get directions for performing an act To outline To summarize To reproduce To analyze thought To remove difficulties of thought or form To supplement thought To solve a problem	When important factual articles are read To search for particular effects To judge literary or other values To supplement thought For spiritual guidance When classical material with unusual words is met To memorize poetry

FIGURE 8.9. Life uses of reading classified according to rate. (Yoakam 1928, p. 69.) Reproduced by permission of the author and the publisher, the Macmillan Publishing Co.

of material and for different purposes is easily demonstrated. The same kind of material can be read at different speeds to determine the rate that seems to bring about the best results. Because rate should be influenced by one's purpose for reading, children should learn to set their own purposes and to adjust their rates accordingly.

Materials for Developing Comprehension and Rate

Assembling Practice Materials Some of the best material for sharpening comprehension skills appears in workbooks. A collection of comprehension exercises, varied in both type and difficulty, can be assembled for use in a nonconsumable fashion. Several appropriate works can be selected, and three copies of each ordered. These workbooks are cut into separate units. Two copies are cut down the center to obtain separate sheets, then each page is mounted inside a transparent plastic folder or envelope, preferably one on which answers may be written and then erased. The third copy serves as the teacher's edition; it may already contain the answers, or the teacher may have to write them in.

The exercises are then classified as to type and difficulty. A simple scheme has the type represented by a number and the difficulty by a letter (inferred main ideas at fourth-reader level might be 2-E). Exercises from a variety of sources can be combined in sequence and filed in drawers, boxes, or cartons.

In selecting and using commercial reading comprehension materials it would be wise to consider the flaws commonly found in them (Axelrod 1974a):

1. It is possible to obtain the answers to some questions correctly:
    a. on the basis of experience alone, without even reading the selection.
    b. by just skimming the material (test-wise children read the question first).
    c. because the alternate choices are so obviously incorrect.
    d. simply by chance, especially if very few choices are available.
    e. by detecting the grammatical construction of an item, the cue being that only one or two choices fit grammatically.
2. Ambiguous questions may induce the child to respond "incorrectly."
3. A logically correct answer other than the one given in the teacher's edition may not be considered as correct.

4. Sometimes not enough information needed for answering the question is given in the material.
5. The child's cultural background may interfere with answering certain questions. For instance, the child may not have had an experience important to understanding the selection; or the child's experience may have led to a concept that is not congruent with the one held by the questioner.

Above all, it should be remembered that most materials give practice, but do not teach. You cannot just give a child some material and expect that reading problems will be overcome.

Commercially Available Materials   Among the increasing number of workbooks available to foster and sharpen the comprehension skills of elementary school pupils are:

New Practice Readers (Webster). Each of the 7 books (grades 2–8) contains short selections with vocabulary introductions and 6 varied comprehension and vocabulary questions.

Gates-Peardon Reading Exercises (Teachers College). Booklets for grades 2 and 3 each contain short selections followed by three types of questions: main idea, following directions, and reading for details. There are separate booklets for main ideas, directions, and details for use in grades 4, 5, and 6.

Specific Skill Series (Barnell Loft). Seven workbooks (reading levels 1–7) in each separate series of primary- and intermediate-grade difficulty: Getting the Main Idea, Getting the Facts, Drawing Conclusions, Following Directions, Locating the Answer, Detecting the Sequence, and Using Context.

New Reading Skill Builder Series (Reader's Digest). Two or three booklets at each of reading levels 1–9. Adapted *Reader's Digest* articles followed by varied comprehension questions.

Macmillan Reading Spectrum: Reading Comprehension (Macmillan). Series of 6 programmed workbooks for grades 3–8.

Gaining Independence in Reading (Charles E. Merrill). Three texts for grades 4–6 containing a wide variety of exercises.

New Diagnostic Reading Workbooks (Charles E. Merrill). Series of workbooks (K–6). Each selection is followed by several types of comprehension questions.

Merrill Skilltexts (Charles E. Merrill). Workbooks for grades 1–6. Each lesson is followed by a variety of questions.

Standard Test Lessons in Reading (Teachers College). Five books, ranging from third- to seventh-grade difficulty, each containing 78 short selections followed by multiple-choice questions. Each exercise administered with a 3-minute limit.

Supportive Reading Skills (Dexter and Westbrook). Separate series of workbooks for developing various comprehension, vocabulary, and study skills. Most of the series range in difficulty from 1–9.

Reading for Concepts (Webster). Series of 8 workbooks ranging in difficulty from approximately second- to seventh-grade level. Selections taken mostly from social studies or science; eight different comprehension skills checked.

Read-Study-Think (Weekly Reader). Series of 5 workbooks for grades 2–6 for developing critical reading.

Reading, Thinking, and Reasoning (Steck-Vaughn). Series of 6 workbooks aimed at building 40 specific critical thinking and reading skills; for grades 1–6.

Reading for Meaning (Lippincott). Workbooks for grades 4–12. Each exercise has questions on word meaning and several types of comprehensive questions.

SRA Reading Laboratory (SRA). There are 10 different kits for use from primary grades through college, with the range in any one being from 2 to 8 grade levels. The "Power Builders" are short selections followed by decoding, vocabulary, and comprehension items. "Rate Builders" are included in the higher level kits.

Reading Practice Program (Harcourt). Over 230 self-explanatory lessons organized by skill areas (decoding, vocabulary, comprehension); includes criterion-referenced tests: For reading levels 3–9.

Reading Development (Addison-Wesley). Three kits (*A* for grades 2 to 4; *B* for 5 to 6; *C* for 7 to 10), each with a series of lesson cards covering decoding, vocabulary, and comprehension skills.

Reading for Understanding (SRA). Three multilevel kits (grades 3–8, 8–12, 5 through college), each containing 400 short selections for developing reading comprehension.

Practice in Critical Reading Skills (Instructor Publications). Intermediate-grade workbooks, each containing 4 self-directing activities on topics such as distinguishing fact from opinion and recognizing generalities.

Following Directions (Curriculum Associates). Forty exercises covering previewing, breaking the task into steps, and finding key words; for grades 4–8.

Multiple Skills Series (Lowell & Lynwood). Workbooks for fifth and sixth reader levels (four for each level) each contains 50 short selections followed by five different types of questions.

UNIT 9

Helping Students Read to Learn

Reading skills acquired in the developmental strand of the total reading program should not be an end in themselves. Such skills should be thought of as laying the foundation for successfully utilizing reading for two main purposes: reading to learn (functional reading) and reading for pleasure (recreational reading). This unit is concerned with the former; recreational reading is covered in unit 10. Functional reading is defined here as including those activities in which reading functions as a tool in the learning process. Synonyms that are often used include *work-study skills, work-type reading,* and *study-type reading.*

Because of the way in which schools typically operate, reading has been the most important tool for intellectual inquiry and learning, and will continue to be so in the foreseeable future. It is very difficult for postprimary-grade children to succeed academically without learning to read for information. Functional reading skills become increasingly important as children progress through the grades; a second grader may survive without such skills, but a sixth or eighth grader will find it almost impossible to do so.

As Catterson (1974a) has pointed out, with the advent of "discovery learning" there have been tremendous changes in content-subject texts and methodology. Formerly most students used only a single text; now they are often faced with independently locating, gathering, and organizing information from a variety of sources. Many texts are no longer written in a simple informational pattern; science texts may contain a proposition-proof pattern, social studies texts contain much graphic material, and many of the problems in the new math are not word problems.

The ability to understand and retain information from the various materials used in the content fields requires more than simply applying the reading skills learned in the developmental strand. For one thing, the materials employed in the developmental strand typically are narrative, whereas in the functional strand they are much more often expository. There are at least twelve ways in which narrative and expository materials differ (Dulin 1973). Although there are general reading skills that apply broadly in content subjects, the application of these skills varies not only from one content area to another, but also among materials in a given field. Furthermore, because retention of information is a necessity, success in the content fields demands adequate study habits as well as study skills.

This unit begins with means of assessing reading and study skills needed in the contents subjects, and then discusses the general reading-skill areas that cut across the content fields, their specific application to three content subjects, how to assist children to obtain the most from reading a content subject text, and how to help children who have difficulty reading the regularly assigned text. Considered next are the skills needed to locate, summarize, and organize information from various sources. This is followed by a discussion of study habits, and the last section deals with materials that may be used for practicing functional reading skills.

ASSESSING FUNCTIONAL READING SKILLS

As in any good teaching, the functional reading program should be geared to the individual needs of the pupils. Therefore each child's skills and abilities should be assessed, both initially and continuously. This involves (1) determining the suitability of material the child is asked to read; and (2) determining the extent to which particular reading and study skills have been mastered. Study-skills programs that center on overcoming the individual's weaknesses seem to be the most efficient and productive (Snoddy 1973).

Determining the Suitability of Material

Ability to comprehend a text can be assessed by selecting three 200- to 300-word passages from it: one that represents the average difficulty of the text as determined by a readability formula; one that represents the easiest material found in it; and one that represents the most difficult level of readability found in the text. After a suitable number of good comprehension questions have been formulated, the selection of average difficulty is given to the class as a silent reading test. Excessively slow readers can easily be noted by the long time it takes them to finish. Those whose comprehension scores are 70 percent or higher are next given the most difficult selection to read; those with scores below 70, the easiest. In this way, the teacher can determine (1) those who probably will have little difficulty using the text on their own (children who score highly on the most difficult passage); (2) those who probably will need varying degrees of guided assistance in using the text (those who scored 70 percent or above on the selection of average difficulty, but poorly on the most difficult selection); and (3) those for whom the text is much too difficult (children who scored poorly on the easiest selection) and for whom alternate ways of learning are needed. Having each child in the latter group read the easiest passage orally may provide some insights about the reading problems the child is encountering.

Alternatively, a procedure similar to that described above, but using three cloze passages, may be employed. The modified group IRI is more difficult to construct and takes more time to administer than a cloze test, but it may yield more useful information since different types of comprehension may be assessed. Use of a single cloze passage has the advantage of being less time-consuming, but has the disadvantage of being less informative. Use of the "three cloze passage" procedure offers more useful information.

Vocabulary (knowledge of word meaning) may be sampled initially by selecting 20–25 important terms from the material and constructing a group test patterned after standardized reading vocabulary tests. For such tests, each word should be set in context appropriate for the meaning it is most likely to have in that subject field.

Even when content subject texts are of a generally suitable level, the child may not have mastered all of the skills related to success in functional reading. The results of standardized achievement tests which contain subtests that purport to measure such skills, at best only provide general information useful in planning a program. Such tests usually contain too few items pertaining to a single skill to provide reliable information about individuals, and the test may not sample the skills called for in the school's curriculum.

Teachers can construct their own content reading tests; the suggestions offered by Shepherd (1973), Thelan (1976), or Clary (1976) can be used as guidelines. Criterion-referenced tests, based upon the skills covered in the school's curriculum, may be employed to assess mastery. Specific skill strengths and weaknesses can be placed on a class analysis chart to help plan the instructional program. Perhaps the best way to assess progress is through observing whether the students make use of the skills in carrying out their content area assignments.

Thelan (1976) recommended the "every-pupil response" that allows all pupils to respond simultaneously and provides immediate feedback to the teacher. In response to a question, the students hold up cards that indicate their responses. As the cards are displayed, the teacher quickly scans them, makes notes, and then provides immediate oral feedback as to the acceptability of the answers. A skill or concept can be retaught to those who have not assimilated it. A square card with numbers from 1 to 4 written one on each side can be used as follows: sides 1 and 2 for True and False or Yes and No; sides 1–3 for three-choice items, and all four sides for four-choice questions. Specific children can be asked to explain their answers.

READING SKILLS THAT CUT ACROSS CONTENT SUBJECTS

The three skill areas found in developmental reading (word recognition, vocabulary, and comprehension) also are found in functional reading, but it is necessary to build upon these skills as taught in developmental reading because even if one could expect them to transfer directly to reading in the content areas, they would not be sufficient.

Word Recognition and Decoding

By the time most children begin to read independently in content subject materials, their basic word-recognition and decoding skills are fairly well developed. The main task in this area becomes one of applying these skills to unknown words found in the content subject materials. Problems in application are occasioned by the fact that content materials often contain many more unknown words per page than the materials used in the developmental strand.

When uniform material is used with a large group, important new words can be introduced and their specific meanings taught before the children read the material. However, since the current emphasis is on the use of multiple sources, children must be proficient in applying word recognition and decoding skills independently. If the material contains too many unknown words, the children with weak word-recognition or decoding skills are likely to get little information from it, either because their attention is focused on "getting the words" or because they are overwhelmed and do not even bother to try to recognize the words, let alone understand them.

Vocabulary

Reading vocabulary in the content areas is of four types (N. B. Smith 1963). First are the readily identifiable words—those technical words that have significance only in a particular field: *divisor, longitude, electrode.* Studies have repeatedly shown that many content-subject texts are loaded with technical words (Dale, Razik, and Petty 1973). Children often lack an understanding of the concepts for which these technical terms are labels. A thorough working understanding of these concepts is required because not only must the concepts be understood on their own, but also in relation to other concepts.

The second type, which usually cause less of a problem, are the "overlap" words whose fundamental meanings do not vary greatly from one field to the next (e.g., *group* has basically the same meaning in mathematics and social studies). A third type may be classified as polysemantic words that have acquired specialized meanings in different subjects: the *product* obtained in multiplication differs from the *product* of a factory. Such differences need to be pointed out to children. Finally there are the little words whose meanings change from one subject to another. In an ordinary English sentence, *are* indicates existence; in arithmetic it means *equals.* Teaching the distinct meanings of such words often is overlooked.

As stressed in unit 8, acquisition of clear, accurate concepts calls for a linking to children's experience and requires careful illustration and development. Knowing which concepts are essential greatly aids in deciding which ones require careful teaching. The teacher can concentrate on them, making certain that the basic concepts of the subject, and the terms representing them, are mastered.

Comprehension

Most of the material used in developmental reading is of a narrative type. As such, it does not lend itself to the development of all the comprehension skills necessary for success in the content subjects. Content-subject materials require that the reader be able to understand expository material. The problems children may encounter are shown by studies that indicate that the readability levels of content-subject texts are often more difficult than the grade-level designations assigned to them by the publishers (Roe 1970, Chester 1974).

Even these readability data may be misleading because none of the formulas considers concept load or density as a factor, and much content-subject material is compact and has high concept density. Many concepts are related and cumulative, and are presented at a much more rapid pace than that encountered in narrative material. It is difficult, if not impossible, to write about complicated ideas without using complex terms, sentences, and paragraphs. The ability to understand and make use of such material requires the application of known basic skills and the acquisition of special reading-study skills.

Most paragraphs in expository material explain and inform, and the reader often must coordinate information from printed and graphic material. Two of the seven types of paragraphs found in content subject materials (H. A. Robinson 1975) are the explanatory and definitional paragraphs. Explanatory paragraphs call for careful analysis; key words cannot be skipped, and because a complete idea is rarely fully explained in one paragraph, the reader must be able to understand the relationships between paragraphs. Instead of explaining a process or an event, definitional paragraphs attempt to clarify the meaning of one or more words, phrases, or clauses which usually contain technical meaning. In reading such paragraphs, the student should make use of typographical aids and graphic materials as aids to interpreting the definition. Strategies for reading other types of paragraph are presented by H. A. Robinson (1975). The most common types of paragraph found in each subject are listed in the next section.

SPECIFIC SKILLS FOR VARIOUS CONTENT AREAS

Some content areas make use of materials that require rather specialized reading procedures. Only three content subjects are considered here, and a fourth in unit 10. Whether the school is organized on a departmental or self-contained classroom basis, it is the teacher's responsibility to help children acquire the additional skills needed for reading the various materials used in the content subjects. While one cannot deny that one of the teacher's major responsibilities is to impart knowledge, at least equally important is helping students to acquire the skills that enable them to learn from texts on their own.

Arithmetic and Mathematics

Success in mathematics is dependent upon a number of specialized reading-study skills; Earle (1976), for example, listed 16 such skills. It also requires the ability to think abstractly. Mathematical material has to be read very carefully and exactly because it is generally characterized by conciseness, abstraction, and complex relationships. Every word may be critical because understanding the precise meaning of each word may be necessary for accurate comprehension. According to Catterson (1974b), there are two major language patterns in recent mathematics texts. The explanation pattern, which is usually several paragraphs long and designed to present a specific math concept, is often followed by a set of exercises or problems to test the students' understanding of the concept. The problem pattern involves two types: (1) word problems; and (2) single-sentence problems intended to test understanding of a concept—problems that children often find difficult because of the density of vocabulary and instructions.

Among the language competencies vital to reading mathematics is understanding noun phrases, which provide much of the numerical and quantitative information needed, and which may be used as adverbs of frequency ("Barb plays tennis *each day*") or rate ("John earns $2 *an hour*") (Knight and Hargis 1977). Within these constructions, the words employed influence meaning. For example, *a* and *an* rarely have the same meaning as *each* and *every*. The most common syntactical structure found in word problems is the comparative construction that may indicate a level of equality (e.g., Rob has *as* much money *as* Sue) or inequality (e.g., Jimmy is old*er than* Amy). Children's ability to deal with mathematical language may be assessed through object manipulation without requiring a verbal response ("Put a block in *each* box") or by requiring yes/no responses to questions posed as the child views simple pictures ("Are there *more* cats *than* there are dogs?").

The ways in which word problems are written influence their difficulty for children. Rosenthal and Resnick (1974) found that the following types were difficult for third graders: (1) problems in which events are out of chronological order; (2) problems that start with an unknown set, rather than end with it; and (3) problems containing verbs denoting a gain (e.g., *bought*) rather than a loss (e.g., *sold*).

Readability studies have shown that the technical math vocabulary load may be the source of some major reading problems. Many words used in math texts appear infrequently in a common reading vocabulary (Willmon 1975, Rupley 1975). Willmon (1971) listed the 473 words most frequently found in eight primary-grade arithmetic series, and found that 69 percent of the technical terms did not appear on the Thorndike-Lorge list of the 1000 words most frequently occurring in print.

Apart from the computational skills required, the student must understand the symbols used in order to perform such number problems as $2 + 2 = \square$. The relationship between reading and mathematics can be demonstrated by writing and discussing equivalent math and English sentences:

$$2 \quad + \quad 2 \quad = \quad 4$$
Two plus two equals four

Units which may be used for relating reading and mathematics have been presented by Lacey and Weil (1975) for use in grades 4–7.

In order to solve word problems, the student must understand the technical vocabulary and abbreviations used; be able to determine which details are significant and to understand their relationship; and be able to focus on the question asked in the word problem because it determines the significance of the facts given in the problem.

Many children find two-step problems such as the following difficult to solve:

Mrs. Smith had nine oranges. She sold five of them and divided the rest equally between Mary and Helen. How many oranges did each girl get?

In order to find the answer, the child has to understand (1) "the rest" means what was left, or the remainder; (2) therefore, the number sold must be subtracted from the original number of oranges; (3) "divided equally between" means that each girl received half of "the rest"; and (4) "the rest," therefore, is divided by two.

Children also often have difficulty solving word problems containing irrelevant facts, such as:

> Mr. Jones had 10 dogs. Five dogs weighed 80 pounds and 5 weighed 90 pounds. If each dog ate 1½ pounds of food each day, how much food did all 10 dogs eat every day?

Many children attempt to use every number found in the word problem, often automatically adding in every number in the problem. Children can be given guided practice in determining which stated facts are and are not relevant in solving a problem. Other exercises might involve presenting problems from which essential information is missing, and having them identify what is needed. Students also must learn to adjust their reading rate and style to the demands of word problems.

There are several possible strategies for solving word problems. One helpful sequence is: (1) read carefully to determine exactly what the question asks you to find (*to find*); (2) read again to find what relevant facts are given (*given*); (3) interpret clues about the operations revealed by such expressions as *all together, each one,* and *was left* (*clues*); (4) decide what operation must be performed, and in problems requiring more than one step, what the sequence ought to be (*steps*); (5) get a trial answer (*solve*); and (6) verify the answer (*check*). If the answer does not make sense, start over again.

Another procedure suggested by Earle (1976) involves the following steps: (1) read the problem quickly to obtain a general grasp of the problem and to visualize the problem as a whole; (2) reexamine the problem to understand what you are asked to find (it may be stated as a question or a command); (3) reread the problem to note what information is necessary, and what is irrelevant; (4) translate the relationship into math terms (one or more math sentences or equations); (5) perform the necessary computations; (6) examine the solution carefully, labeling it to correspond to what you were asked to find; then (7) check the answer against the problem situation to judge if it is reasonable.

A PQ4R (Preview, Question, Read, Reflect, Rewrite, Review) method for solving word problems has been outlined by Maffei (1973).

Incomplete comprehension when reading word problems often results in erroneous or absurd answers. Erroneous solutions are produced in a variety of ways such as giving the answer in the wrong unit of measurement (feet instead of yards) or choosing the wrong operation because the problem was misunderstood.

When arithmetic reasoning is more of a problem than computation, it often can be helped by treating the difficulty as a specialized form of reading difficulty. Leading the child through the word problem sentence by sentence and asking questions that may reveal interpretations and inferences, helps to locate specific mistakes and correct misunderstanding. Guiding the child through the various steps needed for solving the problem and asking for a response at each step also may provide cues.

Catterson (1974b) suggested giving extra practice in solving word problems by providing a study guide in which the child supplies written answers in the blank spaces opposite each question related to the steps necessary for solving the problem. Such a procedure can help the teacher to determine at what step(s) the child is having difficulty. Children who have difficulty providing their own answers may initially be given multiple-choice items. Word problems whose readability is far beyond the reading ability of the child may be rewritten in easier language.

When students are introduced to algebra and geometry, they have to learn a new kind of language. The concepts of mathematics are both abstract and very sharply defined. Some concepts are represented by symbols ($=$ means *equal to,* $<$ means *less than,* $>$ means *greater than*), letters are used to represent both constants and unknowns, and concepts like *congruent, parallel,* and *perpendicular* are specialized ideas that are fundamental to understanding what the operations mean. Therefore concept development is extremely important if students are to do more than simply memorize formulas.

Social Studies

Although earlier studies suggested that the readability of most social studies books was above the grade level designation of the publishers (Johnson and Vardian 1973), there is some recent indication that the overall reading difficulty of elementary school social studies texts, as well as the range of levels within them, is decreasing (R. E. Johnson 1977). Nevertheless, it should be noted that decreasing the readability score does not necessarily make the material more comprehensible. As Shepherd (1973) has pointed out, social studies material contains many ideas that are removed from children's firsthand experiences. The problem may be compounded by the condensation of the subject matter, and the use of complex sentences. Furthermore, many social studies words represent abstract or indefinite concepts (*democracy*) or may be foreign words with unusual pronunciations (*fjord, Marseilles*). As Preston and Herman (1974, pp. 386–87) have stated: "The textbook by its very nature contains an uncommon number of topics. Because of this, some volumes seem like massive outlines, with only sparse paragraphs on each topic. . . . They present concepts and state generalizations, though with only a minimum of explanation and illustrative examples. They lack space for much detail, for their main task is to cover in one easily transportable volume whatever their subject may be."

Four types of paragraph structures are commonly found in social studies materials, with the first being the most frequent: (1) cause-effect or effect-cause; (2) chronological sequence; (3) comparison/contrast; and (4) detailed enumerative statements of fact. Children should be given direct instruction and guided practice in how to read these types of paragraphs, primarily using material they are required to read.

A useful teaching strategy for helping children to organize the information presented in cause-effect paragraphs involves use of a retrieval chart (Mueller 1975). After the students have read the material, an outline chart (see below) is provided, and the students supply the information for the appropriate boxes:

	Clothing	Food	Control of Children
What the Spartans did			
Results			

The social studies also lend themselves quite well to the development of critical or reflective thinking and reading. For example, after understanding the cause-effect relationships of Spartan child-rearing practices and the nature of the finished product, children could be asked such questions as, "Was it right for the Spartans to treat their children in this way? Why or why not?" Since generalizations abound in historical accounts, their accuracy may be examined. Children often are amazed when they first discover that the same topic is treated differently (perhaps even in a contradictory manner) in different sources. Propaganda techniques are readily found in social studies materials, particularly in primary sources.

A great deal of information is provided in social studies materials through the use of pictures, maps, graphs, charts, and tables. These visual aids are not always interpreted correctly by children; nor are they always well utilized. Pie charts, bar graphs, line graphs, and other kinds of data representation may occur in social studies texts long before their interpretation is presented in mathematics. Each chart or graph can be treated as a reading selection, whose structure needs to be understood, whose concepts need to be mastered, and whose meanings and details are worth exploring.

As for reading maps, filling in outlines (a fairly common practice) merely forces attention to details, without ensuring that understandings are developed. If a map is considered to be a form of reading matter, it can be approached in the usual fashion: (1) preparation, including reference to experience, concept development, and motivation; (2) study (silent reading); and (3) comprehension questions and discussion.

Development of the ability to read maps, graphs, etc., should proceed from the relatively simple to the more complex, as with other skills. For example, young children may first make a map of their school neighborhood and then learn to read it as they actually follow it. Later, they can be helped to understand maps by first seeing an aerial photograph of an area and then relating it to a map. As they get older, many children need assistance in understanding the various purposes (e.g., rainfall, population, products, physical) for which a given map is used. If some maps, charts, and tables are given detailed attention as reading material, the chances are good that other illustrations of the same kind will be used and understood.

Use of Trade Books   Reading only social studies and science texts can become dull and uninteresting. Using trade or library books related to the content in ways suggested by Huus (1974) and Billig (1977) not only can make these subjects more interesting to children because the literature puts the material on a personal basis, but it also can help children understand some of the concepts the texts attempt to impart. Troy (1977), who presented ideas for the use of literature in teaching science as well as social studies, stated that use of fiction can help children understand that history is about people rather than just a series of events.

Using the Newspaper   According to L. Johnson (1975b), the values of using the newspaper as an instructional medium are that it offers (1) an up-to-the-minute source for keeping any textbook current; (2) interesting reading material especially for adolescents who will not, or do not, read books or magazines; and (3) a vehicle for teaching reading skills. Newspaper publishers often offer cut-rate prices to schools, and may offer workshops and other assistance. Some textbook publishers have reprinted actual newspaper accounts covering important events in history. Use of such material may make history seem more alive.

Pillar (1974) has outlined a module for teaching the following newspaper skills: (1) differentiating between fact and opinion; (2) the content and arrangement of a newspaper; (3) determining the most important events of the day; (4) analyzing ways in which stories are presented; (5) differentiating among reportorial, editorial, and emotive writing; and (6) interpreting and evaluating pictures and cartoons. Other suggestions for teaching reading skills through using a newspaper have been offered by Cheyney (1971) and Sargent (1975).

Science

Children may have difficulty reading science materials because of the interrelationships of the myriad of details and facts they contain, as well as the high concept density (Shepherd 1973). These details often result in a generalization, abstraction, or theory the child is expected to understand.

The most frequent types of paragraphs found in science materials are enumeration, classification, generalization, problem solving, comparison/ contrast, and sequence. The suggested strategies for reading these types of paragraphs (H. A. Robinson 1975) may be modified for use with elementary school children.

Graphic aids employed in science often differ from those encountered in social studies. Diagrams, schematic drawings, and exploded views that show parts of a system while retaining their actual relationships to each other often are used to depict or clarify scientific concepts or processes. Such graphic aids are not self-explanatory, so time is well spent in discussing them.

When children encounter formulas, they must learn to read them as they would sentences. Accounts of experiments and directions for performing experiments require the ability to read and follow printed directions accurately. If a weakness is found in this area, guided practice can be provided, starting with relatively simple sets of printed directions (see unit 8, p. 343). Reading and carrying out directions for games can also provide motivated practice; and there are workbooks in which all the practice is in following directions (see pp. 356–58).

Because clarity and precision are requirements of scientific writing, many technical terms are employed. Many science concepts are very abstract and therefore difficult for children to understand. Often textbook definitions are not sufficiently clear to children. Children who merely memorize definitions that they do not understand often miss the essential meanings of sentences and paragraphs in which these concepts are the keys to comprehension.

Careful attention must be given to assure that students truly understand key scientific terms. Of possible help in deciding which words might have unknown meanings is a list of selected science words whose meanings were known by at least 75 percent of the children studied in grades 7 through 12, by grade level (Knight and Bethune 1974).

Moretz and Davey (1974) suggested the following strategy for teaching the meaning of terms: (1) say the word for the process being discussed or demonstrated; (2) present the printed word form; (3) assist the students in examining the word parts for meaning (photosynthesis); (4) provide meaningful situations in which students use the term; and (5) reinforce recently presented terms through varied activities. As many facets of meaning as possible should be brought out (e.g., sensory impressions, uses).

HELPING CHILDREN TO READ A TEXTBOOK

Many children, even those who have little or no difficulty comprehending their on-grade reading texts, find it difficult to read on-grade content-subject texts. The possible reasons for this situation have been discussed in the preceding sections. Four general guidelines (Smith and Barrett 1974) may be followed in helping children with at least average reading ability to read content-subject materials: (1) whenever the ideational content or writing style is difficult, give short reading assignments; (2) know each child's reading and study-skill strengths and weaknesses well enough to anticipate any difficulty the child might encounter in dealing with the assignment; (3) be familiar with the material in order to help students overcome possible trouble spots (e.g. vocabulary, figurative language); and (4) prepare students for the ideas they will meet and point out the possible trouble spots.

Guided Lessons

One way to assist children in learning how to read a given text and gain the most from it is to employ a modified version of a directed reading activity (see unit 3, pp. 79–80).

The first step, preparation, involves relating the new concepts to the children's previous experiences, teaching or introducing the printed words that represent the new concepts, and providing a challenging question that gives a purpose for reading. When children lack related experience, visual aids such as movies, filmstrips, and slides often can be used effectively.

The second step, guided reading, usually starts with silent reading. In addition to the purpose-setting questions, additional questions can be asked and the answers discussed following reading. This silent reading is often done in class, especially in the primary grades, but may be assigned as homework. Both the specific skills one is trying to develop and the nature of the material help to determine the kinds of questions to use.

Depending on the maturity of the children, oral or written questions or responses may be used. Written answers, which require all children to provide responses, should be corrected quickly and any errors or misconceptions should be discussed and clarified. Children can be asked to reread orally to defend their answers; this helps to locate possible reasons for their lack of understanding.

For the most part, related practice will involve outlining, note taking, and summarizing. Guided corrective follow-up practice in word recognition, decoding, and vocabulary should be provided on an individual or small group basis.

Enrichment activities are optional, but as previously noted, supplementary reading of such literature as biographies and historical fiction is desirable. Many types of self-expression can be employed periodically: illustrations may be made, models constructed, experiments conducted and evaluated, and historical events dramatized.

Systematic Study Procedures

When one talks about reading in the content areas, one is usually referring to studying; that is, attempting to understand and to remember information found in a given source. Perhaps it is not so surprising to find that students often lack study skills when one considers a study (Askov, Kamon, and Klumb 1977) which found that some teachers themselves did not possess many such skills. You cannot teach what you do not know.

A number of systematic study procedures are currently available, all of which stem from the SQ3R method developed by F. P. Robinson (1962). That procedure has five steps: Survey, Question, Read, Recite, and Review. During the survey, which is a form of skimming, the reader attempts to obtain a quick overview of the material. This preview may involve read-the table of contents (if it is a book); skimming introductory and summary paragraphs, as well as the headings; and briefly studying graphic aids. In order to involve the student actively in the reading process, the second step requires turning headings, subheadings, or topic sentences into questions. This is intended to help the reader to establish a purpose for reading, and to focus reader attention. The next step involves reading to answer the questions, while taking care not to ignore other important information. Reading is then followed by recitation to oneself, which may assume varying forms depending upon individual preferences. What one has read may be summarized by underlining, taking notes, outlining, or reciting aloud or silently. Difficulty in recalling the information needed for recitation suggests that the reader does not have a firm grasp of the content and therefore should reread the material. Recitation also provides an immediate review. The final step involves both immediate and spaced review in order to aid long-term memory for the material.

Pauk (1973) has questioned the value of SQ3R and other such procedures. He believed that most problems in reading a text were caused by difficulty in (1) selecting essential ideas and their supporting details; and (2) remembering them. Pauk suggested the following direct-study approach, which some intermediate-grade students and older children could employ with slight modifications: (1) draw two vertical columns on a sheet of paper; (2) read a page or two, stopping at the end of a section or topic; (3) with the material still fresh in mind, go back to the beginning of the material just read, and select the essential ideas, facts, and supporting details; (4) as these essentials are selected, they are written in the reader's own words in the left-hand column; (5) after the chapter or unit is completed, return to the beginning of the notes, and in the right-hand column opposite each idea, jot down a key word or phrase; and (6) cover the left-hand column, and using only the right-hand column as a cue, recite aloud the full notes which the key words summarize. The sixth step, recitation, is essential. Reflection, a logical follow-through, should involve thinking about what has been read and going beyond the facts (Pauk 1975).

Notes, in whatever form, should be studied by imposing some structure on them through rearranging, reconstructing, synthesizing, conceptualizing, and internalizing the essential information. Once the information has been organized, readers can relate what has been read to their own frames of reference by speculating on the information, and asking themselves such questions as "What do these facts lead to?" or "Why are these ideas important?"

Guiding the Initial Reading Before and during the initial reading the teacher, through relevant questioning, may focus attention on (1) what the introductory paragraph does; (2) the meanings of center headings and their relationship to the topic and each other; (3) the meanings of side and marginal headings and their relationship to center headings and each other; (4) the direction the material takes (e.g., transitional expressions); (5) the thinking skills required (e.g., comparison, cause-effect); (6) how illustrations and typographic aids contribute to obtaining meaning; (7) what the chapter or section conclusions tell; and (8) the use of vocabulary lists, author's questions, and suggested additional readings (Tinker and McCullough 1975).

Tinker and McCullough (1968) also suggested that prior to making the reading assignment, the teacher must decide whether she wants the children to get what the author or the teacher thinks is important. If it is what the author believed to be important, the teacher directs the student to the ways in which the author indicated importance (italics, main headings, amount of space devoted, repeated mention, questions in the text, etc.). If the teacher wants to emphasize something else, she must present specific questions that guide the selection and organization of ideas (e.g., "Compare . . ." or "Summarize . . .").

Study Guides Another way to assist students in understanding content subject texts and recalling important information is to provide them with a study guide to which they may refer as needed to find or to verify an answer. As Tutolo (1977) has suggested, study guides can be designed (1) so that students are asked to respond to questions according to their ability (e.g., less capable students primarily answer literal comprehension questions); (2) to focus the student's attention on the paragraph structure (e.g., "The first two sentences in this paragraph will tell you why [the cause] the men hated the stranger [the effect]"); or (3) to lead the students through a specific skill development (drawing a conclusion). Attention also may be focused on aspects of the material that may cause a problem (e.g., an implied relationship), or of which the students should be aware (e.g., "In this sentence, *however* signals that a contrast is coming"), or use of typographical aids ("The word in the darkest print is very important to understand").

These study guides, which are intended to stimulate and direct the thinking process, are usually typewritten pages that can be duplicated. If the teacher cannot find the time to develop a study guide for a whole text, such guides may be developed cooperatively with other teachers employing the same text. Or the teacher may first wish to develop brief guides covering only the most relevant concepts, and later develop and revise more complete guides through the years.

In the limited-purpose type of study guide described by Cunningham and Shablak (1975), the teacher (1) determines the overall purpose for a particular reading assignment; (2) selects those sections of the reading necessary to achieve that purpose (all irrelevant sections are eliminated from the assignment); and (3) determines step by step what must be done operationally to achieve that purpose. Not only are students told what to look for, they are also specifically told what to do with it when it is found. For example, the guide might state: "Page 42, para. 1: A question is raised in the last sentence that can be answered by reading the next two paragraphs. State the question in your own words before you continue reading." Or, it might state: "Page 19, para. 3: Read this paragraph carefully because it describes how a car engine uses gasoline."

The following procedure (Herber and Nelson 1975), which might aid older students in reading content-subject materials, is based on two assumptions: (1) that because teachers are more skilled than students in perceiving relationships, they can establish an instructional sequence that moves students along a continuum toward independence; and (2) it is easier to recognize information and ideas than to produce them. It involves the following stages: (1) The teacher prepares a number of statements for the pupils' reaction. Exact references are given to indicate where the information supporting the statements may be found in the text. (2) The teacher prepares the statements, but references are to be found by the pupils. (3) The teacher prepares questions for the students to answer. References are given indicating where the information needed for answering the questions may be found in the text. (4) The teacher prepares questions, but no references are given. (5) The pupils survey the material to raise their own questions and then answer them. (6) The students produce statements.

Study guides for use in mathematics have been illustrated by Freeman

(1973). Thomas and Robinson (1972) and many of the references cited in this section contain examples of study guides or offer other helpful suggestions for teaching reading in the content subjects. Those interested in reading further in the area will find the annotated bibliography compiled by Fay and Jared (1975) helpful.

Preinstructional Strategies Among the procedures that have been employed to facilitate learning through reading are advance organizers, which have taken many names and shapes. The purpose of advance organizers, as conceptualized by Ausubel (1963), is to relate material that is to be learned to the already existing cognitive structure of the learner. Advance organizers are supposed to provide a conceptual framework that the learner can use to clarify the learning task. They differ from overviews and summaries. Advance organizers are written at a level of abstraction and generality above that of the material to be learned, while overviews and summaries are written at the same level of abstraction as the material and accomplish their effects through repetition and selective emphasis on key words or central concepts.

In their review of the literature, Barnes and Clawson (1975) found 12 studies that supported the usefulness of advance organizers, and 20 that did not. There was no clear pattern even when variables such as length of the study, the ability and grade level of the subjects, type of organizer, and cognitive level of the learning task were analyzed separately. Barnes and Clawson concluded that as presently constructed, advance organizers do not generally facilitate learning.

The possible effects of providing students with specific behavioral (instructional) objectives are also debatable. For example, Kurtz (1974) found that use of behavioral objectives with sixth-grade students had no significant effect on learning from prose. Using high school students, Kaplan and Simmons (1974) found that although there was no significant difference in the overall performance between subjects who received the objectives before or after reading the material, there was a difference in the type of information learned. Relevant learning (information directly related to the objectives) was facilitated by presenting the objectives before the material was read, and incidental learning by presenting them after the material was read.

As to the relative effectiveness of pretests, behavioral objectives, overviews, and advance organizers, Hartley and Davies (1976) concluded (based on their review of the literature) that the advantage of using any of these preinstructional strategies is not clear cut, and that many of the reported advantages may be due to flaws or inadequacies in research procedures.

HELPING POOR READERS TO LEARN IN THE CONTENT SUBJECTS

When a text is beyond the reading ability of a child, the teacher must seek alternative ways of enabling the child to learn what it contains. Sometimes an easier text or other source covering the same topic can be found. Over the years teachers can acquire a collection of materials that may be used for such a purpose.

Sole reliance on a single text has a number of limitations, not the least of which is its probably excessive difficulty for many of the children. Other drawbacks are the fact that only one point of view is usually presented, and the use by many teachers of deadly whole class lessons in which children take turns reading orally from the text.

Use of a unit or project approach not only helps to overcome these limitations but also allows the teacher to accommodate the wide range of reading abilities typically found in a class. In a project approach the main topic usually is divided into several subtopics, each of which becomes the responsibility of a committee. Ordinarily the committee is structured so that it contains students with a wide range of reading abilities. This not only helps to break down the stigma often attached to low reading groups, but also provides the opportunity for use of varying materials at levels suitable for each child. Each major subtopic is analyzed with the aid of the teacher into specific issues and questions, and these are organized into an outline. The committee members utilize the available sources of information (not all of which may involve reading). Because of the range of reading ability within each committee, a number of pertinent sources covering a wide range of readability must be available to them.

Use of a variety of sources presents the teacher with a natural opportunity for providing meaningful direct instruction and guided practice in reading and study skills. While the children are individually perusing books, pamphlets, and other sources, the teacher should be free to provide help and guidance as needed. Circulating around the room, the teacher can spot children who are having difficulty and confer briefly with each. Thus individual problems in applying previously taught skills can be overcome, and the skills be made functionally effective.

Even when a curriculum is centered around a single text, which serves as a summary and springboard to related activities and discussions, units and projects can be very helpful in providing varied opportunities for putting reading and study skills to use. Research-type reading skills are best developed when there is a real need for their use.

At times it is suggested that teachers rewrite or edit existing material so that children can better comprehend it. Among the editing suggestions offered by Cardinell (1976) for keeping the material as factually accurate and representative of the original as possible are: (1) retain some of the especially appropriate words to maintain the "feel" of the selection, provided their meanings are explained by the context or by the inclusion of an additional paragraph which clarifies a difficult concept; and (2) use shorter sentences, being careful to avoid choppy sentences or eliminating words that indicate the flow of ideas; (3) minimize the use of passive sentences, dependent clauses, participles, inverted sentences, and parenthetical expressions; and (4) attempt to use words that evoke imagery.

Another procedure involves differentiated assignments in which students are assigned tasks at varying levels of difficulty or complexity in an inquiry-based approach (Devon, Klein, and Murphy 1975). For example, the poorest readers (provided of course the text is not far beyond their capabilities) may be asked to read page 10 and to list the three major causes of forest fires; the best readers, to read Chapter 2 and to summarize the economic effects of forest fires (Bader 1974). The assignments may be in a single text or involve reading materials of varying degrees of difficulty.

When it is considered essential for a child to learn what is in a particular text that he or she cannot read, the concepts may be acquired through listening. Although some learning will probably occur from listening to lectures and class discussions, it is also important for the disabled reader to participate in the discussions. Therefore, prior to taking up the topic in class, the material can be read to the child by a family member, who may also discuss and review the information with the child. Lessons also may be taped and used by children. When information is to be acquired through listening, it becomes important to teach children how to listen (see unit 8, p. 321).

Sometimes a text is so difficult that it is at or above the frustration level for the majority of the class. Under these conditions it is advisable to use the text only as a reference and collection of illustrations, centering the main instructional program around other materials as in the unit approach discussed above. Sometimes the main factual material must be presented through lectures and by providing mimeographed material, or putting notes on the board for the children to copy. Such procedures should be accompanied by discussion and clarification of the concepts presented.

When it is necessary for children to acquire concepts in ways other than by reading, adjustments should also be made in determining their knowledge of the concepts. For testing, the teacher must either construct a test which the child can read, or administer the test orally. Children are likely to become discouraged if they are learning, but fail the subject simply because they cannot read the test or lack the written communication skills needed to demonstrate their knowledge.

Many children find that the time available in school for studying their texts is insufficient. Allowing children to take texts home provides them with the opportunity to reread, to look up words, and to write notes or summarize. If the book is too difficult for a child to read, a family member can read it to or with the child. Schools that do not allow children to take texts home lose a valuable amount of potential learning. Many children need more time for reading and studying their content subject texts than the school day provides.

LOCATIONAL SKILLS

The ability to locate desired information is a vitally important tool. Locational skills include knowing which sources to consult, where to find them, and how to discover the needed information efficiently. The discussion begins with the latter.

Alphabetical Sequence

Because so many sources of information (e.g., dictionaries, directories, encyclopedias, indexes) are arranged alphabetically, the ability to locate items quickly in an alphabetical sequence is very useful. Informal work on alphabetizing usually begins in the first grade with arranging word cards by their first letter. Systematic instruction in alphabetization is usually given as an introduction to the use of the dictionary, and may begin with picture dictionaries in the first grade.

Although most first graders can recite the alphabet in correct sequence, wide variations occur as with most skills. Some children will have complete knowledge, while others may not know all the letter names, let alone their alphabetical order. A quick way to assess such knowledge is to ask the class to write the alphabet in "the right order." Because such a task also requires writing skills, those who fail it may be asked, apart from their peers, to recite the alphabet aloud.

Instruction may need to be varied. Some children will first need to learn to associate letter names with their printed symbols. For those who know letter names, but not alphabetical order, instruction may involve placing three to five letters (starting with *a, b, c*) in correct sequence until the complete alphabetical order is learned. Alphabet charts may be helpful and singing the alphabet jingle in unison aids some children.

Once alphabetical sequence is known, children should learn where letters belong without having to recite the sequence from the start. The teacher can ask such questions as "What letter follows (comes after) *m*?" "What letter comes before *h*?" "What letter comes between *b* and *d*?" Of course the sequential concepts (*after, follows, before, between*) must be understood. Written exercises of this type can be used for individual, group, or class practice.

Next children can learn to arrange words in sequence according to first letter. To assess this skill, present about five words, each starting with a different letter, and ask the children to put them in alphabetical order. Individual or group instruction can be provided for those who have trouble with this pretest. After they can alphabetize by the first letter, children can go on to words that have the same first letters, but different second letters. They can start with pairs (*apple, axe*), deciding which should come first in the pair. Then they can be given series of words differing in the second letter (*copper, candle, cute, center, cradle*). When this level of alphabetization has been mastered, the same general procedure can be used with words which differ only in the third letters.

After basic knowledge of alphabetical sequence has been acquired, some guided practice in applying it in specific situations can be provided. The dictionary is the natural place to start. To find words quickly, children should be able to open the dictionary near the entry (alphabetically tabbed dictionaries facilitate this skill); decide whether it is necessary to turn forward or backward; use the guide words to locate the page on which the word appears; and then skim down the columns to find the word.

Practice in these skills can be made interesting by having each child record the time it takes to perform the task, trying to lessen the time with each successive practice session. A list of 10 to 20 assorted words can be placed on the board. At a signal, all start using their dictionaries to locate each word. As each word is located, the child writes down the page number and the word that precedes the one being sought. As each child finishes the list, he or she looks up and copies a number that the teacher has been changing every fifteen seconds. The child's number, divided by four, is the number of minutes it took that child to complete the task.

Once skill in locating words in a dictionary has been achieved, it is usually not necessary to have similar practice sessions in other alphabetical references, except as noted below. Usually it suffices to point out that the same skills can be applied in using any reference that is set up in alphabetical order.

Indexes

Indexes in books can present special problems. Some indexes are carefully made, so that if you want to locate information about the legibility of the letters of the alphabet, the relevant pages can be found under both *legibility* and *letters*. Other indexes contain only the brief notation: *letters, see legibility;* or the item may be represented by one term, not both. Sometimes the only way to be sure of obtaining the necessary information is to check both words. Practice in discussing and solving problems such as the following can promote efficient use of an index: If you need to learn about the value of the annual tobacco crop in Virginia, would you first look under *value, annual, tobacco, crop,* or *Virginia*? Why? What other word(s) might you look under? Why? Exercises such as the one in figure 9.1 also may provide needed practice and can be used to monitor progress.

Using a library card index requires specific information about the ways in which books are indexed. In many such card indexes, books are entered by the author's name, by title, and by topic. Some of the questions that may puzzle children are illustrated by the following: Can you find a book about Abraham Lincoln without knowing the author's name or the exact title? If so, should you look in the *As* or *Ls*? What do you do when many authors have the same last name? Why copy down the number of the book found on the index card? How can you tell from the index card where to find the book in the library?

Certain specific kinds of information about indexing should be explained

INDEX

UNIT 8

Aquarium: home, 26, 27, 29; oceanariums, 41, 42, 44; origin, 33-35, 38; plants in, 43, 45-47; public, 37, 39-41; water filter, 48, 49, 51

Barton, Clara: American Red Cross, 65, 67-69, 71; author, 63, 64, 66; clerk, 61; Johnstown Flood, 70, 71, 73; nurse, 65, 72, 73, 75

Brazil: architecture, 89, 93-95; coffee, 96-98, 101-103; discovery, 86, 87, 89; rain forest, 88, 90-92 (*map*); recreation, 104, 105, 107

Caterpillar: birth, 121, 122, 124; defenses, 123, 127, 129; growth, 125, 126; homes, 130-132, 134, 135

See also Butterfly; Moth

QUESTIONS

1. Which pages would you read to obtain information concerning the earliest aquariums?
   - (A) 37, 39-41
   - (B) 43, 45-47
   - (C) 33-35, 38

2. How many pages probably deal with books Clara Barton wrote?
   - (A) 3
   - (B) 4
   - (C) 5

3. On which pages would you find information on sports and other leisure-time activities in Brazil?
   - (A) 89, 93-95
   - (B) 96-98, 101-103
   - (C) 104, 105, 107

4. Which pages are likely to provide information about the size of caterpillars?
   - (A) 125, 126
   - (B) 121, 122, 124
   - (C) 130-132, 134, 135

5. Which pages would furnish information on the shelters of caterpillars?
   - (A) 121, 122, 124
   - (B) 123, 127, 129
   - (C) 130-132, 134, 135

FIGURE 9.1. Exercise to develop the ability to use an index. Taken from Richard A. Boning, *Using an Index*, p. 10. Copyright © 1975 by Dexter & Westbrook, Ltd. Reproduced by permission of the publisher.

to children, and illustrated for them. For example, *A* and *The* are disregarded in alphabetizing items. With items like *Isle of Wight*, the proper name takes priority (*Wight, Isle of*). Because many children do not discover these details for themselves, they need opportunities to practice locating information through use of an index, and to seek help from the teacher when they encounter difficulty in doing so.

Table of Contents

Use of the table of contents of a book begins early in the primary grades, usually with the book being used for reading instruction. The table of contents allows one to find the page on which a story, chapter, or major topic begins. As such it is a time-saver, but when specific details are sought, the index is more useful.

Reference Works

Encyclopedias are invaluable sources of information, but children need guided practice in learning how to use them for locating answers to specific questions. The index is often very complex, and sometimes the list of subheadings under a topic is a little index in itself. Also, the continuity of pagination from one volume to the next may be confusing. Furthermore, the alphabet guide on the spine of each volume requires a new application of alphabetizing: Is *Mississippi River* to be found in the volume marked LEUX-MEND or MEND-NEER? If you want information about what electrical engineers do, should you look up *electrical, engineering,* or *profession*? The teaching sequence of skills needed in using reference works includes (1) learning what types of information can be found in various reference works; (2) deciding under which headings or entries the information is most likely to be found; (3) locating the correct volume in works of more than one volume; and (4) interpreting commonly used abbreviations. Each of these skills can be organized into a sequence of relatively brief, sequential lessons. At each higher grade these skills should be assessed, reviewed if necessary, and brought to a higher level of efficiency.

Teachers should be aware that the readability level cf many encyclopedias may present difficulties for children. For example, a study of the readability of eight multivolume encyclopedias indicated that 66 percent of the reading matter in them was too difficult for intermediate-grade children, especially for fourth graders (Dohrman 1974). Furthermore, teachers should guard against the mistaken belief that something is an indisputable fact if found in an encyclopedia. As Wehmeyer (1975) has illustrated, encyclopedias can and do report different, and sometimes contradictory, "facts." Children should be aware of this possibility and be encouraged to investigate contradictions and disagreements found in references.

Among the many kinds of reference works with which children should become acquainted prior to senior high school are atlases, almanacs, yearbooks, *Reader's Guide to Periodical Literature,* a biographical dictionary, and a thesaurus. An introduction to each of these by a teacher or librarian can open up a new avenue for independent learning.

A process method for locating information has been suggested and illustrated by Sanacore (1974a). After selecting a problem to solve, the student (1) records the problem; (2) analyzes the problem in terms of key words and the types of information and reference tools that might be helpful; (3) uses basic references (e.g., *How and Where to Look it Up, Guide to Reference Books*) that direct one to more specific sources; (4) indicates where the desired information was found, and notes specific citations; and (5) lists the reference tools he or she became aware of as a result of this project.

Skimming

Skimming techniques are discussed in unit 8 (p. 337). This kind of specialized reading skill finds its greatest use in the search for information in special reference works. As with other skills, skimming is best practiced in using materials in which the skill is naturally employed.

SUMMARIZING AND ORGANIZING IDEAS

Summarizing what one reads is a basic study skill. Whether the purpose is reviewing for a test, or bringing together information from various sources in a report, a good written summary saves time because the original sources need not be reread.

The very act of summarizing requires that one read carefully, thoughtfully, and with the intent of discovering the structure of the author's plans.

One must select main ideas, decide what details are worth noting, understand how ideas are related, and restate the author's words in one's own words. Summarizing forces the employment of comprehension skills, aside from its value as a written record.

Early Beginnings

First-grade children should be introduced to the beginnings of summarizing in a natural way. In planning a trip, the important things to look for are discussed, then listed by the teacher. Each experience story is a summary developed in group discussion, and at first recorded by the teacher. Children get practice in deciding what is important, in stating ideas clearly, and in arranging them in proper sequence.

Whenever a project or activity is planned, additional practice in organizing and recording is gained. Teacher guidance is essential because most young children need help in separating the essential from the nonessential, the important from the inconsequential or irrelevant. The teacher can guide discussion skillfully so that the children have opportunities to evaluate ideas and to decide which of alternate ways of stating an idea is best. General questions are listed, with specific questions listed under each. As answers are found and entered under the questions, an organized summary gradually takes shape. At the same time, practice in reading to locate answers to questions, to select main ideas, and to relate details to them helps to lay the groundwork for outlining and note taking.

Summarizing

The ability to express essential ideas clearly and succinctly is basic to both outlining and note taking. Summarizing has three main features: (1) skill in finding main ideas; (2) deciding whether the main idea is all that should be recorded, or if some amplifying details are also needed; and (3) stating the essential thoughts in one's own words as briefly as possible.

Learning to restate an author's thoughts in one's own words requires considerable effort. Understanding of an idea is demonstrated when the author's particular verbal formulation can be put into one's own language. Analyzing and writing newspaper headlines is one very useful kind of practice in stating ideas briefly. Another is taking well-written prose and paraphrasing it, sentence by sentence, always striving for a sentence briefer than the original but having the same essential meaning. One learns to delete adjectives, adverbs, and nonessential phrases and clauses, cutting sentences down to minimum essentials of subject and predicate. The preceding sentence, for example, could be summarized as: Cut sentences to minimum essentials. Obviously, such a brief representation of an idea is less explicit than the original and cannot convey the full meaning, but it is sufficient to serve as a reminder of the full thought if one has read the original.

Outlining

Factual material in which the structure is easy to identify is best suited for teaching outlining, which may begin in the middle grades. Outlining single paragraphs should come first. The main idea is identified by roman numeral I, and the details are indented and identified by capital letters. Each idea is expressed in a condensed form. At first, completed outlines are presented by the teacher who points out and discusses the importance of outlining and how the outline was derived. Then the teacher and children can outline a few paragraphs together, with the children suggesting the wording of items. Comparing these suggestions and choosing the best ones allows children to learn naturally "telegram style" writing in which only essential words are employed.

The second step is to provide a complete skeleton with a few items (either headings or details) filled in. During the third stage, the structure of the outline is given, and the children fill in both headings and details. In stage four, only the number of main headings is indicated. Finally, the children are to complete an outline without assistance.

When some competence in outlining single paragraphs has been attained, short selections of a few paragraphs each can be provided. For the first few such selections, the teacher does most of the work, getting suggestions from the children. The second step is providing a skeleton outline, with a few headings filled in, the rest to be completed by the children. Figure 9.2 illustrates an exercise of this kind. Finally, children can be asked to outline selections completely on their own.

Next, the material can have a more complex pattern, with headings, subheadings, and sub-subheadings. With such materials, children can be taught a sequence of subordination: Roman numeral, capital letter,

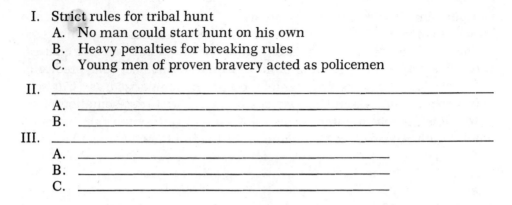

I. Strict rules for tribal hunt
    A. No man could start hunt on his own
    B. Heavy penalties for breaking rules
    C. Young men of proven bravery acted as policemen

II. _____
    A. _____
    B. _____
III. _____
    A. _____
    B. _____
    C. _____

FIGURE 9.2.   Example of a partially completed outlining exercise. A four-paragraph selection about the Plains Indians has been used. A complete outline of the first paragraph is given; only the number of subtopics for the second and third paragraphs is indicated; the fourth paragraph is to be outlined entirely by the student on a separate sheet. Reprinted by permission from *Indians of the Plains* by Eugene Rachlis. Copyright © 1960 by American Heritage Publishing Company, Inc., p. 33.

Arabic number, lower-case letter, Arabic numeral in parentheses, lower-case letter in parentheses. Rarely will children have the occasion to go beyond the fourth, or lower-case letter, level of subordination. A formal outline of this unit, for example, does not need to be carried beyond the fourth level. Thus, the present paragraph would be represented as follows (preceding parts of the outline being omitted).

VII. Summarizing and organizing ideas
    C. Outlining
        3. Introducing finer subdivisions
            a. subheadings can be further subdivided
            b. usual sequence of symbols: I, A, 1, a, (1), (a)
            c. usually 4 levels of subordination sufficient
            d. present paragraph illustrates c

The same instructional sequence listed above can be used with selections containing such subdivisions. The amount of practice needed at each step will vary from child to child and will usually involve a series of learning sessions and later practice in applying outlining in many reading situations.

Note Taking

It is desirable to teach the use of a formal outline before introducing note taking. Once one has learned to think in outline terms, the number-and-letter scheme can be discarded.

Note taking demands selective thoughtful reading. One must select what is worth recording, separate main from subordinate points, consider the relationships among ideas, and briefly put the author's ideas into one's own words. The summarizing and outlining skills needed for note taking are most often put to use in making records of what we read; somewhat less often, in recording lectures. Use of a formal outline is unnecessary when taking notes that are to be used only by oneself in later reviewing.

Brevity can be fostered not only by shortening sentences, but also by using grammatically incomplete sentences and by employing abbreviations. It is advisable to indent subordinate ideas as in a formal outline, without bothering to label them with numbers or letters. Important concepts can be underlined to highlight them.

In underlining the text, a form of note taking, the reader should set up some key whereby main ideas are differentiated from minor or supporting points. For example, main ideas can be double underscored and subpoints underscored, numbered, or lettered. Some readers prefer to underscore entire sentences; others like to underline only key phrases or words. One way to combat the inclination to underline too much is to underline only after a section with a center or side heading has been read. This prevents underlining as one reads along, only to find the material summarized at the end of the section. Moreover, if the material is clearly understood, the reader should have little difficulty in deciding what to underline. If one does have difficulty, rereading is indicated.

Efficient reading notes on the first paragraph of this subsection might look like this (complete words shown in parentheses would not appear; they are shown here to illustrate the possible use of abbreviations):

Note taking
    Tch (Teach) formal outline 1st
    Demands selective thoughtful rdg. (reading)
    Used more in rdg. than lectures
    Be brief—use ungrammatical sent. (sentences) & abbrev. (abbreviations)
    Indent sub-ideas; don't label
    Highlight impt. (important) ideas

Castallo (1976) has described the use of a listening guide as a lead-in to note taking. An incomplete outline (main idea and the first major subheading) is given to the children to look over before the lecture (or reading assignment). As the lecture proceeds, the children fill in the blanks at the appropriate times, while the teacher does the same on an overhead projector or board (this presents a model).

In addition to taking notes on relatively long selections, such as chapters in texts, students often need to assemble information from a variety of sources for a report. For this, some training in using index cards is helpful, both to summarize and to copy desirable quotations. It also is necessary for students to learn how to record the origin of their information (bibliographic data such as found in the Bibliography of this book) so that a footnote citing the reference can be written later, if needed.

Before using a variety of sources to make a report, the student should make at least a general outline of what he hopes to find. The original outline can be modified as additional or unexpected information is uncovered. This provides a framework both in knowing what to look for when reading the sources, and later in writing the report.

STUDY HABITS

Study habits, as distinguished from study skills, refer to the habitual tendencies that individuals develop in regard to the amount of time they spend in studying and the conditions of time, place, and circumstances that determine to a considerable degree how well they use the reading and study skills they have learned.

Teachers are often concerned about helping their students learn the contents of their subjects. It is also important to help the students to become efficient users of time, who can apply sound reading and study skills under self-selected conditions that make for efficient learning.

Assessing Study Habits

Assessing study habits is important for two reasons. One is finding out what does happen when the students study. The second is bringing out the conditions that make it easy or difficult to study efficiently. Perhaps this can be done through appropriate reading, but group discussion and consideration of individual difficulties are more important.

Charting Use of Time   One of the most frequent causes of poor academic work is devoting insufficient time to it. Many children do not realize how much time they waste—time which is used neither for study nor for worthwhile recreation or socialization. The first step in assisting them with this problem is to help them to discover the facts.

In the upper middle school, junior high, or senior high school, a teacher or guidance counselor can recommend keeping a chart of the use of time for a typical week. A page is ruled into seven vertical columns, each headed with a day of the week. Then the page is ruled horizontally into appropriate time intervals. Time outside of school can be ruled in half-hour intervals; school time according to the length of the school periods. For one week, a child records what he or she does each day, from getting up to going to bed.

Some boys and girls manage to waste large amounts of time. They dawdle before starting to work and take excessive time getting a drink or snack, looking out the window, or just daydreaming. The easiest way to take account of this is to fill in the time chart immediately after each period of study, and to rate in percent the proportion of time that was actually spent in studying. One way to keep track of interruptions is to place a check mark on a sheet of paper each time the individual's mind or body strays from the task.

The value of any procedure such as this depends on the interest and cooperation of the group and their motivation for carrying it through honestly. If they are convinced that its purpose is to help them to become better students, and that honest self-ratings will not be used against them, reasonably honest recordkeeping can be expected.

After keeping a time chart for a week, each student can compute the number of hours spent in each of such activities as living routines (e.g., dressing, eating) attending classes, travel, study, chores or work, and recreational and social activities. Many students are genuinely surprised to learn that they actually spent considerably less time studying than they had estimated. At this point the teacher can help to clarify the question of how much time is usually needed to study a subject conscientiously. Each student can then formulate a time plan for the next week and try to carry it out. An example of such a plan is shown in figure 9.3. Of course, no two

	Sun.	Mon. Tues. Weds. Thurs. Fri. Sat.
7:15 – 8:00		Get ready for school ⟶
8:00 – 8:30		Ride school bus ⟶
8:30 – 9:15	Breakfast	Home room/study hall ⟶ Breakfast
9:15 – 12:15	Free	Classes ⟶ Free
12:15 – 1:00	Lunch	⟶
1:00 – 3:00	Free	Classes ⟶ Free
3:00 – 4:00	Free	After school activities ⟶ Free
4:00 – 4:30	Free	Ride school bus ⟶ Free
4:30 – 6:00	Study	Outdoors ⟶ Study
6:00 – 7:00	Dinner	⟶
7:00 – 8:30	Free	Study ⟶ Free
8:30 – 10:00	Free	⟶

FIGURE 9.3.   A one-week plan for use of time.

students will set exactly the same goals for themselves and come out with identical plans. Once a reasonably efficient plan has been established, the pupil can use it to guide study habits.

Teacher Observations

In the upper grades there are usually some supervised study periods, or subject periods in which part of the time is spent in reading for information. During such periods useful observations can be made. All the teacher needs is a seating chart and the willingness to carry out a simple observational plan. Usually two different symbols are enough: one is used when a child interrupts his or her own work in a way that does not disturb others; and the other is used when the child interrupts or disturbs others. Each time a child stops studying, the appropriate symbol is entered in his or her box in the seating chart. At the end of the study period, typically some boxes will be empty; others quite filled.

When there is a pattern of poor concentration and frequent interruptions, the results of study-period observations are best taken up privately with individuals. Of course, a frustratingly difficult text can induce inattentiveness. Those with the least ability to sustain attention during study periods often have other problems as well, and the inability to concentrate is often only part of a larger problem of general adjustment, or is symptomatic of some emotional or physical disability. Children who have serious difficulty in attending to studying should be referred to the school psychologist, guidance counselor, or an appropriate outside agency.

Physical Conditions for Studying

Listing the desirable conditions for studying is relatively easy; providing them is much harder. They include: privacy, freedom from interruptions and distracting sights and sounds, good nonglare lighting, a comfortable straight-backed chair, and a desk of appropriate height with room enough to allow the spreading out of books and papers.

It is possible for students to get work done under highly unfavorable conditions. Some manage to concentrate while working at a kitchen table, with perhaps a phone conversation going on nearby or a television set competing for attention. Some children get so accustomed to studying with the radio playing popular music that they have trouble concentrating when it is quiet. They are somehow able to relegate the noise to the background. These facts testify to human adaptability; they do not contradict the general desirability of freedom from distractions, and a physical setting that provides for a comfortable study posture and freedom from eyestrain.

Completion of a simple questionnaire can reveal quite a bit about a child's study conditions at home. Some disadvantaged children live under crowded and unsatisfactory conditions that make study at home almost impossible. It would be a mistake to assume, however, that children from more advantaged homes necessarily have satisfactory conditions for study at home. Sometimes their parents are either indifferent to their study needs or do not realize what is needed.

Motivating Students to Study

Many children take their schoolwork quite seriously by the time they reach the middle grades. When parents are interested, motivation for improving academic achievement is self-generated and the teacher's role is one of helping to analyze difficulties and suggesting ways in which study habits can be improved. In these cases, motivation is not a real problem.

Some children react against parental overemphasis on academic success by becoming resentful or rebellious, using insufficient study and the resulting unsatisfactory marks as a weapon against their parents. It is best to refer such parent-child problems to a psychologist, counselor, or social worker.

Other children, because of their cultural heritage, see little "payoff" in studying. Therefore, it is most important to convince them of two things: (1) they have the ability to succeed in school, despite their previous records; and (2) better occupations, higher education, and self-fulfillment are open to them. For many of these students, successful attainment of short-term goals is more motivating than long-range goals. When disadvantaged students feel that academic success is worthwhile, they often are as responsive to instruction and guidance as other groups of children.

MATERIALS FOR PRACTICING
FUNCTIONAL READING SKILLS

Among the materials that focus primarily on reading in the content subjects are:

Be a Better Reader (Prentice-Hall). Books A–C for grades 4–6, books 1–6 for grades 7–12. Each contains a variety of word recognition, vocabulary, comprehension, and study skills in 4 content subjects.

Scholastic Go (Scholastic). Designed for students reading below grade level in grades 4–8. In each text, which covers 4 content areas, the readability begins below grade level and gradually increases to grade level.

Reading Comprehension in Varied Subject Matter (Educators). Eight workbooks (grades 3–10), each comprising 31 selections followed by various types of vocabulary and comprehension questions; each book covers a variety of subject areas.

Learning to Use the Library (Xerox Educational). Series of 4 books for grades 3–6 covering the parts of a book, finding a particular book, locating periodicals, and using key reference books.

Study Skills for Information Retrieval Series (Allyn & Bacon). Three workbooks containing exercises on locating, organizing, and summarizing information; for use in fourth grade and up.

Study Skills Library (EDL). Multilevel kits (grades 3–9), one for each of several content areas. Provides practice in applying reading and study skills.

Organizing and Reporting Skills Kit (SRA). Intermediate-grade kit deals with effective note taking, outlining, and reporting.

Children Writing Research Reports (Curriculum Associates). Intermediate-grade program dealing with in-depth research and reporting, and generalizing from research.

Table and Graph Skills (Xerox Educational). Four workbooks for grades 3–6.

Map Skills for Today (Xerox Educational). Five workbooks for grades 2–6 dealing with map terminology, symbols, and various types of maps.

Graph and Picture Study Skills Kit (SRA). Intermediate-grade kit concerned with interpreting graphic data, editorial cartoons, charts, and diagrams.

Map and Globe Skills Kit (SRA). Kit for grades 4–8 covering various map- and globe-reading skills.

Newslab (SRA). Intermediate-grade kit dealing with how to interpret 12 sections of a newspaper.

Actionmap Program (Denoyer-Geppert). Upper-elementary-grade program containing 5 kits (physical feature elements, location and use of natural resources, urban centers and natural resources, historical development of transportation and commerce, and weather).

Design for Reading: Freeways to Reading (Harper & Row). Multilevel kits for reading literature, science, and social studies.

UNIT 10

Instilling the Desire to Read

Although we have been fairly successful in teaching children how to read, our efforts to develop reading as a leisure-time habit leave a great deal to be desired. Surveys continually show that while the American public reads newspapers, and to a lesser extent magazines, relatively few adults read books.

A lasting interest in reading can be developed in various ways, among the most important of which is helping children to enjoy reading. We can also stimulate reader interest by expanding the range of reading material that will attract children. Reading interests and taste can be improved by helping children to progress to more mature preferences, to broaden the scope of what they read, and to recognize and prefer material that has literary merit.

This unit first takes up the nature of interest and the background necessary for understanding and studying the reading interests of children. What can be done to stimulate a desire to read is considered in the second section, which is followed by a discussion on improving the range and maturity of reading interests. The final section is concerned with resources for locating interest-fostering materials.

396

LEARNING ABOUT CHILDREN'S INTERESTS

The word "interest" means a positive feeling for something, a liking of something, as when one says, "I am interested in football." The word also encompasses the object or activity liked, as in "Music is an interest of mine." A particular activity or topic is interesting to someone when it is an activity or topic to which the person chooses to devote some time.

The Inception and Development of Interests

An interest is born in a pleasurable experience, which leads to expectation that if the activity is repeated, the experience will again be pleasurable. Several additional pleasurable experiences of the same sort lead to a relatively lasting disposition to expect pleasure from the activity, and a corresponding inclination to turn to it voluntarily. When most of the experiences are satisfying, an occasional disappointing one can be taken in stride. But in the initial stages, one experience that results in fear, anger, embarrassment, or disappointment can nip the interest in the bud. An interest, therefore, is a learned preference.

Interests develop, deepen, and endure when the conditions necessary for their nourishment are present. This nourishment can be provided in several ways.

1. *Pleasure in the activity itself*. Certain activities are inherently pleasant. The enjoyment of tasty foods, the pleasure of moving rhythmically, the delight of a gentle touch or caress; these are built into our natures. As children develop, this quality of intrinsic pleasantness extends to other actions and activities.
2. *The feeling of ease and security*. Young children tend to enjoy activities that are easy for them and in which they feel safe and secure. The familiar is so reassuring and comforting that they sometimes want to carry repetition far beyond the adult's tolerance.
3. *The feeling of accomplishment*. If it were not for an exploratory tendency that causes children to venture into new activities and topics, the need for security would lead to stagnation. Unless repetition of the activity also involves a challenge, an opportunity to use one's abilities and to test them, interest will wane. Ideally, an interest should involve

an inherently pleasurable type of activity, in which the child feels reasonably secure, yet one that provides an opportunity to improve in repeated efforts. The feeling of satisfaction that results from knowing that one has successfully accomplished something is a very powerful strengthener of interest. The desire to improve is itself a powerful motivation, when there is reason to expect it to be fulfilled.

Knowledge that one is doing well increases interest; realization that one is doing poorly decreases it. Talented people tend to use their abilities and develop them, while the untalented do less and fall further behind. Interest and ability generally go together and reinforce each other.

4. *Social approval.* Children are very responsive to adult approval and disapproval; not only the words used but also the facial expressions, gestures, body language, and tones of voice. The teacher's reactions are often more important than those of the parents. As children get older, peer approval becomes increasingly important. By the middle grades, children tend to form clubs. Whether the group is an antisocial gang or a Girl Scout Troop, their standards and codes of conduct greatly influence behavior, often outweighing the combined influence of parents and teacher.

Factors Influencing Reading Interests

A number of factors interact to influence reading interests. These fall mainly into two categories: personal factors and institutional factors (Purves and Beach 1972).

Personal Factors   The age, sex, intelligence, reading ability, attitudes, and psychological needs of the reader may influence reading interests. Elementary school children show a definite development of interest according to grade level. Most students display an interest in stories that contain characters of their own age. Very young children identify with fantasy figures, usually animals, who have childlike experiences. Older children in the elementary school prefer more realistic stories that portray peers having suspenseful adventures. At the junior and senior high levels, students display a wider range of interests. Adult interests appear to begin at about eighth or ninth grade, with an accompanying shift from reading for entertainment to reading for self-understanding. Unless they are greatly influenced by education or employment, reading interests do not usually change much after age sixteen.

The reader's sex may influence reading interests. In general, girls' reading interests mature earlier than boys', and girls tend to read more. Sex differences in reading preferences are not very strong in the primary grades, and there is likely to be a surprising breadth of choice voiced by first and second graders (Kirsch 1975). Past research has also indicated that intermediate-grade boys and girls tend to express somewhat differing interests that become more pronounced by the junior high school. However, the extent to which such choices are culturally influenced is yet to be determined. It may be that giving children more freedom of choice and encouragement to read in new areas will alter new findings regarding sex differences in reading interests. Regardless of the general trends in reading interests, children should not be limited to such choices.

The relationship between intelligence and reading interests is not clearly established. In general, bright children read more and have a wider range and more mature reading interests than those of lesser intelligence. Mentally slow children do less voluntary reading and prefer material that is slightly immature for their ages (see unit 11, pp. 484–86).

Reading ability is not directly related to reading interests. High interest is more important for comprehension of poor readers than for average or better readers. Good readers are not necessarily avid readers (Lamme 1976a).

Positive attitudes toward reading usually develop if reading fulfills a need. But a positive attitude toward reading does not necessarily lead to an active reading of books. Attitudes, which vary with level of reading ability, background experiences, efforts, and peer influences, are unique, personal, and highly unpredictable.

Satisfaction of psychological needs is one of the major factors involved in reading interests. Needs and interests are not the same thing; the same need can find expression in different interests. Among the needs is the need for a positive self-concept. There are also intellectual, emotional, social, and aesthetic needs. There is, however, little evidence that elementary school children read primarily to satisfy such needs. They seem to regard reading mainly as a recreational activity. It is impossible to generalize about the relationship between needs and interests because individuals vary so considerably. Children turn to other media to satisfy their needs if expectations of reward from reading are not high.

Institutional Factors   Institutional factors influencing reading interests include the availability of books; socioeconomic status and ethnic background; and, peer, parent, and teacher influences. Accessibility and availability of books strongly influence children's choices. Repeated studies
have indicated that the amount and kinds of reading materials found in
the home have a marked relationship to children's reading habits. There
has been an increase in school and classroom library collections. Traveling libraries are often found in rural areas.

Socioeconomic class, in and of itself, does not appear to have a strong
effect on reading interests. For example, Johns (1975) found that urban
middle graders preferred stories depicting middle-class settings and characters with positive self-concepts. This finding seems related to that of
Feeley (1974), who found that lower-class children, like their generations
before them, continued to express the hope of escaping the realities of their
lower-class existence. There also appear to be few differences among the
reading interests of rural, suburban, and urban children.

Research findings regarding differences among the expressed reading interests of children from various ethnic backgrounds are inconclusive. Some
(Lewis 1970, Lickteig 1972) found such differences; others (Bouchard
1971, Barchas 1971, Johns 1973) did not. A wide range of individual interests was found within each group, and there was much overlapping
among groups.

Friends and peers exert some influence on reading interests through discussions and recommendations. Apart from recommending or assigning
reading, teachers can be important in developing interests by serving as
models, particularly when they are enthusiastic about reading.

Competition for Children's Time

For years, reading has faced strong competition from the mass media
for children's time. During the 1920s it was the movies, and in the next
two decades, it was the radio. Since about 1950, television has taken over
much of the time that children previously devoted to movies, radio, and
reading.

Television   Preschoolers spend more time watching TV than on any other
activity; by the time they reach 18, they will have logged some 15,000
hours watching TV, as compared with only 10,000 hours in school (Car-

negie Corporation 1977). Average televiewing time for 6- to 11-year-olds is almost 24 hours per week, and almost 20 hours for teen-agers (Lamb 1976). Yet, only 7 hours per week is spent in reading outside school (Feeley 1973).

The general lack of significant correlations between hours spent watching TV and voluntary reading tends to preclude any generalization regarding the effects of TV watching (Purves and Beach 1972), or its impact on reading (Barth and Swiss 1976). There is even conflicting evidence whether children's TV programs assist in the formation of concepts that are necessary in developing the reading process (Mukerji 1976).

Increased TV viewing has cut into the time formerly spent reading comics and pulp magazines, but newspapers and better magazines seem to have held their own as leisure-time activities. Although there is some indication that TV may influence reading tastes, the extent to which watching TV influences reading tastes is still an open question (Feeley 1974).

The fact is, a child who does not like to read will find other ways to fill his or her spare time. A child who finds reading interesting, easy, and accessible will not let the mass media capture and hold his or her exclusive attention.

There has been a great deal of concern regarding the violence to which children are exposed in TV shows. For example, the Carnegie Corporation (1977) reported that more than 6 of 10 shows contain some violence, and about 3 in 10 are saturated with violent acts. Rothenberg (1975) stated that there is no support for the contention that TV violence has a healthy cathartic effect; in fact, he believed that it was more likely to increase subsequent aggressiveness and to decrease emotional sensitivity to violence. Eron et al. (1974) expressed a similar opinion. There is also the possibility that some individuals who are predisposed toward delinquency will be inspired to commit criminal acts. So there is a need for parental regulation and supervision. Unfortunately, parents generally exert little, if any, control over what and how much TV is watched (Starkey and Swinford 1974, Hamilton 1976).

Occasionally parents and teachers report fatigue, lack of interest in play, school, or reading, increased nervousness, eyestrain, and disturbed mealtimes, which they attribute to television. Research, however, has not demonstrated general damaging effects of heavy TV watching, although undesirable effects do occur in some children. Several studies have shown a relationship between heavy TV watching and low school achievement, but no direct cause-effect relationship has been established (Comstock

1975). Poor or reluctant readers are apt to spend their free time in ways other than reading.

On the other hand, educational television programs such as "Sesame Street" and "The Electric Company" have been at least moderately successful in achieving some of their goals (Lamb 1976). Some critics, such as Feeley (1975), feel that these programs are too narrowly conceived (e.g., teaching symbol-sound associations, interesting children in print) and should be more concerned with conveying a view of reading as a communication process rather than as a decoding process. Be that as it may, one cannot expect more of a program than it was designed to produce.

Television also may have positive effects on the intellectual and educational development of children. Many children enter school with vocabularies and knowledge about current events, science, and foreign lands, which they acquired from TV. A popular TV program can send millions of children to the library for the book upon which the program was based. There are great possibilities in using TV programs as motivation for related reading, and these have not been fully exploited.

In addition to motivating children to read, television can be used for reading-study related activities. Among those listed by Adams and Harrison (1975) are making a simple outline of a TV show, and copying all the abbreviations used in 10 or 20 commercials. Other suggestions for using TV viewing in the teaching of reading may be found in Becker (1973). Solomon (1976) described ways to use videotapes and scripts of popular commercial television programs in developing reading skills and changing the attitudes of inner-city children toward reading. The latter idea has been incorporated into a TV program, "Television Reading Program," that is produced by a major network (*New York Times* 1977).

Comics   Comics enjoy a larger readership than any other printed medium except the daily newspaper, which itself often features comic strips (Ball 1976b). Even about half the adult population reads comics regularly (Leeds 1974). Young children prefer comics with humanized animal characters like those in movie or TV animated cartoons. Older children like adventure stories, superhuman characters, and science fiction. The readability of comics tends to be at the intermediate-grade levels, and many children pay attention only to the pictures. Forbidding comic books just makes them seem more desirable, but attempts should be made to keep those emphasizing sadism and crime out of the hands of children.

One way to handle reading the comics is to help children to learn how to discriminate between the better and poorer types. This will involve setting up standards (the 20 set forth by Ball [1976b] can be written more simply for use by children), and then allowing the children to compare and criticize them. Second, comic books can be used as springboards to reading the books upon which the comic character was based; or the teacher can direct the child to a book on the same or a similar topic. Although some frown upon allowing children to read comic books, if they are well selected and children will read nothing else, they do provide some reading experience.

Radio   Radio is mainly used by children as a source of music and news. Many pupils like to play the radio while they read or study. A background of unobtrusive music does not seem to interfere with concentration (although some may find the loudness and sounds offensive); it may actually help by masking other sounds that would be distracting. The more attention-compelling the program, the more likely it is to disrupt attention to reading or study.

Reading Interests by Age Levels

Definitive statements regarding children's reading interests are difficult to make. In reading this section, it is important to remember that there are tremendous individual differences in interests. These far outweigh group tendencies that are related to age, sex, intelligence, or cultural background. To understand the reading interests of children, it is necessary to consider each child separately. General trends only help the teacher to anticipate the possible interests of their children. The trends indicated below are based primarily on the summary by H. M. Robinson and Weintraub (1973). During the past several years, changes in attitudes concerning sex roles may have brought about changes in children's reading interests that have not yet been researched.

Primary Grades   Investigations continue to reveal that primary-grade children have strong interests in animals and make-believe, and some interest in the activities of children of their age. Peer rather than child-parent interactions, pranks themes over pollyanna themes, and activities related to their own sex are preferred by middle-class first graders (Rose, Zimet, and Blom 1972). Until age eight or nine interest in the fanciful usually increases, but then gradually declines. Humorous poems, poems about animals, and poems related to their own experiences seem to be preferred.

Intermediate Grades   Intermediate-grade children show a greater variety of interests than their younger counterparts. By age 9 or 10, definite sex differences in interests have appeared. Boys generally prefer adventure and mystery, fictionalized history and biography, mechanics, science, inventions, and hobbies. Girls show a preference for sentimental stories, usually developing an interest in romantic fiction between ages 11 and 14. They share the boys' interests in mystery and adventure, but not for science and inventions. Boys tend to refrain from human-interest stories or anything that is considered to be "feminine." Both sexes tend to like stories in which the characters struggle with problems they face in their own lives; and excitement and humor are reasons often stated for liking books (Lauritizen and Cheves 1974). Most children read the comics, children's and even some adult magazines, and newspapers. Ashley (1970) concluded that there was very little chance to encourage good reading habits after the fifth grade, by which time reading tastes have nearly crystallized.

Small and Kenney (1975) suggested that if middle-school libraries were organized in the following 15 sections rather than in the usual manner, students would be better able to find material of interest to them: (1) Animals; (2) Adolescent Life; (3) Adventure; (4) Biography (People); (5) Careers; (6) Cars; (7) Humor; (8) Mystery and the Supernatural; (9) Nonfiction; (10) The Past; (11) Romance; (12) Science Fiction; (13) Social Problems; (14) Sports, and (15) Westerns. To these, one might add "Recreational" which Feeley (1974) found of interest to both sexes.

Poetry is generally not popular with children; but some preference is shown for poems that relate to children's experiences, are humorous, and have strong rhythm and rhyme. Terry's study (1974) found that limericks and narrative poems were the most popular in the intermediate grades; haiku, the least popular. Intermediate graders disliked poems they found difficult to understand or that were sentimental or serious. Marston (1975) speculated that the peculiar difficulty of poetry for children may lie not only in the fact that it often requires a high level of thinking, but also that it does so through the use of devices that make it look easy. Not perceiving its real complexity, the student may decide that poetry is "kid stuff."

Classroom observations have revealed that for the most part the teaching of poetry is unimaginative, burdensome, and joyless (Baskin, Harris, and Salley 1976). The major faults fall into three categories: (1) using poetry as a device to achieve unrelated academic purposes (e.g., hand-writing exercises, celebrating a holiday); (2) overloading children with certain types of poetry (e.g., "haiku overkill"); and (3) assigning memorization as a punishment. Baskin et al. (1976) described a thematic lesson model for teaching poetry that has the following characteristics: (1) choosing poems that have instant appeal; (2) exploiting the developmental interests of children in choosing poems; (3) using poems covering a wide range of difficulty, so that all children will have an opportunity to participate; and (4) involving the children in evaluating and judging the poems.

Junior and Senior High Schools At the junior and senior high school level, studies have repeatedly shown such a tremendous range of individual differences as to almost preclude making any generalizations regarding general reading interests. If forced to select the most popular topics, one would include action, adventure, sports, crime, war, historical novels, and mystery for boys. Girls prefer books about personal and social relationships, romance, humor, and mystery without violence.

Until about age 12 or 13 voluntary reading increases; after that, there is often a marked decline. This seems to coincide with other demands and interests that compete for time at this age. Although fewer books are read, magazine and newspaper reading begins to increase. Many teen-agers seem interested in current events (Kirkland, Clowers, and Wood 1974), an interest that can be utilized in teaching the social sciences.

Gentile and McMillan (1977) believed the following factors to contribute heavily to teen-agers' reluctance to read (possible ways of helping to overcome some of the problems are indicated in parentheses): (1) equating reading with failure and never having experienced the joys of reading (allow them to select from a variety of high interest materials); (2) not getting excited about ideas in books; (3) being unable to "sit still" for prolonged periods of time (get them actively doing something that requires reading); (4) adolescents are preoccupied with themselves (suggest books that might help them with their problems); and (5) strong pressure from the school or home to read, producing resistance.

Determining Reading Interests

Many indications of children's interests can be observed in their everyday behavior and conversations. During show-and-tell periods, children often

THINGS I LIKE TO DO

Name _____

1. After school I like to:

   _____   _____
   _____   _____
   _____   _____

2. When it rains I like to:

   _____   _____
   _____   _____
   _____   _____

3. After supper, I like to:

   _____   _____
   _____   _____
   _____   _____

4. On weekends, I like to:

   _____   _____
   _____   _____
   _____   _____

5. My favorite TV shows are:

   _____   _____
   _____   _____
   _____   _____

6. My favorite kinds of movies are:

   _____   _____
   _____   _____
   _____   _____

7. The best books I have ever read were:

   _____   _____
   _____   _____
   _____   _____

8. I like to read about:

   _____   _____
   _____   _____
   _____   _____

FIGURE 10.1. A simple interest questionnaire for children.

bring in things or talk about their experiences. Some children repeat the same theme over and over in their artwork. Hobby clubs allow them to bring in and talk about all kinds of things from insects and coin collections to magic tricks; others will bring in model rockets or trains they have built. Many children are devoted to pets (which also cover a wide range from the common to the exotic) and are vitally interested in animals. For those not prone to talk in front of the class, the teacher can arrange a quiet private interview during which the child can indicate personal likes and dislikes.

When pupils are old enough to write compositions, topics can be assigned, such as, "What I like to do after school" or "My hobby." This may allow children to express interests they would not openly discuss. Sometimes helpful leads can be gained from writing about a topic such as "I would read more if. . . ."

Interest questionnaires, such as the simple one shown in figure 10.1, may be used. More elaborate ones may be found in A. J. Harris and Sipay (1975). With young children, the questions can be asked during an informal conference, with the teacher recording the responses. Older children can fill in a duplicated copy on their own. Children usually do not hesitate to tell about their interests when provided the opportunity; they like it when the teacher shows a desire to know more about what they enjoy. The more ways of gathering information regarding children's interests that a teacher can employ, the more reliable will be the data.

Interest and the Difficulty of Material

Children are not likely to select reading as a leisure-time activity when the available material is too difficult. There is a tendency for interesting material to be better understood than uninteresting material, if for no other reason than that it is hard to concentrate on dull content. Interest may allow average or above-average readers to comprehend material above their instructional level, and interest has a greater effect on comprehension for average or low-ability students than for high-ability children. As Fry (1975) contended, high motivation can overcome high difficulty, but low motivation demands a low readability level. It should be remembered, however, that interest alone will not overcome the difficulties caused by material which contains a large number of unknown words or concepts.

Estimating Readability   A number of methods are available for estimating the difficulty of reading materials, none of which is perfectly accurate.

Jorgenson (1975) found that teacher's estimates of the readability of reading material above the first-grade level were not particularly reliable. However, experienced teachers often can form a rough estimate of a book's
difficulty by checking the (1) vocabulary employed, (2) load and complexity of the concepts presented, and (3) sentence length and complexity.
References that list the estimated difficulty of the titles they contain can be
helpful in selecting materials.

Research has shown that two factors are consistently valid measures of
readability—vocabulary and sentence length. Unless one is interested
in doing research, the simple two-variable formulas should be sufficient
(Klare 1974–75). Three commonly used formulas employ these factors.
The revised Spache Readability Formula (Spache 1974) is applicable only
to primary-grade materials, and the Dale-Chall Formula (Dale and Chall
1948) to materials from fourth grade up. Burmeister (1976a) has provided
a table that makes the Spache easier to apply. The Harris-Jacobson Readability Formulas (Harris and Sipay 1975, pp. 658–75) cover from the preprimer through the eighth-reader level, and are easier to apply than the
Spache or Dale-Chall formulas. Singer (1975) has developed the SEER technique by which paragraphs of unknown difficulty are simply matched to
paragraphs of known difficulty in order to estimate their readability. Fry's
Readability Graph (1968), which is also easy to apply, is based on the
average number of syllables and sentences in three 100-word samples.

Another measure of readability that has received attention is the cloze
procedure, which is discussed in a different context in unit 6. To summarize the procedure, a certain number of words (usually every fifth

TABLE 10.1.

Criterion Scores for Cloze Readability Tests [a]

Use to Be Made of the Materials	Grade Level of the Student					
	4	5	6	7	8	9
Textbook	58	57	56	55	53	52
Reference	53	52	51	49	48	47
Voluntary	62	54	50	49	46	44

[a] Data from Bormuth (1975).

word) are deleted from a passage, and the reader is to supply the missing words. Bormuth (1975) suggested that different cloze criterion scores be used for different grade levels and purposes. These are shown in table 10.1. Bormuth (1975, p. 81) also believed that "for children below grade four, it is probably as important, or more important to evaluate the word recognition difficulty of the materials as it is to evluate their comprehensibility." Two studies (Sauer 1969, Hodges 1972), however, suggest that cloze test scores do not closely approximate the functional reading levels as determined by other procedures. Nor do cloze scores and readability formulas yield similar results (Schlief and Wood 1974, Froese 1975).

Klare (1976) summarized some of the findings of readability studies:

1. When it has a chance to operate, at times motivation can override the effects of readability upon comprehension; this suggests that it is of great importance to raise motivation and keep it high.
2. Even when improvements in readability do not result in better comprehension scores, they may increase the likelihood that children will continue to read.
3. The need for improved readability may be somewhat reduced by reader interest in the topic.
4. It is more important to improve the readability of low-preferred than high-preferred material.
5. The grade-equivalent scores provided by readability formulas should not be considered to be precise values.
6. Certain editorial changes (e.g., reducing sentence length) can affect formula scores without producing corresponding changes in reading comprehension.
7. Readability is less critical if the reader's background information on that topic is high; when the reader's background is meager, the formula may underestimate the difficulty of the material for that child.
8. Readability formulas may overestimate difficulty for highly intelligent readers.

Both readability formulas and the cloze procedure have their limitations. Readability formulas do not consider the concept load or interest of the material, two factors that may greatly influence the material's difficulty. For example, if a readability formula were applied to the quotation (rarely are formulas applied to sentences) "To be or not to be. That is the question," its readability score would be quite low. Yet the concept behind those words is quite complex. Also, even though sentence length is an important variable, formulas do not consider the type of sentence. Passive sentences are more difficult to process than active sentences. When the conventional word order is rearranged, a degree of difficulty is added. Fry (1975) also has asserted that the nearer the kernel is to the beginning of the sentence, and the less the distance between the subject and the verb, the easier the sentence is to read. As for cloze tests, their results may be influenced because nouns, main verbs, and adjectives are more difficult to "fill in" than are structure words (Hittleman 1973).

CREATING AN INTEREST IN READING

Many procedures can be tried to help children learn to enjoy reading. Basic to them all is teaching children to read well enough so that their reading can be reasonably fluent and accurate and the content understood. Children are likely to shy away from a task that is so difficult as to be distasteful.

Attitudes toward Reading

An individual's attitude toward reading is likely to influence not only his choice of it as a leisure-time activity but also to influence others. It is therefore of interest to note that a study by Davis (1974) revealed that only 8 percent of the 367 teachers queried were of the opinion that reading for pleasure and enjoyment were important uses of reading. Furthermore, less than half of the teachers questioned by Mueller (1973) selected reading over TV, even for obtaining the news! Apparently, the respondents in these studies valued reading only mildly as part of their lives.

In the National Literature Assessment Survey (S. Johnson 1974), approximately four out of five 17-year-olds reported that literature had a great value for them. The most frequently stated reasons were: (1) it exposed them to other points of view; (2) it led to a greater self-awareness; (3) it helped to create an ability to evaluate critically; (4) it taught them to think; (5) it was entertaining, and (6) it helped to build vocabulary and writing skills. Thirteen-year-olds tended to respond that literature improved their language and was important to their future. Of course, one must consider that the results of such a questionnaire are likely to be influenced by what the respondent thinks the teachers want to hear.

The Estes Attitude Scale (Estes 1971) was used in a study with third through seventh graders in an attempt to modify attitudes toward reading (Aaron and Seaton 1976). The researchers concluded that attitudes about reading are apparently too complex to be altered significantly in a more positive direction by short-term teacher reinforcement. There was some indication that more intensive long-term teacher effort might prove successful.

Alexander and Filler (1975) have described and given sample items from eight different measures of reading attitude. Cautioning that it was difficult to make valid generalizations regarding attitudes and reading, Alexander and Filler (1976) drew the following conclusions:

1. There is not always a positive correlation between high reading achievement and a favorable attitude toward reading.
2. Certain instructional practices and special programs can, but do not necessarily, improve attitudes.
3. The student's self-concept and interests, as well as the attitudes and behavior of parents and teachers, may influence attitudes.
4. Girls do not necessarily have more favorable attitudes toward reading than boys.
5. More intelligent students do not necessarily have more favorable attitudes than low-IQ children.
6. Low socioeconomic students do not necessarily have more negative attitudes toward reading than higher-SES children.

Literature Programs

Lists of behavioral objectives (e.g., Peterson 1975) are available for teaching literature. While such objectives may serve a limited purpose by providing guidelines for certain measurable skills, a good literature program should attempt to evoke affective reactions from the readers. It is difficult, however, to measure behaviors in the affective domain.

A study by Karre (1976) indicated that knowledge and skills can be developed while enlivening a lesson with students' personal experiences, appreciations, and attitudes. In her study, upper-grade students responded well to an approach to teaching literature that began with concern with the students' feelings and went from there to evaluate these feelings through an involvement with the piece of literature. There is very little evidence indicating whether teachers engage elementary-school children in an analysis of literature or what the results of such a teaching strategy might be (Cullinan 1974b). The National Assessment of Literature, which was critically reviewed by Grendstaff and Muller (1975), demonstrated that most American students, especially 17-year-olds, can recognize certain literary characters, interpret metaphorical language, and make acceptable inferences (although they often could not give reasons for their choices). They also stated that they had a positive attitude toward literature as both a recreational activity and a school subject; but these responses may simply reflect the persuasive powers of teachers in commenting on the values of literature.

Although various combinations are possible, planned literature programs usually are approached in six different ways (Huus 1975):

1. In *free reading* a certain amount of time is provided weekly for children to read materials of their own choice. Such a program has the advantage of capturing and extending students' interests. Its main disadvantage is that it assumes the availability of a wide range of books as to difficulty and topics from which to choose; often this is not the case. Also, some students may not progress to books of greater depth, or only choose to read superficially.
2. *Reading aloud* for 10 to 15 minutes by the teacher or student can be interesting and enjoyable if the material is well chosen, prepared, and presented. Although it may stimulate interest and aid in developing listening skills, some students are relatively passive participants.
3. In *guided supplementary reading,* the pupils are given help in selecting materials. Consideration can be given to assisting them in choosing appropriate materials; but if the teacher dominates, interest can be deadened.
4. *Topic units* utilize a subject, a type of work, or style of writing as the coordinating theme. They have the advantage of focusing on a common theme which allows the readers to compare and contrast the works of various authors. Their disadvantages lie in finding topics that have equal appeal to all the group members, and the difficulty of synchronizing the various activities of several groups working simultaneously.
5. *Creative sharing* is accomplished through oral reading, story telling,

creative activities, and critiques. Such activities can generate interest, but there is the danger that more time is spent on the creative production than on reading and reacting to the literature.

6. A *total literature program* incorporates the aforementioned in a flexible overall plan.

There has been little written regarding the evaluation of recreational reading programs, but six guidelines have been offered by H. K. Smith (1976): (1) improvement in the status of recreational reading should be one of the school's goals; (2) evaluation should be continuous; (3) various evaluative procedures should be employed; (4) evaluation is more effective when done by a team of parents, teachers, librarians, and students; (5) the student's recreational reading should be compared with his past performance, not with that of others; and (6) evaluation techniques should not diminish the student's interest or enjoyment of reading. Because adequate evaluation instruments are lacking, the recreational reading program has to be evaluated through the use of such informal techniques as interest inventories, reading logs, observations, interviews, and book reports. Interpretation of the findings obtained through such techniques is dependent on the teacher's and students' value judgments.

Developing a Love for Stories

From the simple bedtime story to the finest movie, stage play or television play, a well-presented good story has the power to enthrall its audience. Elementary school children, even far beyond the primary grades, love to have stories read or told to them.

It is helpful for young children to be seated on the floor or mats close together, so they can have a feeling of intimacy. Above the second grade, special seating arrangements are not important.

Stories to be read or told should be selected with the maturity and special interests of the group in mind. The story's language can be considerably more mature than what most of the children could read for themselves, and listening to fine stories and poetry helps to build up the children's understanding of language and the syntactic patterns encountered in "book language" which may differ from their oral language patterns. It also helps to extend their concepts. McCormick (1977a, b) suggested that reading achievement can be aided and an interest in reading developed by reading aloud to children on a regular basis, especially to those from low socioeconomic backgrounds, low achievers, and the young.

Lamme (1976b) found that the following behaviors on the part of the teacher enhanced the children's enjoyment of being read to: (1) the children were actively integrated into the reading by such techniques as "chorally reading the refrain" or predicting what would happen next in the story; (2) frequent eye-contact with the audience; (3) reading expressively; (4) using variety in her voice; (5) pointing to the words and pictures in the book; (6) being familiar with the story; (7) selecting books with pictures that the children could see; (8) grouping the children so all could hear and see; and (9) highlighting the words and language of the story.

If the teacher is ill at ease in reading or telling stories, she can use commercially prepared records or tapes to stimulate interest. Even children can read or tape stories to share with their classmates. Van Metre (1977) described a three-step process for turning stories into oral interpretations of literature. The first step, selecting the material, has eleven guidelines, which can be summarized into one question, "Do the children respond to it and want to share it?" Next, eleven other guidelines are provided for putting the literature into script format, which indicates the various parts for the readers. Lastly, the oral interpretation is staged without scenery or costumes.

Cullinan and Carmichael (1977) have suggested specific stories to read aloud to children, and strategies for using literature for developing language skills. As for storytelling, Groff (1977) was of the opinion that busy average classroom teachers cannot, and should not, try to live up to the difficult standards presented by traditional writers on the art of storytelling, such as the long hours of preparation in which the story is overlearned, and the practice on speech delivery. Rather, he believed that dramatization and drama were needed "to grab" today's TV-minded children.

Bringing Children and Books Together

The more accessible the books, the greater the likelihood that they will be read. In addition to public and school library resources, each classroom should have its own collection. A classroom library should contain a minimum of 50 titles ranging in readability from very easy to quite challenging, and include a wide variety of topics, fictional and factual. There also should be a special collection of materials related to any ongoing project. Good children's magazines should also be placed in the reading corner. These books may be borrowed from the school or public library, and should be changed periodically. Librarians can give invaluable help to teachers in selecting books for classroom collections or for individual children.

Although the principles of seeking and self-selection can be largely followed for independent recreational reading, teachers can help children to save time in browsing. Books can be arranged under a few broad headings, such as "Make Believe," "True Stories about People," or "Animals." The difficulty of the book can be coded by use of color tabs on the book spines: e.g., green = easy, yellow = average, red = hard. Lynch (1976) has suggested a plan whereby the school has a central file on all available books, which would contain not only readability levels and topics, but also comments from the children and teachers concerning the books.

It is helpful to have part of the classroom set up as a reading corner. The furnishing should include book shelves, a table or two, and chairs; or just a carpet to sit on or lie on while reading. Decorations can include posters, book jackets, and children's pictures illustrating some of the books. Having the children help to furnish, decorate and care for the reading corner is likely to increase their interest in it. A simple system for checking books in and out can be set up, with the procedures taken care of by child librarians, who often cherish the one-week privilege.

Time for recreational reading should be provided during the school day, as indicated in the plans set forth in unit 5. In addition to definitely scheduled time, children should have books handy in their desks, to which they can turn when they finish an assignment early. Allotting class time for independent or recreational reading provides evidence to children that the teacher places a high premium on reading. There should be definite periods set aside for uninterrupted silent reading. For example, Petre (1977) has described a daily 35-minute total school reading break in which everyone, including teachers, would read self-selected materials.

An individual conference can be a motivational device for increasing recreational reading. In a detailed plan based on specific behavioral objectives (Sorenson, Schwenn, and Klausmeier 1969), the adult provides models of desired reading behaviors (e.g., telling the child she frequently likes to read; having the child observe her reading while she is waiting for the child to get to the conference) for the child to observe and imitate. Desired reading behaviors and expressed attitudes are reinforced through such responses as smiling, nodding affirmatively, attending closely to the child, or making statements such as "That's fine." The child receives feed-back about his progress by helping him to learn the skills in which he is weak and by telling him how many pages or books he has read.

Book Clubs   Having a book club whose membership is open to the entire class can foster an interest in reading; the only requirement is possessing a library card and being ready to report on a book. Officers can be elected, and meetings can be held weekly. At every meeting, a few members each reports on a book read, perhaps reading aloud a small part of the book.

Use of paperbacks in schools has increased steadily, but despite their relatively low cost, overwhelming endorsement, variety of titles, and appeal to children, the great majority of paperbacks used in the elementary schools are those purchased by children through book clubs (Larrick 1976). For some reason, their purchase by most librarians and schools has been minimal.

A middle-grade book club using paperbacks may be organized in the following manner: (1) build up a collection of paperbacks, with six to eight copies of each; (2) form groups of about six children who would like to read the same book which, in the initial stages of the program, the teacher may briefly describe and invite certain children to read; (3) provide a volunteer adult leader, who may be helped by being given a short general guide, applicable to most books, containing such things as ways of stimulating discussion and guidelines for exploring characterizations or plot structure (the adult should understand, however, that the primary purpose is enjoyment); and (4) set a weekly meeting time for approximately six weeks, the time taking the place of a regular instructional period (D. V. Davis 1975).

There is also a voluntary national program, Reading Is Fun-Damental (RIF), that has distributed millions of free paperbacks to children. Most trade book publishers produce paperbacks and some, such as Scholastic, Weekly Reader, and Xerox Education, have paperback book clubs. As a reference, one may turn to *Paperback Books for Children* (Simmons 1972), which annotates hundreds of books arranged by subject area with suggested grade levels.

Motivating the Reluctant Reader

The first step in getting the reluctant or nonreading child to read voluntarily is to find a brief, easy book that will hold the child's interest. Humorous stories often work well for this purpose. If short books are unavailable, Culyer (1975) described a procedure for cutting up "big books" and stapling the stories into "skinny books" which are placed in folders and color coded as to approximate level of readability (the first letters of the colors can form a mnemonic device; e.g., GROW, Green = preprimer; Red = primer; Orange = first reader; White = low second). Also among his recommendations was assigning homework that required children to read the "skinny books" to younger children.

Johns and Lunt (1975) listed 42 ways to motivate children to read, a number of which are presented in this unit.

Teacher Enthusiasm   Interest in books can be infectious and contagious. A teacher who is an enthusiastic reader and who reads and enjoys many children's as well as adult books, cannot help but convey some of this enthusiasm to children. Such a teacher will read many good stories to the class; will call their attention to new books or books in areas they have not considered, perhaps reading just enough of the story to them to whet their interest; will help children find books that they will enjoy reading; and will ensure that favorable conditions for independent reading are maintained.

Ensuring Enjoyment   Interests are nourished by the pleasure in the act itself; by ease, by security, by the feeling of accomplishment; and by social approval. Pleasure in the act of reading is a natural by-product when the difficulty is suitable for independent reading and the content is absorbing. Readers, even more capable ones, do not always read books which are at their independent or instructional levels. At times they may read books far below their independent levels; and at other times, material above their estimated frustration levels. There is nothing wrong with such behavior. Only when the child consistently reads material that is too easy, or consistently attempts to read material that is too difficult, is there any need for concern. Reluctant readers become less reluctant when they can be guided into selecting books that at first are very easy, as well as interesting for them. For confirmed readers, the ease factor is much less important; at times they will enjoy the challenge of material which contains exciting new ideas even if the material is quite difficult. Encouraging competent readers to read "at their growing points" will allow them to grow in skill and gain the feeling of accomplishment.

Progress Charts   An individual progress chart of independent reading can serve both as a record of reading done and as an incentive to read more.

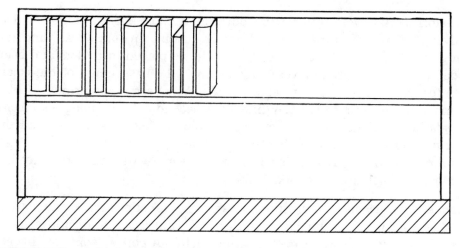

FIGURE 10.2.   A bookcase chart for recording independent reading. A pupil who finishes a book draws another book into the bookcase. The books may be labeled and colored.

In using the bookcase chart shown in figure 10.2, some teachers duplicate the outline; others have the children draw their own. Among the variants of progress charts are, having children add leaves to a tree, fish to a pond, bricks to build a house, or a space shuttle traveling to and from its space station. Usually on this type of chart, there is not enough room to enter such details as the author's name, title, number of pages read, and when the book was started and completed. Therefore it is a good idea also to keep a more complete record on a form like that shown in figure 10.3. Most children enjoy seeing their bookcases fill up and their reading records get longer. The purpose of recording the number of pages is to make it easy for both teacher and pupil to distinguish between such extremes as 20-page picture books and full-length books. This also takes care of books that are started but not finished. A child should not be required to finish every book; a standard that most of us would rebel against because of lack of interest.

These motivational devices, however, must be used cautiously. Stressing group completion often inadvertently places emphasis on quantity rather than quality. Highly competitive youngsters will select only "thin" books to read or will fabricate the number completed. Slow or poor readers tend to feel defeated before they start. Thus, what starts out as a motivational device can result in unproductive competition. If used with individ-

MY READING RECORD

Name _____

Title	Author	Date Began	Date Finished	No. Pgs. Read

FIGURE 10.3. A form for recording independent reading.

uals, progress charts should not be displayed; each child should compete only with himself or herself.

Progress charts have proved especially useful for group participation. In groups, children can make a figure of a favorite storybook character which is mounted. Or, they can add sections, representing the book recently read, to a large "book worm" that stretches around the room or board. A time line can be used to have children place a picture about their book in its proper place, or pictures of the story settings could be placed on a large outline map. Each of these suggestions is not limiting in any way, but instead offers children the opportunity to contribute creatively to a group project. No matter which device is selected, a frequent change of presentation to encourage student participation is recommended.

Book Reports   A written book report usually is regarded as a distasteful chore that often dampens rather than stimulates enthusiasm for reading. But it need not be.

A desirable book report should have the following characteristics: (1) it discloses enough about the book to demonstrate that it was understood; (2) it does not lessen interest in reading or tend to reduce the number of books read; and (3) it gives an opportunity for some form of creative expression. Because most written book reports that are detailed enough to satisfy the first criterion fail on the other two, teachers have explored a variety of other ways of reporting on books:

1. *Oral book reports.* Once a week or so, children can report by telling briefly what the book is about and why they would or would not recommend it. Or, they can prepare a humorous, exciting, or descriptive passage for reading to an audience. When several children have read the same book they can have a panel discussion, or informally dramatize a scene from the book, reading dialogue from the book, or inventing their own; or sometimes they can prepare a puppet show. Individuals who voluntarily report on books can become members of a "reviewers club" or receive some similar honorary recognition.

2. *Artistic book reports.* Children who like to draw or paint often can prepare a visual book report. Several kinds are possible: designing a colorful book jacket illustrating an incident of central importance, making models or puppets of characters, building a diorama of a setting, etc. Fennimore (1977) illustrated other possible creative ways of reporting

on a book, and listed how eight different books might be used to develop "projective book reports."

3. *Shared written reports.* Writing book reports can seem worthwhile when children know that the reports are to be read and used by their classmates. Evaluative book reports can be filed in a loose-leaf notebook which children can use to look up what classmates or former students have said about a book, either before reading it to see if they want to, or after reading it to compare their impressions.

4. *Individual oral reports.* In an individualized reading program, individual conferences provide opportunities for children to discuss what they have been reading. A private discussion of a book between a teacher and a shy child may help the child to display knowledge he or she might not otherwise show, and thus may be useful in any reading program.

5. *Cumulative book reports.* Each student who reads a book may record personal comments in a marked folder that contains only reviews of that book. These folders are available in a central place for all students to consult. Reporting of this type allows children to read what other class members have said about the book and does not force them to respond to a book in a set pattern. Most children are inclined to provide information not covered by other reviewers, or to state their disagreement and cite reasons. Having conflicting reviews may stimulate discussion.

6. *Individual reaction reports.* A child can be asked to make personal critical comments, favorable or otherwise, on a 4" × 6" index card. These comments may be about the funniest, happiest, saddest, etc., part of the book or story character; the details of the setting of the story or an event in the book; whether or not the child liked the book and why; or they may simply state how the story made him or her feel. Not only are the possibilities of this type of reaction report limitless, but they also encourage creativity.

7. *Class or group discussions.* A thematic approach (e.g., courage, overcoming a handicap, making a difficult decision) also may be employed with either a class or group. In this approach, children read different stories (although the same book may be read by a few) with the same central theme, then discuss and compare how the theme developed in the stories they read. Or a group may read the same book and discuss it.

8. *Individualized written reviews.* Pillar (1975) suggested that 30 acceptable ways of writing a book report be typed on individual cards from which a child may choose as many or as few as he or she wishes, writ-

ing as little or as much as he or she chooses. Among the suggestions
are: (1) You are a TV talk-show host who has one of the main story characters as a guest. List the questions you would ask him or her; (2)
Pretend you are a puppy. Tell which of the people in the book you
would want to adopt you, and why. (3) Pick one character to invite to
dinner. Tell why you selected this character above all the others. (4)
You run a computer dating service. Describe the perfect match for the
main character according to looks, personality, etc. (5) You are a
fortuneteller. Predict what the characters will be doing 10 years from
the end of the story. Think about what each is like—their talents, personalities, etc. (6) You have the magical power to transfer the major
characters into animals. Decide upon an animal for each based upon
the character's personality traits.

9. *Other creative alternatives.* Criscuolo (1977) stated that the following
   alternatives to the typical book report are especially appealing to middle-
   grade students:
   a. Rebus reading—the student creates a rebus story to match the book
      by substituting pictures for words in certain spots in sentences or
      paragraphs.
   b. "Lost and Found"—the student writes an ad for an object or person
      from the book.
   c. "Dress-up Day"—the students dress up like the story characters and
      tell the class, or have them guess, the role each is playing.
   d. "Computerized Dating"—the student fills out an application, indi-
      cating name, hobbies, etc., which is posted. If another child spots
      a book of possible interest, he or she brings it to the first child's
      attention.
   e. "Shape it, Scrape it, Drape it"—the students carve soap or balsa
      models, make puppets, design costumes or collages, or make a scale
      model of an important object or location in the story.
   f. "Academy Awards"—the students nominate and then vote on their
      favorite books.
   g. "Book-a-trip"—the student acts as a travel guide, giving an illus-
      trated talk.
   h. "Quiz Show"—a pupil pretends to be a character whom the class
      must identify through questioning.
   i. "It's in the Headlines"—students write headlines illustrating im-
      portant events in the story.

j. Collage—the important main ideas, scenes, characters, etc. are incorporated into a collage.

k. Reading mobilizers—a mobile is made of important quotes, characters, words, and incidents from the book.

Parents Can Help Parents who regularly read stories to preschoolers pave the way for success in learning to read. When children first learn to read, many parents stop reading and telling stories to them. Apparently they are unaware that even the easiest library book is probably above their child's independent reading level. Even for children who read well, sharing books through family reading helps to enhance the pleasure of reading. However, parents do not have to be avid readers themselves in order to have children who are (Hansen 1973).

In addition to sharing reading with children, parents can help them improve their reading ability and interests in other ways.

1. *Providing a model.* The child who grows up in a home in which the parents enjoy reading and spend much of their free time reading, is likely to adopt the family attitude toward reading.

2. *Providing books.* Parents need to be reminded that a fine book makes a fine present, and they need guidance in what kinds and levels of books to buy. As shown in the section on "Learning About Books for Children," there are magazines, book clubs, and individual titles available for children of all ages. The school can help parents by supplying lists of recommended books, by celebrating Book Week with appropriate displays, and by holding Book Fairs.[1] The school also can work with the local parent organization to convey to parents the importance of children's becoming regular visitors to the public library for a story hour and to select books.

3. *Understanding the school's reading program.* Many parents have forgotten how they learned to read, and do not understand what the school is trying to do in the reading program. In addition to parent-teacher discussions of reading instruction (PTA meetings can be devoted to demonstrating how and why certain materials or practices are employed), parents can obtain helpful information from a book written

---

1. Information on organizing and running a Book Fair may be obtained from the Children's Book Council, 67 Irving Place, New York, N.Y. 10003.

directly for them by Larrick (1975). Various programs for helping parents to understand the school's reading program and how they might help their children at home have been described by Criscuolo (1974), Trezise (1975), McWilliams and Cunningham (1976), and Sloan (1976).

Stimulating Summertime Reading   Although some children read a great deal during the summer, the majority do not do so unless special efforts are made to promote reading during the summer vacation. Summertime reading may also aid in maintaining or improving reading skills and lessen the regression in reading ability shown by some children when they reenter school in the fall.

Ingenious teachers and parents can find a variety of ways to encourage summer reading. Himmelsteib (1975) proposed that a minimally trained junior high school student volunteer can take a primary-grade child to the library weekly to help select books, help him with the hard words, and read to him. Another way is to make a class visit to the public library late in the spring, with the librarian giving a "sales talk" and encouraging children to apply for library cards. Yet another is to distribute a recommended reading list, with provision for the children to check the books they read and return the list in September. Many public libraries and schools run special summer recreational reading programs including story hours, book discussions, and movies. Various forms of recognition are provided for those who achieve a particular level. Improving the reading skills of poor readers during the summer is more likely to be successful if the children are given material they find easy and interesting to read, and if direct efforts are made to improve their reading skills.

IMPROVING THE RANGE AND MATURITY OF READING INTERESTS

Opening Up New Avenues

In addition to using interests children have already acquired, teachers should set the stage for the development of new reading interests. It is not difficult to provide conditions in which children become eager to read in previously untouched areas.

If, for example, a class has done little or no reading about pets or other animals, the teacher can stimulate an interest in that area by bringing in a hamster, turtle, or hermit crab, or can invite a few children to bring in their pets. All kinds of questions about pets are likely to arise in a skillfully led discussion. What do they eat? Are there different kinds? How long do they live? Are any of them dangerous? At the strategic moment, the teacher produces some books about pets, and the hunt for answers is initiated. While reading about one kind of pet, children are likely to peruse information about other kinds of pets. This can easily lead to reading fiction or factual books about dogs, cats, tropical fish, horses, and on to wild animals. Another successful approach is to start with a visit to a zoo or animal farm, or to show a movie or filmstrip. Sometimes a television program about animals can be used as a starter.

This interest-building strategy, which can be applied in many areas, involves the following steps: (1) open up a new interesting area with a real or vicarious experience; (2) stimulate the children to ask questions; (3) make available reading material in which answers can be found; and (4) provide books on closely related topics.

Often a curious child will open up a lead to a new interest area. Current news reports keep children excited about a great many science topics and new inventions as well as ecology. Today's teacher must exert effort to keep personally in touch with what is going on in the world; keeping curious children supplied with the information they want is often challenging.

Children's questions can be handled in a variety of ways. One is to write on a card each question that arises, and periodically to distribute one card apiece to a number of children, as an individual research project. Another is to turn a group of related questions over to a committee. Such techniques help children to become active seekers of information and relieve the teacher of the compulsion to try to know all the answers. At times, it is not a bad idea for the teacher to admit that she does not know an answer but that she will obtain it. Before presenting the answer, she may explain how and where she found it.

When the language patterns used by authors are strange to children and hard to grasp, oral reading by the teacher is often necessary. Poetry, for example, uses unfamiliar words (e.g., ne'er), and the arrangements of lines and unusual word sequence often make it difficult for children to obtain the continuity of thought. When they listen to the teacher reading poetry, the children can experience the rhythm and cadence of the language and can develop appropriate images, meanings, and feelings, without having to struggle with the printed representation. Once children have some familiarity with a poem, they are likely to enjoy reading it for them-

selves, and choral reading can also be effective and enjoyable. The usefulness of a teacher presentation or a recording is just as great with older
children as it is with younger ones. Once a taste for poetry and some
familiarity with poetic forms have been acquired, children can proceed to
some independent reading of poetry and often try to write their own
poems.

Providing Reading Ladders

Maturity in taste is never achieved in one giant leap; it comes about
gradually, through reading many books, mediocre and excellent, babyish
and mature, coming gradually to prefer the finer and more mature. Taste
is achieved through discrimination, and to be able to compare and
choose one must sample both literature and trash. Teachers and librarians
who restrict children's reading to what they consider worthwhile are ignoring the psychological principle that personal standards are built from
direct experience in comparing and contrasting works of varying degrees
of merit.

Often there is a marked difference between what adults believe children
ought to like to read, and what children actually prefer. Many books that
have won Newbery or Caldecott awards are not particularly popular with
children. This may be in part due to the wide range of readability found
in these books; some are quite difficult. Yet children do enjoy very much
such series books as The Hardy Boys and Nancy Drew, which librarians and
critics often believe to lack literary merit. Reading such a series one after
the other is excellent for improving fluency and developing a positive reading habit. Sooner or later the child exhausts the series and turns to other
books. Although such books may provide a valuable part of children's early
reading experiences, their taste should not be allowed to stay at that level
(Wertheimer and Sands 1975). For older students, the junior novel can
be used to bridge the gap between children's literature and adult books
effectively as described by Ritt (1976).

To help children raise their levels of taste and broaden their range of
reading interests, it is necessary to start from where they are and to recommend and provide a "ladder" of books of increasing merit and maturity
which they can be encouraged to climb, one rung at a time.

A third grader who loves animal cartoons and comic books, but does not
care to read books, could be started with Harry the Dirty Dog, an easy, thin

book. Next, the child might advance to the various books about the humorous, mischievous adventures of the monkey *Curious George*. This could lead to other easy books in which animals get into ridiculous situations, such as Dr. Seuss's *Horton Hatches the Egg.*

Be patient with the fifth-grade girl who reads nothing but *Black Stallion* books. When she has completed the dozen or so books in this series, one can suggest other stories about horses such as *Black Beauty, Misty of Chincoteague,* and *Justin Morgan Had a Horse.* If *The Wild Heart is* enjoyed, an animal story with a somewhat similar theme like De Jong's *Hurry Home, Candy* can be recommended. This could lead into other animal tales or books, and then into other stories with human-animal relations as the theme, that also deal with the problems of growing up and accepting reality. For such purposes, try *The Yearling, The Red Pony,* or *Dorp Dead.*

Reading and Personal Development

Reading can have a powerful effect on the development of personality and character, as well as on intellect. Children identify strongly with admired heroes and heroines, and look down on the villains. In their imaginative play and daydreams, they often put themselves in the hero's or heroine's role. Whether the characters are real or fictional, they try to emulate them. Thus, reading may have a powerful influence on the formation of their ideals, beliefs, and aspirations, as well as often leading to a career choice.

Stories that become classics appeal to deep and widespread human emotions. A skilled author can evoke these emotions in readers, allowing them to develop a deeper understanding and appreciation for the strengths and foibles of man and thus better understand life. Attitudes are more likely to be modified by reading followed by discussion, than by reading alone.

The reasons why a reader reads and the satisfactions a reader derives from literature are multiple. And because the possible effects of literature on the reader also are multiple and uncertain, children may well react differently to the same story or poem.

Bibliotherapy *Bibliotherapy* involves the deliberate selection of reading material to help the reader solve or gain insights into his particular problem. According to Corman (1975) the dynamics of bibliotherapy may be divided into the processes of identification, catharsis, and insight. As the reader identifies with the character, he begins to lessen his personal sense of isolation and differences from others. Catharsis supposedly occurs when the reader vicariously experiences the motivation, conflicts, and emotions of the character. The identification and catharsis lead to insight through which some of the reader's tensions are relieved and he is more readily able to recognize his own traits in others.

Bibliotherapy attempts to (1) teach the reader to think positively and constructively; (2) encourage the child to talk freely about a problem; (3) help the child to analyze personal attitudes or behavior; (4) suggest that a problem may be solved in various ways; (5) stimulate an eagerness to discover an adjustment to the child's problem that will lessen personal conflict or conflict with society; and (6) assist readers in comparing their problems with those of others (Rongione 1972).

Attempts to use bibliotherapy to help children with various types of problems have been reported. For example, Schubert (1975) has listed specific books that can be used with the handicapped, emotionally disturbed, racially prejudiced, retarded readers, and the socially maladjusted. Recently, with an increasing divorce rate, more attention has been given to helping children handle the problems caused by troubled or broken homes in ways that reassure, comfort, and attempt to give courage to the young reader (Haley 1975). Books that may help children cope with other life crises such as hospitalization and death have been discussed by Hormann (1977).

Within limits bibliotherapy may be helpful, but the idea can produce a misleading oversimplification of the situation. There is no guarantee that a particular book will influence a child. It will not take the place of psychotherapy for the seriously maladjusted, who should be referred for professional help; but if used cautiously, it may not only help troubled children to cope better with their problems but it also may help to sensitize children to the problems faced by others.

The following modified guidelines for using bibliotherapy were offered by Shepherd and Iles (1976): (1) since the majority of children in the classroom do not have serious emotional problems, bibliotherapy is more likely to be used with those who have minor problems or questions with which they need help; (2) do not directly and bluntly mention the problem to the child; (3) in order to be helpful, the book need not deal directly with the problem; (4) select books that are believable; and (5) try to create a situation in which the child will choose to read the book without coercion; if displaying and discussing it does not work, try suggesting that the story has a very interesting plot.

Those wishing to learn more about bibliotherapy may refer to Riggs (1971) and Schultheis (1972). Dreyer (1977) has developed a guide to children's literature that describes over 1000 books for children aged 2 to 15 according to possible needs and problems. Another guide (Baskin and K. Harris 1977) annotates and evaluates over 300 children's books dealing with the handicapped. Books may be used to promote sensitivity and empathy through techniques suggested by V. Reid (1972).

Child Development through Reading   For children who become readers, reading is an open road into an ever-expanding, multidimensional world. It provides new ideas and images for the mind. It offers answers to hundreds of questions about the nature of the world and its contents. Reading allows these children to live vicariously in the lives of all kinds of people, and to experience at least partially some of their times and emotions. It acquaints them with many phases of human behavior: nobility and baseness, generosity and greed, humility and arrogance, courage and cowardice, joy and sorrow. Its heroes and heroines can provide models to admire, emulate, and imitate.

Reading is, then, a way of living many lives in one. Through reading, people can extend their knowledge far beyond the boundaries of their own immediate lives.

Language Arts and Reading

Few would argue that reading is not one of the language arts. From time to time in the history of American education, attempts have been made to incorporate the teaching of reading completely in large blocks of time entitled "The Language Arts" during which all of the communication skills were supposedly taught in an integrated fashion. On the other hand, and perhaps in response to evidence that reading skills were not being well taught, at times the teaching of reading has been almost completely divorced from the other language arts. Neither extreme has been particularly successful.

Certainly the use of a language-experience approach calls for use of listening, speaking, writing, and reading skills. Too often after the initial stages of reading instruction, little is done to take advantage of the interrelatedness of the language arts and the potential for improving skills in one area through incorporating its use with another. Yet the possibilities are there. For example, Donham and Ichen (1977) have described their use of picture books to stimulate creative writing in the intermediate grades. Somewhat similarly, Moss (1977) developed a program of exposing six- and seven-year-olds to literature (stories with a common theme were read to and by the youngsters), which in turn led to the creation of their own stories. Hearing and discussing children's literature helped the children to discover the basic literary elements of plot, characterization, setting, and style, which in turn aided them in their own creative writing. As Murray (1975) pointed out, writing can aid reading skills because the writer must read and reread his own material to discover if he has communicated his intended meaning effectively. He listed 22 reading activities that can help children read as writers do.

The limited available research findings suggest that favorable effects of reading practice on writing skills, and vice versa, can be demonstrated. But until more comprehensive evidence becomes available, our procedures for integrating the language arts will have to rest on assumptions and intuitions (Applebee 1977).

LEARNING ABOUT BOOKS FOR CHILDREN

Teachers should have more than a nodding acquaintance with children's books, including library books (or trade books, as they are often called), as well as reading texts and content area texts. If one has not had a recent course in children's or adolescent literature, books such as those by Arbuthnot (1972) can be helpful. Rudman's book (1976) organizes and discusses children's literature in terms of social issues.

To bring children and books together effectively, one should both understand the children and have a broad acquaintance with the books that might suit them. A vital part of an independent reading program is the teacher's ability to discuss children's readings with them. This requires knowing the book well enough to ask intelligent questions about it and to be able to judge the adequacy and accuracy of the children's responses. It is impossible to know all books this well, but the teacher should be personally acquainted with a sampling of reasonable size. Reading children's books need not be boring; good children's literature can be an enjoyable experience for the adult who has not completely buried childhood interests and enthusiasms.

With approximately three thousand new juvenile books appearing yearly, in addition to older titles, teachers have to be highly selective and must rely heavily on recommendations made by specialists in children's literature. It is very helpful to be able to consult with a knowledgeable librarian, who herself frequently depends on special lists and reviews that can also be used as references by teachers. Among the many sources, the following are especially recommended:

Children's Catalog, twelfth ed. (H. W. Wilson, 1971). Annual supplements. A very comprehensive listing of over 5000 titles, with reviews and a system of cross indexing by author, title, subject matter, and grade level. Highly recommended books are starred.

Best Books for Children (Bowker, 1974). Annually revised paperback covering over 4000 books arranged by topics, levels, with author, title, and series indexes.

The Best in Children's Books, third ed. (University of Chicago Press, 1973). Contains almost 1400 titles of outstanding children's books published between 1966 and 1972. Titles are arranged alphabetically by author, with subject and title indexes and reviews.

Books for Children, Preschool through Junior High School (American Library Association, 1971). Annual supplements. Contain one-paragraph reviews of over 3000 titles; indicate broad grade levels and if primarily for boys or girls.

Adventuring with Books: A Booklist for Pre-K–Grade 8, new ed. (National Council of Teachers of English, 1977). An annotated list of 2500 books, all published since 1970, with suggested interest and difficulty levels by category.

Bibliography of Books for Children (Association for Childhood Education International, 1977). Over 2000 annotated listings (fiction and nonfiction) arranged by general age subject areas; especially useful at the primary level.

Literature and Young Children (National Council of Teachers of English, 1977). Suggests specific books for children and gives practical suggestions for their use. Includes author, illustrator, and title indexes.

Growing up with Books; Growing up with Paperbacks; Growing up with

Science Books (Bowker, 1976, 1977). Each contains nearly 200 titles; entries are grouped by subject with recommended age levels. Small, inexpensive pamphlets, good for parents.

Junior High School Library Catalog, third ed. (H. W. Wilson, 1975). Almost 3800 titles are briefly reviewed; classified by topic, author, and title. Annual supplements.

Your reading: a booklist for junior high students (National Council of Teachers of English, 1975). Over 1600 titles listed so as to be used by the students themselves in choosing from 40 categories.

Other book sources have been listed by Ladley (1970) who also annotated sources of children's magazines. Schulte (1975) listed some 30 sources for use with adolescents. Recent reviews of children's books may be found in such publications as *Language Arts* (Formerly *Elementary English*), the *Reading Teacher, Horn Book, Junior Libraries,* the *Bulletin* of the Center for Children's Books (University of Chicago), the American Library Association's *Booklist and Subscription Books Bulletin,* as well as in the children's book sections of the *New York Times* and *Saturday Review.*

Ethnic and Cultural Materials

In recent years, much material has been published pertaining to various ethnic or cultural backgrounds. Although research does not clearly indicate whether minority group children prefer to read about their own, it is probable that many do. Furthermore, ethnic materials can be of interest to majority-group children and help them to understand ways other than their own. *Reading Ladders for Human Relations* (V. Reid, 1972), which annotates some 1300 books and offers suggestions for their use, is a very helpful source of information about books that may help to extend sensitivity toward others.

Among the materials published for and about minority groups are:

Open Door Books (Children's Press). Thirty-six autobiographies of successful minority-group men and women. Reading level about 5; interest level, grades 5–12.

Toward Freedom (Garrard). Highlights the important contributions made by black Americans. Reading level about 6; interest level, 5–9.

Target Today Series (Benefic). Short story lessons in each book deal with contemporary urban life. Reading level 2–6; interest level, 3–9.

Americans All (Garrard). Biographies of Americans of many races, creeds, and national origins. Reading level, about 4; interest level, 3–6.

We are Black (SRA). Fairly short selections taken from books and periodicals. Reading levels, 2–6; interest levels, 4–8.

Multi-Ethnic Reading Library (Scholastic). Three paperback collections covering a wide range of readability and interest levels.

Our Native Americans Book (Benefic). Customs, lives, etc. of various Indian and Eskimo tribes and Hawaiians. Reading level, 2–3; interest level, 2–5.

Indians (Garrard). American history from the Indian's viewpoint, using biographies. Reading level, about 3; interest levels, 2–5.

Indian Culture Series (Montana). True-life stories of the Indians from the past through the present. Reading levels, 3–5; interest levels, 4–12.

Folk Tales and Legends (Montana). Authentic tribal tales and legends. Reading levels, 1–4; interest level; 1–7.

The Indian Reading Series: Stories and Legends of the Northwest (Educational Systems). Stories and legends show how different tribes explained the world around them. Designed to reinforce pride in cultural heritage. Reading and interest levels: primary grades.

Other books have been listed and annotated by Griffen (1970), Archer (1972), Weber (1972), Strickland (1973b), Stensland (1973), Spache (1975), and Reed (1976). Suggestions for teaching literature to the disadvantaged have been presented by Bachner (1975a, 1975b). Bresnahan (1976) listed criteria for selecting sensitive and sensible books about blacks.

UNIT 11

Assisting Children with Special Needs

For varying reasons, some children have special needs that must be considered in providing reading instruction. The first section of this unit focuses attention on children with reading disabilities. Next, the educationally disadvantaged are considered, with an emphasis on linguistic and cultural variations. The last sections deal with the slow learner and the gifted child.

The chief focus in discussing these various types of children (the categories are not mutually exclusive—a disadvantaged child may also be a disabled reader or a gifted child) is on presenting information that will help teachers to understand, discover, and provide for their needs. There are individual differences that must be accommodated, but almost all children respond to good teaching.

DISABLED READERS

One question a teacher must ask about a child's reading ability is, "Is his general level of achievement reasonably close to what can be expected of him?" In addition to those making normal progress, the teacher should try to identify three basic types: slow learners, underachievers, and disabled readers. A distinction needs to be made among such children so that realistic goals and expectations may be set and their reading programs adjusted accordingly. *Slow learners,* children with limited general intellectual capacity, cannot be expected to function at grade level; they need an adapted academic program. *Underachievers,* those who are reading at or above grade level but significantly below their potential, often need to be better motivated. Many gifted children fall into this category.

A child who is a *disabled reader* has a level of reading ability that is significantly below average for grade placement and potential and is also disparate with the child's cultural, linguistic, and educational experience. In short, a disabled reader functions significantly below what might reasonably be expected for a child of his or her age, mental attainment, and experiental and educational background. Procedures for determining if a child is reading near potential have been explained in unit 6 (pp. 212–14).

Dyslexia and Learning Disabilities [1]

In recent years, a great deal of interest and attention have been focused on children who have extreme difficulty in learning to read. These are the children who, long after their peers have learned to read, and despite at least average intelligence and numerous attempts to teach them, have not yet learned to recognize more than a few words and are extremely deficient in decoding. They not only find it exceedingly difficult to acquire basic mechanical reading skills, but also to retain skills they have apparently "learned." Different labels (e.g., word-blind, minimally brain damaged, primary reading disability) have been attached to these children. More recently the terms *dyslexia* and *learning disability* have become popular, but there is no consensus as to the definition of either of these terms. For this reason, we prefer not to use them.

According to Critchley (1970), The Research Group on Developmental Dyslexia of the World Federation of Neurology in 1968 recommended two definitions: *dyslexia,* "a disorder in children who, despite conventional classroom experience, fail to attain the language skills of reading, writing, and

1. For a more complete discussion refer to Harris and Sipay (1975, pp. 136–40).

spelling commensurate with their abilities"; and *specific developmental dyslexia,* "a disorder manifested by difficulty in learning to read despite conventional instruction, adequate intelligence, and socio-cultural opportunity. It is dependent upon fundamental cognitive disabilities which are frequently of constitutional origin." The first of these definitions is essentially the same as our concept of reading disability, except that it omits mention of sociocultural opportunity. The second adds the notion of a constitutional causation. Unfortunately, most people who use the term dyslexia do not bother to indicate which of these meanings they intend.

Critchley also wrote: "A recent trend has been to avoid precision of thought by including the concept of dyslexia within a medley of other disorders. Thus 'language disability,' 'learning disability,' 'perceptual disorders' are terms which have crept in, and have added confusion to the topic of developmental dyslexia. It would be better to avoid this kind of toponymy" (1970, p. 13). In our opinion, dyslexia has added confusion to the topic of reading disability. "Learning disability" is also ambiguous, sometimes being used in a purely descriptive way, and sometimes with the notion that a constitutional defect or deficiency is involved.

There is little agreement or hard evidence as to what causes what we prefer to refer to as *severe reading disability.* Among the possible causes cited are cerebral dysfunctioning or defects, maturational lag, cerebellar-vestibular dysfunctioning, and perceptual defects. Some believe the condition is inherited. Long lists of symptoms have been proposed, but although some of these symptoms are present in most cases, not all or even most of them are manifested in every case.

Most people who subscribe to the theories of dyslexia and learning disabilities are of the opinion that factors within the child are causing the reading problem and that these must be overcome before the child can learn to read. Thus, the child may be taught such "enabling" skills as visual perception for a long time before any attempts are made at reading instruction. The effectiveness of such procedures in improving reading is yet to be proven. Reading specialists, on the other hand, attempt to determine the status of the child's reading skills, and to teach those skills that are weak or nonexistent. In the last few years, there has been considerable controversy over who should treat the severely disabled readers.

Educators too often seem satisfied with placing a label on a child, and then justifying his lack of progress because of it ("He has a learning disability, so I really can't help him"). Such labels carry a negative connotation that often results in lower expectations of the child by both regular and special-education teachers (Gellung and Rucker 1977).

What needs to be done is to determine the severely disabled reader's strengths and weaknesses, and to devise a highly individualized program so that the child can begin to learn effectively. Such programs are often beyond what can be expected of classroom teachers, but they can play an important role in helping the child by working cooperatively with experts in conducting and evaluating the program. When such assistance is not available, the classroom teacher must do the best he or she can.

At present, no one has a panacea for severe reading disability. It may be that a number of different types of disability exist within this general category. We still have a great deal to learn about reading disability.

Where and by whom should disabled readers be treated? A distinction is frequently made between corrective and remedial reading, the basic difference being the severity of the reading disability. Corrective cases, those who are "mildly disabled," are usually treated in groups by the classroom teacher in the classroom. Remedial cases, those with "more severe reading problems," are usually treated by a reading specialist individually or in small groups outside of the classroom.

Exact criteria for distinguishing between corrective and remedial cases are not available. The reading problems treated differ in degree more than in kind, and where and by whom they are treated often depend more on the availability of resources than on the nature of the problem (Clymer 1967). Furthermore, corrective reading is a normal part of good teaching. Therefore, rather than talking about treating corrective or remedial cases, the following sections discuss how the classroom teacher can work with children who have varying needs. Working with children who have reading problems should include understanding and dealing with the factors that may be contributing to the reading problem, diagnosing specific learning needs, teaching the specific skills needed, and providing effective motivation.

Correlates of Reading Disability

Finding the original cause of a reading disability is often impossible. Usually a number of years have passed since the child entered school, records are incomplete, and memories are faulty. Even if one could discover all the relevant facts, there are usually several potential contributing factors still present, and the relative significance of each in a particular case is likely to arouse disagreement even among experts. Whatever the initial causes, a constellation of interacting factors soon become mutually reinforcing.

For the classroom teacher, it is preferable not to worry about the original causation, but rather to concentrate on trying to determine what is presently preventing or curtailing improvement. There are many factors, other than intellectual, that are correlated with reading disabilities. Only a brief summary of these is possible here; a more detailed coverage may be found in Harris and Sipay (1975). It should be noted that the following factors are referred to as "correlates" because although they are frequently associated with reading disability, a definite causal relationship for a particular child is difficult to establish.

Physical Factors   Uncorrected visual defects are the most common physical handicaps among disabled readers. The kinds of visual defects most apt to be associated with reading disability are farsightedness and various kinds of eye muscle difficulties which result in quick ocular fatigue, difficulty in forming a clear retinal image, and difficulty in fusing the separate images relayed by each eye. These defects often allow a child to pass the Snellen Chart Test that is commonly used to screen vision in schools; they can be detected on more elaborate visual screening tests used in some schools. Failure on a visual screening test indicates the need to refer the child to a visual specialist (optometrists and ophthalmologists often do not agree on the relationship of vision to reading ability). It also should be noted that two children may have exactly the same visual anomalies, but only one may have a reading problem; some children are able to compensate for such handicaps. Even if the child does not have a reading problem, suspected physical or sensory defect should be referred for examination and possible treatment.

Hearing defects, endocrine problems, and neurological defects may contribute to a child's reading problem. A problem with hearing in general (this makes learning difficult since most instruction occurs orally) or with specific sounds can cause problems in learning phonics. Lack of energy may be due to a chronic debilitating condition like asthma, malnutrition, or heart disease. Lack of sufficient sleep because of a late bedtime is sometimes the very simple basis of drowsiness in school. A predisposition to reading disability tends to run in some families; whether or not this is hereditary is still an unsolved question.

Visually impaired children. Visually impaired children range from those who have slight visual problems to the blind. A main objective of teaching reading to severely visually impaired children is to place them in situations that will promote as much learning as possible without harming their vision. Not only should the lighting be adequate and the reading period brief enough to avoid visual fatigue or injury, but the teacher also must consider the use of materials with large print. Books and even some standardized reading tests in large print are available from various publishers. Sources of such sight-saving materials are available from local associations of the blind or visually impaired, or from the American Printing House for the Blind, or the Library of Congress, Division for the Blind and Physically Handicapped. There are also a number of devices for magnifying print for those who, although legally blind, have partial vision. One such device magnifies print as much as sixty times on a television screen. Visually impaired children should be given preferential seating in the classroom.

Hearing impaired. Children who are auditorially impaired range from those having mild hearing losses that interfere somewhat with auditory discrimination and learning some phonic skills, to the congenitally deaf child who has never heard sounds and probably has not developed speech. Hearing-impaired children should be given preferential seating in the classroom (e.g., have the child sit near the teacher) and the teacher should enunciate clearly without exaggerating or slowing her speech, so that the child can make use of whatever lip reading skills he possesses.

Logically, it seems that the deaf would have difficulty learning to read with a program that emphasized phonics; perhaps that is why a whole-word approach is usually employed (Orlando 1973). But, although there are some books devoted to teaching the deaf to read (e.g., Hart 1963, Strong 1964), there is very little evidence as to which method is most effective for the majority. Lane and Baker (1974) have demonstrated that high reading achievement is possible for some deaf children, but that a slower than normal rate of learning should be expected. Use of photography as an aid to teach a sight vocabulary to deaf children has been discussed by Bodner (1975), and Peters and Peters (1974) have presented an annotated bibliography of resource materials and texts for use with the deaf.

Educational Factors   Among the school-related problems that can interfere with progress in reading is frequent or prolonged absence, something that the school cannot prevent. Schools are responsible, however, for the following: starting reading instruction before the child is ready, failing to provide systematic instruction in word recognition and decoding skills, using instructional material that is too difficult for the child, frightening children or habitually using sarcasm and disparagement, failing to arouse the child's interest in reading, and failure to detect and correct difficulties while they are still new and minor. One of the factors often unrecognized as a contributor to reading disability is poor teaching.

Social Factors   The attitudes toward reading of the child's family and peers may influence reading ability. It is difficult to help a child if his parents are uninterested and uncooperative, or if gang influence sets anti-intellectual standards. Aside from interest, the presence or absence of positive educational and cultural stimulation in the home has a pervasive influence on the schoolwork of children.

Disturbed or maladjusted parents sometimes create very distressing conditions for children. Parents often aggravate a reading disability by scolding or punishing the child for his poor reading, disparaging him, comparing him unfavorably with a scholastically competent sibling, or trying to teach him in inappropriate ways. Other parents pressure their children to achieve to the point where the child resists by not learning.

Emotional Factors   In many cases, school failure is intimately connected with the child's total personal and emotional adjustment. An emotional problem may persistently interfere with concentration, attention, and motivation and strongly contribute to a child's reading problem. In other cases, failure in learning to read produces gradually increasing discouragement; after a while the child tends to avoid or evade reading, and is likely to become upset and confused when he cannot escape from reading.

It is of little importance whether the emotional problem or reading problem occurs first. A vicious cycle becomes established in which each bad experience with reading produces unpleasant feelings, and the strong emotions of fear, anger, shame, or embarrassment interfere with clear thinking and attention. This makes it ever more difficult for the child to learn to read; the emotional and reading problems become mutually reinforcing. Difficulty in learning to read may lead to a sense of insecurity, frustration, and a poor self-concept.

What can the teacher do about these possible handicaps? There are very realistic limits to what teachers can do about many of the conditions that may be contributing to the reading disability. The teacher cannot change the child's constitutional makeup. She can recommend a visual or medical examination, but can do nothing except try to persuade the parents to follow the advice. Sometimes it is a major victory just to get a pair of broken eyeglasses repaired. The teacher can do little about neighborhood conditions and has no jurisdiction over the child's playmates or out-of-school activities. Parents often resent inquisitiveness about their own personal problems, or those of their children.

Teachers should try to make use of available specialized personnel both in discovering and dealing with possible contributing factors. Parents are likely to discuss the child's health problems more freely with a school nurse or physician, and to discuss adjustment problems more openly with a school psychologist, social worker, or guidance counselor. The parents also are more likely to accept recommendations from people they regard as specialists. Nevertheless, there are times when only the classroom teacher can take the initiative, and the conscientious teacher will do what she can to help the child.

In taking on a responsibility that would be carried by special personnel in other schools, the teacher should proceed cautiously and with all the tact she can muster. If the teacher can get across the idea that she knows that the parents want to do the best they can to help the child, and that her own interest in helping the child is genuine, a situation in which parents and teacher pool their information and try to think through problems together can sometimes be successfully established. Parents need to feel that the things they know about the child and their opinions are important and respected. Diplomacy is important. Instead of telling parents bluntly, "Johnny should have had a thorough eye examination by now," a teacher is much more likely to succeed if she leads gently into the suggestion; "Mrs. Jones, Gene blinks a lot and his eyes fill with tears and turn pink when he reads. Maybe there is something wrong with his eyes that the school vision tests cannot detect. Has he ever been examined by an eye specialist?"

Tact and patience often bring results in the long run, even if action does not take place quickly. Whether or not action to eliminate possible contributing handicaps can be taken or stimulated, it is up to the teacher to do what she can to teach the child to read.

Analyzing Specific Learning Needs

Just because a child's general level of reading ability is at a particular reader level, all the skills normally taught at that reader level in the developmental reading program need not be introduced. Nor need the skills be introduced at a pace similar to that in the developmental program. One should attempt to determine what the child has already mastered, where the gaps or difficulties are in reading skills, and how the child can best learn.

Initial Testing   With children below the third-reader level, testing can be initiated with an informal reading inventory or standardized oral reading test, followed by a word recognition test and a test covering essential decoding skills, as described in unit 6. For children reading at or above the third-reader level, a silent reading test also is desirable, either a standardized or informal one. Careful analysis and comparison of these tests should make it possible to fill out most of the checklist shown in figure 6.9, or to record the important facts and conclusions about the child's reading in some other suitable form.

One should then be able to form tentative answers to the following questions:

1. Is the child able to read independently at any level? If so, what would be the most suitable level for starting independent reading?
2. What is the child's instructional reading level? Considering the child's feelings about reading, should he be started at this level or below it?
3. What are the outstanding characteristics of the child's sight vocabulary? Is his fund of high-utility words adequate? Does he frequently make certain specific kinds of errors? Is there a particular method of learning words that seems to work best for him?
4. Does he make adequate use of semantic and syntactic cues? What does he know about phonics? Can he separate words into parts that he can recognize or readily decode? Can he make the necessary symbol-sound associations? Can he blend sounds into syllables and syllables into words? Does he need to start with phonics readiness or simply need some polishing and filling in of gaps?
5. Are there any comprehension problems that do not seem to be secondary to word-recognition difficulties? If so, are there any clues that help explain why comprehension is poor?
6. What interests has the child shown that might be useful in the selection of reading materials?

Based on the answers to these questions, a teaching plan is formulated and the remedial program begins.

Continuous Diagnosis   Diagnosis, the development of a thorough knowledge of a problem condition, should be a continuous process. The teacher checks the suitability of the material, both for difficulty and for interest appeal. Each lesson clarifies the picture of what the child does and does not know about word identification, word meanings, and how to read for meaning. When a child is unable to perform a task, the teacher asks herself, "Why? Does the child lack prerequisite skills? If the task were presented in a different way, could the child learn it? Am I moving too quickly? Am I asking him to learn too much at a time, or too soon? Were my directions clear? What information does he need, or what must he understand, in order to be able to answer the comprehension question?" Once a skill has been introduced, ample opportunity for applying it while reading in context should be provided, for often a skill is taught in isolation. It does a child no good to be able to complete a workbook page if he does not apply that skill during reading.

The faster a child improves, the more often it is necessary to reappraise performance and change the instructional program. A nine-year-old may begin at a first-reader level, with a small sight vocabulary and few decoding skills. In a few months the child may have mastered the majority of the word identification skills at the first- and low-second reader levels and be using material at the low-second-reader level for instructional purposes. A child who was required to complete the entire reader level program at the same pace as in a developmental reading program could never catch up. As the child completes each instructional objective, the teacher should plan ahead. Should more reading be done at second-reader level to assure mastery, or is the child ready for instruction at third-reader level? Which high-utility words should be added to the child's sight vocabulary? What remaining decoding or word-recognition skills are still needed? Should the emphasis shift from oral reading to silent reading? Is the child's reading rate increasing satisfactorily or does it need some special attention? Each lesson may yield new evidence that can be used to evaluate and, when necessary, to modify the program.

Teaching the Disabled Reader

Working with Groups   Most of the help that classroom teachers can provide for children with reading problems will be planned for the relatively less serious cases, who generally fit fairly well within the lowest reading group in the class. When the program is highly individualized, these children can be seen somewhat more frequently and for longer conferences than most of their classmates. When developmental reading is taught with groups, as is most typical, special attention can also be given to them.

The lowest reading group is usually a mixture of mentally slow children, who are doing about as well as they can, and brighter children with varying degrees of reading disability. Although the group members are all more or less at the same instructional reading level, there are often marked differences in the particular areas of reading skills in which group members are strong or weak. More often than not, the mentally slow children are fairly good in word recognition and in reading for directly stated details, but tend to read orally slowly and in a monotonous tone and have trouble understanding main ideas, making inferences, seeing implications, anticipating outcomes, or understanding cause-effect relationships. The disabled readers, on the other hand, are very likely to have their main reading problems in word recognition and decoding, and to do relatively well in reading for meaning in material that is at or below their instructional levels.

Teachers who are alert to individual needs can do much during a group session to meet these needs. In preparatory activities, the teacher can check one child's recognition of a word, another's grasp of its meaning, and a third's ability to apply his decoding skills to it. In discussion after reading a selection, the brighter children can more frequently be asked the more searching questions and the mentally slower children the ones dealing with directly stated facts. Related practice in word recognition and decoding can stress the needs of those with particular problems in these areas.

Additional help can be provided for children, regardless of the group in which they normally receive reading instruction, by setting up special needs groups. Children with similar needs meet in such groups once a week or more as long as they need such instruction.

The independent reading program can be used helpfully also. It is worth a special effort to locate books that are mature enough to interest the disabled reader and yet easy enough so that the child can read them unaided. If a child can be successfully launched on a program of independent reading, the benefits to his or her reading may be as great as those from direct instruction. When the child reports about a book during a book review session or reads an excerpt during an audience reading period, the rest of the class can recognize the improvement—and they are usually generous with their compliments. Aside from the fact that a great deal of easy reading helps to automatize sight vocabulary and speed up reading, the resulting strengthening of the child's feeling of being accepted gives morale a boost and encourages further efforts.

Handling Rivalry   Most disabled readers crave social approval. Sometimes they attempt to shine by disparaging the work of their group mates. Such a tendency must be checked, not by reproving or punishing, but by holding up a set of more appropriate standards of behavior to the group. The teacher can emphasize in various ways that a child's reading should be judged in comparison with his or her own past performance, not with that of other group members or other groups. One child's mistakes do not make another child any better. Each child is competing with his or her previous reading performance, and trying to improve it; when he succeeds he deserves praise. Patient reiteration of these ideas usually is successful in reducing the tendency of disabled readers to pick on one another.

It is also vital to avoid the appearance of playing favorites. Within the low group, the teacher may be more hopeful of producing marked improvement in some children than in others; but this should not be at all evident during group activities. Each group member is deserving of teacher attention and needs recognition and approval, whether the child has the potential for improving greatly or not. Special interest in certain individuals can be shown in individual contacts with them.

Working with Individuals   Sometimes a teacher undertakes to help a child whose reading disability is such that he cannot learn much during group lessons, or because his ability is far below that of even the lowest group in the class. Others need individual help because they are highly distractible or tend to disrupt group sessions. Privacy and exclusive attention to the one child sometimes are more essential for progress than what is taught. The presence of other children when he tries to read gives an occasional youngster such stage fright that he becomes mentally paralyzed.

Although such children should be taught by a special teacher of reading, when one is not available, the classroom teacher can try to help. If the child is receiving special help, the reading specialist and classroom teacher should work together to coordinate their efforts. Without such cooperation, the child may become confused by use of differing methods, materials, and goals.

Surprisingly good progress may be made by some seriously disabled readers when they receive 30- to 45-minute sessions, two or more times a week. Time may be found for this before or after school, during a free period, or individualized reading may be scheduled. If it is impossible to find a half-hour block of time, ten to fifteen minute sessions can be used to accomplish a great deal.

The special magic of individual remedial help is that the child receives the total, undivided attention and appreciation of an adult. For many children this is a unique experience; there have always been brothers, sisters, playmates, and classmates. Usually the child values the relationship very much. The rapport that can develop is very much like that in successful psychotherapy, and the personal relationship with the teacher sometimes helps a child to overcome emotional problems as well as educational difficulties. Successful learning serves as additional therapy. Repeated successful experiences on a short-term basis may influence the long-term development of a positive self-concept.

Individualized remedial reading gives teachers the opportunity to use to their maximum effect the basic psychological principles that underlie all good teaching. There is no need to compromise between what one child needs and what another child requires. There is no set curriculum to cover nor any predetermined timetable to set the pace. The teacher can give exclusive attention to discovering the child's needs, establishing readiness for each new step, finding and using established interests, motivating the child to try new directions, presenting facts and principles in the clearest and most understandable way possible, using gamelike reviews, and reteaching as often as necessary to produce permanent learning. There is nothing unique in the learning activities or in the teaching techniques; the special value lies in the personal relationship and in the opportunity to fit the instruction more precisely to the child than is usually achieved in the classroom.

Working with a Small Diverse Group Classroom teachers are sometimes asked to give remedial help to a small group of from two to six children. Quite often the children in such a group are so diverse in reading skills that little group instruction is possible. When this is the case, most of the period must be spent working individually with one child after another, while the rest of the group carries on with assigned reading activities. The entire group is brought together for some activity which they can perform with reasonable equality. With children at primary-grade reading levels, this can be a word-recognition game, an audience reading session, or the teacher reading an installment of an exciting story. With a more advanced group, a short rate-and-comprehension exercise, which group members can take at varying degrees of difficulty, sometimes is suitable. During the brief individual sessions, the teacher can discuss outside reading with the child, listen to some oral reading, review high-utility words, teach a new phonic principle, do some further testing, and so on.

Managing such a group requires careful planning and efficient use of time. The group is like a miniature classroom, with each child a group in himself. With efficient planning of reading activities that require little or no teacher direction, each child's learning goes on when the teacher is with other children as well as when a child is receiving personal attention.

Using Paraprofessionals   There has been increasing use of partially trained adults as aides in the reading program. Paraprofessionals from back- grounds similar to those of the students also can serve to bridge the gap be- tween home and school (Holloway 1976). If favorable results are to be achieved, their selection, training and supervision requires a substantial investment of professional time. They should possess similar personal qual- ities as teachers (e.g., ability to relate well to others, emotional stability), and their training should involve clarifying the role of the paraprofessional, providing some basic information on learning to read, providing informa- tion regarding the social and environmental factors that influence the learning of the students with whom she would be working, and developing the hows and why of cooperative planning (Paraprofessionals and Read- ing Committee, International Reading Association 1973).

The lack of clearly defined roles and responsibilities for both parapro- fessionals and teachers has contributed to the negative and ambivalent attitudes of some teachers toward paraprofessionals. Dauzat (1973) rec- ommends that with proper training and supervision, paraprofessionals may (1) apply readability formulas so teachers can help children select appro- priate materials; (2) prepare teaching materials (word charts, sentence strips, etc.); (3) reinforce specific reading skills through games or exer- cises prescribed by the teacher; (4) tutor a child with a special problem, under the teacher's supervision; (5) supervise the children's independent reading; (6) listen to oral reading, perhaps even noting areas of consistent weakness; (7) extend the pupils' backgrounds by reading to them; (8) pro- vide a supportive environment by giving the child personal attention; (9)

assist in preparing or reproducing experience stories; (10) supervise small group dramatics; (11) supervise peer-tutoring; and (12) prepare media designed to motivate recreational reading (e.g., posters, book fairs).

Using Other Children as Tutors   Older children have successfully tutored younger children (Niedermeyer and Ellis 1971, Willis et al. 1972, Snapp et al. 1972). At times the tutoring also results in reading gains for the tutor (Frager and Stern 1970, Mohan 1971). However, as a result of their critical review of the research on children tutoring children, Devin-Sheehan, Feldman, and Allen (1976) concluded that the evidence supporting the practice is inconclusive, with many questions as yet left unanswered, and that few generalizations could be based on the existing data. A somewhat similar conclusion was drawn by Ellson (1976) who felt that despite the common belief that individualized instruction is almost infallibly effective, the significant variable in producing effective tutoring is what the tutor *does*—there is no magic in individual attention in itself. A ten-unit program for training peer tutors has been outlined by Boraks and Allen (1977). Programmed tutoring, which provides very specific instruction for the tutor using a specific reading series, has been quite successful with children whose readiness for reading is low (Ellson, P. Harris, and Barber 1968).

Motivating the Disabled Reader

Building Rapport   The teacher's first objective, in a corrective or remedial reading situation, is to establish rapport with each child. Establishing a comfortable and unconstrained relationship of mutual confidence can be accomplished by getting across the feeling that the child is liked, appreciated, and understood. Whether the teacher's feelings toward a child are genuine or faked, the child will know. Avoid gushing and making a sentimental fuss over the child. A pleasant but businesslike attitude is desirable, in which the teacher provides learnable tasks, encourages, accepts poor performance without criticism or discouragement, explains or clarifies with inexhaustible patience, never scolds or disparages, and confidently conveys the impression that she believes the child will improve. The teacher, who must believe in her ability to help the child, is not disheartened when the child has an off day and celebrates every sign of real progress.

Ensuring Success   Teachers must be prepared to find that, after years of chronic failure, the disabled reader often feels hopeless and stupid. Activities that might embarrass the child, such as reading orally in front of classmates, should be avoided, and the child should be presented opportunities to be successful in other ways than reading. Because replacing discouragement with hope is most important, it is usually desirable to start with learning activities that are well below the child's instructional level, to make sure that he will succeed. Using material (that the child has not used before) at the child's independent reading level for a while may not provide much new learning, but it can produce a major change in attitude. In the early lessons, the number of new words or skills introduced, the amount of material covered in a lesson, etc., must be far less than what the teacher has become accustomed to in regular classroom instruction. After the child has become convinced that he or she is making progress, the pace and the difficulty can be gradually increased; but the reading material should always be of appropriate difficulty and the activities within the amount that the child can absorb in one lesson. Learning how little to try to cover is one of the hardest tasks for the teacher who is new at remedial teaching.

Dramatizing Progress   Children with reading disabilities have had such a scarcity of praise and successful learning experiences that when they do something worth noting it should be celebrated. Many of these children have such deep-seated feelings of inadequacy and inferiority that visible, dramatic evidence of their improvement needs to be kept before them. Having built up a self-image of chronic failure, these children find it hard to believe that they are finally succeeding unless they see incontrovertible evidence that they are actually learning.

It is desirable to set up three or four major goals for the remedial program and to set up a visually effective progress chart for each. Thus, a disabled reader who is functioning at the first-reader level might have a progress chart that shows each new word learned, a chart for the total number of pages read with 90 percent accuracy, and one for new phonic principles mastered. For a sixth grader reading at third-reader level, it would probably be better to chart stories read or books finished than pages read, and to keep a separate account of independent reading done between lessons. Among the variety of individual progress charts that can be constructed are the two shown in figure 11.1.

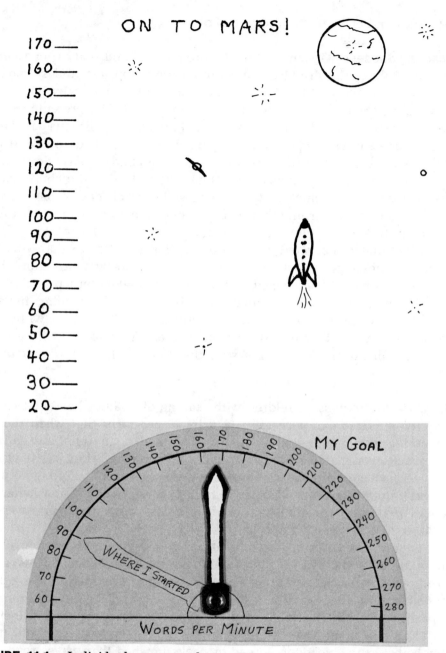

FIGURE 11.1. Individual progress charts. *Top:* spaceship chart for recording the successful completion of a task or unit. The spaceship is held in place by a pin or small piece of tape, and is moved higher as additional tasks are completed or higher scores are made. *Bottom:* a speedometer chart for recording reading rate improvement. One dial hand indicates where the pupil started; the other is moved to indicate progress.

Making Reading Interesting   For children who hate books, a modified experience story approach often works well as a starter. The teacher gets a child to talk about a personal interest or experience, and together they formulate a brief story that the teacher first prints in manuscript and later types. The words that the child cannot recognize are taught, one by one, by whatever method is effective,[2] and the selection is reread orally until it can be read fairly well by the child. Then it can be read to classmates and sent home to be read to the parents. This continues with new selections; gradually the child takes over writing the stories, which can be bound together to form a "book." Usually it does not take very long until the child indicates a desire to try reading a real book.

Sometimes a sales campaign is necessary to get children to accept books that are easy enough for them. The *Begin-Over Approach* is one in which the teacher explains to the child that most words in books that he would like to read are the short words, and it is necessary to learn them before tackling the longer and harder words. Therefore it is desirable to start back near the beginning, with a book in which these words are almost the only ones that have to be learned. Low-difficulty material can be made more palatable when the child is given a genuine and valid reason for using it—a reason that the child can understand and accept. If the child is embarrassed by having a "baby book," a cover can be placed on it so that peers will not recognize its level. Occasionally allowing the child to select, during an independent reading period, books that are obviously too difficult may help the child to maintain "face" with peers.

The availability of many high-interest, low-vocabulary-load books has eased the selection of remedial materials. A sample page from one of these is shown in figure 11.2. Books, some of which are written as low as the preprimer (PP) level, from the following list of series (or others that do not appear in a series) may be useful in working with disabled readers. The indicated reading and interest levels are those provided by the publishers. The reading-grade levels indicate the range of readability of the various books in the series; the interest levels, the range of interests of these books. Where the titles do not clearly indicate the topic(s) covered, they appear in parenthesis. Some of them also may be useful for supplementary reading for those who have difficulty reading the on-grade content subject texts.

2. For children with severe word-recognition problems, it may first be necessary to determine which method(s) a child can learn by. In addition to the whole-word and phonics approaches, a number of others are available (see A. J. Harris and Sipay 1975, pp. 393–404).

Chapter Eight

THE LAST SWIM

Dan opened his eyes. He saw that the sun was going down. Soon they could look for their boat again. He sat up and looked around.

"Something is wrong," he thought. Then he knew what it was. Andy was not there!

"Carlos! Bill!" called Dan. "Andy is gone!"

The men jumped to their feet.

"What did you say?" asked Carlos.

"Andy is gone," said Dan. "But here is his life jacket."

"Where could he be?" asked Bill.

"There is only one answer," said Dan. "Andy must have gone looking for Salty and the *Sea Watch*."

"But why would he go on his own?" asked Carlos.

"Andy knows this island," said Dan. "He must—"

Just then a man crashed through the trees.

"It's Andy!" said the men.

FIGURE 11.2. Page from a book with high interest and low vocabulary. The readability level of this book is second reader; interest level is third grade and up. Taken from *Castaways*, by Frances B. Berres, James C. Coleman, William S. Briscoe, and Frank M. Hewett, p. 54, The Deep-Sea Adventure Series. Copyright © 1971 by Addison-Wesley Publishing Company, Inc. Reproduced by permission of the publisher. All rights reserved.

Title	Reading-grade Level	Interest-grade Level	Publisher
Animal Adventure Series	PP–1	1–4	Benefic
Butternut Bill Series (Ozark Mountain family in 1850s)	PP–1	1–6	Benefic
Button Family Adventures (poor family)	PP–3	1–3	Benefic
Cowboy Sam Series	PP–3	1–6	Benefic
Sailor Jack Series	PP–3	1–6	Benefic
Moonbeam Series (space-aged monkey)	PP–3	1–6	Benefic
Dan Frontier Series (pioneers)	PP–4	1–7	Benefic
Cowboys of Many Races	PP–5	1–6	Benefic
First Reading Books (animals and birds)	1–2	1–4	Garrard
Beginner Books (humorous stories)	1–2	1–4	Random
Basic Vocabulary Books (folktales, animals)	1–2	1–4	Garrard
Jim Forest Readers	1–3	1–7	Field
Space-Age Books	1–3	3–6	Benefic
What Is It Series (science)	1–4	1–8	Benefic
About Books (science and social studies)	1–4	2–8	Childrens
Breakthrough (modern stories, biographies)	1–6	7–12	Allyn
Pacemaker True Adventures	2	5–12	Fearon
Pacemaker Story Books (mystery and adventure)	2	7–12	Fearon
True Books (social studies and science)	2–3	1–6	Childrens
Discovery Books (biographies)	2–3	2–5	Garrard
Boxcar Children Mysteries	2–3	3–8	Whitman

Gateway Books (all content areas)	2–3	3–8	Random
Step-Up Books (action stories)	2–3	3–9	Random
Interesting Reading Series	2–3	7–12	Follett
The Wildlife Adventure Series	2–4	3–9	Field
Sports Mysteries Series	2–4	4–9	Benefic
Racing Wheels Series	2–4	4–9	Benefic
The Morgan Bay Mysteries	2–4	4–11	Field
Checkered Flag Series (racing)	2–4	6–12	Field
The Deep Sea Adventure Series	2–5	3–11	Field
World of Adventure Series	2–6	4–9	Benefic
American Adventure Series	2–6	4–9	Harper
Space Science Fiction Series	2–6	4–9	Benefic
Mystery Adventure Series	2–6	4–9	Benefic
First Books	2–9	3–12	Watts
Junior Science Books	3	2–5	Garrard
Holidays	3	2–5	Garrard
Folklore of the World Books	3	2–8	Garrard
Pacemaker Folktale Series	3	3–6	Fearon
Frontiers of America Series	3	3–8	Childrens
American Folktales	3–4	2–6	Garrard
Story of Series (biographies)	3–4	3–9	Hale
Warner Mystery Stories	3–6	4–6	Scott F.
Hi-Lo Reading Series	3–8	5–12	Pyramid
Regional America Stories	4	3–6	Garrard
Sports	4	3–6	Garrard
Explorers	4	3–6	Garrard
Pleasure Reading Books	4	3–6	Garrard
Americans All Series	4	3–9	Field
Exploring and Understanding Series (science)	4	4–9	Benefic
Signal Books (sports, careers, etc.)	4	5–9	Doubleday
Everyreader Series (simplified classics)	4	7–12	Webster

Childhood of Famous Americans Series	4–5	4–9	Bobbs
How and Why Series (science, social studies)	4–5	4–9	Hale
Getting to Know Series (countries)	4–5	4–9	Hale
The Reading-Motivated Series (history)	4–5	4–10	Field
Rally Series (racing)	4–5	7–10	Childrens
We Were There Books (history)	4–6	5–9	Hale
Allabout Books	4–6	5–11	Random
Turner-Livingston Reading Series (basic social behavior)	4–6	7–9	Follett
Vocational Reading Series	4–6	9–12	Follett
Rivers	5	4–7	Garrard
Creative People in the Arts and Sciences	5	4–7	Garrard
Myths, Tales, and Legends	5	4–7	Garrard
World Landmark Books (history)	5–6	5–11	Random
Landmark Books (history)	5–7	5–11	Random
Turner-Livingston Communications Series	5–6	8–10	Follett
Turner Career Guidance Series	5–6	11–12	Follett
Fun to Read Classics	5–8	5–12	Childrens

Initial teaching and learning of a skill is best done with straightforward techniques, but word recognition and decoding practice can be made fun through the use of games or contests. The materials listed in unit 7, pp. 290–93, can be used in remedial teaching as well as with normal readers. An annotated list of books useful for skill building has been provided by Adams (1976). Additional materials are listed and annotated by Spache (1974), White (1972), Leibert (1971), and Cramer and Dorsey (1970). Even the lyrics of contemporary music can provide a source of reading material for older children reading from the preprimer to fourth-reader levels (Klink 1976).

Allowing older children to be active participants both in studying their learning needs and in selecting reading activities often works very well. The child can be told that he is a reading detective, helping to discover clues by identifying his strengths and weaknesses and listing specific skills which need to be improved. Sometimes the child knows quite well what his trouble is; all you have to do is ask him. Reading activities for these problem areas are selected, and as each problem is cleared up, it is crossed off the list. When the first problems have been solved, new higher level ones are discovered.

Wilhoyte (1977) has suggested the use of a learning contract, a written agreement between the student and teacher, which describes a specific objective, the activities that will help meet that objective, and an estimated length of time for its completion. After the student's needs have been determined, they are discussed and the teacher and pupil negotiate specific objectives (this involves the child in decision making). The necessary materials are placed in a work folder, with the teacher providing time and support as needed. At the end of the contract period, or before that if the child feels he is ready, his mastery is evaluated. If the criteria for mastery are met, he gets an "award letter" which can be shared with parents and peers.

Enlisting Parental Cooperation   It is highly desirable to get parents to work cooperatively with the teacher, not only in eliminating or lessening possible handicaps, but also in carrying forward a positive remedial program. There are two aspects of this: the positive one of getting them to do things that are helpful, and the negative one of trying to get them to stop doing things that are harmful.

Most parents are eager to have a part in helping their children. If they are not given something to do, they are likely to follow their own ideas, and these often do more harm than good. They are particularly apt to keep home teaching a secret from a teacher when they think she would disapprove of the practice. A training program designed to help parents become "teaching partners" such as that described by Breiling (1976) can be productive.

Parents can be helpful in many ways, and these should be emphasized. They include (1) attending to health problems, getting any special examinations that may be recommended, and following through with treatment when indicated; (2) showing more appreciation of the child's talents and positive qualities, helping to build his morale; (3) helping to build his experiential background by taking him on trips and visits to museums and other places of interest, by including him in conversations about interesting topics, and by encouraging him to watch some educational television programs; (4) taking him regularly to the public library, and enlisting the librarian's help in finding books that he can read and enjoy; and (5) showing real pleasure in any indications that his reading is really improving.

Whether it is wise to encourage parents to help in teaching reading is a debatable issue. Some remedial teachers spend considerable time with parents, showing them exactly what to do and how to do it. Others try to keep parents out of the teaching role as much as possible. Still others provide short review exercises that parents can use with the child at home, on which a successful performance is almost guaranteed by the child's previously demonstrated level of mastery. If the parents are involved at all in teaching, it is important for the teacher to guide and supervise what they do. Whether or not parents can help with reading depends on their ability and patience, and on the emotional relationship between parents and child. Some parents are so emotionally involved, they want the child to succeed so badly, that they react excessively to the slightest sign of failure.

On the negative side are a number of common practices that parents should be requested, as tactfully as possible, to stop. Before doing this, it is wise to indicate that you realize they have been trying to help the child, and that these practices have been done with the best of intentions, but that it is time to try something else because these practices have just not worked with their child. The common list of "don'ts" includes: calling the child dumb or stupid; comparing a child unfavorably with a sibling, or holding up some other child as a model; punishing the child for poor school grades (beatings and deprivation of play are not uncommon); and going over the child's reading in long emotional sessions that usually end with the parent angry and the child in tears.

EDUCATIONALLY DISADVANTAGED CHILDREN

Disadvantaged children are not all the same. Their success in school varies greatly, and depends not only on their characteristics, but also on the school's attitude toward them and what is done to assist them in learning.

Educationally disadvantaged children do not represent any single race, culture, or nationality. They speak various dialects of American English, or their first language may be Spanish, Oriental, or that of one of the various American Indian peoples. Whipple (1966) aptly referred to them as "children without." They often lack adequate food, clothing, shelter, medical and dental care, language skills, conceptual development, motivation to learn, and a positive self-image. Children living in crowded conditions and surrounded by activities that bombard them with stimuli learn to shut them out in order to have peace of mind. However, this habit becomes a hindrance in school because they then shut out the teacher's instructional stimuli (Jenkins 1976). These children usually come from cultures that differ greatly from the culture of the school they attend.

The disadvantaged primarily live in urban centers or rural areas. They may be migrant children whom Jassoy (1976) has called the most disadvantaged of all. Their nomadic existence forces migrant children to adjust to constant changes in environment and a disorganized, rootless existence. Changing schools four to five times a year makes it difficult to provide them with a sequential reading program, and often by the time the teacher obtains information about their reading skills and abilities, they have moved on. Migrant children often do not have enough opportunities to apply their new knowledge, so that it is not retained.

There is ample evidence that the disadvantaged tend to have low school achievement. Studies have indicated that economically and educationally disadvantaged children typically perform more poorly in reading than children of other socioeconomic classes right from the beginning of their academic careers, and that the gap widens as they progress through the grades (Barton 1963, Dyer 1968).

The one factor that the disadvantaged have in common is economic poverty (K. Johnson 1977). But it is not likely that the school can or will eradicate poverty, and there is no guarantee that more money alone will positively influence learning. Two factors frequently cited as possible causes of the problems disadvantaged children have in learning to read are their dialect or language, and denigration of their culture.

Materials that are conceptually attuned to the cultures of disadvantaged children have been developed in the hope that they would be more interesting and understandable for the children, as well as reflect their cultural heritage. Most commercial reading program materials use multiracial and multicultural characters. Although there is little research evidence that their use or the structure of the accompanying instructional program facilitates reading ability, there may be some accrued benefits (e.g., easier identification with the story characters, awareness of other cultures and their contributions to society) that cannot be readily measured by tests.

Dialect Speakers

No language is spoken in exactly the same way by all its speakers, but certain linguistic features are more socially stigmatized than others. Although the term standard English is commonly used, there is no single standard of pronunciation in standard English (McDavid 1968). But, with certain minor exceptions, a standard syntax does exist; educated speakers throughout the United States follow the same syntactic rules (Cazden 1972). Even within a given dialect, not all speakers pronounce words in the same way. We each have our own *ideolect*—a distinct way in which an individual pronounces words.

Usually variations of a language are understood by other speakers of that language. Dialect speakers often switch dialects, depending upon the particular situation. Thus, many black English speakers can be classified as bidialectal in that they use black English when communicating with their peers and families, and a version closer to standard English in school. Even when a speaker is truly bidialectal, however, there are marked individual differences. Some speakers are very competent in both dialects, others are more competent in either black English or standard English; and yet others are barely competent in either.

Furthermore, there are variations in language competence among speakers of a given dialect. Even when speakers have the same degree of language competence, there are variations in verbal fluency, creativeness, reasoning power, and social perception. It seems very probable that dialect speakers can be helped to reach a higher level of competence, but we do not know how this can be best accomplished, nor do we know how to predict the maximum level a child can achieve after such teaching (Carroll 1973).

Speakers of Black English   There is disagreement among linguists and sociolinguists as to what term should be used to describe the dialect of English spoken by many blacks and some nonblacks. Some prefer the term "black dialect," others "nonstandard English" or "Negro nonstandard English"; many employ the term "black English." We prefer the latter because it reflects the fact that it is a variation of English, and as such constitutes a legitimate dialect. It should be understood that not all blacks speak black English (BE); the speech of many blacks is indistinguishable from that of other speakers of the same region and social class. Nor do all speakers of black English use exactly the same dialect.

Black English is not a "deficient" dialect; it is a "different" dialect because it has a fully formed linguistic system, with its own consistent pronunciation and grammatical rules (Fasold and Wolfram 1970). Although BE shares many features with standard English (SE), it can be distinguished from SE, as will be pointed out below.

Speakers of BE may give the incorrect impression that they are intellectually inferior, or that their language development is retarded. However, their oral responses reflect the phonological and syntactic rules of their dialect. Their culture does not always emphasize or reward verbal ability, therefore, they may possess undeveloped expressive language facility (Anastasiow 1971).

Since it is extremely difficult to separate a dialect from the culture in which it is spoken, the teacher must be careful not to disparage a child's language, and thus denigrate his or her way of life. Teachers should be familiar with the child's language or dialect not only in order to facilitate communication and impart a feeling of security in the child, but also in order to be able to distinguish dialectal rendition from word recognition errors.

The following contrastive analysis between features of BE and SE is based on the writings of Shuy (1973), Fryburg (1974), Ruddell (1974), Kleederman (1975), K. Johnson (1975) and R. J. Smith and Johnson (1976). For a more complete, relatively nontechnical description of black English refer to Fasold and Wolfram (1970). BE has phonological and syntactical features that differ from SE. Some of these BE features often are found in the speech of many non-blacks who reside in the same area. Also, it should be noted that many BE speakers do not use all these features.

Phonological Feature	SE	BE
1. Deletion of /r/ in medial and final positions (often results in homonymns); however /r/ retained before front vowels	hard more tree	hod mow tree

2. Deletion of /l/ in certain word endings	tool help	too hep
3. Devoicing of initial /th/ = /d/	then	den
4. Simplification of some initial consonant clusters		
a. /thr/ = /tr/	thread	tread
b. /shr/ = /sr/ or /sw/	shrimp	srimp; swimp
c. /pr/ = /p/ in un-stressed syllables	protect	p'otect
5. Devoicing or deletion of some final consonants [3]		
a. Final voiceless /th/ = f	lath	laugh
b. Final voiced /th/ = v	lathe	lave
c. Deletion of /t/	suit	sue
d. Deletion of /d/ or weakening to /t/	rode	roe; rote
e. Deletion of /g/	log	law
f. Deletion of /k/	back	baa
6. Simplification or modification of some final consonant clusters		
a. /sk/ = /s/	desk	dess
b. /sks/ = /ss/ [4]	masks	masses
c. /st/ = /s/	past	pass
d. /sp/ = /s/	gasp	gas
e. /nt/ = /n/	meant	men
f. /ng/ = /n/	sing	sen
g. /skt/ = /kst/	asked	axed

3. In SE, especially in casual speech, the final consonant sound of a word preceding a word beginning with a vowel sound, will usually be articulated. Thus "west end," but "wes' side." In BE, the devoicing or deletions are fairly consistent.
4. In SE, words ending in /s/ plus /p/, /t/, or /k/ take the s plural form. But because /p/, /t/, and /k/ are so often deleted in BE in final consonant clusters, the plural is formed as though the words ended in /s/. Thus, "ghosses" instead of "ghosts."

h. /dn't/ = /tn/   didn't   dit'n
i. /nd/ = /n/   mind   mine

7. Vowel modifications
  a. /ī/ = /ä/   find   fän
  b. /oi/ before /l/ = /ô/ toil   taw
  c. /i/ before nasals =
      /e/   pin   pen
  d. /ē/ before /l/ or /r/
      = /ā/   seal   say
  e. /o͝o/ = /ô/   poor   paw
  f. /ou/ = /o/   found   fon

8. First syllable stress on
   words that usually have
   second syllable stress   ho tel'   ho' təl

Grammatical Features

1. Nouns
   a. Deletion of plural
       markers when
       pluralization sig-
       naled by preceding
       word   ten cents   ten cen'
   b. Plural overgenerali-
       zation   men   mens

2. Lack of noun-verb   Pam runs fast   Pam run fas'
   agreement   They run fast   Day runs fas'
                            She has a pan   She have a pan

3. Pronouns
   a. Use of pronominal
       apposition   Peg walks slowly.   Peg *she* walk slow.
   b. Use of objective in
       place of nominative
       pronouns   *We* have to go.   *Us* got to go.
   c. Substitution of *them*
       for *these*   See these cans.   See *dem* cans.

d. Use of *here* with *this*	The can _____.	Dis here can _____.
e. Substitution of *which* for *who*	Mark, who is _____.	Mark, which is _____.
f. Use of existential *it*	There are a lot of people out front.	It's a lot of people ot fron.

4. Verbs
   a. Copula (linking verb) *to be*

1) Deletion of *be* when the action occuring is present and momentary.	He is talking.	He talkin.
2) Use of *be* to indicate the present habitual	He usually is working.	He be workin.
3) Use of *been* to indicate the past habitual	He always has worked.	He *ben* work.
4) Standard use in tag question	Is he here?	He ain't here, *is* he?
5) Different conjunction of irregular verbs		
a) present	I do — I take	I do — I take
b) past	I did — I took	I done — I taken
c) perfect	I have done — I have taken	I have did — I have take

   b. Past tense

1) Deletion of marker when *ed* = /t/ or /d/ but not /ed/	Yesterday, Ted walked home.	Yesterday, Ted walk home.
2) Changes in verb form	I drank the soda.	I drunk d' pop.
3) Addition of *ed* to present tense form of irregular verbs	I rode my bike.	I rided my bäk.

c. Future tense

    1) Deletion of *will*   I will go home.   I'ma go home.

    2) Deletion of *'ll*   She'll be there.   She be dere.

d. Double negative   I don't have any.   I don't got none.

e. Perfective aspect

    1) Use of *done* to indicate the action is completed   I went.   I done go.

    2) Use of *been* to indicate the distant past   He went.   He done been gone.

f. Deletion of *have* in perfect present tense   He has taken it.   He taken it.

g. Deletion of *would*   If he didn't have to go, he would be home.   If he didn't have to go, he be home.

h. Use of *ain't*

    1) To signal past tense when past tense form not used   I didn't see it.   I ain't see it.

    2) In place of *doesn't, don't hasn't, isn't*   He isn't here.   He ain't here.

5. Possessives

    a. Deletion of markers   Ann's cat is lost.   Ann cat los'.

    b. Substitution of *they* for *their* and *you* for *your*   Your pin is gone.   You pen gone.

    c. Use of different markers   It is mine.   It is mines.

6. Indefinite article

    a. Simplification of *an*   I want an egg.   I wan' a egg.

    b. Deletion of *a* with nouns that have plural forms.   Hand me a mop.   Han' me mop.

c.	Addition of *a* with nouns without plural forms	Give me cash.	Give me a cash.
7.	Adjectives and adverbs		
	a. Use of *more* with comparative forms using—*er*	He is bigger.	He be more bigga.
	b. Omission of—*ly*	She ran quickly.	She ran quick.
8.	Substitution of prepositions	He is at the store.	He be to da stow.
9.	"If" construction	I asked if he did it.	I aks did he do it.
10.	Sentence patterns		
	a. Inversion of question form	Can he see it?	He see it?
	b. Omission of *do* forms	How did he see me?	How he see me?
	c. Use of *at* in "where" questions	Where are you?	Where you at?

BE and SE also have lexical differences. Different words are used to indicate the same meaning (e.g., *greens* for *salad, tote* for *carry, kin* for *family*). Similar differences occur between regional variations of SE (*pop* for *soda, bag* for *sack*).

Those interested in learning more about BE may refer to Brasch and Brasch (1974), Kocher (1974), Labov (1972), Fasold and Shuy (1970), and Wolfram and Clarke (1971). Some of the BE features are also found in the speech of southern rural whites and may represent regional dialect features common to both races.

Does Use of Black English Adversely Influence Reading Ability?   There is sufficient evidence that, on the average, speakers of BE and other "non-standard" dialects score below SE speakers on reading tests. However, whether this factor is a direct cause of poor reading ability is a complex debatable issue. Speaking BE may simply be a small part of a syndrome associated with lower reading performance. BE is a social-class dialect whose speakers often are classified as "disadvantaged" economically, educationally, and otherwise. All the factors associated with poverty (inadequate neo- and perinatal care, inadequate nutrition, etc.) are inextricably interwoven, thus making it impossible to isolate specific factors.

The "different language" explanation has led to the belief that the phonological and grammatical differences between BE and SE are significant enough to interfere with reading acquisition and ability. Research, however, has shown that there is rarely a direct causal relationship between speaking BE and reading achievement. Many deviations from SE made during oral reading by dialect speakers can be traced to their variety of speech; for the most part, their responses conform to the grammatical and semantic constraints of the preceding structure of the sentence (Weber 1973, Hunt 1974–75). As for word recognition, children who speak BE did not recognize significantly more homophones whose spelling was closer to their dialectal pronunciations than those spelled in SE (Simons 1974b). Although they may delete sounds in final consonants in their speech, they apparently understand the meanings of the printed forms of many of these words (Karlsen and Blocker 1974). It may be the same for other phonological features of BE. For example, BE speakers usually comprehend the effect of the printed past tense marker -ed, even though they delete its sound in pronunciation. It may be wise to point out such visual cues to these children, and to check their understanding of such morphological cues. Other researchers (Rystrom 1973, Walker 1975) have found that speaking a nonstandard dialect does not adversely influence word recognition. In fact, Rystrom (1970) found that training BE speaking children to speak SE not only did not significantly increase reading achievement, but also had a negative effect on learning to decode.

It is not always clear during oral reading whether a deviation from the printed stimuli is a dialect translation or a reading error. K. Johnson (1975) offered some suggestions for determining whether a response is a "dialect shift" or a reading error. In order to be able to use these suggestions, the teacher must be familiar with BE and its differences from SE. A phonological change such as replacing /t/ with /z/ (walked-walks) would be an error because it is not a direct translation. A dialect shift would delete the /t/ (walked-walk) because that is consistent with the rules of BE. A double negative such as "He is not no smart," or an omission of a plural marker ("two boy") are other examples of dialect shifts.

The main question regarding use of dialect is whether it adversely influences reading comprehension. Research does not show that speaking BE presents any unique problem in comprehending written SE (Hall and

Turner 1974, Simons and Johnson 1974, Liu 1975–76). BE speakers are usually no more successful in understanding material written in their dialect than in SE (Nolen 1972, I. Ramsey 1972). The effects of being a dialect speaker upon listening comprehension of SE also seems limited (Gantt, Wilson, and Dayton 1974–75). In fact, in one study (Cagney 1977), first-grade BE speakers understood orally presented stories better in SE than in BE. Thus, it seems that the nonstandard speaker is usually able to derive the deep meaning of an SE communication despite the surface-structure differences which characterize their dialect.

Learning to comprehend SE is important for learning to read; learning to speak SE does not seem to be, although it has social and economic values later in life. But, as Venezky and Chapman (1973) pointed out, although there is little direct evidence of dialect effect on learning to read, there is the potential for indirect interference. Problems may arise if the teacher considers the child's language to be inferior (and thereby the child and his culture) and often corrects his speech in a derogatory manner.

Teaching Reading and SE to BE Speakers   The various opinions concerning the teaching of beginning reading have been covered in unit 3. Research evidence does not show that any of these approaches is more effective than the others; there is still a need for well-designed research in this area. Theoretically, use of a language-experience approach in the initial stages of reading instruction can help to avoid problems that might be created by using commercially prepared materials which contain mismatches between the language presented and that of the children. But inner-city black first-grade children made more progress in reading comprehension using basal readers than with a language-experience approach (A. J. Harris and Serwer 1966).

At any level, teachers should accept dialect renditions as correct in oral reading. This will require teachers to know the phonological, syntactical, and lexical rules of the child's dialect.

Such knowledge also will allow teachers to employ what Seymour (1973b) referred to as the "avoidance technique." For example, in teaching auditory discrimination, the children would not be asked to listen for the difference between "pin" and "pen" which are homonyms in their dialect. Or, when testing, a distractor that is a homonym for the correct response in the child's dialect would not be employed (e.g., *lass* would not be used if *last* were the expected response). Rather, the teacher should provide choices that all contain the element under consideration (e.g., *worked, talked, walked;* rather than *work, works, worked*). Exercises to focus the child's attention on the desired element would be similar to the following:

1. Add *ft* or *lt* or *pt* to finish the word
                 They le_____ the party.
2. Add *d* to one of these words and put it in the sentence: nine name pole
                 They _____ the cat Tab.

Many of the above suggestions can also be used with non-English speakers and bilingual children.

Not only should the child's language be accepted in the classroom and the child not be made to feel ashamed of it, but also children should be made aware that differences exist between BE and SE, and be given the opportunity to learn SE. Dialects do not all have equal prestige. The hard facts of life are that SE carries prestige, and its use facilitates access to certain social groups; proficiency in SE is educationally, socially, and economically helpful. If the classroom atmosphere is accepting of language variations, and instruction in SE is handled carefully and tactfully, it need not alienate the child.

Primary-grade BE speakers can be taught SE through a combined use of children's literature and pattern practice as described in the lesson plans set forth by Cullinan, Jaggar, and Strickland (1974). In the middle grades, the teacher can start building an awareness of the grammatical differences between BE and SE (Mantell 1974). Starting with single sentences which differ in only one feature and gradually leading to use of sentences encompassing more than one feature, the following types of exercises can be used:

1. *Discover the difference.* After the children listen to recorded samples of BE and SE, they are given mimeographed copies of the script and asked to identify the specific differences between the two ways in which the idea was expressed. Responses are discussed.
2. *Most people say.* The children collect samples of speech which show how they, their friends, family, teachers, and TV announcers express such ideas as negation and plurality. These samples are then categorized as a chart under the appropriate heading (*I say, My friends say, Most people say,* etc). In a game involving about five students, a

card containing one of those samples may be chosen and the child must describe a situation appropriate for its use.

Junior high school students may benefit from use of a contrastive analysis program similar to the one described by Crowell and Kolba (1974). The program involves twenty taped lessons with accompanying activity books and Language Master Cards. At the beginning of each lesson, the student is instructed about the specific contrast for which he is to listen in the dialogue between a SE speaker and a BE speaker. Making the child aware of the areas of possible interference between two dialects or language through contrasts is also recommended for bilinguals by Oñativea and Donoso (1977), who described a visual analogy program for providing the learner with clear visual cues to syntactic patterns. Other suggestions for guiding BE speakers may be found in T. Wilson (1976).

Bilingual or Monolingual Children

Children whose first language is not English have special problems in school. When they begin formal reading instruction, the written form of English causes problems because it differs greatly from their native language. In learning to decode, they may encounter difficulty because the phonemes in their language, particularly vowel and final consonant sounds, differ from those of standard American English. Teachers often spend a great deal of time and energy trying to get these children to "pronounce the sounds properly." The purpose of phonics is to assist readers in decoding words that are not recognized at sight. If they can recognize or decode the words, they probably will pronounce them using their own pronunciation; speakers of SE do the same.

The key question is whether or not the reader understands what the words mean. This is not to say that children should not be helped in acquiring standard English, but rather that perhaps this should not be attempted through teaching phonics in the reading program. The same is true for dialect speakers.

Spanish-speaking Children   Most Spanish-speaking children in the United States belong to families that have come from Mexico, Puerto Rico, or Cuba, and speak Andalusian Spanish, not the Castilian dialect. Certain

English vowel sounds (e.g., /a/,/u/) are difficult for Spanish speakers to produce, and certain consonant sounds (e.g., /v/,/th/,/z/,/zh/, and /j/) do not occur in Spanish, so the Spanish speaker often replaces them with sounds he perceives as similar in his language. English relies on voiced and voiceless sounds (*bit* vs. *pit*) to establishing meaning contrast; Spanish does not. Blends of /s/ plus /t, p, k, f, m, n, l/ do not occur in Spanish; nor does any Spanish word begin with /s/ plus a consonant sound. In Spanish, a vowel precedes /s/, and the following consonant begins the second syllable. Thus, *star* is often pronounced as "es tar" (Ching 1976).

The following contrastive analysis of English and Spanish was compiled from Frey (1970), Ruddell (1974), Pacheco (1975), and R. J. Smith and Johnson (1976).

Phonological features	English word(s)	Spanish speaker may say something that sounds like
1. Vowel modifications		
a. /i/ = /ē/	sit; it is	seat; ēt ēz
b. /a/ = /e/ or /o/	mat, sat	met, sot
c. /u/ = /e/ or /o/	but, hut	bet, hot
d. /ā/ = /e/	late	let
e. /o͝o/ = /o͞o/	full	fool
2. Consonant modifications		
a. /b/ = /p/	ban	pen
b. /b/ = /v/ (between vowels)	babies	bevies
c. /g/ = /k/	gold	cold
d. /j/ = /ch/ or /y/	jar, jello	char, yellow
e. /sh/ = /ch/	sheep	cheap
f. final /m/ = /n/	comb	cone
g. voiceless /th/ = /s,t,f/	thigh	sigh
h. voiced /th/ = /d,z,v/	them, this	dem, zis
i. /w/ = /gw/	way	gway
j. /z/ = /s/	zip	seep
k. /zh/ = /ch/	closure	cloture
l. Deletion of final consonant sound in words ending in /r/ plus /d,t,l,p/ and /s/	card	car

Grammatical Features

1. Nouns
   a. Deletion of plural markers   two cars   two car
   b. Lack of noun-verb   the boy walks   the boy walk
      agreement   the boys walk   the boys walks

2. Pronouns
   a. Deletion in questions   Is he here?   Is here?
   b. Deletion in statements   It is ready.   Is ready.

3. Verbs
   a. Copula (linking verb) *be*
      (1) Substitution of *have*   I am ten years   I have ten year.
          for *am*   old.
   b. Past tense
      (1) Use of present for past   Mel said she   Mel said she ēz let
          form   was late   yesterday.
                                    yesterday.
      (2) Deletion of *-ed* marker Yesterday I   Yesterday I want
                                    wanted help.   help.
   c. Negation
      Substitution of *no* for *not* Jane is not   Chen is no talk.
                                      talking.
                                      Don't talk.   No talk.

4. Indefinite article
   Deletion in certain contexts   He is a teacher. He is teacher.

5. Adjectives
   a. Use of *more* instead of
      comparative form *-er*   It is smaller.   Is more small.
   b. Use of *most* instead of   It is the   Is most small.
      superlative form *-est*   smallest.
   c. Placement after noun   The blue ball is The ball blue is
                                    nice.   nice.

6. Sentence patterns
   Inversion of question form   Is the door   Is open the door?
                                    open?

Certain "mispronunciations" by Spanish speakers are the result of a linguistic problem created by attempting to transfer their native language information to English. Thus, "ēz" for "is" is a linguistic problem because Spanish phonic rules indicate that *i* represents /ē/. Linguistic problems are treated by teaching the child that (1) English letters (especially vowels) represent more sounds than in Spanish and, (2) many Spanish language phonics rules do not apply to English, and transferring these rules to English makes it difficult to pronounce English words.

Pronunciation problems are also created by attempts to approximate an English sound which does not occur in Spanish. Thus, *junk* pronounced as "chunk" would indicate a pronunciation problem because there is no Spanish phonics rule that associates /j/ with /ch/. Pronunciation problems are caused by (1) the Spanish speaker's difficulty adjusting his speech organs (lips, tongue, teeth) because their placement differs in pronouncing Spanish and English; and (2) the speaker has had little practice in pronouncing the sounds foreign to his language.

The teacher may attempt to help the child by providing practice in auditory discrimination between the two sounds, and by modeling the sounds and having the child imitate them. Axelrod (1974) provided specific examples that can be used as guidelines in making the distinction between linguistic errors and pronunciation problems.

Chicano Spanish is a blend of sixteenth-century Spanish, Mexican Spanish, Indian, and American English (Ziros 1976). The English spoken by speakers of this dialect often is affected by its polylinguistic origins. For example, "Yeah, no?" which means "This is true, isn't it?" is taken from the Spanish "Si, no?" When a Chicano speaks Spanish or English, phonemic and morphemic features from one language may intrude on the other. The Chicano is aware of this blending of two languages which he refers to as "anglicismos" (anglicisms).

Two basic approaches to teaching non-English speakers to read have been briefly discussed in unit 3 (p. 115). One approach is to teach the children to read first in their native language, teaching receptive and expressive oral language skills in English as a second language, with the reading of English delayed until some skill in reading the native language has been developed. The other is to introduce oral English from the beginning of school, and to delay reading until a reasonable degree of listening and speaking competence has been established. Both these approaches have their advocates, and present research does not clearly favor either of them (Hatch 1974).

The key, as with BE, may be the degree to which the child has command of the English language. It seems sensible not to attempt to teach children to read *in English* until they have some degree of competence in that language. Children who are monolingual in a language other than English, may learn to pronounce English words by rote, but understand little of what they are asked to read.

Regardless of the difficulties their language may cause in learning to read, non-English speakers and bilinguals have needs that should be considered in their educational programs. Once a child is identified as a non-English-speaker or as having limited English-language skills, he may be enrolled in an English as a Second Language program.

The bilingual or monolingual child's ability to communicate should be assessed in both of his languages or his only language. Of course, this will require that the examiner be knowledgeable in the child's native language. Language competence may be assessed through the use of commercially available tests, structured question and answer interviews, communicative tasks (a two-person game or task that requires the child to use oral language), or through observation in various natural situations. As Geniski and Chambers (1977) demonstrated, no single test or procedure is sufficient. The only reliable way to assess communication competence is by listening to the child in a variety of settings. A quick assessment of a child's ability to handle English phonology may be obtained by asking him or her to repeat, one at a time, the following three sentences (Jolly and Jolly 1974):

1. Victor William *w*alked slowly through the house.
2. *Ch*arles *s*aid, "*Sh*ame on you! Are you too *y*oung to *w*alk fast?"
3. *It is* easy to *j*ump over the *sch*ool.

It is very important that teachers be sensitive to the child's cultural values. Teachers should help these children learn to set attainable goals in which achievement through effort is rewarded. When the culture stresses group performance rather than individual competition, as in many Indian tribes, the school should also place more emphasis on group than on individual achievement.

Children whose culture differs from that of the school should be helped to feel secure and accepted, and should be provided with an educational program that allows them to be successful. Their language or dialect must be accepted, and in learning to speak and to read English they will need help in overcoming problems that may be created by the phonological, grammatical, and lexical differences between their native tongue or dialect and standard English.

The following teaching strategies (Ching 1976) may help the children develop motivation and positive self-concepts:

1. Develop a bond of trust and friendship with the children; using a few words in their language helps them to feel welcome and comfortable (Allen 1977).
2. Provide an atmosphere that encourages the children to talk about themselves and their experiences; allow them to teach some of their native language to the English-speaking children.
3. Develop a unit on their culture, and have a place in class displaying books, pictures, and artifacts relating to their cultural heritage. Such efforts not only demonstrate a positive attitude toward their culture, but it may help them and other children learn more about their culture. Books often portray incorrect stereotypes of minority groups. Their coverage may not be openly hostile, but very often they omit the culture's positive features and contributions. Therefore, books about Latin Americans should be chosen wisely; see Schon (1976).
4. Use photographs of them to motivate oral, writing and reading activities.
5. Have people from the children's culture, who have succeeded in various endeavors, talk to the children (to provide models of achievement).
6. Give them many opportunities to be recognized by their peers, through both sharing and academic accomplishment.
7. Involve the parents and siblings in class activities whenever possible (e.g., to share information regarding their culture or a hobby).

Among the ways suggested by Zintz (1975) and Ching (1976) for developing English syntactic ability are:

1. Use of an audio-lingual approach in which the teacher produces a sentence structure model and repeats it several times. Then, the teacher provides cues to which first the whole class, then small groups, and finally individuals respond. Ample opportunities to use these structure models in a variety of situations should be provided.

2. Various drills
   a. Substitution. *Teacher:* Ray is here. *Response:* He is here.
   b. Replacement. The replacement items are placed on the board. After the teacher presents an oral sentence, she points to one of the words and a child replaces the equivalent in the sentence (*T:* "I ate the *apple*." Teacher points to *orange*. *R:* "I ate the *orange*.")
   c. Cued answer. The teacher asks a question that requires a specific response (*T:* "What did Mike do?" *R:* "Mike went to sleep.")
   d. Transformations. The children change or modify the basic structure of the sentence provided by the teacher into other types of structures.
      (1) "There": A bird is in the cage. = There is a bird in the cage.
      (2) Question: Mary is at home. = Is Mary at home?
      (3) Question, supplying the question word: Jan was here. = *Who* was here?
      (4) Passive: Tom built a cart. = A cart was built by Tom.
      (5) Changing the verb to a noun: Frank swims. = Frank is a swimmer.
      (6) Combining kernel sentences into one sentence
          (a) Coordination of simple sentences: It is cloudy. Soon it will rain. = It is cloudy and soon it will rain.
          (b) Coordination omitting repeated words: Barbara is beautiful. Barbara is intelligent. = Barbara is beautiful and intelligent.
          (c) Subordination of a clause: Fred has read many books about magic. He can tell you how tricks are done. Fred, who has read many books about magic, can tell you how tricks are done.
      (7) Combining parts of sentences using *because, until, when,* etc.: I ate. I was hungry. = I ate because I was hungry.
      (8) Changing tense: I have a book = I had a book.
   e. Pattern. The child uses the same sentence structure as in the teacher's model (*T:* Birds can fly. *R:* Fish can swim.)
   f. Expansion sentences. Starting with a kernel sentence, more information is added gradually:
      Dogs bark.
      Dogs bark loudly.
      The mean dogs bark loudly.
      The mean dogs bark loudly all day.
   g. The children's nonstandard renditions are translated into SE, and

the differences in the statements which carry the same meaning (I no go; I am not going.) are discussed.

Oral/aural instruction should initially stress functional vocabulary such as the names of objects and activities in the room (Yawkey et al. 1974). Among the ways oral English language skills may be developed are (Ching 1976):

1. Conversation. At first the main purpose is to make the child feel comfortable and to encourage the child to participate in conversation. After the child is able to converse naturally and spontaneously, the teacher can gradually guide the improvement of the quality of expression.
2. Discussion. There are many classroom opportunities for discussion to gain information, to solve problems, and to share ideas. The teacher should not criticize the child's speech, but his rendition may be repeated casually in SE. Or the teacher may say, "Another way of saying that is _____."
3. Storytelling
4. Dramatization
5. Oral reports on topics of personal interest
6. Choral speaking is an excellent way to help children learn to be relaxed and comfortable when speaking in front of others.

In developing teaching strategies for Mexican-American children, five key cultural values should be considered (Dixon 1976):

1. The children's identities tend to be closely tied to their families in which older siblings frequently act as parent substitutes.
2. Motivation tends to be more related to group or family achievement than to strong self-emphasis.
3. Achievement is greater in an atmosphere in which the task is carried out cooperatively rather than in a competitive manner.
4. The children perform best when placed in a setting in which they can relate directly to the teacher or other children.
5. The children are apt to have a field-dependent cognitive style.

These values suggest that activities emphasizing skill improvement of all group members may be more successful than activities where only individual improvement is emphasized. In general, it is better to stress cooperation rather than competition. Mexican-American children are likely to profit from experiences in which there is direct contact with the teacher or another child; the use of other children as tutors is natural and desirable.

If possible, the non-English-speaking child should initially be seated next to bilingual peers to provide an avenue for immediate communication so that classroom routines can be readily explained. After a few months, the child should be seated near, or surrounded by, monolingual English speakers to prevent excessive reliance on his bilingual peers, and to require him to converse in English (Cortez 1976). Cortez also suggested that in determining which English words to teach, the teacher should consider whether the words represent concepts appropriate for the child's age level and maturity, and whether they will be useful and relevant in the child's new environment. When preparing instructional tapes, the teacher should speak at a normal speed without any exaggeration or distortion, and the Spanish expression should precede the English equivalent (*Mi nombre es Margarita*. My name is Margaret).

Those who wish to read more about teaching language and reading to Spanish-speaking children may refer to the sources cited in this section and to Rosen and Ortego (1969), Horn (1970), and Hatch (1974). Further information regarding materials and sources for bilingual and bicultural education may be found in L. Johnson (1975a) or obtained from the Center for Applied Linguistics. Cornejo (1974) has developed a criterion-referenced assessment system for bilingual reading.

American Indian Children

According to Narang (1974), there are approximately 150,000 Indian schoolchildren in the United States, many of whom come from economically disadvantaged homes. Verbal interaction between parents and children is very limited, and the short incomplete English sentences spoken by adults are often nonstandard and contain a limited vocabulary. The effects of such an environment on readiness for school learning are obvious.

Approximately half to two-thirds of the Indians who enter school have little or no English language skill (Fox 1976). Adjustments to this handicap are often not made. For example, Ramstad and Potter (1974) found that although Nez Percé kindergarteners were significantly lower than their

English-speaking classmates in the ability to understand and use English, they were receiving the same instructional program.

Tribal cultures often are very strong and quite different from that of the school. Therefore, it is quite important for teachers to understand and accept the children's culture, and to help them gain pride in themselves and their cultural heritage. Building an Indian home living area in the classroom, as described by Hakes (1975), can help the young child bridge the gap between home and school life.

As with other minorities, Indians generally have not received fair treatment in texts and trade books. An examination of Canadian social studies texts by Kirkness (1977) indicated that Indians received the worst treatment by far of any minority group, both by commission and omission. Although Stoodt and Ignizio (1976) reported that not one of the 70 children's books they evaluated presented a flawless representation of the Indian, there is some indication of a changing attitude toward the American Indian in children's fiction (Townsend 1976), with this literature falling mainly into one of three types: (1) stories that retell, in fictional terms, well-known historical events from the Indian point of view; (2) conflict roles built around Indian identity problems; and (3) descriptions primarily concerned with past and present Indian way of life.

When compared with whites, American Indian children score especially low in reading (Fox 1976). Greene and Kersey (1975) found that the Seminoles they studied were initially functioning one and a half standard deviations below the national median. There is little evidence about the possible interference the various Indian languages may have on learning to read English. M. Fry and C. Johnson (1973) found a minimal relationship between oral language production and the reading achievement of two groups of American Indians. But, as the studies with speakers of black English and Spanish have shown, phonological and morphemic feature differences are probably not greatly contributory to the reading problems these children show.

Since there is a wide diversity of Indian languages (there are at least 200 different groups of Indian peoples in the United States) it would be impossible to present an adequate contrastive analysis between the Indian languages and English. Such a contrast for Navaho has been presented by Tinker and McCullough (1975). Illustrations of the kinds of problems Indians and Eskimos may have with reading comprehension have been given by Griese (1971).

Chinese-American Children

The Cantonese dialect is spoken by most Chinese-Americans, who for the most part are bilingual and often are not economically disadvantaged. There are a number of differences between Chinese and English (Ching 1976):

1. English has many more vowel sounds. Chinese speakers have difficulty producing certain vowel sounds (e.g., /ē/, /ā/) so their attempts often result in homophones for a significant number of English words.
2. Some Chinese dialects do not have a number of English consonant sounds: /th/ (voiced and voiceless), /sh/,/n/,/r/,/j/,/zh/,/v/.
3. Many English words end in consonants, but not in Chinese, so *off* may be pronounced as *offu*, an extra vowel being added to the final /f/.
4. Consonant clusters do not occur in Cantonese; so Cantonese speakers have difficulty forming plurals and past tenses using /s, t, d, z/. Also, Chinese does not show plurality in a noun ending and has only one form of the verb (Tinker and McCullough 1975).
5. In Chinese, most grammatical relationships are indicated by word order and auxiliary words (He gave me two books = Yesterday he give I two book).
6. Plurality is indicated in Chinese by numerical designation or auxiliary words (two books = two book).
7. Verb tense in Chinese is indicated by a time word or phrase. An action verb followed by "jaw" indicates past tense (He went = He go jaw).
8. English articles, prepositions, and some conjunctions are reduced or absent in Chinese.
9. In Chinese questions, the noun and verb are not inverted. The order is similar to a statement with *ma* and *la* added at the end (Are you happy? = You are happy *ma*?).
10. When the context is sufficient for meaning, a subject and predicate are not required in Chinese (The dog is small = Dog small).
11. In Chinese, tone or pitch distinguishes word meaning; in English, pitch combines with intonation to convey sentence meaning.

The following contrastive analysis of English and Chinese was taken mainly from Ruddell (1974):

Phonological features	English word	Chinese speaker may say something that sounds like
1. Vowel "modifications"		
a. /ē/ = /i/	feet	fit
b. /ā/ = /e/ or /a/	mate	met, mat
c. /o͞o/ = /o͝o/	fool	full
2. Consonant "modifications"		
a. final /b/ = /p/	cab	cap
b. final /g/ = /k/	rag	rack
3. initial /z/ = /s/	zip	sip
4. initial /v/ = /w/	vest	west
5. final /v/ = /f/	loave	loaf
6. /zh/ = /s/	leisure	lisser
7. voiceless /th/ = /t/ or /s/	thin	tin, sin
8. voiced /th/ = /d/	than	dan
9. /sh/ = /s/	ship	sip
10. final /ch/	church	churchi
11. final /j/	judge	judgi
12. /n/ = /l/	net	let
13. /r/ = /l/	right	light
14. /w/ = /v/	went	vent
Grammatical features		
1. Nouns		
a. Deletion of plural markers	six cats	six cat
b. Lack of noun-verb agreement	She walks.	She walk.
2. Pronouns; no shift in person	I know her.	I know she.
3. Articles deleted	Tom is the captain.	Tom captain.
4. Verbs		
a. Copula *be* deleted	He is here.	He here.
b. *Be* substitution	Yesterday, I was here.	Yesterday, I at here.

	c. Tense		
	(1) Substitution	I am talking.	I right at talk.
5.	Proposition deleted	I live in Kansas.	I lif Kansas.
6.	Conjunction deleted	Bill and I are friends.	Bill I friends.

The suggestions made for teaching English to Spanish-speaking children also apply to working with Chinese-American students who need such instruction. Like other cultures mentioned in this unit, books often neglect or present a stereotype of the Chinese or Chinese-Americans. The understanding of Chinese-American children can be promoted by using materials similar to those annotated by Sue (1976).

SLOW-LEARNING CHILDREN

Slow-learning children make up approximately the bottom 25 percent on measures of general intelligence. Those with IQ scores of 80 to 90 are usually classified as "dull normal" and those with scores in the 70s are labeled as "slow learners." The more seriously mentally retarded often are subdivided into the educable mentally retarded (EMR) having IQs of 50 to 69, and the trainable mentally retarded (TMR) with IQs below 50. Although most seriously retarded children are educated in special classes, there are increasing efforts to "mainstream" slow learners and EMRs; that is, to place them in regular classrooms. The same is true for physically and emotionally handicapped children. There is some evidence that special-class EMRs achieve significantly lower than comparable children in regular classrooms (Lazar 1971).

No child should be considered mentally retarded unless he or she has been tested individually by a qualified psychologist. At times, teachers have misjudged children as being retarded when the real problem was a severe emotional difficulty, a sensory defect such as a severe hearing loss, a speech defect, a receptive or expressive language handicap, or a severe reading disability.

Teachers who have slow learners in their classes must understand the limits of their learning ability so as not to expect the impossible of them. Pressure for achievement far beyond their capacity has made the lives of many slow learners and retarded children miserable. On the other hand, they should not be treated as though it is impossible for them to learn. The goals set for the mentally handicapped should be realistic and attainable.

In any situation, the teacher's attitude toward the child's capabilities and performance influences not only the child's desire to learn but his self-concept as well.

Knowing what can reasonably be expected academically of slow learners can help teachers understand their limitations. In this way, the teacher is relieved of guilt feelings when the child cannot perform "at grade level" and the child is relieved of pressure to catch up with the mythical "average child."

The determining of reading expectancy (the level of reading performance that may reasonably be expected of a particular child) has been discussed in unit 6 (pp. 212–14). There it was pointed out that two alternative procedures are to compare the child's reading grade with his mental grade, or with a combination of mental and chronological measures called a reading expectancy grade. Table 6.2 (p. 213) can be used to find a child's reading expectancy grade if one knows the child's age and IQ. The mental grade is the child's present mental age minus 5.2 years. (The average age for entering first graders is 6.2 years, and the grade score for the first month of the first grade is 1.0; $6.2 - 1.0 = 5.2$). With regular promotion the difference between mental age and mental grade remains 5.2 years through the elementary school. Several other more complex ways to estimate reading expectancy have also been advocated; research has not yet determined which is the most accurate.

For children with below-average intelligence the mental grade provides a somewhat lower expectancy than the reading-expectancy grade; the lower the child's IQ, the bigger the difference. It may be that the reading-expectancy grade is preferable for estimating potential for rote learning tasks such as word recognition and spelling, while the mental grade may be more appropriate for tasks stressing reasoning such as reading comprehension and mathematical reasoning. As shown in table 11.1, it takes those with IQs below 80 quite a long time to reach the general mental maturity level of an average beginning first grader. Readiness for beginning reading is probably better estimated from table 6.2.

Slow learners are unlikely to learn unless attempts are made to teach them. The mentally retarded need programs that are adapted to their limited learning ability and that consider their special needs. They may need prolonged reading readiness experiences, during which specific readiness skills are developed. Some of them do comparatively well in learning to recognize words, while many are slow in building a sight vocabulary and learning phonics.

TABLE 11.1.

Approximate Mental Grades for Children of Below-average Intelligence

IQ	Chronological Age												
	7.2	7.7	8.2	8.7	9.2	9.7	10.2	10.7	11.2	11.7	12.2	12.7	13.2
90	1.3	1.7	2.2	2.6	3.1	3.5	4.0	4.4	4.9	5.3	5.8	6.2	6.7
85	1.0	1.3	1.8	2.2	2.6	3.0	3.5	3.9	4.3	4.7	5.2	5.6	6.0
80	kgn	1.0	1.4	1.8	2.2	2.6	3.0	3.4	3.8	4.2	4.6	5.0	5.4
75	kgn	kgn	1.0	1.3	1.7	2.1	2.5	2.8	3.2	3.6	4.0	4.3	4.7
70	kgn	kgn	kgn	kgn	1.2	1.6	1.9	2.3	2.6	3.0	3.3	3.7	4.0
65	pre [a]	pre	kgn	kgn	kgn	1.1	1.4	1.8	2.1	2.4	2.7	3.1	3.4
60	pre	pre	pre	kgn	kgn	kgn	kgn	1.2	1.5	1.8	2.1	2.4	2.7

[a] Indicates that in terms of general mental maturity and reasoning ability, the child is functioning at a prekindergarten level.

There is no demonstrated best method for teaching the mentally handicapped to read (Cegelka and Cegelka 1970). It is likely that although some may learn better through a whole-word or a phonic approach, extreme reliance on either is eventually likely to curtail the child's reading ability.

Woodcock (1967) reported a three-city study in which several methods of teaching beginning reading (including a basal-reader series, a phonic method, i.t.a., and *Words in Color*) were used with comparable groups of EMR children. There were no significant differences among the results of the methods; all groups made about a half-year of progress, on the average, in two years of instruction. This seems representative of what can be expected when the teaching is good. It should be noted that all the methods compared had been developed originally for normal learners.

Fuller (1974) has reported success using her Ball-Stick-Bird program in teaching subjects with IQs between 33 and 72 to read. Only three basic forms are used to construct all the letters: a circle (ball), line (stick), and angle (bird). The children are first taught to form letters, then letter sounds, with blending introduced after two symbol-sound associations have been learned. Simplicity of learning is said to be achieved by using only capital letters and using consistent symbol-sound associations. Fifteen books accompany the program.

Mentally retarded children have limitations in comprehension. This is most evident when the task requires making an inference, drawing a conclusion, anticipating an outcome, or finding a main idea that is not directly stated. Research studies on the reading comprehension of the mentally handicapped have generally found that these children have more success with directly stated facts than with inferences (Hurley 1975). Their concepts are usually quite specific and narrow, and they have trouble with abstract ideas and generalizations.

The reading interests of slow learners tend to be a little immature, but closer to those of average children of their age than to those of younger children of equal mental maturity. For independent reading, they do best with books of interest to children of their chronological age, in which the language structure is clear and simple and the ideas easy to understand.

In some schools, slow learners are required to spend an extra year in the primary grades; this is usually based more on their slow progress in reading than on their IQs. The retention, which preferably occurs at the end of first grade, provides the opportunity to lessen the gap between their performance and the grade norm. For children with IQs near 90, this gives them the opportunity to function at or near grade level. For many with IQs well below 90, an extra year may reduce the discrepancy but it will not allow them to function near grade level; in the middle and upper grades, they are likely to fall further behind. Repeating more than one year in the elementary school may induce disruptive conduct or personality disturbances that are more undesirable than the academic difficulties created by keeping a child with an age group in which he or she is always below average. Even if we help each child to read as well as potential allows, slow-learning children will remain with us and will require the continuation and improvement of efforts to help them to learn at their own paces.

There are some practical suggestions that are generally applicable in teaching slow learners:

1. Make certain that the material used for reading instruction is not above their instructional levels.
2. Introduce new skills at a pace that allows assimilation.
3. Break down the skill into as small steps as possible. This requires a task analysis to find exactly what a child must be able to do, in sequence, in order to perform the task.
4. Provide extra repetition. Mentally retarded children often accept and enjoy repetition. For example, the same story may be reread for several different purposes, thus providing additional exposures to the printed words. There also should be ample planned, spaced review.

5. Important concepts need to be carefully developed from many experiences and illustrations, and understanding of these concepts needs to be checked (they often resort to memorizing verbal formulations which they do not understand). Whenever possible, concepts should be related to practical concrete examples that fall within the children's experiences.

6. Considerable use of audiovisual aids is helpful in making up for their lack of real experiences.

7. Watch for signs of special talent or interest in such nonverbal areas as art, music, athletics; look for ways to use these interests to develop their self-concepts and create an interest in recreational reading.

8. Slow learners do not have any uniquely different ways of learning; the teaching procedures that work with other children are also effective with them, provided that care is taken regarding their readiness for learning a given skill or concept, and their generally slower pace in learning.

9. In content areas, their limitations in grasping ideas and in being able to read texts make it highly desirable to try to provide less difficult reading material and to keep the curriculum to minimum essentials; often projects can be used to provide simpler tasks for the slow learner. Some materials for teaching content subjects and reading skills to slow learners are available from Follett.

Interest in learning to read can be increased by teaching slow learners common words that are important signals in their environment. Sign words like *stop, go, wait, danger, keep out, poison, entrance, exit, men, women* (many of which appear only in capital letters), if recognized and understood, can sometimes save them from embarrassment or serious danger. C. T. Wilson (1963) provided a comprehensive list of such words and phrases, and McMullen (1975) discussed teaching EMRs to recognize and understand "protection words" and testing their understanding of them. Names of local streets, bus routes, and frequently purchased products can be used for word recognition and decoding practice. Even classified ads may be used for slow learners who are reading at approximately the fifth-reader level (Hirshoren, Hunt, and Davis 1974).

The more that reading can be related to their own lives, the more slow learners are likely to recognize it as worth the effort to learn. For example, McIntyre (1977) has outlined a survival kit on cars that can be used to teach sixteen reading skills to poor readers in general. Exercises for developing reading skills needed for functioning in an adult society (Wilson and Barnes 1974) may be used for the mentally handicapped, although they were designed for seriously disabled readers in general. With older students, reading matter that relates to daily living and occupations is often well received. Among such materials are those published by Follett (*Vocational Reading Series, Turner-Livington Reading Series, Turner Communications Series*) and SRA (*New Rochester Occupational Reading Series*).

GIFTED AND CREATIVE CHILDREN

In a large group of children, about 15 percent have IQs between 110 and 120; another 7 percent between 120 and 130, and an additional 3 percent above 130. Most of these children, who will supply the bulk of the future college population, tend to be one to three years ahead of the average child of their age in achievement, and are usually at least average in physical and social development. From their ranks will come our future leaders— the scholars, scientists, professional persons, educational, religious, political and military leaders, business executives, and creators of the arts and literature.

At one time the sole criterion for "giftedness" was an IQ score; but now the more flexible definition devised by an advisory panel to the United States Office of Education is more frequently used (Labuda 1974b): "gifted and talented pupils are those who by virtue of outstanding abilities are capable of high performance." Witty (1971a) has distinguished between verbally gifted children and creative children, noting that the latter have a much higher incidence of social maladjustment and that their nonconformity may make them disturbing elements in the class. Highly creative students may be less regardful of convention and authority, display more independent thinking and judgment, and be more temperamental (Nelson and Cleland 1971). Witty (1971) suggested the following for teaching reading to creative students: (1) replace the basal program with a balanced program adapted to their needs; (2) encourage them to enjoy and write poetry; (3) provide ample opportunities to enjoy humorous presentations; and (4) work closely with their parents and the school librarian.

Recognizing superior potentiality involves more than just looking at test scores; other kinds of evidence are available. Superior potentiality may be shown in academic areas like science or mathematics or in an unusual gift for writing, art, or music. The child's expressive language skills, particularly vocabulary usage and sentence structure, quickness in grasping new concepts, unusual powers of concentration, a keen sense of humor, exceptional powers of observation, and effective problem-solving ability can be quite revealing (Furr 1971).

Underachievers

Underachieving in very bright children varies greatly in its significance. A 10-year-old fifth grader who has a mental age of 14 and is reading at seventh-reader level (corresponding to a mental age of 12) is not reading up to potential, but the problem is really not serious. But if this same child were reading at a fifth-reader level (average for age ten), the problem *would be* serious. The child may have persistent difficulties in word recognition, may be an unusually slow reader, or just may not be interested in reading. The reading problem may also be related to an emotional disturbance.

When reading ability is above average but considerably below potential, the problem is sometimes one of lack of motivation or lack of teacher guidance in attaining high-level reading proficiency. The literature on gifted children may be somewhat misleading because it tends to stress their achievements but fails to mention the problems they may encounter. Often they are so far advanced above the on-grade materials and program that they find the work too easy and so may become bored, restless, and disruptive, or may withdraw into fantasy to escape (Swiss and Olsen 1976).

When lack of interest or motivation is the real problem, an extra effort to apply the interest-arousing principles described in unit 10 is in order. In addition, it is advisable to help underachievers to set higher goals for themselves. They should know that although their reading ability is "satisfactory," the teacher thinks that they have the ability to raise their reading levels substantially.

When there are no persisting gaps in basic skills, a program to upgrade the reading level of a bright underachiever does not have to be elaborate. An effective program need have only two major components: (1) rate and comprehension exercises with which reading can be sharpened, with a progress chart kept on all scores; and (2) effective motivation to increase the amount and quality of independent reading, including the use of appropriate progress charts. In addition, there should be continuing expression of genuine interest and encouragement by the teacher; this is probably the most important requirement.

When the reading progress of a gifted child is held to a mediocre level by the persistence of interfering handicaps or by incompletely mastered basic reading skills, the principles described in this unit for treating disabled readers also apply.

Fostering Superior Reading

Many bright children can read at levels commensurate with their capacity, or close to it. The school has a very real obligation to help these children to continue their accelerated rate of growth in reading abilities and interests. In the past, concern for the average child and especially with the disabled reader has at times blinded teachers to the needs of their best readers. Often, little attention is paid to their needs. For example, Rubin (1975) found that there were only minimal adjustments made for children who scored two to three grade levels above their grade placement.

Some educational practices tend to prevent superior children from improving in reading as much as they could. One of them is exclusive reliance on whole-class instruction or on a rigid instructional plan in which all reading is done in two or three groups; the rate of progress of the top group may seem very slow to a very bright child. Another is failing to provide a rich and varied diet of reading materials that bright children can consume at a rapid rate; a meager library collection is costly in wasted opportunities for growth. A third is in failing to free the gifted child from much of the review and repetition that slow and average children need. A fourth is failing to excite their curiosity about many things that there is not time for the class to explore, but which the very bright child can look into on his own. A final one is extensive use of the bright child as a helper, class librarian, or tutor to such an extent that the child's own time for reading is seriously curtailed.

Freeing the Gifted from Lockstep Boredom

In some schools, gifted students are accelerated (skip grades) or are placed in special classes. More commonly, they receive enrichment programs while remaining with their age group for most of the school week. If an eight-year-old is already comprehending material at the fifth-reader level, little is gained by requiring the child to spend a year on two third readers and their related workbooks.

Such a child should be given a reading program better adapted to individual needs. It might include (1) a variety of vocabulary and comprehension exercises difficult enough to challenge the child and selected to help develop higher-level reading skills; (2) large blocks of time for individualized reading, including much of the time spent by classmates in group developmental reading lessons; and (3) both individual and group projects that entice the child into extensive research reading. When reading comprehension is being developed or checked, the questions should penetrate, probe, and provoke.

Witty (1974) strongly recommended creative reading for the gifted. Creative reading is a thinking process in which new ideas are originated, evaluated, and applied. Questions that call for divergent thinking should be posed: asking for information not in the story, requesting the reader's personal ideas, requiring inferences to be made, and focusing on what the reader can add.

According to R. Smith (1974b), the key to fostering the habit of reading creatively probably lies in (1) selecting material that has interesting characterization and situations, vivid descriptions, well-chosen words, and other features that allow the reader to empathize, visualize, and think through an idea with the author; and (2) structuring reading-related instructional activities that provide direction for the student but do not focus thinking so sharply that the process of synthesizing information is stifled or the emergence of personal feelings is repressed. He also cited the following conditions as necessary to develop creative reading: (1) the material must be suitable for creative thinking; (2) the students must be given time for the synthesizing process to work; (3) students and teachers must realize that the products resulting from creative reading cannot be graded or evaluated as correct or incorrect; and (4) the assigned questions or tasks must reflect reasonable expectations of the students (don't ask students to write an original opera).

Suggestions for fostering early creative reading have been provided by Turner and Alexander (1975). On the basis of the belief that the teacher should act as a resource for learning rather than as a dispenser of information, Nelson and Cleland (1971) suggested the following ideas for facilitating the education of gifted and creative students:

1. Develop learning experiences around the students' natural curiosity by dealing with problems relevent to their needs and interests.
2. Allow them to engage in organizing and planning activities.

3. Keep the program flexible so as to encourage exploration and innovation.
4. Encourage and reward initiative, inquisitiveness, originality, and a
   questioning attitude.
5. Be as concerned with fostering the learning process as with the end
   product.
6. Provide feedback instead of making judgments (e.g., instead of giving
   a grade on a paper, point out how it could be improved).

Barbe et al. (1971) suggested that many primary-grade gifted children enjoy the challenge of locating the origins and meanings of new words
and preparing word and picture displays. The primary-grade program also
can integrate reading mythology and folklore with oral and written activities and can include a literature club.

Intermediate-grade programs for the gifted tend to emphasize the critical
and creative reading of literature, and adjusting rate to purpose. Children
at this level enjoy holding imaginary telephone conversations with historical persons, writing and telling exaggerated stories and tall tales,
building stories from lists of randomly selected characters, events, and
places, developing lists of similes, metaphors, and picturesque language,
and writing different endings to stories they have read. They can learn to
analyze the motives of fictional characters, to follow the development of a
plot, to interpret the author's mood and purpose, and to interpret various
types of poetry.

Gifted junior high students may be placed in humanities programs that
have understanding of humankind as the central theme. In such programs,
they may explore such topics as communication and its influence on our
culture, or attempt to discover creative solutions to environmental problems.
At this age level, the Junior Great Books Program is frequently employed.

Among the 95 activities listed by Issacs (1974) for tying in the other
language arts and reading for the gifted are (1) keeping a diary of
memorable experiences; (2) compiling a bibliography of interesting books
other members of the class might want to read during the summer, and
(3) converting a short story into a play.

If school policy requires that every child complete the basal-reader program for the grade, this can be done without spending the whole year on
it. If there are one or two gifted children in a class, they can be allowed to
progress through the basal program at their own rates, with the teacher
checking periodically in individual conferences.

If there are enough gifted children to form a group, the group can cover the basal program at a rapid rate. They do not need much preparation for stories; they can read the stories quickly; discussion does not have to be lengthy; and rereading can often be eliminated. Some workbook exercises can be assigned, especially those introducing new skills, but many pages can be skipped. In this way, the basal program can be covered in half the usual time or even less, freeing the remainder for the kinds of reading activities listed above. The basal program can be completed before such activities are initiated. Alternatively, the activities can be interspersed with the basal program; for example, the basal program may be used on Tuesdays and Thursdays, with the other days devoted to other reading activities.

Gifted children should be allowed to use above-grade-level material for instructional purposes, particularly when it involves advanced skills, and if corresponding adjustments are made in their future instruction. If serious objections are raised by the teachers who might normally use these materials in the next grade, other procedures can be employed. One plan allows the child to progress above grade level in a basal or supplementary reading program other than the one normally used for instruction. The main objection to this plan is that it eventually requires the superior reader to "go through" the on-grade text even though he already possesses the skills at that level. Another plan allows the child to pursue an individualized reading program, using self-selected materials that are above the child's age level in difficulty and maturity.

Mentally superior children are our nation's most precious natural resource. They are usually curious and interested in learning, if the school does not blunt this interest by stressing conformity and repetitive drill. The best policy with such children is to make the finest books available and accessible to them, and to assist them in making as much progress as possible.

The teacher is the key. Gifted children benefit from having bright knowledgeable teachers, but the most frequently cited attributes of successful teachers of the gifted are the same as those for any good teacher (Nelson and Cleland 1971). The teacher's attitude toward the gifted or creative child is no less important than for other types of children. If the teacher is threatened by the child's knowledge or questions and acts accordingly, problems are likely to occur. Gifted children (and average children too) need teachers who are not afraid to say, "I don't know the answer; let's find out."

Paul E. Kotler

MODULES FOR COMPETENCY-BASED LEARNING

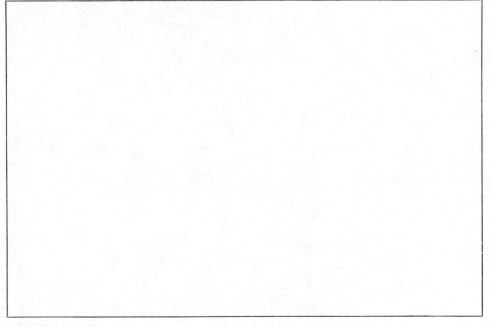

Introduction

Courses on the teaching of reading can be organized in several ways. The eleven units of this textbook can be used as required or optional reading with any plan for course procedure. They can, for example, serve quite well as a text in a course taught by the lecture/discussion/assigned-reading pattern that is widely used in college and university courses.

During the past few years there has been a tremendous growth of interest in what has come to be called competency-based education. The eleven modules that follow provide the framework for a competency-based course on how to teach reading in the elementary school. Depending on the preferences of the instructor and the availability of the many kinds of accessories needed for a competency-based course, the instructor may decide to use the modules much as they are; may use only selected parts of the modules; or may make the use of the modules optional with the student, as a guide to study and to possible applications of ideas gained in the course.

The term "competency-based" refers to forms of course organization that have some essential characteristics in common and other characteristics that are frequently included but are not essential.

The essential characteristics of such an approach are as follows:

1. The particular knowledge, understanding, attitudes, and skills that the student is expected to have attained by the end of the course are made explicit at the beginning of the course.
2. The criteria to be applied in evaluating the student's achievement are also made clear in advance.
3. The course provides varied activities in which the student can apply the knowledge gained.
4. Students are evaluated on what they can do as well as on what they know.

Other characteristics that are often part of the procedure for a competency-based course are as follows:

1. Alternative ways of learning may be provided. Lectures may be attended live or may be listened to at the student's convenience in a library or media center. Group discussions may be arranged, either with or without the presence of the instructor. Demonstrations and observations may be live or recorded on videotape for later viewing. Varied kinds of application exercises may be offered.
2. Alternative ways of demonstrating competence are provided. These are discussed in the Postassessment section (p. 501).
3. Students who show that they have already mastered a module (or part of it) may be excused from further work on it.
4. Students may be allowed considerable flexibility in the time it takes them to complete the modules.
5. When suitable arrangements can be made, some of the student's observations and practice with children may be carried out in a cooperating school.
6. A student who fails to demonstrate satisfactory performance on a module or part of a module is given opportunity for further preparation and reassessment.

The Nature of a Module

A module may be defined as a segment of a total program that (1) specifies the knowledge and skill competencies that are the expected outcomes of the program segment; (2) describes appropriate learning experiences for developing these competencies; and (3) indicates procedures that can be used in determining whether or not a student has satisfactorily mastered the knowledge and skills specified.

A module typically has five main elements:

1. A statement of the objectives, usually framed in terms of the competencies that the student should have developed as a result of work on the module.
2. A plan for assessing the student's knowledge and skills prior to beginning the module. This may be for one of two purposes:

   a. determining if the student has the background needed for successful work in this module

   b. determining if the student has sufficient knowledge of the ideational content and skills, on the basis of prior study and experience, to be credited with completion of the module.

3. A list of the alternative appropriate ways of demonstrating achievement of each objective, often with a specification of the minimum level of performance that is acceptable evidence of mastery.

4. Required and optional kinds of learning experiences are listed. The varied kinds of such experiences are described in the Learning Activities section (p. 500).

5. A plan for continuing assessment during work on the module and final assessment upon completion of the module. Types of assessment are described in the Postassessment section (p. 501).

In a competency-based course it is necessary to schedule an orientation session at the beginning of the course, which students are required to attend. At this session the instructor will explain the nature of the course procedures and will probably distribute some duplicated material. Ordinarily this information will include the following:

1. A calendar of course meetings, both required and optional

2. A procedure for turning in reports and other written material and receiving them back from the instructor

3. Procedures for signing up for such activities as viewing a film or listening to a tape, a small-group meeting, an individual conference with the instructor, a visit to a school for a specific purpose

4. Due dates for completion of modules, with information on the degree of flexibility that can be allowed

5. Procedures for taking tests and for arranging to be observed at a particular activity

Additional orientation sessions may be scheduled at intervals during the course, as needed. These details of course procedure will vary from one school and course to another and therefore are not specified in the modules that follow.

Modules are of varying lengths and take varying times to complete. The modules that follow can usually be completed in from one to three weeks each.

Three of the 11 modules may be treated as optional in some courses, or for some students in a particular course. Module 2, dealing with reading readiness, may not be required by some instructors of students who plan to teach above the primary grades. Module 9, which treats study skills and study habits, may be treated as optional for students who do plan to teach in the primary grades. Module 11, which is concerned with the special instructional needs of different groups of untypical children, may be made optional for all students, or part of it may be required and the rest optional. The remaining modules (1, 3, 4, 5, 6, 7, 8, and 10) are usually required of all students.

Objectives

The heart of each module is a carefully formulated set of objectives, which describe what the student should know and be able to do after studying the module. The ways of making knowledge available to students do not have to be much different from those used in conventionally taught courses. "While modern technologies certainly may be utilized, it is also possible to involve students in text and reference reading, in small and large group discussions, in lectures, and in whatever other instructional media and styles each professor finds to be most productive" (Sartain 1974, p. 51).

How specifically should objectives be worded? Some reading specialists favor the use of highly specific behavioral objectives, especially for the teacher to use in guiding pupil learning. Thus a teacher concerned about knowledge of the alternative sounds represented by *c* can formulate a behavioral objective such as: Given five printed words in which *c* is followed by *a, o,* or *u,* intermingled with five words in which *c* is followed by *e, i,* or *y,* the pupil pronounces at least nine words with the correct sound for *c.* Such a behavioral objective specifies the task, the means of responding, and the minimum acceptable score.

A behavioral objective specifies what the pupil should be able to do after instruction. It does not indicate what the teacher can or should do to bring about this result, although with the goal specified, the teacher should be able to devise a teaching procedure. In doing so, the teacher will probably describe the task as: To teach that *c* represents the sound of /s/ before *e, i,* and *y,* and represents the sound of /k/ before *a, o,* and *u.* Such an objective may be called a *process objective.* The process objective indicates what the teacher wants to do; the behavioral objective, what the pupils should be able to do after learning.

The extreme specificity that characterizes most behavioral objectives is neither necessary nor desirable in the modules that follow, although a strong effort has been made to make clear what the student is expected to learn, to know, and to do. Advanced-level students may be handicapped by too much specificity; they may be tempted to concentrate exclusively on what is covered in the objective as stated and to ignore other helpful information. Furthermore, some of the important objectives—the development of positive attitudes and feelings about children, about books, and about the importance of reading—are very difficult to state in behavioral terms or to evaluate with any degree of accuracy.

A simple system is used in the modules for identifying objectives. Each listed objective is identified by the number representing the number of the module, and the place of the objective in sequence within that module. Thus the third objective in module 1 is numbered 1.3. Objectives that call for knowledge are identified with a K; those which call for application are marked A. Required objectives are marked R; optional objectives are Opt. Thus the objective identified above is fully labeled as 1.3 K R, indicating that it is concerned with knowledge and is required. These ratings are suggested; the instructor may sometimes change them.

Preassessment

Possession of the prerequisite background for taking the course can usually be assumed for all students who enter it. Undergraduates will nearly always have had courses in educational psychology and general elementary methods. Students in a basic graduate course will usually have completed an undergraduate sequence that included some introduction in methods of teaching reading and student teaching; and will have varying amounts of experience. Such students have the prerequisite background for module 1, and module 1 is a prerequisite for the subsequent modules.

One of the features of many competency-based programs is that a student can be given credit for knowledge and skills acquired prior to entering the course. A student who requests advance credit for a module should be prepared to demonstrate accomplishment of the objectives of that module. Achievement of the knowledge objectives can be determined by either a written or an oral test. Achievement of application objectives can usually be judged by the instructor on the basis of an interview. Credit can be given for all or part of the module.

Learning Activities

Reading is an essential source of the knowledge to be learned in this course. The text has been written to provide a common base of useful information, theory, and teaching suggestions. Unless otherwise specified, each unit of the text is required reading for the corresponding module. Other readings that are listed are usually optional. It is advisable to make written notes on readings, especially those that must be consulted in a library. Completing optional reading may be accepted as one form of work for additional credit.

Listening is another avenue for learning. In a competency-based course students may have an option of attending a live lecture or listening to a recorded lecture at their convenience. Discussions among students may be informal, may be scheduled as small-group discussions without the instructor, or may be held with the instructor participating.

Observing may take many forms. Relevant films may be part of large-group meetings. Depending on local resources, videotapes of expert teachers conducting specific types of activities may be available for viewing. The instructor may demonstrate testing or teaching techniques. Live observations may be possible in school classrooms. The instructor will indicate, for each module, what the facilities are for observing.

Developing a collection of teaching ideas and materials is a useful form of application for certain modules. These may be borrowed from published sources, or devised by the student. They may be kept in a notebook, a scrapbook, or a large envelope.

Simulation is a useful way to learn practical techniques. Usually about five students take part as a group. Each prepares a plan for a brief lesson and teaches it with the others acting as pupils. Afterward the group analyzes and evaluates each of the lessons. If the students are not satisfied with their performance, they can reschedule and try again.

The final practical application for a module should, when feasible, include experience with a child or children. Usually a request for a group of children has to be filed well in advance. The instructor will ordinarily require an acceptable written lesson plan before approving such a request. The availability of cooperative schools varies greatly and direct experience with children may not always be feasible.

The study of commercial reading materials is closely related to the study of teaching procedures. These materials include published readiness and reading tests, basal readers and teachers guides, workbooks, kits and collections of specific types of exercises, and trade and reference books.

The construction of teaching materials is frequently carried on by teachers and provides another form of practical application. Among the types of materials that students may construct are informal tests, practice exercises for specific skills, and learning games. These may then be used with one or more children or evaluated by fellow students or the instructor.

Postassessment

Mastery of the knowledge objectives of a module may be determined in a variety of ways. A written objective, short-answer, or essay-type test may be given on completion of the module, or shorter quizzes may be given as specific objectives are completed. Alternatives to the written test include the following: preparation of a written paper or report, oral interview, and instructor observation of participation in a prepared small-group discussion. The forms of knowledge evaluation may vary from module to module, or from objective to objective. Unless otherwise specified, a grade of 80 percent is the minimum evidence of satisfactory mastery on written tests. Other forms of evaluation may use the ratings of superior, satisfactory, and unsatisfactory.

A student in a competency-based course is given more than one chance to be successful. A student who fails to meet the minimum standard for part of a module or the entire module is ordinarily given the opportunity for further preparation and reassessment.

Application objectives may be assessed in ways appropriate to their different natures. Products, such as a lesson plan, a test scored and interpreted, a critique of a workbook, or a one-page exercise devised by the student, may be submitted in writing and returned with comments. Activities such as teaching a lesson to student peers, administering a test to a child, or teaching a lesson to a child or group of children may be evaluated by a qualified observer, either the instructor or someone (e.g., a cooperating classroom teacher or course assistant) empowered to do so. For certain limited activities, self-ratings or ratings by fellow students may be acceptable.

Suggestions for Students

The following method for doing the reading assignments as a way of meeting the objectives is recommended:

1. In the text, read the introduction to the unit and quickly turn the pages, noting the headings and subheadings, to get an overview of what the unit covers.
2. Give the entire unit a careful reading, without taking notes or underlining.
3. Read the objectives of the module. Starting with the first objective, reread the part of the unit that is relevant to it, this time taking written notes or underlining points that you wish to use.
4. Do the same for each of the other required objectives.
5. Skim at least one of the recommended readings for information that is specifically relevant to one or more of the objectives. When such information is found, make written notes on points that disagree with the text or supplement it.
6. Test yourself on the "K" objectives by answering each without consulting notes or references. Then reread the notes or underlined material to check the adequacy of your performance.

For objectives that call for written reports, students may find it helpful to have at least one other student read a draft of the report critically and revise it in the light of the comments before submitting it.

For objectives that call for teaching, a preliminary rehearsal of the lesson with one or more fellow students may help to produce a good performance.

When there is some flexibility in the time schedule for completing modules, there is a strong temptation to let assignments for other courses take priority and thus fall well behind the recommended schedule. This puts pressure on the student during the latter part of the term or semester, when other courses are likely to have extra work, such as term papers. As a result, the quality of the student's work may deteriorate and the course may become a matter of just barely satisfying minimum requirements, instead of a rich opportunity to develop competence for teaching reading. Students are therefore advised not to fall more than one week behind the recommended time schedule.

Module 1

Reading: Who Needs It? What Is It?

PREREQUISITES

The only prerequisites for this module are those required for admission to the course.

OBJECTIVES

1.1   K R   The student can cite evidence of the continuing importance of reading.

1.2   K R   The student shows understanding of the relation of reading to the other three main aspects of language.

   1.21   The student can compare development of oral language to the development of reading and writing.

   1.22   The student can define or explain and illustrate the meanings of the following terms: deep and surface structure; semantics; syntax; phoneme, grapheme, morpheme, morphophoneme; pitch, stress, and juncture; orthography.

1.3   K R   The student can summarize the relationship of each of the following to learning to read: intelligence, linguistic development, physical and physiological factors, sociocultural factors, maturation, learning.

1.4   K R   The student can compare two models of the reading process and indicate similarities and differences in their implications for reading instruction.

1.5   K R   The student can offer an acceptable definition of reading, and defend it.

1.6   K R   The student can briefly describe the three main components of a comprehensive reading program and can state three major objectives for each component.

1.7   K R   The student can state the three basic features of a behavioral objective and can write both a behavioral objective and a process objective for a specific reading skill (not the one used in the text).

1.8   K Opt   The student reads (a) Reed (1965) or Walcutt (1961) and (b) K. Goodman (1976b) or Gibson (1970); and writes a paper comparing and evaluating the two definitions of reading.

1.9   K Opt   Two or more students prepare and present a debate on the nature of reading, each taking the part of an author mentioned as a reference on pages 21–26 of unit 1.

1.10   K Opt   Two or four students prepare and present a debate on the topic *Resolved,* That the adoption of an alphabet with consistent grapheme-phoneme correspondences is both necessary and inevitable.

1.11   A Opt   The student asks five children individually "What is reading?" and "Why is it important?" and presents and discusses their replies in an oral or a written report.

1.12   A Opt   The student interviews three adults representing different occupations to find out what they read and how much they read in a typical week, and reports orally or in writing.

1.13   A Opt   The student keeps a personal diary of all reading done during seven consecutive days and submits a tabular summary listing each kind of reading, the amount of each on each day, and totals for the week.

PREASSESSMENT

A student who wishes to be given advance credit for all or part of module 1 should request an early interview with the instructor and be prepared to demonstrate mastery of the required objectives.

LEARNING ACTIVITIES

Reading

Text, unit 1
Barnett (1969)
Fry (1977, pp. 3–19)
Guszak (1972, pp. 187–94)
L. A. Harris and Smith (1976, pp. 1–45)
Hodges and Rudorf (1972)
Otto et al. (1974, pp. 5–28, 97–120)
Ruddell (1974, pp. 1–107)
Savage (1973)
Zintz (1975, pp. 3–72)

Listening and Discussing

Details to be provided by the instructor.

Observing

No observations are planned for this module.

Other

The activities required for each of the optional objectives are indicated in the statement of the objective.

POSTASSESSMENT

The student passes a written test prepared by the instructor with a grade of at least 80 percent.

or

The student constructs and submits a 20-item test sampling the information relevant to objectives 1.1 through 1.7. Each item should be on a separate 3″ × 5″ or 4″ × 6″ index card, with the student's name on the top line and a model answer on the back. The items may be multiple-choice, fill-in (completion), or single-sentence items, or may include some of each. At least 15 of the items must be acceptable in terms of relevant content, clarity and freedom from ambiguity, and requiring relevant knowledge.

Module 2

Reading Readiness: What, Why, and How

PREREQUISITES

The prerequisite is satisfactory completion of module 1.

OBJECTIVES

2.1   K R   The student can effectively evaluate the statement "A child is either ready for reading or he isn't; there are no two ways about it."

2.2   K R   The student can explain and illustrate the statement "Correlation does not imply causation."

2.3   K R   The student can discuss the bearing of each of the following on readiness for reading:

general intelligence
cognitive clarity
specific concepts
visual perception and discrimination
visual-motor ability
auditory perception and discrimination
retarded speech development
chronological age
sex differences
neurological status
speaking a divergent dialect or foreign language

socioeconomic status

emotional and social development

interest in reading

2.4   K R   The student can evaluate the following statement: "A readiness program for all first graders will ensure that all will learn to read."

2.5   K R   The student compares two standardized reading readiness tests with respect to ease of administration and scoring, clarity of directions, freedom from cultural bias, abilities measured, evidence of reliability and validity, and usefulness to a teacher in forming decisions about children.

2.6   K R   The student analyzes a reading readiness workbook and evaluates its usefulness in kindergarten and first grade.

2.7   A R   The student can write an acceptable lesson plan for a lesson on one component of reading readiness.

2.8   A R   The student can teach a reading readiness lesson acceptably to a small group of fellow students.

2.9   K Opt   Two or four students prepare and present a debate on the topic *Resolved,* That all five-year-olds should be taught to read.

2.10   A Opt   The student obtains a reading readiness test that has been taken by a child, scores it, and writes a report that summarizes and interprets the results.

2.11   A Opt   The student teaches a reading readiness lesson, using a lesson plan that has been approved, to two or more children of appropriate age.

PREASSESSMENT

A student who wishes to be given advance credit for all or part of module 2 should request an interview with the instructor before beginning the module and be prepared to demonstrate mastery of the required objectives.

LEARNING ACTIVITIES

Reading

Text, unit 2

Burns and Roe (1976, pp. 73–125)

Downing and Thackray (1971)

Durkin (1974, pp. 106–89)
Heilman (1972, pp. 25–55; 109–61)
Otto et al. (1974, pp. 73–96)
Raven and Salzer (1971)
R. J. Smith and Johnson (1976, pp. 69–87)
Spache and Spache (1977, pp. 142–225)

Listening and Discussing

Details to be provided by the instructor.

Observing

Details to be provided by the instructor.

Other

For objective 2.5, several specimen sets of each of three or four standardized reading readiness tests should be available in the Reserve Reading Room.

For objective 2.6, several teachers' editions of reading readiness workbooks (pupil book plus teachers guide) should be available in the Reserve Reading Room.

For objective 2.10, several record forms of a reading readiness test, each taken by a child but not visibly scored, should be available in the Reserve Reading Room. In scoring the test, the student should make no marks of any kind on the record form.

POSTASSESSMENT

The student passes a written test prepared by the instructor.

or

The student constructs and submits a 20-item test sampling the information relevant to objectives 2.1 through 2.4. Each item should be on a separate 3″ × 5″ or 4″ × 6″ index card, with the student's name on the top line and a model answer on the back. The items may be multiple-choice, fill-in, or single-sentence items or may include some of each. At least 15 of the items must be acceptable in terms of relevant content, clarity and freedom from ambiguity, and requiring relevant knowledge.

For objectives 2.5, 2.6, and 2.10, written reports are to be submitted to the instructor. In preparing the report, the appropriate form of those found at the end of this module may be used as a guide.

For objectives 2.8, 2.9, and 2.11, the instructor or a delegate may observe and evaluate, or alternatively, peer evaluation may be used. In the latter case, each participant in a group rates each other participant, using the Form for Evaluating Participation in a Group Activity. The student being rated collects the ratings and turns them in, accompanied by a self-rating on the activity. For objective 2.11 it is suggested that students work in pairs, using the same children, each rating the lesson taught by the other.

Guide for Comparing and Evaluating
Standardized Tests

Student's name, and date of submission of report, should be on the top line.

State the exact name, publisher, and date of publication of each test.

List the subtests for each test, and the number of items in each subtest.

To what extent do the tests seem to be measuring the same abilities? Different abilities?

What abilities, other than those indicated by subtest names, seem to be required for successful performance?

Does each test seem to be free of cultural bias? If not, give one or more examples of biased items.

Are directions and sample items clear and easy to follow? What specific concepts seem to be assumed? How does a child mark his or her chosen answer? What help is given for keeping the place?

Are there time limits? If so, do they seem to be reasonable?

What aids are provided for scoring the test? Is scoring quick and easy?

Are the norms based on a satisfactory sample of the relevant child population?

What evidence is there of the test's validity? Which test seems to have higher validity?

Is the reliability of each subtest high enough for interpreting an individual's performance?

How helpful are the sections in the Manual of Directions on interpreting and using the scores on the test?

What is your overall evaluation of each test?

Guide to Evaluation of
Reading Readiness Workbooks

Student's name, and date of submission of report, should be on the top line.

Give title, author, publisher, and date of publication of each workbook being evaluated.

Go through the pages of the pupil book and tabulate the main kinds of skills that the pages are intended to develop. How many pages for each skill? Does each page teach only a single skill? How are the skills sequenced?

What abilities or skills seem to be required in addition to those on which practice is given?

In comparing two workbooks, note similarities and differences in regard to:

1. Physical features, illustrations, etc.
2. Skills covered
3. Types of responses called for
4. Suitability of difficulty level of items
5. Probable interest appeal to school beginners
6. Relevance to beginning reading
7. Degree of self-direction required

Which of these workbooks would you prefer to use? Why?

How can workbooks like these be used to good advantage in a reading readiness program?

Guide for Writing
a Reading Lesson Plan

Student's name, and date of submission of plan, should be on the top line. Give the number of the course objective.

State the lesson topic, the grade level of the pupils, and the intended grade level of the lesson.

State the main objective(s) of the lesson (1) in behavioral terms and (2) as a process objective.

Specify the materials to be used. List textbook, other reading material, visual or audiovisual aids, arts and crafts materials. Give title, author, publisher, and date of publication of published materials. Indicate the specific pages to be used.

Preparation. What prerequisite abilities, knowledge, and skills do the pupils need in order to be able to participate successfully? Can the prerequisites be assumed or must there be some readiness preparation included in the lesson?

Lesson development. Describe the expected step-by-step development of the lesson. Include at least two of the more important questions to ask. How is the lesson to be summarized at its conclusion?

Evaluation. How is pupil learning to be checked? How is your performance in teaching to be assessed?

Note: If the lesson plan is used, the Form for Evaluating the Teaching of a Lesson is to be used by the evaluator.

Form for Evaluating Participation
in a Group Activity

Student being evaluated: _____

Evaluator: _____   Date of activity: _____

Objective of activity:

Nature of activity:

Other participants: _____ fellow students
                    _____ children (give ages or grades)

Describe briefly the student's performance:

    Strong points:

    Weak points:

The student's participation is rated as:
    _____ Superior   _____ Satisfactory   _____ Unsatisfactory

    Signed: _____

Form for Evaluating
the Teaching of a Lesson

Person being observed: _____

Place: _____ Date: _____ Duration: _____

Observer: _____

Lesson objective:

Brief description of the learners:

Brief description of the lesson:

Was the lesson appropriate for these learners?

Were satisfactory motivation and attention obtained and maintained?

Was the lesson as presented relevant to the stated objectives?

Was the teacher well prepared for the lesson?

Was the step-by-step development of the lesson satisfactory?

Was the lesson summarized or "tied together"?

Did the teacher get every pupil to respond?

Were the varying needs of individuals attended to?

Was the objective of the lesson achieved?

What means was used to check achievement?

Rating of the lesson as a whole:

      _____ Superior   _____ Satisfactory   _____ Unsatisfactory

                                                  Signed: _____

Note: The evaluator should be given a copy of the lesson plan in advance. The lesson plan has previously been evaluated as satisfactory. Any serious defects in the plan that become obvious during the lesson should be reported. However, this evaluation is concerned primarily with the way in which the plan is carried out.

Module 3

Learning to Read

PREREQUISITES

Satisfactory completion of module 1 and of module 2 when that module has been required.

OBJECTIVES

3.1 K R The student will be able to describe the important characteristics of each of the following approaches in beginning reading instruction: eclectic basal reader, language-experience, individualized developmental reading, phonic, linguistic, special alphabet, individualized skill-emphasis.

3.2 K R The student will show understanding of both the strong points and the possible limitations of six approaches used in beginning reading instruction.

3.3 K R The student will be able to describe the materials and teaching plan for one first-grade level of a reading series.

3.4 K R The student will show understanding of the special problems of teaching reading to children who speak a minority dialect or a foreign language.

3.5 A R The student, working cooperatively with two other students, will prepare a satisfactory written lesson plan for teaching one story unit of a first-grade reading text.

3.6 A R The student will teach part of a first-grade lesson to two other students, taking the part of first-grade children.

3.7 K Opt The student will compare a preprimer or primer teaching plan for an eclectic basal series with a teaching plan for a code-emphasis text at the same level.

515

3.8   K Opt   The student shows knowledge of the historical development
                of beginning reading approaches in the United States.

3.9   A Opt   The student will teach a reading lesson to a small group of
                first-grade children.

PREASSESSMENT

A student who wishes to be given advance credit for all or part of module
3 should request an interview with the instructor before beginning the
module and be prepared to demonstrate mastery of the required objectives.

LEARNING ACTIVITIES

Reading

Text, Unit 3
Various approaches and viewpoints: *Individualized reading:*
Aukerman (1971)   A. J. Harris and Sipay (1972,
Barrett and Johnson (1973)   pp. 184–205)
Durkin (1974, pp. 11–50)   Hunt (1971)
Kerfoot (1965)   Reid (1970)
Southgate and Roberts (1970)   R. C. Wilson and James (1972)
Vilscek (1968)
                                             Language experience:
                                             Hall (1970)
                                             Humphrey and Redden (1972)
                                             Stauffer (1970)
                                             Veatch (1973)

For objective 3.8 the following references are particularly helpful:
N. B. Smith (1965)
Mathews (1966)

Listening and Discussing

Details to be provided by the instructor.

Observing

Details to be provided by the instructor.

Other

For objectives 3.3, 3.5, 3.6, 3.7, and 3.9, several sets of eclectic and code-emphasis readers should be available for time-limited circulation, including the pupil books, teachers manuals or teachers annotated editions, and pupil and teacher copies of the workbooks.

POSTASSESSMENT

For objectives 3.1, 3.2, and 3.4, the student passes a written test prepared by the instructor.

or

The student constructs and submits a 20-item test sampling the information that is relevant to objectives 3.1, 3.2, and 3.4, using the format described for module 1.

For objective 3.3, the Guide for Evaluation of Reading Textbooks (p. 518) should be followed. For objective 3.7 the same guide may be used, adding a final section comparing the two series.

For objective 3.5 the Guide for Writing a Reading Lesson Plan (p. 512) should be followed. Three students may cooperate in preparing the report.

For objective 3.6 each group of three students may cooperate in teaching the lesson plan prepared for objective 3.5. One student teaches the preparatory part of the lesson, another the guided reading part, and the third teaches one follow-up skill. As each teaches, the others act the parts of first-grade children.

For objective 3.8 the student prepares a written report of about 500 words.

For objective 3.9 the Form for Evaluating the Teaching of a Lesson (p. 514) is to be filled out by the observer, who may be the instructor or someone delegated by the instructor.

Guide for Evaluation of
Reading Textbooks

Student's name and date should be above the title of the report.

Give title, author, publisher, date of publication, and publisher's designated grade level for each item being evaluated.

The pupil book, teachers guide (may be called a manual or teachers annotated edition), and correlated workbook (if available) should be studied together.

In regard to the pupil book, the following should be described:

1. Physical features, type, illustrations
2. Types of story content
3. Variety of characters; fairness in regard to race, ethnic, socioeconomic status, sex
4. Naturalness of language used
5. Interest appeal to children

In regard to the teachers guide, the following should be described:

1. The emphasis in the skills program (most guides contain an index of skills, showing the pages on which each skill is treated)
2. A brief outline of a typical lesson plan
3. The specific procedure(s) used in introducing new words
4. The specific procedure(s) used in teaching decoding skills
5. Amount of attention given to comprehension; kinds of comprehension questions emphasized
6. Convenience features for the teacher

In regard to the correlated workbook the following should be described:

1. Physical features
2. Provisions, if any, for self-direction by the pupils
3. Emphasis in the skills program (the teachers edition of the workbook usually has an index of skills)

4. Relevance of the workbook exercises to the skills taught with the reader
5. Interest appeal of exercise content
6. Suitability of difficulty level and types of responses required
7. Ease of scoring and diagnostic evaluation

If one series is being studied, the concluding portion of the report should present the student's conclusions about strong and weak points and how the student would feel if required to use those materials in teaching.

If two series are being compared, each should be described separately and the differences, strong and weak points of each, and judgment of over-all teachability should be summarized in the final part of the report.

Module 4

An Overview of the Elementary School Reading Program

PREREQUISITES

Satisfactory completion of modules 1 and 3.

OBJECTIVES

4.1   K R   The student will be able to explain how each of the following approaches changes above first grade: basal reader, language-experience, individualized developmental reading, phonic, linguistic, diagnostic/prescriptive.

4.2   K R   The student can explain the uses of oral and silent reading in the elementary grades.

4.3   K R   The student can compare the emphases in primary-grade reading programs with those in middle-grade programs; or in middle-grade and upper-grade reading programs.

4.4   K R   The student will select one grade (2–6) at which he or she may teach and describe the materials and teaching plan provided at that grade level in one reading series.

4.5   A R   The student will prepare a satisfactory lesson plan, using an appropriate reading selection, for teaching a reading lesson to an average group in a particular grade (chosen by the student).

4.6   A R   The student will teach a short lesson to a small group of fellow students, who simulate an appropriate group of pupils; each in turn teaches a lesson with the others as pupils.

4.7 K Opt The student will study two levels of a reading series that are two or more levels apart (2–6), and will describe the similarities and differences in types of selections, teaching plans, and workbooks.

4.8 K Opt The student will prepare a report comparing the McGuffey reader for a particular grade with a reader currently used in that grade.

4.9 A Opt The student, using an approved lesson plan, will teach a reading lesson to a group of children of appropriate age (grades 2–6).

PREASSESSMENT

A student who wishes to be given advance credit for some or all of module 4 should request an interview with the instructor before beginning the module and be prepared to demonstrate mastery of the required objectives.

LEARNING ACTIVITIES

Reading

Text, Unit 4
Burns and Roe (1976, pp. 237–43)
Dallman et al. (1974, pp. 287–323)
Duffy (1974)
Durkin (1974, pp. 83–105)
Heilman (1972, pp. 413–45)
Quandt (1975, pp. 124–44)
R. J. Smith and Barrett (1974)
Tinker and McCullough (1975, pp. 476–538)
One or more series of elementary school readers, with accompanying teachers guides and workbooks

Listening and Discussing

Details to be provided by the instructor.

Observing

Details to be provided by the Instructor.

Other

Representative sets of readers for the appropriate grades should be available for limited-time circulation; these are necessary for objectives 4.4 through 4.9.

POSTASSESSMENT

For objectives 4.1, 4.2, and 4.3, the student passes a test prepared by the instructor.

or

The student constructs a 20-item test sampling the information that is relevant to objectives 4.1, 4.2, and 4.3. Conditions are the same as in preceding modules.

For objective 4.4 the student will submit a written report, following the Guide for Evaluation of Reading Textbooks (p. 518).

For objective 4.5 the Guide for Writing a Reading Lesson Plan (p. 512) should be followed.

For objective 4.6, each student should be rated on the Form for Evaluating Participation in a Group Activity (p. 513) by each other member of the group and should also submit a self-evaluation.

For objective 4.7 the student may follow the Guide for Evaluation of Reading Textbooks (p. 518) but may devise another form of organization.

For objective 4.8, if McGuffey readers are not available, another series at least 30 years old may be substituted. Only the pupil books need be compared.

For objective 4.9, the Form for Evaluating the Teaching of a Lesson (p. 514) should be filled out by the designated observer.

Module 5

Planning and Organizing for Differentiated Reading Instruction

PREREQUISITES

Satisfactory completion of modules 1, 3, and 4.

OBJECTIVES

5.1   K R   The student will be prepared to discuss the significance of the following for good progress in reading: instructional time, motivation, attention, planning, readiness.

5.2   K R   The student will be able to describe four types of reading groups and indicate appropriate functions for each.

5.3   K R   The student will be able to discuss seven issues that influence the effectiveness of group instruction.

5.4   K R   The student will be able to describe four types of individualization that may be employed in a reading program.

5.5   K R   The student will be able to describe four types of reading activity in which whole-class instruction may be appropriate.

5.6   A R   The student will submit a one-week plan for reading instruction for a second-grade, fourth-grade, or sixth-grade class, including an explanation or justification of the plan.

5.7   K Opt   The student will describe and evaluate one published diagnostic/prescriptive reading program.

5.8   K Opt   The student will evaluate individualized developmental reading on the basis of the published research concerning its effectiveness.

5.9   A Opt   The student will describe and evaluate the provisions made for individual differences in one elementary school classroom after observing reading lessons in that classroom.

5.10   A Opt   Given a set of reading scores for a class, the student will formulate a grouping plan for the class, assign children to groups, and prepare a one-week reading plan that is appropriate for that class.

PREASSESSMENT

A student who wishes to be given advance credit for all or part of module 5 should request an interview with the instructor before beginning the module and be prepared to demonstrate mastery of the required objectives.

LEARNING ACTIVITIES

Reading

Text, Unit 5
Hafner (1977, pp. 17–56)
A. J. Harris and Sipay (1972, pp. 159–83)
L. A. Harris and C. B. Smith (1976, pp. 367–95)
Kerber (1974, pp. 100–111)
May (1973, pp. 1–18, 67–89, 289–341)
Silvaroli and Wheelock (1975, pp. 129–78)
R. J. Smith and Johnson (1976, pp. 45–67; 291–369)
Zintz (1975, pp. 91–145)
For objective 5.7, see Stallard (1977) for a list of such programs
For objective 5.8, see Sartain (1969) and Duker (1968)

Listening and Discussing

Details to be provided by the instructor.

Observing

Details to be provided by the instructor.

Other

For objective 5.10 to be feasible, the instructor should have available the reading scores for several classes at different grade levels, with pupil names disguised. A different class sheet should be provided to each student who wishes to work on this objective.

POSTASSESSMENT

For objectives 5.1 through 5.5, the student passes a test prepared by the instructor.

or

The student prepares a 20-item test sampling the information relevant to objectives 5.1–5.5, conditions the same as in preceding modules.

For objective 5.6, the plan may be organized using the general format of figures 5.2, 5.3, and 5.4, supplemented by a verbal description and an explanation of the rationale employed.

For objective 5.7, use of the Guide for Evaluation of Reading Textbooks (p. 518) is not obligatory since some of the items in it may not apply.

For objective 5.8, a written report of 500 to 750 words may be submitted.

Objective 5.9 can be attempted only if arrangements for observing in classrooms can be made. The written report should include a description of the class and the teacher's provisions for individual differences in reading, with an evaluation of how these provisions seem to be working.

For objective 5.10, the student should obtain a data sheet on a class from the instructor. The report should include (1) the number of groups formed, the children assigned to each group, with an explanation of the rationale employed; and (2) a one-week plan presented similarly to that in objective 5.6.

Module 6

Determining Needs and Assessing Progress

PREREQUISITES

Satisfactory completion of modules 1, 3, and 4.

OBJECTIVES

6.1   K R   The student will show understanding of the following terms:

standardized test	grade equivalent
criterion-referenced test	percentile
informal reading inventory	stanine
screening test	analytical test
cloze test	survey test
norms	diagnostic test
standards	reading capacity
independent level	underachiever
instructional level	checklist
frustration level	miscue
reliability	context reader
validity	segmentation

6.2   K R   The student will be able to explain the similarities and differences between a screening test and an informal reading inventory.

6.3   K R   The student will be able to compare the purposes, good points, and limitations of (1) standardized reading tests, (2) informal reading inventories, and (3) cloze tests.

6.4   A R   The student will be able to score and interpret a child's performance on an IRI that has been prerecorded.

6.5   K R   The student will be able to describe a procedure for determining whether or not a child is reading in accordance with capacity.

6.6   A R   The student will be able to describe and evaluate a specific standardized reading test.

6.7   A Opt The student will be able to administer a standardized reading test to a child, and score and interpret the results.

6.8   A Opt The student will administer an IRI (or a published test similar in makeup to an IRI) to a child and will score and interpret the results.

6.9   A Opt The student will apply miscue analysis to a suitable sample of a child's reading.

PREASSESSMENT

A student who wishes to be given advance credit for all or part of module 6 should request an interview with the instructor before beginning the module and be prepared to demonstrate mastery of the required objectives.

LEARNING ACTIVITIES

Reading

Text, Unit 6
Barrett (1967, pp. 53–96)
Farr (1970, pp. 1–125, 167–310)
Fry (1977, pp. 231–75)
Hafner (1974, pp. 197–222)
M. S. Johnson and Kress (1965)
MacGinitie (1973a, pp. 1–35)
May (1973, pp. 117–92)
Quandt (1977, pp. 224–46)
Silvaroli and Wheelock (1975, pp. 61–102)
Womer (1974)

Listening and Discussing

Details to be provided by the instructor.

Observing

Details to be provided by the instructor.

Other

Specimen sets of several representative standardized silent and oral reading tests should be available for study by the students. Several recordings of children taking an IRI should be available, along with copies of the selections. If objective 6.8 is to be used, the testing materials needed should be available.

POSTASSESSMENT

For objectives 6.1, 6.2, 6.3, and 6.5, the student will pass a test devised by the instructor.

or

The student will construct a 20-item test sampling the information relevant to objectives 6.1, 6.2, 6.3, and 6.5; other conditions the same as for module 3.

For objective 6.4, the student will obtain a recorded IRI and the selections it is based on, and using the Listing/Tally Form in figure 6.2 as a model, will record and score the child's performance and will submit the scored record accompanied by an interpretation of the instructional implications.

For objective 6.6, the student may report on either an oral or a silent standardized reading test. The Guide for Evaluating Standardized Tests (p. 510) may be followed, omitting the questions relating to a comparison of tests.

For objective 6.7, the instructor will provide information about how the needed materials can be obtained. The scored test blank should be submitted along with a report that includes a description of the child's behavior while taking the test, and an interpretation of the results in relation to the child's age, grade, and reading program.

For objective 6.8, the instructor will provide information about how the needed materials can be obtained. Scoring may be done using either a printed record form (if available) or a Listing/Tally Sheet. The record form used should be submitted along with an explanation and interpretation of the results.

For objective 6.9, the student may reanalyze the recorded IRI used for objective 6.4 or the IRI used for objective 6.8, using the system described by Y. Goodman and Burke (1972).

Module 7

Word Recognition

PREREQUISITES

Satisfactory completion of modules 1, 3, 4, 5, 6.

OBJECTIVES

7.1   K R   The student will be able to define or describe and illustrate the following:

closure	visual-motor method
flash card	reversal
configuration	homograph
tachistoscope	homophone
syntactic cue	affix
semantic cue	digraph
graphic cue	diphthong
segmentation	whole-word phonics
blending	cluster
sight vocabulary	blend

7.2   K R   The student will be able to pass a test covering the basic principles of decoding.

7.3   K R   The student will be able to state reasons for and against the use of a whole-word method in beginning reading.

7.4   K R   The student will be able to state reasons for and against a decoding emphasis in beginning reading.

7.5   K R   The student will be able to explain the significance of attention, perception, and memory in acquiring a reading vocabulary.

7.6   K R   The student can describe an alternative procedure for use with children who had difficulty in acquiring a sight vocabulary.

7.7   K R   The student can describe the main principles followed in teaching phonics in meaning-emphasis programs.

7.8   K R   The student can compare two procedures for teaching blending to beginning readers.

7.9   A R   The student can prepare an acceptable lesson plan for teaching a specific decoding skill to children of a specified reading level.

7.10   A R   The student can teach a decoding lesson to a small group of fellow students simulating children.

7.11   K Opt   The student reads several references on the subject of phonic generalizations and prepares a report showing why some are worth teaching and others are not.

7.12   K Opt   The student reads several references on the subject of syllabication and prepares a report on the value of syllabication in decoding.

7.13   A Opt   The student will observe a decoding lesson being taught and will prepare a report describing and evaluating the lesson.

7.14   A Opt   The student will teach a lesson on one decoding procedure to an appropriate small group of children.

PREASSESSMENT

A student who wishes to obtain advance credit for all or part of module 7 should make an appointment with the instructor prior to starting the module and be prepared to demonstrate mastery of the required objectives.

LEARNING ACTIVITIES

Reading

Text, Unit 7
Burmeister (1975)
Dawson (1971)
Duffy and Sherman (1972, pp. 36–211)
Durkin (1976)
Fry (1972, pp. 48–134)
L. A. Harris and Smith (1976, pp. 158–232)

Moretz and Davey (1974)
Wallen (1972, pp. 19–231)

Listening and Discussing

Details to be provided by the instructor.

Observing

Details to be provided by the instructor.

Other

Several kinds of decoding teaching and practice materials in addition to those found in reader series should be available for inspection and study.

POSTASSESSMENT

For objective 7.2, the student will pass a test on decoding prepared by the instructor. In addition to the material in Unit 7, Appendix B will be helpful in preparing for this test.

For objectives 7.1, 7.3, 7.4, and 7.5, the student will pass a written test prepared by the instructor.

or

The student will construct a 20-item test sampling the information relevant to objectives 7.1, 7.3, 7.4, and 7.5.

For objectives 7.6, 7.7, and 7.8, the student will pass a written test prepared by the instructor.

or

The student will take part in a small-group prepared discussion meeting covering objectives 7.6, 7.7, and 7.8. The instructor or a delegate may observe and evaluate, or alternatively, peer evaluation may be used. In the latter case, each participant rates each other participant using the Form for Evaluating Participation in a Group Activity (p. 513). The student being rated collects the ratings and turns them in, accompanied by a self-rating on the activity.

For objective 7.9, a written lesson plan is to be submitted. The Guide for Writing a Lesson Plan (p. 512) should be followed.

For objective 7.10, each student in the small group teaches a lesson to the others, who simulate children of appropriate reading level, and is rated by the others using the Form for Evaluating the Teaching of a Lesson (p. 514).

For objective 7.11 or 7.12, a report of 500–750 words should be submitted.

For objective 7.13, the student will fill out the Form for Evaluating the Teaching of a Lesson, supplemented by any additional comments.

For objective 7.14, the Form for Evaluating the Teaching of a Lesson is to be filled out by the observer, who may be the instructor or someone delegated by the instructor.

Module 8

Helping Children to Improve Comprehension

PREREQUISITES

Satisfactory completion of modules 1, 3, 4, 5, 6, and 7.

OBJECTIVES

8.1 K R The student will be able to define or describe and illustrate the following:

verbalism	prefix
second-level abstraction	suffix
meaningful vocabulary	antonym
homonym	phrasing
definition	chunk
root word	pattern marker
figure of speech	pronoun referent
metaphor	passive construction

8.2 K R The student will be able to describe at least four kinds of context clues.

8.3 K R The student will be able to describe and evaluate the vocabulary development procedure employed in one basal reader and accompanying teachers guide.

8.4 K R The student can describe and compare the teaching implications of logical analyses as compared to statistical analyses of reading comprehension.

8.5   K R   The student will be able to list and discuss seven factors that are related to reading comprehension.

8.6   K R   The student will be able to describe four features that affect the difficulty of a sentence.

8.7   A R   Given a nonfiction passage, the student will be able to construct seven different kinds of comprehension questions on it, including factual, inferential, and critical questions.

8.8   A R   The student will be able to prepare a lesson plan for teaching one reading comprehension skill to a group of children.

8.9   A R   The student will be able to teach a comprehension skill to a small group of fellow students simulating children.

8.10   K Opt   The student will, in cooperation with one or three other students, prepare and present a debate on the following: *Resolved*, That the best way to improve reading comprehension is to develop the language and thinking skills of children with nonreading materials.

8.11   K Opt   The student will be able to compare the procedures for introducing technical vocabulary in two content texts in the same subject at the same grade level.

8.12   A Opt   The student will be able to analyze and compare two sets of independent materials intended for use in developing reading comprehension.

8.13   A Opt   The student will be able to prepare a lesson plan for teaching a Directed Reading-Thinking Activity for a basal-reader selection. See Stauffer (1969, pp. 35–86) for suggested procedures.

8.14   A Opt   The student will be able to teach a reading comprehension lesson to a small group of children.

PREASSESSMENT

A student who wishes to obtain advance credit for all or part of module 8 should make an appointment with the instructor prior to starting the module and be prepared to demonstrate mastery of the required objectives.

LEARNING ACTIVITIES

Reading

Text, Unit 8
Dallman et al. (1974, pp. 165–245)

Fry (1972, pp. 135–202)
Hafner (1977, pp. 95–160)
L. A. Harris and Smith (1976, pp. 46–97, 261–97)
Henry (1974)
Lee, Bingham, and Woelfel (1968)
Ruddell (1974, pp. 361–408)
F. Smith (1975)
Taschow (1976)
Zintz (1975, pp. 268–304, 335–51)

Listening and Discussing

Details to be provided by the instructor.

Observing

Details to be provided by the instructor.

Other

For this module, samples of workbooks and reading kits or laboratories intended for developing comprehension and vocabulary should be available for student inspection, in addition to sets of basal readers. For objective 8.11, elementary texts in content subjects should also be available.

POSTASSESSMENT

For objectives 8.1 through 8.6, the student will pass a written test prepared by the instructor.

or

The student will construct a 20-item test sampling the information relevant to objectives 8.1 through 8.6. This test may include short essay questions in addition to objective and completion or single-sentence questions.

or

The student will take part in a prepared small-group discussion meeting covering objectives 8.1 through 8.6. The instructor or a delegate may observe and evaluate, or alternatively, peer evaluation may be used. In the latter case, each participant rates each other participant using the Form for Evaluating Participation in a Group Activity (p. 513). The student being rated collects the ratings and turns them in, accompanied by a self-rating on the activity.

For objective 8.7, the instructor will make available several passages that may be used. The student will submit questions on 8½″ × 11″ paper, indicating which selection has been used, and labeling the questions according to the type of comprehension involved.

For objective 8.8, a written lesson plan is to be submitted. The Guide for Writing a Lesson Plan (p. 512) should be followed.

For objective 8.9, groups of four to six students should be formed. Each group member teaches a short (5–10 minutes) lesson to the others, who simulate children of the appropriate reading level, and is rated by the others on the Form for Evaluating the Teaching of a Lesson (p. 514).

For objective 8.10, 8.11, or 8.12, the student should submit a written report of not more than 500 words.

For objective 8.13, the Guide for Writing a Lesson Plan need not be followed closely if the student prefers a different organization; however, the main points in it should be covered.

For objective 8.14, the lesson plan should first be approved by the instructor. The teaching should be observed and evaluated by the instructor or a delegate, using the Form for Evaluating the Teaching of a Lesson.

Module 9

Helping Students Read to Learn

PREREQUISITES

Satisfactory completion of modules 1, 3, 4, 5, 6, and 8.

OBJECTIVES

Note: Since in a particular course this module may not be required, or only part of it may be required, the objectives listed below are not labeled R or Opt, leaving the designation of what is required to the instructor.

9.1   K   The student will be able to explain the meanings of the following terms:

every-pupil response	graphic aid
overlap words	SQ3R
readability	advance organizer
definitional paragraph	unit approach
explanatory paragraph	differentiated assignment
problem pattern	alphabetization
two-step problem	telegram style
study guide	listening guide
retrieval chart	time chart

9.2   K   The student will be able to describe a procedure for determining the suitability of a particular textbook for a particular class.

9.3   K   The student will be able to describe a diagnostic procedure for determining the reasons for a pupil's faulty comprehension when reading a particular content textbook.

9.4   K   The student will be able to describe sequential steps in teaching alphabetical order, the use of an index, or outlining.

9.5   A   The student will be able to prepare a lesson plan for a directed reading activity in a content area, assuming that the textbook to be used is suitable in difficulty for the pupils.

9.6   A   The student will be able to teach a directed reading activity in a content area to a small group of fellow students simulating children.

9.7   A   Using the same subject matter as in objective 9.5, the student will be able to prepare a lesson plan suitable for pupils for whom the textbook is frustratingly difficult.

9.8   A   The student will be able to teach a content lesson, using the plan from objective 9.5 or 9.7, to an appropriate group of children.

9.9   A   The student will prepare a study guide for a fifth- or sixth-grade science or social studies assignment.

9.10 A   The student will be able to analyze a use-of-time chart kept for one week.

9.11 A   The student will be able to compare the concept density in 3 pages of a basal reader and 3 pages of a content textbook designated for the same grade.

9.12 A   The student will be able to make a diagnostic analysis of the comprehension difficulties experienced by a pupil when reading a textbook at or above his designated grade level.

PREASSESSMENT

A student who wishes to obtain advance credit for all or part of module 9 should make an appointment with the instructor prior to starting the module and be prepared to demonstrate mastery of the required objectives.

LEARNING ACTIVITIES

Reading

Text, Unit 9
Burns and Roe (1976, pp. 292–344)
Dallman et al. (1974, pp. 247–85, 327–58)

Earle (1976)
Hafner (1977, pp. 161–325)
A. J. Harris and Sipay (1972, pp. 284–310)
Howes (1970)
H. A. Robinson and Thomas (1969)
H. A. Robinson (1975, pp. 1–210)
Thelan (1976)
Thomas and Robinson (1972, pp. 9–250)

Listening and Discussing

Details to be provided by the instructor.

Observing

Details to be provided by the instructor.

Other

Reference material that should be available for this module includes many of the materials listed on pages 394–95 of unit 9, as well as representative content area textbooks and reference works.

POSTASSESSMENT

Note: The instructor will determine which of these suggested forms of assessment are applicable.

For objectives 9.1, 9.2, 9.3, and 9.4, the student will pass a written test provided by the instructor.

or

The student will construct a 20-item test sampling the information covered in unit 9.

or

The student will take part in a prepared small-group discussion meeting covering objectives 9.1 through 9.4. The instructor or a delegate may observe and evaluate, or alternatively, peer evaluation may be used. In the latter case, each participant rates each other participant using the Form for Evaluating Participation in a Group Activity (p. 513). The student being evaluated collects the ratings and turns them in, accompanied by a self-rating on the activity.

For objective 9.5, the student may choose a selection from a text in any content subject at any elementary grade level. A written lesson plan following the Guide for Writing a Lesson Plan (p. 512) is to be submitted.

For objective 9.6, small groups of students should be formed. Each group member teaches a short lesson (5–10 minutes) to the others, who simulate children of the appropriate level, and is rated by the others on the Form for Evaluating the Teaching of a Lesson (p. 514).

For objective 9.7, a written lesson plan is to be submitted. If objective 9.5 has been completed, objective 9.7 should be on the same topic.

For objective 9.8, the lesson plan must be approved in advance, and the lesson is to be observed and evaluated by the instructor or a delegate.

For objective 9.9, a written study guide should be submitted, accompanied by a copy of the material it is intended to cover.

For objective 9.10, it is recommended that each student working on this objective construct and keep a use-of-time chart for one calendar week, and then exchange with another student, turning in a written analysis of the facts revealed by the chart along with the (anonymous) chart.

For objective 9.11, the student will submit a written report which includes a definition of "concept density," a list of the concepts found in each sample, and a discussion of the implications for teaching with each book.

For objective 9.12, the student will first have completed objective 9.3 acceptably. The text to be read by the child should be at or slightly above the child's instructional reading level. Errors or miscues should be tabulated and analyzed for the insight they may provide about comprehension difficulties, and the results presented in a written report.

Module 10 _____

Instilling
the Desire
to Read

PREREQUISITES

Satisfactory completion of modules 1, 3, 4, 5, 6, 7, and 8.

OBJECTIVES

10.1 K R   The student will be able to explain the following as they relate to reading interests and attitudes:

security	RIF
reading ability	SEER
SES	progress chart
free reading	reading ladder
creative sharing	bibliotherapy
book club	

10.2 K R   The student will be able to discuss the similarities, differences, and interrelationship between reading interests and
reading attitudes.

10.3 K R   The student will be able to discuss the influence of five kinds
of institutional factors on reading interests.

10.4 K R   Given two grades that are three years apart, the student will
be able to describe similarities and differences in the reading interests of representative children in those grades.

10.5 K R   The student will be able to describe the characteristics that
make a type of book report suitable or unsuitable for de-

veloping a positive attitude toward reading, giving one or more examples of suitable and unsuitable types.

10.6   A Opt   The student will be able to interview a child to determine a major interest area and plan a "reading ladder" for that child.

10.7   A Opt   The student will be able to plan a campaign for "selling" recreational reading to a class containing several unmotivated readers.

10.8   A Opt   The student will be able to plan a 50-book classroom library for a second-grade, fourth-grade, or sixth-grade class, indicating the categories to be represented and the desirable readability levels.

10.9   A Opt   The student will be able to report on the five books that made the greatest impression on him or her during pre-college years.

10.10   A Opt   The student will describe the recreational reading program in a classroom under observation and evaluate its effectiveness.

10.11   A Opt   The student will read, abstract, and evaluate five children's books at different levels of maturity.

PREASSESSMENT

A student who wishes to obtain advance credit for all or part of module 10 should make an appointment with the instructor prior to starting the module and be prepared to demonstrate mastery of the required objectives.

LEARNING ACTIVITIES

Reading

Text, Unit 10
Catterson (1970)
Dallman et al. (1974, pp. 361–94)
Hafner (1974, pp. 433–46)
A. J. Harris and Sipay (1972, pp. 311–33)
Heilman and Holmes (1972)
Painter (1971)
H. A. Robinson (1975, pp. 233–46)
Ruddell (1974, pp. 455–516)
J. A. Smith (1967, pp. 89–101, 208–59)

Sebesta and Wallen (1972, pp. 303–51)
Tanyzer and Karl (1972)

Listening and Discussing

Details to be provided by the instructor.

Observing

Details to be provided by the instructor.

Other

Several references on children's books, such as those listed on pp. 431–33 of unit 10, should be available in the reserve collection for use during work on this module.

POSTASSESSMENT

For objectives 10.1 through 10.5, the student will pass a written test prepared by the instructor.

or

The student will construct a 20-item test sampling the information that is relevant to objectives 10.1–10.5.

or

The student will take part in a prepared small-group discussion meeting covering objectives 10.1 through 10.5. The instructor or a delegate may observe and evaluate, or alternatively, peer evaluation may be used. In the latter case, each participant rates each other participant using the Form for Evaluating Participation in a Group Activity (p. 513). The student being rated collects the ratings and turns them in, accompanied by a self-rating on the activity.

For objective 10.6 the student may use the interest questionnaire in figure 10.1 to explore the child's interests or may rely on an interview covering similar topics. The child's responses should be reported as recorded, with an interpretation. The reading ladder should contain at least five books, with reasons given for the choices made and the sequence in which they are arranged.

For objective 10.7, a written report of 500 to 750 words should be submitted.

For objective 10.8, the references consulted to determine appropriate categories should be listed. Examples of suitable easy, average, and difficult books should be given for three categories, citing the reference or references in which each is listed.

For objective 10.9, the student should attempt to include books read during the primary, intermediate, junior high, and senior high years. The characteristics of each book that account for the strong personal impression it made should be discussed, and the particular way in which it influenced the student's life should be described.

For objective 10.10, the student should have had several opportunities to observe the particular class, and should interview the teacher concerning her objectives and plans in the area of recreational reading. A written report of 500 to 750 words is to be submitted.

For objective 10.11, the abstract and evaluation for each book should not exceed 150 words.

Module 11

Assisting Children with Special Needs

PREREQUISITES

Satisfactory completion of modules 1, 3, 4, 5, 6, 7, 8, and 10.

OBJECTIVES

Note: Since in a particular course this module may not be required, or only part of it may be required, the objectives listed below are not labeled R or Opt, leaving the designation of what is required to the instructor.

11.1   K   The student will be able to explain the meanings of the following terms used in unit 11:

reading-expectancy grade	bidialectal
mental-grade equivalent	dialect shift
underachiever	avoidance technique
reading disability	anglicismos
corrective reading case	slow learner
dyslexia	EMR
learning disability	mainstreaming
continuous diagnosis	

11.2   K   The student will be able to show an understanding of factors related to reading disability: intellectual, perceptual, physical, neurological, sociocultural, educational, emotional.

11.3   K   The student will be able to describe similarities and differences among developmental, corrective, and remedial instruction.

11.4	K	The student will be able to describe two contrasting approaches for teaching a severely disabled reader.
11.5	K	The student will be able to list several phonological and grammatical differences between standard English and (a) black English, (b) English influenced by Spanish, (c) English influenced by Chinese.
11.6	A	The student will be able to listen to a tape of a BE speaker (or Spanish speaker, or Chinese speaker) reading an IRI and classify the miscues as dialect shifts or reading errors, citing a reason for each decision.
11.7	A	Given the age, M.A., and average reading grade of a child, the student will be able to classify the child as a normal reader, an underachiever, a disabled reader, or a slow learner.
11.8	A	The student will be able to interview a child with deviant reading ability concerning the child's reading attitudes and interests and develop instructional implications from the results of the interview.
11.9	K	The student will be able to describe two policies concerning when to teach the reading of English to children for whom English is a second language and point out the arguments for and against each policy.
11.10	A	After several observations of reading instruction in an elementary school classroom, the student will be able to describe and evaluate the provisions made for children with special needs.
11.11	A	The student will be able to formulate a plan for teaching reading to an EMR child in a class in which most reading instruction is in three groups.
11.12	A	A student who has had the opportunity to tutor a child with special needs in reading will be able to report on the experience and what was learned from it.
11.13	K	The student will be able to explain the following statement using other terminology, and explain its bearing on the teaching of reading to gifted children: A superior reader reads the lines, reads between the lines, and reads beyond the lines.
11.14	A	The student will be able to describe one intellectually gifted person and one creatively gifted person whom he or she has

known, and compare the educational adjustment, problems, and needs of the two.

PREASSESSMENT

A student who wishes to obtain advance credit for all or part of module 11 should make an appointment with the instructor prior to starting the module and be prepared to demonstrate mastery of the required objectives.

LEARNING ACTIVITIES

Reading

Text, Unit 11

On Reading Disabilities:
Burns and Roe (1976, pp. 477–514)
Dallman et al. (1974, pp. 439–55)
A. J. Harris and Sipay (1975, pp. 131–59)
Heilman (1972, pp. 549–621)
Ruddell (1974, pp. 577–620)
Schell and Burns (1972, pp. 10–17, 138–58, 166–256, 466–68, 483–98)
R. J. Smith and Barrett (1974, pp. 152–68)
Tinker and McCullough (1975, pp. 580–97)

On Children with Different Sociocultural and Language Backgrounds:
Ching (1976)
Cullinan (1974a)
Figurel (1970)
Figurel (1972)
Horn (1970)
Laffey and Shuy (1973)
Ruddell (1974, pp. 263–91)
Zintz (1975, pp. 397–437, 438–56)

On Slow-learning Children:
Cegelka and Cegelka (1970)
Dallman et al. (1974, pp. 437–39)
Lazar (1971)
Tinker and McCullough (1975, pp. 110–13)
Zintz (1972, pp. 491–97)

On Reading for the Gifted:
Dallman et al. (1974, pp. 431–37)
A. J. Harris and Sipay (1972, pp. 383–98)
Labuda (1974a)
Tinker and McCullough (1975, pp. 113–16)
Witty (1971b)
Zintz (1972, pp. 483–91)

Listening and Discussing

Details to be provided by the instructor.

Observing

Details to be provided by the instructor.

Other

For objective 11.6, tapes of IRIs given to children who speak a dialect other than SE should be available for listening and analysis.

For objectives 11.8, 11.10, and 11.12, arrangements to observe repeatedly, to interview, or to tutor a child must have been made several weeks prior to beginning this module.

POSTASSESSMENT

Note: The student will be assessed only on objectives that are required, or that are undertaken voluntarily.

For objectives 11.1 through 11.5, the student will pass a written test prepared by the instructor.

or

The student will construct a 20-item test sampling the information relevant to objectives 11.1 through 11.5.

or

The student will take part in a prepared small-group discussion meeting covering objectives 11.1 through 11.5. The instructor or a delegate may observe and evaluate, or alternatively, peer evaluation may be used. In the latter case, each participant rates each other participant using the Form for Evaluating Participation in a Group Activity (p. 513). The student being evaluated collects the ratings and turns them in, accompanied by a self-rating on the activity.

For objective 11.6, each miscue will be listed (said ——— for ———) and classified as dialect shift or not, citing the example of dialect shift given in the text that applies.

For objective 11.7 the instructor will provide the data and the student will utilize table 6.2 in finding the answers.

For objective 11.8, arrangements must be made in advance by the instructor. The student should submit a tape of the interview, or if taping is not possible, a detailed account of the interview; in either case, accompanied by a discussion of possible instructional implications.

For objective 11.9, some additional reading should be done and a written report of about 500 words is to be submitted.

For objective 11.10, the student's observations should be supplemented by an interview with the teacher, and the results summarized in a paper of 500 to 750 words.

For objective 11.11, some additional reading should be done to locate specific suggestions that can be used as illustrative material for a written report of 500 to 750 words.

For objective 11.12, the student should describe the first session, last session, and two intermediate sessions with the child. What the student has learned from the experience should be illustrated with citations of specific occurrences. There is no set limit to the length of the report.

For objective 11.13, some additional reading on teaching reading to gifted children should be done to provide illustrative examples. A written report of 500 to 750 words should be submitted.

For objective 11.14, identities of the two people should not be disclosed, but they should be people whom the student has known over a period of time. A written report of 500 to 750 words is to be submitted.

Appendix A _____

List of Selected Publishers and Their Addresses

Addison-Wesley Publishing Co.,
   Inc.,
   Jacob Way,
   Reading, Mass. 01867

Allyn. Allyn & Bacon, Inc.,
   470 Atlantic Avenue,
   Boston, Mass. 02210

American Book Co.,
   450 West 33rd Street,
   New York, N.Y. 10001

Ambassador Publishing Co.,
   Box 3524,
   Saint Paul, Minn. 55165

American Heritage Publishing Co.,
   Inc.,
   See McGraw-Hill Book Co.

American Library Association,
   50 East Huron Street,
   Chicago, Ill. 60611

American Printing House for the
   Blind,
   P.O. Box 6085,
   Louisville, Ky. 40206

Appleton-Century-Crofts,
   292 Madison Avenue,
   New York, N.Y. 10017

Association for Childhood Education International,
   3615 Wisconsin Avenue N.W.,
   Washington, D.C. 20016

Barnell Loft, Ltd.,
   958 Church Street,
   Baldwin, N.Y. 11510

Beckley-Cardy Co.
   See Benefic Press

BRL. Behavioral Research Labora-
   tories,
   Box 577,
   Palo Alto, Calif. 94302

Bell and Howell Co.,
   Audio Products Division,
   7100 McCormick Road,
   Chicago, Ill. 60645

Benefic Press,
   10300 West Roosevelt Road,
   Westchester, Ill. 60153

Bobbs. Bobbs-Merrill Co.,
    4300 West 62nd Street,
    Indianapolis, Ind. 46206

Borg-Warner Educational Systems,
    600 West University Drive,
    Arlington Heights, Ill. 60004

R. R. Bowker Co.,
    1180 Avenue of the Americas,
    New York, N.Y. 10036

Bowmar Publishing Co.,
    4563 Colorado Blvd.,
    Los Angeles, Calif. 90039

William C. Brown Co.,
    2460 Kerper Boulevard,
    Dubuque, Iowa 52001

CTB. California Test Bureau/
    McGraw-Hill,
    Del Monte Research Park,
    Monterey, Calif. 93940

Center for Applied Linguistics,
    1611 North Kent Street,
    Arlington, Va. 22289

Childrens Press, Inc.,
    1224 West Van Buren Street,
    Chicago, Ill. 60607

Communacad,
    Box 541,
    Wilton, Conn. 06897

Council for Exceptional Children,
    1920 Association Drive,
    Reston, Va. 22091

Curriculum Associates, Inc.,
    6 Henshaw Street,
    Woburn, Mass. 08101

DLM. Developmental Learning
    Materials,
    7440 Natchez Avenue,
    Niles, Ill. 60648

Dexter and Westbrook, Ltd.,
    958 Church Street,
    Baldwin, N.Y. 11510

Dome, Inc.,
    1169 Logan Avenue,
    Elgin, Ill. 60120

Doubleday and Co., Inc.,
    277 Park Avenue,
    New York, N.Y. 10017

Dreier Educational Systems, Inc.,
    300 Raritan Avenue,
    Highland Park, N.J. 08904

The Economy Co.,
    Box 25308,
    1901 West Walnut Street,
    Oklahoma City, Okla. 73125

EDL. Educational Developmental
    Laboratories, Inc.,
    1221 Avenue of the Americas,
    New York, N.Y. 10020

Educational Service, Inc.,
    P.O. Box 219,
    Stevensville, Mich. 49127

Educational Solutions, Inc.,
  80 Fifth Avenue,
  New York, N.Y. 10011

Educational Systems, Inc.,
  2360 South West 170th Avenue,
  Beaverton, Ore. 97005

ETS. Educational Testing Service,
  Princeton, N.J. 08540

Educators Publishing Service,
  75 Moulton Street,
  Cambridge, Mass. 02138

Electronics Futures, Inc.,
  57 Dodge Avenue,
  North Haven, Conn. 06473

EBE. Encyclopaedia Britannica
  Educational Corp.,
  425 North Michigan Avenue,
  Chicago, Ill. 60611

ERIC/RCS. Clearinghouse on Reading and Communication Skills,
  1111 Kenyon Road,
  Urbana, Ill. 61801

Essay Press, Inc.,
  P.O. Box 2323,
  La Jolla, Calif. 92037

Fearon-Pitman Publishers,
  6 Davis Drive,
  Belmont, Calif. 94002

Field Enterprise Educational Corp.,
  510 Merchandise Mart Plaza,
  Chicago, Ill. 60654

Follett Educational Corp.,
  1010 W. Washington Boulevard,
  Chicago, Ill. 60607

Garrard Publishing Co.,
  1607 North Market Street,
  Champaign, Ill. 61820

Ginn and Co.,
  191 Spring Street,
  Lexington, Mass. 02173

Gryphon Press,
  220 Montgomery Street,
  Highland Park, N.J. 08904

E. M. Hale and Co.,
  1201 South Hastings Way,
  Eau Claire, Wisc. 54701

Harcourt. Harcourt Brace Jovanovich, Inc.
  757 Third Avenue,
  New York, N.Y. 10017

Harper. Harper & Row, Inc.,
  10 East 53rd Street,
  New York, N.Y. 10022

D. C. Heath & Co.,
  125 Spring Street,
  Lexington, Mass. 02173

Holt. Holt, Rinehart and Winston,
  Inc.,
  383 Madison Avenue,
  New York, N.Y. 10017

Houghton Mifflin Co.,
  One Beacon Street,
  Boston, Mass. 02107

Ideal School Supply Co.,
   11000 South Lavergne Avenue,
   Oak Lawn, Ill. 60453

International Reading Association,
   800 Barksdale Road,
   Newark, Del. 19711

ISS. Interpretive Scoring Systems
   See NCS/Educational Systems
   Division

Instructor Publications,
   7 Bank Street,
   Dansville, N.Y. 14437

Kenworthy Educational Service,
   Inc.,
   Box 3031, 138 Allen Street,
   Buffalo, N.Y. 14205

Kingsbury Center, Inc.,
   2138 Bancroft Place N.W.,
   Washington, D.C. 20008

Klamath Printing Co.,
   320 Lowell Street,
   Klamath Falls, Ore. 97601

Language. Language Research
   Associates,
   175 East Delaware Place,
   Chicago, Ill. 60611

Library of Congress, Division for
   the Blind and Physically
   Handicapped,
   1291 Taylor Street N.W.,
   Washington, D.C. 20542

J. B. Lippincott Co.,
   East Washington Square,
   Philadelphia, Penn. 19105

Longman Inc.,
   19 West 44th Street,
   New York, N.Y. 10036

Lowell & Lynwood, Ltd.,
   965 Church Street,
   Baldwin, N.Y. 11510

Lyons. Lyons and Carnahan
   See Rand McNally

The Macmillan Publishing Co.,
   866 Third Avenue,
   New York, N.Y. 10022

Mast/Keystone. Mast Development
   Co.,
   2212 East 12th Street,
   Davenport, Iowa 52803

McCormick. McCormick-Mathers
   Publishing Co.,
   450 West 33rd Street,
   New York, N.Y. 10011

McGraw-Hill Book Co.,
   1221 Avenue of the Americas,
   New York, N.Y. 10020

McGraw-Hill Ryerson Ltd.,
   330 Progress Avenue,
   Scarborough, Ontario
   Canada, M1P 2Z5

McKay. David McKay
   See Longman Inc.

Merrill. Charles E. Merrill Publishing Co.,
1300 Alum Creek Drive,
Columbus, Ohio 43216

G. & C. Merriam Co.,
47 Federal Street,
Springfield, Mass. 01101

Milton Bradley Co.,
Springfield, Mass. 01101

Montana. Montana Reading Publications,
517 Remrock Road,
Billings, Mont. 59102

National Association for the Deaf,
814 Thayer Avenue,
Silver Springs, Md. 20910

NCS/Educational Systems Division,
4401 West 76th Street,
Minneapolis, Minn. 55435

National Council of Teachers of English,
1111 Kenyon Road,
Urbana, Ill. 67801

Nelson. Thomas Nelson & Sons Ltd.,
36 Park Street,
London, England W1Y 4DE

Open Court Publishing Co.,
Box 599,
La Salle, Ill. 61301

Personnel Press,
191 Spring Street,
Lexington, Mass. 02173

Phonovisual Products, Inc.,
12216 Parklawn Drive,
Rockville, Md. 20852

Plays, Inc.,
8 Arlington Street,
Boston, Mass. 02116

Prentice-Hall, Inc.,
Englewood Cliffs, N.J. 07632

The Psychological Corp.,
757 Third Avenue,
New York, N.Y. 10017

Pyramid Books,
919 Third Avenue,
New York, N.Y. 10022

Rand McNally and Co.,
Box 7600,
Chicago, Ill. 60680

Random. Random House,
201 East 50th Street,
New York, N.Y. 10022

Reader's Digest Services, Inc.,
Educational Division,
Pleasantville, N.Y. 10570

Reading Is Fundamental, Inc.,
Smithsonian Institute,
L'Enfant 2500,
Washington, D.C. 20560

The Reading Laboratory,
    55 Day Street,
    Norwalk, Conn. 06858

Right to Read,
    400 Maryland Avenue S.W.,
    Washington, D.C. 20202

Scarecrow Press, Inc.,
    52 Liberty Street,
    Box 656,
    Metuchen, N.J. 08840

Scholastic Magazines and Book
    Services,
    50 West 44th Street,
    New York, N.Y. 10036

SRA. Science Research Associates,
    Inc.,
    259 East Erie Street,
    Chicago, Ill. 60611

Scott F. Scott Foresman and Co.,
    1900 East Lake Avenue,
    Glenview, Ill. 60025

L. W. Singer, Inc.,
    201 East 50th Street,
    New York, N.Y. 10022

Steck. Steck-Vaughn Co.,
    Box 2028,
    Austin, Texas 78767

Strine Publishing Co.,
    P.O. Box 149
    York, Penn. 17405

Teachers. Teachers College Press,
    Columbia University,
    1234 Amsterdam Avenue,
    New York, N.Y. 10027

TTC. Teaching Technology Corp.,
    2103 Green Spring Drive,
    Timonium, Md. 21093

University of Chicago Press,
    1130 South Langley Avenue,
    Chicago, Ill. 60628

Walch. J. Weston Walch, Publisher,
    321 Valley Street,
    Portland, Maine 04104

Watts. Franklin Watts, Inc.,
    845 Third Avenue,
    New York, N.Y. 10022

Webster Division of McGraw-Hill
    Book Co.,
    1221 Avenue of the Americas,
    New York, N.Y. 10020

Weekly Reader,
    245 Longhill Road,
    Middletown, Conn. 06457

Westinghouse Learning Corp.,
    100 Park Avenue,
    New York, N.Y. 10017

Albert Whitman and Co.,
    560 West Lake Street,
    Chicago, Ill. 60606

H. W. Wilson Co.,
  950 University Avenue,
  Bronx, N.Y. 10452

Richard L. Zweig Associates,
  20800 Beach Boulevard,
  Huntington Beach, Calif. 92648

Xerox Educational Publications,
  191 Spring Street,
  Lexington, Mass. 02173

Appendix B

A Concise Summary of Grapheme-Phoneme Relationships

A *grapheme* is a letter (*c, a*) or group of letters (*tr, sh, wr, ea*) that represents a *phoneme*, which is a unit of sound in spoken language (/k/ + /a/ + /t/ = /kat/). Linguists and phoneticians do not all agree about the number of phonemes in American English, but the most commonly used number is 44. Because our alphabet does not have enough symbols to represent this number of phonemes, practically every letter, singly and in combinations, has to represent more than one sound. Of the 26 letters, 5 are vowels (*a, e, i, o, u*), 3 are semivowels (*h, y, w*, which sometimes represent a consonant and sometimes a vowel sound), and 18 are consonants. Three consonant graphemes are superfluous because they duplicate sounds already represented by other graphemes (*c* = /k/ or /s/, x = /ks/ or /gs/, qu = /kw/ or /k/).

Many graphemes represent different phonemes in different words. For example, although *t* usually represents /t/ as in *tot*, it can also signal /ch/ as in *nature*, /sh/ as in *mention*, or be silent as in *pitcher*. Each vowel grapheme can represent several different phonemes. All letters except *j, q, v,* and *x* are silent in some words.

Regional and cultural dialects also can create some problems in teaching phonics. For instance, in most of the United States, *path* and *laugh* have the same vowel sound as in *sat;* but in much of New England and the British Commonwealth, these and many other "short *a*" words are pronounced like the sound /ä/ in *father*. In several localities, it is impossible to hear the difference between /a/ and /e/ in many words, and in the South the "long i" tends to sound like /ä/ as in *ah*. The /r/'s in *Harvard* are not sounded by or audible to most Bostonians. Speakers of black English dialects usually do not differentiate between /i/ and /e/. Difficulties arise when teachers do not take into account the differences between their pronunciation (or the ones indicated in the teachers manual) and those of the children, or when the children do not hear any differentiation between two sounds that are different to a teacher's ears.

Many vowels that occur in unstressed syllables are not as clearly sounded as the same vowels in accented syllables. Long vowel sounds are shortened

558

in duration but are not changed much in quality. Short unstressed vowels tend to lose their distinctive sounds; instead a schwa /ə/ sound is heard (see p. 280). Good usage permits considerable variation in the clarity with which these unstressed vowels are pronounced but tends toward diminishing them enough so that a listener cannot usually be sure, from the sound alone, which letter is used in spelling the word.

To complicate matters further, nearly every phoneme can be represented by more than one grapheme. The "long e" sound has 11 spellings as in *be, Caesar, quay, team, see, deceive, people, key, machine, field,* and *amoeba.* The "short e" sound is also represented in 11 different ways, 8 of which sometimes represent /ē/, and 9 of which also represent other vowel sounds as well. The /sh/ phoneme can be represented in 13 ways, as in *she, ocean, machine, official, pshaw, sugar, schist, conscience, nauseous, tension, issue, mission,* and *action.* The only phonemes that do not have two or more spellings are the voiced and unvoiced *th* sounds. The name of a vowel represents its "long sound," and the name of a consonant usually combines the consonant phoneme with a preceding vowel (em) or following vowel (bee). Altogether, the 44 phonemes recognized by one college dictionary are represented by 251 spellings.

There are many irregularities in the grapheme-phoneme and phoneme-grapheme relationships in English. Almost every phonic generalization has exceptions. This makes the teaching and learning of English phonics considerably more difficult than it could be if each grapheme represented just one phoneme, and vice versa.

Because there are so many irregularities, alternatives, and exceptions, it is important that children learn and regularly apply two basic principles in decoding unknown words: (1) try every tentative pronunciation, starting with the most probable sound, in the context of the sentence to see if it makes sense; and (2) when use of the grapheme's most usual phoneme does not produce a meaningful word that fits the context, try alternative phonemes and alternative accent patterns.

Consonants

A consonant is a phoneme produced with more or less obstruction of the breath by tongue, teeth, and lips; also a grapheme that represents a consonant phoneme.

Single consonants. There are 18 consonant letters and three semivowels (*h, w, y*). They are often classified as *voiced* (*j, l, m, n, r, v, w, y, z*) or *unvoiced* (*b, g, h, p, d, k, s, t*). Or they can be classed as *sonorants,* with little obstruction of the breath (*f, h, l, m, n, r, v, w, y*); *fricatives,* with substantial obstruction (*ch, j, sh, s, z, zh, th*); and *stops,* with complete obstruction (*b*, *d*, *g*, *k*, *p*, *t*). They can also be classified according to the part of the mouth where obstruction takes place: *labial* (the lips), *dental* (the teeth), or *glottal* (the tongue). Thus, /k/ is an unvoiced glottal stop, /g/ is a voiced glottal stop, and /j/ is a voiced glottal fricative.

The letter *v* is the only letter that does not represent more than one sound, by itself or in digraphs; but most single consonants are fairly consistent in their symbol-sound associations. Several consonants that at times represent phonemes other than their most common sounds are: [1]

c usually represents /k/ (hard c) before *a, o,* and *u* (cat, came, cup) or before a consonant (club) at the end of a syllable (critic)

c usually represents /s/ (soft c) before *e, i,* and *y* (cent, city, icy)

c represents /sh/ before *ious* (vivacious)

d usually represents /d/ (did)

d followed by *u* sometimes represents /j/ (individual)

d followed by *ge* is usually silent (judge)

f usually represents /f/ (fife)

f occasionally represents /v/ (of)

g usually represents /g/ (hard *g*) before *a, o,* or *u* (gave, go, gun) or before a consonant (glow) or at the end of a syllable (rag)

g usually represents /j/ (soft *g*) before *e, i,* or *y* (gem, giant, gym); but many common words are exceptions to this generalization (get, girl, give)

s usually represents /s/ (see, caps)

s usually represents /z/ after a vowel or voiced consonant (goes, falls, hers); exceptions include bus and purse

s may represent /zh/ or /sh/ when followed by *u* (sugar, treasure); exceptions include such, sue

t usually represents /t/ (tot)

t usually represents /sh/ when followed by *ion, ial, ious,* or *ient* (portion, partial, cautious, patient)

t followed by *u* often represents /ch/ (virtue, picture)

x usually = /ks/ (fox, axe)

x may signal /g/ + /z/ when preceded by *e* and followed by a vowel (exact)

x usually = /z/ in the initial position (xylophone)

z usually = /z/ (zoo), but occasionally = /zh/ (azure)

Double consonants. When a consonant is doubled, the grapheme usually represents a single sound (sitting, stopper, pass); usually the sound ends a syllable. There are three exceptions:

1. It is not suggested that children learn all these associations.

When *cc* is followed by *e* or *i*, sometimes the first *c* = /k/ and the second = /s/ (a*cc*ent); not a*cc*ording

When *gg* is followed by *e*, sometimes the first g = /g/ and the second = /j/ (su*gg*est); not ru*gg*ed

When followed by *ion*, *ss* = /sh/ (pa*ss*ion)

Consonant digraphs. The common consonant digraphs represent one sound that is not represented by either letter by itself.

ch usually = /ch/ (*ch*urch), but may represent /k/ in words of Greek origin (*ch*ord), or /sh/ (ma*ch*ine)

gh = /g/ in the initial position (*gh*ost)

gh is usually silent (hi*gh*,[2] ti*gh*t, nei*gh*bor, throu*gh*)

gh occasionally represents /f/ (rou*gh*, cou*gh*)

ph = /f/ (*ph*one, gra*ph*)

qu although usually a blend, sometimes = /k/ (uni*qu*e)

sc although usually a blend, sometimes = /s/ or /sh/ when followed by *e* or *i* (*sc*ience, cre*sc*endo)

sh = /sh/ (*sh*e, wi*sh*)

th = unvoiced /th/ (*th*in, mo*th*)

th = voiced /th/ (*th*en, wi*th*)

wh = /hw/ or /w/ depending on regional dialect (*wh*en)

wh = /h/ when followed by o (*wh*o, *wh*ole)

Silent consonants. When two or more consonants occur together, sometimes one of them is silent. Some programs list these as consonant digraphs.

bt = /t/ (dou*bt*)

ck = /k/ (ba*ck*); generally used at the end of syllables with short vowels

dge = /j/ (ju*dge*)

gn = /n/ (*gn*aw, ali*gn*)

kn = /n/ (*kn*ow)

lk = /k/ (wa*lk*)

lm = /m/ (ca*lm*)

mb = /m/ (co*mb*)

mn = /n/ (*mn*emonic, sole*mn*); rarely occurs

pn = /n/ (*pn*eumonia)

ps = /s/ in the initial position (*ps*ychology)

---

2. In the spelling pattern *igh*, the *i* usually = /ī/.

sl = /l/ occasionally (ai*sl*e, i*sl*and)
tch = /ch/ (i*tch*)
wr = /r/ (*wr*ite)

Consonant blends. A consonant blend or cluster is a combination of two or more consonant letters representing separate phonemes that are slightly merged but still distinguishable. Some occur only in the initial or final position; others in both. Three letters are often found in blends and the combinations they produce are often referred to as "l," "r," or "s" blends.

bl, cl, fl, gl, pl, sl [3] (*bl*ue, *cl*ap, *fl*y, *gl*ow, *pl*ay, *sl*im)
br, cr, dr, fr, gr, pr, tr (*br*ag, *cr*y, *dr*aw, *fr*y, *gr*ab, *pr*y, *tr*y)
sc = /sk/, *sk, sl, sm, sn, sp, st, sw* (*sc*ar; *sk*y, a*sk*; *sl*ip; *sm*ell; *sn*ap; *sp*ot, a*sp*; *st*ay, mi*st*; *sw*im)
tw (*tw*in)
qu = /kw/ (*qu*een)
scr = /skr/ (*scr*ap)
sch usually = /sk/ (*sch*ool), but occasionally = /sh/ in some words of foreign origin (*sch*ist)
squ = /skw/ (*squ*are)
shr, spl, spr, str, thr, (*shr*ed, *spl*it, *spr*ing, *str*ap, *thr*ee)
ct = /kt/, *ft, ld, lk, lp, lt, mp, nd, ng, nk* = /ngk/, *nt, pt* (a*ct*, li*ft*, mi*ld*,[4] mi*lk*, he*lp*, me*lt*, ca*mp*, a*nd*, si*ng*, si*nk*, a*nt*, we*pt*)

Semivowels. Three letters are commonly listed as semivowels. At times, they represent vowel sounds; at other times, consonant sounds.

h in the initial position usually represents a consonant sound /h/ (*h*ave), but occasionally is silent (*h*onor)
h combines with *o* to represent /ō/ (O*h*!)
h combines with *a* to represent /ä/ (a*h*ah!)
w in the initial position usually represents a consonant sound /w/ (*w*as)
w following a vowel is part of a vowel combination (sa*w*, fe*w*, co*w*); it never occurs as a single vowel letter
y in the initial position usually represents a consonant sound /y/ (*y*es)
y as a vowel may (1) represent•/ī/ (fl*y*) at the end of a monosyllable;

3. When any of these letter combinations except *sl* appears in the final position followed by *e* (e.g., a*ble*), a schwa sound is heard in between (e.g., ā′ bəl).
4. Single vowels preceding *ld* often do not represent their short sound (e.g. old, bald).

(2) represent /ē/ or /i/ (baby) depending on regional dialect; (3) represent /i/ (gyp, bicycle) in the middle position; and (4) be part of a vowel digraph or diphthong (play, they, coy)

Vowels

A vowel sound is a phoneme produced without obstructing the breath. Each vowel letter may occur singularly or in combination with other vowel or semivowel letters, and can represent alternative phonemes. Vowel symbol-sound associations are much more inconsistent than consonant associations. Thus, they are more likely to be difficult for children to learn. Generalizations concerning the sounds that vowel letters are most likely to represent are discussed in unit 7, pages 280–83.

Single vowels. Each of the five regular vowel letters usually represents one of two sounds, its long sound or its short sound. Their long sounds are the same as their alphabet names:

a = /ā/ (ape, bake)
e = /ē/ (eve, mete)
i = /ī/ (ivy, ripe)
o = /ō/ (over, hole)
u = /ū/ or /ōō/ [5] (unit, mule)

The short vowel symbol-sound associations are:

a = /a/ (ant)
e = /e/ (egg)
i = /i/ (ink)
o = /o/ (ox)
u = /u/ (umbrella)
a also may represent /ä/ (father) or /ô/ when followed by *l, ll,* or *lk* (ball, walk)
o also may represent /u/ (son) or /ōō/ (do)
u also may represent /oo/ (put) [6]

Schwa. A schwa /ə/ is a "blurred" vowel sound that occurs in unaccented syllables. It may be represented by a single vowel letter (ago, agent, sanity, comply, focus) or some vowel combinations (humorous, ancient).

Vowels followed by r. The sounds of vowels are somewhat modified

---

5. The "long u" represents /ōō/ (rule) almost as frequently as /ū/ (mule).
6. Words containing these "exceptions" are often learned through a whole-word approach.

when they are followed by *r*. Single vowel phonemes are considerably altered. The sounds represented by *er*, *ir*, and *ur* are often indistinguishable (h*er*, f*ir*, f*ur*). Some dictionaries use a macron (-) to indicate long vowel sounds (followed by *r*); others use special symbols especially â and ê (c*are*, sev*ere*).

ar most often represents /är/ (c*ar*), but also may represent /a/ (c*ar*et), /â/ (v*ar*y) or /ə/ (prim*ar*y)
er usually represents /û/ (h*er*) occasionally /er/ (v*er*y)
ir usually represents /ûr/ (f*ir*), but may also represent /ir/ (sp*ir*it)
or usually represents /ôr/ (f*or*), but in unaccented syllables /ər/ (act*or*)
ur usually represents /ûr/ (f*ur*) and occasionally /oor/ or /ūr/ (d*ur*ing)
air = /âr/ or /ār/ (f*air*)
ear usually represents /êr/ or /ēr/ (*ear*), but may also represent /ûr/ (*ear*n), /är/ (h*ear*t), or /âr/ (b*ear*)
eer = /êr/ or /ēr/ (b*eer*)
ier = /êr/ or /ēr/ (p*ier*)
oar = /ôr/ or /ōr/ (*oar*)
oor = /ôr/ or /ōr/ (d*oor*) or /oor/ (p*oor*)
our may represent /ûr/ (j*our*ney), /ōr/ or /ôr/ (f*our*), or /oor/ (y*our*), or /our/ (*our*)
are = /âr/ or /ār/ (c*are*)
ere = /âr/ or /ār/ (th*ere*) or /êr/ or /ēr/ (h*ere*)
ire = /īr/ (f*ire*)
ore = /ôr/ or /ōr/ (m*ore*)
ure = /ūr/ (c*ure*) or /ûr/ (inj*ure*)

Vowel combinations. There are two types of vowel combinations. A vowel digraph is a two-letter combination that represents one sound. A diphthong is a two-letter combination that represents a vowel blend that neither letter alone would signal. Most commonly *oi, oy, ou,* and *ow* /ou/ are listed as diphthongs; occasionally, *au, aw, ew,* and *ey* are also.

Most common and consistent vowel digraphs:
ee = /ē/ (f*ee*d); rarely /i/ (b*ee*n)
ai = /ā/ (f*ai*l); rarely /e/ (s*ai*d), /a/ (pl*ai*d) or /i/ (mount*ai*n)
ay = /ā/ (s*ay*); rarely /e/ (s*ay*s) or /ī/ (kay*ay*k)
oa = /ō/ (c*oa*t); rarely /ô/ (br*oa*d)
Most common and consistent diphthongs:
ou = /ou/ (*ou*t); rarely /o͞o/ (s*ou*p), /u/ (t*ou*ch), or /ô/ (br*ou*ght)
au = /ô/ (h*au*l, c*au*ght); rarely /a/ or /ä/ (l*au*gh)
oi = /oi/ (*oi*l); rarely /ə/ (porp*oi*se)

oy = /oi/ (b*oy*); rarely /ī/ (c*oy*ote)

aw = /ô/ (s*aw*)

Vowel combinations that usually represent one of two phonemes:

ea = /ē/ (h*ea*l) or /e/ (h*ea*d); occasionally /ā/ (st*ea*k)

oo = /ōō/ (r*oo*m) or /oo/ (b*oo*k); occasionally /u/ (bl*oo*d)

ow = /ō/ (l*ow*) or /ou/ (c*ow*)

Less common and less consistent vowel combinations:

ew = /ū/ (f*ew*) or /ōō/ (fl*ew*); rarely /ō/ (s*ew*)

ey = /ē/ or /i/ (hon*ey*), /ā/ (th*ey*), or /ē/ (k*ey*)

ie = /ē/ (th*ie*f), /ē/ or /i/ (coll*ie*), or /ī/ (p*ie*) in one-syllable words; rarely /e/ (fr*ie*nd)

ei = /ā/ (v*ei*n) particularly when followed by *gh* (w*ei*gh), or /ē/ or /ī/ (*ei*ther); rarely /i/ (forf*ei*t)

oe = /ō/ (t*oe*), /ōō/ (sh*oe*) or /ē/ (am*oe*ba)

ue = /ū/ (c*ue*) or /ōō/ (cl*ue*)

ui = /i/ (g*ui*lt) or /ōō/ (fr*ui*t)

eu = /ū/ (f*eu*d) or /ōō/ (sl*eu*th)

eo = /ə/ (pig*eo*n), /e/ (l*eo*pard), or /ē/ (p*eo*ple)

Generalizations that may be helpful to students in determining vowel values (e.g., what sound a vowel letter or letters most probably represents), syllabication and morphemic analysis, and accenting are presented in unit 7.

Bibliography _____

Aaron, Robert L. & Seaton, Hal. W. Modification of pupil attitude toward reading through positive reinforcement scheduling. In Wallace D. Miller & G. M. McNinch (Eds.), *Reflections and investigations on reading*. Clemson, S.C.: National Reading Conference, 1976. Pp. 219–20.

Adams, Anne H. & Harrison, Cathy B. Using television to teach specific reading skills. *The Reading Teacher*, October 1975, 29, 45–51.

Adams, Ernest. A technique for teaching word identification in the content areas. In Gerald G. Duffey (Ed.), *Reading in the middle school*. Newark, Del.: International Reading Association, 1974. Pp. 112–16.

Adams, Irene. Children's books for the remedial reading laboratory. *The Reading Teacher*, December 1976, 30, 266–70.

Alexander, J. Estill & Filler, Ronald C. Measures of reading attitude. *Elementary English*, March 1975, 52, 376–78.

Alexander, J. Estill & Filler, Ronald C. *Attitudes and reading*. Newark, Del.: International Reading Association, 1976.

Allen, R. Van. How a language-experience program works. In Elaine C. Vilscek (Ed.), *A decade of innovations: approaches to beginning reading*. Newark, Del.: International Reading Association, 1968. Pp. 1–8.

Allen, Virginia G. The non-English speaking child in your classroom. *The Reading Teacher*, February 1977, 30, 504–8.

American Heritage Dictionary of the English Language. New York: American Heritage Publishing Co., 1969.

Anastasiow, Nicholas. *Oral language: expression of thought*. Newark, Del.: International Reading Association, 1971.

Applebee, Arthur N. ERIC/RCS: Writing and Reading. *Journal of Reading*, March 1977, 20, 534–37.

Arbuthnot, May Hill. *Children and books*. 4th ed. Chicago, Ill.: Scott Foresman, 1972.

Archer, Marguerite P. Minorities in easy reading through third grade. *Elementary English*, May 1972, 49, 746–49.

Arnold, Richard D. Class size and reading development. In John E. Merritt (Ed.), *New horizons in reading*. Newark, Del.: International Reading Association, 1976. Pp. 413–21.

Ashley, L. F. Children's reading interests and individualized reading. *Elementary English*, December 1970, 47, 1088–96.

Asimov, Isaac. The ancient and the ultimate. *Journal of Reading*, January 1974, 17, 264–71.

Askov, Eunice N.; Kamon, Karlyn; Klumb, Roger, and Pienaar, Peter T.   Study skill mastery among elementary school teachers. *The Reading Teacher,* February 1977, *30,* 485–88.

Athey, Irene J.   Language models and reading. *Reading Research Quarterly,* Fall 1971, *7,* 16–110. (a)

Athey, Irene J.   Synthesis of papers on language development and reading. *Reading Research Quarterly,* Fall 1971, *7,* 9–15. (b)

Atkinson, Richard C. & Fletcher, John D.   Teaching children to read with a computer. *The Reading Teacher,* January 1972, *25,* 319–27.

Aukerman, Robert C.   *Approaches to beginning reading.* New York: John Wiley & Sons, 1971.

Aulls, Mark W.   Relating reading comprehension and writing competency. *Language Arts,* September 1975, *52,* 808–12.

Ausubel, D. P.   *The psychology of meaningful verbal learning.* New York: Grune & Stratton, 1963.

Axelrod, Jerome.   Some flaws in commercial reading comprehension materials. *Journal of Reading,* March 1974, *17,* 474–79. (a)

Axelrod, Jerome.   Some pronunciation and linguistic problems of Spanish-speaking children in American classrooms. *Elementary English,* February 1974, *51,* 203–6. (b)

Bachner, Saul. Teaching reading and literature to the disadvantaged, part V; practice: materials. *Journal of Reading,* January 1975, *18,* 292–97. (a)

Bachner, Saul.   Teaching reading and literature to the disadvantaged, part VII, specific practices: an assignment. *Journal of Reading,* March 1975, *18,* 481–85. (b)

Bader, Lois A.   Involving content teachers in the reading program. In Gerald G. Duffy (Ed.), *Reading in the middle school.* Newark, Del.: International Reading Association, 1974. Pp. 65–70.

Bailey, Mildred H.   The utility of phonic generalizations in grades one through six. *The Reading Teacher,* February 1967, *20,* 413–18.

Ball, Howard G.   Standards for materials selection. *Journal of Reading,* December 1976, *20,* 208–11. (a)

Ball, Howard G.   Who is Snoopy? *Language Arts,* October 1976, *53,* 798–802. (b)

Balmuth, Miriam.   Phoneme blending and silent reading achievement. In Robert C. Aukerman (Ed.), *Some persistent questions on beginning reading.* Newark, Del.: International Reading Association, 1972. Pp. 106–11.

Bamman, Henry A., et al.   *Oral interpretation of children's literature.* Dubuque, Iowa: William C. Brown, 1971.

Banks, Enid M.   The identification of children with potential learning disabilities. *Slow Learning Child: The Australian Journal on the Education of Backward Children,* 1970, *17,* 27–38.

Baratz, Joan C.   Beginning readers for speakers of divergent dialects. In J. Allen Figurel (Ed.), *Reading goals for the disadvantaged.* Newark, Del.: International Reading Association, 1970. Pp. 77–83.

Barbe, Walter B., et al.   Innovative reading programs for the gifted and creative.

In Paul A. Witty (Ed.), *Reading for the gifted and the creative student.* Newark, Del.: International Reading Association, 1971. Pp. 19–32.

Barchas, Sarah E. Expressed reading interests of children of differing ethnic groups. Doctoral dissertation, University of Arizona, 1971.

Barnes, Buckley R. & Clawson, Elmer U. Do advance organizers facilitate learning? Recommendations for further research based on an analysis of 32 studies. *Review of Educational Research,* Fall 1975, 45, 637–59.

Barnett, Lincoln. *The treasure of our tongue.* New York: Alfred A. Knopf, 1969.

Barr, Rebecca C. The influence of instructional conditions on word recognition errors. *Reading Research Quarterly,* Spring 1972, 7, 509–29.

Barr, Rebecca C. Instructional pace differences and their effect on reading acquisition. *Reading Research Quarterly,* 1973–74, 9, No. 4, 526–54.

Barr, Rebecca. The effect of instruction on pupil reading strategies. *Reading Research Quarterly,* 1974–75, 10, No. 4, 555–82.

Barr, Rebecca. Influence of reading materials on response to printed words. *Journal of Reading Behavior,* Summer 1975, 7, 123–35.

Barrett, Thomas C. The relationship between measures of pre-reading visual discrimination and first-grade reading achievement: a review of the literature. *Reading Research Quarterly,* Fall 1965, 1, 51–76.

Barrett, Thomas C. (Ed.). *The evaluation of children's reading achievement.* Newark, Del.: International Reading Association, 1967.

Barrett, Thomas C. & Johnson, Dale D. *Views on elementary reading instruction.* Newark, Del.: International Reading Association, 1973.

Barth, Rodney J. & Swiss, Thom. ERIC/RCS: The impact of television on reading. *The Reading Teacher,* November 1976, 30, 236–39.

Barton, Allen H. Reading research and its communication: the Columbia-Carnegie project. In J. Allen Figurel (Ed.), *Reading as an intellectual activity.* Newark, Del.: International Reading Association, 1963. Pp. 246–50.

Baskin, Barbara H.; Harris, Karen H.; & Salley, Coleen C. Making the poetry connection. *The Reading Teacher,* December 1976, 30, 259–65.

Baskin, Barbara H. & Harris, Karen H. *Notes from a different drummer: a guide to juvenile fiction portraying the handicapped.* New York: R. R. Bowker, 1977.

Batinick, Mary Ellen. Curtain going up. *Language Arts,* September 1975, 52, 836–38.

Beatty, Ross, Jr. Reading comprehension skills and Bloom's taxonomy. *Reading World,* December 1975, 15, 101–8.

Beck, Isabel L. & Bolvin, John O. A model for non-gradedness: the reading program for individually prescribed instruction. *Elementary English,* February 1969, 46, 130–35.

Becker, George J. *Television and the classroom reading program.* Newark, Del.: International Reading Association, 1973.

Bell, Anne E.; Switzer, Fred; & Zipursky, Myrna A. Open-area education: an advantage or disadvantage for beginners. *Perceptual and Motor Skills*, August 1974, *39*, 407–16.

Belmont, Ira & Birch, Herbert G.   The effect of supplemental intervention on children with low reading-readiness scores. *The Journal of Special Education*, Spring 1974, *8*, 81–89.

Benenson, Thea F.   Prediction of first-grade reading achievement: criterion validation of a measure of visual recognition memory. *Educational and Psychological Measurement*, Summer 1974, *34*, 423–27.

Berger, Allen & Peebles, James D. (Eds.).   *Rates of Comprehension: an annotated bibliography*. Newark, Del.: International Reading Association, 1976.

Betts, Emmett A.   *Foundations of reading instruction*. New York: American Book Co., 1946.

Biemiller, Andrew.   The development of the use of graphic and contextual information as children learn to read. *Reading Research Quarterly*, Fall 1970, *6*, 75–96.

Bilka, Loisanne P.   An evaluation of the predictive value of certain readiness measures. In Robert C. Aukerman (Ed.), *Some persistent questions on beginning reading*. Newark, Del.: International Reading Association, 1972. Pp. 43–49.

Billig, Edith.   Children's literature as a springboard to content areas. *The Reading Teacher*, May 1977, *30*, 855–59.

Blanton, William E. & Bullock, Terry.   Cognitive style and reading behavior. *Reading World*, May 1973, *12*, 276–87.

Bleil, Gordon.   Evaluating educational materials. *Journal of Learning Disabilities*, January 1975, *8*, 19–26.

Blom, Gaston E.; Waite, Richard R.; & Zimet, Sara G.   A motivational content analysis of children's primers. In Harry Levin & Joanna P. Williams (Eds.), *Basic studies on reading*. New York: Basic Books, 1970. Pp. 188–221.

Bloom, Benjamin S. et al.   *Taxonomy of educational objectives, handbook I, cognitive domain*. New York: David McKay, 1956.

Bodner, Barbara A.   The eye of the beholder: photography for deaf preschoolers. *Teaching Exceptional Children*, Fall 1975, *8*, 18–23.

Bond, Guy L. & Dykstra, Robert.   The cooperative research program in first-grade reading instruction. *Reading Research Quarterly*, Summer 1967, *2*, 5–142.

Boraks, Nancy & Allen, Amy R.   A program to enhance peer tutoring. *The Reading Teacher*, February 1977, *30*, 479–84.

Bormuth, John R.   The cloze readability procedure. In John R. Bormuth (Ed.), *Readability in 1968, a research bulletin prepared by a committee of the National Conference on Research in English*. Champaign, Ill.: National Council of Teachers of English, 1968. Pp. 40–47.

Bormuth, John R.   The cloze procedure: literacy in the classroom. In William D. Page (Ed.), *Help for the reading teacher: new directions in research*. Urbana, Ill.: National Conference on Research in English and ERIC/RCS, March 1975. Pp. 60–89.

Botel, Morton & Granowsky, Alvin. A formula for measuring syntactic complexity. *Elementary English,* April 1972, *49,* 513–16.

Bouchard, Louisa-May D. A comparative analysis of children's independent reading interests and the content of stories in selected basal reading texts, grades 4–6. Doctoral dissertation, Marquette University, 1971.

Bougere, Marguerite B. Vocabulary development in the primary grades. In J. Allen Figurel (Ed.), *Forging ahead in reading.* Newark, Del.: International Reading Association, 1968. Pp. 75–78.

Brash, Ila W. & Brash, Walter M. *A comprehensive annotated bibliography of American Black English.* Baton Rouge: Louisiana State University Press, 1974.

Breen, L. C. Vocabulary development by teaching prefixes, suffixes, and root derivations. *The Reading Teacher,* November 1960, *14,* 93–97.

Breiling, Annette. Using parents as teaching partners. *The Reading Teacher,* November 1976, *30,* 187–92.

Brekke, Gerald. Actual and recommended allotments of time for reading. *The Reading Teacher,* 1963, *16,* 234–37.

Bresnahan, Mary. Selecting sensitive and sensible books about blacks. *The Reading Teacher,* October 1976, *30,* 16–20.

Britton, Gwyneth E. Danger: state adopted texts may be hazardous to our future. *The Reading Teacher,* October 1975, *29,* 52–58.

Bruton, Ronald W. Individualizing a basal reader. *The Reading Teacher,* October 1972, *26,* 59–63.

Bryen, Diane N. Speech-sound discrimination ability on linguistically unbiased tests. *Exceptional Children,* January 1976, *42,* 195–201.

Buchanan, Cynthia D. Programed reading. In Elaine C. Vilscek (Ed.), *A decade of innovation: approaches to beginning reading.* Newark, Del.: International Reading Association, 1968. Pp. 227–33.

Burke, Carolyn. Oral reading analysis: a view of the reading process. In William D. Page (Ed.), *Help for the reading teacher: new directions in research.* Urbana, Ill.: National Conference on Research in English and ERIC/RCS, 1975. Pp. 23–33.

Burie, Audry Ann & Heltshe, Mary Ann. *Reading with a smile: 90 reading games that work.* Washington, D.C.: Acropolis Books, 1975.

Burmeister, Lou E. Usefulness of phonic generalizations. *The Reading Teacher,* January, 1968, *21,* 349–56.

Burmeister, Lou E. Contents of a phonics program based on particularly useful generalizations. In Nila B. Smith (Ed.), *Reading methods and teacher improvement.* Newark, Del.: International Reading Association, 1971. Pp. 27–39.

Burmeister, Lou E. *Words—from print to meaning: classroom activities for building sight vocabulary, for using context clues, morphology, and phonics.* Reading, Mass.: Addison-Wesley, 1975.

Burmeister, Lou E. A chart for the new Spache Formula. *The Reading Teacher,* January 1976, *29,* 384–85. (a)

Burmeister, Lou E. Vocabulary development in content areas through the use of morphemes. *Journal of Reading,* March 1976, *19,* 481–87. (b)

Burns, Paul C. & Roe, Betty D. *Teaching reading in today's elementary schools.* Chicago: Rand McNally, 1976.

Buros, Oscar K. (Ed.). *Reading: tests and reviews.* Highland Park, N.J.: Gryphon Press, 1968.

Buros, Oscar K. (Ed.). *The seventh mental measurements yearbook.* Vols. I & II. Highland Park, N.J.: Gryphon Press, 1972.

Buros, Oscar K. (Ed.). *The eighth mental measurements yearbook.* Vols. I & II. Highland Park, N.J.: Gryphon Press, 1978.

Cagney, Margaret A. Children's ability to understand standard English and black dialect. *The Reading Teacher,* March 1977, *30,* 607–10.

Calder, C. R. & Zalatimo, S. D. Improving children's ability to follow directions. *The Reading Teacher,* December 1970, *24,* 227–31.

Calfee, Robert C.; Chapman, Robin S.; & Venezky, Richard L. *How a child needs to think to learn to read.* Technical Report No. 131. Madison, Wis.: Center for Cognitive Development, University of Wisconsin, July 1970.

Cardinell, C. F. Rewriting social studies materials to lower reading levels. *The Reading Teacher,* November 1976, *30,* 168–72.

Carnegie Corporation of New York. Making television better for children: the challenge of ACT. *Carnegie Quarterly,* Spring, 1977, *25,* 1–3.

Carner, Richard L. Reading forum. *Reading News,* August 1973, *2,* 1.

Carroll, John B. Language and cognition: current perspectives from linguistics and psychology. In James L. Laffey & Roger Shuy (Eds.), *Language differences: do they interfere?* Newark, Del.: International Reading Association, 1973. Pp. 173–85.

Carroll, John B. and Chall, Jeanne S. (Eds.). *Toward a literate society.* New York: McGraw-Hill, 1975.

Carroll, John B.; Davies, Peter; & Richman, Barry. *American Heritage word frequency book.* Boston: Houghton Mifflin, 1971.

Castallo, Richard. Listening guide—a first step toward notetaking and listening skills. *Journal of Reading,* January 1976, *19,* 289–90.

Cattell, J. M. The time it takes to see and name objects. *Mind,* 1886, *11,* 63–65.

Catterson, Jane H. (Ed.). *Children and literature.* Newark, Del.: International Reading Association, 1970.

Catterson, Jane H. Problems and principles in teaching middle school reading. In Gerald G. Duffy (Ed.), *Reading in the middle school.* Newark, Del.: International Reading Association, 1974. Pp. 94–102. (a)

Catterson, Jane H. Techniques for improving comprehension in mathematics. In Gerald G. Duffy (Ed.), *Reading in the middle school.* Newark, Del.: International Reading Association, 1974. Pp. 153–65. (b)

Cazden, Courtney B. *Child language and education.* New York: Holt, Rinehart and Winston, 1972.

Cegelka, Patrician A. & Cegelka, Walter J. A review of the research on reading and the educable mentally retarded. *Exceptional Children,* November 1970, *37,* 187–200.

Chall, Jeanne S. *Learning to read: the great debate. An inquiry into the science, art, and ideology of old and new methods of teaching children to read 1910–1965.* New York: McGraw-Hill, 1967.

Chall, Jeanne S.; Roswell, Florence; & Blumenthal, Susan H. Auditory blending ability; a factor in success in beginning reading. *The Reading Teacher,* 1963, *17,* 113–18.

Chance, Larry L. Using a learning stations approach to vocabulary practice. *Journal of Reading,* December 1974, *18,* 244–46.

Cheek, Martha. Objective-based teaching of word-analysis skills in middle and secondary schools. In Lawrence E. Hafner (Ed.), *Inmproving reading in middle and secondary schools: selected readings.* 2nd ed. New York: Macmillan, 1974. Pp. 62–76.

Cherry, Louise J. *Sex differences in child speech: McCarthy revisited.* Research Bulletin RB–75–3. Princeton, N.J.: Educational Testing Service, February 1975.

Chester, Robert D. The psychology of reading. *The Journal of Educational Research,* May–June 1974, *67,* 403–11.

Chester, Robert D. Reading comprehension: a pragmatic approach to assessment and instruction. In Robert T. Williams (Ed.), *Insights into why and how to read.* Newark, Del.: International Reading Association, 1976. Pp. 76–89.

Cheyney, Arnold B. *Teaching reading skills through the newspaper.* Newark, Del.: International Reading Association, 1971.

Ching, Doris C. *Reading and the bilingual child.* Newark, Del.: International Reading Association, 1976.

Chomsky, Noam. Phonology and reading. In Harry Levin & Joanna P. Williams (Eds.), *Basic studies on reading.* New York: Basic Books, 1970. Pp. 3–18.

Clark, Margaret M. *Reading difficulties in schools.* Baltimore: Penguin Books, 1970.

Clary, Linda M. Tips for testing reading informally in the content areas. *Journal of Reading,* November 1976, *20,* 156–57.

Clymer, Theodore. The utility of phonic generalizations in the primary grades. *The Reading Teacher,* January 1963, *16,* 252–58.

Clymer, Theodore. Research in corrective reading: findings, problems, and observations. In Marjorie S. Johnson & Roy A. Kress (Eds.), *Corrective Reading in the elementary classroom.* Newark, Del.: International Reading Association, 1967. Pp. 1–10.

Clymer, Theodore. What is reading? Some current concepts. In Helen M. Robinson (Ed.), *Innovation and change in reading instruction.* Sixty-seventh Yearbook Part 2. Chicago: National Society for the Study of Education, 1968. Pp. 7–29.

Cohen, Alice & Glass, Gerald G. Lateral dominance and reading ability. *The Reading Teacher,* January 1968, *21,* 343–48.

Cole, Luella. *The Improvement of reading.* New York: Farrar & Rinehart, 1938.

Committee on Reading, National Academy of Education. Report of the Committee on Reading. In John B. Carroll & Jeanne S. Chall (Eds.), *Toward a literate society.* New York: McGraw-Hill, 1975. Pp. 3–44.

Comstock, George. The effects of television on children and adolescents, a symposium: the evidence so far. *Journal of Communication,* 1975, 25, 25–34.

Coomber, James E. Perceiving the structure of written materials. *Research in the Teaching of English,* Winter 1975, 9, 263–66.

Cooper, J. Louis. The effect of adjustment of basal reading materials on reading achievement. Doctoral dissertation, Boston University, 1952.

Corder, R. *The information base for reading.* Final Report, Project No. 0–9031. Berkeley, Calif.: Educational Testing Service, 1971.

Corman, Cheryl. Bibliotherapy—insight for the learning handicapped. *Language Arts,* October 1975, 52, 935–37.

Cornejo, Ricardo J. A criterion-referenced assessment system for bilingual reading. *California Journal of Educational Research.* November 1974, 25, 294–301.

Cortez, Emilio G. The Puerto Rican non-English speaking child: what can I do? *Language Arts,* October 1976, 53, 767–69, 804.

Cramer, R. L. Dialectology—a case for language experience. *The Reading Teacher,* October 1971, 25, 33–39.

Criscuolo, Nicholas P. Reaching unreachable parents. *Journal of Reading,* January 1974, 17, 285–87.

Criscuolo, Nicholas P. May bags, peg sheds, crafty crannies, and reading. *The Reading Teacher,* January 1976, 29, 376–78.

Criscuolo, Nicholas. Book reports: twelve creative alternatives. *The Reading Teacher,* May 1977, 30, 893–95.

Critchley, Macdonald. *The dyslexic child.* London: William Heinemann. Medical Books Ltd., 1970.

Cromer, Ward. The effects of "pre-organizing" reading material on two levels of poor readers. Doctoral dissertation, Clark University, 1968.

Cromer, Ward & Dorsey, Suzanne. *Read-ability books for junior and senior high students.* Portland, Me.: Walch, 1970.

Crosby, R. M. N. & Linton, R. A. *The waysiders: a new approach to reading and the dyslexic child.* New York: Delacorte Press, 1968.

Crowell, Sheila C. & Kolba, Ellen D. Contrastive analysis in the junior high school. In Bernice E. Cullinan (Ed.), *Black dialect and reading.* Urbana, Ill.: ERIC/RCS and National Council of Teachers of English, 1974. Pp. 69–84.

Cullinan, Bernice E. (Ed.). *Black dialects and reading.* Urbana, Ill.: ERIC/RCS and National Council of Teachers of English, 1974. (a)

Cullinan, Bernice E. Teaching literature to children, 1966–1972. In H. A. Robinson & A. T. Burrows (Eds.), *Teacher effectiveness in elementary language arts: a progress report.* Urbana, Ill.: National Conference on Research in English and ERIC/RCS, 1974. Pp. 25–37. (b)

Cullinan, Bernice E. & Carmichael, Carolyn W. (Eds.), *Literature and young children.* Urbana, Ill.: National Council of Teachers of English, 1977.

Cullinan, Bernice E.; Jaggar, Angela M.; & Strickland, Dorothy S. Oral language expansion in the primary grades. In Bernice E. Cullinan (Ed.), *Black dialects and reading.* Urbana, Ill.: ERIC/RCS and National Council of Teachers of English, 1974. Pp. 43–54.

Culyer, Richard C.   Skinny books for reading. *Language Arts*, September 1975, 52, 793–96.

Cunningham, Dick & Shablok, Scott L.   Selective reading guide-o-rama: the content teacher's best friend. *Journal of Reading*, February 1975, *18*, 380–82.

Cunningham, Patricia M.   Transferring comprehension from listening to reading. *The Reading Teacher*, November 1975, *29*, 169–72.

Cushenbery, Donald C.   The Joplin plan and cross grade grouping. In Wallace Z. Ramsey (Ed.), *Organizing for individual differences*. Newark, Del.: International Reading Association, 1967. Pp. 33–46.

Dale, Edgar.   Vocabulary measurement: techniques and major findings. *Elementary English*, December 1965, *42*, 895–901, 948.

Dale, Edgar.   Reading as communication. In Robert T. Williams (Ed.), *Insights into why and how to read*. Newark, Del.: International Reading Association, 1976. Pp. 3–13.

Dale, Edgar & Chall, Jeanne S.   A formula for predicting readability. *Educational Research Bulletin*, Ohio State University, 1948, 27, 11–20, 28, 37–54.

Dale, Edgar & O'Rourke, Joseph. *Techniques of teaching vocabulary*. Palo Alto, Calif.: Field Educational Publications, 1971.

Dale, Edgar & O'Rourke, Joseph. *The living word vocabulary: the words we know*. Elgin, Ill.: Dome, 1976.

Dale, Edgar; Taher, Razik; & Petty, Walter.   *Bibliography of vocabulary studies*. 5th ed. Columbia, Ohio: Ohio State University Press, 1973.

Dallman, Martha et al.   *The teaching of reading*. 4th ed. New York: Holt, Rinehart and Winston, 1974.

Dauzat, Sam V.   Wise utilization of human resources: the paraprofessional in the reading program. In Thomas C. Barrett & Dale D. Johnson (Eds.), *Views on elementary reading instruction*. Newark, Del.: International Reading Association, 1973. Pp. 91–97.

Davey, Beth.   Cognitive styles and reading achievement. *Journal of Reading*, November 1976, 20, 113–19.

Davino, Antoinette C.   Reading program for the Afro-American. In Helen K. Smith (Ed.), *Meeting individual needs in reading*. Newark, Del.: International Reading Association, 1971. Pp. 94–100.

Davis, Dorothy V.   Book clubs in the middle grades. *Journal of Reading*, November 1975, *19*, 150–53.

Davis, Frederick B.   Research in comprehension in reading. *Reading Research Quarterly*, Summer 1968, *3*, 499–545.

Davis, Frederick B.   Psychometric research in comprehension in reading. Mimeographed, Graduate School of Education, Rutgers University, New Brunswick, N.J., 1971.

Davis, John.   Why do you teach reading? *Indiana Reading Quarterly*, Winter 1974, *6*, 5–6.

Davis, O. L. & Personke, Carl R., Jr.   Effects of administering the Metropolitan Readiness Test in English and Spanish to Spanish-speaking school entrants. *Journal of Educational Measurement*, 1968, 5, 231–34.

Dawson, Mildred A. (Ed.). *Teaching word recognition skills.* Newark, Del.: International Reading Association, 1971.

DeLawter, Jayne A. The relationship of beginning reading instruction and miscue patterns. In William D. Page (Ed.), *Help for the reading teacher; new directions in research.* Urbana, Ill.: National Conference on Research in English and ERIC/RCS, March 1975. Pp. 42–51.

Della-Piana, Gabriel & Hogben, Michael. Research strategies for maximizing the effectiveness of programmed reading. Paper presented at Association for Programmed Learning, Glasgow, Scotland, April 1968.

Department of Education and Science. *A language for life (The Bullock Report).* London: Her Majesty's Stationery Office, 1975.

DeStefano, Johanna S. Register: a concept to combat negative teacher attitudes toward black English. In Johanna S. DeStefano (Ed.), *Language, society, and education; a profile of black English.* Worthington, Ohio: Charles A. Jones, 1973. Pp. 189–95.

Devin-Sheehan, Linda; Feldman, Robert S.; & Allen, Vernon L. Research on children tutoring children: a critical review. *Review of Educational Research,* Summer 1976, *46,* 355–85.

Devon, Steven; Klein, Rozalyn; & Murphy, Terrence V. Priming—a method to equalize differences between high and low achievement students. *Journal of Reading,* November 1975, *19,* 143–46.

Di Lorenzo, Louis T. & Salter, Ruth. Co-operative research on the nongraded primary. *Elementary School Journal,* 1965, *65,* 269–77.

Dixon, Carol N. Teaching strategies for the Mexican-American child. *The Reading Teacher,* November 1976, *30,* 141–45.

Dohrman, Mary H. The suitability of encyclopedias for social studies reference in the intermediate grades. *The Journal of Educational Research,* December 1974, *68,* 149–52.

Dolch, Edward W. *Teaching Primary Reading.* 3rd ed. Champaign, Ill.: Garrard, 1960.

Dolch, E. W. & Bloomster, M. Phonic readiness. *Elementary School Journal,* 1937, *38,* 201–5.

Donham, Jean & Ichen, Mary L. Reading to write: an approach to composition using picture books. *Language Arts,* May 1977, *54,* 555–58.

Dorsey, Mary E. *Reading games and activities.* Belmont, Calif.: Fearon, 1972.

Downing, John. A summary of evidence related to the cognitive clarity theory of reading. In Phil L. Nacke (Ed.), *Diversity in mature reading: theory and research.* Boone, N.C.: National Reading Conference, 1973. Pp. 178–84.

Downing, John. Children's views of language. In Lloyd O. Ollila et al. (Eds.), *Learning to read, reading to learn.* Victoria, Can.: University of Victoria Press, 1974. Pp. 1–10.

Downing, John. Language arts in open schools. *Elementary English,* January 1975, *52,* 23–29.

Downing, John. The Bullock Commission's judgment of i.t.a. *The Reading Teacher,* January 1976, *29,* 379–82.

Downing, John & Oliver, Peter.   The child's conception of "a word." *Reading Research Quarterly*, No. 4, 1973–74, *9*, 568–82.

Downing, John & Thackray, Derek.   *Reading readiness*. London: University of London Press, 1971.

Dreyer, Sharon S.   *The bookfinder: a guide to children's literature about the needs and problems of youth*. Circle Pines, Minn.: American Guidance Service, 1977.

Du Bois, Nelson F. & Brown, Foster L.   Selected relationships between Frostig scores and reading achievement in a first grade population. *Perceptual and Motor Skills*, October 1973, *37*, 515–19.

Duffy, Gerald G.   Current themes and problems in middle school reading. In Gerald G. Duffy (Ed.), *Reading in the middle school*. Newark, Del.: International Reading Association, 1974. Pp. 2–6. (a)

Duffy, Gerald G. (Ed.).   *Reading in the middle school*. Newark, Del.: International Reading Association, 1974. (b)

Duffy, Gerald G. & Sherman, George B.   *Systematic reading instruction*. New York: Harper & Row, 1972.

Duker, Sam.   *Individualized reading: an annotated bibliography*. Metuchen, N.J.: Scarecrow Press, 1968.

Dulin, Kenneth L.   Teaching and evaluating reading in content areas. In Thomas C. Barrett & Dale D. Johnson (Eds.), *Views on elementary reading instruction*. Newark, Del.: International Reading Association, 1973. Pp. 73–80.

Dulin, Ken L.   The sociology of reading. *The Journal of Educational Research*, May–June 1974, *67*, 392–96.

Dulin, Ken L. & Greenwald, M. Jane.   Mature readers' affective responses to three specific propaganda devices: loaded words, name-calling and borrowed prestige/borrowed dislike. In G. H. McNinch & W. D. Miller (Eds.), *Reading: convention and inquiry*. National Reading Conference, 1975. Pp. 267–72.

Durkin, Dolores.   *Children who read early*. New York: Teachers College Press, 1966.

Durkin, Dolores.   *Teaching them to read*. 2nd ed. Boston: Allyn & Bacon, 1974.

Durkin, Dolores.   A six year study of children who learned to read in school at the age of four. *Reading Research Quarterly*, 1974–75, *10*, No. 1, 9–61.

Durkin, Dolores.   The little things make a difference. *The Reading Teacher*, February 1975, *28*, 473–77.

Durkin, Dolores.   *Strategies for identifying words*. Boston: Allyn & Bacon, 1976.

Dwyer, Carol A.   Sex differences in reading: an evaluation of current theories. *Review of Educational Research*, Fall 1973, *43*, 455–67.

Dwyer, Carol A.   Influence of children's sex role standards on reading and arithmetic achievement. *Journal of Educational Psychology*, December 1974, *66*, 811–16.

Dyer, Henry S.   Research issues on equality of educational opportunity: school factors. *Harvard Education Review*, 1968, *38*, 38–56.

Dykstra, Robert.   Summary of the second-grade phase of the cooperative research program in primary reading instruction. *Reading Research Quarterly,* Fall 1968, *4,* 49–70. (a)

Dykstra, Robert. The effectiveness of code- and meaning-emphasis beginning reading programs. *The Reading Teacher,* October 1968, 22, 17–23. (b)

Earle, Richard A. *Teaching reading and mathematics.* Newark, Del.: International Reading Association, 1976.

Eberwein, Lowell. Does pronouncing unkown words really help? *Academic Therapy,* Fall 1975, *11,* 23–29.

Edwards, Peter. Idioms and reading comprehension. *Journal of Reading Behavior,* September 1974, 6, 287–93.

Edwards, Peter. The effect of idioms on children's reading and understanding of prose. In Bonnie S. Schulwitz (Ed.), *Teachers, tangibles, techniques: comprehension of content in reading.* Newark, Del.: International Reading Association, 1975. Pp. 37–46.

Ehly, Stewart & Larsen, Stephen C. Peer tutoring in the regular classroom. *Academic Therapy,* Winter 1975–76, *11,* 205–8.

Ekwall, Eldon E. *Diagnosis and remediation of the disabled reader.* Boston: Allyn & Bacon, 1976.

Ellson, Douglas G. Tutoring. In N. L. Gage (Ed.), *The psychology of teaching methods.* Chicago: National Society for the Study of Education, 1976. Pp. 120–65.

Ellson, Douglas G; Harris, Phillip; & Barber, Larry. A field test of programed and directed tutoring. *Reading Research Quarterly,* Spring 1968, 3, 307–68.

Emans, Robert. When two vowels go walking and other such things. *The Reading Teacher,* December 1967, *21,* 262–69.

Emans, Robert & Fox, Sharon. Teaching behaviors in reading instruction. In H. Alan Robinson & Alvina T. Burrows (Eds.), *Teacher effectiveness in elementary language arts: a progress report.* Urbana, Ill.: National Conference on Research in English and ERIC/RCS, 1974. Pp. 50–58.

Engin, Ann. W.; Wallbrown, Jane D.; & Wallbrown, Fred H. The relative importance of mental age and selected assessors of auditory and visual perception in the Metropolitan Readiness Test. *Psychology in the Schools,* 1974, *11,* 136–43.

Entwhistle, Doris R. Young children's expectations for reading. In John T. Guthrie (Ed.), *Aspects of reading acquisition.* Baltimore: Johns Hopkins University Press, 1976. Pp. 37–88.

Erickson, Frederick D. F'get you honky!: a new look at black dialect and the school. *Elementary English,* April 1969, *46,* 495–99, 517.

Eron, Leonard, et al. How learning conditions in early childhood, including mass media, relate to aggression in late adolescence. *American Journal of Orthopsychiatry,* 1974, *44,* 412–23.

Esposito, Dominick. Homogeneous and heterogeneous ability grouping: principal findings and implications for evaluating and designing more effective educational environments. *Review of Educational Research,* Spring 1973, *43,* 163–79.

Estes, Thomas H.   A scale to measure attitudes toward reading. *Journal of Reading*, November 1971, *15*, 135–38.

Evans, Howard M. & Touner, John C.   Sustained silent reading: does it increase skills? *The Reading Teacher*, November 1975, *29*, 155–56.

Farr, Roger (Ed.).   *Measurement and evaluation of reading*. New York: Harcourt Brace Jovanovich, 1970.

Farr, Roger & Anastasiow, Nicholas.   *Tests of reading readiness and achievement: a review and evaluation*. Newark, Del.: International Reading Association, 1969.

Fasold, Ralph & Shuy, Roger (Eds.).   *Teaching Standard English in the inner city*. Washington, D.C.: Center for Applied Linguistics, 1970.

Fasold, Ralph & Wolfram, Walt.   Some linguistic features of Negro dialect. In Ralph Fasold & Roger Shuy (Eds.), *Teaching Standard English in the inner city*. Washington, D.C.: Center for Applied Linguistics, 1970. Pp. 41–86.

Fay, Leo & Jared, Lee Ann (Comps.).   *Reading in the content fields: an annotated bibliography*. Newark, Del.: International Reading Association, 1975.

Feeley, Joan T.   Television and children's reading. *Elementary English*, January 1973, *50*, 141–50.

Feeley, Joan T.   Interest patterns and media preferences of middle-grade children. *Reading World*, March 1974, *13*, 224–37.

Feeley, Joan T.   Television and reading in the seventies. *Language Arts*, September 1975, *52*, 797–801, 815.

Feitelson, Dina.   Sequences and structure in a system with consistent sound-symbol correspondence. In John E. Merritt (Ed.), *New horizons in reading*. Newark, Del.: International Reading Association, 1976. Pp. 269–77.

Feldhusen, Hazel J.; Lamb, Pose; & Feldhusen, John.   Prediction of reading achievement under programmed and traditional instruction. *The Reading Teacher*, February 1970, *23*, 446–54.

Fennimore, Flora.   Projective book reports. *Language Arts*, February 1977, *54*, 176–79.

Ferinden, William E., Jr.; Jacobson, Sherman; & Linden, N. J.   Early identification of learning disabilities. *Journal of Learning Disabilities*, November 1970, *3*, 589–93.

Fernald, Grace M.   *Remedial techniques in basic school subjects*. New York: McGraw-Hill, 1943.

Figurel, J. Allen (Ed.).   *Reading goals for the disadvantaged*. Newark, Del.: International Reading Association, 1970.

Figurel, J. Allen (Ed.).   *Better reading in urban schools*. Newark, Del.: International Reading Association, 1972.

Fisher, Sharon.   Conceptual tempo and oral reading performance. Doctoral dissertation, State University of New York at Albany, 1977.

Fitzgibbon, Thomas J.   Reading tests and the disadvantaged. In William E. Blanton et al. (Eds.), *Measuring reading performance*. Newark, Del.: International Reading Association, 1974. Pp. 15–33.

Flanagan, John C.   The PLAN system for individualizing education. *NCME Measurement in Education,* January 1971, *2,* 1–8.

Flesch, Rudolf.   *Why Johnny can't read.* New York: Harper & Row, 1955.

Forester, Leona M.   Idiomagic! *Elementary English,* January 1974, *51,* 125–27.

Fowler, Elaine D.   Predicting reading achievement of Spanish-speaking first grade children. *Reading Improvement,* Winter 1973, *10,* 7–11.

Fox, Sandra J.   Implications for the teaching of reading to American Indian students in the elementary grades. In Wallace D. Miller & George H. McNinch (Eds.), *Reflections and investigations on reading.* Clemson, S.C.: National Reading Conference, 1976. Pp. 170–74.

Frager, Stanley & Stern, Carolyn.   Learning by teaching. *The Reading Teacher,* February 1970, *23,* 403–5, 417.

Francis, W. Nelson.   Linguistics and reading: a commentary on chapters 1 to 3. In Harry Levin & Joanna P. Williams (Eds.), *Basic studies on reading.* New York: Basic Books, 1970. Pp. 43–56.

Freeman, George F.   Reading and mathematics. *The Arithmetic Teacher,* November 1973, *20,* 523–29.

Frey, Betty J.   *Basic helps for teaching English as a second language.* Tucson, Ariz.: Palo Verde Publishing Co., 1970.

Fries, C. C.   *Linguistics and reading.* New York: Holt, Rinehart and Winston, 1963.

Froese, Victor.   IRI's at the secondary level re-examined. In Phil L. Nacke (Ed.), *Interaction: research and practice for college-adult reading.* Clemson, S.C.: National Reading Conference, 1974. Pp. 120–23.

Froese, Victor.   Cloze readability versus the Dale-Chall formula. In Bonnie S. Schulwitz (Ed.), *Teachers, tangibles, techniques: comprehension of content in reading.* Newark, Del.: International Reading Association, 1975. Pp. 23–31.

Fry, Edward B.   A readability formula that saves time. *Journal of Reading,* April 1968, *11,* 513, 516.

Fry, Edward B.   *Reading instruction for classroom and clinic.* New York: McGraw-Hill, 1972.

Fry, Edward B.   A kernel distance theory for readability. In G. H. McNinch & W. D. Miller (Eds.), *Reading: convention and inquiry.* Clemson, S.C.: National Reading Conference, 1975. Pp. 252–54.

Fry, Edward B.   *Elementary reading instruction.* New York: McGraw-Hill, 1977.

Fry, Maurine & Johnson, Carole S.   Oral language production and reading achievement among selected students. *Journal of American Indian Education,* October 1973, *13,* 22–27.

Fryberg, Estelle L.   Black English: a descriptive guide for teachers. In Bernice E. Cullinan (Ed.), *Black dialects and reading.* Urbana, Ill.: ERIC/RCS and National Council of Teachers of English, 1974. Pp. 190–96.

Fuller, Renee.   Breaking down the IQ walls: severely retarded people can learn to read. *Psychology Today,* October 1974, *8,* 97–102.

Furr, Oneta R.   Improving flexibility in reading for the advanced student. In Helen K. Smith (Ed.), *Meeting individual needs in reading.* Newark, Del.: International Reading Association, 1971. Pp. 124–32.

Gadway, Charles J. National assessment of educational progress. Reading: summary. Preliminary Report 02–R–00. Denver, Colo.: Education Commission of the States, May 1972.

Gagné, R. M. *The conditions of learning.* 2nd ed. New York: Holt, Rinehart and Winston, 1970.

Gainsburg, Joseph C. *Advanced skills in reading,* book 1. Rev. ed. New York: Macmillan, 1978.

Gantt, Walter N.; Wilson, Robert M.; & Dayton, C. Mitchell. An initial investigation of the relationship between syntactical divergency and the listening comprehension of black children. *Reading Research Quarterly,* 1974–75, *10,* No. 2, 193–211.

Garcia, Ricardo L. Mexican-Americans learn through language experience. *The Reading Teacher,* December 1974, *28,* 301–5.

Gellung, Tom B. & Rucker, C. N. Labels and teacher expectation. *Exceptional Children,* April 1977, *43,* 464–65.

Geniski, Celia & Chambers, Richard. Informal assessment of the bilingual child. *Language Arts,* May 1977, *54,* 496–500.

Gentile, Lance M. & McMillan, Merna M. Why won't teenagers read? *Journal of Reading,* May 1977, *20,* 649–54.

Gerhard, Christian. *Making sense: reading comprehension improved through categorizing.* Newark, Del.: International Reading Association, 1975.

Geyer, John J. Perceptual systems in reading: the prediction of a temporal eye-voice span. In Helen K. Smith (Ed.), *Perception and reading.* Newark, Del.: International Reading Association, 1968. Pp. 44–52.

Geyer, John J. Comprehensive and partial models related to the reading process. *Reading Research Quarterly,* Summer 1972, 7, 541–87.

Gibson, Eleanor J. The ontogeny of reading. *American Psychologist,* 1970, 25, 136–43.

Gibson, Eleanor J. & Levin, Harry. *The psychology of reading.* Cambridge, Mass.: M.I.T. Press, 1975.

Gladney, Mildred R. A teaching strategy. In R. E. Hodges & E. H. Rudorf (Eds.), *Language and learning to read: What teachers should know about language.* Boston: Houghton Mifflin, 1972. Pp. 73–83.

Glasner, Robert. Adapting the elementary school curriculum to individual performances. *Proceedings of the 1967 invitational conference on teaching problems.* Princeton, N.J.: Educational Testing Service, 1968.

Glass, Gerald G. *Teaching decoding as separate from reading.* Garden City, N.Y.: Adelphi University Press, 1973.

Glass, Gerald G. & Burton, Elizabeth H. How do they decode? verbalizations and observed behaviors of successful decoders. *The Reading Teacher,* March 1973, 26, 645.

Gleitman, Lila R. & Rozin, Paul. Teaching reading by use of a syllabary. *Reading Research Quarterly,* Summer 1973, 8, 447–83.

Golub, Lester S. A computer assisted literacy development program. *Journal of Reading,* January 1974, *17,* 279–84.

Gomberg, Adeline W.   Freeing children to take a chance. *The Reading Teacher*, February 1976, *29*, 455–57.

Gonzales, Phillip C. & Elijah, David V. Jr.   Rereading effect on error patterns and performance levels on the IRI. *The Reading Teacher*, April 1975, 28, 647, 652.

Goodman, Kenneth S.   Dialect barriers to reading comprehension. *Elementary English*, December 1965, 42, 853–60.

Goodman, Kenneth S.   Analysis of reading miscues: applied psycholinguistics. *Reading Research Quarterly*, Fall 1969, 5, 9–30.

Goodman, Kenneth S.   The reading process: theory and practice. In R. E. Hodges & E. H. Rudorf (Eds.), *Language and learning to read: what teachers should know about language*. Boston: Houghton Mifflin, 1972. Pp. 143–59.

Goodman, Kenneth S. (Ed.).   *Miscue analysis: application to reading instruction*. Urbana, Ill.: National Council of Teachers of English and ERIC/RCS, 1973. (a)

Goodman, Kenneth S.   Miscues: windows on the reading process. In K. S. Goodman (Ed.), *Miscue analysis: applications to reading instruction*. Urbana, Ill.: National Council of Teachers of English and ERIC/RCS, 1973. Pp. 3–14. (b)

Goodman, Kenneth S.   Do you have to be smart to read? Do you have to read to be smart? *The Reading Teacher*, April 1975, 28, 625–32.

Goodman, Kenneth S.   Miscue analysis: theory and reality in reading. In John G. Merritt (Ed.), *New horizons in reading*. Newark, Del.: International Reading Association, 1976. Pp. 15–26. (a)

Goodman, Kenneth S.   Reading: A psycholinguistic guessing game. In H. Singer & R. B. Ruddell (Eds.), *Theoretical models and processes of reading*. 2nd ed. Newark, Del.: International Reading Association, 1976. Pp. 497–508. (b)

Goodman, Yetta M.   Reading strategy lessons: expanding reading effectiveness. In William D. Page (Ed.), *Help for the reading teacher: new directions in research*. Urbana, Ill.: National Conference on Research in English and ERIC/RCS, March 1975. Pp. 34–41.

Goodman, Yetta M.   Miscues, errors, and reading comprehension. In John E. Merritt (Ed.), *New horizons in reading*. Newark, Del.: International Reading Association, 1976. Pp. 86–93.

Goodman, Yetta & Burke, Carolyn.   *Reading miscue inventory*. New York: Macmillan, 1972.

Goodman, Yetta & Greene, Jennifer.   Grammar and reading in the classroom. In Roger Shuy (Ed.), *Linguistic theory: what can it say about reading?* Newark, Del.: International Reading Association, 1977. Pp. 18–31.

Goodman, Yetta & Sims, Rudine.   Whose dialect for beginning readers. *Elementary English*, September 1974, 51, 837–41.

Goolsby, T. M. & Frary, R. B.   Effect of massive intervention on achievement of first grade students. *Journal of Experimental Education*, 1970, 39, 46–52.

Gough, Pauline B.   Sexism in basal readers: a continuing trend. *Indiana Reading Quarterly*, Spring 1974, 6, 27–30.

Gove, Mary K.   Using the cloze procedure in a first grade classroom. *The Reading Teacher*, October 1975, *29*, 36–38.

Gray, William S. The major aspects of reading. In Helen M. Robinson (Ed.), *Sequential development of reading abilities.* Supplementary Educational Monographs, No. 90. Chicago: University of Chicago Press, 1960. Pp. 8–24.

Greene, H. Ross & Kersey, Harry A. Upgrading Indian education: a case study of the Seminoles. *School Review,* February 1975, *83,* 345–61.

Grendstaff, Faye L. & Muller, Al. The National Assessment of Literature: two reviews. *Research in the Teaching of English,* Spring 1975, *9,* 80–106.

Griese, Arnold A. Focusing on students of different cultural backgrounds—the Eskimo and Indian pupil—special problems in reading comprehension. *Elementary English,* April 1971, *48,* 229–34.

Griffen, Louise (Comp.). *Multi-ethnic books for young children: annotated bibliography for parents and teachers.* Washington, D.C.: National Association for the Education of Young Children, 1970.

Groff, Patrick. *The syllable: its nature and pedagogical usefulness.* Portland, Ore.: Northwest Regional Educational Laboratory, April 1971.

Groff, Patrick. Let's update storytelling. *Language Arts,* March 1977, *54,* 272–77, 286.

Grommon, Alfred H. Problems and recommendations. In Alfred H. Grommon (Ed.), *Reviews of selected published tests in English.* Urbana, Ill.: National Council of Teachers of English, 1976. Pp. 141–65.

Gronlund, Norman E. *Stating behavioral objectives for classroom instruction.* New York: Macmillan, 1970.

Gronlund, Norman E. *Preparing criterion-referenced tests for classroom instruction.* New York: Macmillan, 1973.

Guinet, Lynne. Evaluation of DISTAR materials in three junior learning assistance classes. Vancouver, Canada: Department of Planning and Evaluation, Board of School Trustees, July 1971. Pp. 2–4.

Gunderson, Doris V. Are linguistic programs different? In Robert C. Aukerman (Ed.), *Some persistent questions on beginning reading.* Newark, Del.: International Reading Association, 1972. Pp. 115–25.

Guralnick, Michael J. Alphabet discrimination and distinctive features: research review and educational implications. *Journal of Learning Disabilities.* August/September 1972, *5,* 428–34.

Guszak, Frank J. Teacher questioning and reading. *The Reading Teacher,* December 1967, *21,* 227–34.

Guszak, Frank J. *Diagnostic reading instruction in the elementary school.* New York: Harper & Row, 1972.

Guthrie, John T. Reading comprehension and syntactic responses in good and poor readers. *Journal of Educational Psychology,* December 1973, *65,* 294–99.

Guthrie, John T. et al. The maze technique to assess, monitor reading comprehension. *The Reading Teacher,* November 1974, *28,* 160–68.

Hafner, Lawrence E. (Ed.). *Improving reading in middle and secondary schools: selected readings.* 2nd ed. New York: Macmillan, 1974.

Hafner, Lawrence E. *Developmental reading in middle and secondary schools.* New York: Macmillan, 1977.

Hakes, Judith.   Home living Navajo style. *Language Arts*, September 1975, *52*, 870–71, 901.

Haley, Beverly.   Once upon a time—they lived happily. *Language Arts*, November/December 1975, *52*, 1147–53.

Hall, Maryanne.   *Teaching reading as a language experience*. Columbus, Ohio: Charles E. Merrill, 1970.

Hall, Maryanne.   *The language experience approach for the culturally disadvantaged*. Newark, Del.: International Reading Association, 1972.

Hall, Vernon C. & Turner, Ralph R.   The validity of the "different language explanation" for poor scholastic performance by black students. *Review of Educational Research*, Winter 1974, *44*, 69–81.

Hall, Vernon C.; Turner, Ralph R.; & Russell, William.   Ability of children from four subcultures and two grade levels to imitate and comprehend crucial aspects of standard English: a test of the different language explanation. *Journal of Educational Psychology*, April 1973, *64*, 147–58.

Hamilton, Harlan.   TV tie-ins as a bridge to books. *Language Arts*, February 1976, *53*, 129–30.

Hammill, Donald; Goodman, Libby; & Wiederholt, J. Lee.   Visual-motor processes: can we train them? *The Reading Teacher*, February 1974, *27*, 469–78.

Hammill, Donald & Larsen, Stephen C.   The relationship of selected auditory perceptual skills and reading ability. *Journal of Learning Disabilities*, *47*, August/September 1974, 429–35.

Hammill, Donald & Mattleman, Marciene. An evaluation of a programmed reading approach in primary grades. *Elementary English*, March 1969, *46*, 310–12.

Hansen, Harlan S.   The home literacy environment—a follow-up report. *Elementary English*, January 1973, *50*, 97–98, 122.

Hardy, Madeline; Stennett, R. G.; & Smythe, P. C.   Word attack: how do they "figure them out"? *Elementary English*, January 1973, *50*, 99–102.

Hardy, Madeline; Stennett, R. G.; & Smythe, P. C.   Development of auditory and visual language concepts and relationship to instructional strategies in kindergarten. *Elementary English*, April 1974, *51*, 525–32.

Harker, W. John.   Classroom implications from models of reading comprehension. In Bonnie S. Schulwitz (Ed.), *Teachers, tangibles, techniques: comprehension of content in reading*. Newark, Del.: International Reading Association, 1975. Pp. 2–9.

Harrigan, John E.   Initial reading instruction: phonemes, syllables, or ideographs. *Journal of Learning Disabilities*, February 1976, *9*, 74–80.

Harris, Albert J.   Lateral dominance, directional confusion, and reading disability. *Journal of Psychology*, 1957, *44*, 283–94.

Harris, Albert J.   The effective teacher of reading. *The Reading Teacher*, December 1969, *23*, 195–204.

Harris, Albert J.   New dimensions in basal readers. *The Reading Teacher*, January 1972, *22*, 310–15.

Harris, Albert J.   Develop administrative and supervisory competence in teaching reading. *Reading Improvement*, Spring 1976, *13*, 48–52.

Harris, Albert J. & Jacobson, Milton D.   *Basic elementary reading vocabularies.*
New York: Macmillan, 1972.

Harris, Albert J. & Jacobson, Milton D.   Some comparisons between Basic
Elementary Reading Vocabularies and other word lists. *Reading Research
Quarterly,* No. 1, 1973–74, *9,* 87–109.

Harris, Albert J.; Morrison, Coleman; Serwer, Blanche L.; & Gold, Lawrence.   A
continuation of the CRAFT Project: comparing reading approaches with disadvantaged urban Negro children in primary grades. Final Report, USOE.
Project No. 5–0570–2–12–1. New York: Selected Academic Readings, 1968.

Harris, Albert J. & Serwer, Blanche L.   The CRAFT Project: instructional time
in reading research. *Reading Research Quarterly,* Fall 1966, 2, 27–56. (a)

Harris, Albert J. & Serwer, Blanche L.   *Comparison of reading approaches in
first-grade teaching with disadvantaged children* (The CRAFT Project). Final
Report, Cooperative Research Project No. 2677. New York: Division of
Teacher Education, The City University of New York, 1966. (b)

Harris, Albert J. & Sipay, Edward R.   *The Macmillan Reading Readiness Test,
RE: manual for administering, scoring, and interpreting.* New York: Macmillan, 1970.

Harris, Albert J. & Sipay, Edward R. (Eds.).   *Readings on reading instruction.*
2nd ed. New York: David McKay, 1972.

Harris, Albert J. & Sipay, Edward R.   *How to Increase Reading Ability.* 6th ed.
New York: David McKay, 1975.

Harris, Larry A. & Smith, Carl B.   *Reading instruction through diagnostic
teaching.* 2nd ed. New York: Holt, Rinehart and Winston, 1976.

Harris, Louis T. & Associates.   Survival literacy study. *Congressional Record,*
18 November 1970. Pp. E9719–23.

Harris, Theodore L.   Reading flexibility: a neglected aspect of reading instruction. In John E. Merritt (Ed.), *New horizons in reading.* Newark, Del.: International Reading Association, 1976. Pp. 27–35.

Harris, Theodore L.; Creekmore, Mildred; & Matteoni, Louise.   Teacher's
manual to accompany *Pug.* Oklahoma City: Economy Company, 1975.

Hart, B.   *Teaching reading to deaf children.* Washington, D.C.: Volta Bureau,
1963.

Hartley, James & Davies, Ivor K.   Preinstructional strategies: the role of pretests, behavioral objectives, overviews and advance organizers. *Review of
Educational Research,* Spring 1976, 46, 239–65.

Hatch, Evelyn.   Research on reading a second language. *Journal of Reading
Behavior,* April 1974, 6, 53–61.

Hayes, Robert B. & Wuest, Richard C.   *Factors affecting learning to read.* Final
Report, Project No. 6–1752. Harrisburg, Pa.: State Education Department,
1967.

Heilman, Arthur W.   *Principles and practices of teaching reading.* 3rd ed. Columbus, Ohio: Charles E. Merrill, 1972.

Heilman, Arthur W. & Holmes, Elizabeth Ann.   *Smuggling language into the
teaching of reading.* Columbus, Ohio: Charles E. Merrill, 1972.

Helfeldt, John P. & Lalik, Rosary.   Reciprocal student-teacher questioning. *The Reading Teacher*, December 1976, *30*, 283–87.

Henderson, Norman B., et al.   Will the IQ test ban decrease the effectiveness of reading prediction? *Journal of Educational Psychology*, December 1973, *65*, 345–55.

Henning, Kathleen.   Drama reading, an on-going classroom activity at the elementary school level. *Elementary English*, January 1974, *51*, 48–51, 65.

Henry, George H.   *Teaching reading as concept development: emphasis on affective thinking.* Newark, Del.: International Reading Association, 1974.

Herber, Harold L. & Nelson, Joan B.   Questioning is not the answer. *Journal of Reading*, April 1975, *18*, 512–17.

Herr, Selma E.   *Learning activities for reading.* 3rd ed. Dubuque, Iowa: William C. Brown, 1977.

Hill, Walter R.   Reading testing for reading evaluation. In William E. Blanton et al. (Eds.), *Measuring reading performance.* Newark, Del.: International Reading Association, 1974. Pp. 1–14.

Hillerich, Robert L.   Word lists—getting it all together. *The Reading Teacher*, January 1974, *27*, 353–60.

Himmelsteib, Carol.   Buddies read in a library program. *The Reading Teacher*, October, 1975, *29*, 32–35.

Hirshoren, Alfred; Hunt, Jacob T.; & Davis, Caroline.   Classified ads as reading material for the educable retarded. *Exceptional Children*, September 1974, *41*, 45–47.

Hittleman, Daniel R.   Seeking a psycholinguistic definition of readability. *The Reading Teacher*, May 1973, *26*, 783–89.

Hockman, Carol H.   Black dialect reading tests in the urban elementary school. *The Reading Teacher*, March 1973, *26*, 581–83.

Hodges, Elaine J.   A comparison of the functional reading levels of selected third grade students of varying reading abilities. Doctoral dissertation, University of Northern Colorado, 1972.

Hodges, Richard E.   Theoretical frameworks of English orthography. *Elementary English*, November 1972, *49*, 1089–97.

Hodges, Richard E. & Rudorf, E. Hugh (Eds.).   *Language and learning to read: what teachers should know about language.* Boston: Houghton Mifflin, 1972.

Hoffman, M. S.   Early indications of learning problems. *Academic Therapy*, Fall 1971, *7*, 23–35.

Holden, M. & MacGinitie, Walter.   Metalinguistic ability and cognitive performance in children from five to seven. Paper presented at the American Educational Research Association meeting, New Orleans, February 1973.

Hollander, Sheila K.   Why's a busy teacher like you giving an IRI? *Elementary English*, September 1974, *51*, 905–7.

Holloway, Ruth L.   Professional and paraprofessional roles in an industrial society. In John E. Merritt (Ed.), *New horizons in reading.* Newark, Del.: International Reading Association, 1976. Pp. 524–29.

Hood, Joyce.   The effect of readability of stories on oral reading error scores. In

Abstracts: literacy & beyond. Newark, Del.: International Reading Association, 1976. P. 69.

Hood, Joyce & Kendall, Janet R.   A qualitative analysis of oral reading errors of reflective and impulsive second graders: a follow-up study. *Journal of Reading Behavior,* Fall 1975, *7,* 269–81.

Hoover, M. E. R.   Appropriate use of black English by black children as rated by parents. *Dissertation Abstracts International,* 1975, *36,* 2079A.

Hormann, Elizabeth.   Children's crisis literature. *Language Arts,* May 1977, *54,* 559–66.

Horn, Thomas D. (Ed.).   *Reading for the disadvantaged: problems of linguistically different learners.* New York: Harcourt Brace Jovanovich, 1970.

Hoskisson, Kenneth.   "False" questions and "right" answers. *The Reading Teacher,* November 1973, *27,* 159–62.

Howes, Virgil M. (Ed.).   *Individualizing instruction in reading and social studies: selected readings on programs and practices.* New York: Macmillan, 1970.

Huey, Edmund B.   *The psychology and pedagogy of reading.* New York: Macmillan, 1908. Reprinted by M.I.T. Press, Cambridge, Mass., 1968.

Humphrey, Jack W. & Redden, Sandra R.   Encouraging young authors. *The Reading Teacher,* April 1972, *25,* 643–51.

Hunkins, Francis P.   *Questioning strategies and techniques.* Boston: Allyn & Bacon, 1972.

Hunkins, Francis P.   *Involving students in questioning.* Boston: Allyn & Bacon, 1976.

Hunt, Barbara C.   Black dialect and third and fourth graders' performance on the *Gray Oral Reading Test. Reading Research Quarterly,* No. 1, 1974–75, *10,* 103–23.

Hunt, Lyman C., Jr.   The effect of self-selection, interest, and motivation upon independent, instructional, and frustration levels. *The Reading Teacher,* November 1970, *24,* 146–51.

Hunt, Lyman C., Jr.   Six steps to the individualized reading program (IRP). *Elementary English,* January 1971, *48,* 27–32.

Hurley, Oliver J.   Reading comprehension skills vis-à-vis the mentally retarded. *Education and Training of the Mentally Retarded.* February 1975, *10,* 10–14.

Huus, Helen.   Antidote for apathy—acquiring reading skills for social studies. In Lawrence E. Hafner (Ed.), *Improving reading in middle and secondary schools.* 2nd ed. New York: Macmillan, 1974. Pp. 374–85.

Huus, Helen.   Approaches to the use of literature in the reading program. In Bonnie S. Schulwitz (Ed.), *Teachers, tangibles, techniques: comprehension of content in reading.* Newark, Del.: International Reading Association, 1975. Pp. 140–49.

Ingram, T. T. S.   The nature of dyslexia. *Bulletin of the Orton Society,* 1969, *19,* 18–50.

Issacs, Ann F.   Creative reading can be a balance and an anchor in guiding the gifted. In M. Labuda (Ed.), *Creative reading for the gifted learner: a design for excellence.* Newark, Del.: International Reading Association, 1974. Pp. 110–22.

Jacobs, Leland.   Individualized reading is not a thing. In Alice Miel (Ed.), *Individualizing reading practices.* Practical Suggestions for Teaching, No. 14. New York: Bureau of Publications, Teachers College, Columbia University, 1958. Pp. 1–17.

Jamison, Dean; Suppes, Patrick; & Wells, Stuart.   The effectiveness of alternative instructional media: a survey. *Review of Educational Research,* Winter 1974, *44,* 1–67.

Jansky, Jeanette & de Hirsch, Katrina.   *Preventing reading failure: prediction, diagnosis, intervention.* New York: Harper & Row, 1972.

Jassoy, Mary E.   Migrant children: we can teach them. In Brother Leonard Courtney (Ed.), *Reading interaction: the teacher, the pupil, the materials.* Newark, Del.: International Reading Association, 1976. Pp. 67–74.

Jenkins, William A.   Elementary school language tests. In Alfred H. Grommon (Ed.), *Reviews of selected published tests in English.* Urbana, Ill.: National Council of Teachers of English, 1976. Pp. 52–75.

Johns, Jerry L.   What do inner city children prefer to read? *The Reading Teacher,* February 1973, *26,* 462–67.

Johns, Jerry L.   Reading preferences of urban students in grades four through six. *The Journal of Educational Research,* April 1975, *68,* 306–9.

Johns, Jerry L.   Some comparisons between the Dolch Basic Sight Vocabulary and the Word List for the 1970's. *Reading World,* March 1976, *15,* 144–50.

Johns, Jerry L. & Lunt, Linda.   Motivating reading: professional ideas. *The Reading Teacher,* April 1975, *28,* 617–19.

Johnson, Dale D.   Sex differences in reading across cultures. *Reading Research Quarterly,* No. 1, 1973–74, *9,* 67–86.

Johnson, Dale D.   The teaching of reading. *The Journal of Educational Research,* May–June 1974, *67,* 412–20.

Johnson, Dale D. & Pearson, P. David.   Skills management systems: a critique. *The Reading Teacher,* May 1975, *28,* 757–64.

Johnson, Kenneth R.   Black dialect shift in oral reading. *Journal of Reading,* April 1975, *18,* 535–40.

Johnson, Kenneth R.   Accountability and educating black children in reading and the language arts. *Language Arts,* February 1977, *54,* 144–49.

Johnson, Laura S.   Bilingual bicultural education: a two-way street. *The Reading Teacher,* December 1975, *29,* 231–39. (a)

Johnson, Laura S.   The newspaper as an instructional medium. In Bonnie S. Schulwitz (Ed.), *Teachers, tangibles, techniques: comprehension of content in reading.* Newark, Del.: International Reading Association, 1975. Pp. 76–82. (b)

Johnson, Marjorie S. & Kress, Roy A.   *Informal reading inventories.* Newark, Del.: International Reading Association, 1965.

Johnson, Roger E.   The reading level of elementary social studies textbooks is going down. *The Reading Teacher,* May 1977, *30,* 901–6.

Johnson, Roger E. & Vardian, Eileen B.   Reading, readability and social studies. *The Reading Teacher,* February 1973, *26,* 438–88.

Johnson, Ronald J.   The effect of training in letter names on success in begin-
ning reading for children of differing abilities. Paper presented at the Amer-
ican Educational Research Association convention, 1970.
Johnson, Simon S.   How students feel about literature. *American Education,*
April 1974, *10,* 6–10.
Jolly, Constance & Jolly, Robert.   *When you teach English as a second language.*
Brooklyn, N.Y.: Book-Lab, 1974.
Jones, Virginia W.   *Decoding and learning to read.* Portland, Ore.: Northwest
Educational Laboratory, 1970.
Jongsma, Eugene.   An analysis of the language patterns of standardized read-
ing comprehension tests and their effect on student performance. *Journal of
Reading Behavior,* December 1974, *6,* 353–66.
Jorgenson, Gerald W.   An analysis of teacher judgment of reading level. *Amer-
ican Educational Research Journal,* Winter 1975, *12,* 67–76.
Kagan, Jerome, Reflection-impulsivity and reading abilities in primary grade chil-
dren. *Child Development,* 1965, *36,* 609–28.
Kaplan, Robert & Simmons, Francine G. Effects of instructional objectives as
orienting stimuli or as summary/review upon prose learning. *Journal of Edu-
cational Psychology,* August 1974, *66,* 614–22.
Karlsen, Bjorn & Blocker, Margaret.   Black children and final consonant blends.
The Reading Teacher, February 1974, *27,* 462–63.
Karre, Idahlynn.   The response of middle school students to affective and cogni-
tive approaches to teaching literature: an experimental study. Reported in
Jane Porter, Research report. *Language Arts,* March 1976, *53,* 341–44.
Kennedy, Delores K. & Weener, Paul.   Visual and auditory training with the
cloze procedure to improve reading and listening comprehension. *Reading
Research Quarterly,* Summer 1973, *8,* 524–41.
Keogh, Barbara K. & Becher, Lawrence D.   Early detection of learning prob-
lems: questions, cautions and guidelines. *Exceptional Children,* September
1973, *40,* 5–11.
Keogh, Barbara K. & Smith, C. E.   Early identification of educationally high-
potential and high-risk children. *Journal of School Psychology,* 1970, *8,* 285–90.
Keogh, Barbara K.; Tchir, Cheryl; & Windeguth-Behn, Adele.   Teacher's percep-
tion of educationally high risk children. *Journal of Learning Disabilities,*
June/July 1974, *7,* 367–74.
Kerber, James E.   *Tasks of teaching reading.* Worthington, Ohio: Charles A.
Jones, 1974.
Kerber, James E.   The tasks of teaching reading. *Language Arts,* April 1976,
53, 414–15, 421.
Kerfoot, James F. (Ed.).   *First grade reading programs.* Newark, Del.: Inter-
national Reading Association, 1965.
Kilty, Ted K.   The readability of commonly encountered materials. Mimeo-
graphed, Western Michigan University, Kalamazoo, Mich., 1976.
King, Martha; Ellenger, Bernice D.; & Wolf, Willavene (Eds.).   *Readings in
critical reading.* Philadelphia: J. B. Lippincott, 1967.
Kingston, Albert J.; Weaver, Wendell W.; & Figa, Leslie E.   Experiments in

children's perceptions of words and word boundaries. In F. P. Greene (Ed.), *Investigations relating to mature reading*. Boone, N.C.: National Reading Conference, 1972. Pp. 91–99.

Kiraly, John Jr. & Furlong, Alexandra. Teaching words to kindergarten children with picture, configuration, and initial sound cues in a prompting procedure. *The Journal of Educational Research*, March 1974, 67, 295–98.

Kirkland, Lorraine; Clowers, Wilda; & Wood, Betsy. What do teenagers read? In Lawrence E. Hafner (Ed.), *Improving reading in middle and secondary schools: selected readings*. 2nd ed. New York: Macmillan, 1974, Pp. 434–38.

Kirkness, Verna J. Prejudice about Indians in textbooks. *Journal of Reading*, April 1977, 20, 595–600.

Kirsch, Dorothy. From athletes to zebras—young children want to read about them. *Elementary English*, January 1975, 52, 73–78.

Klare, George R. Assessing readability. *Reading Research Quarterly*, 1974–75, 10, No. 1, 62–102.

Klare, George R. A second look at the validity of readability formulas. *Journal of Reading Behavior*, Summer 1976, 8, 129–52.

Kleederman, Frances F. Black English and reading problems: sociolinguistic considerations. *Reading World*, May 1975, 14, 256–67.

Klein, Helen A.; Klein, Gary A.; & Bertino, Mary. Utilization of context for word identification decisions in children. *Journal of Experimental Child Psychology*, February 1974, 17, 79–86.

Klein, Maro. A stab at teaching comprehension of the conditional. *Journal of Reading*, November 1975, 19, 154–59.

Klein, Stephen P. & Kosecoff, Jacqueline. Issues and procedures in the development of criterion referenced tests. TM Report 26. Princeton, N.J.: ERIC Clearinghouse on Tests, Measurement and Evaluation, September 1973.

Klesius, Stephen E. Perceptual motor development and reading—a closer look. In Robert C. Aukerman (Ed.), *Some persistent questions on beginning reading*. Newark, Del.: International Reading Association, 1972. Pp. 151–59.

Klink, Howard. Words and music. *Language Arts*, April 1976, 53, 401–3.

Knight, David W. & Bethune, Paul. Science words students know. In Laurence E. Hafner (Ed.), *Improving reading in middle and secondary schools*. 2nd ed. New York: Macmillan, 1974. Pp. 304–7.

Knight, Lester N. & Hargis, Charles H. Math language ability: its relationship to reading in math. *Language Arts*, April 1977, 54, 423–28.

Kocher, Margaret. Annotated bibliography. In Bernice E. Cullinan (Ed.), *Black dialects and reading*. Urbana, Ill.: ERIC/RCS and National Council of Teachers of English, 1974. Pp. 155–89.

Kolcznski, Richard. Boys' right to read: sex factors in learning to read. In Jerry L. Johns (Ed.), *Literacy for diverse learners: promoting reading growth at all levels*. Newark, Del.: International Reading Association, 1974. Pp. 39–45.

Kreider, Barbara. *Index to children's plays in collection*. Metuchen, N.J.: Scarecrow Press, 1972.

Kulhavy, R. W. & Swenson, I. Imagery instruction and the comprehension of text. *British Journal of Educational Psychology*, 1975, 45, 47–51.

Kurtz, P. D.   The effect of instructional objectives on student learning. *The Alberta Journal of Educational Research*, December 1974, 20, 327–33.

Labov, William.   *Language of the inner city: studies in Black English vernacular*. Urbana, Ill.: National Council of Teachers of English, 1972.

Labov, William & Cohen, Paul.   Some suggestions for teaching standard English to speakers of nonstandard and urban dialects. In Johanna S. DeStefano (Ed.), *Language, society; and education: a profile of black English*. Worthington, Ohio: Charles E. Jones, 1973. Pp. 218–37.

Labuda, Michael (Ed.).   *Creative reading for gifted learners: a design for excellence*. Newark, Del.: International Reading Association, 1974. (a)

Labuda, Michael. Gifted and creative pupils: reasons for concern. In M. Labuda (Ed.), *Creative reading for gifted learners: a design for excellence*. Newark, Del.: International Reading Association, 1974. Pp. 2–7. (b)

Lacey, Patricia A. & Weil, Philip E.   Number-reading-language! *Language Arts*, September 1975, 52, 776–82.

Ladley, Winifred C.   *Sources of good books and magazines for children: an annotated bibliography*. Newark, Del.: International Reading Association, 1970.

Laffey, James L.   *Methods of reading instruction: an annotated bibliography*. Newark, Del.: International Reading Association, 1971.

Laffey, James L. & Shuy, Roger (Eds.).   *Language differences: do they interfere?* Newark, Del.: International Reading Association, 1973.

Lake, Mary L.   First aid for vocabularies. *Elementary English*, November 1967, 44, 783–84.

Lake, Mary L.   Improve the dictionary's image. *Elementary English*, March 1971, 48, 363–66.

Lamb, Pose.   Reading and television in the United States. In John E. Merritt (Ed.), *New horizons in reading*, Newark, Del.: International Reading Association, 1976. Pp. 370–82.

Lamme, Linda L.   Are reading habits and abilities related? *The Reading Teacher*, October 1976, 30, 21–27. (a)

Lamme, Linda L.   Reading aloud to young children. *Language Arts*, November/December 1976, 53, 886–88. (b)

Lane, Helen S. & Baker, Dorthea.   Reading achievement of the deaf: another look. *The Volta Review*, November 1974, 76, 489–99.

Larrick, Nancy.   *A parent's guide to children's reading*. 4th ed. New York: Doubleday, 1975.

Larrick, Nancy.   The paperback bonanza. In Brother Leonard Courtney (Ed.), *Reading interaction: the teacher, the pupil, the materials*. Newark, Del.: International Reading Association, 1976. Pp. 101–5.

Larson, Martha L.   Reader's theatre: new vitality for oral reading. *The Reading Teacher*, January 1976, 29, 359–60.

Lauritizen, Carol & Cheves, Deborah.   Children's reading interests classified by age level. *The Reading Teacher*, April 1974, 27, 694–700.

Lazar, Alfred L.   Reading programs and materials for the educable mentally retarded. In Helen K. Smith (Ed.), *Meeting individual needs in reading*. Newark, Del.: International Reading Association, 1971. Pp. 74–84.

Lee, Dorris; Bingham, Alma; & Woelfel, Sue. *Critical reading begins early.* Newark, Del.: International Reading Association, 1968.

Leeds, Donald S. Content, interest, and role as sociological factors affecting reading performance. *Reading World,* December 1974, *14,* 149–59.

Leibert, Robert E. (Ed.). *A place to start.* Kansas City, Mo.: University of Missouri Reading Center, 1971.

Lenneberg, E. H. *Biological foundations of language.* New York: John Wiley & Sons, 1967.

Lessler, Ken & Bridges, Judith S. The prediction of learning problems in a rural setting: can we improve on readiness tests? *Journal of Learning Disabilities,* February 1973, *6,* 90–94.

Levin, Joel R. Comprehending what we read: an outsider looks in. In H. Singer & R. B. Ruddell (Eds.), *Theoretical models and processes of reading.* 2nd ed. Newark, Del.: International Reading Association, 1976. Pp. 320–30.

Levin, Harry & Turner, E. A. Sentence structure and the eye-voice span. Studies in oral reading IX, preliminary draft. ED 011 957. Project No. B.R. 5–1213–9–OEC–6–10, September 1966.

Levin, Harry & Watson, J. The learning of variable grapheme-to-phoneme correspondence. In Harry Levin et al., *A basic research program on reading.* Final Report, Cooperative Research Project No. 639, 1962.

Lewis, Jeneva B. A comparison of kindergarten teachers' perceptions of children's preferences in books with the children's actual preferences. Doctoral dissertation, East Texas State University, 1970.

Liberman, Isabelle Y., et al. Letter confusion and reversals of sequence in the beginning reader: implication for Orton's theory of developmental dyslexia. *Cortex,* June 1971, *7,* 127–42.

Liberman, Isabelle Y., et al. Explicit syllable and phoneme segmentation in the young child. *Journal of Experimental Child Psychology,* October 1974, *18,* 201–12.

Lickteig, Mary Jane. A comparison of book selection preferences of innercity and suburban fourth and sixth graders. Doctoral dissertation, University of Oregon, 1972.

Liu, Stella S. F. An investigation of oral reading miscues made by nonstandard dialect speaking black children (abstract). *Reading Research Quarterly,* 1975–76, *11,* No. 2, 193–97.

Lohnes, Paul R. Evaluating the schooling of intelligence. *Educational Researcher,* February 1973, *2,* 6–11.

Lohnes, Paul R. & Gray, Marian M. Intelligence and the cooperative reading studies. *Reading Research Quarterly,* Spring 1972, *7,* 466–76.

Long, Barbara H. & Henderson, Edmund H. Certain determinants of academic expectancies among Southern and non-Southern teachers. *American Educational Research Journal,* Spring 1974, *11,* 137–47.

Lopardo, Genevieve S. LEA-cloze reading material for the disabled reader. *The Reading Teacher,* October 1975, *29,* 42–44.

Loret, Peter G., et al. *Anchor test study: equivalence and norms tables for*

selected reading achievement tests (grades 4, 5, 6). Stock# 1780–01312.
Washington, D.C.: U.S. Department of HEW, USOE, 1974.

Lowe, A. J. & Follman, John. Comparison of the Dolch list with other word
lists. *The Reading Teacher,* October 1974, 28, 40–44.

Lumsden, D. Barry. Programed instruction: buyer beware! *Journal of Reading,*
October 1975, 19, 52–54.

Lundahl, Flemming. Split-half classes. In John E. Merritt (Ed.), *New horizons
in reading.* Newark, Del.: International Reading Association, 1976. Pp. 428–
33.

Lundsteen, Sara W. *Listening: its impact on reading and the other language
arts.* Urbana, Ill.: National Council of Teachers of English, 1971.

Lynch, Lorraine. Open to suggestion: designing a reading file. *Journal of
Reading,* May 1976, 19, 668–69.

MacDonald, James B.; Harris, Theodore L.; & Marin, John S. Individual versus group instruction in first grade reading. *The Reading Teacher,* May 1966,
19, 643–46.

MacGinitie, Walter H. Evaluating readiness for learning to read: a critical review and evaluation of research. *Reading Research Quarterly,* Spring 1969, 4,
396–410.

MacGinitie, Walter H. (Ed.). *Assessment problems in reading.* Newark, Del.:
International Reading Association, 1973. (a)

MacGinitie, Walter H. Testing reading achievement in urban schools. *The
Reading Teacher,* October 1973, 27, 13–21. (b)

MacGinitie, Walter H. Difficulty with logical operations. *The Reading Teacher,*
January 1976, 29, 371–75.

Mackworth, Jane F. Some models of the reading process: learners and skilled
readers. *Reading Research Quarterly,* Summer 1972, 7, 701–33.

Mackworth, Jane F. & Mackworth, Norman H. How children read: matching
by sight and sound. *Journal of Reading Behavior,* September 1974, 6, 295–303.

Mackworth, Norman H. The line of sight approach. In Stanley F. Wanat (Ed.),
Language and reading comprehension. Arlington, Va.: Center for Applied
Linguistics, May 1977. Pp. 1–22.

Maffei, Anthony C. Reading analysis in mathematics. *Journal of Reading,*
April 1973, 16, 546–49.

Malicky, Grace V. The effect of deletion produced structures on word identification and comprehension of beginning readers (abstract). *Reading Research
Quarterly,* No. 2, 1975–76, 11, 212–16.

Mallett, Jerry J. Add spice to vocabulary study. *Language Arts,* September
1975, 52, 843–46.

Mann, Lester. Review of the Frostig Developmental Tests of Visual Perception.
In Oscar K. Buros (Ed.), *The seventh mental measurements yearbook,* Vol. II.
Highland Park, N.J.: Gryphon Press, 1972. Pp. 871–73.

Mantell, Arlene. Strategies for language expansion in the middle grades. In
Bernice E. Cullinan (Ed.), *Black dialects and reading.* Urbana, Ill.: ERIC/
RCS and National Council of Teachers of English, 1974. Pp. 55–68.

Manzo, Anthony V.   Guided reading procedure. *Journal of Reading*, January 1975, *18*, 287–91.

Marcus, Albert.   Diagnosis and accountability. *Elementary English*, May 1974, *51*, 731–35.

Marston, Emily.   Children's poetry preferences: a review. *Research in the Teaching of English*, Spring 1975, *9*, 107–10.

Marwit, Samuel J. & Neumann, Gail.   Black and white children's comprehension of standard and nonstandard English passages. *Journal of Educational Psychology*, June 1974, *66*, 329–32.

Mathews, Mitford M.   *Teaching to read: historically considered.* Chicago: University of Chicago Press, 1966.

Mattleman, Marciene.   *101 activities for teaching reading.* Portland, Me.: Walch, 1973.

Mavrogenes, Nancy A.; Hanson, Earl F.; & Winkley, Carol K.   A guide to tests of factors that inhibit learning to read. *The Reading Teacher*, January 1976, *29*, 343–58.

May, Frank B.   *To help children read.* Columbus, Ohio: Charles E. Merrill, 1973.

Mays, Deril K.   The experimental analysis of error behavior in oral reading. In Phil L. Nacke (Ed.), *Interaction: research and practice for college-adult reading.* Clemson, S.C.: National Reading Conference, 1974. Pp. 140–52.

Mazurkiewicz, Albert J.   What do teachers know about phonics. *Reading World*, March 1975, *14*, 165–77. (a)

Mazurkiewicz, Albert J.   What the professor doesn't know about phonics can hurt! *Reading World*, December 1975, *15*, 65–86. (b)

McCormick, Sandra.   Choosing books to read to preschool children. *Language Arts*, May 1977, *54*, 543–48. (a)

McCormick, Sandra.   Should you read aloud to your children? *Language Arts*, February 1977, *54*, 139–43, 163. (b)

McCracken, Glenn & Walcutt, Charles C.   *Basic Reading, book A, teacher's edition.* Philadelphia: J. B. Lippincott, 1975.

McDaniels, Garry L.   The evaluation of Follow Through. *Educational Researcher*, December 1975, *4*, 7–11.

McDavid, Raven I., Jr.   Variations in standard American English. *Elementary English*, May 1968, *45*, 561–64, 608.

McFeeley, Donald C.   Syllabication usefulness in a basal and social studies vocabulary. *The Reading Teacher*, May 1974, *27*, 809–14.

McGraw-Hill Book Company.   Guidelines for equal treatment of the sexes. *Elementary English*, May 1975, *52*, 725–33.

McIntyre, Virgie M.   Survival kits for stragglers. *Journal of Reading*, May 1977, *20*, 661–68.

McLoughlin, William P.   *The non-graded school: a critical assessment.* Albany, N.Y.: State Education Department, September 1967.

McMullen, Darlene A.   Teaching protection words. *Teaching Exceptional Children*, Spring 1975, *7*, 74–77.

McNeil, John D. False prerequisites in the teaching of reading. *Journal of Reading Behavior*, December 1974, 6, 421–27.

McWilliams, David R. & Cunningham, Patricia M. Project PEP. *The Reading Teacher*, April 1976, 29, 653–55.

Medley, Donald M. *Teacher competence and teacher effectiveness: a review of process-produce research.* Washington, D.C.: American Association of Colleges for Teacher Education, 1977.

Menyuk, Paula. Relations between acquisition of phonology and reading. In John T. Guthrie (Ed.), *Aspects of reading acquisition.* Baltimore: Johns Hopkins University Press, 1976. Pp. 89–110.

Merryman, Edward P. The effects of manifest anxiety on the reading achievement of fifth grade students. *The Journal of Experimental Education*, Spring 1974, 42, 36–41.

Meskauskas, John A. Evaluation models for criterion-referenced testing: views regarding mastery and standard-setting. *Review of Educational Research*, Winter 1976, 46, 133–58.

Messmore, Peter B. Multi-ethnic reading texts: the role of inferred story character identification and reading comprehension. *Journal of Reading Behavior*, Spring 1972–73, 5, 126–33.

Meyer, Ron & Cohen, S. Alan. A study of general reading compared to direct instruction to increase vocabulary achievement. *Reading World*, December 1975, 15, 109–13.

Miller, Wilma H. The Joplin plan—is it effective for intermediate-grade reading instruction? *Elementary English*, November 1971, 46, 951–54.

Mishra, S. P. & Hurt, M., Jr. The use of the Metropolitan Readiness Test with Mexican-American children. *California Journal of Educational Research*, 1970, 21, 182–87.

Mitchell, Addie S. Should dialectical differences be considered in reading instruction? In Howard A. Klein (Ed.), *The quest for competency in teaching reading.* Newark, Del.: International Reading Association, 1972. Pp. 151–57.

Mohan, M. Peer tutoring as a technique for teaching the unmotivated. *Child Study Journal*, Summer 1971, 1, 217–25.

Monteith, Mary K. A whole word list catalog. *The Reading Teacher*, May 1976, 29, 844–47.

Moore, Omar K. & Anderson, Alan R. The responsive environments project. In R. Hess & R. M. Bear (Eds.), *The challenge of early education.* Chicago: Aldine, 1967. Chap. 13.

Moretz, Sara & Davey, Beth. Process and strategies in teaching decoding skills to students in middle and secondary schools. In Lawrence E. Hafner (Ed.), *Improving reading in middle and secondary schools: selected readings.* 2nd ed. New York: Macmillan, 1974. Pp. 76–101.

Mork, Theodore. The ability of children to select reading material at their own instructional level. In Walter H. MacGinitie (Ed.), *Assessment problems in reading.* Newark, Del.: International Reading Association, 1973. Pp. 87–95.

Morphett, Mabel & Washburne, Carlton.   When should children begin to read? *Elementary School Journal*, March 1931, *31*, 496–503.

Moss, Joy F.   Growth in reading in an integrated day classroom. *Elementary School Journal*, March 1972, 72, 304–20.

Moss, Joy F.   Learning to write by listening to literature. *Language Arts*, May 1977, *54*, 537–42.

Mueller, Doris L.   Teacher attitudes toward reading. *Journal of Reading*, December 1973, *17*, 202–5.

Mueller, Ruth G.   Utilizing social studies content to develop critical reading. In Bonnie S. Schulwitz (Ed.), *Teachers, tangibles, techniques: comprehension of content in reading*. Newark, Del.: International Reading Association, 1975. Pp. 158–67.

Mukerji, Rose.   TV's impact on children: a checkerboard scene. *Phi Delta Kappan*, January 1976, *57*, 316–21.

Murray, Donald M.   Write to read: creative writing in the reading program. In Bonnie S. Schulwitz (Ed.), *Teachers, tangibles, techniques: comprehension of content in reading*. Newark, Del.: International Reading Association, 1975. Pp. 134–39.

Narang, H. L.   Improving reading ability of Indian children. *Elementary English*, February 1974, *51*, 190–92.

Narang, H. L.   Self-evaluation of a reading lesson for reading teachers. *Elementary English*, March 1975, 52, 338–39.

National Council of Teachers of English.   New NCTE guidelines, encourage nonsexist use of language. *Language Arts*, March 1976, *53*, 329–35.

Nekas, George B.   The anxiety levels of first grade children prior to and during formal reading instruction. *The Reading Teacher*, March 1973, *26*, 645.

Nelson, Joan B. & Cleland, Donald L.   The role of the teacher of gifted and creative children. In Paul A. Witty (Ed.), *Reading for the gifted and the creative student*. Newark, Del.: International Reading Association, 1971. Pp. 45–57.

Nelson, Rosemary O.   The effect of different types of teaching methods and verbal feedback on the performance of beginning readers. *Journal of Reading Behavior*, 1974, *6*, No. 3, 305–26.

Neuwirth, Sharyn E.   A look at intersentence grammar. *The Reading Teacher*, October 1976, *30*, 28–32.

Nevius, John R., Jr.   Teaching for logical thinking is a prereading activity. *The Reading Teacher*, March 1977, *30*, 641–43.

Newport, John F.   The Joplin plan: the score. *The Reading Teacher*, November 1967, *21*, 158–62.

New York Times.   CBS-TV plans a program to aid reading in school. 25 June 1977.

Niedermeyer, F. C. & Ellis, Patricia. Remedial reading instruction by trained pupil tutors. *Elementary School Journal*, 1971, *71*, 400–405.

Niles, Olive.   System for objective-based assessment—reading (SOBAR). *The Reading Teacher*, November 1973, 27 203–4.

Nolen, Patricia A.   Reading nonstandard dialect materials: a study at grades two and four. *Child Development*, September 1972, *43*, 1092–97.

Oakan, Robert; Wiener, Morton; & Cromer, Ward.   Identification, organization and reading comprehension for good and poor readers. *Journal of Educational Psychology*, 1971, *62*, 71–78.

O'Donnell, Roy C. & King, F. J.   An exploration of deep structure recovery and reading comprehension skills. *Research in the Teaching of English*, Winter 1974, *8*, 327–38.

Ogletree, Earl J. and Dipasalegne, Rosalee W.   Innercity teachers evaluate DISTAR. *The Reading Teacher*, April 1975, *28*, 633–37.

Oliver, Marvin E.   The effect of high intensity practice on reading comprehension. *Reading Improvement*, Fall 1973, *10*, 16–18.

Ollila, Lloyd.   Pros and cons of teaching reading to four- and five-year-olds. In Robert C. Aukerman (Ed.), *Some persistent questions on beginning reading*. Newark, Del.: International Reading Association, 1972. Pp. 53–61.

Olshavsky, Jill; Andrews, Nancy; & Farr, Roger.   Convergent and discriminant validity of informal assessment of reading skills. In Phil L. Nacke (Ed.), *Interaction: research and practice for college-adult reading*. Clemson, S.C.: National Reading Conference, 1974. Pp. 226–31.

Olson, Willard C.   *Child development*. Boston: D. C. Heath, 1949.

Oñativia, Oscar V. & Donoso, Maria A. R.   Basic issues in establishing a bilingual method. *The Reading Teacher*, April 1977, *30*, 727–34.

Orlando, Charles P.   Review of reading research. In Lester Mann & David A. Sabatino (Eds.), *The first review of special education*. Vol. 1. Philadelphia: JSE Press, 1973. Pp. 261–83.

Otto, Wayne.   Developing a skills-based approach to reading comprehension. In W. D. Miller & G. H. McNinch (Eds.), *Reflections and investigations on reading*. Clemson, S.C.: National Reading Conference, 1976. Pp. 251–57.

Otto, Wayne & Askov, E.   *Rationale and guidelines: the Wisconsin Design for Reading Skill Development*. Minneapolis: National Computer Systems, 1972.

Otto, Wayne, et al.   *Focused reading instruction*. Reading, Mass. Addison-Wesley, 1974.

Pacheco, Manuel T.   Linguistic understandings for the teacher of Spanish-speaking children. In *Reading and the Spanish-speaking child*. Austin, Tex.: Texas State Council of the International Reading Association, 1975. Pp. 13–21.

Page, William D. & Carlson, Kenneth L.   The process of observing oral reading scores. *Reading Horizons*, Spring 1975, *15*, 147–50.

Painter, Helen W. (Ed.).   *Reaching children and young people through literature*. Newark, Del.: International Reading Association, 1971.

Paradis, Edward E.   The appropriateness of visual discrimination exercises in reading readiness materials. *Journal of Educational Research*, February 1974, *67*, 276–78.

Paraprofessionals and Reading Committee, International Reading Association.   Paraprofessionals and reading. *The Reading Teacher*, December 1973, *27*, 337–44.

Pauk, Walter.   Two essential study skills for the community college student. *Reading World*, May 1973, *12*, 239–45.

Pauk, Walter.   The study skills corner: the R that educates. *Reading World,* March 1975, *14,* 188–90.

Pearson, P. David.   The effects of grammatical complexity on children's comprehension, recall, and conceptions of certain semantic relations. *Reading Research Quarterly,* 1974–75, *10,* No. 2, 155–92.

Pearson, P. David.   A psycholinguistic model of reading. *Language Arts,* March 1976, *53,* 309–14.

Pehrsson, Robert S. V.   The effect of teacher interference during the process of reading or how much of a helper is Mr. Gelper? *Journal of Reading,* May 1974, *17,* 617–21.

Peters, Nathaniel A. & Peters, Juanita I.   Better reading materials for the content areas. *The Volta Review,* November 1974, *76,* 500–507.

Peterson, Gordon.   Behavioral objectives for teaching literature. *Language Arts,* October 1975, *52,* 968–71, 991.

Peterson, J.; Greenlaw, M. Jean; & Tierney, Robert J.   Assessing instructional placement with an IRI. In *Abstracts: literacy and beyond.* Newark, Del.: International Reading Association, 1976. Pp. 112–13.

Petre, Richard M.   On the job reading for teachers. *Journal of Reading,* January 1977, *20,* 310–11.

Petty, Walter T.; Herold, Curtis P.; & Stoll, Earline.   *The state of knowledge about the teaching of vocabulary.* Cooperative Research Project No. 3128. Champaign, Ill.: National Council of Teachers of English, 1968.

Petty, Walter T.; Murphy, J. Brien; & Mohan, Madan.   Spelling achievement and the initial teaching alphabet: analysis of errors. *The Elementary School Journal,* February 1974, *74,* 309–13.

Pikulski, John J.   Predicting sixth grade achievement by first grade scores. *The Reading Teacher,* December 1973, *27,* 284–87.

Pikulski, John J.   Linguistics applied to reading instruction. *Language Arts,* April 1976, *53,* 373–77, 384. (a)

Pikulski, John J.   Using the cloze procedure. *Language Arts,* March 1976, *53,* 317–18, 328. (b)

Pikulski, John J. & Jones, Margaret B.   Writing directions children can read. *The Reading Teacher,* March 1977, *30,* 598–602.

Pillar, Arlene M.   A module for teaching newspaper skills. *Elementary English,* April 1974, *51,* 571–77.

Pillar, Arlene.   Individualizing book reviews. *Elementary English,* April 1975, *52,* 467–69.

Platts, Mary E.   *Anchor: a handbook of vocabulary discovery techniques for the classroom teacher.* Stevensville, Mich.: Educational Services, 1970.

Popp, Helen M.   Current practices in the teaching of beginning reading. In John B. Carroll & Jeanne S. Chall (Eds.), *Toward a literate society.* New York: McGraw-Hill, 1975. Pp. 101–46.

Powell, William R.   Acquisition of a reading repertoire. *Library Trends,* October 1973, *22,* 177–96.

Prager, Barton B. & Mann, Lester.   Criterion-referenced measurement: the world of gray versus black and white. *Journal of Learning Disabilities,* February 1973, *6,* 72–84.

Preston, Ralph C. & Herman, Wayne L., Jr.   *Teaching social studies in the elementary school.* 4th ed. New York: Holt, Rinehart and Winston, 1974.

Purves, Alan C.   Literature tests. In A. H. Grommon (Ed.), *Reviews of selected published tests in English.* Urbana, Ill.: National Council of Teachers of English, 1976. Pp. 127–37.

Purves, Alan C. & Beach, Richard.   *Literature and the reader; research in response to literature, reading interests, and the teaching of literature.* Champaign, Ill.: National Council of Teachers of English, 1972.

Pyrczak, Fred.   Passage-dependence of reading comprehension questions: examples. *Journal of Reading,* January 1975, *18,* 308–11.

Pyrczak, Fred & Axelrod, Jerome.   Determining the passage-dependence of reading comprehension exercises: a call for replication. *Journal of Reading,* January 1976, *19,* 279–83.

Quandt, Ivan J.   *Teaching reading: a human process.* Chicago: Rand McNally, 1977.

Quorm, Kerry.   A comparison of four methods of developing reading readiness skills. In Lloyd O. Ollila et al. (Eds.), *Learning to read reading to learn.* Victoria, Can.: University of Victoria Press, 1974. Pp. 196–203.

Ramsey, Imogene.   A comparison of first grade Negro dialect speakers' comprehension of standard English and Negro dialect. *Elementary English,* May 1972, *49,* 688–96.

Ramstad, Vivian V. & Potter, Robert E.   Differences in vocabulary and syntax usage between Nez Percé Indian and white kindergarten children. *Journal of Learning Disabilities,* October 1974, 7, 491–97.

Rankin, Earl F.   Grade level interpretation of cloze readability scores. In Frank Greene (Ed.), *The right to participate.* Milwaukee: National Reading Conference, 1971. Pp. 30–37.

Rankin, Earl F.   The cloze procedure revisited. In Phil L. Nacke (Ed.), *Interaction: research and practice for college-adult reading.* Clemson, S.C.: The National Reading Conference, 1974. Pp. 1–8 (a)

Rankin, Earl F.   *The measurement of reading flexibility.* Newark, Del.: International Reading Association, 1974. (b)

Rankin, Earl F. & Overholser, Betsy M.   Reaction of intermediate grade children to contextual clues. *Journal of Reading Behavior,* Summer 1969, *1,* 50–73.

Raths, James & Katz, Lilian G.   Review of *CIRCUS: Comprehensive Program of Assessment Services for Pre-primary Children. Journal of Educational Measurement,* Summer 1975, *12,* 144–47.

Raven, Ronald J. & Salzer, Richard.   Piaget and reading instruction. *The Reading Teacher,* April 1971, *24,* 630–39.

Recht, Donna R.   The self-correction process in reading. *The Reading Teacher,* April 1976, *29,* 632–36.

Reed, David W.   A theory of language, speech, and writing. *Elementary English,* December 1965, *42,* 845–51.

Reed, Linda.   ERIC/RCS report: multi-ethnic literature and the elementary school curriculum. *Language Arts*, March 1976, *53*, 256–61.

Reid, Virginia M.   *Individualizing your reading program*. New York: Resources for Learning, 1970.

Reid, Virginia M. (Ed.).   *Reading ladders for human relations*. 5th ed. Urbana, Ill.: National Council of Teachers of English, 1972.

Reiss, Steven & Dyhalo, Nestor.   Persistence, achievement, and open-space environments. *Journal of Educational Psychology*, August 1975, *67*, 506–13.

Rentel, Victor M.   Concept formation and reading. *Reading World*, December 1971, *11*, 111–19.

Rentel, Victor M. & Kennedy, John J.   Effects of pattern drill on the phonology syntax, and reading achievement of rural Appalachian children. *American Educational Research Journal*, Winter 1972, *9*, 87–100.

Resnick, Lauren B. & Beck, Isabel L.   Designing instruction in reading: interaction of theory and practice. In John T. Guthrie (Ed.), *Aspects of reading acquisition*. Baltimore: Johns Hopkins University Press, 1976. Pp. 180–204.

Richards, I. A.   *Design for escape: world education through modern media:* New York: Harvest Books, Harcourt Brace Jovanovich, 1968. Pp. 70–71.

Richardson, Ellis; Di Benedetto, Barbara; & Bradley, C. Michael.   The relationship of sound blending to reading achievement. *Review of Educational Research*, Spring 1977, *47*, 319–34.

Riggs, Corinne W. (Comp.).   *Bibliotherapy: an annotated bibliography*. Newark, Del.: International Reading Association, 1971.

Ritt, Sharon I.   Journeys: another look at the junior novel. *Journal of Reading*, May 1976, *19*, 627–34.

Robbins, Melvyn P.   The Delacato interpretation of neurological organization. *Reading Research Quarterly*, Spring 1966, *1*, 57–78.

Robertson, Douglas J. & Trepper, Terry S.   The effects of i.t.a. on the reading achievement of Mexican-American children. *Reading World*, December 1974, *14*, 132–38.

Robertson, Jean E.   Pupil understanding of connectives in reading. *Reading Research Quarterly*, Spring 1968, *3*, 387–417.

Robinett, Ralph F.   A "linguistic" approach to beginning reading for bilingual children. In James F. Kerfoot (Ed.), *First grade reading programs*. Newark, Del.: International Reading Association, 1965. Pp. 132–49.

Robinson, Francis P.   *Effective reading*. New York: Harper & Row, 1962.

Robinson, H. Alan.   A study of the technique of word identification. *The Reading Teacher*, January 1963, *16*, 238–41.

Robinson, H. Alan.   *Teaching reading and study strategies: the content areas*. Boston: Allyn & Bacon, 1975.

Robinson, H. Alan & Thomas, Ellen L. (Eds.).   *Fusing reading skills and content*. Newark, Del.: International Reading Association, 1969.

Robinson, Helen M.   Perceptual training—does it result in reading improvement? In Robert C. Aukerman (Ed.), *Some persistent questions on beginning reading*. Newark, Del.: International Reading Association, 1972. Pp. 135–50. (a)

Robinson, Helen M.   Visual and auditory modalities related to methods for beginning reading. *Reading Research Quarterly*, Fall 1972, 8, 7–39. (b)

Robinson, Helen M. & Weintraub, Samuel.   Research related to children's interests and to developmental values of reading. *Library Trends*, October 1973, 22, 81–108.

Robinson, Richard D.   *An introduction to the cloze procedure: an annotated bibliography.* Newark, Del.: International Reading Association, 1972.

Rodgers, Denis.   Which connectives? Signals to enhance comprehension. *Journal of Reading*, March 1974, 6, 462–66.

Roe, Betty D.   Readability of elementary school text books. *Journal of the Reading Specialist*, May 1970, 9, 163–67.

Roettger, Doris.   Effects of early intervention programs. In John E. Merritt (Ed.), *New horizons in reading.* Newark, Del.: International Reading Association, 1976. Pp. 464–71.

Rogers, Janette S.   Reading practices in open education. *The Reading Teacher*, March 1976, 29, 548–54.

Rongione, Louis A.   Bibliotherapy: its nature and uses. *Catholic Library World*, May–June 1972, 43, 495–500.

Rose, Cynthia; Zimet, Sara G.; & Blom, Gastone E.   Content counts: children have preferences in reading textbooks stories. *Elementary English*, January 1972, 49, 14–19.

Rosen, Carl L. & Ortego, Philip D.   *Issues in language and reading instruction of Spanish-speaking children: an annotated bibliography.* Newark, Del.: International Reading Association, 1969.

Rosenshine, Barak V.   Classroom instruction. In N. L. Gage (Ed.), *The psychology of teaching methods.* Seventy-fifth yearbook, Part 1. Chicago: National Society for the Study of Education, 1976. Pp. 335–71.

Rosenshine, Barak V. & Berliner, David C.   Academic engaged time. Paper presented at the annual convention of the American Education Research Association, April 1977.

Rosenthal, Daniel J. A. & Resnick, Lauren B.   Children's solution processes in arithmetic word problems. *Journal of Educational Psychology*, December 1974, 66, 817–25.

Rosner, Jerome.   Auditory analysis training with prereaders. *The Reading Teacher*, January 1974, 27, 379–84.

Ross, Alan O.   *Psychological aspects of learning disabilities & reading disorders.* New York: McGraw-Hill, 1976.

Rothenberg, Michael.   The effect of television violence on children and youth. *Journal of the American Medical Association*, 1975, 234, 1043–46.

Roundabush, Glen E.   An empirical structure for reading objectives. *Journal of Reading Behavior*, December 1974, 4, 403–19.

Rowell, E. H.   Do elementary students read better orally or silently? *The Reading Teacher*, January 1976, 29, 367–70.

Rubin, Rosalyn.   Reading ability and assigned materials: accommodation for the slow but not the accelerated. *Elementary School Journal*, 1975, 75, 374–77.

Ruddell, Robert B. *Reading-language instruction: innovative practices.* Englewood Cliffs, N.J.: Prentice-Hall, 1974.

Ruddell, Robert B. Language acquisition and the reading process. In H. Singer & R. B. Ruddell (Eds.), *Theoretical models and processes of reading.* 2nd ed. Newark, Del.: International Reading Association, 1976. Pp. 22–38.

Ruddell, Robert B. and Williams, Arthur C. *A research investigation of a literacy teaching model, Project DELTA.* EPRA Project No. 005262. Washington, D.C.: U.S. Department of HEW, 1972.

Rude, Robert T. Objective-based reading systems: an evaluation. *The Reading Teacher,* November 1974, 28, 169–75.

Rudman, Masha K. *Children's literature: an issues approach.* Lexington, Mass.: D. C. Heath, 1976.

Rupley, William H. ERIC/RCS report: content reading in the elementary grades. *Language Arts,* September 1975, 52, 802–7.

Russell, David H. & Russell, Elizabeth F. *Listening aids through the grades.* New York: Teachers College Press, Columbia University, 1959.

Russell, David; Karp, Etta E.; & Mueser, Anne Marie. *Reading aids through the grades.* 2nd ed. New York: Teachers College Press, Columbia University, 1975.

Rystrom, Richard. Dialect training and reading: a further look. *Reading Research Quarterly,* Summer 1970, 5, 581–99.

Rystrom, Richard. Reading, language, and nonstandard dialects: a research report. In James L. Laffey & Roger Shuy (Eds.), *Language differences: do they interfere?* Newark, Del.: International Reading Association, 1973. Pp. 86–90.

Samuels, S. Jay. Letter-name versus letter-sound knowledge in learning to read. *The Reading Teacher,* April 1971, 24, 609–15, 662.

Samuels, S. Jay. Automatic decoding and reading comprehension, *Language Arts,* March 1976, 53, 323–28.

Samuels, S. Jay & Dahl, Patricia R. Relationships among IQ, learning ability, and reading achievement. In Jerry L. Johns (Ed.), *Literacy for diverse learners: promoting reading growth at all levels.* Newark, Del.: International Reading Association, 1974. Pp. 31–38.

Samuels, S. Jay & Dahl, Patricia R. Establishing appropriate purpose for reading and its effect on flexibility of reading rate. *Journal of Educational Psychology,* February 1975, 67, 34–43.

Samuels, S. Jay & Turnure, James E. Attention and reading achievement in first-grade boys and girls. *Journal of Educational Psychology,* February 1974, 66, 29–32.

Sanacore, Joseph. A checklist for the evaluation of reading readiness. *Elementary English,* September 1973, 50, 858–60, 870.

Sanacore, Joseph. Locating information: the process method. *Journal of Reading,* December 1974, 18, 231–33. (a)

Sanacore, Joseph. The tutor: an asset to the reading program. *Elementary English,* April 1974, 51, 563–64. (b)

Sargent, Eileen E. *The newspaper as a teaching tool.* Norwalk, Conn.: Reading Laboratory, 1975.

Sartain, Harry W.   The research base for individualized reading instruction. In J. Allen Figurel (Ed.), *Reading and realism*. Newark, Del.: International Reading Association, 1969. Pp. 523–30.

Sartain, Harry W.   The modular content of the professional program. In Harry W. Sartain & Paul E. Stanton (Eds.), *Modular preparation for teaching reading*. Newark, Del.: International Reading Association, 1974. Pp. 31–59.

Sauer, Freda M.   The designation of reading instructional level of disabled fourth grade readers utilizing cloze testing procedure. Doctoral dissertation, Oklahoma State University, 1969.

Savage, John F. (Ed.).   *Linguistics for teachers: selected readings*. Chicago: Science Research Associates, 1973.

Scanlon, Robert G.   Individually prescribed instruction: a system of individualized instruction. *Educational Technology*, December 1970, *10*, 44–46.

Schaefer, Paul J.   Effective use of questioning. *Reading World*, May 1976, *15*, 226–29.

Schaer, Hildgard F. & Crump, W. Donald.   Teacher involvement and early identification of children with learning disabilities. *Journal of Learning Disabilities*, February 1976, *9*, 91–95.

Schell, Leo M. & Burns, Paul C.   *Remedial reading: classroom and clinic*. 2nd ed. Boston: Allyn & Bacon, 1972.

Schiffman, Gilbert B.   Special programs for underachieving children. In Darrell B. Carter (Ed.), *Interdisciplinary approaches to learning disorders*. Philadelphia: Chilton, 1970. Pp. 69–79.

Schlief, Mable & Wood, Robert W.   A comparison of procedures to determine readability level of non-text materials. *Reading Improvement*, Fall 1974, *11*, 57–64.

Schnell, Thomas R. & Sweeney, Judith.   Sex role bias in basal readers. *Elementary English*, May 1975, 52, 737–42.

Schon, Isabel.   Looking at books about Latin Americans. *Language Arts*, March 1976, *53*, 267–71.

Schubert, Delwyn.   The role of bibliotherapy in reading instruction. *Exceptional Children*, April 1975, *41*, 497–99.

Schulte, Emerita S.   Resources for adolescent literature: a selected bibliography. *Journal of Reading*, November 1975, *19*, 117–20.

Schultheis, Sister Miriam.   *A guidebook for bibliotherapy*. Glenview, Ill.: Psychotechics, 1972.

Schwartz, Elaine & Sheff, Alice.   Student involvement in questioning for comprehension. *The Reading Teacher*, November 1975, *29*, 150–54.

Schwartz, Judy I.   An investigation of attitudes on the use of black dialect materials for beginning reading instruction. *Research in the Teaching of English*, Fall 1975, *9*, 200–209.

Sebesta, Sam L. & Wallen, Carl J.   *The first R: readings on teaching reading*. Chicago: Science Research Associates, 1972.

Seidman, Miriam R.   Comparing physical openness and climate openness of elementary schools. *Education*, Summer 1975, *95*, 345–50.

Seifort, Mary.   Research views: reading comprehension and speed of decoding. *The Reading Teacher*, December 1976, *30*, 314–15.

Serwer, Blanche L.   Linguistic support for a method of teaching reading to black children. *Reading Research Quarterly*, Summer 1969, *4*, 449–67.

Serwer, Blanche L. & Stolurow, Lawrence M.   Computer-assisted learning in language arts. *Elementary English*, May 1970, *47*, 641–50.

Seymour, Dorothy Z.   Word division for decoding. *The Reading Teacher*, December 1973, *27*, 275–83. (a)

Seymour, Dorothy Z.   Neutralizing the effect of the nonstandard dialect. In James L. Laffey & Roger Shuy (Eds.), *Language differences: do they interfere?* Newark, Del.: International Reading Association, 1973. Pp. 149–62. (b)

Sharon, Amiel T.   What do adults read? *Reading Research Quarterly*, 1973–74, *9*, No. 2, 148–69.

Shepherd, David L.   *Comprehensive high school reading methods.* Columbus, Ohio: Charles E. Merrill, 1973.

Shepherd, Terry & Iles, Lynn B. What is bibliotherapy? *Language Arts*, May 1976, *53*, 569–71.

Shohen, Sam.   A language experience approach to reading instruction. In Thomas C. Barrett & Dale D. Johnson (Eds.), *Views on elementary instruction.* Newark, Del.: International Reading Association, 1973. Pp. 43–48.

Shohen, Sam.   An extended first and second grade readiness class: context and outcomes. In Jerry L. Johns (Ed.), *Literacy for diverse learners: promoting reading growth at all levels.* Newark, Del.: International Reading Association, 1974. Pp. 49–55.

Shuman, R. Baird.   Open-ended stories and basic reading skills. *Journal of Reading*, October 1976, *20*, 18–22.

Shuy, Roger W.   Nonstandard dialect problems: an overview. In James L. Laffey & Roger Shuy (Eds.), *Language differences: do they interfere?* Newark, Del.: International Reading Association, 1973. Pp. 3–16.

Silvaroli, Nicholas J. & Wheelock, Warren H.   *Teaching reading: a decision making process.* Dubuque, Iowa: Kendall/Hunt, 1975.

Simmons, Beatrice (Ed.).   *Paperback books for children.* Chicago: American Library Association, 1972.

Simons, Herbert D.   Reading comprehension: the need for a new perspective. *Reading Research Quarterly*, Spring 1971, *6*, 338–63.

Simons, Herbert D.   Black dialect and learning to read. In Jerry L. Johns (Ed.), *Literacy for diverse learners: promoting reading growth at all levels.* Newark, Del.: International Reading Association, 1974. Pp. 3–13. (a)

Simons, Herbert D.   Black dialect phonology and word recognition. *The Journal of Educational Research*, October 1974, *68*, 67–70. (b)

Simons, Herbert D. & Johnson, Kenneth R.   Black English syntax and reading interference. *Research in the Teaching of English*, Winter 1974, *8*, 339–58.

Singer, Harry.   The SEER technique: a non-computation procedure for quickly estimating readability level. *Journal of Reading Behavior*, Fall 1975, *7*, 255–67.

Singer, Harry & Ruddell, Robert B. (Eds.). *Theoretical models and processes of reading.* 2nd ed. Newark, Del.: International Reading Association, 1976.

Singer, Harry; Samuels, S. Jay; & Spiroff, Jean. The effect of pictures and contextual conditions on learning responses to printed words. *Reading Research Quarterly,* No. 4, 1973–74, *9,* 555–67.

Sipay, Edward R. A comparison of standardized reading scores and functional reading levels. *The Reading Teacher,* January 1964, *17,* 265–68.

Sipay, Edward R. The effect of prenatal instruction on reading achievement. *Elementary English,* April 1965, *42,* 431–32.

Sipay, Edward R. Interpreting the USOE cooperative reading studies. *The Reading Teacher,* October 1968, *22,* 10–16.

Sloan, Margaret. Increasing parent-teacher interaction. In Brother Leonard Courtney (Ed.), *Reading interaction: the teacher, the pupil, the materials.* Newark, Del.: International Reading Association, 1976. Pp. 58–63.

Small, Robert C., Jr., & Kenney, Donald J. Reading interests and library organization. *Language Arts,* November/December 1975, *52,* 1127–29.

Smith, Frank. *Understanding reading.* New York: Holt, Rinehart and Winston, 1971.

Smith, Frank. The learner and his language. In R. E. Hodges & E. H. Rudorf (Eds.), *Language and learning to read: What teachers should know about language.* Boston: Houghton Mifflin, 1972. Pp. 35–43.

Smith, Frank. *Comprehension and learning: a conceptual framework for teachers.* New York: Holt, Rinehart and Winston, 1975.

Smith, Frank & Goodman, Kenneth S. On the psycholinguistic method of teaching reading. *Elementary School Journal,* January 1971, *71,* 177–81.

Smith, Helen K. Evaluating progress in recreational reading. In John E. Merritt (Ed.), *New horizons in reading.* Newark, Del.: International Reading Association, 1976. Pp. 208–14.

Smith, James A. *Creative teaching of reading and literature.* Boston: Allyn & Bacon, 1967.

Smith, Lewis B. & Morgan, Glen D. Cassette tape recording as a primary method in the development of early reading material. *Elementary English,* April 1975, *52,* 534–38.

Smith, Nila B. *Reading instruction for today's children.* Englewood Cliffs, N.J.: Prentice-Hall, 1963. Pp. 342–44.

Smith, Nila B. *American reading instruction.* Rev. ed. Newark, Del.: International Reading Association, 1965.

Smith, Nila B. The quest for increased reading competency. In Howard A. Klein (Ed.), *The quest for competency in teaching reading.* Newark, Del.: International Reading Association, 1972. Pp. 45–56.

Smith, Richard J. The physiology of reading. *The Journal of Educational Research,* May–June 1974, *67,* 397–402. (a)

Smith, Richard J. Using reading to stimulate creative thinking in the intermediate grades. In M. Labuda (Ed.), *Creative reading for gifted learners: a design for excellence.* Newark, Del.: International Reading Association, 1974. Pp. 51–59. (b)

Smith, Richard J. & Barrett, Thomas C.   *Teaching reading in the middle grades.* Reading, Mass.: Addison-Wesley, 1974.

Smith, Richard J. & Johnson, Dale D.   *Teaching children to read.* Reading, Mass.: Addison-Wesley, 1976.

Snapp, Matthew, et al.   A study of individualizing instruction by using elementary school children as tutors. *Journal of School Psychology,* March 1972, *10,* 1–8.

Snoddy, James F.   Improving study skills: a review of selected research. In Thomas C. Barrett & Dale D. Johnson (Eds.), *Views on elementary reading instruction.* Newark, Del.: International Reading Association, 1973. Pp. 81–87.

Solomon, Bernard.   The television reading program. *Language Arts,* February 1976, *53,* 135–36.

Sorenson, Juanita S.; Schwenn, Elizabeth A.; & Klausmeir, Herbert J.   The individual conference—a motivational device for increasing independent reading in the elementary grades. Practical Paper No. 8. Madison, Wis.: Wisconsin Research and Development Center for Cognitive Learning, The University of Wisconsin, October 1969.

Southgate, Vera & Roberts, Geoffrey R.   *Reading—which approach?* London: University of London Press, 1970.

Southwell, P. R.   The initial teaching alphabet. *Developmental Medicine and Child Neurology.* December 1973, *15,* 794–99.

Spache, Evelyn B.   *Reading activities for child involvement.* 2nd ed. Boston: Allyn & Bacon, 1976.

Spache, George D.   *Good reading for poor readers.* Rev. ed. Champaign, Ill.: Garrard, 1974.

Spache, George D.   *Good reading for the disadvantaged reader and multi-ethnic resources.* Champaign, Ill.: Garrard, 1975.

Spache, George D., et al.   A longitudinal first grade reading readiness program. *The Reading Teacher,* May 1966, *19,* 580–84.

Spache, George D. & Spache, Evelyn B.   *Reading in the elementary school.* 3rd ed. Boston: Allyn & Bacon, 1973.

Spache, George D. & Spache, Evelyn B.   *Reading in the elementary school.* 4th ed. Boston: Allyn & Bacon, 1977.

Spearitt, Donald.   Identification of subskills of reading comprehension by maximum likelihood factor analysis. *Reading Research Quarterly,* Fall 1972, *8,* 92–111.

Staats, A. W.   *Learning, language and cognition.* New York: Holt, Rinehart and Winston, 1968.

Stallard, Kathy.   Comparing objective-based reading programs. *Journal of Reading,* October 1977, *21,* 36–44.

Stanley, Julian C. (Ed.).   *Preschool programs for the disadvantaged: five experienced approaches to early childhood education.* Baltimore: Johns Hopkins University Press, 1972.

Starkey, John D. & Swinford, Helen L.   Reading? Does television viewing time affect it? ED. 090 966. Unpublished paper. Northern Illinois University, DeKalb, Ill., 1974.

Stauffer, Russell G.   A study of prefixes in the Thorndike list to establish a list of prefixes that should be taught in the elementary school. *Journal of Educational Research*, 1942, 35, 453–58.

Stauffer, Russell G. (Ed.).   *The first grade reading studies: findings of individual investigations.* Newark, Del.: International Reading Association, 1967.

Stauffer, Russell G.   *Directing reading maturity as a cognitive process.* New York: Harper & Row, 1969.

Stauffer, Russell G.   *The language-experience approach to the teaching of reading.* New York: Harper & Row, 1970.

Stauffer, Russell G. & Cramer, Ronald.   *Teaching critical reading at the primary level.* Newark, Del.: International Reading Association, 1968.

Stauffer, Russell G. & Harrell, Max M.   Individualizing reading-thinking activities. *The Reading Teacher*, May 1975, 28, 765–69.

Stanchfield, Jo M.   Development of prereading skills in an experimental kindergarten program. In Robert C. Aukerman (Ed.), *Some persistent questions on beginning reading.* Newark, Del.: International Reading Association, 1972. Pp. 20–30.

Stensland, Anna Lee.   *An annotated bibliography of literature by and about the American Indian.* Champaign, Ill.: National Council of Teachers of English, 1973.

Stephens, W. E.; Cunningham, E.; & Stigler, B. J.   Reading readiness and eye hand preference pattern in first grade children. *Exceptional Children*, 1967, 33, 481–88.

Sticht, Thomas G., et al.   Project REALISTIC: determination of adult functional literacy skill levels. *Reading Research Quarterly*, Spring 1972, 7, 424–65.

Stoodt, Barbara D.   The relationship between understanding grammatical conjunctions and reading comprehension. *Elementary English*, April 1972, 49, 502–5.

Stoodt, Barbara D. & Ignizio, Sandra.   The American Indian in children's literature. *Language Arts*, January 1976, 53, 17–21.

Strickland, Dorothy S.   A program for linguistically different, black children. *Research on the Teaching of English*, Spring 1973, 7, 79–86. (a)

Strickland, Dorothy S.   The black experience in paperback (kindergarten through grade 6). In M. Jerry Weiss et al. (Eds.), *New perspectives in paperbacks.* York, Pa.: Strine, 1973. Pp. 20–23. (b)

Strong, A.   *Reading for deaf children.* Washington, D.C.: Volta Bureau, 1964.

Sucher, Floyd.   Use of basal readers in individualizing reading instruction. In J. Allen Figurel (Ed.), *Reading and realism.* Newark, Del.: International Reading Association, 1969. Pp. 136–43.

Sue, Paulina Wee.   Promoting understanding of Chinese-American children. *Language Arts*, March 1976, 53, 262–66.

Swalm, James E.   Is listening really more effective for learning in the early grades? *Elementary English*, November/December 1974, *51*, 1110–13.

Swalm, James E. & Kling, Martin.   Speed reading in the elementary school. *The Elementary School Journal*, December 1973, *74*, 158–64.

Swineford, Edwin J.   The perils of reading. *Language Arts*, September 1975, *52*, 816–19, 851.

Swiss, Thom & Olsen, Turee.   ERIC/RCS: reading and gifted children. *The Reading Teacher*, January 1976, *29*, 428–31.

Tanyzer, Harold & Karl, Jean (Eds.).   *Reading, children's books, and our pluralistic society*. Newark, Del.: International Reading Association, 1972.

Taschow, Horst G.   How to teach critical reading. In Robert T. Williams (Ed.), *Insights into why and how to read*. Newark, Del.: International Reading Association, 1976. Pp. 90–97.

Tatham, Susan M.   Reading comprehension of materials written with select oral language patterns, a study of grades two and four. *Reading Research Quarterly*, Spring 1970, *5*, 402–26.

Terry, Ellen.   *Children's poetry preference: a national survey of upper elementary grades*. Research Report No. 13. Urbana, Ill.: National Council of Teachers of English, 1974.

Thelan, Judith.   *Improving reading in science*. Newark, Del.: International Reading Association, 1976.

Thomas, Ellen L. & Robinson, H. Alan.   *Improving reading in every class*. Boston: Allyn & Bacon. 1972.

Thomas, Richard A. & Dziuben, Charles D.   Criterion-referenced reading tests in perspective. *The Reading Teacher*, December 1973, *27*, 292–94.

Thompson, Richard A.   *Energizers for reading instruction*. West Nyack, N.Y.: Parker, 1973.

Thorndike, Robert L.   Reading as reasoning. *Reading Research Quarterly*, 1973–74, *9*, No. 2, 135–47.

Tinker, Miles A. & McCullough, Constance M.   *Teaching elementary reading*. 3rd ed. New York: Appleton-Century-Crofts, 1968.

Tinker, Miles A. & McCullough, Constance M.   *Teaching elementary reading*. 4th ed. Englewood Cliffs, N.J.: Prentice-Hall, 1975.

Towner, John C. & Evans, Howard M.   The effect of three-dimensional stimuli versus two-dimensional stimuli on visual form discrimination. *Journal of Reading Behavior*, December 1974, *4*, 395–402.

Townsend, Mary Jane.   Taking off the war bonnet: American Indian literature. *Language Arts*, March 1976, *53*, 236–44.

Tovey, Duane R.   Relationship of matched first grade phonics instruction to overall reading achievement and the desire to read. In Robert C. Aukerman (Ed.), *Some persistent questions on beginning reading*. Newark, Del.: International Reading Association, 1972. Pp. 93–101.

Trezise, Joan.   Parents read aloud to children. *Language Arts*, September 1975, *52*, 881–82, 888.

Troy, Anne.   Literature for content area learning. *The Reading Teacher*, February 1977, *30*, 470–74.

Tuinman, J. Jaap.   Determining the passage dependency of comprehension questions in 5 major tests. *Reading Research Quarterly*, 1973–74, *9*, No. 2, 206–23.

Tuinman, J. Jaap & Blanton, B. Elgit.   Problems in the measurement of reading skills. In Lawrence E. Hafner (Ed.), *Improving reading in middle and secondary schools*. 2nd ed. New York: Macmillan, 1974. Pp. 212–22.

Tuinman, J.J. ; Rowls, Michael; & Farr, Roger.   Reading achievement in the United States: then and now. *Journal of Reading*, March 1976, *19*, 455–63.

Turner, Thomas N.   Figurative language: deceitful mirage or sparkling oasis for reading? *Language Arts*, October 1976, 53, 758–61, 775.

Turner, Thomas N. & Estill, Alexander J.   Fostering early creative reading. *Language Arts*, September 1975, 52, 786–89.

Tutolo, Daniel J.   Teaching critical listening. *Language Arts*, November/December 1975, 52, 1108–12.

Tutolo, Daniel J.   The study guide—types, purpose and value. *Journal of Reading*, March 1977, 20, 503–7.

Vacca, Jo Anne L. & Vacca, Richard T.   Learning stations: how to in the middle grades. *Journal of Reading*, April 1976, *19*, 563–67.

Valmont, William J.   Creating questions for informal reading inventories. *The Reading Teacher*, March 1972, 25, 509–12.

Van Blarecom, Ginger & White, Sandra.   Testing comprehension of the central thought: selecting versus generating main ideas. In W. D. Miller & G. H. McNinch (Eds.), *Reflections and investigations on reading*. Clemson, S.C. National Reading Conference, 1976. Pp. 317–23.

Van Metre, Patricia D.   Oral interpretation, a path to meaning. *Language Arts*, March 1977, 54, 278–82.

Vaughn, Joseph L., Jr.   The effect of interest on reading comprehension among ability groups and across grade levels. In G. H. McNinch & W. D. Miller (Eds.), *Reading: convention and inquiry*. Clemson, S.C.: National Reading Conference, 1975. Pp. 172–76.

Veatch, Jeanette.   *Reading in the elementary school*. New York: Ronald Press, 1966.

Veatch, Jeannette, et al.   *Key words to reading: the language experience approach begins*. Columbus, Ohio: Charles E. Merrill, 1973.

Venezky, Richard L.   Nonstandard language and reading. *Elementary English*, March 1970, 47, 334–45.

Venezky, Richard L.   *Testing in reading: assessment and instructional decision making*. Urbana, Ill.: National Council of Teachers of English and ERIC/RCS, 1974.

Venezky, Richard L. & Chapman, Robin S.   Is learning to read dialect bound? In James L. Laffey & Roger Shuy (Eds.), *Language differences: do they interfere?* Newark, Del.: International Reading Association, 1973. Pp. 62–69.

Vilscek, Elaine C. (Ed.).   *A decade of innovation: approaches to beginning reading*. Newark, Del.: International Reading Association, 1968. (a)

Vilscek, Elaine C.   What research has shown about the language-experience program. In Elaine C. Vilscek (Ed.), *A decade of innovation: approaches to beginning reading.* Newark, Del.: International Reading Association, 1968. Pp. 9–23. (b)

Vukelich, Carol.   A language process for use with disadvantaged children. *Elementary English,* January 1974, *51,* 119–24, 141.

Wagner, Guy & Hosier, Max.   *Strengthening reading skills with educational games.* Riverside, N.J.: Teachers Publishing, 1970.

Wagner, Guy; Hosier, Max; & Blackman, Mildred.   *Listening games: building listening skills with instructional games.* Darien, Conn.: Teachers Publishing, 1962.

Wagner, Guy; Hosier, Max; & Cesinger, Joan.   *Word power games.* Riverside, N.J.: Teachers Publishing, 1972.

Walcutt, Charles C. (Ed.).   *Tomorrow's illiterates: the state of reading instruction today.* Boston: Little, Brown, 1961.

Walcutt, Charles C.; Lamport, Joan; & McCracken, Glenn.   *Teaching reading: a phonic/linguistic approach to developmental reading.* New York: Macmillan, 1974.

Walker, Laurence.   Newfoundland dialect interference in oral reading. *Journal of Reading Behavior,* Spring 1975, *7,* 61–78.

Wallen, Carl J.   *Competency in teaching reading.* Chicago: Science Research Associates, 1972.

Warburton, F. W. & Southgate, Vera.   *ITA: an independent evaluation.* London: Murray & Chambers, 1969.

Wardhaugh, Ronald.   Is the linguistic approach an improvement in reading instruction? In Nila B. Smith (Ed.), *Current issues in reading.* Newark, Del.: International Reading Association, 1969. Pp. 254–67.

Washburne, Carleton.   Individualized plan of instruction in Winnetka. In William S. Gray (Ed.), *Adjusting Reading Programs to Individuals.* Supplementary Educational Monographs, No. 52. Chicago: University of Chicago Press, 1941. Pp. 90–95.

Watson, Billy & Van Etten, Carlene.   Materials analysis. *Journal of Learning Disabilities,* August/September 1976, *9,* 408–16.

Watters, Elisabeth.   Reading in a family-grouped primary school. In Helen K. Smith (Ed.), *Meeting individual needs in reading.* Newark, Del.: International Reading Association, 1971. Pp. 29–35.

Waugh, R. P. & Havel, K. W.   Teaching modern syllabication. *The Reading Teacher,* October 1975, *29,* 20–25.

Weber, Rose-Marie.   Dialect differences in oral reading: an analysis of errors. In James L. Laffey & Roger Shuy (Eds.), *Language differences: do they interfere?* Newark, Del.: International Reading Association, 1973. Pp. 47–61.

Weber, Rosemary.   Bibliography. In Harold Tanyzer and Jean Karl (Eds.), *Reading, children's books, and our pluralistic society.* Newark, Del.: International Reading Association, 1972. Pp. 81–89.

Wehmeyer, Lillian M.   It must be right . . . I read it in the encyclopedia! *Language Arts,* September 1975, *52,* 841–42.

Weiger, Myra.   Puppetry. *Elementary English,* January 1974, *51,* 55–65.

Wertheimer, Barbara S. & Sands, Carol.   Nancy Drew revisited. *Language Arts*, November/December 1975, *52*, 1131–34, 1161.

Whaley, W. Jill.   Closing the blending gap. *Reading World*, December 1975, *15*, 97–100.

Whipple, Gertrude.   The special needs of children without. In G. Whipple & Millard Black (Eds.), *Reading for children without—our disadvantaged youth*. Newark, Del.: International Reading Association, 1966. Pp. 1–7.

Whisler, Nancy G.   Visual-memory training in first grade: effects on visual discrimination and reading ability. *The Elementary School Journal*, October 1974, *75*, 51–54.

Whisler, Nancy G.   Pupil partners. *Language Arts*, April 1976, *53*, 387–89.

White, Marian E.   *High interest—easy reading for junior and senior high school students*. 2nd ed. New York: Citation Press, 1972.

Wiener, Roberta.   A look at reading practices in the open classroom. *The Reading Teacher*, February 1974, *27*, 438–42.

Wilhoyte, Cheryl H.   Contracting: a bridge between the classroom and resource room. *The Reading Teacher*, January 1977, *30*, 376–78.

Williams, Joanna P.   Learning to read: a review of theories and models. *Reading Research Quarterly*, Winter 1973, *8*, 121–46.

Williamson, Leon E. & Young, Freda.   The IRI and RMI diagnostic concepts should be synthesized. *Journal of Reading Behavior*, July 1974, *6*, 183–94.

Willis, Perry W., et al.   A remedial reading technique for disabled readers that employs students. *Psychology in the Schools*, January 1972, *9*, 67–70.

Willmon, Betty.   Reading in the content area: a new math terminology list for the primary grades. *Elementary English*, May 1971, *50*, 463–71.

Willmon, Betty.   Readability interference in reading mathematics texts. In Bonnie S. Schulwitz (Ed.), *Teachers, tangibles, techniques: comprehension of content in reading*. Newark, Del.: International Reading Association, 1975. Pp. 313–16.

Wilson, Corlett T.   An essential vocabulary. *The Reading Teacher*, November 1963, *17*, 94–96.

Wilson, Richard C. & James, Helen J.   *Individualized reading: a practical approach*. Dubuque, Iowa: Kendall-Hunt, 1972.

Wilson, Robert M. & Barnes, Marcia M.   *Survival learning materials: suggestions for developing*. York, Pa.: Strine, 1974.

Wilson, Robert M. & Ribovich, Jerilyn K.   Ability grouping? Stop and reconsider! *Reading World*, December 1973, *13*, 84–91.

Wilson, Thomasyne L.   Guiding black children's "speaking." *Language Arts*, March 1976, *53*, 251–55, 261.

Witty, Paul A.   Characteristics of gifted and creative pupils and their needs for reading experience. In Helen K. Smith (Ed.), *Meeting individual needs in reading*. Newark, Del.: International Reading Association, 1971. Pp. 108–23. (a)

Witty, Paul A. (Ed.).   *Reading for the gifted and the creative student*. Newark, Del.: International Reading Association, 1971. (b)

Witty, Paul A.   Rationale for fostering creative reading in the gifted and the creative. In M. Labuda (Ed.), *Creative reading for gifted learners: a design for excellence*. Newark, Del.: International Reading Association, 1974. Pp. 8–24.

Wolfram, Walter A.   Extended notions of grammar and reading comprehension. *Journal of Reading Behavior*, Fall 1976, *8*, 247–58.

Wolfram, Walter A. & Clarke, Nona H.   *Black-white speech relationships*. Arlington, Va.: Center for Applied Linguistics, 1971.

Womer, Frank B.   What is criterion-referenced measurement? In W. Blanton, R. Farr, & J. J. Tuinman (Eds.), *Measuring reading performance*. Newark, Del.: International Reading Association, 1974. Pp. 34–43.

Woodcock, Richard W.   The Peabody-Chicago-Detroit reading project—a report of the second-year results. Paper presented at the Fourth International i.t.a. Conference, Montreal, Canada, 11 August 1967.

Wright, James A.   A taxonomy of thinking skills for young readers. *Reading Horizons*, Fall 1965, *6*, 20–25.

Wright, Robert J.   The affective and cognitive consequences of an open education elementary school. *American Educational Research Journal*, Fall 1975, *12*, 448–68.

Yoakman, Gerald A.   *Reading and study*. New York: Macmillan, 1928.

Yawkey, Thomas D., et al.   Teaching oral language to young Mexican-Americans. *Elementary English*, February 1974, *51*, 198–202, 238.

Young, Kan-Hua and Jamison, Dean T.   The economic benefits of schooling and reading competence. RB–75–19. Princeton, N.J.: Educational Testing Service, May 1975.

Zintz, Miles V.   *The reading process: the teacher and the learner*. 2nd ed. Dubuque, Iowa: William C. Brown, 1975.

Ziros, Gail I.   Language interference and teaching the Chicano to read. *Journal of Reading*, January 1976, *19*, 284–88.

Name Index

618

Shepherd, D. L., 362, 368, 371
Shepherd, T., 428
Sherman, G. B., 532
Shohen, S., 66, 86
Shuman, R. B., 331
Shuy, R., 460, 465, 548
Silvaroli, N. J., 524, 527
Simmons, B., 416
Simmons, F. G., 377
Simons, H. D., 114, 327, 466, 467
Sims, R., 114
Singer, H., 26, 244, 316, 408
Sipay, E. R., 17, 43, 57, 59, 94, 116, 135, 197, 198, 213, 229, 257, 324, 338, 351, 407, 408, 438, 451, 516, 425
Sloan, M., 424
Small, R. C., 404
Smith, C. B., 505, 524, 531, 536
Smith, C. E., 59
Smith, F., 104, 249, 297, 317, 344, 536
Smith, H. K., 413
Smith, J. A., 543
Smith, L. B., 89
Smith, N. B., 74, 318, 363, 516
Smith, R. J., 46, 47, 50, 131, 180, 317, 343, 372, 460, 470, 489, 508, 521, 524, 548
Smythe, P. C., 39, 283
Snapp, M., 448
Snoddy, J. E., 360
Solomon, B., 402
Sorenson, J. S., 415
Southgate, V., 75, 107, 516
Southwell, P. R., 107
Spache, E., 92, 263, 508
Spache, G. D., 72, 92, 408, 433, 455, 508
Spearitt, D. 318
Spiroff, J., 244
Statts, A. W., 22
Stallard, K., 112, 524
Stanchfield, J. M., 72
Stanley, J. C., 53
Starkey, J. D., 401
Stauffer, R. G., 116, 306, 345, 348, 516
Stennett, R. G., 39, 283
Stensland, A. L., 433

Stephens, W. E., 48
Stern, C., 448
Sticht, T. G., 4
Stigler, B. J., 48
Stoll, E., 299
Stolurow, L. M., 111
Stoodt, B. D., 328, 478
Strickland, D. S., 67, 433, 468
Strong, A., 439
Sucher, F., 160
Sue, P. W., 481
Suppes, P., 111
Swalm, J. E., 321, 351
Sweeney, J., 83
Swenson, I., 349
Swineford, E. J., 347
Swinford, H. L., 401
Swiss, T., 401, 487
Switzer, F., 181

Tanyzer, H., 54
Taschow, H. G., 536
Tatham, S. M., 325
Tchir, C., 59
Telegdy, G. A., 52
Terry, E., 404
Thackray, D., 36, 37, 507
Thelan, J., 362, 540
Thomas, E. L., 377, 540
Thompson, R. A., 112, 210, 263
Thorndike, R. L., 318
Tierney, R. J., 188
Tinker, M. A., 321, 375, 478, 479, 521, 548, 549
Tovey, D. R., 288
Towner, J. C., 69, 135
Townsend, M. J., 478
Trepper, T. S., 107
Trezise, J., 424
Troy, A., 370
Tuinman, J. J., 4, 208, 330
Turner, E. A., 129
Turner, R. R., 114, 467
Turner, T. N., 308, 489
Turnure, J. E., 147
Tutolo, D. J., 347, 375

Vacca, J. A., 177
Vacca, R. T., 177
Valmont, W. J., 188
Van Blarecom, G., 335
Van Etten, C., 264
Van Metre, P. D., 414

Vardian, E. B., 368
Vaughn, J. L., 320
Veatch, J., 92, 516
Venezky, R. L., 41, 114, 467
Vilscek, E. C., 75, 88, 516
Vukelich, C., 67

Wagner, G., 263, 306, 322
Waite, R. R., 77
Walcutt, C. C., 22, 98, 99
Walker, L., 208, 466
Wallbrown, F. H., 54
Wallbrown, J. D., 54
Wallen, C. J., 532, 544
Warburton, F. W., 107
Wardhaugh, R., 104
Washburne, C., 36
Watson, B., 264
Watson, J., 104
Watters, E., 181
Waugh, R. P., 280
Weaver, W. W., 39
Weber, R., 433
Weber, R-M., 466
Weber, R. M., 466
Weener, P., 317
Wehmeyer, L. M., 385
Weiger, M., 126
Weil, P. E., 366
Weintraub, S., 403
Wells, S., 111
Wertheimer, B. S., 426
Whaley, W. J., 286
Wheelock, W. H., 524, 527
Whipple, G., 458
Whisler, N. G., 42, 155
White, M. E., 455
White, S., 335
Wiederholt, J. L., 68
Wiener, M., 324
Wiener, R., 181
Wilhoyte, C. H., 456
Williams, A. C., 331
Williams, J. P., 27
Williamson, L. E., 230
Willis, P. W., 448
Willmon, B., 366
Wilson, C. T., 485
Wilson, R. C., 516
Wilson, R. M., 152, 467, 486
Wilson, T. L., 469
Windeguth-Behn, A., 59
Winkley, C. K., 54
Witty, P. A., 486, 489, 549
Woelfel, S., 345, 536
Wolf, W., 345

Subject Index

ability groups, 151, 154
abstraction, levels of, 296
academic engaged time, 145
acceleration, 178
accenting, 281
accuracy, silent reading, 220
achievement tests, 203; *see also* standardized tests
adapted reading program, 435
additions, 218
administrative procedures for dealing with individual differences, 178–182
advance organizers, 377
affix, 265, 306
age levels, and reading interests, 398
allophone, 9
alphabet reform, 13–14
alphabetical order, 85, 380–382
American Indian children, 477–478
analogies, 310
analysis skills, in decoding, 276–281
analytic phonics, 266
analytical tests, 203
Anchor Test Study, 207
answers to specific questions, finding, 338
antonyms, 301, 309
anxiety, 51
aptitude-treatment interaction, 117
arithmetic, reading skills in, 365–368
assessing progress, 183–236; functional reading skills, 360–362; study habits, 390
attention, 38; securing and maintaining, 147; and studying, 392
attitudes toward reading, 399, 410–411
audience reading, 127, 163
auding, 321; *see also* listening comprehension
audiovisual materials, 176; for teaching decoding, 292
auditory acuity, 49

auditory blending, 43, 228, 275
auditory defects, 49
auditory discrimination, 43; suggestions for teaching, 71, 269
auditory perception, 42–44
author's outline, 336
author's plan and intent, grasping, 338
automatic word recognition, 467
avoidance technique, 467

basal reader programs: in first grade, 76–83; in grades 2 and 3, 119–122; instructional procedures, 79–81; individualized progress in, 161; materials, 76–79, 119–121, 131–132; in middle grades, 132–133; in upper grades, 138; variations in methodology, 80
basal readers, content of, 76, 77, 82–83, 119, 131
basal series, using different, 81–82
Basic Elementary Reading Vocabularies, 254–255
beginning reading instruction: basal reader programs, 76–83; code-emphasis approaches, 95–108; color systems, 108; comparison of approaches, 115–117; computer-assisted instruction, 110–111; diagnostic and prescriptive reading instruction, 111–113; for dialect speakers and non-English speakers, 113–115; individualized developmental reading, 89–95; individualized skills-emphasis program, 108–113; language-experience programs, 83–89; linguistic programs, 101–105; meaning-emphasis approaches, 75–95; phonic programs, 95–101; programmed materials, 108–110; special alphabet programs, 105–108
begin-over approach, 451
behavioral objectives, 31, 318, 377, 411
bibliotherapy, 427–429
bidialectal, 459

FT. MYERS

H